Theorizing Composition

Theorizing Composition

A Critical Sourcebook of Theory and Scholarship in Contemporary Composition Studies

EDITED BY

Mary Lynch Kennedy

Emmanuel S. Nelson, *Advisory Editor*

GREENWOOD PRESS
Westport, Connecticut • London

Library of Congress Cataloging-in-Publication Data

Theorizing composition : a critical sourcebook of theory and
  scholarship in contemporary composition studies / edited by Mary
  Lynch Kennedy.
       p.   cm.
    Includes bibliographical references and index.
    ISBN 0–313–29927–7 (alk. paper)
       1. English language—Rhetoric—Study and teaching—Theory, etc.
    2. Academic writing—Study and teaching—Theory, etc.   3. Report
    writing—Study and teaching—Theory, etc.   4. Interdisciplinary
    approach in education.   I. Kennedy, Mary Lynch, 1943– .
    PE1404.T473   1998
    808'.042'07—dc21   97–32005

British Library Cataloguing in Publication Data is available.

Library of Congress Catalog Card Number: 97–32005
ISBN: 0–313–29927–7

First published in 1998

Greenwood Press, 88 Post Road West, Westport, CT 06881
An imprint of Greenwood Publishing Group, Inc.

Printed in the United States of America

The paper used in this book complies with the
Permanent Paper Standard issued by the National
Information Standards Organization (Z39.48–1984).

10 9 8 7 6 5 4 3 2 1

To Bill

Contents

Preface

The last twenty-five years have witnessed extraordinary changes in the academic specialization variously described as Composition Studies or Rhetoric and Composition. What was noticeable about the field in its infancy was a preoccupation with practice, a de-emphasis on theory, and an exclusive reliance on writing process. As its disciplinary status has grown, Composition Studies has expanded its focus, reconceptualized the writing process, and embraced a wide range of contemporary critical perspectives, with the result that constructs like poststructuralism, social constructionism, gender, and genre, which were largely unknown in 1965, now dominate discussion. Louise Phelps characterizes the newly emerging field of Composition Studies as having already passed through "a purely pragmatic phase, aimed at establishing the most effective teaching methods" (45), and arriving now at a phase that is "fully theoretical." Some critics have complained about a theory glut and argued that the field has become preoccupied with theory.

As the intellectual context of Composition has changed to give theory a new legitimacy and a privileged position, journal articles and conference presentations are filled with "theory talk," some of it highly complex and confusing. One cause of puzzlement is that the new interpretations and visions of the field and the language in which they are expressed are contingent upon a multiplicity of theories, not a universally acceptable framework. Some of these theories, such as reader-response criticism, have been grafted onto traditional curricula and have informed practice; others, such as social constructionism, have only begun to take hold of the field; and some, such as genre theory, are too new for us to judge their effect. The result of this theory boom is that Composition Studies has emerged as a highly interdisciplinary field that draws on the scholarship of many other specialties and has a discourse in which multiple perspectives find expression. It has rejected a central, objective representation; instead, it proposes a plurality of possible approaches, with different vocabularies, different metaphors, and different frames of reference.

Today there is no mainstream theory, no dominant approach or monolithic school of thought, dominating Composition Studies, nor is the field grounded in any one method. Furthermore, teachers and scholars are coming to theory at different times and in different ways. Some espouse theories of postmodernism; others still align themselves with current-traditional rhetoric. Theories are intertwined, and theoretical perspectives overlap. Composition Studies does not have a single, stable, critical identity. Diverse and complex, it resists affiliation with any particular critical movement or camp.

This turn of events has left many members of the field bewildered and unprepared for the current scholarly discussion, which has become a conversation overheard. Teachers and students have difficulty catching even the gist of broad theoretical arguments and reflecting on their relevance to the field, let alone entering into the conversation, which is extremely diverse and further complicated by a plurality of theoretical positions.

This book has grown out of my experiences teaching "Theory and Practice in Composition," a graduate course for students in the Master's Program at the State University of New York College at Cortland. My students are baffled by the complex array of theories in Composition Studies. In their undergraduate careers, many of these students feared and resisted theory; most ignored it. They complain that the articles I assign are sometimes impenetrable because they are "too theoretical." The authors of these articles assume that their readers have a backgound in theory, which my students lack. Thus this book is intended to help students like mine. Readers can use it as a valuable orientation to the major theories that have influenced contemporary Composition Studies and helped shape the field over the past 25 years and as a base for exploring these theories further. I hope the book will serve a wide audience of students and teachers, including specialists who are looking for a quick overview as well as nonspecialists who are encountering theory for the first time.

The aim of *Theorizing Composition: A Critical Sourcebook of Theory and Scholarship in Contemporary Composition Studies* is to help readers become conversant with the field's new intellectual currents. To that end, it presents clear explanations of the many theories that underpin Composition Studies and have permeated the work of influential writers in the field during the past 25 years. It introduces readers to what Composition Studies means in terms of abstract, speculative theories; ideological formations; and new modes of interpretation; and it thus enables them to evaluate recent trends, learn from their insights, and see how they diverge, mesh, intersect, complement, and compete with one another.

The book consists of 66 essays, each of which focuses on a particular theory or group of theories. The essays show how various individuals contribute to theoretical movements, but very few concentrate only on the work of a single theorist. There are, for example, several discussions of Jacques Derrida, briefly in connection with collaborative/social process theory, and more substantially in connection with deconstruction and poststructuralism. All of the essays situate the theories, many of which derive from other disciplines, within the larger context of Composition Studies, giving adequate attention to the various concepts that bear on the field to any significant degree.

In compiling this book, my task was difficult because I had to select a defined number of theories from a body of work that is continually expanding. I don't claim to have covered every theory that has had an impact on Composition Studies, but I have attempted to include most of the important ones. Admittedly, readers will discover that some thought-provoking theories have been overlooked. This may be due to oversight on my part or simply the result of lack of space. Certainly, this work was not intended to be encyclopedic; Theresa Enos has already done an admirable job in that area.

Each essay first provides an interpretive and critical summary of a particular theory or theories, including key elements, basic concepts and claims, and information about the seminal or most influential works. It then reviews the theory's critical reception in Composition Studies and discusses its significance in the field by evoking scholarship that relates the theory to composition. For example, Timothy W. Crusius's entry, "Hermeneutics," explains philosophical concepts of Martin Heidegger, Hans-Georg Gadamer, and Paul Ricoeur and then goes on to discuss how such composition specialists as James Kinneavy have offered comments or applied hermeneutics to the field of Composition Studies. Each essay is followed by a bibliography, which invites readers to pursue a more in-depth investigation of the particular theory. The bibliography lists primary texts and the major scholarship using the theory in composition and provides additional suggestions for further reading. In addition, a selected general bibliography appears toward the end of the book. The penultimate section of this volume, the index, provides a veritable Who's Who of distinguished theorists, critics, and composition scholars. It also allows readers to compare instances in the volume in which a particular figure is mentioned. Finally, "About the Contributors" contains biographical information about the editor and the authors of each of the essays.

This sourcebook of theory and scholarship in contemporary Composition Studies will enable readers to sort out what many perceive as a bewildering array of theories in modern composition. It is not a volume devoted to "theory talk." It does not extol the virtues of theory or explain its limitations; question what theory can and cannot do; present the debate between theory and practice; differentiate among theories, categorize them, or show the relationships among them; or discuss the theoretical divides and camps within the composition community. Other volumes, including some written by the contributors to this book, have covered these areas quite well. In the 1980s, we have the scholarly works of C. H. Knoblauch and Lil Brannon, Louise Phelps, Stephen H. North, and William A. Covino. And recently there has been a remarkable number of articles and books devoted to these topics. The connection between critical theory and writing theory is explored in *Writing Theory and Critical Theory*, a series of essays edited by John Clifford and John Schilb, and the relationships among Platonism, Aristoteleanism, New Criticism, and modern poststructuralism are discussed in W. Ross Winterowd and Jack Blum's *A Teacher's Introduction to the Rhetorical Tradition*. In *The Practice of Theory: Teacher Research in Composition*, Ruth E. Ray analyzes how theory has contributed to the development of Composition Studies. John Schilb, in *Between the Lines: Relating Composition Theory and Literary Theory*, and the contributors to Patricia Harkin and John Schilb's *Contending with Words: Composition and Rhetoric in a Postmodern Age* examine the encounter of Composition Studies with postmodernism. Lee Odell, in *Theory and Practice in the Teaching of Writing: Rethinking the Discipline*; Joseph Harris, in *A Teaching Subject: Composition Since 1966*; and Sidney I. Dobrin, in *Constructing Knowledges: The Politics of Theory-Building and Pedagogy in Composition*, discuss and question the relationship beween theory and classroom practice. Other books offer readers overviews of particular theories: for example, Sharon Crowley's *A Teacher's Introduction to Deconstruction*, Timothy W. Crusius's *A Teacher's Introduction to Philosophical Hermeneutics*, Richard Beach's *A Teacher's Introduction to Reader-Response Theories*, and Ray Linn's *A Teacher's Introduction to Postmodernism*. The sources mentioned in this preface, as well as some major texts, are listed in the Selected General Bibliography.

Unlike scholarly works, which target experienced readers by focusing either on particular aspects of theoretical movements or providing in-depth coverage of single theories, this volume is an invaluable resource for a broad spectrum of users: students of Composition, of course, but also scholars engaged in other fields who need to verify information as well as teachers, graduate students, undergraduates, and general readers.

I wish to sincerely thank the contributors to this book. I am deeply grateful to my Advisory Editor, Emmanuel S. Nelson, for his encouragement and enthusiasm for this publication. It has been a pleasure working with George Butler at Greenwood. I also owe special thanks to William McCleary, Alan Smith, and my secretaries, Karen Knapp and Patricia Hazard. My greatest debt is to Bill, whose love and support make projects like this possible.

BIBLIOGRAPHY

Beach, Richard. *A Teacher's Introduction to Reader-Response Theories*. Urbana, IL: NCTE, 1993.

Clifford, John, and John Schilb, eds. *Writing Theory and Critical Theory*. New York: MLA, 1994.

Covino, William A. *The Art of Wondering: A Revisionist Return to the History of Rhetoric*. Portsmouth, NH: Boynton, 1988.

Crowley, Sharon. *A Teacher's Introduction to Deconstruction*. Urbana, IL: NCTE, 1989.

Crusius, Timothy W. *A Teacher's Introduction to Philosophical Hermeneutics*. Urbana, IL: NCTE, 1991.

Dobrin, Sidney I. *Constructing Knowledges: The Politics of Theory-Building and Pedagogy in Composition*. Albany, NY: State U of New York P, 1997.

Enos, Theresa, ed. *Encyclopedia of Rhetoric and Composition: Communication from Ancient Times to the Information Age*. New York: Garland, 1995.

Harkin, Patricia, and John Schilb, eds. *Contending with Words: Composition and Rhetoric in a Postmodern Age*. New York: MLA, 1991.

Harris, Joseph. *A Teaching Subject: Composition Since 1966*. Upper Saddle River, NJ: Prentice-Hall, 1997.

Knoblauch, C. H., and Lil Brannon. *Rhetorical Traditions and the Teaching of Writing*. Upper Montclair, NJ: Boynton, 1984.

Linn, Ray. *A Teacher's Introduction to Postmodernism*. Urbana, IL: NCTE, 1996.

North, Stephen M. *The Making of Knowledge in Composition: Portrait of an Emerging Field*. Upper Montclair, NJ: Boynton, 1987.

Odell, Lee. *Theory and Practice in the Teaching of Writing: Rethinking the Discipline*. Carbondale: Southern Illinois UP, 1993.

Phelps, Louise. ''Images of Student Writing: The Deep Structure of Teacher Response.'' In *Writing and Response: Theory, Practice, and Research*. Ed. Chris M. Anson. Urbana, IL: NCTE, 1989, 37–67.

Ray, Ruth E. *The Practice of Theory: Teacher Research in Composition*. Urbana, IL: NCTE, 1993.

Schilb, John. *Between the Lines: Relating Composition Theory and Literary Theory*. Portsmouth, NH: Boynton, 1996.

Winterowd, W. Ross, and Jack Blum. *A Teacher's Introduction to the Rhetorical Tradition*. Urbana, IL: NCTE, 1994.

Theorizing Composition

A

AUDIENCE AND DISCOURSE COMMUNITY THEORY
Summary/Reception and Significance in Composition Studies

Audience Theory

A key underlying question for understanding theories of audience and discourse community in composition studies is this: How is *audience*, a concept associated with oratorical rhetoric and the physical presence of a speaker and listeners, transformed by written rhetoric? For Aristotle, audience is the primary concern in the rhetorical act: "Of the three elements in speech-making—speaker, subject, and person addressed—it is the last one, the hearer, that determines the speech's end and object" (*Rhetoric* 1.3). However, compositionists have had to contend with a different set of relationships in which classical concepts of orator, speech, and audience do not translate directly to writer, text, and reader.

Book 2 of Aristotle's *Rhetoric* is the primary classical source for the "audience analysis" mode of theorizing audience, in which the rhetor identifies key characteristics—for Aristotle, these are age and status—of the audience in order to tailor the speech to appeal to that audience. Porter notes that Aristotle is the principal source for the classical theory of audience; other classical rhetoricians treat the concept of audience in passing or not at all (*Audience* 19). As the intervening centuries shaped the legacy of classical rhetoric, audience theory was eclipsed by attention to other concerns, particularly organization and style, as can be seen in our century in current-traditional rhetoric (Porter, *Audience* 30).

Ong identifies the lack of attention in literary theory in "The Writer's Audience Is Always a Fiction," a widely cited articulation of audience theory for written texts. Ong objects not only to the New Critics' denial of the importance

of the reader role in literary texts, but also to speech-communication theory
(also derived in part from classical rhetoric), which assumed a direct and unproblematic relationship among speaker, message, and receiver. In response,
Ong posits a fictionalized audience constructed by the writer.

As the discipline of composition studies emerged, its theorists paid more
attention to the rhetorical concept of audience. Ede offers an overview of theoretical resources and recent research work in a wide-ranging bibliographic essay, "Audience: An Introduction to Research." While the variety of sources
overwhelms the potential for synthesis in Ede's essay, it contains useful pointers
to relevant work in cognitive psychology, composition, speech communication,
rhetoric, and philosophy.

Responding directly to Ong as well as the new interest in audience within
composition studies, Ede and Lunsford's influential article, "Audience Ad-
dressed/Audience Invoked," foreshadows the turn to discourse community theory. Ede and Lunsford argue that the Ongian conception, "audience invoked,"
must be balanced by an alternate view, "audience addressed," in which audiences are quite real. They posit a synthesis in which "the term *audience* refers
not just to the intended, actual, or eventual readers of a discourse, but to all
those whose image, ideas, or actions influence a writer during the process of
composition" (168).

The Turn to Discourse Community Theory

In current composition theory, the term *discourse community* encompasses
both writers and their potential readers. A discourse community is defined
loosely by shared knowledge, goals, and interests. Discourse communities, according to Porter (*Audience*), are messy and discontinuous, with shifting borders
and memberships; however, they can be identified by their *forums*—the means
through which participants communicate with each other. In this scheme, neither
audience nor author is an autonomous body; rather, audience, author, and texts
(as well as speech) are woven together in a larger governing discourse. Sources
of discourse community theory have been identified particularly in social constructionism (see Bruffee); in reader-response theory, in Fish's notion of the
interpretive community; and in sociolinguistics, in research into speech communities (see Swales). In developing this theory, compositionists have focused
much attention on its implications for writing instruction, particularly instruction
in "academic writing."

Bizzell's 1982 essay, "Cognition, Convention, and Certainty: What We Need
to Know about Writing," contains important early statements for discourse community theory. She poses two theories of writing, one "inner-directed" and the
other "outer-directed," and she critiques Flower and Hayes's inner-directed
cognitive process research by illustrating some ways in which outer-directed
theory could inform gaps in its model. Bizzell argues that the writer's position
in a discourse community both motivates and constrains her or his work.

Bartholomae's essay, "Inventing the University," also reveals emerging ideas about discourse communities. Much like Bizzell, Bartholomae argues that the writer's position in the discourse defines the writing situation: "It is the discourse with its projects and agendas that determines what writers can and will do" (139). Bartholomae also critiques Flower and Hayes's exclusive focus on the inner process of the writer, pointing out that successful composing takes place when writers locate themselves in "a familiar and established territory—one with insiders and outsiders; one with set phrases, examples, and conclusions" (143).

Porter's essay, "Intertextuality and the Discourse Community," focuses attention on the text/intertext relationship to a writer's composing. Porter describes a view of writing that highlights the relationship between the work of intertextual critics and discourse community theory: "Authorial intention is less significant than social context; the writer is simply a part of a discourse tradition, a member of a team, and a participant in a community of discourse that creates its own collective meaning" (35). As he responds to what he believes is an "anti-rhetorical" emphasis on creativity and originality in first-year writing textbooks, Porter argues that instruction should be refocused away from "audience analysis" toward a consideration of the discourse community in which the writer is working. Evaluation should be tied not only to the conventions of the community, but also to the writer's success in making a contribution (42–43).

Critics of discourse community theory express various concerns but do not refute its central claims or offer a theory with greater explanatory power. Joseph Harris, in "The Idea of Community in the Study of Writing," debunks the notion of a unified "academic discourse community," pointing to the variety of discourse forms and agreements and disagreements—from committee meetings and hallway conversations to conferences, articles, and books—that characterize academic life. Particularly in response to Bartholomae, Harris argues for revising the metaphor of discourse community:

Rather than . . . romanticizing academic discourse as occurring in a kind of single cohesive community, I would like to urge, instead, that we think of it as taking place in something more like a city. That is, instead of presenting academic discourse as coherent and well-defined, we might be better off viewing it as polyglot, as a sort of space in which competing beliefs and practices intersect with and confront one another. (20)

Despite this critique, Harris does not throw out the notion of academic discourse or deny that there are ways of identifying how it is carried out or by whom. Rather, he complicates an oversimplified or static picture, insisting that we always see multiple communities and multiple discourses interacting even within a single setting.

Another critic of discourse community theory is Cooper, who locates her discomfort in the danger that a discourse community can become an exclusionary and static artifact of social and institutional arrangements: "In this sense a discourse community is a way of regulating who has access to resources, power, even to discourse itself, and it creates gatekeepers to make sure that the right people get in and all others are excluded" (205). Thus Cooper argues that the notion of an academic discourse community has an exclusionary function and teaching academic discourse is a gatekeeping activity. In her view, we should think of discourse communities as more provisional, being formed around specific projects, and composed of people working on those projects.

According to Miller's essay, "Rhetoric and Community: The Problem of the One and the Many," scholars in many disciplines have identified the notion of community as missing from the liberal tradition, which defines the relations between individual and state or institution in our culture: "Community is offered as the missing dimension of contemporary political and social life, the dimension that provides commitment, connectedness, solidarity, and meaning" (83). Drawing in part from Cooper's reservations about discourse community theory, Miller offers certain cautions to those attracted by theories of community—in particular, the normative circularity that results when discourse that is constrained and generated within a community is judged by that same community (86).

Despite these critiques, discourse community theory is well established as a powerful way of conceptualizing and contextualizing the problematic relationship between writer and reader in written discourse.

BIBLIOGRAPHY

Primary Texts

Aristotle. *Rhetoric*. Trans. Rhys Roberts. New York: Modern Library, 1954.
Fish, Stanley. *Is There a Text in This Class? The Authority of Interpretive Communities*. Cambridge, MA: Harvard UP, 1980.
Ong, Walter. "The Writer's Audience Is Always a Fiction." *PMLA* 90 (1975): 9–21.
Swales, John. *Genre Analysis*. New York: Cambridge UP, 1990.

Major Scholarship in Composition

Bartholomae, David. "Inventing the University." In *When a Writer Can't Write*. Ed. Mike Rose. New York: Guilford, 1985, 134–65.
Bizzell, Patricia. "Cognition, Convention, and Certainty: What We Need to Know about Writing." *Pre/Text* 3 (1982): 213–43.
Bruffee, Kenneth. "Social Construction, Language, and the Authority of Knowledge: A Bibliographic Essay." *College English* 48 (1986): 773–90.
Cooper, Marilyn. "Why Are We Talking about Discourse Communities? Or, Foundationalism Rears Its Ugly Head Once More." In *Writing as Social Action*. Eds. Marilyn M. Cooper and Michael Holzman. Portsmouth, NH: Heinemann, 1989, 202–20.
Ede, Lisa. "Audience: An Introduction to Research." *College Composition and Communication* 35 (1984): 140–54.
Ede, Lisa, and Andrea Lunsford. "Audience Addressed/Audience Invoked: The Role of Audience in Composition Theory and Pedagogy." *College Composition and Communication* 35 (1984): 155–71.
Harris, Joseph. "The Idea of Community in the Study of Writing." *College Composition and Communication* 40 (1989): 11–22.

Miller, Carolyn R. "Rhetoric and Community: The Problem of the One and the Many."
In *Toward Defining the New Rhetorics*. Ed. Stuart Brown and Theresa Enos.
Newbury Park, CA: Sage, 1992, 79–94.

Porter, James. *Audience and Rhetoric: An Archaeological Composition of the Discourse
Community*. Englewood Cliffs, NJ: Prentice-Hall, 1992.

———. "Intertextuality and the Discourse Community." *Rhetoric Review* 5 (1986): 34–
47.

KARIN EVANS

AUTHORSHIP THEORIES

Summary

For most of the twentieth century, textual scholarship has proceeded on the assumption that an author is autonomous, originary, proprietary, normatively male, and moral: that he can write alone, uninfluenced by others; that he can invent new ideas and express them in fresh words; that he has a right to own those words and make financial profit from them; that he is probably male (though plausibly female); and that an author's accomplishing autonomy and originality is a demonstration of his high personal character. This representation of the author is a legacy of Romanticism: its canonization can be seen in Young (1759), Wordsworth (1815), and Emerson (1836). Its hold on twentieth-century thought is demonstrated in Bloom (1973) and is legitimated in copyright legislation and in academic policies outlawing plagiarism.

Just after the mid-twentieth century, critical challenges to the autonomous, originary, proprietary, normatively male, and moral author became commonplace; see especially Barthes (1968), Foucault (1969), and Gilbert and Gubar (1979). These challenges led scholars to question whether the received notion of the author was a description of the true nature of authorship or a constructed product of its society. From this line of questioning came the scholarly field of theory of authorship, represented in the work of Stewart (1991), Woodmansee (1994), Woodmansee and Jaszi (1994), and Meltzer (1994). In 1995 Burke edited the first anthology of readings in the theory of authorship.

Reception and Significance in Composition Studies

Most contemporary theorists of authorship come from the disciplines of law and letters, and an increasing number of them come from composition and rhetoric. The first extended applications of the theory of authorship to composition studies were LeFevre (1987), Gere (1987), and Lunsford and Ede (1990). These three books work with the pedagogy of collaboration and peer response, which by 1987 was an established field within composition studies, and use the tenets of that field to redefine the definitions of student authorship in composition studies. All three offer a history of authorship theory specific to the discipline of composition and rhetoric. Gere articulates a key premise upon which the new assertions are made: "*Learning*, when conceived in collaborative terms, assumes a socially derived view of knowledge and opposes a fixed and hierarchical one"

(75) (italics added). LeFevre suggests that collaboration is not just an advanced stage of the writing process but occurs in the invention stage, as well; thus her work challenges the autonomy of the student writer. Lunsford and Ede continue in the same vein, asserting the status of author for student writers and thereby challenging long-standing hierarchies of authorship.

Miller's 1992 book applies the methods of contrastive rhetoric to composition studies' representations of authorship and plagiarism in composition studies. Miller argues that the plagiarisms of Martin Luther King, Jr., are not so much a transgression against textual morality as they are a demonstration of alternative textual standards—in this case, the standards of the American Protestant ministry, and in particular African-American preaching, in which neither proprietorship nor autonomy prevail as textual values. Matalene's 1985 essay takes a similar line of inquiry abroad, demonstrating that neither autonomy nor originality obtain in Chinese textual values.

Brody's 1993 contribution focuses on the gendering of the student author. Like Gere, LeFevre, and Lunsford and Ede, she offers a history of that gendering, exploring the ways in which composition studies, in its early years, drew on classical rhetorical theory and contemporaneous texts to offer up a student author who must be masculine, autonomous, and chaste. That so many major contributions to the theory of authorship in composition and rhetoric include a history of authorship is itself a demonstration of the newness of this line of inquiry; theorists of authorship in composition and rhetoric must assume that their readers are unfamiliar with that history.

As that line of inquiry continues, it diversifies. Two forthcoming books, one by Howard and the other a collection of essays edited by Roy and Buranen, apply the theory of authorship to the representations of plagiarism in composition studies. These works ask whether the plagiarist will continue to be treated as a moral transgressor and whether plagiarism will continue to be posited in texts rather than in writers and readers.

A caucus on intellectual property has been established at the annual Conference on College Composition and Communication. Although no books on intellectual property have yet been published in composition studies, two important articles—by Woodmansee and Jaszi (1995) and Lunsford and West (1996)—may lead scholars in that direction.

The conjunction of hypertext and the postmodern theory of authorship provides evidence for the argument that all writing is collaborative and that intellectual property is arbitrarily legislated and increasingly difficult to sustain. Digitized composition and hypertext constitute an exponentially expanding field of inquiry in the theory of authorship. Scholars argue about the causal connection between hypertext and postmodern theory—whether hypertext is made possible by the theory, or whether the theory enabled the development of hypertext—but that there is a connection between the two is a widely accepted assertion. Faigley (1992) explores that connection, especially in his Chapter 6, "The Achieved Utopia of the Networked Classroom." Lanham's 1994 book and Landow's 1994 collection of essays are important resources, and much of Tuman's 1992 collection is specific to composition studies.

Scholarly attention to the theory of authorship in composition studies is in a period of expansion and diversification. Scholarship asserts that every composition pedagogy is propelled by a theory of authorship and, further, that the theory of authorship that guides a pedagogy also establishes the possible subject positions for students and teachers alike. Whether student writers are treated as authors or as error makers has long been a topic of discussion in composition studies, and recent work in the theory of authorship provides fresh perspectives for this established conversation.

BIBLIOGRAPHY

Primary Texts and Major Scholarship in Composition

Barthes, Roland. "The Death of the Author." 1968. Rpt. In *Image, Music, Text*. Trans. Stephen Heath. New York: Hill and Wang, 1977.

Bloom, Harold. *The Anxiety of Influence: A Theory of Poetry*. New York: Oxford UP, 1973.

Brody, Miriam. *Manly Writing: Gender, Rhetoric, and the Rise of Composition*. Carbondale: Southern Illinois UP, 1993.

Burke, Séan. *Authorship: From Plato to the Postmodern*. Edinburgh, Scotland: Edinburgh UP, 1995.

Emerson, Ralph Waldo. *Nature*. 1836. Rpt. in *Selected Writings of Emerson*. Ed. Brooks Atkinson. New York: Modern Library, 1950, 3–44.

Faigley, Lester. *Fragments of Rationality: Postmodernity and the Subject of Composition*. Pittsburgh, PA: U of Pittsburgh P, 1992.

Foucault, Michel. "What Is an Author?" *Bulletin de la Société Française de Philosophie* 63.3 (1969): 73–104. Rpt. In *Language, Countermemory, Practice: Selected Essays and Interviews*. Ed. Donald F. Bouchard. Trans. Donald F. Bouchard and Sherry Simon. Ithaca, NY: Cornell UP, 1977, 113–38.

Gere, Anne Ruggles. *Writing Groups: History, Theory, and Implications*. Carbondale: Southern Illinois UP, 1987.

Gilbert, Sandra M., and Susan Gubar. "Infection in the Sentence: The Woman Writer and the Anxiety of Authorship." In *The Madwoman in the Attic: The Woman Writer and the Nineteenth-Century Literary Imagination*. New Haven, CT: Yale UP, 1979. Rpt. in *Feminisms: An Anthology of Literary Theory and Criticism*. Ed. Robyn R. Warhol and Diane Price Herndl. New Brunswick, NJ: Rutgers UP, 1991, 289–300.

Howard, Rebecca Moore. *Standing in the Shadow of Giants: Plagiarists, Authors, Collaborators*. Norwood, NJ: Ablex, forthcoming.

Landow, George P., ed. *Hyper/Text/Theory*. Baltimore, MD: Johns Hopkins UP, 1994.

Lanham, Richard. *The Electronic Word: Democracy, Technology, and the Arts*. Chicago: U of Chicago P, 1994.

LeFevre, Karen Burke. *Invention as a Social Act*. Carbondale: Southern Illinois UP, 1987.

Lunsford, Andrea A., and Lisa Ede. *Singular Texts/Plural Authors: Perspectives on Collaborative Writing*. Carbondale: Southern Illinois UP, 1990.

Lunsford, Andrea A., and Susan West. "Intellectual Property and Composition Studies." *College Composition and Communication* 47.3 (October 1996): 383–411.

Matalene, Carolyn. "Contrastive Rhetoric: An American Writing Teacher in China." *College English* 47.8 (December 1985): 789–808.

Meltzer, Françoise. *Hot Property: The Stakes and Claims of Literary Originality.* Chicago: U of Chicago P, 1994.

Miller, Keith D. *Voice of Deliverance: The Language of Martin Luther King, Jr., and Its Sources.* New York: Free P, 1992.

Roy, Alice, and Lise Buranen, eds. *Perspectives on Plagiarism and Intellectual Property in a Postmodern World.* Albany: State U of NewYork P, forthcoming.

Stewart, Susan. *Crimes of Writing: Problems in the Containment of Representation.* New York: Oxford UP, 1991.

Tuman, Myron C., ed. *Literacy Online: The Promise (and Peril) of Reading and Writing with Computers.* Pittsburgh, PA: U of Pittsburgh P, 1992.

Woodmansee, Martha. *The Author, Art, and the Market: Rereading the History of Aesthetics.* New York: Columbia UP, 1994.

Woodmansee, Martha, and Peter Jaszi. "The Law of Texts: Copyright in the Academy." *College English* 57.7 (November 1995): 769–87.

Woodmansee, Martha, and Peter Jaszi, eds. *The Construction of Authorship: Textual Appropriation in Law and Literature.* Durham, NC: Duke UP, 1994.

Wordsworth, William. "Essay, Supplementary to the Preface." 1815. Rpt. In *The Prose Works of William Wordsworth.* Ed. W. J. B. Owen and Jane Worthington Smyser. Vol. 3. Oxford, U.K.: Clarendon P, 1974.

Young, Edward. *Conjectures on Original Composition.* 1759. Rpt. Leeds, U.K.: Scolar P, 1966.

REBECCA MOORE HOWARD

B

BURKEAN THEORIES OF RHETORIC

Summary

Kenneth Burke developed his theory of language as symbolic action from the 1920s into the 1990s. This theory must be understood in the context of his theory on theory. It is critical to understand both as rhetorical theories before examining each and how they have influenced composition studies.

Burke's key term is *rhetoric*. This selection means that he deals with matters of doubt and uncertainty in human relations. He defines human beings as *animal symbolicum*, symbol-using, symbol-misusing, and symbol-abusing animals; inventors of the negative, we are separated from our natural condition by instruments we make, goaded by the spirit of hierarchy, and rotten with perfection (1966, 16). Burke's overall motive is to help people come to terms, not to war— *ad bellum purificandum* ([1945] 1962).

What follows from his definition and key term is, first, his attention to motives, symbols and forms, scenes, and the consequences of symbolic actions and, then, his attention to the dialectical relationships among these terms. He assumes, simply and profoundly, that "getting along with people is one devil of a task, but that, in the last analysis, we should all want to get along with people (and do want to)" (1984, 1).

Burke's Theory of Theory

Burke's rhetorical approach to language in general, and theory in particular, reveals the following attitudes toward theory: No theory is true across all time, space, and cultures. Rhetors choose among theories in order to be effective in particular contexts. Theories are abstractions from situations and strategies for encompassing situations; in other words, they are motivated and purposeful actions or practices. Theories, which may also be called *terministic screens* or *perspectives by incongruity*, are also consequential in that, as they provide a focus on the subject, they dictate a focus off of it. Burke's own theory of theory and his theory of language as symbolic action are not true. Rather, they are rhetoric; that is, they are motivated and consequential and must be judged on the basis of how well they work in particular contexts.

Burke's theory of theory can be summarized in several quotes and a representative anecdote. He begins with the fact that "all living things are Critics" in that they can revise their "critical appraisals" and "interpret the signs about them" (1954, 5). He then explains that "the experimental, speculative technique made available by speech would seem to single out the human species as the only one possessing an equipment for going beyond criticism of experience to a criticism of criticism" (1954, 5). On a daily basis, all humans theorize and practice.

Second, Burke argues:

We must keep trying anything and everything, improvising, borrowing from others, developing from others, dialectically using one text as comment upon another, schematizing; using the incentive to new wanderings, returning from these excursions to schematize again, being oversubtle where the straining seems to promise some further glimpses, and making amends by reduction to very simple anecdotes. (1950, 265)

Burke does not restrict himself to any one school, mode, or period of criticism: the theorist, like the rhetorician, uses whatever will work in a given context. The "main ideal of criticism" is "to use all that there is to use" ([1941] 1967, 23).

Third, Burke says that "the universe would appear to be something like a cheese; it can be sliced in an infinite number of ways—and when one has chosen his own pattern of slicing, he finds that other men's cuts fall at the wrong places" (1954, 103). Theories are matters for debate and argument, collaboratively constructed and reconstructed within discourse communities to get things done. Our theories are motivated cuts with real consequences, and, therefore, we must learn to work out how to divide and distribute the cheese without resorting to war and famine.

Theory of Language as Symbolic Action

Burke's action theory of language can be placed productively in many contexts, from Ernst Cassirer's theory of symbolic forms to J. L. Austin's speech act theory and to modernism in the 1920s (the subject of Jack Selzer's recent book, *Kenneth Burke in Greenwich Village: Conversing with the Moderns, 1915–1931*). Locating Burke's theory of language in these contexts provides a perspective by incongruity and implicit critique.

Situating Burke's theory, fully elaborated in *Language as Symbolic Action* (1966), in the context of his first work of criticism, *Counter-Statement* ([1931]

1968), shows how Burke revises terms, such as "form," "symbol," and "art," for his own rhetorical purposes. Most people know Burke by his Pentad, consisting of the five terms of dramatism—act, scene, agent, agency, and purpose. What is not heeded often enough is how Burke, immediately recognizing the limitations of his Pentad, does what he does with any formulation—he revises it. He recommends the ratios among the terms for analysis, so that, for example, instead of looking only at the act, he looks at the act/scene ratio. Burke thus revises his 5-term analytical machine into a 25-term apparatus.

But he does not stop there, lest his critical machine might be too reductive or be used reductively. He explains that the Pentad resulted from the fact he had five children and then adds a sixth term, attitude, thereby multiplying his perspectives dramatically. Although Burke's dramatism will be discussed elsewhere in this volume, it is critical to realize a principle here about Burkean theories: Burke's Pentad has been adopted because, unlike most of his work, it is relatively explicit, static, and transportable across contexts, (even though Burke's revisions of the Pentad were attempts to prevent such arhetorical uses).

In sum, Burke's theory of language as action is primarily a theory of language as action, revisionary in two senses of that term. Whatever Burke sets up—whatever becomes "rotten with perfection"—he revises. He translates what *is* into what *might be*, and he always looks at matters *as if* they were other than they appear to be. He argues that language and literature should be understood as equipment for living and strategies for coping.

In *Counter-Statement*, Burke outlines a rhetorical writing process: first the poet selects a symbol (defined by Burke as an abstraction from a situation); the poet then individuates that form, which readers later reindividuate, according to their motives and to the constraints of the situation. There must be some margin of overlap, some identification, between writer and reader for communication and persuasion to occur. In his rhetoric, forms, symbols, and words are not self-contained entities removed from the world; they are shared strategies for encompassing a situation.

With his shift from language as an abstract object to the *act* of abstraction, Burke redefines it. While he believes that language constructs our worlds and ourselves, Burke has no doubt that the world also exists apart from us: "And our 'Lexicon' would not for the world make literature and life synonymous since, by comparison in such terms, the meanest life is so overwhelming superior to the noblest poem that illiteracy becomes almost a moral obligation" ([1931] 1968, x).

While Burke might seem to be contradicting himself in saying that language is individual and social, that forms can be understood in isolation or in contexts, and that identity is intact and multiple, what he assumes as a rhetorician is that we use the particular definitions and perceptions that will persuade and help people get along. Burke's rhetoric is grounded in situations in which the " 'collective revelation' of testing and discussion" (1941, 4) determines whether or not language works and is persuasive.

The ultimate test, for Burke, is how useful language is in providing equipment for living and strategies for coping. He locates the hope for peace in people's abilities to use language. Questions of ideology, gender, race, and class are understood as rhetorics. Burke's choices both extend and limit what he can do.

Reception and Significance in Composition Studies

It is difficult to say whether or not Burkean theories have permeated the work of writers in the field of composition because it is not clear whether Burkean theories are exactly, originally, or specifically Burkean. What I mean is that general aspects of Burke's theory of language as symbolic action are shared diversely by many, some of whom never seem to have heard of Burke. It is as William Faulkner said, in response to a question of literary influence, that there seems to be a "pollen of ideas" in the air and that many (including Burke) were similarly pollinated, some of whom (like Burke) reacted allergically: he could not stop acting and reacting in response to the sting of rhetoric.

But what distinguishes Burke from others who share his views of language (as performance, social, constitutive of knowledge, and changing), is his constant dedication to rhetoric and to using language to help people get along. What distinguishes him from most contemporary scholars in composition and rhetoric is that his work has influenced scholars in many other disciplines, notably, Frank Lentricchia, Rene Girard, Wayne Booth, Clifford Geertz, Dell Hymes, and Hayden White.

We in composition have interpreted and cited Burke and claimed him our own, and he has served our profession well. He has helped us understand how writing crosses cultures, professions, disciplines, texts, genres, and people; Burke has demonstrated persuasion across the disciplines. We have used his Pentad and notions of identification, attitude, and forms to support both personal and academic writing, to emphasize invention, style, arrangement, and argument; and to examine issues of race, class, gender, sexual orientation, and health. We have asked of Burke what he asks of his readers: "Now, where are we?"

Burkean theories have most directly influenced the work of W. Ross Winterowd, Richard M. Coe, James A. Berlin, Susan Wells, Tilly Warnock, William A. Covino, and Michael Hassett, among others.

BIBLIOGRAPHY

Primary Texts

Burke, Kenneth. *Attitudes toward History*. 3rd ed. Berkeley: U of California P, 1984.
———. *Counter-Statement*. 1931. Rpt. Berkeley: U of California P, 1968.
———. *A Grammar of Motives*. 1945. Rpt. Berkeley: U of California P, 1962.
———. *Language as Symbolic Action: Essays on Life, Literature, and Method*. Berkeley: U of California P, 1966.
———. *Permanence and Change: An Anatomy of Purpose*. 3rd ed. Berkeley: U of California P, 1954.
———. *The Philosophy of Literary Form*. 1941. Berkeley: U of California P, 1967.
———. *A Rhetoric of Motives*. Berkeley: U of California P, 1950.

————. *The Rhetoric of Religion: Studies in Logology*. Berkeley: U of California P, 1961.

Major Scholarship in Composition

Berlin, James A. *Rhetorics, Poetics, and Cultures: Refiguring College English Studies*. Urbana, IL: NCTE, 1996.

Coe, Richard M. *Process, Form, and Substance: A Rhetoric for Advanced Writers*. 2nd ed. Englewood Cliffs, NJ: Prentice-Hall, 1990.

Covino, William A. *Forms of Wondering: A Dialogue on Writing, for Writers*. Portsmouth, NH: Boynton/Cook, 1990.

————. *Magic, Rhetoric, and Literacy: An Eccentric History of the Composing Imagination*. Albany: State U of NewYork P, 1994.

Hassett, Michael. "Sophisticated Burke: Kenneth Burke as Neosophistic Rhetorician." *Rhetoric Review* 13 (1995): 371–90.

Warnock, Tilly. *Writing Is Critical Action*. Glenview, IL: Scott, Foresman and Company, 1989.

Winterowd, W. Ross. *The Contemporary Writer: A Practical Rhetoric*. 3rd ed. Orlando, FL: Harcourt Brace Jovanovich, 1989.

Wells, Susan. *Sweet Reason: Rhetoric and the Discourse of Modernity*. Chicago: U of Chicago P, 1996.

TILLY WARNOCK

C

CLASSICAL RHETORIC

Summary

Although Western rhetorical practice goes back at least to Homer, classical rhetorical theory began with the ideas and practices of the fifth-century Greek Sophists, a diverse collection of itinerate intellectuals, teachers, and orators who thought of themselves as philosophers or "seekers of wisdom" rather than as rhetoricians.

The "older," or fifth-century, Sophists, whose era extended from approximately 460 to 380 B.C.E., were concerned with a wide range of subjects and influenced by a variety of intellectual, cultural, and political factors—including the philosophical and scientific inquiries begun by the sixth-century natural philosophers, the emergence of literacy, the humanistic challenge to traditional polytheistic beliefs, and the political shift from oligarchy and tyranny to democracy. What they all shared, however, was a philosophical and pedagogical concern with language. In many ways, the Older Sophists' inquiries about language were shaped by the questions raised by natural philosophers such as Parmenides and Empedocles, who were trying to answer basic ontological and epistemological questions—What is? How do we know? Whatever debt the Older Sophists owe to these predecessors, they can be credited with inaugurating a dialogue about the nature of language, its relationship to reality and truth, its social utility, and its educational importance that continues to our day. While the Sophists differed in their theoretical views—and some contemporary scholars argue against group identification—the major Older Sophists shared interconnected beliefs in the contingency of all truth, the incommensurability of language and reality, and the centrality of *logos* (speech, word, thought, reason) in shaping human beliefs and community life. Together they can be said to have invented "rhetorical self-consciousness" (Kerferd, 78).

Although many of the Older Sophists' texts have been lost and those that remain are often fragmentary, their inquiries into *logos* laid the conceptual groundwork for what later became rhetorical theory. Of those usually identified as noteworthy—Protagoras, Gorgias, Antiphon, Hippias, Prodicus, Critias, and Thrasymachus—Protagoras and Gorgias were the most important contributors to later rhetorical theories. Protagoras's fragments (*Fragments* 18–28) and Gorgias's *Encomium on Helen, Defense of Palamedes*, and *On the Nonexistent* or *On Nature* (42–46, 50–63) illustrate the commonalities and distinctions among sophistic thinkers and articulate many of the seminal rhetorical concepts found in sophistic thought.

Protagoras of Abdera (ca. 490–420 B.C.E.) was a friend and confidant of Pericles even though he was a foreigner in Athens. This close association with Athenian democracy at its height influenced Protagoras's views about the nature and purpose of discourse. Three interconnecting fragments suggest Protogoras's philosophy of language and explain his educational approach: the two, or *dissoi*, *logoi*; human measure, and stronger/weaker *logoi*. Protagoras believed that there were always contrary or contradictory versions (*logoi*) regarding phenomena and that the "measure" of each version's truth was a matter of human perspective or frame of reference: "Of all things the measure is human, of things that are, that they are, and of the things that are not, that they are not" (Sprague, 13). Thus, truths varied according to perception and circumstance, the latter being a matter of time (*kairos*) and cultural codes or "laws" (*nomos*).

The discursive practices "invented" by Protagoras—eristics, antilogic debate, the so-called Socratic method of question and answer (Schiappa, *Protagoras and Logos* 162–63)—followed from these notions about the centrality of human perception and the role of language in arriving at contingent truths. Since there were always contrary versions of the truth, these debating techniques were essential to democracy in that they permitted minority opinions to be competitive and to challenge "stronger" or dominant opinions. By teaching ordinary citizens to forward their opinions in the public sphere, Protagoras believed he was teaching *arete*, or virtue, understood by him to mean concrete skills or excellence and to be a necessary and preeminent quality in a democratic society (Schiappa, *Protagoras and Logos* 168–71).

Gorgias of Leontini (ca. 480–375 B.C.E.), a student of Empedocles and the Older Sophist most familiar to contemporary scholars, came as an ambassador to Athens in 427 B.C.E. A consummate orator, he was immediately popular, eventually achieving great financial success as a teacher of Athenian youth. Like Protagoras, Gorgias believed that absolute truth was inaccessible to humans and that probable or contingent truth was knowable yet limited by human perception and circumstance. What distinguished Gorgias's theory from Protagoras's was his concept of *apate*, the deceptive and irrational power of *logos*. Unlike Protagoras, he made no claim to teach *arete* but rather claimed to teach the art of powerful speech.

For Gorgias, external phenomena were incommensurable with *logos*: "For that by which we reveal is *logos*, but *logos* is not substances and existing things. Therefore, we do not reveal existing things to our neighbors, but *logos*, which is something other than substances" (*On the Nonexistent* 46). Thus, *logos* worked by deception in that words "appear to be synonymous with experiences actually perceived and not their mere symbolic representation" (Richard Enos, 78). Since Gorgias saw no clear distinction between the rational and irrational powers of language, his theories regarding *logos* and his oratorical practices drew on both. He advanced antithetical arguments in order to reach probable or "reasonable" conclusions, and he exploited the irrational properties of language—its sound effects and ability to produce evocative mental pictures—to induce *psychagogia* (enchantment of the soul or altered emotional states in listeners). Gorgias contended that most beliefs were based on opinion, not knowledge, and that, given people's inaccurate memory of the past, unreliable apprehension of the present, and ignorance of the future, these opinions could be altered readily through the power of *logos* (*Ecomium on Helen* 52).

Encomium on Helen not only articulates Gorgias's theory of language but also enacts it. In this declamation, Gorgias sets out to replace the culturally dominant, or "stronger," opinion about Helen's responsibility for the Trojan War with the "weaker" opinion that she was not responsible. He does so by analyzing the four possible explanations for Helen's actions and exempting her from responsibility in each case, thus leading listeners to conclude that she is not to be blamed. One of the possible causes considered is Paris's persuasive speech. If this was the cause for her actions, argues Gorgias, then she is blameless since "[s]peech is a powerful lord, which by means of the finest and most invisible body effects the divinest works: it can stop fear and banish grief and create joy and nurture pity" (*Encomium* 52). For Gorgias, *logos* was powerful because it worked on both reason and the emotions; it enabled listeners to consider alternative opinions by "deceptively creat[ing] verbal realities" (Richard Enos, 79). *Encomium on Helen* illustrates the deceptive power of *logos* by matching style to matter: multiple *logoi* are presented syntactically through antithesis and parataxis; the intoxicating or druglike effects of *logos* are effected through rhyme, rhythm, and various tropes and schemes.

In Gorgias's theory and practice, the analytical structuring of multiple *logoi* and the stylistic creation of multiple realities were ways of coming to know. Gorgias's recognition that *logos*, like a drug, could be used for good or ill and his attempts to understand and explicate its "technology" through performance and instruction can be read as an ethical concern for ensuring that the most probable or best available version of truth at a given time will prevail.

Rather than an abrupt break between the Sophists and their successors, we find an evolution in rhetorical theory, with Isocrates and Plato developing separate strands of sophistic thought (Bizzell and Herzberg, 24). While Plato took on and attacked their philosophical notions about the relationship between language and knowledge/truth, Isocrates, the student of Gorgias, took up and extended the sophistic concern with the role of *logos* in civic life.

Isocrates (436–338 B.C.E.) began as a logographer or speech writer but is best known as an educator, who founded one of the most successful schools in Athens. In *Against the Sophists*, he attempts to distinguish himself from the excesses of those who taught verbal tricks and pyrotechnics and who engaged in eristic wrangling about abstruse matters far removed from the practical concerns of civic life. By contrast, he dedicated his career to advocating the ethical use of "eloquence" in civic life and to preparing civic leaders through training in *logos*. Despite his condemnation of some sophistic practices, he shared many of the Older Sophists' beliefs and practices. Isocrates believed in the impossibility of absolute knowledge, the necessity of fitting discourse to the kairotic moment, and the persuasive power of style. His educational philosophy is best articulated in the *Antidosis*, where he argues that natural talent, instruction, and practice work together to produce educated citizens (Isocrates, 291, 293).

Plato (ca. 428–47 B.C.E.), who is often represented in histories of rhetoric as the great enemy of rhetoric, actually plays an important role in the history of rhetorical theory, offering, as he does, a contrasting *logos* regarding rhetoric, which George Kennedy calls "philosophic rhetoric" (41–60). While Plato agreed with the Sophists about the unreliability of human sense perception, he did not agree that human beings had no access to higher truth. For Plato, higher or absolute truth was accessible, however imperfectly, through reason or the soul's recollection of past existence in the metaphysical realm of Ideal Forms. The mode of recollection was dialectical reasoning, a technique that he saw as the antidote or replacement for various forms of sophistic debate, particularly antilogy, which led, in Plato's view, to only probable or uncertain truths.

Plato's method of discrediting various sophistic beliefs and replacing them with his own philosophical framework is through dissociation, that is, through differentiating terms and marking one term as positive, the other as negative (Richard Enos, 78). Thus, in the *Gorgias*, the character of Socrates establishes distinctions between belief and knowledge and true and false art, the former, of course, being associated with Gorgias, the representative Sophist, the latter with Socrates. Plato's objections to sophistic rhetoric were its concern with conventional wisdom or opinion rather than transcendent truth, its aim to create belief rather than certain knowledge, its failure to distinguish between false and true *logoi*, and its belief that morality, or the "good," was a matter of perspective, contingent on the historical moment and cultural location.

In the *Phaedrus*, Plato rehabilitates and redefines rhetoric as the servant of philosophy, thus appropriating its power to forward the true knowledge discovered or recovered through dialectic. As an epistemological method, dialectic first sought agreed-upon definitions from which to proceed, whereas antilogy proceeded from contrary definitions or accounts. So, for example, the case of Helen's guilt or innocence in Plato's dialectical method would be determined only after a definition of responsibility had been established from which to judge her guilt or innocence. As articulated in the *Phaedrus*, dialectic is a method of cross-examination or question and answer that operates by division and collection to arrive at "true" definitions, which allow the philosopher to make distinctions between the concept and its opposite, the concept and its component parts, and so on. Thus, the true or ideal orator must first discover the truth before engaging in rhetoric:

A man must first know the truth about every single subject on which he speaks or writes. He must be able to define each in terms of a universal class that stands by itself. . . . He must then discover the kind of speech that matches each type of nature. . . . Not until a man acquires this capacity will it be possible to produce speech in a scientific way, in so far as its nature permits such treatment, either for purposes of instruction or of persuasion. (72)

Related to Plato's subordination of rhetoric to dialectic was his attack on the new technology of writing. For Plato, writing was even further removed from the face-to-face dialectical encounter between two philosophers than "true" rhetoric, which Plato describes as the "living, animate discourse of a man who really knows" (*Phaedrus* 70). Ironically, Plato had to use both rhetoric and writing to critique the two, and for that reason he wrote dialogues, the closest written simulation of dialectic. By positioning rhetoric as posterior and subservient to dialectic or philosophy, Plato reserved his "philosophic rhetoric" for the privileged few, claiming for its province the quest for eternal, metaphysical truths and dismissing its role as a democratic art concerned with the discovery of contingent truths regarding civic and social policies.

Undoubtedly the best known of the classical rhetoricians, Aristotle (384–322 B.C.E.) drew on both the rhetorical theories of the Sophists and the philosophy of his teacher, Plato, to create a comprehensive theoretical framework in *On Rhetoric*. For Aristotle, transcendent truth, or what Plato would call knowledge, was available through scientific demonstration and formal logic. However, Aristotle, with the Sophists, believed that there were other matters having to do with civic life about which only probable truth or knowledge was possible. In Aristotle's view, this was rhetoric's proper province.

Book 1 of Aristotle's *On Rhetoric* can be read as a direct response to Plato's critique of rhetoric in the *Gorgias* and his proposal of a "scientific" methodology for producing philosophic rhetoric in the *Phaedrus*. Specifically, Aristotle counters Plato's claim that rhetoric is not an art by pointedly calling it a "true art" and the counterpart of dialectic, not its inferior. Like dialectic, Aristotle argues, rhetoric has no subject of its own; rather it is a method of discovering probable truths about a range of subjects. For Aristotle, dialectic was distinguished from rhetoric in that the former proceeded interactively to make genus/species distinctions about general subjects like "justice," while the latter proceeded to discover the "available means of persuasion" regarding particular subjects or cases. Indeed, Aristotle defines rhetoric as "an ability, in each [particular] case, to see the available means of persuasion" (*On Rhetoric* 36–37).

Importantly, then, Aristotle's definition of rhetoric turned on invention or strategies of inquiry. In Aristotle's system of beliefs, knowledge of subject matter lay outside of rhetoric and was something the rhetorician brought to the rhetorical situation. What the art of rhetoric provided was a "scientific" method of analyzing knowledge of a subject matter and the rhetorical situation (exigence and audience) for the "available means of persuasion." Although part of Aristotle's contribution to rhetorical theory lies in his systematization of prior rhetorical practices and concepts such as the three common rhetorical situations (political deliberation, legal deliberation, and ceremonial occasions), his chief contribution is his theory of invention.

Although a complete discussion of Aristotle's theory of invention is beyond the scope of this entry, requiring as it would a discussion of Aristotle's related writings on analytics, ethics, politics, and metaphysics, his concept of the *topoi*, the three artistic appeals (*ethos, pathos, logos*), and the enthymeme deserve mention. The *topoi*, a metaphorical term referring to the "places" or "haunts" where the rhetor searches for effective arguments, were, for Aristotle, a central and teachable part of rhetorical *techne* (art). His contribution was to systematize potential lines of reasoning and potential ethical and emotional appeals so that rhetors might acquire the "ability" of discovering all "available means of persuasion" in a given case.

Notable about the artistic appeals—the appeal based on the rhetor's character, the appeal to the audience's emotions regarding the subject, and the appeal to the audience's reason—are their consideration of the whole person and their dependence on the rhetor's knowledge of the audience as well as of the subject. To "invent" artistic appeals or proofs, the rhetor needed to understand what the audience respected and valued in a speaker, what range of emotions were possible regarding the topic, and what the audience would accept as premises from which to draw conclusions or make judgments. Thus, implicit in Aristotle's theory of rhetoric was dialogic engagement between rhetors and audiences.

Equally central to Aristotle's theory of invention was his concept of the enthymeme or deductive argument, which, with example or inductive argument, comprised the two bases for logical proof in *On Rhetoric*. The enthymeme, sometimes defined as a rhetorical or abbreviated syllogism, was geared to general audiences who have difficulty following a complicated chain of reasoning. Often enthymemes drew their premises from maxims or conventional wisdom and commonsense probabilities, thereby invoking the audience's prior beliefs and assumptions in order to persuade them to accept the rhetor's conclusions or judgment about a given case. Thus, the culturally bound knowledge that was so central to sophistic epistemology was tacitly acknowledged in Aristotle's rhetorical theory. In short, the enthymeme encapsulated Aristotle's epistemological beliefs regarding probable knowledge, working not only "locally as a formal structure for [a particular] argument'' but also ''teleologically, as the theoretical basis for inquiry into probable knowledge'' (Gage 157).

Although the Roman rhetoricians contributed little new to rhetorical theory, they preserved, codified, and expanded the theories generated by the Greek rhetoricians. Perhaps the most significant Greek rhetorical concept passed down through the Romans was *stasis* theory, developed by the Greek rhetorician Hermagoras, whose texts were lost but whose ideas survived in the anonymously authored *Rhetorica ad Herennium* (ca. 84 B.C.E.); Cicero's *De inventione* (84 B.C.E.); and Quintilian's *Institutio oratoria* (95 C.E.). Stasis theory extended Aristotle's notion that rhetors needed to understand the ''elements'' in question in any case by developing a sequence of four questions (conjectural, definitional, qualitative, and procedural) for determining the point at issue, the position on which the rhetor must take a stand.

Other Roman contributions to the preservation and elaboration of rhetorical theory include *Rhetorica ad Herennium*'s comprehensive treatment of all five canons of rhetoric; Cicero's urbane portrayal of the liberally educated, ideal rhetorician in *De Oratore* (55 B.C.E.); and Quintilian's twelve-book, detailed curriculum (the *Institutes*) for the training of orators, ''good men speaking well,'' from birth through adulthood.

Reception and Significance in Composition Studies

Dissatisfied with college writing instruction and its lack of a conceptual framework, Albert Kitzhaber, in a 1962 *College English* essay, identified the problem as a loss of the classical rhetorical tradition and proposed as a solution an approach to instruction based on the 2,500-year-old rhetorical tradition. Taking up this call for a revival of classical rhetoric were such scholars as Edward P. J. Corbett, Wayne Booth, and James Kinneavy. Probably the most influential of these early revivalist texts in composition studies was Edward P. J. Corbett's *Classical Rhetoric for the Modern Student* ([1965] 1990), which offered students and writing instructors an updated textbook version of Aristotelian rhetoric.

Early reception of classical rhetoric in composition studies was often reverential and shaped by the pedagogical imperative implicit in Kitzhaber's call for its revival. These responses, which Kathleen Welch labels the ''Heritage School'' (6–33), treated ancient texts as artifacts that could be objectively interpreted without regard for cultural context or the problems of translation. The resulting interpretations often reduced complex classical concepts to formulas and taxonomies that could be easily imported into teaching practice. Welch contends that this formulaic and reductionist approach explains the reaction against classical rhetorical theory by some composition scholars, most notably C. H. Knoblauch and Lil Brannon, whose *Rhetorical Traditions and the Teaching of Writing* describes classical rhetoric as ''old-time religion'' and blames it for the emergence of current-traditional approaches to writing instruction.

An alternative to Heritage School reception is what Welch calls the Dialectical School of reception, which ''resist[s] the lure of transforming classical rhetoric

into accessible information'' and instead contextualizes classical texts, acknowledges multiple translations of key terms, identifies historiographic methods, and
draws on interdisciplinary scholarship from philosophy, speech communications,
and classics to produce self-consciously interpretative accounts (25–26).

Since the early to mid-1980s, the reception of classical rhetoric in our field
has taken a decidedly critical and political turn, resulting in four strands of
scholarship: debates about historiography, critical reconsiderations of canonical
figures, rehistorization of classical rhetoric to incorporate the Sophists, and feminist and gender-studies interrogations and reformulations of rhetorical
traditions.

Beginning with John Schilb's 1986 ''The History of Rhetoric and the Rhetoric
of History,'' which was followed the next year by an issue of *Pre/Text* devoted
to historiography, the debate about historiography has invigorated and productively complicated composition's reception of the classical tradition. Some
scholars have drawn on the theoretical work of Nietzsche, Foucault, Marx, Hayden White, and Dominick LaCapra to call into question history's truth claims,
linearity, and supposed disinterestedness. Others, like Susan Jarratt and Victor
Vitanza, propose subversive methods of history writing that defy the notion of
linearity, play with style, and expand the texts and artifacts considered rhetorical.
Still others, notably Edward Schiappa, argue for the continuing validity of traditional hermeneutic methods such as ''*ipsissima verba* primacy, triangulation,
linguistic density, and resonance'' on the grounds that though all history is
interpretation, some interpretations are more ''defensible'' than others (*Protagoras and Logos* 32–35). Perhaps the most influential critical reconsideration of
major figures is Jasper Neel's work on Plato and Aristotle. By providing deconstructive readings of these canonical figures, Neel aims to ''neutralize'' what
he considers their deleterious effects on rhetoric generally and composition studies particularly. In the case of Plato, he directly takes on the philosopher's
attempt to forever subordinate rhetoric and writing to philosophy and speech
and in his thoroughgoing interrogation of Aristotle's work, he attempts to undo
the stranglehold that the Aristotelian system, with its privileging of hierarchical
and colonial ideologies, continues to have on composition studies.

Whether or not the rehabilitation of the Sophists is a ''mirage'' or an ''oasis''
as Edward Schiappa suggests (*Protagoras and Logos*) the important work on
sophistic rhetorics by Susan Jarratt, John Poulakos, Richard Enos, and Schiappa
himself has changed forever the way we see the whole of classical rhetoric. As
Cheryl Glenn would have it, the work on the Sophists, along with other new
scholarship, has remade the rhetorical map. Not only has this work offered us
rich alternative theories of rhetoric, it has provided a critical lens for rereading
the work of their more famous successors, Plato and Aristotle.

Similarly, the work of feminist and gender-studies scholars has remapped the
territory of classical rhetoric. This diverse and provocative strand of scholarship
includes work that ''writes'' women into the history of rhetoric (Glenn, ''Sex,
Lies, and Manuscript''; Jarratt and Ong; Swearingen); work that reinterprets

canonical texts using gender as an analytic category (duBois; Jarratt and Ong); work that identifies new genres of rhetorical practice such as women's speech performances in religious festivals (Jarratt, "Speaking to the Past," 204); and work that challenges the earlier-mentioned efforts to include women in classical historical accounts, recommending rather a "*radical* contextualization of all rhetorical acts . . . to forge a new storying of our tradition" (Biesecker, 147). Theoretical and methodological disagreements aside, as a whole, this work is "revitalizing rhetorical theory by shaking the conceptual foundations of rhetorical study itself" (Glenn, "Remapping Rhetorical Territory," 294).

For those who initiated the revival of classical rhetoric in the 1960s, the significance of this tradition was in its potential for disciplinary legitimation and foundational knowledge. While the study of classical rhetoric may have offered some of the former, providing us as it does with never-ending topics for scholarly inquiry and linking our field with work in other disciplines, it certainly did not supply the latter. Indeed, instead of producing foundational knowledge, the study of rhetoric has called into question the status of knowledge and led to a view of knowledge as rhetorically constituted. Thus, its value to contemporary composition lies in its resistance to univocal, authoritative knowledge and in its encouragement of continual inquiry and critique.

As an adaptable framework for producing and analyzing all forms of discourse, classical rhetoric offers a rich heuristic for teaching and scholarship. Sharon Crowley's *Ancient Rhetorics for Contemporary Students* and the recent call for undergraduate courses in historical rhetoric are testimony to the renewed interest in classical rhetoric's pedagogical potential. Similarly, the interdisciplinary interest in the rhetoric of inquiry and in rhetoric as a critical method testifies to its value as a scholarly tool. Finally, the multiple and contested historical narratives that constitute classical rhetoric offer us a valuable, dialectical perspective on the present. In both their resonance and their dissonance with the present, these narratives instruct, provoke, and enlighten. As Nietzsche said of classical study in *The Use and Abuse of History*: "I do not know what meaning classical scholarship may have for our time except in its being 'unseasonable'— that is, contrary to our time, and yet with an influence on it for the benefit, it may be hoped, of a future time"(60).

BIBLIOGRAPHY

Primary Texts

Aristotle. *On Rhetoric*. Trans. George A. Kennedy. New York: Oxford UP, 1991.

Cicero. *De Oratore*. Vol. III, trans. E.W. Sutton and H. Rackham. Vol. IV, trans. H. Rackham. Loeb Classical Library. Cambridge, MA: Harvard UP, 1942.

———. *De inventione*. Trans. H. M. Hubbell. Cambridge, MA: Harvard UP, 1949.

Dissoi Logoi. Rpt. in *The Older Sophists*. Ed. Rosamond Kent Sprague. Columbia: S Carolina UP, 1987, 279–93.

Gorgias. *Defense of Palamedes*. Rpt. in *The Older Sophists*. Ed. Rosamond Kent Sprague. Columbia: S Carolina UP, 1987, 54–63.

————. *Encomium on Helen*. Rpt. in *The Older Sophists*. Ed. Rosamond Kent Sprague. Columbia: S Carolina UP, 1987, 50–54.

————. *"On the Nonexistent,"* or *"On Nature."* Rpt. in *The Older Sophists*. Ed. Rosamond Kent Sprague. Columbia: S Carolina UP, 1987, 42–46.

Isocrates. *Isocrates in Three Volumes*. Vol. 2. Trans. George Norlin. Loeb Classical Library. Cambridge, MA: Harvard UP, 1929.

Plato. *Gorgias*. Trans. W. C. Hembold. New York: Macmillan, 1952.

————. *Phaedrus*. Trans. W. C. Hembold and W. G. Rabinowitz. New York: Macmillan, 1956.

Protagoras. *Fragments*. Rpt. in *The Older Sophists*. Ed. Rosamond Kent Sprague. Columbia: S Carolina UP, 1987, 18–24.

Quintilian. *On the Teaching of Speaking and Writing*. Ed. James J. Murphy. Trans. John Selby Watson. Carbondale: S Illinois UP, 1987.

Rhetorica ad Herennium. Trans. Harry Kaplan. Cambridge, MA: Harvard UP, 1954.

Sprague, Rosamond Kent, ed. *The Older Sophists*. Columbia: S Carolina UP, 1972.

Major Scholarship in Composition

Biesecker, Barbara. "Coming to Terms with Recent Attempts to Write Women into the History of Rhetoric." *Philosophy and Rhetoric* 25 (1992): 140–61.

Bizzell, Patricia, "Opportunities for Feminist Research in the History of Rhetoric." *Rhetoric Review* 11.1 (1992): 50–58.

Bizzell, Patricia, and Bruce Herzberg. *The Rhetorical Tradition*. Boston: Bedford/St. Martin's, 1990.

Booth, Wayne C. *The Rhetoric of Fiction*. 2nd ed. Chicago: U of Chicago P, 1983.

————. "The Rhetorical Stance." *College Composition and Communication* 14 (1963): 139–45.

Connors, Robert, Lisa S. Ede, and Andrea A. Lunsford, eds. *Essays on Classical Rhetoric and Modern Discourse*. Carbondale: S Illinois UP, 1984.

Corbett, Edward P.J. *Classical Rhetoric for the Modern Student*. 1965. Rpt. 3rd ed. New York: Oxford UP, 1990.

Covino, William A. *The Art of Wondering: A Revisionist Return to the History of Rhetoric*. Portsmouth, NH: Boynton/Cook, 1988.

Crowley, Sharon. *Ancient Rhetorics for Contemporary Students*. New York: Macmillan, 1994.

————. "Of Gorgias and Grammatology." *College Composition and Communication* 30 (1979): 279–84.

duBois, Page. "The Platonic Appropriation of Reproduction." In *Sowing the Body: Ancient Representations of Women*. Chicago: U of Chicago P, 1988, 169–81.

Enos, Richard. *Greek Rhetoric before Aristotle*. Prospect Heights, IL: Waveland P, 1993.

Enos, Theresa, ed. *Learning from the Histories of Rhetoric*. Carbondale: S Illinois UP, 1993.

Gage, John. "An Adequate Epistemology for Composition." In *Essays on Classical Rhetoric and Modern Discourse*. Ed. Robert Connors, Lisa S. Ede, and Andrea A. Lunsford. Carbondale: S Illinois UP, 1984, 152–69.

Glenn, Cheryl. "Remapping Rhetorical Territory." *Rhetoric Review* 13 (1995): 287–303.

————. "Sex, Lies, and Manuscript: Refiguring Aspasia in the History of Rhetoric." *College Composition and Communication* 45 (1994): 189–99.

Horner, Winifred. *Historical Rhetoric: An Annotated Bibliography of Selected Sources in English.* Boston: G. K. Hall, 1980.

———. *The Present State of Scholarship in Historical and Contemporary Rhetoric.* Columbia: U of Missouri P, 1983.

Jarratt, Susan. *Rereading the Sophists: Classical Rhetoric Refigured.* Carbondale and Edwardsville: S Illinois UP, 1991.

———. "Speaking to the Past: Feminist Historiography in Rhetoric." *Pre/Text* 11.3–4 (1990): 189–209.

———. "Toward a Sophistic Historiography." *Pre/Text* 8.12 (1987): 9–26.

Jarratt, Susan, and Rory Ong. "Aspasia: Rhetoric, Gender, and Colonial History." In *Reclaiming Rhetorica.* Ed. Andrea A. Lunsford. Pittsburgh, PA: U of Pittsburgh P, 1995, 9–23.

Kennedy, George. *Classical Rhetoric and Its Christian and Secular Traditions.* Chapel Hill: U of N Carolina P, 1980.

Kerferd, G. B. *The Sophistic Movement.* London: Cambridge UP, 1981.

Kinneavy, James. *A Theory of Discourse.* Englewood Cliffs, NJ: Prentice-Hall, 1971.

Kitzhaber, Albert R. "New Perspectives of Teaching Composition." *College English* 23 (1962): 440–44.

Knoblauch, C. J., and Lil Brannon. *Rhetorical Traditions and the Teaching of Writing.* Upper Montclair, NJ: Boynton/Cook, 1984.

Lunsford, Andrea A., ed. *Reclaiming Rhetorica.* Pittsburgh, PA: U of Pittsburgh P, 1995.

Murphy, James, ed. *The Rhetorical Tradition and Modern Writing.* New York: MLA, 1982.

Murphy, James, et al. *A Synoptic History of Classical Rhetoric.* 2nd ed. Davis, CA: Hermagoras P, 1995.

Neel, Jasper. *Aristotle's Voice.* Carbondale: Southern Illinois UP, 1994.

———. *Plato, Derrida, and Writing.* Carbondale: Southern Illinois UP, 1988.

Nietzsche, Friedrich. "On the Uses and Disadvantages of History for Life." In *Untimely Meditations.* Trans. R. J. Hollingdale. Cambridge: Cambridge UP, 1983, 57–123.

Ong, Walter. *Orality and Literacy.* London: Methuen, 1982.

Peaden, Catherine. "Feminist Theories, Historiographies, and Histories of Rhetoric: The Role of Feminism in Historical Studies." In *Rhetoric and Ideology: Compositions and Criticisms of Power.* Ed. Charles Kneupper. Arlington, TX: Rhetoric Society of America, 1989, 116–25.

Poulakos, John. "Rhetoric, the Sophists, and the Possible." *Communications Monographs* 51 (1984): 215–25.

———. *Sophistical Rhetoric in Classical Greece.* Columbia: U of S Carolina P, 1995.

———. "Towards a Sophistic Definition of Rhetoric." *Philosophy and Rhetoric* 16 (1983): 35–48.

Poulakos, Takis, ed. *Rethinking the History of Rhetoric: Multidisciplinary Essays on the Rhetorical Tradition.* Boulder, CO: Westview P, 1993.

Pre/Text 8 (1987).

Schiappa, Edward. *Protagoras and Logos.* Columbia: U of S Carolina P, 1991.

———. ed. *Landmark Essays on Classical Rhetoric.* Davis, CA: Hermagoras P, 1994.

———. "Sophistic Rhetoric: Oasis or Mirage?" *Rhetoric Review* 10.1 (1991): 5–18.

Schilb, John. "The History of Rhetoric and the Rhetoric of History." *Pre/Text* 7.1–2 (1986): 11–34.

Swearingen, C. Jan. "A Lover's Discourse: Diotima, Logos, and Desire." In *Reclaiming*

98-863

Rhetorica. Ed. Andrea A. Lunsford. Pittsburgh, PA: U of Pittsburgh P, 1995, 25–51.

Vitanza, Victor. " 'Notes' Towards Historiographies of Rhetorics." *Pre/Text* 8.1–2 (1987): 63–125.

————, ed. *Writing Histories of Rhetoric*. Carbondale: Southern Illinois UP, 1994.

Welch, Kathleen. *The Contemporary Reception of Classical Rhetoric*. Hillsdale, NJ: Erlbaum, 1990.

ALICE GILLAM

COGNITIVE DEVELOPMENTAL THEORY

Summary

Cognitive developmental theory emerges as a deviation from the lines of thought preceding it. The eighteenth century may generally be seen as the dividing line between the so-called philosophical and psychological approaches to rhetoric (Barritt and Kroll, 49). The shift to the psychological approach spawned at least two divergent lines of inquiry. One thread, the more dominant approach, focused research on the study of the listener-reader. Both psychological and communication research during much of the twentieth century continued this emphasis with studies of audience response and speaker reaction to feedback.

An alternative tradition, which has had more promise for research on composing, shifted the focus from the mind of the receiver of the stimuli to the study of the cognitive processes of the mind itself. The cognitive developmental strand, with its roots in Europe, especially in the work of Piaget, was concerned with the nature of knowledge and with the structures and processes by which it is acquired. David Elkind credits Piaget with creating a new discipline, genetic epistemology, which he termed an "experimental philosophy which seeks to answer epistemological questions through the developmental study of the child" (v). Elkind claims that Piaget's theory, "in the most general sense, is that mental growth is governed by a continual activity aimed at balancing the intrusions of the social and physical environment with the organism's need to conserve its structural systems" (v).

In both methods and theories, Piaget is a seminal influence in the understanding of cognitive growth. Piaget's methods, with their reliance on close and careful observation, came as a protest against "armchair epistemology." Cognition, according to Piaget's model, is highly active, with knowledge being constructed rather than copied directly. Contributions from Piaget's work significant to composition include his theories of constructivism, adaptation, developmental stages, and egocentrism.

Constructivism is expressed in Piaget's notion of adaptation, with its two complementary and simultaneous aspects: assimilation and accommodation. Assimilation describes the ways in which humans as active knowers, "reconstrue and reinterpret the environment to make it fit with [their] own existing framework" (Flavell, Miller, and Miller, 4). Accommodation is the process of adjusting one's own knowledge to external events and objects. Flavell, in explaining Piaget's idea, claims that "in any cognitive encounter with the environment, assimilation and accommodation are of equal importance and must always occur together in a mutually dependent way" (5). Piaget's explanation of cognitive maturation describes it as a slow and gradual process occurring each time the child's mind attempts to assimilate a new object and its associated concepts, thereby stretching a little. This leads to accommodation and, thus, in slow incremental steps, there is mental growth.

According to Piaget, this gradual development leads to definable stages of development. Piaget sees these stages as fixed and argues that children have to proceed through them all. Much of his work focuses on describing these stages: the sensorimotor, occurring in infancy; the preoperational, occurring in ages 2 to 7; the concrete operational, occurring in ages 7 to 11; and the formal operational, occurring in ages 11 to 15. Piaget did not consider cognitive development beyond the stage of formal operations.

Piaget uses the term *cognitive egocentrism* to designate the initial inability of a child to decenter, that is, to differentiate or distinguish clearly between one's own point of view and another's. This is characterized in young children as an inability to shift the given cognitive perspective and the tendency to instead assume that the perspective of others is the same as one's own (Flavell, Miller, and Miller, 197). However, researchers have questioned the assumption that the inability is outgrown by identifying a tendency to return to egocentric thought thoughout our lives when in an unfamiliar environment or engaged in an especially difficult task.

While Piaget's later work de-emphasizes developmental stages, much of his work was devoted to their study and description. Critics of Piaget's work find the question of how cognitive growth is best described and explained still unsettled. Although considered controversial at the time he proposed them, several of Piaget's assumptions are now widely accepted: knowledge is highly organized; learning involves the assimilation of new ideas to previous knowledge; and intellectual development is an active construction on the part of the knower (Moshman and Franks, 13).

In his third edition of *Cognitive Development* (1993), Flavell claims the main strategy for studying cognitive development to be the information-processing approach, a shift from his 1977 position, when he argued that the Piagetian view appeared more promising than the information-processing view. By 1993 Flavell argues for a broad definition of cognition that recognizes the "complex interweaving" (3) of the many aspects of cognitive functioning. He claims four main strands of cognitive development research at this time: the Piagetian, information processing, neo-Piagetian, and contextual.

Generally, the information-processing model imagines the mind as a complex cognitive system. Work from several fields has been influential: from psychology, Bruner, Goodnow, and Austin in A *Study of Thinking*; from linguistics, Miller in "The Magic Number Seven," as well as Chomsky's work; and from computer science, the work of Newell and Simon. Newell and Simon suggest that the new common emphasis "was not the investigation of problem solving, but rather the exploration of complex processes and the acceptance of the need to be explicit about internal, symbolic mechanisms" (4).

In an attempt to provide an explanation of what the mind does as it processes information, this approach makes use of observations of behaviors to determine which strategy is being used. For instance, the time it takes to answer a question can provide evidence of how much processing is taking place. Errors in performance can be studied. Verbal responses such as hesitations, pauses, becoming inarticulate, and verbal contradictions can be studied for evidence of cognitive activity. The researcher attempts to break the cognitive processes into units and then make inferences about which cognitive procedures are being used. No stages are posited. However, changes from one strategy to another are qualitative.

The neo-Piagetians are researcher-theorists who generally agree with much of Piaget's work, but who also recognize problems in his theories, which they address using the information-processing model. Problematic for this group is Piaget's concept of stages of development, since children within a certain stage often do not demonstrate the behavior of that stage, as well as his lack of systematic data on the contexts within which his experiments were conducted.

Case (as explained by Flavell) accounts for the unevenness of cognitive development by adding a multilevel cognitive system. He also includes new emphases for cognitive change, including mental ability and problem solving procedures (Flavell, Miller, and Miller, 14). For both the information-processing model and the neo-Piagetians, cognitive development comes with "improved procedures for problem solving and increased processing capacity, speed and efficiency" (17). Voss, considering problem-solving by experts and novices, studies informal reasoning and ill-defined problems, and suggests ways in which such research may enhance our understanding of complex tasks such as writing.

The contextual approach finds its roots in the work of Vygotsky. The difference between this approach and the three others has to do with social context. The three preceding approaches "assign some role to social influences on cognitive change" (15), while contextualists focus attention on the social. While there are variations of contextualism, there is a shared belief "that the cognitive and the social are inextricably connected" (Flavell, Miller, and Miller, 15).

There are two general levels of social context. The first is the social-cultural-historical moment in which a child exists. The second level connects to the day-to-day interactions that a child has with significant figures in his or her life. The metaphor used by the contextualists is "child as apprentice" (Flavell, Miller, and Miller, 16). Vygotsky's "zone of proximal development" is an important concept for contextualists, with cognitive change resulting from assistance by a competent peer or adult and with engagement in increasingly more difficult tasks.

Several researchers have sought to develop theories of cognitive development in late adolescence and adulthood since Piaget's claim for formal operations as the final stage of development presents a problem in Piagetian theory. Perry developed a model of intellectual development based on a study of students at Harvard in the 1950s. Belenky and colleagues articulated a similar cognitive developmental theory focusing on the intellectual development of women. Basseches proposed dilectical thinking as a third alternative to universalistic thought and relativistic thought. Dialectic builds upon, but is more complex than, the concept of system. While formal thinking is systematic, dialectic thinking is metasystematic. Basseches's work on dialectical thinking is best defined as a developmental possibility rather than as a specific stage that all adults will attain. Neimark identifies difficulties in defining a mature thinker. Her idealized mature thinker is "an individual who transforms experience in thought in a systematic, deliberate manner in order to organize it and evaluate it within a coherent broader framework" (56).

Despite differences in terminology, researchers on adult development associate mature thinking with metacognitive and metasystematic qualities, defined by an ability to both recognize and reflect on the constraints of alternative paradigms of knowledge making. Basseches locates higher education as one of the primary sites for the development of mature thinking.

Reception and Significance in Composition Studies

Although the emergence of composition studies is not easily tied to a specific date or event, the early 1970s is seen as the start of serious, scholarly investigation of writing. Prior to that time, theoretical and social developments emerging in the 1960s made cognitive development particularly welcome in composition studies. Dixon's *Growth through English*, a 1967 report that emerged from the Dartmouth Conference (which had been influenced by the work of Piaget, Vygotsky, and George Kelly [Berlin, 163]), shifted the concern to "learning," that is, to the processes through which children acquire competence or expressiveness in language. The conceptualizations of Moffett in 1968, as well as the emergence of compensatory education programs and open admissions in colleges, highlighted the need for research on composing. In response to dissatisfaction with the simplification of rhetoric as it was appearing in composition textbooks (which had collapsed it to simply the modes of narration, description, and argumentation, all with a common purpose and illustrated with models from the literary tradition), efforts were made to reclaim classical rhetoric and thereby acknowledge different aims in writing with their respective logics (Kinneavy, 178). Jakobson's "Linguistics and Poetics," published in 1967, provided a theoretical model for the functions of language. Britton and his colleagues also disclaimed the modes approach and argued for the primacy of the functions of language. Kinneavy's *A Theory of Discourse* argued for the validity of the aims of discourse model in various fields of language study (178). D'Angelo's *A Conceptual Theory of Rhetoric* addressed the relationship between writing and thinking. Larson recommended the use of heuristic questioning growing from Young, Becker, and Pike's interest in tagmemics. As composition studies reclaimed its rhetorical traditions, it acknowledged connections between cognition and writing.

In early composition research, Rohman and Wlecke suggested three stages in composing: prewriting, writing, and editing. Rohman further suggested that student prewriting activities such as meditations and journal keeping could be taught. Cognitive developmental psychology offered a way to study the invisible process of composing more systematically. Emig, in the United States, began studying the composing process of eight students, while Britton and colleagues, at nearly the same time, were studying the composing processes of students in Great Britain. Both sets of researchers found composing processes to vary depending on the kind of writing being done. Emig found that the composing process described in texts was not consistent with the composing processes of writers. Studying writers at work thus provided a window on composing, which is a cognitive process.

Cooper and Odell, in their *Research in Composing: Points of Departure*, set a new research agenda by moving away from the comparison group studies that had been recommended by Braddock and his coauthors in 1963 in *Research in Written Composition*, a work that sought to bring rigor to composition studies by outlining basic problems in composition research. Odell and Cooper argued that the basic research in composition—the research that would provide a thorough understanding of both writing processes and written products—had yet to be done. Hairston and Emig both claimed that the writing-as-process approach constituted a paradigm shift away from the current-traditional views of writing. Lauer, in "Heuristics and Composition," urged composition researchers to explore theory in areas outside of English studies and rhetoric and suggested cognitive psychology as a particularly fruitful source for the further study of invention.

Numerous studies reflected connections between cognition and writing by studying the writing process. Flower and Hayes used protocol analysis, a methodology borrowed from the social sciences, asking writers to describe their thought processes as they composed aloud. By measuring pause time, a concept from information processing using time spent as an indication of complexity of thought, they developed linguistic and rhetorical hypotheses about composing suggesting a hierarchical rather than a linear process. All writers planned at the sentence level, but experienced writers paused to consider content and rhetorical goals such as audience and the nature of the task. Flower and Hayes created a comprehensive model of composing and pointed to a recursive process in which planning, generating, translating, and editing need to be "juggled" (Flower and Hayes, "The Dynamics of Composing," 31). Such studies have provided new perspectives on invention strategies.

Pianko found that poor writers were unsuccessful because of their failure to reflect on what they were writing. Perl claimed the single most important aspect of successful composing to be rereading a text as one produces it to develop a sense of the emerging structure. The studies of Sommers and Bridwell, both in

1980, focused on revision. In 1981, Matsuhashi studied writers as they paused and planned during composing.

Berlin claims that the influence of cognitive psychology was strong for the ten years from 1975 to 1985. During this time a number of researchers studied texts as a demonstration of cognitive processes (Faigley and Witte; Williams; Hirsch; Gere; Odell; Cooper and Holzman; and Daiker, Kerek, and Morenberg). Cognitive psychology influenced the work describing composing, notably Lunsford; Barritt and Kroll; and Rose (186). Shaughnessy studied "error" in writing as evidence of a larger cognitive process.

While Piaget's strict stages of development have been discredited, the cognitive developmental model suggesting that children's thinking was not simply quantitatively different from adult thinking but also qualitatively different led to other research questions. Graves has argued for the importance of audience in the composing of very young children. Bissex has researched the "natural" cognitive inclination of children to write. Other aspects of development of writing in children were studied by researchers such as Wells, Dyson, and Hull.

Bereiter and Scardamalia (1985) made a case for the ability of writers to attain reflective knowledge or metacognitive awareness of their own processes. They identified behaviors of expert and novice writers and made a distinction between knowledge telling, which is "serviceable" for routine tasks, and knowledge transforming, which "is not fully realized until four ideas at a time can be coordinated" (156).

Flower and Hayes (1977) investigated distinctive features of the expert process, finding that first, experts shift into active awareness when a problem demands it, and second, that experts flexibly shift among various ways of representing knowledge. Metacognition is associated with more experienced writers.

Maimon, Nodine, and O'Connor, in *Thinking, Reasoning, and Writing*, defined writing as thinking made visible. The editors claimed that writing had been redefined as the act of composition, that is, "the creative act of forming and arranging linguistic elements that generate and express thought" (161). They set directions for future research questions, including: Is thinking or reasoning a unitary subject or multiple? Are there levels of knowledge? To what degree are knowledge and learning social rather than individual?

The possibilities of studying cognitive processes relating to writing were consistent with the field's pursuit of basic information on the thought processes related to writing. The cognitive developmental model, however, has more recently been criticized by composition theorists such as Bizzell, who acknowledges the importance of the contributions of such work, but advocates for other approaches that more directly acknowledge the social aspects of writing. She refers to the research of Heath, which indicates that "students' readiness to develop their writing in school is greatly influenced by their social and cultural backgrounds" (Bizzell, "Cognition, Convention, and Certainty," 187). Bizzell characterizes the first school of contemporary research as focusing on the individual's mind, but suggests that "more recently a second school has developed to research the social and cultural factors that influence a writer's perform-ance"(188).

Flower has acknowledged the importance of the social aspect, incorporating it into her more recent work, notably *The Construction of Negotiated Meaning*. In "Cognition, Context, and Theory Building," she addresses the current debate between the roles of cognition and context, arguing for work that "can explain how context cues cognition" rather than "build theoretical positions that po-larize cognitive and cultural positions" (282).

Studies based on cognitive development have yielded significant changes in the way composition is understood. Cognitive developmental theory has pro-vided composition with a theoretical basis, a research direction, and a method-ology. The epistemology that developed from Piaget has offered composition studies ways to consider the writer and writing, thus constituting a worldview that has shaped the field. Piaget offered two important concepts: first, that knowledge is constructed; and second, that individuals must accommodate the external world, modifying their mental world to assimilate new information to their existing mental structures. Development, viewed as individuals' construc-tion of knowledge, is now more significant than the generally discredited Pi-agetian "stages" in understanding how writers develop, becoming able to handle more aspects of the complexities of writing with increasing age and experience.

Perhaps the most obvious contribution of cognitive-processing theory is the research direction leading to study of writing as process—close observations of writers in the act of composing making the choices and decisions that move text forward. Cognitive studies has influenced the use of methodologies that include empirical methods, as well as qualitative methods such as case study, ethnog-raphy, ethnomethodology, process tracing, and protocol analysis. The "thinking-aloud protocol" used by Flower and Hayes (1977) to obtain a window on writing processes, while criticized by, for example, Cooper and Holzman for the inferences about thinking, is defended by Steinberg and has yielded fruitful insights. While composition studies has historically welcomed ways of knowing from a variety of disciplines, criticism of methodology that has centered on the contrast between the hermeneutical/humanities-based approach and the psycho-logical/social science approach may be, in part, the result of a lack of what Basseches might term dialectical tolerance.

The influence of cognitive studies has been felt in the establishment of the writing across the curriculum movement in schools and colleges throughout the country. Writing as thinking made visible moved to the center of courses across disciplines: writing products gave some evidence of students' thinking; and writ-ing as a way to construct meaning became a central component in the teaching of such courses. A less positive implication may be found in the tendency of some textbooks and some instructors in both writing courses and writing-intensive courses to reduce the complexity of writing to simplistic instruction in a reified "process writing."

The relation between cognitive developmental theorists and those who focus on the social-cultural context is problematic in assessing the significance of the cognitive theories on composition. In response to criticism from those arguing for the need to include the social influence in any models of composing, empirical researchers such as Flower have responded by acknowledging the significance of the social context. In "Cognition, Context, and Theory Building," Flower builds a case for constructing an interactive theory of cognition and context. She argues for an observation-based theory that will "help pose questions, structure the search and frame hypotheses" (297). Other researchers, such as Brandt, are moving toward making connections between the social and the cognitive by recommending ethnomethodology.

The future of cognitive developmental studies as one line of inquiry within composition scholarship may depend upon the discipline's willingness to become a "community of observers working from different points of view, with different methods, and in different contexts of observation" (Flower, "Cognition, Context, and Theory Building," 309).

BIBLIOGRAPHY

Primary Texts

Basseches, Michael. *Dialectical Thinking and Adult Development*. Norwood, NJ: Ablex, 1984.

Belenky, Mary F., et al. *Women's Ways of Knowing: The Development of Self, Voice, and Mind*. New York: Basic–Harper, 1986.

Bruner, Jerome S., Jacqueline J. Goodnow, and George Austin. *A Study of Thinking*. New York: Wiley, 1956.

Case, Robbie. *Intellectual Development: Birth to Adulthood*. New York: Academic P, 1985.

———. *The Mind's Staircase: Exploring the Conceptual Underpinnings of Children's Thought and Knowledge*. Hillsdale, NJ: Erlbaum, 1992.

Chomsky, Noam. Rev. of *Verbal Behavior*, by B. F. Skinner. *Language* 35 (1959): 26–58.

Flavell, John, Patricia Miller, and Scott Miller. *Cognitive Development*, 3rd ed. Englewood Cliffs, NJ: Prentice-Hall, 1993.

Miller, George A. "The Magic Number Seven." *The Psychology of Communication*. New York: Basic, 1975, 14–44.

Newell, Allen, and Herbert A. Simon. *Human Problem Solving*. Englewood Cliffs, NJ: Prentice-Hall, 1972.

Perry, William G. *Forms of Intellectual and Ethical Development in the College Years*. New York: Holt, 1968.

Piaget, Jean. *The Language and Thought of the Child*. Trans. Marjorie Gabain. Cleveland, OH: Meridian-World, 1955.

———. *Six Psychological Studies*. Intro. David Elkind. Trans. Anita Tenzer. New York: Vintage-Random, 1967.

Siegler, Robert S. *Children's Minds*. Englewood Cliffs, NJ: Prentice-Hall, 1986.

Sternberg, Robert. *Mechanisms of Cognitive Development*. New York: Freeman, 1984.

Voss, James F. "On the Composition of Experts and Novices." In *Thinking, Reasoning, and Writing*. Ed. Elaine Maimon, Barbara Nodine, and Finbar O'Connor. New York: Longman, 1989, 69–84.

Vygotsky, Lev Semenovich. *Thought and Language*. Trans. Eugenia Hanfmann and Gertrude Vaker. Cambridge, MA: MIT P, 1962.

Major Scholarship in Composition

Barritt, Loren S., and Barry M. Kroll. "Some Implications of Cognitive-Developmental Psychology for Research in Composing." In *Research on Composing: Points of Departure*. Ed. Charles R. Cooper and Lee Odell. Urbana, IL: NCTE, 1978, 49–57.

Berkenkotter, Carol. "Paradigm Debates, Turf Wars, and the Conduct of Sociocognitive Inquiry in Composition." *College Composition and Communication* 42 (1991): 151–69.

Bereiter, Carl. "Development in Writing." In *Cognitive Processes in Writing*. Ed. Lee W. Gregg and Erwin R. Steinberg. Hillsdale, NJ: Erlbaum, 1980, 73–93.

Bereiter, Carl, and Marlene Scardamalia. *The Psychology of Written Composition*. Hillsdale, NJ: Erlbaum, 1987.

Berlin, James A. *Rhetoric and Reality; Writing Instruction in American Colleges, 1900–1985*. Carbondale, IL: Southern Illinois UP for the Conference on College Composition and Communication, 1987.

Bissex, Glenda. *Gnys at Wrk: A Child Learns to Write and Read*. Cambridge, MA: Harvard UP, 1980.

Bizzell, Patricia. "Cognition, Convention, and Certainty: What We Need to Know about Writing." In *Academic Discourse and Critical Consciousness*. Pittsburgh, PA: U of Pittsburgh P, 1992.

———. "Composing Processes: An Overview." In *The Teaching of Writing; Eighty-fifth Yearbook of the National Society for the Study of Education*. Ed. Anthony R. Petrosky and David Bartholomae. Chicago: National Society for the Study of Education, 1986.

Braddock, Richard, Richard Lloyd-Jones, and Lowell Schoer. *Research in Written Composition*. Champaign, IL: NCTE, 1963.

Brandt, Deborah. "The Cognitive as the Social: An Ethnomethodological Approach to Writing Process Research." *Written Communication* 9 (1992): 315–35.

Bridwell, Lillian S. "Revising Strategies in Twelfth Grade Students' Transactional Writing." *Research in the Teaching of English* 14 (1980): 197–222.

Britton, James N., Tony Burgess, Alex McLeod, and Harold Rosen. *The Development of Writing Abilities (11–18)*. London: Macmillan, 1975.

Charney, Davida. "Empiricism Is Not a Four-Letter Word." *College Composition and Communication* 47 (1996): 567–93.

Cooper, Charles R., and Lee Odell. *Research in Composing: Points of Departure*. Urbana, IL: NCTE, 1978.

Cooper, Marilyn, and Michael Holzman. "Talking about Protocols." *College Composition and Communication* 34 (1983): 284–93.

Daiker, Donald A., Andrew Kerek, and Max Morenberg, eds. *Sentence Combining: A Rhetorical Perspective*. Carbondale: Southern Illinois UP, 1985.

D'Angelo, Frank. *A Conceptual Theory of Rhetoric*. Cambridge, MA: Winthrop, 1975.

Dixon, John. *Growth through English*. Reading, England: National Association for the Teaching of English, 1967.

Dyson, Anne Haas. "Individual Differences in Beginning Composing; An Orchestral Vision of Learning to Compose." *Written Communication* 4 (1987): 411–42.

Elkind, David. Introduction. In Jean Piaget, *Six Psychological Studies*. New York: Vintage–Random House, 1967, v–xviii.

Emig, Janet. *The Composing Processes of Twelfth Graders*. Urbana, IL: NCTE, 1971.

Faigley, Lester, and Stephen Witte. "Analyzing Revision." *College Communication and Composition* 32 (1981): 400–414.

Flower, Linda S. "Cognition, Context, and Theory Building." *College Composition and Communication* 40 (1989): 282–311.

———. *The Construction of Negotiated Meaning; A Social Cognitive Theory of Writing*. Carbondale: Southern Illinois UP, 1994.

———. "Writer-Based Prose: A Cognitive Basis for Problems in Writing." *College English* 41 (1979): 19–37.

Flower, Linda S., and John R. Hayes. "The Cognition of Discovery: Defining a Rhetorical Problem." *College Composition and Communication* 31 (1980): 21–32.

———. "A Cognitive Process Theory of Writing." *College Composition and Communication* 32 (1981): 365.

———. "The Dynamics of Composing: Making Plans and Juggling Constraints." In *Cognitive Processes in Writing*. Ed. Lee W. Gregg and Edwin R. Steinberg. Hillsdale, NJ: Erlbaum, 1980, 31–50.

———. "Images, Plans, and Prose. The Representation of Meaning in Writing." *Written Communication* 1 (1984): 229–44.

———. "The Pregnant Pause: An Inquiry into the Nature of Planning." *Research in the Teaching of English* 15 (1981): 229–44.

———. "Problem-Solving Strategies and the Writing Process." *College English* 39 (1977): 449–61.

Fulkerson, Richard. "Composition Theory in the Eighties: Axiological Consensus and Paradigmatic Diversity." *College Composition and Communication* 41 (1990): 409–29.

Gere, Anne Ruggles. "Insights from the Blind: Composing without Rewriting." In *Revising: New Essays for Teachers of Writing*. Ed. P. A. Sudol. Urbana, IL: NCTE, 1982.

Graves, Donald. "An Examination of the Writing Processes of Seven Year Old Children." *Research in the Teaching of English* 9 (1975): 227–41.

Gregg, Lee W., and Edwin R. Steinberg, eds. *Cognitive Processes in Writing*. Hillsdale, NJ: Erlbaum, 1980.

Hairston, Maxine. "The Winds of Change: Thomas Kuhn and the Revolution in the Teaching of Writing." *College Composition and Communication* 33 (1982): 76–86.

Hayes, John R., and Linda Flower. "Identifying the Organization of Writing Processes." In *Cognitive Processes in Writing*. Ed. Lee Gregg and Edwin R. Steinberg. Hillsdale, NJ: Erlbaum, 1980, 3–30.

Heath, Shirley Brice. *Ways with Words: Language, Life, and Work in Communities and Classrooms*. New York: Cambridge UP, 1983.

Hirsch, E. D., Jr. *The Philosophy of Composition*. Chicago: U of Chicago P, 1977.

Hull, Glynda. "The Editing Process in Writing: A Performance Study of More Skilled and Less Skilled College Writers." *Research in the Teaching of English* 21 (1987): 8–29.

Jakobson, Roman. "Linguistics and Poetics." In *Essays on the Language of Literature.* Ed. Seymour Chathman and Samuel R. Levin. Boston: Houghton, 1967, 296–322.

Kinneavy, James. *A Theory of Discourse.* Englewood Cliffs, NJ: Prentice-Hall, 1971.

Kroll, Barry M. "Cognitive Egocentrism and the Problem of Audience Awareness." *Research in the Teaching of English* 12 (1978): 269–81.

———. "Developmental Perspectives and the Teaching of Composition." *College English* 41 (1980): 741–52.

Larson, Richard. "Discovery through Questioning: A Plan for Teaching Rhetorical Invention" In *Contemporary Rhetoric.* Ed. W. Ross Winterowd. New York: Harcourt, 1975, 144–154.

Lauer, Janice. "Heuristics and Composition." *College Composition and Communication* 21 (1970): 396–404.

Lunsford, Andrea A. "Cognitive Development and the Basic Writer." *College English* 41 (1979): 38–46.

Maimon, Elaine, Barbara Nodine, and Finbar O'Connor, eds. *Thinking, Reasoning, and Writing.* New York: Longman, 1989.

Matsuhashi, Ann. "Pausing and Planning: The Tempo of Written Discourse Production." *Research in the Teaching of English* 15 (1981): 113–34.

Moffett, James. *Teaching the Universe of Discourse.* Boston: Houghton, 1968.

Moshman, David, and Bridget A. Franks. "Intellectual Development: Formal Operations and Reflective Judgment." In *Thinking, Reasoning, and Writing.* Ed. Elaine Maimon, Barbara Nodine, and Finbar O'Connor. New York: Longman, 1989, 9–22.

Neimark, Edith D. "A Model of the Mature Thinker." In *Thinking, Reasoning, and Writing.* Ed. Elaine Maimon, Barbara Nodine, and Finbar O'Connor. New York: Longman, 1989, 47–68.

Nystrand, Martin, ed. *What Writers Know; The Language, Process, and Structure of Written Discourse.* New York: Academic P, 1982.

Nystrand, Martin, Stuart Greene, and Jeffrey Wiemelt. "Where Did Composition Studies Come From? An Intellectual History." *Written Communication* 10 (1993): 267–333.

Odell, Lee. "Measuring the Effect of Instruction in Pre-Writing." *Research in the Teaching of English* 8 (1974): 228–40.

Perl, Sondra. "The Composing Processes of Unskilled College Writers." *Research in the Teaching of English* 13 (1979): 317–36.

Pianko, Sharon. "A Description of the Composing Processes of College Freshman Writers." *Research in the Teaching of English* 13 (1979): 5–22.

Rohman, D. Gordon. "Pre-Writing: The Stage of Discovery in the Writing Process." *College Composition and Communication* 16 (1965): 106–12.

Rohman, D. Gordon, and Albert O. Wlecke. "Pre-writing: The Construction and Application of Models for Concept Formation in Writing." U.S. Office of Education Cooperative Research Project no. 2174. East Lansing: Michigan State U, 1964.

Rose, Mike, ed. *When a Writer Can't Write.* New York: Guilford, 1985.

Rubin, Donald L. "Social Cognition and Written Communication." *Written Communication* 1 (1984): 211–45.

Shaughnessy, Mina. *Errors and Expectations; A Guide for the Teacher of Basic Writing*. New York: Oxford UP, 1977.

Sommers, Nancy. "Revision Strategies of Student Writers and Experienced Adult Writers." *College Composition and Communication* 31 (1980): 378–88.

Steinberg, Edwin R. "Protocols, Retrospective Reports, and the Stream of Consciousness." *College English* 48 (1986): 697–712.

Wells, Gordon. *The Meaning Makers: Children Using Language and Using Language to Learn*. Portsmouth, NH: Heinemann, 1986.

Williams, Joseph. "The Phenomenology of Error." *College Composition and Communication* 32 (1981): 152–68.

Young, Richard, Alton Becker, and Kenneth L. Pike. *Rhetoric: Discovery and Change*. New York: Harcourt, 1970.

CAROL JAMIESON AND DENISE DAVID

COLLABORATIVE/SOCIAL PROCESS THEORY

Summary

Kenneth Bruffee is generally identified as the first compositionist to advocate for what is now known as "socially constructed" knowledge and a pedagogy to enact it. Borrowing from philosophers and language theorists like Lev Vygotsky and Richard Rorty, Bruffee, in "Collaborative Learning and the 'Conversation of Mankind,' " located his own theory in the practice of peer tutoring, where he observed that "knowledge is established and maintained in the normal discourse of communities of knowledgeable peers" (640). Partly because of the role the concept of community plays in rescuing meaning from the deconstructionists like Jacques Derrida, and partly because compositionists had already been using groups in their pedagogy, Bruffee's theory and practice were warmly received in composition studies. In addition, contemporaneous historical and theoretical works on collaborative dimensions of literacy and composing provided a larger context for a Bruffean pedagogy, thus enhancing its appeal. For instance, Anne Gere, in *Writing Groups: History, Theory, and Implications*, showed that literacy has been fostered in various extra-institutional groups for over a century, and Karen LeFevre showed that even invention is primarily a social process.

Since the publication of Bruffee's "Conversation," work in collaboration has exploded, with some (e.g., Reagan, Fox, and Bleich, *Writing With*) continuing to apply and refine the work pedagogically, with some gathering what we know both professionally and pedagogically into standard references (e.g., Ede and Lunsford, *Singular Texts/Plural Authors*; Forman, *New Visions of Collaborative Writing*) and others offering rebuttals and critiques (e.g., Stewart, Trimbur, Schilb). More recent applications deriving from networked environments (e.g., Smith, Landow) sometimes seek to rewrite our notion of collaboration altogether. However, thus far, there is basic agreement on the nature of collaboration: it is thought to allow a collective creation of knowledge consistent both with Bakhtinian notions of multivocality and with more recent notions of situatedness, which we associate with postmodernism.

Reception and Significance in Composition Studies

What one means by the term "collaborative writing," as Lisa Ede and Andrea Lunsford suggest, has varied. Charlotte Thralls, for instance, claims that "all writing is inherently collaborative" (64), even writing composed by an individual, while Melanie Sperling limits the reference to two or more individuals working together—"The term collaboration," she says, "implies a conscious mutuality by which individuals of somewhat equal standing work in conjunction with one another toward a unified purpose" (227). Others, like Deborah Bosley, shift the focus to the document produced, which involves "people working together to produce one written document in a situation in which a group takes responsibility for having produced the document" (6). Likewise, the practices from which these definitions are produced are not of a piece: some researchers focus on the workplace and the experienced writer—what the experts do—while others cast their gaze on the classroom.

The processes of collaboration, both print and, more recently, on-line, are likewise still being articulated. James Reither and Douglas Vipond, for instance, articulate three forms of collaboration: coauthoring, workshopping, and knowledge-making. Lisa Ede and Andrea Lunsford, in the most frequently cited general text on collaboration in composition studies, *Singular Texts/Plural Authors*, identify two modes of collaboration. Defining collaboration as "group writing" (14), Ede and Lunsford categorize their two modes: (1) the hierarchical, "carefully, and often rigidly structured, driven by highly specific goals, and carried out by people playing clearly defined and delimited roles"; and (2) the dialogic, "loosely structured, and the roles enacted within it are fluid: one person may occupy multiple and shifting roles as a project progresses" (133).

Working from electronic contexts, George Landow and John Smith elaborate yet other dimensions and understandings of collaborative processes. In *Hypertext: The Convergence of Contemporary Critical Theory and Technology*, Landow identifies four variations of collaboration: (1) "the form of two or more scientists, songwriters or the like continually conferring as they pursue a project in the same place at the same time"; (2) " 'versioning,' in which one worker produces a draft that another person then edits by modifying and adding"; (3) "the assembly-line or segmentation model of working together, according to which individual workers divide the overall task and work entirely independently"; and (4) networked "hypertext systems," which combine elements of the earlier versions by linking texts: "Any document placed on any networked system that supports electronically linked materials potentially exists in collaboration with any and all other documents on that system; . . . any document electronically linked to any other document collaborates with it" (88–89). (This last point regarding the inherent Bakhtinian intertextuality of on-line texts was earlier made concerning print texts: see Porter.)

John Smith, also working from an understanding of collaboration located in electronic environments, distinguishes in *Collective Intelligence in Computer-*

based Collaboration between collaboration and cooperation: whereas cooperation requires that people complete their tasks satisfactorily, Smith says, they can work apart from their partners; collaboration, on the other hand, "carries with it the expectation of a singular purpose and a seamless integration of parts, as if the conceptual object were produced by a single good mind" (2–3). The agency of Smith's collaboration, then, is singular, a concept we hear sounded in Charles Moran's review, "Computers and English: What Do We Make of Each Other?":

So in writing this review I am less the lone reviewer that I once was, speaking from the mountain or the garret; I am much more the voice of, yes, myself, but of others too, a corporate, collaborative, collective "self" that is more social and therefore more knowledgeable than the old. (193)

At the same time that collaboration has been defined and parsed, another, more critical and cautionary body of literature has developed as well, most of it addressing the relationship of collaborative identity and how it effaces difference and can be used for ill. In an early critique, Donald Stewart reminds us of the history of the word—its reference to Nazi sympathizers during World War II—as he also reminds us that collaborative pedagogy is only one pedagogy among many. John Schilb, citing Stewart, urges us to consider the ethics of collaboration. Joseph Harris suggests that the notion of community is neither so unified nor so innocent as we sometimes project. John Trimbur points to the individual differences within a group and how those can be allied with differential power structures. Gesa Kirsch suggests that even within multivocal, collaborative texts, differential power structures obtain, and—worse, perhaps—are often masked. Gregory Clark also focuses on difference within collaboration, arguing that without an explicit understanding of difference, no consensus is even possible. Working toward a resolution of this identity-difference issue, Susan Miller looks toward four characteristics of urban societies. She argues for a collaboration that

would allow for differentiation without exclusion; appreciate variety; encourage erotic attraction to novel, strange, and surprising encounters; and value publicity in public spaces . . . where people stand and sit together, interact and mingle, or simply witness one another, without becoming unified in a community of "shared final ends." (299)

Authorship and assessment comprise a final two topics within collaboration. The "experts" (e.g., scientists and professors) concern themselves with how credit is awarded for scholarship, typically by way of authorial attribution and institutional acknowledgment of collaborative work, especially in the humanities. The latter point is taken up by Judith Entes: as she suggests, producing collaborative scholarship requires a kind of authority that presumably one is still seeking to demonstrate. A similar but more pragmatic approach is taken by

Genny McNenny and Duane Roen: they point out that to "work," collaboration brings with it specified requirements—well-chosen partners, for instance, and a willingness to compromise. Given that authorial attribution in composition studies tends to follow the first author, they also recommend that authors with less prestige (e.g., graduate students) be awarded that place and that more senior scholars take the initiative in explaining our collaborative practices to our colleagues in other disciplines.

The student side of the authorship question tends to play out in assessment practices, though this is both an undertheorized and an underresearched area. Deborah Holdstein, one of the few voices to consider implications of collaboration for student assessment, locates a kind of "false" collaboration used to support institutional agendas:

They [college testing programs] perpetuate a myth of democracy, collaboration, at the expense of student writers whose performance must not only anticipate "what it is that we want," but whose act of writing and whose product must reflect the principle of the solitary, individual writer, even though teachers reject this principle. (78)

How we account for collaborative work in a systematic method of assessment has yet to be addressed.

Collaboration is widely accepted within the field of composition studies: it provides a stage for discussions about knowledge, identity politics, and pedagogical practice. Also, as electronic writing becomes ubiquitous, larger issues regarding authorship and assessment will keep collaboration in the foreground.

BIBLIOGRAPHY

Primary Texts and Major Scholarship in Composition

Anderson, Worth, Cynthia Best, Alycia Black, John Hurst, Brandt Miller, and Susan Miller. "Cross-Curricular Underlife." *College Composition and Communication* 41 (1990): 11–36.

Bosley, Deborah. "A National Study of the Uses of Collaborative Writing in Business Communication in Courses among Members of the ABC." Ph.D. diss., Illinois State U, 1989.

Bruffee, Kenneth. "Collaborative Learning and the 'Conversation of Mankind.' " *College English* 46 (1984): 635–52.

Clark, Gregory. "Rescuing the Discourse of Community." *College Composition and Communication* 45 (1994): 61–75.

Ede, Lisa, and Andrea Lunsford. *Singular Texts/Plural Authors*. Carbondale: Southern Illinois UP, 1990.

Entes, Judith. "The Right to Write a Co-Authored Manuscript." In *Writing With*. Ed. Sally Barr Reagan, Thomas Fox, and David Bleich. Albany: State U of New York P, 1995, 47–61.

Forman, Janis, ed. *New Visions of Collaborative Writing*. Portsmouth, NH: Boynton/Cook–Heinemann, 1992.

Gere, Anne Ruggles. *Writing Groups: History, Theory, and Implications*. Carbondale: Southern Illinois UP, 1957.

Harris, Joseph. "The Idea of Community in the Study of Writing." *College Composition and Communication* 40 (1989): 11–22.

Holdstein, Deborah. "The Institutional Agenda, Collaboration, and Writing Assessment." In *Writing With.* Ed. Sally Barr Reagan, Thomas Fox, and David Bleich. Albany: State U of New York P, 1995, 77–89.

Kirsch, Gesa. "Multi-Vocal Texts and Interpretive Responsibility." *College English* 59 (1997): 191–202.

Landow, George. *Hypertext.* Baltimore, MD: Johns Hopkins UP, 1992.

LeFevre, Karen. *Invention as a Social Act.* Carbondale: Southern Illinois UP, 1987.

McNenny, Genny, and Duane Roen. "The Case for Collaborative Scholarship in Rhetoric and Composition." *Rhetoric Review* 10 (1992): 291–310.

Miller, Susan. "New Discourse City." In *Writing With.* Ed. Sally Barr Reagan, Thomas Fox, and David Bleich. Albany: State U of New York P, 1995, 283–301.

Moran, Charles. "Computers and English: What Do We Make of Each Other?" *College English* 54 (1992): 193–98.

Porter, James. "Intertextuality and the Discourse Community." *Rhetoric Review* 5 (1986): 34–47.

Reagan, Sally Barr, Thomas Fox and David Bleich, eds. *Writing With: New Directions in Collaborative Teaching, Learning, and Research.* Albany: State U of New York P, 1995.

Reither, James, and Douglas Vipond. "Writing as Collaboration." *College English* 51 (1989): 855–68.

Schilb, John. "The Sociological Imagination and the Ethics of Collaboration." In *New Visions of Collaborative Writing.* Ed. Janis Forman. Portsmouth, NH: Boynton/Cook–Heinemann, 1992, 105–20.

Smith, John B. *Collective Intelligence in Computer-based Collaboration.* Hillsdale, NJ: Erlbaum, 1994.

Sperling, Melanie. "Speaking of Writing." In *Writing With.* Ed. Sally Barr Reagan, Thomas Fox, and David Bleich. Albany: State U of New York P, 1995, 227–246.

Steward, Donald C. "Collaborative Learning and Composition: Boon or Bane?" *Rhetoric Review* 7 (Fall 1988): 58–83.

Thralls, Charlotte. "Bakhtin, Collaborative Partners, and Published Discourse." In *New Visions of Collaborative Writing.* Ed. Janis Forman. Portsmouth, NH: Boynton/Cook–Heinemann, 1992, 63–81.

Trimbur, John. "Consensus and Difference in Collaborative Learning." *College English* 51 (1989): 602–16.

KATHLEEN BLAKE YANCEY AND MICHAEL SPOONER

COMMUNICATION THEORY

Summary

An umbrella term for a body of heterogeneous, diverse, multidisciplinary research, contemporary communication theories born in American speech and communication departments emphasize social science methodologies and perspectives. In general, the analysis highlights the social and political purposes of discourse rituals, specifically discourse-in-use, where interpersonal communication is grounded in beliefs about individualism, "upward" mobility, and independent interaction in society. With a tendency to focus on the psychological, communication theories investigate multiple levels of discourse (economical, social, material, institutional, and cultural); knowledge about the production of messages is a result of objective study through quantitative methods of observation, standardization, and replication. In the late nineteenth and early twentieth centuries, many theorists rejected the view that language can accurately represent the social world, focusing instead on the measurement of linguistic parts and their relationships to each other. Because communication theories draw from a variety of disciplines such as rhetoric, sociology, anthropology, philosophy, linguistics, literary theory, and psychology, there are many ways to codify and arrange the theoretical frameworks or taxonomies that inform the discipline. The most useful approach, identified by Stephen Littlejohn, is the use of genre, which highlights the differences as well as similarities among communication theories.

First, structural and functional theories understand human communicative behavior to be part of a system of social structures. Building on research in biology, linguistics, and sociology, these theories stress synchrony or stability over time, thus investigating the birth and unintended consequences of behavior. Viewing language as separate from reality and acknowledging the arbitrary relationship between language and events, these theories focus on accurately and carefully representing reality. For example, network theory is the study of the ways in which a system of connected individuals forms a social structure that is maintained by sophisticated communication rituals. Therefore, theorists investigate how networks in institutions are formed, their influence on work efficiency, the expectations placed on individuals, and the structures for sharing ideas and negotiating conflict.

Second, cognitive and behavioral theories, building on psychology, focus primarily on individuals, their cognitive processes, and the interaction of information, cognition, and human behavior. For example, research on message reception and information processing concentrates on how individuals react, adjust, and assimilate through social interaction. In composition studies, Janet Emig's analysis of students' composing processes or Linda Flower and John Hayes's research on writers' protocol analysis, task environment, long-term memory, and comparisons of expert and novice problem-solving repertoires can be categorized in this genre.

Third, interactional and conventional theories view communication as a consequence of social interaction; therefore, it is not always rule- or ritual-governed, predictable, or stable. Rather than predict or represent reality, these theories attempt to describe the ways in which human knowledge making is a result of interaction, social structures, and institutional negotiations. See, for example, Patricia Bizzell's work on academic discourse, its place in the institution, and its role in underscoring literacy in the composition classroom.

Fourth, another set of interpretive theories that emerge from work in phenomenology (the study of humans' conscious experiences) and hermeneutics (the study of meanings and contexts) teach that knowledge is always a product of human interaction and interpretation. Therefore, these theories investigate the process by which interpretation occurs, focusing on how people experience and understand reality through language. Building on Hans-Georg Gadamer's theories, Timothy Crusius advocates for a "hermeneutical rhetoric," where dialogue and argumentation in public discourse are the primary focus of writing instruction. Another dimension is ethnography (the interpretation of cultures), where researchers endeavor to understand how language and social processes influence the life and rituals of a culture. Refer to research by Shirley Brice Heath, Tom Fox, and Sondra Perl and Nancy Wilson.

Fifth, critical theories unite in their common concern for improving the quality of human social life. Identified as conflict based (i.e., involving the struggle to subvert and overturn the interests of dominant ideologies), critical theorists, including feminists, Marxists, and Freireans, emphasize the importance of bringing to the center the interests and concerns of minorities. Showing how language offers a framework in which the practices of daily life are supported by cultural forms, systems, and rituals, the theorists uncover the structures that maintain and perpetuate any institution's power relations. This genre includes the work of feminists like bell hooks and Susan Jarratt, Marxists like James Berlin, and Freireans like Henry Giroux and Ira Shor.

Reception and Significance in Composition Studies

Speech and communication departments draw from a social science paradigm, while English builds on a humanities framework. In understanding the relationship between communication theory and composition studies, one must recognize that while there is no direct connection between the research on discourse done in the two disciplines, many parallels exist, since both place discourse at the center of attention. Thus, current research in both disciplines focuses on the following three areas: agency, domains of discourse, and praxis and organizational power.

The study of agency underscores the relationship between the knower and the known, including an analysis of the constraints on the reproduction of action. Here, agents are generally understood as active participants in the construction of knowledge, as typified in the work of James Kinneavy and Walter Fisher. Kinneavy's classification of the aims of discourse (expressive, persuasive, referential, and literary) and description of the utility of the communication triangle have influenced composition pedagogy. Similarly, Fisher's theories of narratology accentuate the importance of integrating personal with public knowledge.

In investigating the domains of discourse, Michel Foucault emphasizes "perspective-in-speech-use," where discourse represents both a worldview and a system of meanings. Because discourse can only be understood within a local context, ethnography by Heath and Fox contributes to the understanding of classroom cultures. In addition, Lauer and Asher identify a broad spectrum of composition research designs, including case study, ethnography, quantitative description, experiment, and meta-analysis. The main purpose, as articulated by Jürgen Habermas, is the development of a critical theory of society, grounded in language and human interaction, that privileges a rational, egalitarian public dialogue resulting from mutual comprehensibility and understanding.

Finally, praxis that emphasizes social intervention is the key to critical communication. By recognizing that they produce knowledge and meaning through social interaction, citizens must take active roles in the maintenance of the public sphere. It is the role of the intellectual in a democratic society to advocate for the improvement of human social life. Besides the feminists, Marxists, and Freireans, this is the realm of cultural studies, which seeks to examine cultural texts and their effects in structuring the discursive practices of a society.

BIBLIOGRAPHY

Primary Texts

Berger, Charles, and Steven Chaffee. *Handbook of Communication Science*. Newbury Park, CA: Sage, 1987.

Bizzell, Patricia. *Academic Discourse and Critical Consciousness*. Pittsburgh, PA: U of Pittsburgh P, 1992.

Gardiner, Alan Henderson. *A Theory of Speech and Language*. Oxford: Clarendon, 1951.

Fisher, Walter. *Human Narration as Communication: Toward a Philosophy of Reason, Value, and Action*. Columbia: U of South Carolina P, 1987.

Kincaid, D. Lawrence. *Communication Theory: Eastern and Western Perspectives*. San Diego, CA: Academic P, 1987.

Littlejohn, Stephen W. "Communication Theory." In *Encyclopedia of Rhetoric and Composition*. Ed. Theresa Enos. New York: Garland, 1996, 117–21.

———. *Theories of Human Communication*. 5th ed. Belmont, CA: Wadsworth, 1996.

Rogers, Everett. *A History of Communication Study: A Biographical Approach*. New York: Free P, 1994.

Scollon, Ron, and Suzanne Wong Scollon. *Intercultural Communication*. Cambridge: Blackwell, 1995.

Spitzack, Carole, and Kathryn Carter. *Doing Research on Women's Communication*. Norwood, NJ: Ablex, 1989.

Major Scholarship in Composition

Berlin, James. *Rhetorics, Poetics, and Cultures: Refiguring College English Studies*. Urbana, IL: NCTE, 1996.

Caywood, Cynthia, and Gillian Overing. *Teaching Writing: Pedagogy, Gender, and Equity*. Albany: State U of New York P, 1987.

Cintron, Ralph. "Wearing a Pith Helmet at a Slight Angle, or Can Writing Researchers Do Ethnography in a Postmodern Era?" *Written Communication* 10 (1993): 371–412.

Crusius, Timothy W. *A Teacher's Introduction to Philosophical Hermeneutics*. Urbana, IL: NCTE, 1991.

Emig, Janet. *The Composing Processes of Twelfth Graders*. Urbana, IL: NCTE, 1971.

Fitts, Karen, and Alan France. *Left Margins: Cultural Studies and Composition Pedagogy*. Albany: State U of New York P, 1995.

Flower, Linda, and John Hayes. "A Cognitive Process Theory of Writing." *College Composition and Communication* 32 (1981): 365–87.

Fontaine, Sheryl, and Susan Hunter. *Writing Ourselves into the Story: Unheard Voices from Composition Studies.* Carbondale: Southern Illinois UP, 1993.

Foucault, Michel. *The Archaeology of Knowledge and the Discourse on Language.* Trans. A. M. Sheridan Smith. New York: Pantheon, 1972.

Fox, Tom. *Social Uses of Language in the Classroom.* Norwood: Ablex, 1990.

Gere, Anne Ruggles, ed. *Into the Field: Sites of Composition Studies.* New York: MLA, 1993.

Giroux, Henry. *Theory and Resistance in Education: A Pedagogy for the Opposition.* South Hadley, MA: Bergin, 1983.

Habermas, Jürgen. *Communication and the Evolution of Society.* Trans. Thomas McCarthy. Boston: Beacon, 1979.

Heath, Shirley Brice. *Ways with Words: Language, Life, and Work in Communities and Classrooms.* Cambridge: Cambridge UP, 1983.

hooks, bell. *Teaching to Transgress: Education as the Practice of Freedom.* New York: Routledge, 1994.

Jarratt, Susan. "Feminism and Composition Studies: The Case for Conflict." In *Contending with Words.* Ed. Patricia Harkin and John Schilb. New York: MLA, 1991, 105–23.

Kinneavy, James. *A Theory of Discourse.* New York: Oxford UP, 1981.

Kirsch, Gesa, and Patricia A. Sullivan. *Methods and Methodology in Composition Research.* Carbondale: Southern Illinois UP, 1992.

Lauer, Janice M., and J. William Asher. *Composition Research: Empirical Designs.* New York: Oxford UP, 1988.

Perl, Sondra, and Nancy Wilson. *Through Teachers' Eyes: Portraits of Writing Teachers at Work.* Portsmouth, NH: Heinemann, 1986.

Shor, Ira. *Freire in the Classroom: A Sourcebook for Liberatory Teaching.* Portsmouth, NH: Boynton/Cook, 1987.

SUE HUM

CONSTRUCTIVIST THEORY

Summary

Jean Piaget, the Swiss psychologist, developed a theory of learning to explain the nature of human knowledge known as constructivism. The theory, based on his scientific study of children's knowledge formation, is described in the *Construction of Reality in the Child* and in Inhelder and Piaget's *The Growth of Logical Thinking from Childhood to Adolescence.* Piaget describes three kinds of knowledge—physical, social, and logico-mathematical—based on source of experience and on modes of structuring in the brain, which correspond to developmental levels of thinking. Experiences are interpreted and categorized into relationships (schemata) that are used to predict and understand future experience. For Piaget, learning occurs in two ways. Either an experience fits into the structure of knowledge (relationships of meaningful experiences, or schemata) that an individual has previously constructed and is assimilated into that structure, or it creates dissonance and the need to change, or accommodate, cognitive structure. In each case, the child actively participates in bringing meaning to experience in developmentally sequenced ways that enable him or her to construct knowledge. Thus, the active search for meaning within experience is the impetus for learning to occur. In cognitive constructivist terms, the environment provides experience, but the brain constructs learning. (This notion contrasts with a behaviorist or associationist view of learning, wherein the environment provides the stimulus and the stimulus provokes the learning.)

Lev Vygotsky is an important contributor to the current understanding of constructivist theory. Vygotsky, a Russian psychologist and contemporary of Piaget's whose work was not well known in the West until after the 1960s publication of his books in English, argued that development is a function of sociohistorical and interpersonal social factors as well as of the child's individual development. Piaget argued that environmental/learner influences are bidirectional; Vygotsky argued that they are transactive. A child who engages or collaborates with a more competent person can reach greater understanding than Piaget's development levels alone would predict. This increased understanding is not outside the child and taken in, but rather is created in the process of collaboration and is inherently social. Scaffolding, or the support a learner receives when collaborating with a more experienced peer or an adult, can help him or her construct knowledge within a zone of proximal development. Although Piaget recognizes social and cultural factors that contribute to development, Vygotsky views them as essential to development.

Essentially, constructivist understanding of literate activity assumes an interactivity or a transactivity between the reader/writer and the text and context. Meaning is not an independent reality, but is constructed by the reader based on understandings that are cognitive, developmental, social, and cultural. Thus, constructivist models for composing are likely to stress interaction among knowledge, intention, context, and strategies, as they meet in the composer's mind. Constructivist models include those evolved from information-processing theory (Anderson), writer as composer (deBeaugrande, Kucer), and writer as expert or novice problem solver (Chi, Feltovich, and Glasser; Flower and Hayes; Kucer). Prior knowledge as it influences the creation of meaning has been studied by Branscombe and Taylor, Hull and Rose, and van Dijk and Kinstch. Branscombe and Taylor show how a kindergartner variously constructs meanings of letter formation, story grammar, and the function of written discourse in and out of school as he or she learns to create a written text. Thus prior knowledge is not just cognitive, but task related and social as well.

Reception and Significance in Composition Studies

The pedagogical response to constructivism in composition studies is generally traceable through the shift from transmission-based strategies of instruction to strategies that are "interpretation based" or "meaning based." The Dartmouth Conference is a focal point for tracing this change, as it introduced the work of Dixon, Barnes, and Britton, British scholars who were redefining con-

ceptions of growth in writing and how to teach it. Douglas Barnes (1976) identified two concepts of instruction: "transmission," wherein teachers establish
themselves as experts who dispense existing knowledge to students, and "interpretation," wherein teachers act as facilitators of students' cognitive development through the discovery of knowledge through active learning and social
interaction. According to Barnes, teachers who viewed themselves as facilitators
of student learning were more concerned with the process whereby students
generated meaning and less concerned with the product. This constructivist view
of student knowledge development recognizes that the control of learning belongs with the learner, not the teacher.

Dixon describes the necessity of meaningful engagement in order for knowledge to be constructed and, therefore, for language learning to happen when he
reminds teachers that "language is learnt in operation, not in dummy runs"
(13). This shift, from a belief that knowledge about language is transmitted by
teacher to student to a belief that language knowledge is constructed through
meaningful language use, ran counter to the view that the teacher controls isolated practice, which in turn fosters language learning. According to Maxine
Hairston, such epistemological changes mirrored pedagogical changes in composition, which she described as moving away from the current-traditional model
to a process-oriented approach.

Constructivist pedagogy narrowly conceived is neither content centered nor
student centered; it is meaning centered. The social dimension of the construction of meaning adds a necessary layer to the cognitive dimension. Cognitive
constructivist and social constructivist approaches to teaching in composition
are generally characterized by a focus on understanding, inquiry, and relevance
to students' interests and background knowledge. These approaches can be
found in pedagogical models for all grades. Donald Graves and Lucy Calkins
outline a process approach for writing instruction in the elementary grades,
wherein the teacher prompts and directs student writers to internalize the norms
of good writing. Calkins couples composition instruction with genre study and
helps students determine the characteristics of good writing by learning how to
read like writers. Peer response and teacher conferencing are designed to help
children internalize a reader's response to their work. Peer response works both
to provide an external executive function for children who are at Piaget's concrete operational stage and to provide the social scaffolding Vygotsky predicts
will move learners through the zone of proximal development.

Nancie Atwell describes how a meaning-centered approach to writing using
the writing workshop—which provides students with time, ownership, and feedback—motivates middle-school students and enables them to become better
writers. Atwell argues that writing exercises will not help students to develop
the thinking necessary to make the choices that real writers make. Only real
writing for real purposes will provide the requisite learning experiences.

John Mayher, in his book *Uncommon Sense*, argues against what he calls the
commonsense approach of American education—transmission-based teaching,

which views knowledge as external to the knower and defines learning as mastering discrete skills. Mayher posits instead a classroom organized around teacherless small groups, learning logs, and student-defined projects, which focuses on the learner and the active construction of meaning with language.

While cognitive constructivism remains a strong model for the teaching of writing, a related model based on the social construction of meaning (influenced by the work of Richard Rorty and Thomas Kuhn, as well by Berger and Luckman), has emerged. Social constructionism critiques cognitive constructivism's focus on the individual as the site of meaning. Instead it emphasizes the role that language plays in negotiating cultural, social, and academic knowledge and the power it provides those who can negotiate within the discourses. Social constructionism does not necessarily ground specific pedagogies; however, it focuses composition classrooms on facilitating students' entry into the academic discourse community by teaching them to read and write in the language of the academy. Learning to write as a person (an expressionist goal) or to master form (a current-traditional goal) is subsumed by learning to write as, for example, a chemist or a historian and thus becoming immersed in the discourse of the discipline or in understanding the relationship of language and meaning.

David Bartholomae explains the goal of the introductory college composition course as systematically introducing the student to the rules for generating meaning in the university. In order to be empowered within the system, the student must own these unwritten rules. Bazerman also argues for active participation and reflective practice by both teacher and students in the rhetoric of the disciplines, which involves examining the language and textual practices that shape meaning and knowledge. While examining the individual as knower, Bazerman situates knowing within social action.

Linda Flower connects the personal and the social, the cognitive and the contextual, in composition instruction. She examines Piagetian and Vygotskyian theories of cognitive constructivism to describe a cognitive rhetoric and to outline instructional practices, including collaborative planning, negotiated meaning, and self-reflection.

As composition pedagogy changed to reflect a constructivist orientation, so too did research and inquiry. In 1982 Janet Emig described three "governing gazes" for inquiry, each of which provides a set of assumptions for theory and methodology. She situated transactional/constructivist inquiry with a gaze that "knows the interplay between the knower and the known, and the mutually transforming effects of that interaction" (74); it is an interplay between positivism and phenomenological inquiry, paradigms she considered fundamentally opposed. In 1993 Richard Larson suggested that constructivist research was perhaps the culmination of the paradigm shift in composition first described by Hairston.

BIBLIOGRAPHY

Primary Texts and Major Scholarship in Composition

Anderson, Richard C. *The Architecture of Cognition*. Cambridge, MA: Harvard UP, 1983.

Atwell, Nancie. *In the Middle: Writing, Reading and Learning with Adolescents*. Upper Montclair, NJ: Boynton/Cook, 1987.

Barnes, Douglas. *From Communication to Curriculum*. Harmondsworth, England: Penguin, 1976.

———. "Language in the Secondary Classroom." In *Language, the Learner and the School*. 4th ed. Ed. D. Barnes, J. Britton, and M. Torbe. Portsmouth, NH: Boynton/Cook, 1990. 9–87.

Bartholomae, David. "Inventing the University." In *When a Writer Can't Write: Studies in Writer's Block and Other Composing Process Problems*. Ed. Mike Rose. New York: Guilford P, 1985, 134–65.

Bazerman, Charles. *Constructing Experience*. Carbondale: Southern Illinois UP, 1994.

Berger, Peter L., and Thomas Luckman. *The Social Construction of Reality: A Treatise in the Sociology of Knowledge*. New York: Anchor, 1967.

Branscombe, N. Amanda, and Janet B. Taylor. "The Development of Scrap's Understanding of Written Language." *Childhood Education* 72 (1996): 278–82.

Britton, James. *Language and Learning*. New York: Penguin, 1970.

Calkins, Lucy M. *The Art of Teaching Writing*. 2nd ed. Portsmouth, NH: Heinemann, 1995.

Chi, M., P. Feltovich, and R. Glasser. "Categorization and Representation of Physics Problems by Experts and Novices." *Cognitive Science* 5 (1981): 121–52.

deBeaugrande, Robert. *Text, Discourse and Process: Toward a Multi-disciplinary Science of Texts*. Norwood, NJ: Ablex, 1980.

Dixon, James. *Growth through English: A Record Based on the Dartmouth Seminar*. Reading, England: National Association for the Teaching of English, 1967.

Emig, Janet. "Inquiry Paradigms and Writing." *College Composition and Communication* 23 (1982): 64–75.

Flower, Linda. *The Construction of Negotiated Meaning: A Social Cognitive Theory of Meaning*. Carbondale: Southern Illinois UP, 1994.

Flower, Linda S., and John. R. Hayes. "Images, Plans and Prose: The Representation of Meaning in Writing." *Written Communication* 1 (1984): 120–60.

Graves, Donald, *Writing: Teachers and Children at Work*. Exeter, NH: Heinemann, 1983.

Hairston, Maxine. "The Winds of Change: Thomas Kuhn and the Revolution in the Teaching of Writing." *College Composition and Communication* 23 (1982): 76–88.

Inhelder, B., and Jean Piaget. *The Growth of Logical Thinking from Childhood to Adolescence*. New York: Basic, 1958.

Hull, G., and M. Rose. " 'This Wooden Shack Place': The Logic of an Unconventional Reading." *College Communication and Composition* 42 (1990): 299–329.

Kucer, Stephen. "The Making of Meaning: Reading and Writing as Parallel Processes. *Written Communication* 2 (1985): 317–36.

Kuhn, Thomas. *The Structure of Scientific Revolutions*. Chicago: U of Chicago P, 1962.

Larson, Richard. "Competing Paradigms for Research and Evaluation in the Teaching of English." *Research in the Teaching of English* 27 (1993): 283–92.

Mayher, John S. *Uncommon Sense: Theoretical Practice in Language Education*. Portsmouth, NH: Boynton/Cook, 1991.

Piaget, Jean. *The Construction of Reality in the Child*. New York: Ballantine, 1954.

Rorty, Richard. *Consequence of Pragmatism*. Minneapolis: U of Minnesota P, 1982.

van Dijk, Teun A., and Walter Kinstch. *Strategies of Discourse Comprehension*. New York: Academic P, 1983.

Vygotsky, Lev S. *Mind in Society: The Development of Higher Psychological Processes*. Ed. Michael Cole. Cambridge, MA: Harvard UP, 1978.

———. *Thought and Language*. Cambridge, MA: MIT P, 1962.

A. LEE WILLIAMS

CONTACT ZONE THEORY

Summary

The term *contact zone* was first introduced by Mary Louise Pratt in a keynote address at the 1990 MLA Responsibilities for Literacy conference. The address was published subsequently in MLA's *Profession 91* under the title, "Arts of the Contact Zone." Contact zones, or arts of the contact zone, denotes not so much a full-blown theory of writing or of writing pedagogy but a way of viewing literacy, that is, a way of re-envisioning the models of writing and community that now form the basis of literacy teaching and theorizing (34). More specifically, Pratt defines contact zones as "social spaces where cultures meet, clash, and grapple with each other, often in contexts of highly asymmetrical relations of power such as colonialism, slavery, or their aftermaths as they are lived out in many parts of the world today" (34).

Within such social spaces or contexts, Pratt envisions several types of literate art: autoethnography, transculturation, critique, collaboration, bilingualism, mediation, parody, denunciation, imaginary dialogue, and vernacular expression ("Arts of the Contact Zone," 37). These various arts, she explains, often constitute a marginalized person or group's "point of entry into the dominant circuits of print culture" (35). That is, autoethnographic writings like American slave autobiographies or transcultural texts like Andean Guaman Poma's letter to King Philip III of Spain represent an oppressed culture's critical engagement with the literate practices of the dominant culture. Pratt's example of her son Manuel, a fourth grader, suggests that the arts of the contact zone can also be found in the classroom. But she ponders, "What is the place of unsolicited oppositional discourse, parody, resistance, critique in the imagined classroom community?" (Arts, 39) In Manuel's actual classroom, there wasn't a place for them, for, as Richard Miller puts it in "Fault Lines in the Contact Zone," the teacher's usual star on Manuel's unconventional paragraph "labors to conceal a conflict in the classroom over what work is to be valued and why, presenting instead the image that everything is under control—students are writing and the teacher is evaluating" (390).

An example of a classroom that would instead focus on such sites of conflict is the "Cultures, Ideas, Values" course at Stanford. Centering on the Americas and the multiple cultural histories that have intersected there, the course "functioned not like a homogenous community or a horizontal alliance but like a contact zone'' (Pratt, ''Arts of the Contact Zone,'' 39). In this contact zone, according to Pratt, the formal lecture became anomalous; teacher and students instead had to work in the knowledge that whatever one said was going to be systematically received in radically heterogeneous and nonprescriptive ways (39).

Although Pratt offers little in the way of practical approaches to teach writing in a contact zone, she clearly sees the contact zone as a site of learning, one that includes a broad range of pedagogical arts like exercises in storytelling, experiments in collaborative work, and ways for people to move into and out of rhetorics of authenticity (''Arts of the Contact Zone,'' 40).

Reception and Significance in Composition Studies

For a theory or concept that has so far been expressed in very few primary sources, Pratt's notion of the contact zone has had an exceptionally profound influence on composition studies. Besides the plethora of conference papers on this relatively new and hot topic in the field, several articles on contact zones have appeared in the major composition journals: *College English, College Composition and Communication, Teaching English in the Two-Year College, Journal of Basic Writing*, and *Journal of Advanced Composition*. Interest in the theory has furthermore prompted two leading scholars in the field to publish a book, an anthology, entirely based on contact zone theory (see Bizzell and Herzberg's *Negotiating Difference*).

Many of the published articles attempt, in various ways, to apply contact zone theory to writing instruction. One scholar, for instance, uses the theory to work with students' writing styles (Lu, 447), while another uses it to modify and enhance her use of portfolio assessment (Lewiecki-Wilson, 267–68). Although Miller criticizes Pratt for not offering specific examples of how her students negotiated their ideas and identities in the contact zone, he also applies contact zone theory to the composition classroom, especially as it pertains to hate speech that could surface in the classroom (391).

While such applications of contact zone theory have been crucial to its development and potential usefulness, some of them have been criticized for failing to offer in their view of the classroom as contact zone a compelling view of public discourse as a forum expressing and negotiating cultural and political differences (Harris, 27). Two very recent works on contact zone theory may, however, begin to provide the more nuanced view of public discourse for which Harris calls. First, Phyllis van Slyck's article in *College English* directs teachers to think more critically about the way they position themselves, not just their students, in the classroom (152). Second, Patricia Bizzell and Bruce Herzberg''s anthology, *Negotiating Difference*, addresses the need to negotiate the differences among cultures through the study of what they call six contact zones in American history. Both of these works offer to the field of composition studies important developments in contact zone theory and pedagogy.

BIBLIOGRAPHY

Primary Texts and Major Scholarship in Composition

Bizzell, Patricia. " 'Contact Zones' and English Studies." *College English* 56.2 (1994): 163–69.

Bizzell, Patricia, and Bruce Herzberg. *Negotiating Difference: Cultural Case Studies for Composition.* Boston: Bedford Books of St. Martin's P, 1996.

Harris, Joseph. "Negotiating the Contact Zone." *Journal of Basic Writing* 14.1 (1995): 27–42.

Lewiecki-Wilson, Cynthia. "Teaching in the 'Contact Zone' of the Two-Year College Classroom: Multiple Literacies/'Deep Portfolio.' " *Teaching English in the Two-Year College* 21.4 (1994): 267–76.

Lu, Min-Zhan. "Professing Multiculturalism: The Politics of Style in the Contact Zone." *College Composition and Communication* 45.4 (1994): 442–58.

Miller, Richard. "Fault Lines in the Contact Zone." *College English* 56 (1994): 389–408.

Pratt, Mary Louise. "Arts of the Contact Zone." In MLA, *Profession 91.* New York: MLA, 1991. 33–40.

———. "Criticism in the Contact Zone: Decentering Community and Nation." In *Critical Theory, Cultural Politics, and Latin American Narrative.* Ed. Steven Bell and Leonard Orr. Notre Dame, IN: U of Notre Dame P, 1993. 83–102.

Slyck, Phyllis van. "Repositioning Ourselves in the Contact Zone." *College English* 59.2 (1997): 149–70.

Sullivan, Francis. "Critical Theory and Systemic Linguistics: Textualizing the Contact Zone." *Journal of Advanced Composition: A Journal of Composition Theory* 15.3 (1995): 411–34.

KERMIT ERNEST CAMPBELL

CONTRASTIVE RHETORIC

Summary

From its origins in applied linguistics, contrastive rhetoric is emerging as an independent discipline in composition scholarship. Contrastive, or comparative, rhetoric studies what constitutes writing well in different cultures and languages. Research in contrastive rhetoric has examined the formal differences between texts written by native and nonnative speakers of English, and these textual differences have been related to cultural differences in rhetorical expectations and conventions.

Contrastive rhetoric arose to meet the challenges of teaching English composition to increasing numbers of people who speak English as a second language (ESL). It was, as Ulla Connor states it in her book, *Contrastive Rhetoric*, "the first serious attempt by applied linguists in the United States to explain second language writing" (5). Robert Kaplan coined the term *contrastive rhetoric* and articulated its basic notion in his 1966 article "Cultural Thought Patterns in Intercultural Education," published in *Language Learning*. Kaplan, an applied linguist, was influenced by the Sapir-Whorf hypothesis and theories of second language (L2) acquisition. Benjamin Lee Whorf hypothesized that thought is inseparable from language and that language is inseparable from culture. L2 research comparing L1 and L2 learning began to examine how the former influences the latter. Kaplan argued that logic and rhetoric are generally culturally determined and specifically influenced by the social conventions of a culture. He discussed these social conventions as "thought patterns" that condition the way people think, speak, and write. Drawing on theories of cultural relativism and research on language acquisition, Kaplan hypothesized that L2 writing performance is inescapably influenced by the rhetorical conventions of students' native languages.

To substantiate his hypothesis, Kaplan examined some 600 English writing samples written by college ESL students. His focus was principally on patterns of paragraph organization. He found that students with different linguistic backgrounds constructed English paragraphs according to the "thought patterns" that are typical of their native cultures. Kaplan delineated these thought patterns in a famous set of diagrams. For example, a solid, straight arrow was used to represent the American thought pattern to suggest that American students write paragraphs in a linear progressive manner. In contrast, a spiral that gradually closes in on a point but never reaches it was used to characterize the "Oriental" sequence of thought. Kaplan was convinced that Asian students treat topics in totality and focus on the interrelatedness rather than deal with them directly. In his own words, "Things are developed in terms of what they are not, rather than in terms of what they are" (10).

Kaplan's theory of contrastive rhetoric has drawn waves of responses, with perhaps more criticism than praise from L2 writing teachers and researchers. Foremost among the criticism has been the claim that contrastive rhetoric, as proposed by Kaplan, adopted a narrow view of rhetoric, reducing it merely to formal patterns of development. In Kaplan's original study, rhetoric was explicitly reduced to paragraph organization. Second, Kaplan's study was limited to the expository texts written by ESL students, overlooking other text genres, developmental factors of student writers, and the complexity of discursive conventions within cultures. Third, according to Ilona Leki in her article, "Twenty-Five Years of Contrastive Rhetoric," Kaplan's study helped confine contrastive rhetoric within the current-traditional approach to teaching ESL writing, which emphasizes written products over writing processes. Fourth, Kaplan's notion of contrastive rhetoric ignored cultural contexts of writing in different languages. In short, embedded in theories of applied linguistics and language acquisition, Kaplan's theory of contrastive rhetoric emphasized textual analyses that reduced broader rhetorical contexts to cultural stereotypes by ignoring relevant work in rhetoric and composition on such important factors as purpose, audience, and situation.

Much of subsequent research in contrastive rhetoric has taken a similar text-based approach but avoided its limitations by attending to the pragmatics of writing. Connor's "Argumentative Patterns in Student Essays: Cross-Cultural Differences," in Connor and Kaplan's *Writing across Languages*, is a case in point. Connor decided to study persuasive writing because it "requires the writer to be aware of both audience and personal constructs" (58). Using a multilevel analysis system that focused on the processes of composing, she examined argumentative patterns in essays written in L1 by students from England, Finland, Germany, and the United States. She found that there was some cross-cultural variation in "the writer's reasons for selecting ideas and on how they are presented" (65). Though Connor did not find apparent cultural differences with regard to audience considerations, she concluded her study by reiterating the importance of teaching audience awareness in ESL composition.

Like any new field of inquiry, the field of contrastive rhetoric has since its inception expanded by drawing on neighboring disciplines, such as rhetoric and composition studies, genre studies, text linguistics, and the ethnography of communication. Insights from research in these disciplines have helped change the textual orientation of contrastive rhetorical studies. The most notable is perhaps a study by Muriel Saville-Troike and Donna Johnson entitled "Comparative Rhetoric: An Integration of Perspectives." In this article in *Pragmatics and Language Learning*, Saville-Troike and Johnson argued that contrastive rhetoric should adopt an ethnography of communication perspective that emphasizes "a text and its production as a socially situated communicative event," that is, "text as praxis" (231). An ethnography of communication perspective, as Saville-Troike and Johnson maintained, defines contrastive rhetoric as the study of "skilled language use in different speech communities" and gives priority to the functions of language within cultural, social, and political settings, as well as physical ones (241).

Reception and Significance in Composition Studies

As work in contrastive rhetoric has developed a more sophisticated sense of such rhetorical factors as audience, purpose, and situation, it has enjoyed an increasing reception within composition studies, particularly among ESL teachers and researchers. The theory of contrastive rhetoric has begun to shape the basic approach to the teaching of L2 writing. With its emphasis on the relations of texts to cultural contexts, contrastive rhetoric has provided teachers with a practical, nonjudgmental framework for analyzing and evaluating ESL writing and helping students see the rhetorical differences between English and their native languages as a matter of social convention, not cultural superiority. ESL writing teachers can further use the framework, as Connor points out in *Contrastive Rhetoric*, to explicate "problems in composition encountered by second language writers" as attributable to differences in rhetorical strategies of their native languages (5). In doing so, they will eventually not only teach ESL students textual conventions of English composition, but also explain the broader sociocultural contexts in which these conventions are embedded and valued.

Work in contrastive rhetoric has established the groundwork for comparative studies of discursive conventions. Research has begun on differences in genres, modes of composing, author-audience relations, and ways of configuring purposes and defining topics, including comparative studies of English and Chinese, Japanese, Korean, Thai, Hindi, Arabic, Spanish, German, and French. Such research has been well documented by Connor in *Contrastive Rhetoric*, Alan Purves in *Writing across Languages and Cultures*, and Connor and Kaplan in *Writing across Languages*. Research in contrastive rhetoric has also been attentive to pedagogical implications and begun to generate practical suggestions for teachers. For example, in "Contrastive Rhetoric: An American Writing Teacher in China," Carolyn Matalene reminded teachers that Chinese ESL students may not only write but also think in a characteristically Chinese way in their English classes. She exhorted fellow teachers to take the initiative to explain their comments such as, "Be original" and "Use new language." These students, Matalene noted, "are too puzzled and too polite to point . . . out [their need for clarification]—and they are certainly not in the habit of questioning teachers" (792).

As an emerging discipline, contrastive rhetoric has already made its impact felt in the field of composition studies. As the numbers of international students in English-speaking countries continue to increase and educated people increasingly are challenged to communicate across cultures, contrastive rhetoric has the potential to foster a growing awareness of and positive attitude toward the fact that people write differently in different languages and cultures. Rhetoricians and composition teachers are coming to understand rhetorical conventions as sociocultural constructs. The norms for writing well that may seem self-evident within a culture are soon seen not to be universal when one looks to other languages and cultures, and what is deemed as adequate writing in one language is not by any means either superior or inferior to that in another.

It is fair to say that as a result of contrastive rhetorical studies, rhetoricians and composition scholars have realized the need to fight against the lingering exclusionism in the field and expand the boundaries of (Western) rhetoric and composition scholarship. Mary Garrett, a featured speaker at a recent convention of the Rhetoric Society of America, reminded us that we in the field of rhetorical and composition studies ought to understand the rhetorics of others and commit attention to research in contrastive rhetoric (45–46). We must, as Patricia Bizzell and Bruce Herzburg pledge in their multicultural reader, *Negotiating Difference: Cultural Case Studies for Composition*, "develop effective rhetorical strategies for communicating both within and across cultural boundaries" (v). Research on the historical development and sociocultural diversity of rhetorical conventions is needed to move contrastive rhetoric beyond stereotypical models of other cultures so that it may contribute to cross-cultural understanding.

BIBLIOGRAPHY

Primary Texts and Major Scholarship in Composition

Bizzell, Patricia, and Bruce Herzberg. *Negotiating Difference: Cultural Case Studies for Composition*. Boston: Bedford Books of St. Martin's P, 1996. v–xi.

Blumler, Jay G., Jack M. McLeod, and Karl Erik Rosengren, eds. *Comparatively Speaking*. Newbury Park, CA: Sage, 1992.

Carbaugh, Donald, ed. *Cultural Communication and Intercultural Contact*. Hillsdale, NJ: Erlbaum, 1990.

Connor, Ulla. "Argumentative Patterns in Student Essays." In *Writing across Languages*. Ed. Ulla Connor and Robert B. Kaplan. Reading, MA: Addison-Wesley, 1987, 57–71.

———. *Contrastive Rhetoric*. New York: Cambridge UP, 1996.

Connor, Ulla, and Robert B. Kaplan, eds. *Writing across Languages*. Reading: Addison-Wesley, 1987.

Fox, Helen. *Listening to the World*. Urbana, IL: NCTE, 1994.

Garrett, Mary. "How Far We've Come: How Far We Have to Go." In *Making and Unmaking Prospects for Rhetoric*. Ed. Theresa Enos. Mahwah, NJ: Erlbaum, 1997, 43–48.

Hinds, John. "Contrastive Rhetoric: Japanese and English." *Text: An Interdisciplinary Journal for the Study of Discourse* 3 (1983): 183–95.

Jensen, Vernon J. "Teaching East Asian Rhetoric." *Rhetoric Society Quarterly* 17 (1987): 135–49.

Johnson, Donna M., and Duane H. Roen, eds. *Richness in Writing: Empowering ESL Students*. New York: Longman, 1989.

Kachru, Braj B., ed. *The Other Tongue*. Urbana: U of Illinois P, 1982.

Kaplan, Robert B. "Cultural Thought Patterns in Intercultural Education." *Language Learning: A Journal of Applied Linguistics* 17 (1966): 1–20.

Leki, Ilona. "Twenty-Five Years of Contrastive Rhetoric: Text Analysis and Writing Pedagogies." *TESOL Quarterly* 25 (1991): 123–43.

———. *Understanding ESL Writers*. Portsmouth, NH: Boynton/Cook, 1992.

Matalene, Carolyn. "Contrastive Rhetoric: An American Writing Teacher in China." *College English* 47 (1985): 789–808.

Oliver, Robert T. *Communication and Culture in Ancient India and China*. Syracuse, NY: Syracuse UP, 1971.

Péry-Woodley, Marie-Paule. "Contrasting Discourses." *Language Teaching* 23 (1990): 143–51.

Purves, Alan C., ed. *Writing across Languages and Cultures*. Newbury Park, CA: Sage, 1988.

Saville-Troike, Muriel, and Donna M. Johnson. "Comparative Rhetoric: An Integration of Perspectives." *Pragmatics and Language Learning* 5 (1994): 231–45.

Shen Fan. "The Classroom and the Wider Culture: Identity as a Key to Learning English Composition." *College Composition and Communication* 40 (1989): 459–66.

Smith, Larry K., ed. *Discourse across Cultures*. New York: Prentice-Hall, 1987.

GUANJUN CAI

CRITICAL THEORY OF THE FRANKFURT SCHOOL

Summary

The Neo-Marxian social theorists associated with the Institute of Social Research, founded in Germany in 1923 in affiliation with the University of Frankfurt, have been known both as "The Frankfurt School" and as "critical theorists." Their goal has been to reread Marx in light of the historical development of capitalism in late modernity. The most influential of the first generation were Theodor Adorno (1903–1969), Walter Benjamin (1892–1940), Max Horkheimer (1895–1973), and Herbert Marcuse (1898–1979). Of the second generation, Jürgen Habermas (born 1929) is preeminent.

All Frankfurt School theorists have been dialectical thinkers who studied the interpenetration of the economic, political, social, and cultural spheres. Their studies critique domination and explore possibilities for liberation. Critical theory sustains the hope that reflection itself has emancipatory force. Hence, critical theory is both social theory and a reflection on critique.

The first generation of critical theorists produced empirical studies, historical interpretation, literary exegesis, and philosophical analysis. Identifying sources of authoritarianism, elaborating new forms of dialectic, unmasking ideologies, critiquing the Enlightenment, and theorizing history were shared concerns.

The Frankfurt School's commitment to Marxism and opposition to fascism resulted in their forced exile from Nazi Germany. The institute continued its work in New York City from 1934 until 1953, when it was reestablished in Frankfurt. The first-generation theorists were deeply affected by the failure of communism to create a just society and by the rise of fascism; those who escaped to the United States were equally struck by consumerism's restrictions on democracy. Orthodox Marxism's inability to assess these developments motivated these theorists to synthesize Marxist insights, such as Marx's theory of commodification and Lukacs's rethinking of reification, with other resources, including Kant's aesthetics, Hegel's theory of history, Nietzsche's analysis of knowledge and interests, Weber's concept of rationalization, and Freud's psychoanalysis.

Instrumental reason, a major focus of critique, was identified by Horkheimer and Adorno in *Dialectic of Enlightenment* as a form of reason that equates rationality with means/ends calculation. They argued that reducing human reason to quantification expanded the reach of technologies that dominate nature, including human nature. Since the Renaissance, more and more domains of action and knowledge had come under the rule of instrumental reason, until positivism and scientism convinced many that meaning could be conferred only on empirically verifiable knowledge. In late capitalism, instrumental reason exerts its power by insinuating itself within administrative-bureaucratic systems and by rendering other forms of reason unthinkable, so that the very possibility of critical reflection is restricted.

Instrumental reason invaded mass culture. Horkheimer and Adorno developed the concept of the culture industry to emphasize that the entertainment marketed to the public served the profit motive, commodified leisure time, and standardized "the good life" (*Dialectic*). The culture industry used methods of mass communication so effectively that the individual's sense of self came to be structured by its messages.

For Horkheimer and Adorno, popular art forms constructed an ideology that inculcated values congruent with capitalism. In *Aesthetic Theory*, Adorno contrasted popular literature, music, and art with "authentic" avant-garde art, the structure of which confronted audiences with the tragic distance between the possibility of justice and the actuality of suffering. Only such complex works could elicit critical reflection. Adorno opposed Benjamin, who had refused to exempt high art from complicity with suffering (*Illuminations* 253–64) or to condemn popular art forms such as photography and film for their dependency on technologies of standardization (217–51).

As instrumental reason came to structure workplace relations, education, and leisure time, these domains replaced the family as the primary factor in identity formation. Horkheimer, Adorno, and Marcuse concurred with Freud: repressed sexual energy produced an ego that confronted the pressures of socialization by restricting libido to the unconscious. Adorno and Horkheimer argued that the erosion of family influence only strengthened instrumental reason's control of social relations. In contrast, Marcuse argued that the very "surplus-repression" exerted by instrumental reason, whereby erotic energies were diverted away from pleasure and into labor, would so advance technological progress that the need for human labor would cease (*Eros and Civilization*). In Marcuse's dialectical prognosis, instrumental reason must expand until it erases its own need for being and thereby releases libidinal energies to transform social relations.

Other first-generation critical theorists also devised forms of dialectic. Benjamin's "Dialectical Images" defamiliarized everyday objects to impel observers to take a critical stance (*Gesämmelte Schriften* 4, Vol. 1). Horkheimer's "unconcluded" dialectic replaced a "revelatory" final assessment with a search for limitations in existing knowledge (*Eclipse of Reason*). Adorno's "negative dialectics" located possibilities locked within the "forcefield" between an object and its concept. The goal for all was "immanent criticism," in which the object of thought was assessed according to principles and possibilities interior to it (*Eclipse* 182).

Unlike the first generation of theorists, Jürgen Habermas has not developed a distinctive dialectic. Instead he elaborates taxonomies of social institutions, knowledge modes, and discourse forms. He is committed to foundationalist systematization. His approach to instrumental reason reflects these commitments. In *Knowledge and Human Interests*, Habermas assigns instrumental reason a positive role: it is a "knowledge-constitutive" interest in controlling nature, a beneficial form of rationality when restricted to empirical-analytical knowledge. To offset its power, Habermas recommends developing forms of rationality inherent in two other "knowledge-constitutive" interests: a practical interest in mutual understanding and an emancipatory interest in freedom (301–17). He claims that a preoccupation with instrumental reason derailed the project of the first-generation Frankfurt theorists (*The Theory of Communicative Action*, vol. 1).

In *The Theory of Communicative Action*, Habermas identifies two forms of rationality, communicative rationality, which is a positive resource for negotiating in the "lifeworld" of family, workplace, and political affiliations, and functionalist rationality, which coordinates state administration and the market economy. If freedom is to be expanded, communicative rationality within the lifeworld must be increased and the invasion of functionalist rationalities of money and power must be resisted. Habermas attributes the loss of control and meaning experienced in late modernity to this "colonization" of the lifeworld by functionalist rationality.

Habermas's solution to colonization is to expand multiple public spheres within which individuals resolve conflict and negotiate consensus concerning just action. The discursive conditions that would strengthen these public spheres include understanding intersubjectivity as the ground of discourse and acknowledging that the concept of an ideal speech community regulates discourse.

Reception and Significance in Composition Studies

Frankfurt School theorists and cultural studies advocates share motives, themes, and methods. However, first-generation critical theorists have been sparingly referenced in composition studies. Adorno's "negative dialectic" is summarized by James Berlin to defend modes of historicizing that attempt to account for all historical data while acknowledging the impossibility of accessing final historical truth (149–50). Kurt Spellmeyer draws on Adorno, Horkheimer, and Marcuse (throughout *Common Ground*) and on Benjamin and Horkheimer (in "After Theory") to describe relationships among writing, pedagogy, and culture. Other scholars have evoked first-generation critical theory in citations at the beginning and end of articles (Freedman, Kinneavy, McComiskey).

Uses of Habermas in composition studies include similar forms of citation and synopsis. Kurt Spellmeyer draws on Habermas as he discusses how discourse is obstructed in contemporary culture. Louise Phelps identifies Habermas as a figure relevant to contextualist composition theory (115). Victor Vitanza (144–59) and Lester Faigley (39–44) use a debate between Habermas and Jean-Francois Lyotard, the contemporary French theorist of postmodernism, to contrast modernist with postmodernist philosophy.

However, since the mid-1980s, Habermas's work has received more attention. By including one of his essays in *Professing the New Rhetorics*, Theresa Enos and Stuart C. Brown identify Habermas's theory as applicable to composition studies. In composition journals, his theory has been applied to rhetorical invention, collaborative learning, technical and public writing, and pedagogy. Most recently, Susan Wells articulated a rhetoric of intersubjectivity grounded in the theory of Habermas and Jacques Lacan, the Freudian poststructuralist theorist.

In "Toward a Rhetoric of Intersubjectivity," Hugh Grady and Susan Wells affirm Habermas's claim that to speak in the public sphere, interlocutors must assume that rationality is achievable and that there are mechanisms for judging how fully it has been realized. Grady and Wells also transpose Habermas's discourse taxonomy (theoretical, practical, aesthetic, therapeutic, and explicative) into a heuristics classification based on audience information needs.

In "Habermas . . . and the Teaching of Technical Discourse," Susan Wells argues that students of technical writing must learn how knowledge and power are distributed differentially, with many audiences having a stake in restricting access to information. By keeping Habermas's consensus-oriented speech situation available as a counterfactual norm, the instructor can incorporate a "what if" principle among technical writers' rhetorical resources even as they learn to work within the limits of workplace relations.

In "Consensus and Difference in Collaborative Learning," John Trimbur recommends that the concept of an ideal speech community should regulate classroom communication. He too argues that the ideal speech community—one in which no one is coerced, all are accorded equal respect, and ideas are exchanged without distortion—is regulative, counterfactual, and anticipatory, not empirical. Seen as an ideal, consensus is transformed from an endpoint to a working tool for opening up communication. Dialogue can be examined for its approximation toward relations of nondomination. Differences in perspective, knowledge, and social location can be experienced in a relatively dehierarchized space, and reasons for the uneven distribution of power can be explored.

In "Habermas' . . . Communicative Action," Patricia Roberts assumes that consensus is an empirical dimension of successful speech acts and that Habermas's focus on consensus discourse warrants privileging persuasive discourse and value-oriented audience analysis.

In "Rogue Cops and Health Care," Susan Wells uses Habermas's conception of the public sphere to generate options for connecting classrooms to civic space: constructing the classroom as a public sphere, analyzing discursive exchanges produced beyond the classroom, assigning public sphere writing, and creating multidisciplinary writing teams to simulate how differentiated knowledge practices are coordinated in public writing.

In "Composition, Philosophy, and Rhetoric: The 'Problem of Power,' " David Sebberson recommends Habermas's discourse theory as a corrective to Louise Phelps's contextualist theory. Claiming that Phelps emphasizes the generative force of language but leaves power untheorizable, Sebberson claims that Habermas's distinctions between strategic action and communicative action and between open and covert strategic action keep power in focus and retain critique as a genre.

The first work to use Habermas as a resource in theory building in composition studies is Susan Wells's *Sweet Reason*. Coordinating Habermas's social theory and Lacan's psychoanalytic theory, Wells argues for a rhetoric of intersubjectivity that can analyze texts and writing from the perspectives of language, narrative, and action. Habermas articulates rhetoric's relationship to reason, defined as a form of intelligibility commensurate to the tasks of establishing common ground and coordinating action. Lacan provides counterinsights on rhetoric's relationship to desire, which he terms a drive impervious to reason, but, like reason, implicated in textual labor. By calling on Lacan to illuminate the aspects of language, narrative, and action that Habermas ignores, and vice versa, Wells highlights both theorists' strengths and rhetoric's capacious scope. Wells's text inaugurates a new stage in the reception of critical theory in composition studies.

BIBLIOGRAPHY

Primary Texts

Adorno, Theodor. *Aesthetic Theory*. 1970. Rpt. Ed. Gretel Adorno and Rolf Tiedemann. Trans. Robert Hullot-Kentor. Minneapolis: U of Minnesota P, 1997.

———. *Minima Moralia: Reflections from Damaged Life*. 1951. Rpt. Trans. E. F. N. Jephcott. London: Verso, 1974.

Benjamin, Walter. *Gesämmelte Schriften*. 6 vols. Ed. Rolf Tiedemann and Jermann Schweppenhauser. Frankfurt, Germany: Suhrkamp Verlag, 1972–.

———. *Illuminations*. 1955. Rpt. Ed. Hannah Arendt. Trans. Harry Zohn. New York: Schocken Books, 1969.

Habermas, Jürgen. *Communication and the Evolution of Society*. 1976. Rpt. Trans. Thomas McCarthy. Boston: Beacon P, 1979.

———. "Intermediate Reflections: Social Action, Purposive Activity, and Communication." In *Professing the New Rhetorics: A Sourcebook*. Ed. Theresa Enos and Stuart C. Brown. Englewood Cliffs, NJ: Prentice-Hall, 1994, 204–20.

———. *Knowledge and Human Interests*. 1968. Boston: Beacon P, 1971.

———. *The Theory of Communicative Action*. Trans. Thomas McCarthy. Vol. 1, *Reason and the Rationalization of Society*. Vol. 2, *Lifeworld and System: A Critique of Functionalist Reason*. Boston: Beacon P, 1981, 1987.

Horkheimer, Max. *Critique of Instrumental Reason*. 1967. Trans. Matthew J. O'Connell et al. New York: Continuum, 1994.

———. *Eclipse of Reason*. New York: Oxford UP, 1947.

Horkheimer, Max, and Theodor W. Adorno. *Dialectic of Enlightenment*. 1944. Trans. John Cumming. New York: Continuum, 1994.

Marcuse, Herbert. *Eros and Civilization*. New York: Random House, 1955.

———. *One-Dimensional Man*. Boston: Beacon P, 1964.

Major Scholarship in Composition

Berlin, James A. "Revisionary History: The Dialectical Method." In *Rethinking the History of Rhetoric: Multidisciplinary Essays on the Rhetorical Tradition*. Ed. Takis Poulakos. Boulder, CO: Westview P, 1993, 135–51.

Enos, Theresa, and Stuart C. Brown. "Introduction." In *Professing the New Rhetorics: A Sourcebook*. Ed. Theresa Enos and Stuart C. Brown. Englewood Cliffs, NJ: Prentice-Hall, 1994, ix–xii.

Faigley, Lester. *Fragments of Rationality: Postmodernity and the Subject of Composition*. Pittsburgh, PA: U of Pittsburgh P, 1992.

Freedman, Carl. "Marxist Theory, Radical Pedagogy, and the Reification of Thought." *College English* 49 (1987): 70–82.

Grady, Hugh and Susan Wells. "Toward a Rhetoric of Intersubjectivity: Introducing Jürgen Habermas." *Journal of Advanced Composition* 6 (1985–86): 33–47.

Kinneavy, James. "Restoring the Humanities: The Return of Rhetoric from Exile." In *The Rhetorical Tradition and Modern Writing*. Ed. James R. Murphy. New York: MLA, 1982, 19–28.

McComiskey, Bruce. "Neo-Sophistic Rhetorical Theory: Sophistic Precedents for Contemporary Epistemic Rhetoric." *RSQ* 24.3–4 (1994): 1–24.

Phelps, Louise Weatherbee. *Composition as a Human Science: Contributions to the Self-Understanding of a Discipline*. New York: Oxford UP, 1988.

Roberts, Patricia. "Habermas' Varieties of Communicative Action: Controversy without Combat." *Journal of Advanced Composition* 11 (1991): 409–24.

Sebberson, David. "Composition, Philosophy, and Rhetoric: The 'Problem of Power.' " *Journal of Advanced Composition* 13 (1993): 199–216.

Spellmeyer, Kurt. "After Theory: From Textuality to Attunement with the World." *College English* 58 (1996): 893–913.

———. *Common Ground: Dialogue, Understanding and the Teaching of Composition*. Englewood Cliffs, NJ: Prentice-Hall, 1993.

Trimbur, John. "Consensus and Difference in Collaborative Learning." *College English* 51 (1989): 602–616.

Vitanza, Victor. "Three Countertheses: Or, A Critical In(ter)vention into Composition Theories and Pedagogies." In *Contending with Words: Composition and Rhetoric in a Postmodern Age*. Ed. Patrica Harkin and John Schilb. New York: MLA of America, 1991, 139–72.

Wells, Susan. "Habermas, Communicative Competence, and the Teaching of Technical Discourse." In *Theory in the Classroom*. Ed. Cary Nelson. Urbana: U of Illinois P, 1986, 245–69.

———. "Rogue Cops and Health Care: What Do We Want From Public Writing?" *College Composition and Communication* 47 (1996): 325–41.

———. *Sweet Reason: Rhetoric and the Discourses of Modernity*. Chicago: U of Chicago P, 1996.

                                                                                  SUSAN BROWN CARLTON

CULTURAL STUDIES

Summary

Cultural studies designates a web of overlapping practices that have influenced research and teaching across various academic disciplines, especially in the humanities and social sciences. Work in cultural studies seems to be dependent upon a growing body of "key" texts distributed largely through a set of anthologies and reference works. As a result, no one method of analysis can be identified with the practice of cultural studies. Instead, the inquiries of cultural studies borrow techniques of analysis from a variety of disciplines: interview and survey techniques from sociology; archival research from history; cinematic analysis from film studies; critique from the Frankfurt School; textual analysis from semiotics. As a consequence, the concepts used in cultural studies are derived from the modes of analysis employed, rather than vice versa. The pattern of a given cultural studies inquiry, therefore, is not so much one of the conscious development of an interdisciplinary practice as the development of an ongoing conversation about a lexicon in which crucial terms such as "culture," or "intervention," or "signifying practices" are contested. Discussions of the term "culture," for example, usually begin with Raymond Williams's gloss on the term in *Culture and Society* (pp. 317ff) and that book's sequel, *The Long Rev-olution* (pp. 41–71), which is then redefined in order to alter the scope of the subject matter under investigation so that a new analysis can be admitted to the conversation (see, for example, Bennett's "Putting Policy into Cultural Stud-ies"). From these contested definitions comes a library of analyses from which new keywords and analyses emerge.

Although these practices do not lend themselves to easy codification and many advocates decline to discuss an all-encompassing "theory," it may be said cul-tural studies entails:

- resistance to essential notions of the self; cultural studies practitioners see identity as a product of interactions between, and among, various subcultures and dominant cul-tures and as mediated by the conflicting discourses of class, gender, and race
- an active engagement with political issues that intersect with pedagogical concerns
- a strict attention to the ordinary struggles of everyday life (whether the struggles are contemporary or historical)
- a critical intervention in the construction of meaning

Whether studying punk rock, lyric poetry, the fashion industry, youth culture, or stock car racing, cultural studies advocates do not assume that "meaning" is inherent in the text, artifact, or social practice under discussion. For instance, the meaning of a TV show is understood to be a product of struggle and ne-gotiation between the text, the text's producer, and the text's consumer. While cultural studies seems at times to be synonymous with the study of "popular culture," its practices are also useful for studying various issues outside the domain of the popular. Illnesses such as AIDs, ethics, scientific practices, and institutional critique are common cultural studies projects.

Reception and Significance in Composition Studies

Many of the cultural studies practices that became connected with composi-tion studies were associated with the Birmingham School, which may be said to have emerged from a set of unrelated inquiries undertaken by Oxford- and Cambridge-trained scholars who found that Arnoldian/Leavisite notions of "cul-ture" had little to do with—and tended to devalue—the experiences of the mostly working-class students in the extramural education programs in which they taught. These encounters led such scholars as Raymond Williams, Richard Hoggart, and E. P. Thompson (independently of one another) to rethink the idea of "culture" in their scholarship and pedagogy. Williams's *Culture and Society* and *The Long Revolution*, Hoggart's *Uses of Literacy*, and Thompson's *Making of the English Working Class* provided new ways of thinking about culture as the "lived experience" of ordinary people, especially those who had little access to "high" culture.

By the early 1960s, these books had proved influential in changing prevailing notions of culture that focused on the productions of an elite. In 1965 Richard

Hoggart, after accepting an appointment in the Department of English at Birmingham University, founded the Centre for Contemporary Cultural Studies. In the face of indifference from his colleagues in English and hostility from those in sociology, Hoggart and his first assistant (fresh from his own stint of extramural teaching and a thesis about Henry James), Stuart Hall, developed the most mythologized academic project since the postwar era. Cultural studies scholars examined the many ways in which working-class people resisted forces of domination and made sense of their lives from whatever was available, ranging from ''elite'' texts (see Thompson, *Making of the English Working Class*) to mass-produced ones. Early research includes Dick Hebdige's examination of punk fashion, *Subculture: The Meaning of Style*; and Paul Willis's ethnographic inquiry into the ways working-class boys resist middle-class education, entitled *Learning to Labor*. Much important work from this early period was collectively produced: the Women's Studies Interest Group published *Women Take Issue: Aspects of Women's Subordination*, and Stuart Hall edited, with various colleagues, such collections as *Policing the Crisis: Mugging, the State, and Law and Order*, as well as a work on youth culture called *Resistance through Rituals* (Hall and Jefferson).

Its emergence from a specific pedagogical context made British cultural studies especially appealing to composition teachers working in the United States. Part of the appeal, no doubt, stems from a recognition of the innovative work undertaken by Willis, Hall, and others whose ethnographic and/or politicized inquiries seemed appropriate to the times. Some compositionists turned to cultural studies as part of a response to pedagogical approaches that view the writing classroom as a neutral, apolitical site for students to express their feelings. To connect cultural studies with composition studies is to assume that teaching has political consequences and that neither pedagogy nor course content is neutral (see Ohmann, 325). Most importantly, much of the work in British cultural studies—ethnographic inquiries into the nature of subcultures, studies of media and the popular, and examinations of other aspects of everyday life—paralleled interests that were independently developing in U.S. composition circles. For example, *Errors and Expectations*, Mina Shaughnessy's path-breaking work with basic writers, which is based on a specific rethinking of the role of ''error'' in student-produced texts, makes it possible to view literacy not as a skill, but as a site of struggle over meaning and identity. Similarly, Shirley Brice Heath's ethnography, *Ways with Words*, studies the social and political context of language skills as they develop among rural school children. These are just two works which, while hardly indebted to British cultural studies, helped to create a receptive context for work—theoretical and practical—from overseas. Since the mid-1980s, cultural studies programs and courses have begun to spread in universities across the United States, as a search on the World Wide Web will show.

In surveying the work done in English composition, it is difficult and problematic to draw boundaries demarcating when a scholar or a teacher is or is not practicing cultural studies. As C. Mark Hurlbert and Michael Blitz argue, ''[W]e can say that cultural studies is an academic lie we tell ourselves. There's no such thing as non-cultural studies. There is only a vast array of distinctions among levels of attention to cultural phenomena and cultural events'' (e-mail interview). On the other hand, the range of composition practices clearly demarcates people philosophically and politically; some teachers define their pedagogical goals as being at odds with cultural studies (see, for example Maxine Hairston's ''Required Courses Should Not Focus on Politically Charged Social Issues''). It is also difficult to decide what actually constitutes work in cultural studies. Rather than assume a position of authority to decide whose work in composition should be identified with cultural studies and whose should not, we have decided to include work in the field that is self-identified as cultural studies.

Scholarship That Articulates Cultural Studies and Composition

As Patricia Harkin (e-mail interview) explains, connecting composition studies and cultural studies is an especially complex task because both formations are themselves multidisciplinary and because both enterprises specifically call upon practitioners to engage problems of pedagogy as part of their project. Following Fredric Jameson, Harkin gives the label ''articulation'' to the ''punctual and ephemeral'' connections among aspects of the several inquiries and pedagogies that these local and contingent efforts entail.

In a series of influential texts, James Berlin explained the conceptions of the Birmingham School and applied their techniques of analysis to the concerns of the composition teacher in the United States. In ''Composition Studies and Cultural Studies: Collapsing Boundaries,'' Berlin traces theories of rhetoric in English departments that approximate, but fall short of, the promise of cultural studies to ''provide a comprehensive program that can critique the production and reception of discourse within the realm of power and politics'' (130). Liberal expressionism and social constructionist rhetorics, he argues, fail to take into account aspects of power and subjectivity working on individuals in societies. Social epistemic rhetoric comes closer to mirroring the development of cultural studies put forth by Terry Eagleton, which Berlin paraphrases as ''the examination of the ways discursive formations are related to power or, alternately, the study of language's uses in the service of power'' (100). In ''Composition Studies and Cultural Studies,'' Berlin describes the purposes and goals of a composition course that

[is organized] around an examination of the cultural codes, the social semiotics, that are working themselves out in shaping consciousness in our students. . . . Our effort is to make students aware of the cultural codes—the various competing discourses—that attempt to influence who they are. Our larger purpose is to encourage our students to resist and negotiate these codes—these hegemonic discourses—in order to bring about more personally humane and socially equitable economic and political arrangements. (50)

Berlin's theory for a cultural studies–inflected composition program was instituted at Purdue University. Composition teachers trained by Berlin admit some difficulties with this approach, which were related to resistance from the university's mostly white, mostly conservative undergraduate students (see Downing and Sosnoski, *Conversations in Honor of James Berlin*, a special issue of *Works and Days*). Since Berlin's death in 1994, Patricia Harkin has maintained the program's focus on cultural studies but has shifted away from an exclusive emphasis on critique. In a recent e-mail interview, she described the current focus as follows:

I consider [cultural studies at Purdue] in a context of "commodity capitalism," . . . a stage of capitalism in which . . . absolutely everything . . . has become a commodity to be purchased and consumed. In such a context, many students no longer think of schooling as a process of learning, but rather as a commodified "credit," or degree, which they purchase much as they purchase auto insurance. . . . And—in such a context, "cultural studies" as MERELY critique is not a particularly desirable commodity. Therefore . . . I'm inclined to offer Cultural Studies/Composing as an instance of AGENCY that comes from being an informed producer and consumer of writing. So we "teach" the explanation paper, for example, as a genre that the culture values but we also question why the culture values this genre enough to think that it should be taught in first year writing instead of (say) the Haiku, a genre that culture says it values but does not enjoin. . . . In this way, cultural studies can fulfill its responsibility to critique disciplinarity but do so homeopathically—by going through the cultural behavior it examines, rather than simply demanding resistance to it.

While Berlin is the most widely recognized proponent of cultural studies in the teaching of writing, some of the other key figures are: Michael Blitz, Karen Fitts, Alan France, Diana George, C. Mark Hurlbert, John Schilb, Diana Shoos (George and Shoos), and John Trimbur.

Michael Blitz and C. Mark Hurlbert have collaborated to write extensively about cultural studies and the politics of composition. Their work often traces ways in which institutional and corporate settings of the university influence how and what one teaches. In "The Institution('s) Lives!" (Hurlbert and Blitz), they describe their project as being about "the university as the script-making machinery that it is, . . . how any of us goes about writing our own scripts, about finding our own ways of interacting with students and colleagues and with the institution itself in meaningful and more socially responsible ways." In "Cults of Culture" (Blitz and Hurlbert) they examine the institutional script of "cultural studies" and argue for a more critical reading than it typically gets in the textbooks and essay collections that explain and authorize it. In "Rumors of Change: The Classroom, Our Classrooms, and Big Business" (Hurlbert and Blitz), they bring to the surface the many ways in which educational institutions and corporations work together and competitively in "the business of maintaining or transforming culture." And in the essay collection they edited, *Composition and Resistance* (Hurlbert and Blitz), they write about the possibilities of class projects that amount to collective "culture making." They claim, "Finally that's where cultural studies has to go—it has to take on multiple projects of culture-making that take into account the very well-being of cultures and communities" (Blitz and Hurlbert, e-mail interview).

Karen Fitts and Alan France describe their goal for cultural studies and composition as wanting to make "students aware of the presence of ideology in their lives, to enable their reading and writing of powerful cultural texts, and to flag these texts as constructed, as not a part of the a natural world, and therefore as susceptible to being reconstructed" (ix). Fitts and France's 1995 anthology, *Left Margins: Cultural Studies and Composition Pedagogy*, focuses on the conflict and student resistance typically generated by this teaching approach, and its essays explore classroom practices for turning that oppositional moment into a fruitful one pedagogically. Henry Giroux, in that collection, claims that it is necessary to see pedagogy as a central aspect of cultural studies, as a way of connecting theory and practice, form and content (7). Writing assignments, he claims, should be designed to get "students to theorize their own experiences rather than articulate the meanings of other people's theories" (11). Gerald Graff critiques *Left Margins* for being caught in a "classic double bind": "The only way oppositional pedagogy can avoid being authoritarian is by ceasing to be oppositional" ("The Dilemma of Oppositional Pedagogy," 275). He claims this contradiction cannot be overcome at the level of a single course, but only when looking at the organization and interrelation of courses in the curriculum (275).

Diana George and Diana Shoos endorse the cultural studies approach for its relevance in engaging students in writing related to memory, experience, observation, and research, while also insisting on the relevance of all texts for cultural analysis and engaging the complexity and contradictions of student and teacher responses to cultural texts (210). George and Shoos warn, however, that all courses in popular culture are not cultural studies: "Cultural studies . . . is about critiquing institutions, especially at those institutions that embody power relations. . . . [A] course that attempts to use cultural studies without acknowledging its domain as an interrogator of institutions is simply a course in pop culture" (201). However, many persons whose work concerns film, popular music, TV, technoculture, or the World Wide Web continue to describe themselves as cultural studies practitioners, much to the consternation of earlier proponents (see Nelson, "Always Already Cultural Studies").

A focus on the popular, nonetheless, is often a prominent feature of cultural studies approaches to composition, as many textbooks (like George and Trimbur's *Reading Culture*) demonstrate. John Trimbur argues in "Composition Studies: Postmodern or Popular" that a cultural studies that focuses on the reader's reception of the popular can act as a response to the "privatizing and depoliticizing effects" of postmodernism (119). He conceives of cultural studies as "the popular practices individuals and groups have devised to negotiate the discursive maze of urban life" (127). Cultural studies infused into composition, he argues, would demand consideration not just of cultural texts, but of the reader's active engagement with them: "to connect rhetoric both to sign systems and lived experience" (130).

Like Trimbur, John Schilb, in "Cultural Studies, Postmodernism, and Composition," claims that composition as an institutional formation is well suited to investigate cultural studies and postmodernism (177). An inquiry into cultural studies and postmodernism, argues Schilb, could help "composition become what it deserves to become: not a plodding servant of other disciplines but a key force in the diagnosis of the contemporary world" (188). For this to happen, Schilb claims, composition needs to lose its focus on the individual course and open up composition students to "team teaching, joint section meetings, programs colloquia, letters between classes, and even program publications" (188). To some extent, this has been happening. (See, for example, the range of essays on intersections between culture and composition in Hurlbert and Totten's *Social Issues in the English Classroom*.)

The first-year writing course at Carnegie Mellon University is taught, according to David Shumway, as an entry into issues like American identities or politics of the media. In it, he says, "students are taught to discover and interpret cultural narratives, stories that help communities and individuals within them organize and articulate their social and moral values, and which reappear in many texts and media" (e-mail interview).

Graduate programs in composition and rhetoric are adding cultural studies emphases, for example, at the University of Utah. Susan Miller writes that

composition pedagogy based on cultural studies accents the production of texts, not their interpretation. It emphasizes reading rhetorically, to determine the purpose, readership, selection of evidence, language, and form of specifically situated acts of writing, and teaches heuristics for writing in awareness of each of these elements of analysis. (e-mail interview)

In a recent e-mail interview, Linda Brodkey said:

My take on cultural studies is decidedly ethnographic, that is, a matter of teaching students to imagine themselves as cultural actors whose performances in cultural events— such as their writing and reading practices—are available to cultural analysis and critique by way of systematic observation, interview, and analysis.

In "Writing about Difference: Hard Cases for Cultural Studies," Penticoff and Brodkey explain the rationale for the controversial "Writing about Difference" course taught at the University of Texas at Austin. The mandatory freshman writing course focused on the issue of cultural difference by asking students to engage in a "sustained rhetorical inquiry" framed around U.S. District and Supreme Court opinions on cases involving issues of race, gender, physical disability, bilingualism, and sexual orientation.

This course and many similar courses that draw on cultural studies to teach composition have come under heavy fire from the academic right. In "Diversity, Ideology, and Teaching Writing," Maxine Hairston delivers a jeremiad against any teacher who advocates politicized theory or social change in the composition class. She emphatically renounces such practice as "radical," "regressive," "silly, simplistic," and basically a coercive tool of the "cultural left" (183). First, Hairston claims that a composition course drawn from Marxist political theory will alienate the students and threaten to silence their writing. Secondly, she argues that political courses lack a student-centered focus and that the teacher becomes a dictatorial authority in the classroom.

From a different political position, Kurt Spellmeyer, in "Out of the Fashion Industry: From Cultural Studies to the Anthropology of Knowledge," views cultural studies as a fashionable trend in the composition field that suffers a tendency by some teachers to prioritize arcane theory, while disregarding or disdaining students. While he seems to overstate the theoretical rigidity of cultural studies, he usefully reminds compositionists that all innovative work on culture need not originate in Britain. He mentions Shirley Brice Heath's *Ways with Words* and Mike Rose's *Possible Lives* as works that provide complex portraits of people interacting with culture.

Finally, a few writers whose work concerns teaching locate themselves outside of the composition tradition described here. James Sosnoski argues that cultural studies is given too restrictive a history in the textbooks that authorize it. He proposes alternatives to the "negative" form of critique characteristic of cultural studies work and is concerned with cultural agency in Cyberspace. Gerald Graff, in *Beyond the Culture Wars*, is concerned with many of the issues that propel cultural studies but deliberately distinguishes himself from—and often writes critically about—the Birmingham trajectory of cultural studies. In "Cultural Studies, Postmodernism, and Composition," John Schilb makes a case for Graff's views in the teaching of writing. David Shumway, Anne Balsamo, Kathleen McCormick, and Paul Smith write about the problems of teaching cultural studies to first-year college students in courses that have writing components but focus on literary issues.

BIBLIOGRAPHY

Primary Texts

Aronowitz, Stanley. *Roll over Beethoven*. Hanover, CT: Wesleyan UP, 1993.

Bennett, Tony. *Outside Literature*. London: Routledge, 1990.

———. "Putting Policy into Cultural Studies." In *Cultural Studies*. Ed. Lawrence Grossberg, Cary Nelson, and Paula Treichler. New York: Routledge, 1992, 23–37.

Bennett, Tony, Colin Mercer, and Janet Wooacot. *Popular Culture and Social Relations*. London. Open UP, 1986.

Berube, Michael. "Pop Goes the Academy: Cultstuds Fight the Power." In *Public Access*. Ed. Michael Berube. New York: Verso, 1994, 137–160.

Davies Ioan. *Cultural Studies and Beyond*. London: Routledge, 1995.

Eagleton, Terry. *Literary Theory: An Introduction*. Minneapolis: U of Minnesota P, 1983.

Easthope, Anthony. *Literary into Cultural Studies*. London: Routledge, 1991.

Fiske, John. *Power Plays, Power Works*. London: Verso, 1993.

Franklin, Sarah, et al. *Off-Centre: Feminism and Cultural Studies*. New York: Harper, 1991.

Frow, John. *Cultural Studies and Cultural Value*. Oxford, U.K.: Oxford UP, 1995.

Gilroy, Paul. *There Ain't No Black in the Union Jack*. London: Hutchinson, 1987.

Giroux, Henry A. "Who Writes in a Cultural Studies Class? or, Where Is the Pedagogy?" In *Left Margins*. Ed. Karen Fitts and Alan W. France. Albany: State U of New York P, 1995, 3–16.

Giroux, Henry, David Shumway, Paul Smith, and James J. Sosnoski. "The Need for Cultural Studies: Resisting Intellectuals and Oppositional Public Spheres." *Dalhousie Review* 64 (1984): 472–86.

Grossberg, Lawrence. *We Gotta Get Out of This Place*. London: Routledge, 1992.

Grossberg, Lawrence, Cary Nelson, and Paula Treichler. *Cultural Studies*. New York: Routledge, 1992.

Hall, Stuart. *Policing the Crisis: Mugging, the State, and Law and Order*. New York: Holmes and Meier, 1978.

Hall, Stuart, Dorothy Hobson, Andrew Lowe, and Paul Willis. *Culture, Media, Language*. London: Hutchinson, 1980.

Hall, Stuart and Tony Jefferson. *Resistance through Rituals*. London: Hutchinson, 1976.

Harris, David. *From Class Struggle to the Politics of Pleasure: The Effects of Gramscianism on Cultural Studies*. London: Routledge, 1992.

Hebdige, Dick. *Cut 'n' Mix*. London: Commedeia, 1987.

———. *Hiding in the Light*. London: Commedeia, 1988.

———. *Subculture. The Meaning of Style*. London: Methuen, 1979.

Hoggart, Richard. *The Uses of Literacy*. London: Chatto and Windus, 1957.

Jameson, Fredric. "On Cultural Studies." *Social Text* 34 (1993): 17–54.

———. Reification and Utopia in Mass Culture." *Social Text* 1 (1979): 130–48.

Johnson, Richard. "What Is Cultural Studies Anyway?" *Social Text* 16 (1986–87): 38–80.

MacCabe, Colin. *High Theory/Low Culture*. Manchester, UK: Manchester UP, 1986.

McRobbie, Angela, "New Times in Cultural Studies." *New Formations* 13 (1991) 1–18.

———. "Settling Accounts with Subcultures: A Feminist Critique." In *On Record: Rock, Pop, and the Written Word*. Ed. Simon Firth and Andrea Goodwin. New York: Pantheon, 1990, 66–80.

McRobbie, Angela, and Mica Nava, eds. *Gender and Generation*. London: Macmillan, 1984.

Morris, Meaghan. "Banality in Cultural Studies." *Discourse* 10.2 (1988): 3–29.

Nelson, Cary. "Always Already Cultural Studies: Two Conferences and a Manifesto." *Journal of the Midwest Modern Language Association* (special issue on cultural studies and new historicism) 24 (Spring 1991): 24–38.

Nelson, Cary, et al., eds. *Cultural Studies*. New York: Routledge, 1992.

Radway, Janice. *Reading the Romance*. Chapel Hill: U of North Carolina P, 1984.

Ross, Andrew. *No Respect: Intellectuals and Popular Culture*. London: Routledge, 1989.

Smith, Dorothy. *The Everyday World as Problematic*. Toronto, Canada: U of Toronto P, 1987.

Storey, John. *What Is Cultural Studies? A Reader*. London: Arnold, 1996.

Thompson, E. P. *The Making of the English Working Class*. New York: Vintage, 1963.

————. *The Poverty of Theory*. London: Merlin, 1978.

————, ed. *Warwick University Ltd.: Industry, Management, and the University*. Harmondsworth, UK: Penguin, 1970.

Turner, Graeme. *British Cultural Studies*. London: Unwin Hyman, 1990.

Williams, Raymond. *Culture and Society*. London: Chatto and Windus, 1958.

————. *Keywords*. New York: Oxford UP, 1984.

————. *The Long Revolution*. London: Chatto and Windus, 1963.

————. *Politics of Modernism: Against the New Conformists*. London: Verso, 1989.

————. *Problems in Materialism and Culture*. London: Verso, 1989.

Major Scholarship in Composition

Balsamo, Anne. "Cultural Studies and the Undergraduate Literature Curriculum." In *Cultural Studies in the English Classroom*. Ed. James Berlin and Michael Vivion. Portsmouth, NH: Boynton, Cook, Heinemann, 1992, 145–64.

Berlin, James. "Composition and Cultural Studies." In *Composition and Resistance*, Ed. C. Mark Hurlbert and Michael Blitz. Portsmouth, NH: Boynton/Cook, 1991, 47–56.

————. "Composition Studies and Cultural Studies: Collapsing Boundaries." In *In the Field: Sites of Composition Studies*. Ed. Anne Ruggles Gere. New York: MLA, 1993, 99–116.

————. *Rhetorics, Poetics, and Cultures: Refiguring College English Studies*. Urbana, IL: NCTE, 1996.

Berlin, James A., and Michael J. Vivion, eds. *Cultural Studies in the English Classroom*. Portsmouth, NH: Boynton/Cook–Heinemann, 1992.

Blitz, Michael, and C. Mark Hurlbert. "Class Actions." In *Composition and Resistance*. Ed. C. Mark Hurlbert and Michael Blitz. Portsmouth, NH: Boynton/Cook–Heinemann, 1991, 167–74.

————. "Cults of Culture." In *Cultural Studies in the English Classroom*. Ed. James A. Berlin and Michael J. Vivion. Portsmouth, NH: Boynton/Cook–Heinemann, 1992.

————. Interview by author, E-mail, 13 February 1997.

Brodkey, Linda. Interview by author, E-mail, 15 February 1997.

Downing, David, and James Sosnoski, eds. *Conversations in Honor of James Berlin*, A Special Issue of *Works and Days* 27/28 (Fall 1997).

Fitts, Karen, and Alan W. France. *Left Margins: Cultural Studies and Composition Pedagogy*. Albany: State U of New York P, 1995.

Foreman, Joel, and David R. Shumway. "Cultural Studies: Reading Visual Texts." In *Cultural Studies in the English Classroom*. Ed. James A. Berlin and Michael J. Vivion. Portsmouth, NH: Boynton/Cook–Heinemann, 1992.

George, Diana, and Diana Shoos. "Issues of Subjectivity and Resistance: Cultural Studies in the Composition Classroom." In *Cultural Studies in the English Classroom*. Ed. James A. Berlin and Michael J. Vivion. Portsmouth, NH: Boynton/Cook–Heinemann, 1992, 200–210.

Gere, Anne Ruggles, ed. *Into the Field: Sites of Composition Studies*. New York: MLA, 1993.

Graff, Gerald. *Beyond the Culture Wars: How Teaching the Conflicts Can Revitalize American Education*. New York: Norton, 1992.

————. "The Dilemma of Oppositional Pedagogy: A Response." In *Left Margins: Cultural Studies and Composition Pedagogy*. Ed. Karen Fitts and Alan France. Albany: State U of New York P, 1995, 275–82.

Hairston, Maxine. "Diversity, Ideology, and Teaching Writing." *College Composition and Communication* 42 (1994): 179–93.

———. "Required Courses Should Not Focus on Politically Charged Social Issues." *Chronicle of Higher Education* 23 (January 1991): B1, B2.

Harkin, Patricia. Interview by author. E-mail, 11 February 1997.

———. "In the Crossfire: (After) Jim Berlin." *Works and Days* 27/28 (Spring/Fall 1996): 291–98.

Harkin, Patricia, and John Schilb, eds. *Contending with Words: Composition and Rhetoric in a Postmodern Age*. New York: MLA, 1991.

Heath, Shirley Brice. *Ways with Words*. Cambridge: Cambridge UP, 1983.

Hurlbert, C. Mark, and Michael Blitz. "The Institution('s) Lives!" *Pre/Text* 13 (Spring/Summer 1992): 59–78.

———. "Rumors of Change: The Classroom, Our Classrooms, and Big Business." In *Social Issues in the English Classroom*. Ed. C. Mark Hurlbert and Samuel Totten. Urbana, IL: NCTE, 1992, 269–82.

Hurlbert, C. Mark, and Samuel Totten, eds. *Social Issues in the English Classroom*. Urbana, IL: NCTE, 1992.

McCormick, Kathleen. *The Culture of Reading and the Teaching of English*. Manchester: Manchester UP, 1994.

Miller, Susan. E-mail interview, 16 February 1997.

Ohmann, Richard. "Afterword." In *Left Margins: Cultural Studies and Composition Pedagogy*. Ed. Karen Fitts and Alan France. Albany: SUNY P, 1995, 325–31.

Penticoff, Richard, and Linda Brodkey. " 'Writing about Difference': Hard Cases for Cultural Studies." In *Cultural Studies in the English Classroom*. Ed. James A. Berlin and Michael J. Vivion. Portsmouth, NH: Boynton/Cook–Heinemann, 1992, 123–44.

Rose, Mike. *Possible Lives*. Boston: Houghton-Mifflin, 1995.

Schilb, John. "Cultural Studies, Postmodernism, and Composition." In *Contending with Words: Composition and Rhetoric in a Postmodern Age*. Ed. Patricia Harkin and John Schilb. New York: MLA, 1991, 173–88.

Shaughnessy, Mina. *Errors and Expectations: A Guide for Teachers of Basic Writing*. New York: Oxford UP, 1977.

Shumway, David. Interview by author. E-mail, 15 February 1997.

Smith, Paul. "A Course in Cultural Studies." In *Cultural Studies in the English Classroom*. Ed. James A. Berlin and Michael J. Vivion. Portsmouth, NH: Boynton/Cook–Heinemann, 1992, 169–81.

Sosnoski, James. *Modern Skeletons in Postmodern Closets: A Cultural Studies Alternative*. Charlottesville: U of Virginia P, 1995.

Spellmeyer, Kurt. "Out of the Fashion Industry: From Cultural Studies to the Anthropology of Knowledge." *College Composition and Communication* 47.3 (1996): 424–36.

Trimbur, John. "Composition Studies: Postmodern or Popular." In *Into the Field: Sites of Composition Studies*. Ed. Anne Ruggles Gere. New York: MLA, 1993, 117–32.

Trimbur, John, and Diana George. *Reading Culture*. New York: HarperCollins, 1995.

Willis, Paul. *Learning to Labor*. New York: Columbia UP, 1981.

PAULA MATHIEU, JAMES J. SOSNOSKI, AND DAVID ZAUHAR

CURRENT-TRADITIONAL RHETORIC

Summary

Current-traditional rhetoric traces its theoretical grounding to eighteenth-century thinking articulated by the "British new rhetoricians": George Campbell, Hugh Blair, and Richard Whatley (Crowley, "The Current-Traditional Theory of Style," 233; *The Methodical Memory* 56, xi).

The term "current-traditional" was first used by Daniel Fogarty in 1959 and was clearly a philosophy of writing instruction that emphasized form over content. Fogarty compares current-traditional rhetoric to the rhetorical approaches articulated by Aristotle, Kenneth Burke, and I. A. Richards, and as he summarizes their views in a chart, Fogarty notes that Aristotle's rhetoric includes Deliberative oratory and Epideictic oratory, a central theme in Burke is "identification," and so on. Under the "current-traditional" section, Fogarty starts with

GRAMMAR—SYNTAX—SPELLING—PUNCTUATION—MECHANICS

and moves through the "modes" (Exposition, Description, Narration, and Argument—commonly known as EDNA) to "style qualities" (where "clearness" is the first entry) and into the atomistic division of a text—words, sentences, paragraphs, and so on (118–19). Current-traditional rhetoric is clearly rule governed to the extent that a writer would *begin* by learning the rules (an approach modeled on how Latin had always been taught) and, once the rules were known, the actual writing might start.

In the current-traditional view, as Sharon Crowley puts it, the individual author's mind is seen "as a storehouse filled with treasures" which, on demand, creates clear and "grammatical sentences [that] literally represent complete thoughts," ideas so clearly presented that anyone with a good mind can understand their meaning (*Methodical Memory* 59, 174). Perspicuity is what matters; language is only a medium to translate the mind's thoughts into words. Such a focus shifts attention from a text's *content* to center only on the text's form—how the ideas are being (re)presented—an arhetorical approach that removes considerations of audience, purpose, and so on from the composition.

The current-traditional approach also represents a way of writing instruction that posits an isolated and individual author whose mind clearly sees and understands a topic and is capable of articulating that vision perfectly in words (words that are chosen after the idea has been "discovered" and prior to any language that might encapsulate the notion). Those words clearly and completely convey the idea to the reader, who will see and understand that idea or image in exactly the same way. Because all minds operate in the same manner, text produced by the author's mind will perfectly represent what is *in* that mind and all readers will easily understand what the author put into words. And since the words clearly and "naturally" represent the ideas inside the mind, something of a "mind fusion" occurs, with reader and writer perfectly understanding one another. Words have to be used for communication, of course, but they act only as the clear lens through which ideas are transmitted.

The current-traditional approach also insists on coherence, both in each paragraph and in the essay as a whole; each "theme," therefore, can have only one central idea—and that main topic is determined before the writing begins and often formalized in an outline the author follows while writing (see Crowley, "Current-Traditional Rhetoric," 156; *Methodical Memory* 68). Further, the gist of any "theme" is presented as moving from the general to the specific, for the general is always determined before any words are put on paper.

Reception and Significance in Composition Studies

Current-traditional rhetoric in America was grounded in Alexander Bain's 1888 text, *English Composition*, and dominated textbooks published throughout this century. Many current texts continue to focus on the "four modes" of discourse (EDNA). Current composition texts often insist that students using those texts approach their own writing through what Richard Young classifies as other features of the current-traditional approach:

- a focus on the product instead of the process
- an atomistic way of looking at a text, seeking always to work with its smallest elements
- a strong focus on surface features
- a concentration on the research paper. (31)

We can still see the current-traditional mind-set at work in composition programs that divide their first-year writing courses into an expository/argument writing class followed by a research-based class—as if one cannot incorporate the other and as if one were better and more advanced in some way than the other (Crowley, "Current-Traditional Rhetoric," 157).

Teachers in current-traditional classrooms do a lot of lecturing in order to discuss how effectively "model" (often professional) essays follow the many prescriptions for correct writing that are outlined in the textbook. Student writing and student texts are secondary.

The current-traditional approach to writing instruction presents writing, not as a messy, recursive procedure, but as "a neat linear progression: select, narrow, and amplify" (Crowley, *Methodical Memory* 148). Assignments, since they ignore rhetorical considerations, often ask students to select a topic in which they are interested, organize their ideas, create a thesis statement, write an outline, and compose the draft—in exactly that sequence.

Over the last 20 or so years, "process pedagogy" has attempted to challenge the current-traditional model of writing instruction, seeking to replace what has been known as Paulo Freire's "banking method" of teaching with a more student-centered classroom, where the teacher acts as a "facilitator" who often asks students to work in collaborative groups as they peer-review one another's texts. Student writing is central to such classrooms, and writing is presented as an often-disorderly, recursive activity. However, for the most part, assignments still ask students to "select a topic and decide what you want to write before you start writing"; writing is seen as a linear process where each isolated activity follows the previous part of the sequence; student writers continue to see themselves as isolated, individual authors who move into the university writing community only when they can somehow author(ize) a text; creating an outline before writing any "text" is commonplace; and teachers often still read and evaluate only the product that is produced.

BIBLIOGRAPHY

Primary Texts and Major Scholarship in Composition

Berlin, James. *Rhetoric and Reality: Writing Instruction in American Colleges, 1900–1985.* Carbondale: Southern Illinois UP, 1987.

———. *Writing Instruction in Nineteenth-Century American Colleges.* Carbondale: Southern Illinois UP, 1984.

Connors, Robert J. "Mechanical Correctness as a Focus in Composition Instruction." *College Composition and Communication* 36 (1985): 61–72.

———. "The Rise and Fall of the Modes of Discourse." *College Composition and Communication* 32 (1981): 444–55.

Crowley, Sharon. "Around 1971: Current-Traditional Rhetoric and Process Models of Composing." In *Composition in the 21st Century.* Ed. Lynn Z. Bloom, Donald A. Daiker, and Edward M. White. Carbondale: Southern Illinois UP, 1996, 64–74.

———. "Current-Traditional Rhetoric." *Encyclopedia of Rhetoric and Composition.* Ed. Theresa Enos. New York: Garland, 1996, 156–57.

———. "The Current-Traditional Theory of Style: An Informal History." *Rhetoric Society Quarterly* 16 (1986): 233–50.

———. *The Methodical Memory.* Carbondale: Southern Illinois UP, 1990.

Fogarty, Daniel. *Roots for a New Rhetoric.* New York: Columbia Teachers' College P, 1959.

Kitzhaber, Albert R. *Rhetoric in American Colleges, 1850–1900.* Dallas, TX: Southern Methodist UP, 1990.

Young, Richard. "Paradigms and Problems: Needed Research in Rhetorical Invention." In *Research on Composing: Points of Departure.* Ed. Charles R. Cooper and Lee Odell. Urbana, IL: NCTE, 1978, 29–47.

GREGORY R. GLAU

D

DECONSTRUCTION

Summary

In order to attempt to define "deconstruction" in a manner true to the theory itself, one must view the term "deconstruction," like any other term, as ultimately indeterminate and contextualized. According to the theory, one can never claim to have a "whole" sense of a text because its meaning constantly shifts as both readers and writers move through different contexts, such as history, time, place, and other works and aspects of the culture. As we suggest various basic claims and concepts within deconstruction, then, the reader must keep in mind the free-floating, ever-shifting nature of this particular strand of postmodernism, which has impacted contemporary composition. Within the disciplines of literary and cultural studies in the United States, deconstruction is often grouped with postmodernism and poststructuralism because, like these movements, it is characterized as "a growing awareness of randomness, ambiguity and chaos" (Faigley, 3). Of these, postmodernism is the umbrella, encompassing aesthetics, philosophical theories, and a sociohistorical assertion about the state of Western cultures (Faigley, 3). Poststructuralism is a subset of postmodernism and includes theorists who argue against a structured notion of both language itself and literary texts. Unlike structuralists, poststructuralists, including especially Michel Foucault, see, among other things, a looser connection between word (signifier) and referent (signified). Deconstruction in turn is one strand of poststructuralism based primarily on Jacques Derrida's theories.

Much of Derrida's work critiques the Platonic base of philosophy by pointing to those moments when the canonical texts have systematically ignored the epistemic nature of language by claiming a direct connection between pure thought and nature. Logocentrism is an aspect included in Derrida's attack on Western philosophy, which he calls metaphysics of presence. He uses the term *logocentrism* to refer to the assumption that we can find a word or concept that will be a stable foundation, a final word. Derrida asserts that we can only know our world through language and there is no central, fixed presence in language, unlike logocentrism, which privileges mind over language. Derrida calls into question the hierarchy apparent in all binary pairs, challenging the very nature of dualistic thinking within Western tradition. Binaries such as signified/signifier, good/evil, subjectivity/objectivity, and speech/text trap the speaker/writer into choosing between two extremes rather than integrating multiple possibilities or seeing that situations are multifaceted and that those facets interact. For Derrida, the binary is a false dichotomy because each member of the pair depends on the other for its own definition—could not in fact exist without the other. In this way, he topples the binary hierarchy of structuralism, in which the signified is privileged over the signifier.

Derrida focuses on the relationship of language, thought, and culture most directly in *Dissemination, Of Grammatology*, and *Writing and Differance*. His arguments about the relationship of presence and language can be demonstrated in his treatment of language itself. He coined his key term, *differance*, to illustrate at least three simultaneous movements in language. First, meaning is made only through *differance*; that is, we notice that the letter C differs from the letter B, and therefore that CAT is a different word from BAT. The meaning is contained only within the relationship among these words/letters and is not inherent in the signifier. Second, meaning is not made in a linear sense, as *differance* also refers to a scattering or dispersal. We can visualize a signification bouncing in a random fashion as it intersects with multiple words/letters. Third, meaning is always deferred: because we only know a thing by comparing it to those things from which it differs, we must hold meaning at bay as we collect and process these various differences. One of these differences is the binary opposite of presence or absence, which is also included in every term. For example, as one reads a word, one defers meaning until reaching the end of the sentence, and in turn defers the meaning of the paragraph until reaching its end. Thus, meaning is never fixed and continues to react with and within the context as well as within the reader.

Another important aspect of deconstruction is "play," which Derrida calls "the disruption of presence" ("Structure," 93). Play undermines a structure, and in a centerless situation is more generative and positive. He sees two sides of play:

Turned toward the lost or impossible presence of the absent origin, this structuralist thematic of broken immediacy is therefore the saddened, *negative*, nostalgic, guilty, Rousseauistic side of the thinking of play whose other side would be the Nietzschean *affirmation*, that is the joyous affirmation of the play of the world and of the innocence of becoming, the affirmation of a world of signs without fault, without truth, and without origin which is offered to an active interpretation. ("Structure," 93)

The play, often interpreted as invention within composition, is located not within the "inventor" but within the language itself. Derrida both "plays" with the words and also sees how the words themselves play within the text, which opens up all possibilities.

These assertions lead Derrida to a method of reading that looks for those places where a text works against itself. Deconstruction is desystematizing— taking a small gap, inconsistency, or "snag" and using it to interrupt the main structure, or "unity," of the text. As Derrida says, "Language bears within itself the necessity of its own critique" ("Structure," 87). Because all terms and concepts have within them a dependence on their opposites, all claims inevitably rely on their opposites as well. Thus, deconstructive readings do not try to tie a text to some signified that existed prior to and outside of the text itself. Rather, deconstruction recovers the repressed and exposes the contradictions, the uneven surfaces that an apparent unity attempts to erase. To deconstruct a text, Derrida says, is to work through the structured genealogy of its concepts in the most scrupulous and immanent fashion. At the same time one must discover what is at stake in that repression. Gerald Graff suggests that deconstruction is a method of "reading against the grain" that resembles psychoanalysis, "which proceeds by going beyond the surface or 'manifest content' of our dreams and actions, to the repressed or unconscious 'latent content' that is presumed to lurk below" (171).

Reading deconstructively demands a new view of authorship as well. Derrida claims, "The reading must always aim at a certain relationship, unperceived by the writer, between what he commands and what he does not command of the patterns of the language he uses" (quoted in Crowley, *A Teacher's Introduction* 7). Deconstruction tears apart traditional notions of "authors" as stable, fixed, autonomous subjects, and writers cannot be said to "control" the meaning of their texts. Likewise, they cannot claim to "know" their audiences, which are also indeterminate. Thus we understand the looseness and indeterminate nature of a theory in which the words themselves, the text, the audience, and even the author continue to be destabilized in an interactive process that defies both set meaning and methodology.

Reception and Significance in Composition Studies

In American English departments, deconstruction theory was first embraced by literary critics. Compositionists were not usually exposed to its primary texts. Rather, early encounters with deconstruction came through the American (Yale) school of literary theorists, which included Paul de Man, Geoffrey Hartman, and J. Hillis Miller. These theorists were denounced by compositionists as further evolutions of the New Critics, self-absorbed nihilists who contributed to elitist movements within the academy and further marginalized the compositionists.

Ironically, perhaps, Paul de Man had much to say about rhetoric, but his interpretation has largely been ignored by compositionists and rhetoricians alike. The reasons for this reluctance could range from a perception that he narrows rhetoric again to style as figures and tropes to his own personal involvement with fascism in Germany. De Man examines the history of English studies, seeking to uncover the institutional resistances to theory, especially deconstruction. He calls his version of the deconstructive project "rhetorical reading or, simply, 'reading' " (Esch, 385). De Man elevates or recovers philology and rhetoric as prerequisites for both historical understandings of texts and also for effective critiques of ideology (Esch, 385). De Man suggests literature "should be taught as a rhetoric and a poetics prior to being taught as a hermeneutics and a history" (*Resistance* 25–26). He especially invokes the *trivium* and the tradition of humane letters to show the hierarchical order of language, and he sees rhetoric as the disrupter or potentially deconstructive force (*Resistance* 14). Thus he delays the traditional interpretive project by first having readers examine the text in question as a construction of writing and rhetoric (Esch, 386).

Compositionists distrusted deconstruction, not only because of its ties to potentially elitist literary theory, but also because the Derridean concepts of language and critiques of metaphysics of presence threaten traditional assumptions of composition. Deconstruction not only disrupts time-honored concepts such as "unity and coherence," "organization or structure," "voice," "smooth transitions," and other theories such as "expressivism," but also disrupts the sense that meaning, authors, texts, and audiences are stable concepts. As Doug Brent points out, the 1970s saw rhetors like Wayne Booth "devote quite a bit of time . . . to insisting that meaning is shareable" because the deconstructive view of language "if sincerely held, would make rhetoric impossible by denying its most fundamental postulate: that we can deliberately and predictably influence each other through language" (19).

However, the changes within compositionists' reception of deconstruction can be seen in W. Ross Winterowd's range of responses. In 1987 he characterized Derrida's theorizing as "dillettante, if not downright anti-social" (cited in Crowley, *A Teacher's Introduction* 24). But more recently, in his 1994 NCTE publication, *A Teacher's Introduction to Composition in the Rhetorical Tradition*, Winterowd invites Jack Blum to contribute the culminating chapter, placing poststructural and deconstructive theories squarely in the rhetorical tradition. Winterowd does seem to exemplify the compositionist's reluctant embrace of a theory that refuses to be ignored. Others, like Sharon Crowley and James Berlin, see deconstruction as a worldview that reintroduces the importance of analyzing all discourse. As Berlin explains, "If the perceiving subject, the object perceived, and the community of fellow investigators are all in large part the effects of linguistic practices, then every discipline must begin with a consideration of the shaping of discourse in its activities" (*Rhetorics* 68). No longer can rhetoric be subordinated to either literature or philosophy because all knowledge is understood as rhetorical.

Crowley's 1989 *A Teacher's Introduction to Deconstruction* performs deconstructive readings "of what might be called the academic ideology that governs a good deal of literacy instruction in American schools" (xvi). Rather than seeing the indeterminacy of authors and texts as an end of composition, she instead seeks to move composition pedagogy away from the idea of the "sovereign author: and towards readers and the common language of community" (35). Composition theory, in other words, should shift its center of focus from writers to the larger context in which meaning is made, that is, to the play between writers and readers and communities and language. Berlin, whose project was to make composition a tool for democratic education, draws on the concept of *differance* to point out that the discussions of "subjects"—authors and readers alike—should account not only for what is thought to be present, but also "to what is left out of dominant discourses, the overlooked margins. We are asked to locate heretofore silenced voices" (*Rhetorics* 71). Thus, he calls for rhetoric to more fully acknowledge the contexts in which we make meaning: "The economic, social, and political conditions of a historical period can be known and acted upon only through discourses of the moment" (72). Like Derrida, Berlin asserts that meaning is always deferred and is defined by particular—not universal—moments.

In addition to Crowley and Berlin, other compositionists such as Lester Faigley, William Covino, and Victor Vitanza, among others, have embraced deconstruction. In his recent *Fragments of Rationality*, Lester Faigley has led the movement toward the most open embrace of deconstruction, in which he attempts to interpret the theory under a wider umbrella of "postmodernism" and apply it to present-day composition studies. That his book was widely praised and well received is another indication of a shift in perspective among compositionists. Faigley argues that most movements in composition contain within them both modernist and postmodernist tendencies. Furthermore, he uses postmodernism's critique of the "free" individual to explain why pedagogical movements to promote social equity through education have failed.

William Covino saw the significance of "play" within deconstruction as akin to rhetoric's notion of "invention." At the same time he wrote movingly in support of an open-ended writing process that allows language to generate possibilities within itself. Using a writing style that mirrors certain deconstructive moves within texts, Victor Vitanza also applies deconstructive theory to the writing process, successfully modeling how such deconstructive writing might be attempted. Although he uses deconstruction in his own writing, he is reluctant to make pedagogical claims. He argues that a deconstructive pedagogy is in fact a contradiction in terms and warns against a type of "pedagogy hope" in which compositionists falsely assume that theories can be enacted in pedagogy. Such claims, he says, deny the particularity of classrooms and reveal an underlying (and false) belief in the universality of a theory, which is a form of logocentrism.

Starting from Derrida's claim that no stable, fixed meaning exists, compositionists are led to continuous interrogation into their reading, writing, and teaching practices. This self-reflexivity and questioning attitude may be the key for future implications of deconstruction for compositionists. We must constantly question claims, too, that link a theory with an action, for as both Vitanza and

Crowley point out, a claim for deconstructive pedagogy leads to both "pedagogy hope" and impossible juxtapositions or "oxymorons." Vitanza suggests that if we declare a moratorium on attempting to turn theory into praxis at this point, we will gain enough time to realize that theory both "can, but cannot, be employed to critique and to found theoretical praxis" (160). His concern is that in composition, will to theory becomes unified and totalizing, fixed and immutable, based again upon the Greek model of pedagogy in which students are not empowered, but oppressed. This desire for mastery over a student is what Vitanza calls "pedagogy hope."

On the other hand, because of the many binaries extant in our field, which privilege one concept above the other, deconstructive theory becomes an important "tool" to explode those binaries. When we consider, for example, the binaries of teacher/student, theory/practice, and academic discourse/"real-world" writing, deconstructive theory would seem to support pedagogical trends that undermine what have long been the privileged concepts and explore, instead, the value of their opposites. Thus, deconstruction would seem to support pedagogies that decenter authority in composition classrooms, promote collaborative learning and writing, define writing assignments as open-ended and view writing processes as recursive. As writing teachers, we more often teach and acknowledge the recursivity of writing, backed up not only by deconstruction, but also by empirical research within the field. As writing teachers we also question the current traditional approach to writing in which genre boundaries were once firmly established. Instead, in some composition programs, we see one assignment merging with and influencing the next without traditional respect for modes. Crowley maintains:

On the deconstructive account (and in process pedagogy as well) writing is conceived as continuous and dynamic. For pragmatic reasons, readers and writers entertain the illusion that the flow of writing is halted by its being stapled or paper-clipped. . . . But this illusion of closure is only a convenient fiction. (*Teacher's Introduction* 41)

This resistance toward closure spills over into classroom praxis, decentering, destabilizing, and reconfiguring student-to-student and teacher-student interactions.

In addition to questioning their writing and classroom practices, compositionists have begun to question institutional practices. Examining claims for writing within the institutional context leads compositionists to examine the constraints upon the kinds of practices they institute. Deborah Esch points out that Derrida himself insisted that deconstruction was not just for "engaging texts," but also a way of engaging institutional structures:

Deconstruction goes *through* certain social and political structures, meeting with resistance and displacing institutions as it does so . . . to deconstruct traditional sanctions—theoretical, philosophical, cultural—effectively, you have to displace . . . "solid" structures, not only in the sense of material structures, but "solid" in the sense of cultural, pedagogical, political, economic structures. (379)

While some compositionists appear to embrace many of the underlying assumptions of deconstruction, it would be inappropriate (and at odds with deconstructive theory itself) to claim that changes in composition originated from deconstruction, since pressure toward these perspectives also originated from social construction, feminism, postmodernism, postcolonialism, and other theoretical bases. Given Vitanza's admonition about theory/pedagogy hope, we cannot claim to apply deconstructive theory directly. But "applying" theory to the classroom is something very different from "reading" how a theory has inverted, subverted, oozed, or woven itself into praxis. The difference lies in the flexible, questioning, and open approach we adopt. Because of the shifting and fluctuating nature of this particular theory, our analyses are simply snapshots, temporarily finding ways in which deconstruction has unraveled certain current traditional practices, yet knowing the oxymoronic nature of snapshots as freezing time and movement.

These ironies are part of the nature of deconstruction itself. Derrida is aware that his own works will, or do, deconstruct themselves. He invites us to participate—or not, opening up our own writing praxis, our classrooms, and our institutions to a playful, destabilizing, potentially transformational inquiry.

BIBLIOGRAPHY

Primary Texts

de Man, Paul. *Allegories of Reading: Figural Language in Rousseau, Nietzsche, Rilke, and Proust*. New Haven, CT: Yale UP, 1979.
———. *Blindness and Insight: Essays in the Rhetoric of Contemporary Criticism*. New York: Oxford UP, 1971.
———. *The Resistance to Theory*. Minneapolis: U of Minnesota P, 1986.
Derrida, Jacques. *Dissemination*. Trans. Barbara Johnson. Chicago: U of Chicago P, 1981.
———. *Writing and Differance*. Chicago: U of Chicago P, 1978.
———. *Of Grammatology*. Trans. Gayatri Chakravorty Spivak. Baltimore, MD: Johns Hopkins UP, 1976.
———. *The Margins of Philosophy*. Trans. Alan Bass. Chicago: U of Chicago P, 1982.
———. *Negotiations*. Ed. Deborah Esch and Thomas Keenan. Minneapolis: U of Minnesota P, forthcoming.
———. *Positions*. Chicago: U of Chicago P, 1981.
———. "Structure, Sign and Play in the Discourse of Human Sciences." In *Critical Theory since 1965*. Ed. Hazard Adams and Leroy Searle. Tallahassee: Florida State UP, 1986, 83–94.
Miller, J. Hillis. "Composition and Decomposition: Deconstruction and the Teaching of Writing." In *Composition and Literature: Bridging the Gap*. Ed. Winifred Bryan Horner. Chicago: U of Chicago P, 1983, 38–56.
———. "The Critic as Host." *Critical Inquiry* 3 (1977): 439–47.

Major Scholarship in Composition

Atkins, G. Douglas, and Michael Johnson, eds. *Writing and Reading Differently: Deconstruction and the Teaching of Composition and Literature*. Lawrence: UP of Kansas, 1985.

Berlin, James A. *Rhetorics, Poetics, Cultures: Refiguring College English Studies*. Urbana, IL: NCTE, 1996.

Brent, Doug. *Reading as Rhetorical Invention: Knowledge, Persuasion, and the Teaching of Research-based Writing*. Urbana, IL: NCTE, 1992.

Covino, William. "Making Differences in the Composition Class: A Philosophy of Invention." *Freshman English News* 10 (1981): 1–13.

Crowley, Sharon. "Derrida, Deconstruction, and Our Scene of Teaching." *Pre/Text* 8 (1987): 169–83.

———. *A Teacher's Introduction to Deconstruction*. Urbana, IL: NCTE, 1989.

Culler, Jonathan. *On Deconstruction: Theory and Criticism after Structuralism*. Ithaca, NY: Cornell UP, 1982.

Esch, Deborah. "Deconstruction." In *Redrawing the Boundaries*. Ed. Stephen Greenblatt and Giles Gunn. New York: MLA, 1992, 374–391.

Faigley, Lester. *Fragments of Rationality: Postmodernity and the Subject of Composition*. Pittsburgh, PA: U of Pittsburgh P, 1992.

Flax, Jane. "Postmodernism and Gender Relations in Feminist Theory." In *Feminism/Postmodernism*. Ed. Linda J. Nicholson. New York: Routledge, 1990, 39–62.

Graff, Gerald. "Determinancy/Indeterminancy." In *Critical Terms for Literary Study*. Ed. Frank Lentricchia and Thomas McLaughlin. Chicago: U of Chicago P, 1990, 163–76.

Harkin, Patricia, and John Schilb, eds. *Contending with Words: Composition and Rhetoric in a Postmodern Age*. New York: MLA, 1991.

Harned, Jon. "Post-Structuralism and the Teaching of Composition." *Freshman English News* 15 (1986): 10–16.

Johnson, Barbara, ed. *The Pedagogical Imperative*. Yale French Studies, no. 63. New Haven, CT: Yale UP, 1981.

Leitch, Vincent. *Deconstructive Criticism: An Advanced Introduction*. New York: Columbia UP, 1983.

Miller, Susan. *Rescuing the Subject: A Critical Introduction to Rhetoric and the Writer*. Carbondale: Southern Illinois UP, 1989.

Myers, Greg. "Reality, Consensus, and Reform in the Rhetoric of Composition Teaching." *College English* 48 (1986): 154–74.

Neel, Jasper. *Plato, Derrida, Writing*. Carbondale: Southern Illinois UP, 1988.

Poster, Mark. *The Mode of Information: Poststructuralism and Social Context*. Chicago: U of Chicago P, 1990.

Schilb, John. "Composition and Poststructuralism: A Tale of Two Conferences." *College Composition and Communication* 40 (1989): 422–43.

———. "Deconstructing Didion: Poststructuralist Rhetorical Theory in the Composition Class." In *Literary Nonfiction: Theory, Criticism, Pedagogy*. Ed. Chris Anderson. Carbondale: Southern Illinois UP, 1989, 262–86.

Scholes, Robert. "Deconstruction and Criticism." *Critical Inquiry* 14 (1988): 278–95.

Soper, Kate. "Postmodernism, Subjectivity, and the Question of Value." *New Left Review* 186 (March/April 1991): 120–28.

Vitanza, Victor. "Three Countertheses: Or, A Critical In(ter)vention into Composition Theories and Pedagogies." In *Contending with Words*. Ed. Patricia Harkin and John Schilb. New York: MLA, 1991, 139–72.

White, Edward M. "Post-Structural Literary Criticism and the Response to Student Writing." *College Composition and Communication* 35 (1984): 186–95.

Winterowd, W. Ross. "Post-structuralism and Composition." *Pre/Text* 4 (1983): 85–95.

———. "The Purification of Literature and Rhetoric." *College English* 49 (1987): 257–73.

Winterowd, W. Ross, and Jack Blum. *A Teacher's Introduction to Composition in the Rhetorical Tradition*. Urbana, IL: NCTE, 1994.

BARBARA HEIFFERON AND PHYLLIS MENTZELL RYDER

DIALOGISM/BAKHTINIAN THEORY

Summary

The Russian philosopher Mikhail Mikhailovich Bakhtin (1895–1975) has been recognized by many as one of this century's most original thinkers. Oddly enough, this characterization is not inconsistent with the many introductions to Bakhtinian theory that caution readers that Bakhtin is elusive and his work too diverse, enigmatic, or contradictory to collect within a unified theory. Indeed, Bakhtin would be likely to concur with such a characterization, not because a common denominator cannot be located within his work, but because a common denominator, or a single or unitary self, is antithetical to Bakhtin's understanding of the "dialogic" nature of language and meaning. Dialogism expresses the social or "shared" nature of language use. "The word," according to Bakhtin, "is a two-sided act. It is determined equally by whose word it is and for whom it is meant" (Bakhtin and Volosinov, *Marxism* 85). As such, speakers or writers *and* listeners or readers shape discourse. Thus, the diverse strains of Bakhtin's work can be understood as a function of, and a response to, various critical and political movements of his time, such as aesthetic theory, phenomenology, structuralism, formalism, Freudianism, and Marxism.

Not only did Bakhtin engage a diversity of readers and writers of his time, but a diversity of contemporary readers from literary, rhetorical, composition, feminist, and cultural studies have embraced Bakhtinian theory. In each case the needs of individual disciplines shape and define the profile and meaning of the work. Indeed, despite much overlap, scholars and writers within the field of composition studies construe Bakhtinian theory in ways that are distinct from those of scholars in literary studies. In many ways, composition studies' conception of Bakhtinian theory results from an understanding of where the study of composition goes beyond literary concerns of textual interpretation. Clearly, many of Bakhtin's key ideas lend support to current explanations of the writing process, as well as to the study of the contexts in which individuals practice and gain expertise in writing.

The understanding that language is inherently "dialogic" is key to understanding the essence of much of Bakhtinian theory and its relevance for composition studies. "Bakhtin believed that a fundamental fact of human existence was the relation between the 'I' and 'the other,' an irreducible duality conceived in terms of the need to *share* being" (Holquist 5). In effect, our relationship with the world, including people, ideas, and objects, is entirely social. Our relationship is mediated by others' languages and perspectives that are "already" a part of our perceptual landscape. Our "discourse finds the object at which it was directed already as it were overlain with qualifications, open to dispute, charged with value, already enveloped in an obscuring 'light' of alien words. . . . It is entangled, shot through with shared thoughts, points of view, alien value judgments and accents" (Bakhtin, *Dialogic* 276).

Because words travel not to and from individual to object, but "through" others' words, there is no such thing as a "neutral" word. Bakhtin explains: "All words have the 'taste' of a profession, a genre, a tendency, a party, a particular work, a particular person, a generation, an age group, the day and hour. Each word tastes of the context and contexts in which it has lived its socially charged life" (*Dialogic* 293). As I speak or write, I do so "through" others' words; I make meaning in relation to what others have said. It is this dialogic or intersubjective nature of language use that insures that language users participate in the sociohistorical consciousness of a particular historical moment.

Bakhtin's basic unit of analysis is the "utterance." As such, he sees the primary language relationship as dyadic: language production is "the product of the reciprocal relationship between speaker and listener, addresser and addressee" (Bakhtin and Volosinov, *Marxism* 85–86). It is, however, important to understand that utterance between speaker/writer and listener/reader occurs within a context of multiplicity: what Bakhtin refers to as "dialogized heteroglossia." Heteroglossia is a key concept, as it represents "[t]he authentic environment of an utterance, the environment in which it lives and takes shape" (*Dialogic* 272). The concept of heteroglossia elaborates the complicated and multiple context in which language users participate in the process of making meaning. In effect, speaking or writing involves navigating a sea of languages, voices, and accents.

The heteroglossic context from which language evolves makes language use dynamic. It accounts for the "push and pull" within language that language users engage as they speak or write. Bakhtin conceptualizes this tension within language as "centripetal" and "centrifugal" forces, forces that aspire to cancel difference and operate within a unified language or, on the other hand, disperse language and operate within a multiplicity.

Bakhtin's concepts of *dialogism* and *heteroglossia* are particularly useful for identifying and discussing the multiple accents and voices that inhere in language, as well as for explaining how a particular word or utterance achieves meaning in relation to another's word. Indeed, making meaning is a process that involves distinguishing one's own voice against a background of other voices, other languages. This process requires a speaker or writer to "appropriate [others' words], adapting [them] to his own semantic and expressive intention"

(*Dialogic* 293). In effect, as writers we need to "take" another's word and make it our own. Motivation to populate another's language with one's own intentions comes from an understanding, tacit or conscious, that language is essentially valuative. Because the heteroglossic context is "a dialogically agitated and tension-filled environment of alien words, value judgments and accents," our words struggle not simply with the alphabet of others' prose, but with the values enacted by others' language *(Dialogic* 276). Making meaning within this valuative context is, as Bakhtin provides, "a difficult and complicated process" (*Dialogic* 294).

What heteroglossia offers is a promise that our language will struggle with others' language. Language is produced or propelled by coming into contact with other languages, languages that express how other voices or speakers regard or value an object. This "social evaluation," as Bakhtin calls it, shapes individual expression, as it "determines the choice of objects for cognition . . . [and] organizes how we see and conceptualize the event being communicated" (*Formal Method* 395). In this sense, Bakhtin helps us understand how meaning is "molded" around value. Value guides the process of making meaning; it accounts for the shape that our speaking or writing takes. Moreover, as an individual struggles with the values that exist within her or his own and others' language, her or his writing becomes richer, more significant (*Formal Method* 123). Bakhtin's understanding of the dialogic nature of language makes expression and communication dynamic. What individual speakers or writers must do is figure out "how to enter and sustain the flow of discourse that is 'always already' there" (Nystrand, *Structure* 34).

Reception and Significance in Composition Studies

As Bakhtin's concepts of dialogism and heteroglossia define and reinforce the "shared" nature of language, making meaning becomes a truly intersubjective act. Composition scholars in the 1970s and 1980s who sought to explain the writing process in terms of the social environment from which it evolves were quick to recognize the value of Bakhtin's work. Indeed, heteroglossia promises the kind of conversation that social constructionism suggests is central to collaborative learning and the process of reaching consensus. A basic premise of social constructionism is that for one to think well, one "must learn to think well collectively—that is, [one] must learn to converse well" (Bruffee, 640). In effect, talk describes the parameters of both social and individual thought. The range and complexity of our thought is in direct proportion to the degree to which we have been initiated into public conversation. Bakhtin's work, particularly his concept of heteroglossia, refines our understanding of "public conversation," representing it as an enriched, socially active medium that naturally complements the goals of collaborative learning.

Many of the premises of collaborative learning theory are founded on the work of a contemporary of Bakhtin's, the Russian developmental psychologist L. S. Vygotsky. Vygotsky's discussion of intellectual growth focuses on "mastering the social means of thought, that is, language'' (51). His contribution is widely understood to be his explanation of how development proceeds from the public to private as individuals internalize external public discourse. In this way, Vygotsky's work provided a blueprint for the social nature of human development. Bakhtin's theoretical work in language complements Vygotskian theory as it amplifies the complicated nature of public discourse. It makes sense that a theory of language, such as heteroglossia, that multiplies the available pool of influence as it multiplies language, voice, and perspective, would gain acceptance with collaborative learning theorists who understand the process of learning to write as a matter of being initiated into the conversation and consensual habits of community. In a sense, heteroglossia promises to hasten the process of socialization, as writers join ''larger, more experienced communities of knowledgeable peers through assenting to those communities' interests, values, language, and paradigms of perception and thought'' (Bruffee, 646).

In addition to being understood as a heuristic for initiation into the consensual process, the multitude of voices guaranteed by heteroglossia has come to represent the kind of heterogeneous environment that promotes dialogic activity. This understanding follows Bakhtin's depiction of the vigorous social life of language: ''[A]ll languages of heteroglossia . . . may be juxtaposed to one another, mutually supplement one another, contradict one another and be interrelated dialogically. As such they encounter one another and co-exist. . . . As such, these languages live a real life, they struggle and evolve in an environment of social heteroglossia'' (*Dialogic* 292).

An advocate of the dialogic activity generated by heteroglossia, John Trimbur argues that heteroglossia promotes what he calls ''dissensus'' (''Consensus and Difference''). Trimbur views the social context as a ground (a heteroglossic ground) against which writers can develop and distinguish their own voices, their difference, and in this way make a contribution to larger conversations.

Bakhtin's concept of heteroglossia is also valued by theorists who believe that learning to write is not so much a matter of asserting difference as much as it is a process of finding ''a common ground,'' a place where the writer's own language might ''intersect'' with other forms, such as academic discourse (see Spellmeyer; Ritchie). The fact that language is saturated with multiple voices allows an individual to use personal voice to ''get a foot in the door.''

Bakhtin's concept of heteroglossia has also been welcomed by theorists who need a language for talking about how writers must learn to move between languages (see Goelman; Blair). Arguing a similar line, some writers have suggested that the work of writing involves learning how to juxtapose voices and speech genres, which allows language to function as an analytical tool that helps a writer free consciousness from the ''prison-house of language.''

In general, for most composition theorists and educators, the promise of Bakhtin's work resides in the promise of dialogic ''struggle.'' Adopting Bakhtin is adopting the hope that heteroglossia will become a dialogic force in the classroom as members of the class infuse the conversation with their different voices.

The belief is that different perspectives will animate the conversation, and in the push and pull of a multitude of perspectives a writer's language will develop. In effect, the hope is that, thrown into a sea of language, a writer will not only learn to swim, but swim well.

Bakhtinian theory was welcomed into composition studies as it featured a force—heteroglossia—that supported the individual writer's processes. Moreover, the theory was attractive because it contextualized the writing process, placing it within and making it responsible to the social context from which, social theories suggest, language evolves. At the same time, an emphasis on multiple languages elevated the value of talk, which paralleled a growing understanding within the field of the importance of talk to learning to write (see, for example, Moffett; Britton; Nystrand, "Sharing Words").

Understanding the stratified and dynamic nature of language as described by the concepts of dialogism and heteroglossia has stimulated new questions. Theorists want to know more about "how writers resolve the conflicting claims of the voices in their heads [and] . . . how writers forge a voice and way of speaking from the conflicting social forces and polyphony of voices that converge in their mental experience" (Trimbur, "Beyond Cognition" 278). New questions focus, not so much on an explication of "languages used," as instigated by the concept of heteroglossia, but "language use," which focuses more on the nature of the writing process itself. Pairing Vygotskian and Bakhtinian theory, the cognitive psychologist James Wertsch proposes that the process of speaking is an act of "choosing" or "privileging" one language or "tool" from a user's "tool kit" over another (124). Wertsch's analysis follows from both his understanding of heteroglossia as a diversity of languages available to individuals, which thus constitute a "kit," and his understanding that Bakhtin "viewed social languages and speech genres as the means by which communication and mental action are organized" (104).

Based on Bakhtin's emphasis on the valuative nature of heteroglossia, writing has been described as a process of "valuing." According to the composition scholar Jerry Mirskin, "not only is the *context* for making meaning valuative, as well as the actual language that inhabits that context, but in addition the *act* of speaking or writing itself is an activity that involves taking a social attitude or valuative stance toward the world" (391). Accordingly, writing involves negotiating not others' language per se, as suggested by Wertsch's analysis, but the valuative perspectives that inhere within and are communicated by others' words.

In a recent essay, Michael Bernard-Donals observed that "[t]he Bakhtin industry continues to grow in the 1990s much as it did in the seventies and eighties" ("Mikhail Bakhtin," 170). In some ways Bakhtinian theory arrived on the scene when we, as composition scholars and teachers, were learning to value the diversity of voices we were finding among our students and in our culture as a whole. The work extended Vygotskian theory as it refined our understanding of the social context in which writers practice making meaning.

The theory has remained a resource within the field as its application has evolved from a theory that supported collaborative learning initiatives to one that enriches our understanding of individual writing processes. New work on the horizon is beginning to detail how teachers of writing can take an active role in structuring classrooms to enhance dialogic activity between students, as well as between teachers and students (see Nystrand and Gamoran; Nystrand, *Opening Dialogue*).

BIBLIOGRAPHY

Primary Texts

Bakhtin, Mikhail M. *The Dialogic Imagination*. Ed. Michael Holquist. Trans. Caryl Emerson and Michael Holquist. Austin: U of Texas P, 1981.

————. *Speech Genres and Other Late Essays*. Ed. and trans. Caryl Emerson. Minneapolis: U of Minnesota P, 1984.

Bakhtin, M. M., and Pavel N. Medvedev. *The Formal Method in Literary Scholarship*. Trans. A. J. Wehrle. Cambridge, MA: Harvard UP, 1978.

Bakhtin, M. M., and V. N. Volosinov. *Marxism and the Philosophy of Language*. Trans. L. Matejka and I. R. Titunik. Cambridge, MA: Harvard UP, 1973.

Clark, Katerina, and Michael Holquist. *Mikhail Bakhtin*. Cambridge, MA: Harvard UP, 1984.

Holquist, M. *Dialogism: Bakhtin and His World*. New York: Routledge, 1990.

Todorov, Tzvetan. *Mikhail Bakhtin: The Dialogic Principle*. Minneapolis: U of Minnesota P, 1984.

Major Scholarship in Composition

Bernard-Donals, Michael. *Mikhail Bakhtin: Between Phenomenology and Marxism*. Cambridge: Cambridge UP, 1994.

Nystrand, Martin. "A Social-Interactive Model of Writing." *Written Communication* 6 (1989): 66–85.

Recchio, Thomas. "A Bakhtinian Reading of Student Writing." *College Composition and Communication* 42.4 (1991): 446–54.

Trimbur, John. "Beyond Cognition: The Voices in Inner Speech." *Rhetoric Review* 5.2 (1987): 211–21.

————. "Consensus and Difference in Collaborative Learning." *College English* 51.6 (1989): 602–16.

Wertsch, James V. *Voices of the Mind: A Sociocultural Approach to Mediated Action*. Cambridge, MA: Harvard UP, 1991.

Works Cited

Bernard-Donals, Michael. "Mikhail Bakhtin: Between Phenomenology and Marxism." *College English* 56.2 (1994): 170–88.

Blair, Catherine P. "Only One of the Voices: Dialogic Writing across the Curriculum." *College English* 50.4 (1988): 383–95.

Britton, James. "Talking to Learn." In *Language, the Learner, and the School*. Ed. Douglas Barnes, James Britton, and H. Rosen. Harmondsworth, UK: Penguin, 1971. 79–115.

Bruffee, Kenneth A. "Collaborative Learning and the Conversation of Mankind." *College English* 46.7 (1984): 635–52.

Goelman, Judith. "The Dialogic Imagination: More Than We've Been Taught." In *Only Connect*. Ed. Thomas Newkirk. Upper Montclair, NJ: Boynton/Cook, 1986, 131–42.

Holquist, Michael. "The Politics of Representation." *Quarterly Newsletter of the Laboratory of Comparative Human Cognition* 5.1 (1983): 2–9.

Mirskin, Jerry. "Writing as a Process of Valuing." *College Composition and Communication* 46.3 (October 1995): 387–410.

Moffett, James. *Teaching the Universe of Discourse*. Boston: Houghton, 1983.

Nystrand, Martin. *Opening Dialogue: Understanding the Dynamics of Language and Learning in the English Classroom*. New York: Teachers College P, 1997.

Nystrand, Martin. "Sharing Words: The Effects of Readers on Developing Writers." *Written Communication* 7.1 (1990): 3–24.

———. *The Structure of Written Communication: Studies in Reciprocity between Writers and Readers*. Orlando and London: Academic P, 1986.

Nystrand, Martin, and Adam Gamoran. "Student Engagement: When Recitation Becomes Conversation." In *Contemporary Research on Teaching*. Ed. H. Waxman and H. Walber. Berkeley, CA: McCutchan, 1991, 257–76.

Ritchie, J. "Beginning Writers: Diverse Voices and Individual Identity." *College Composition and Communication* 40.2 (1989): 152–74.

Spellmeyer, Kurt. "A Common Ground: The Essay in the Academy." *College English* 51.3 (1989): 715–29.

Trimbur, John. "Consensus and Difference in Collaborative Learning." *College English* 51.6 (1989): 602–16.

———. "Beyond Cognition: The Voices in Inner Speech." *Rhetoric Review* 5.2 (1987): 211–21.

Vygotsky, Lev S. *Thought and Language*. Trans. Eugenia Hanfmann and Gertrude Vakar. Cambridge, MA: MIT P, 1962.

Wertsch, James V. *Voices of the Mind: A Sociocultural Approach to Mediated Action*. Cambridge, MA: Harvard UP, 1991.

JERRY MIRSKIN

DISCOURSE THEORY

Summary

The term "discourse theory" has several meanings. We will use it to mean a theory of discourse types, recognizable by the use of such familiar terms as *narration*, *description*, *persuasion*, and *information*. However, it is often claimed that a full theory of discourse would also include a theory of the composing process (how discourse is created), a theory of pedagogy (how discourse should be taught), a theory of how children develop the ability to discourse, and, most recently, a theory of the political and social assumptions underlying discourse. There is also the problem of whether we ought to combine a theory of discourse, from the field of rhetoric/composition, with the growing field of textlinguistics, that branch of linguistics that deals with utterances beyond the level of the individual sentence.

However useful it would be to create a theory that combined all of these elements, it is much too large a task for the present purpose. Besides, the other elements are covered elsewhere in this volume. We shall go beyond discourse types only when the features of a type can be used for other purposes, as when the logic of a discourse type has implications for the thought processes that must occur during composing.

Until the 1960s, the only widely used theory of discourse types was based on the work of Alexander Bain, who in the mid-1800s wrote a textbook, *English Composition and Rhetoric*, that established what he called the "forms" of discourse: narration, exposition, description, argumentation, and persuasion. (The modern term for "forms" is "modes.") This scheme became widely used, though other textbook writers often eliminated persuasion and added other forms such as definition, process analysis, and comparison/contrast. Despite modern advances, Bain's forms can still be seen in many composition textbooks. For instance, the widely used college textbook *The Norton Reader* includes in the ninth, shorter edition what it calls an "Index of Rhetorical Modes." In this index are four primary modes—narration, description, exposition, and persuasion/argument—and exposition is broken down into what are apparently regarded as submodes: compare and contrast, classify and divide, define, analyze a process, and cause/effect.

The main difficulty with Bain's theory can be seen in *The Norton Reader*'s list. Why must exposition be subdivided into other forms while narration and description are not? Why is persuasion apparently equated with argument when we know that a mouth-watering description of, say, a pumpkin pie would be at least as effective in persuading consumers to buy the pie as any argument about why they should buy it?

Within a few years of each other, four proposals were made that were referred to as theories of discourse and that showed potential for clearing up the confusion. Though some may doubt that one or two of these are actual theories of discourse, they are so treated in *Discourse: A Critique and Synthesis of Major Theories*, by Timothy W. Crusius, and will be taken into account here. These theories are as follows:

- *The Development of Writing Abilities (11–18)*, by James Britton et al. As part of a massive study of papers written by adolescents, Britton and colleagues developed a system of classifying the papers that became, for many, a de facto theory of discourse. Britton proposed a continuum of discourse, with "transactional" discourse at one end, "poetic" discourse at the other, and "expressive discourse" in the middle. Transactional discourse includes the persuasive and informative, expressive discourse involves writing about oneself, and poetic discourse is literary.

- *Teaching the Universe of Discourse*, by James Moffett (which on the cover is described as "a theory of discourse—a rationale for English teaching used in a student-centered language arts curriculum"). Applying concepts from developmental psychology, Moffett worked out a theory of the kinds of discourse that students should be able to do at each stage of growth, beginning with concrete, interactive, and egocentric types of discourse and working up to the abstract, monologual, and public forms of the adult writer. His theory then became the basis for his textbook on pedagogy, titled, *A Student-Centered Language Arts Curriculum Grades K–13: A Handbook for Teachers.*

- *A Conceptual Theory of Rhetoric*, by Frank J. D'Angelo. Discourse forms like narration and description were originally cast as forms of thought, not forms of discourse, and were used to help orators think up arguments. They were called the *topoi*, or topics. D'Angelo attempted to create and systematize a modern theory of topics, and thus his theory is more a theory of rhetoric than of discourse. However, because of the historical connection between topics and discourse forms, and because D'Angelo made some attempt to turn his topics into organizational patterns for discourse, his book has been included with other theories of discourse.

- *A Theory of Discourse*, by James L. Kinneavy. This will be discussed in the following paragraphs.

Of these four, I would agree with Crusius that the most complete is Kinneavy's *A Theory of Discourse*. As Crusius says, "In scope, depth, and simultaneous concern with detail and integration, it still has no rival, remaining indisputably at the center of our thought about the universe of discourse" (36). Therefore, the following explanation of what a theory of discourse should look like is drawn from Kinneavy.

A Theory of Discourse cleared up the confusions of Bain's system of discourse to a large extent. Kinneavy theorized that discourse exists in two levels, aims and modes. Persuasion and exposition are "aims" of discourse, not modes or forms. An aim can be carried out in any of the forms or in several forms in the same discourse. Thus, we can persuade by narrating, describing, arguing, or comparing and contrasting, or we can use all of these modes in the same persuasive discourse.

To establish his theory of the aims, Kinneavy used the communications triangle with *encoder*, *decoder*, and *reality* at the three apexes and *signal* in the center (*Theory* 61). He posited that each aim resulted from an emphasis on one component of the triangle. *Persuasive discourse* emphasizes the decoder and results when the discourse is focused on moving the decoder to act or change belief. *Expository discourse* (which Kinneavy renamed *referential discourse*) results from an emphasis on reflecting reality as accurately as possible. The other two aims in his theory are *literary discourse*, which results when something creative and delightful is done with the signal (language, in the case of text), and *expressive discourse*, which results when the identity of the encoder is the uppermost concern in the discourse. Kinneavy also subdivided the referential aim into *informative*, *scientific*, and *exploration* and the expressive aim into *individual* and *group* expression.

For his modes, Kinneavy kept Bain's narration and description. He added classification, and replaced argument with evaluation. He did not develop a theory of the modes much beyond this, but his textbooks show that each mode can have subdivisions. For instance, in Kinneavy, McCleary, and Nakadate's *Writing in the Liberal Arts Tradition* (first edition), narration is said to come as history, plot, process analysis, and others—in short, any form that uses chronological order. The modes are considered to be different ways to reflect reality and are established along two dimensions. The first is static/dynamic, with narration and evaluation being considered the dynamic modes—narration being dynamic across time and evaluation being dynamic as one moves from one standard of evaluation to another. Description and classification/division are static, in that we must "freeze" something in time to describe it or classify it. At an earlier or later time, it might look different or belong to a different class. (A butterfly may always be an insect, for instance, but at an earlier time in its life it was an egg, larva, and chrysalis and thus had to be described differently and placed into some different classes.) The other dimension is concrete/abstract. Narration and description are considered concrete because we narrate a particular event or describe a particular object. For classification, we describe a category of objects rather than an individual, and for evaluation, we apply standards that express abstract qualities like "good, better, best"; a specific fact about an object (e.g., it weighs ten pounds) has no evaluative function until we apply an abstract standard like "light" or "heavy."

The entire scheme, therefore, looks as follows:

Aims of Discourse
    Encoder-oriented: Expression
        Individual
        Group
    Decoder-oriented: Persuasion
    Reality-oriented: Reference
        Information
        Science
        Exploration
    Signal-oriented: Literature
Modes of Discourse
    Static/Concrete: Description
    Static/Abstract: Classification
    Dynamic/Concrete: Narration
    Dynamic/Abstract: Evaluation

Use of the term "aim" implies that we are referring here to the writer's aim—saying that the writer aims to persuade, to inform, to express, and so on. However, we can all think of discourses in which it was clear that the writer intended one thing (e.g., to inform us of the difference between a Macintosh and an IBM computer) but ended up doing something else (such as trying to persuade us that one is better than the other). Therefore, to avoid this practical problem,

Kinneavy assumes that the aim lies in the discourse, not in the writer, and that it can be discerned in certain features of the discourse. These features have to do with the *logic*, *structure*, and *style* employed in the discourse. Of these, logic is probably most important, for it refers to *what the writer must logically do* to carry out the aim. In other words, it refers not to logic per se but to what Kinneavy sometimes calls the *logical strategies* of discourse.

For instance, Kinneavy (following Aristotle) would say that the successful persuader uses certain strategies, presenting him- or herself as a sensible, trustworthy, likable person (*ethical proof*), engaging the emotions of the reader in a manner to support the thesis (*pathetic proof*), and presenting the semblance of a logical support (*logical proof*). The organization of the discourse may take several forms but most likely will be recognized as a traditional essay that has an introduction, including the thesis; a refutation of opposing arguments; several arguments (or reasons) to support the thesis; and a conclusion that includes a thesis restatement. The style will be clear, correct, impressive, and appropriate to the occasion and the target audience.

Persuasion occurs in several common genres and subgenres. The traditional persuasive essay structure just described is one genre; two subgenres of it are the essay to prove the existence of the problem and the essay to prove the efficacy of a proposed solution to a problem. Other genres of persuasion are advertising, sermons, and letters to the editor.

In various articles and textbooks written since the original publication of *A Theory of Discourse*, Kinneavy and various coauthors have tinkered with the terminology and definitions of the theory. For instance, at one point he returned to using *exposition* instead of *reference* for the reality-oriented aim. And for all practical purposes, the three subaims within reference have been treated as actual aims. Thus, a full outline of the theory is open to some dispute. Perhaps the most up-to-date version would go as follows:

Persuasive Discourse (intended to influence the decoder)

Logical Strategies: ethical proof, pathetic proof, logical proof

Structure: introduction (with thesis); body (with refutations and reasons); conclusion (with thesis restatement)

Style: clear, correct, impressive; appropriate

Examples: persuasive essays, advertising, sermons, letters to the editor

Expressive Discourse (intended to establish the identity of the encoder)

Logical Strategies: being-for-self, being-for-others, being-in-the-world

Structure: introduction; body (usually a story of personal experience); conclusion (repudiation of one's past and plans to be different in the future)

Style: connotative, individualistic, filled with superlatives, one-sided, ambiguous

Examples: personal essays, diaries, autobiography, declarations of independence, creeds, manifestos

Literary Discourse (intended to entertain or delight the reader)

Logical Strategies: creativity and craft; esthetic pleasure and interpretation; plot (with complication, conflict, resolution)

Structure: exposition, rising action, climax, resolution

Style: nonnormal, consciously patterned; figurative; dramatic

Examples: poetry, drama, short stories, novels, jokes

Reference Discourse (intended to reflect reality)

Informative Discourse (intended to reflect the known facts about a reality)

Logical Strategies: comprehensiveness, surprise value, factuality

Structure: pyramid of surprise or inverted pyramid of surprise, often with an introduction that is not part of the pyramid

Style: matter-of-fact, documented, readable. interesting, nonpersonal

Examples: news stories, feature articles, reference materials, textbooks, many magazine articles

Scientific Discourse (intended to present an objective proof about the nature of a reality)

Logical Strategies: definitions of key terms, axioms of the system, evidence

Structure:

> Of inductive science: introduction (problem); procedures; results; conclusions and discussion

> Of deductive science: introduction (issue); description of the facts of the case; specific issue and thesis; direct argument; refutation of opposing arguments

Style: objective, jargonistic, dense, passive (as in passive voice), impersonal

Examples: scientific journal articles; judicial decisions, philosophical treatises, recommendation reports

Exploratory Discourse (intended to record a search for the truth about reality; more often oral than written)

Logical Strategies: rejecting the dogma, search for a new model, testing the new model

Structure: for the oral, tends to be dialogic and wandering; for the written, tends to be a ''factitious'' (Kinneavy's term) step-by-step reconstruction of the oral

Style: tentative, sometimes personal and emotional, sometimes even humorous, nonliteral, ambiguous

In establishing the aims and defining them in terms of logic, structure, and style, Kinneavy was trying to create a system that is more general than the notion of genre. That is, each aim would subsume many well-established genres, as the aim of literature includes poetry, drama, novels, and so forth. A genre, thus, is an established, conventional way of carrying out an aim. In theory, the aims would be the same for all cultures everywhere, but each culture would have its own genres. Examples of genres from non-Western cultures would be the Chinese eight-legged theme and the Japanese poetic form of haiku. Crusius, however, thinks that the logic, structure, and style posited by Kinneavy also owe much to the conventions of Western culture and may not necessarily be inherent in the aim. Certainly the notion that a successful discourse must carry out all three logical strategies of its aim seems doubtful. An encyclopedia, for example, might be almost entirely composed of informative discourse, but it would be hard to claim that surprise value (the principle that the facts presented should be "new" to the reader) is necessary.

Another issue is the obvious overlap between aims. Satire, for instance, is both literary and persuasive; much persuasion has a strong component of information; and it is often difficult to know whether a story written in the first person is true, and thus a personal essay (expressive discourse), or fictional, and thus a short story. Kinneavy addresses this issue at length but in the end affirms that such overlap does not vitiate his theory. He writes, "But the norms of scientific proof are not the norms of information or of persuasion or of literature or of express. Consequently, it is important to abstract the different norms and consider them in isolation, even if, in practice, aims do overlap" (*Theory* 63).

For the modes of discourse, Kinneavy has not provided the complete theory that he promised in *A Theory of Discourse*. A readable and competent theory of modes can be found in *Modes of Rhetoric* by Leo Rockas, and nearly every textbook in technical writing also has a thorough treatment of some of the modes. However, let us continue with Kinneavy, just to finish out his theory.

A mode is, as we have seen, considered as one dimension of a subject, a way of viewing the subject as static or dynamic, abstract or concrete. A typical discourse, then, may make use of all the modes. For instance, to write about a monarch butterfly we may narrate about the butterfly (e.g., trace its migration north in the spring or its life cycle), describe the butterfly (orange and black, about three inches wide), classify it (species *Danaus Plexippus*, belonging to the family *Danaidae*, the milkweed butterflies, order *Lepidoptera*); and evaluate it ("one of the most beautiful and best-known of the butterflies"). However, even though the discourse may include all of the modes, it is common to use one of the modes to organize the discourse, as is suggested by the title of one of Kinneavy's textbooks: *Writing—Basic Modes of Organization*, by Kinneavy, Cope, and Campbell. For example, one could use the monarch butterfly's life cycle (narration) as the overall organization for a discourse and cover everything else within this structure. That is, at appropriate points within the narration of the life cycle one could describe the egg, larva, chrysalis, and adult; describe habitat and food plants; summarize migration, mating, flight patterns, and growth of the larva; discuss how it fits into the scheme of classifying all butterflies; and evaluate its appearance, commonness, and prospects for long-term survival now that its primary place of hibernation has been discovered.

Reception and Significance in Composition Studies

All of the four theorists mentioned here are well known in the field, and their theoretical books are considered seminal texts in composition studies. Neither Moffett nor D'Angelo has given actual theories of discourse, so they can be somewhat discounted here, but Kinneavy's theory has achieved wide acceptance at the college level, while Britton's is more commonly used at the secondary level. At the same time, discourse theory itself never evolved as an area of primary study. For example, if we define a text on discourse theory as an argument to establish a category of discourse, to explain the history of a category of discourse, or to describe the nature of a particular category, a search of the *Longman Bibliography of Composition and Rhetoric, 1984–85* turns up only 14 articles on discourse theory in the first 200 articles listed in the section entitled, "Rhetorical Theory, Discourse Theory, and Composing." Clearly, rhetorical theory and composing were the dominant subjects. Also, a popular book on how to teach writing, Calkins's *The Art of Teaching Writing* (new edition), mentions none of our four theorists.

In fact, it is likely that interest in the composing process has stifled interest in discourse theory. The trend is expressed in the title of an article by Donald Murray, "Teach Writing as a Process Not Product." Discourse theory comes out on the losing end because it deals with products—the end results of composing—not with process. A second problem may be the power of Bain's theory. As was the case with *The Norton Reader*, it seems that most textbooks are still based on the modes or on a confusion of aims and modes. The majority of composition teachers majored in literature in college and are not aware that a field of composition exists or that great changes occurred in the field in modern times. They want traditional textbooks, which is what textbook writers give them. The two textbooks most faithful to the Kinneavy theory (*Writing in the Liberal Arts Tradition*, by Kinneavy, McCleary, and Nakadate, and *Four Worlds of Writing*, by Janice Lauer, et al.) have not had a new edition since 1990, which suggests that they have not been best-sellers.

On the other hand, discourse theory has clearly had some lasting influence. The argument over whether this or that compositionist is an "expressivist" could not have occurred without the establishment of a theory of expressive discourse. There now is also a specialty in scientific discourse, which seems based on Kinneavy's theory of inductive scientific discourse.

Moreover, the current popularity of assessing student writing and establishing standards for the English language arts depends heavily on being able to give a name to the desired outcomes and to describe the features of each type of writing to be assessed. The National Assessment of Educational Progress (NAEP), for example, assesses three kinds of writing: informative, persuasive, and narrative. While this might seem a confusion of aims and modes, it is clear that the NAEP understands the difference. In assessing narrative-writing ability, the NAEP gives assignments that are either literary or expressive but evaluates them on narrative criteria rather than on whether they are successful literature or expression. That is, successful narratives are those in which the student has provided enough stages of the event being narrated and has linked those stages causally.

And if that is not sufficient evidence of the dependence of assessment on discourse theory, in the three chapters of the *NAEP 1992 Writing Report Card* that explain the nature of the three kinds of discourse and how the student papers were evaluated, there were six footnotes in total; five of the six referred to our four theorists—two to Kinneavy, one to Moffett, one to D'Angelo, and one to Britton (National Center for Education Statistics, report no. 23-W01, 1994, 25, 45, 67)(Applebee et al.). The NAEP studies writing at three grade levels— fourth, eighth, and twelfth—and evaluates all three according to adult standards in order to observe progress. Theories of discourse provide the standards.

It should be noted, though, that a standard also has implications for process as well as progress. If we are to teach students to write information, for example, and we know that student papers will be judged on the standards of being surprising (or interesting), comprehensive, and factual, we can teach students to think along these lines as they find material for their papers and compose and revise their drafts. We might express the problems in this way:

Issues of factuality: How can I determine the truth value of what I'm finding? How can I write so as to distinguish between what I know or can verify personally, what I assume to be widely accepted as fact, and what are opinions or reports of others that I can't verify?

Issues of comprehensiveness: How can I determine the scope of this subject? Is the subject too large or too small to fit my assignment? Have I found all of the information that I need?

Issues of surprise value: What do my readers already know about this subject and what will be new to them? Which aspects of this information have the most relevance to my readers? How can I bring out the relevance and thus make my paper interesting?

Such questions are relevant regardless of the age of the student, though there is probably a developmental sequence to students' abilities to attend to them. One would guess that children would have the easier time with comprehensiveness at first, then develop an ability to emphasize relevance, and only in late adolescence be able to see the importance of documentation. Regardless, however, in these ways a theory of discourse is more than a static theory of endpoints to use in composing.

BIBLIOGRAPHY

Primary Texts and Major Scholarship in Composition

Applebee, Arthur, et al. *NAEP 1992 Writing Report Card.* National Center for Education Statistics Report No. 23–101. Office of Educational Research and Improvement, U.S. Department of Education. Washington, DC: USGPO, 1994.

Britton, James, et al. *The Development of Writing Abilities (11–18).* Urbana, IL: NCTE, 1975.

Calkins, Lucy McCormick. *The Art of Teaching Writing*, New ed. Portsmouth, NH: Heinemann, 1994.

Crusius, Timothy W. *Discourse: A Critique and Synthesis of Major Theories.* New York: MLA, 1989.

D'Angelo, Frank J. *A Conceptual Theory of Rhetoric*. Cambridge, MA: Winthrop, 1975.

Kinneavy, James L. *A Theory of Discourse*. Englewood Cliffs, NJ: Prentice-Hall, 1971; New York: Norton, 1980.

Kinneavy, James L., John Q. Cope, and J. W. Campbell. *Writing—Basic Modes of Organization*. Dubuque, IA: Kendall/Hunt, 1976.

Kinneavy, James L., William J. McCleary, and Neil Nakadate. *Writing in the Liberal Arts Tradition*. 1985. New York: Harper, 1990; 2nd ed., 1990.

Lauer, Janice, et al. *Four Worlds of Writing*. 3rd ed. New York: Harper, 1990.

Lindemann, Erika, ed. *Longman Bibliography of Composition and Rhetoric, 1984–85*. White Plains, NY: Longman, 1987.

Moffett, James. *A Student-Centered Language Arts Curriculum Grades K–13: A Handbook for Teachers*. Boston: Houghton, 1968. Rpt. Boston: Houghton, 1973.

———. *Teaching the Universe of Discourse*. Boston: Houghton, 1968.

Murray, Donald. "Teach Writing as a Process Not Product." *Leaflet* 71.4 (1972): 11–14.

Rockas, Leo. *Modes of Rhetoric*. New York: St. Martin's P, 1964.

WILLIAM J. McCLEARY

DRAMATISM

Summary

Kenneth Burke's dramatism is a method for analyzing and discussing human acts, relations, and motives in fields such as philosophy, political science, economics, religion, literature, and the arts. These acts—thinking as well as concretely observable motion—include speech, writing, and artistic performance. Burke exercises his dramatism primarily upon acts that create written texts, although he approaches all human actions as essentially dramatic and active, having a dynamic and being analyzable in the same terms. Like a drama created by a playwright, even phenomena of thought and speech, which are conventionally perceived as static or immutable, are seen to be dynamic, changeable, and elusive. Burke sometimes applies his method of analysis by examining an act/text from a pair of philosophical or conceptual positions that are opposing and linked in a dichotomy. But more often he examines particular acts/texts, human relations, and motives in light of a pentad: Act, Scene, Agent, Agency, and Purpose. Burke explains how his central question—"What is involved, when we say what people are doing and why they are doing it?" (*Grammar* xv)—involves these five terms:

In a rounded statement about motives, you must have some word that names the *act* (names what took place, in thought or deed), and another that names the *scene* (the background of the act, the situation in which it occurred); also, you must indicate what person or kind of person (*agent*) performed the act, what means or instruments he used (*agency*), and the *purpose*. . . . [A]ny complete statement about motives will offer *some kind* of answers to these five questions: what was done (act), when and where it was done (scene), who did it (agent), how he did it (agency), and why (purpose). (*Grammar* xv)

Each term of the pentad may be used alone or as a pair in a "ratio," such as the "Scene-Act Ratio" or the "Scene-Agent Ratio," which calls attention to the interrelatedness of the terms. Burke's copious examples and allusions, including references to the ancient Greeks, Aquinas, Duns Scotus, Hobbes, Spinoza, Darwin, Marx, Kant, and Jimmy Durante, put dramatism in the intellectual tradition of inquiry starting in Classical Greece and extending through the mainstream of Western European culture to contemporary elite, as well as popular, culture. Burke's 1945 *A Grammar of Motives* is the basic presentation of dramatism. He subsequently elaborated the method in *A Rhetoric of Motives* and in *Language as Symbolic Action* (see "Burkean Theories of Rhetoric" for additional theoretical context).

Reception and Significance in Composition Studies

Dramatism is routinely placed alongside classical rhetoric and tagmemics as one of the standard heuristic methods of invention. The pentad's apparent simplicity has tempted a number of scholars to adapt it to instructional use with college composition students. It has also met with strong resistance. Compositionists of romantic principle, because they privilege the innate creativity of the individual student writer over devices that they believe lead too easily into stale or predictable thought, distrust the pentad. Alternately, they distrust the potential of a dramatistic heuristic for directing student writers to ideas that are preferred by the teacher, acting as agent for the dominant and possibly exploitive culture. Other compositionists question the instructional value of dramatism because the superficial simplicity of the pentad fades as its possibilities are pursued; Burke designed it to work back and forth between simplicity and complexity. Moreover, heuristic use of the pentad and dramatism risks serious compromise of the richness and flexibility of the analytical approach that Burke developed over a very long, busy, and productive intellectual career. Trying to simplify dramatism for beginning students can easily violate the ebullient spirit of Burke's work. Still, Burke himself was not completely adverse to the idea that student texts could adapt the pentad along with the rest of dramatism. In "Questions and Answers about the Pentad," he wrote: "Having seen a 'contemporary handbook of rhetoric, language and literature,' *The Holt Guide to English* by William F. Irmscher and having noted that it puts to good use some of the terms I worked with in my *Grammar of Motives*, I see a feasible point of departure there" (330). Consequently, some compositionists embrace dramatism, some ignore it, and some purposely reject it.

Considering Burke's volume and range of output, it is not surprising that his method has a Protean aspect. Scholars have found in Burke's method diverse qualities, depending on what they seek. Thus, dramatism has a rare synthesizing potential in the diverse and fragmented field called composition. For compositionists in the classical tradition, dramatism has the appeal of corresponding to the topics, using dialectic much as Plato used it and being readily adaptable to social contexts. For the romantics, dramatism supplies a catalyst for the thought processes of writers getting in touch with their own thoughts rather than thoughts of the heuristic's maker. For compositionists concerned with freeing students from dominating or ossifying intellectual systems, dramatism offers the appeal of built-in subversiveness and self-subversiveness. For those who embrace the process approach, dramatism works well as prewriting and as a tool in revision. For deconstructionists, dramatism offers limitless possibilities for the questioning, transformation, and discovery of underlying implications. Deconstructionists and New Critics both emphasize close reading, which is an essential aspect of Burke's method. For postmodernists in general, dramatism's rejection of both authority and of the determinacy of meaning is congenial. The range of student ability levels, subject areas, course objectives, and teaching philosophies that dramatism accommodates is far greater than is widely realized.

BIBLIOGRAPHY

Primary Texts

Burke, Kenneth. *A Grammar of Motives*. 1945. Rpt. Berkeley: U of California P, 1969.
———. *Language as Symbolic Action: Essays on Life, Literature, and Method*. Berkeley: U of California P, 1966.
———. "Questions and Answers about the Pentad." *College Composition and Communication* 29 (1978): 330–35.
———. *A Rhetoric of Motives*. 1950. Rpt. Berkeley: U of California P, 1969.

Major Scholarship in Composition

Comprone, Joseph. "Kenneth Burke and the Teaching of Writing." *College Composition and Communication* 29 (1978): 336–40.
Irmscher, William. *The Holt Guide to English*. 3rd ed. New York: Holt, 1981.
Winterowd, W. Ross., and Geoffrey R. Winterowd. *The Critical Reader, Thinker, and Writer*. 2nd ed. Mountain View, CA: Mayfield, 1997.

RONALD G. ASHCROFT

E

EPISTEMIC RHETORIC AND THEORIES

Summary

Epistemic rhetoric is complex; for ever since communication scholar Robert L. Scott first coined the term in 1967, rhetorical theorists have used it in a number of conflicting ways. As a result, the term has become a rubric for individual theories arguing for rhetoric as a way of knowing. Put differently, theories falling under the heading of rhetoric-as-epistemic all subscribe to the same general idea: Rhetoric is epistemic since it is through language that knowledge is constructed. As James Berlin summarizes it, "In epistemic rhetoric [theories] there is never a division between experience and language, whether the experience involves the subject, the subject and other subjects, or the subject and the material world" (*Rhetoric and Reality* 16). Language gives our experiences form and structure, allowing us to form "conceptions of ourselves, our audiences, and the very reality in which we exist" (166). Thus, an epistemic rhetoric holds that language both embodies and generates knowledge. The differences in the individual theories arise in how each one comes to define the methodology by which humans use language in the epistemic process.

The first instances of epistemic rhetoric research in composition studies are reflected in the works of Richard Young, Alton Becker, and Kenneth Pike (1970), Ann Berthoff (1978), Kenneth Dowst (1980), and James Berlin (1982). Although these scholars' theories can be located earlier in the rhetorics of I. A. Richards, Kenneth Burke, and Richard Ohmann, their theories represent some of the first pedagogical expressions of an epistemic rhetoric (Berlin, "Contemporary Composition," 773). As Berlin states, their "approaches most comprehensively display a view of rhetoric as epistemic, as a means of arriving at truth'' (773).

In *Rhetoric: Discovery and Change*, Young, Becker, and Pike apply the linguistic notion of tagmemics to rhetorical theory, arguing that humans conceive the world in terms of repeatable units. Despite the ever-changing nature of events, there are always recognizable, recurring units of experience that enable humans to maintain certain identities. One way to study how people conceive of the world in terms of these units is through language; for language is a set of symbols that allows us to label these chunks of experience (27). A rhetoric founded upon this notion is epistemic, for a tagmemic rhetoric does not treat language apart from the persons who use it.

Similar to Young, Becker, and Pike, Berthoff argues that it is through language that we ''unitize'' experiences and thus generate knowledge. In *Forming/ Thinking/Writing*, Berthoff claims that meaning is the function of relationships, that is, ''making sense of the world is to see something with respect to, in terms of, in relation to something else'' (44). For Berthoff, rhetoric is the art of representing that ''seeing.'' It is the art of naming, opposing, and defining in order to articulate relationships. Given this definition, rhetoric is epistemic since it is an art of clarifying and articulating relationships as a composer transforms information into meaning.

In contrast to the previous two scholars, Dowst does not offer any specifics as to how we ''unitize'' experiences. In his article ''The Epistemic Approach,'' Dowst argues that knowledge is dialectical, the result of a process involving the interaction of opposing elements. For Dowst, these elements include the writer, reality, and language. He argues that language comes between the writer and reality and therefore filters, shapes, or distorts reality (74; see also Fulkerson, 195). Again, rhetoric is epistemic since it is through language that we are able to learn and discover truths.

Berlin argues along the same lines as Dowst in asserting that truth is dialectical and dynamic. Knowledge is posited as a product of the dialectic in which ''the observer, the discourse community in which the observer is functioning, and the material world conditions of existence'' come together (''Rhetoric and Ideology,'' 488). Moreover, language becomes the agency of mediation in this dialectical interaction. Studying rhetoric (i.e., the ways in which discourse is generated) is equivalent to studying the ways in which knowledge is constructed. For Berlin, rhetoric is epistemic since it is the act involving ''the dialectical interaction engaging the material, the social, and the individual writer'' (488).

Although implicit in all these theories is the epistemological view that through language one comes to know, the discrepant meanings among the particular theories illustrate an essential point about epistemic rhetoric research: It is not a fixed or stable tradition. To borrow John Trimbur's summary of social constructionism, epistemic rhetoric ''is by no means a finished or codified intellec-

tual tradition, and the issues surrounding it remain volatile and open ended''
(*Encyclopedia of Rhetoric and Composition* 677).

Reception and Significance in Composition Studies

Prior to epistemic rhetoric theories, current-traditional rhetoric dominated our
theoretical and pedagogical discussions. Current-traditional rhetoric, as Sharon
Crowley reconstructs it, was "characterized by its emphasis on the formal features of the finished product of composing" (*Encyclopedia* 156). With emphasis
on product, rhetoric became the study of how to adapt one's discourse to one's
audience. Rhetoric's province, therefore, was limited to the ability to convey
knowledge to an audience.

One of the outcomes of current-traditional rhetoric was that composition was
seen as a mere service industry, carrying no scholastic weight of its own. With
no apparent subject matter or methodology, composition theory was not considered a worthy intellectual pursuit. However, with the introduction of this new
rhetoric, composition saw itself as having new importance and new significance
in academia; for epistemic rhetorical theories created a legitimate place for composition in the academy by redefining it as a study of not only the transmission
of knowledge, but also the making of knowledge. Since rhetoric is one of the
intellectual traditions of composition studies, composition could now be seen as
more than just a service industry; rather, it is a field that could claim to share
with the hard sciences a pursuit of defining and critiquing the epistemic process.

Given the outcome of such a new rhetoric, it is not surprising that the notion
of an epistemic rhetoric was well received in composition. In his 1987 book on
the history of composition in American colleges from 1900 to 1985, *Rhetoric
and Reality*, Berlin states that rhetorics displaying epistemic features are one of
the few schools of rhetoric to continue to attract proponents. Since the introduction of epistemic rhetoric in the works mentioned here, influential scholars
such as W. Ross Winterowd, Wayne Booth, Charles Kneupper, James Kinneavy,
Charles Bazerman, and Patricia Bizzell have all appropriated various tenets of
an epistemic rhetoric into their own theories (see Berlin, *Rhetoric*). Given the
prolific nature of epistemic rhetoric theories, its reception has become so significant to the field that claiming rhetoric as epistemic today seems redundant.

Whereas the individual theories are the pedagogical expressions of an epistemic rhetoric, one of its theoretical expressions is reflected in the postmodern
idea of social constructionism. Social constructionism holds the idea that humans
"draw upon linguistic resources available within particular cultures and specialized social milieux in order to constitute reality . . . and position themselves
within those realities" (Trimbur, *Encyclopedia of Rhetoric* 675). In other words,
it is through one's discursive practices that knowledge is constructed. As composition comes to adopt social constructionism as one of its primary theoretical
frameworks—as books like Patricia Harkin and John Schilb's *Contending with
Words* argue—our field accepts the very notion that epistemic rhetoric theories

put forth: Knowledge is constructed through one's language practices. Current rhetorical theory, then, is largely based on and situated within a social-constructionist framework—a framework that implies and gives rise to a rhetoric that is epistemic. Linking the two terms together, therefore, seems repetitive.

Despite the fact that through social constructionism epistemic rhetoric theories have permeated much of the discourse in composition studies, epistemic rhetoric is still an important line of inquiry to pursue for several reasons. First, although scholars, theoretically, accept that knowledge is generated through one's discursive practices, pedagogically it is still taught that all thinking and thought processes occur before writing. Language, therefore, is limited to the medium from which truths are communicated. This is evident through the emphasis on product, namely, current-traditional rhetoric. Because we have not entirely implemented the theoretical notions of an epistemic rhetoric, this is a crucial line of research.

In *Fragments of Rationality*, Lester Faigley illustrates this idea in his discussion of postmodernism in composition. Faigley argues that despite the field's profession of postmodern ideologies—ideologies that situate knowledge within one's discursive practices—we still implement modernist ideas of rationalism and objectivity. These principles imply that knowledge exists independently of discourse. Faigley makes this argument based on the idea that despite our profession to value process, "it is not process for its own sake but rather process [toward a] teleological development" of a product (14). By asking student writers to occupy the modernist position of producing a rational, coherent student subject, the postmodern theory that meaning arises out of our historical, social, and political discursive practices is thus denied. Although Faigley's critique of the field's pedagogical practices is being challenged, scholars continue to work on ways of developing and implementing epistemic rhetorical theories in the classroom.

BIBLIOGRAPHY

Primary Texts and Major Scholarship in Composition

Bazerman, Charles. "What Written Knowledge Does: Three Examples of Academic Discourse." *Philosophy of the Social Sciences* 11 (1981): 361–87.

Berlin, James. "Contemporary Composition: The Major Pedagogical Theories." *College English* 44 (1982): 765–77.

———. "Rhetoric and Ideology in the Writing Class." *College English* 50 (1988): 477–494.

———. *Rhetoric and Reality: Writing Instruction in American Colleges, 1900–1985*. Carbondale: U of Southern Illinois P, 1987.

Berthoff, Ann. *Forming/Thinking/Writing: The Composing Imagination*. 1987. Rpt. 2nd ed. Portsmouth, NH: Heinemann, 1988.

Bizzell, Patricia. *Academic Discourse and Critical Consciousness*. Pittsburgh, PA: U of Pittsburgh P, 1992.

Booth, Wayne C. *Modern Dogma and the Rhetoric of Assent*. Notre Dame, IN: U of Notre Dame P, 1974.

Bruffee, Kenneth A. "Collaborative Learning and the 'Conversation of Mankind.' " *College English* 46 (1984): 635–52.

Burke, Kenneth. "Language as Symbolic Action: Essays on Life, Learning." In *Eight Approaches to Teaching Composition*. Ed. Timothy R. Donovan and Ben W. McClelland. Urbana, IL: NCTE, 1980, 65–86.

Crowley, Sharon. "Current-Traditional Rhetoric." In *Encyclopedia of Rhetoric and Composition*. Ed. Theresa Enos. New York: Garland, 1996, 156–57.

Dowst, Kenneth. "The Epistemic Approach: Writing, Knowing, and Learning." In *Eight Approaches to Teaching Composition*. Ed Timothy R. Donovan and Ben W. McClelland. Urbana, IL: NCTE, 1980, 65–86.

Faigley, Lester. *Fragments of Rationality: Postmodernity and the Subject of Composition*. Pittsburgh, PA: U of Pittsburgh P, 1992.

Foucault, Michel. *The Archaeology of Knowledge*. Trans. A. M. Sheridan Smith. New York: Pantheon, 1972.

Fulkerson, Richard. "On Theories of Rhetoric as Epistemic: A Bi-Disciplinary View." In *Oldspeak/ Newspeak: Rhetorical Transformations*. Ed. Charles Kneupper. Arlington, TX: Rhetoric Society of America, 1985, 194–207.

Harkin, Patricia, and John Schilb, eds. *Contending with Words*. New York: MLA, 1991.

Kinneavy, James L. "The Relation of the Whole to the Part in Interpretation Theory and in the Composing Process." *Visible Language* 17 (1983): 120–45.

Kneupper, Charles W. "The Tyranny of Logic and the Freedom of Argumentation." *Pre/Text* 5 (1984): 113–21.

Knoblauch, C. H., and Lil Brannon. *Rhetorical Traditions and the Teaching of Writing*. Upper Montclair, NJ: Boynton/Cook, 1984.

Ohmann, Richard. "In Lieu of a New Rhetoric." *College English* 26 (1964): 17–22.

Richards, I. A. *The Philosophy of Rhetoric*. New York: Oxford UP, 1936.

Scott, Robert L. "One Viewing Rhetoric as Epistemic." *Central States Speech Journal* 18 (1967): 9–16.

Trimbur, John. "Social Construction." In *Encyclopedia of Rhetoric and Composition*. Ed. Theresa Enos. New York: Garland, 1996, 675–77.

Winterowd, W. Ross. *Contemporary Rhetoric: A Conceptual Background with Readings*. New York: Harcourt, 1975.

Young, Richard L., Alton L. Becker, and Kenneth L. Pike. *Rhetoric: Discovery and Change*. New York: Harcourt, 1970.

RICHARD McNABB

EXPRESSIVISM

Summary

Expressivist rhetoric weaves together several sources: nontraditional textbooks offering new practices for teaching writing, commentaries by first-generation expressivists that began to articulate theory, theorizing in reaction to scholarly and ideological attacks, and recent syntheses that integrate expressivism with social and liberatory rhetorics. Sometimes called expressionism, the movement originated in the 1960s and 1970s as a set of values and practices opposing current-traditional rhetoric.

Current-traditional teaching emphasized academic writing in standard forms and "correct" grammar. It reinforced middle-class values, such as social stability and cultural homogeneity, and supported the meritocracy associated with the military-industrial complex. Graduate studies in English concentrated on literary criticism, ignoring or devaluing pedagogy. Nontraditional textbooks presented expressivist practices as alternatives to current-traditional teaching for an audience of teachers as much as for students. Though radical departures for the time, many of these methods now constitute mainstream writing instruction.

Alternative Textbooks

Murray's *A Writer Teaches Writing* (1968) organizes the writing course as a workshop and still exemplifies the process approach. Murray's use of nondirective feedback from both teacher and students turns the responsibility for writing back to the student. In *Telling Writing* (1970) and elsewhere, Macrorie insists that individual writers recreate their original experience in "telling" details. He protests the bureaucratic language of the schools, what he calls "Engfish." He instructs students to keep a journal as a reflective exercise for documenting individual experience and personal development.

Elbow's *Writing without Teachers* (1973) values the act of writing as a means for both making meaning and creating identity. The "teacherless" classroom returns the responsibility for and control over learning back to students. The book attends mostly to invention. Freewriting helps students discover ideas and their significance, center-of-gravity exercises develop and focus these ideas, and peer response groups allow writers to test their writing on an actual audience and revise based on that response. In an appendix, "The Doubting Game and the Believing Game—An Analysis of the Intellectual Enterprise," Elbow critiques conventional Western skepticism and encourages writers to engage a dialectic of perspectives—self and others, the familiar and the strange—to make themselves better writers, thinkers, and citizens.

In *Writing with Power* (1981), Elbow shows how objective as well as subjective evaluation criteria can aid writers to revise for specific audiences to accomplish specific purposes. His approach becomes more rhetorical and the emphasis on process continues. The context is social and active; the writer is concerned with having an impact on an actual audience. Elbow instructs writers to maintain a productive paradoxical tension between individual and group. Equipped with well-developed personal identities, individuals can function effectively in groups or cultures. Interdependence is both the source and locus of power. Voice is a central concern in *Writing with Power*, as it symbolizes the expressivist value system. Elbow and the expressivists, anticipating feminist pedagogy, work to subvert teaching practices and institutional structures that oppress, appropriate, or silence individual voices.

In collaboration with Pat Belanoff, Elbow further elaborates the role of groups in *A Community of Writers* (1989) and a companion pamphlet developed for teachers, *Sharing and Responding*. The expressivist use of groups anticipates Trimbur's critique of collaborative writing. Trimbur champions dissensus, which recognizes, celebrates, and explores difference in order to reestablish social autonomy. Moreover, dissensus concedes the power of groups and culture to shape the individuals, but maintains individual's potential for agency. Expressivism shares this belief and purpose. The proof of dissensus, for Elbow and the expressivists, is voice, the individual identity of the writer working in a community.

Elbow's "A Method for Teaching Writing," reflects the flavor and intensity of the early expressivists. He argues that voice empowers individuals to act in the world. He recounts his experience counseling applicants for conscientious objector (CO) draft status during the Vietnam conflict. Elbow, a CO himself, sees writing as a means of political action. He teaches those he counsels that they must do more than just make sense when writing applications for CO status, they must communicate intense belief through voice. Writing, thus, becomes a form of political or social activism.

Expressivist Commentaries and Background Theory

Most first-generation expressivists were not inclined to theorize. They considered themselves teachers. When necessary they provided anecdotal narrative, metadiscourse rather than theory, to rationalize their practices. Macrorie's *Uptaught* and *A Vulnerable Teacher* serve as good examples. Expressivist metadiscourse shows the influence of various disciplines, especially linguistics, cognitive and developmental psychology, phenomenology, and existential philosophy.

The theoretical background includes two major sources: Britton's expressive function in language and Kinneavy's expressive discourse. The combination creates something of an ambiguity. Expressivists do not distinguish between the expressive function of language and expressive discourse, which is a type of text. This eventually causes a problem for some critics, especially Harris, who dismisses expressivism entirely. However, expressivists reject dualistic thinking, viewing ambiguity as a source for productive dialectic. In "Expressive Rhetoric: A Source Study," I examine Britton, Kinneavy, and commentary by Murray, Coles, and Elbow to construct an expressivist theory of language and epistemology.

Murray attends to epistemology in "Writing as Process: How Writing Finds its Own Meaning" in Donovan and McClelland's *Eight Approaches to Teaching Composition* (1980), an anthology with a strong expressivist bent. In his "speculation upon the composing process" (3), Murray proposes an instrumental relation between composing and meaning making. He examines three related activities: rehearsing, drafting, and revising. These involve complex interactions between contrary impulses: exploring and clarifying; collecting and combining; and writing and reading. Through these interactions, meaning evolves. Murray's commentary resembles Britton's analysis of the function of expressive language in *Writing and Learning*: writing is a process of discovering meaning through shifting back and forth from participant to spectator modes, and writing involves an interaction between self and subject. Through several iterations, writers use language to generate, connect, shape, and then evaluate for a purpose. According to Murray: "The writer is constantly learning from the writing what it intends to say. The writer listens for evolving meaning. . . . The writing itself helps the writer see the subject" (7). Murray includes a social element in the process, insisting that his students work within a writing community. Meaning results from the interaction of teacher and students, writers and readers, process and product—all accomplished through language.

Expressivist pedagogy is systematic and purposeful, based on a theory of relations between language, meaning making, and self-development. Elbow's freewriting, based originally on his own journal writing, requires self-conscious language processing. In "Toward a Phenomenology of Freewriting," Elbow notes that the initial "experimental form of freewriting" occurred in a personal journal (190). He describes a process similar to the generating/structuring/evaluating movement in Murray's model of the writing process and posits an analytic urge based in writing that results in understanding leading to action. Through the process he gains control of his subject, whether himself or an intellectual concept. He mentions Progoff, a student of Jung, whose work in depth psychology culminated in the "Journal Workshop" method, a formal journal program.

Expressive writing exercises require students, in a sense, to write a phenomenology of self. In *A Theory of Discourse*, Kinneavy argues that the expressive aim is psychologically prior to all others. Using Sartre and the phenomenologists, Kinneavy argues that through expressive discourse the self moves from a private meaning to a shared meaning that results ultimately in some action. Rather than a "primal whine," expressive discourse moves away from solipsism toward accommodation with the world and accomplishes purposeful action. As a consequence, Kinneavy elevates expressive discourse to the same order as referential, persuasive, and literary discourse.

But expressive discourse is not the exclusive province of the individual; it also has a social function. Kinneavy's analysis of the Declaration of Independence makes this clear. Contesting the claim that the purpose of the declaration is persuasive, Kinneavy traces its evolution through several drafts to prove that its primary aim is expressive: to establish an American group identity (410). Kinneavy's analysis suggests that, rather than being individualistic and otherworldly or naive and narcissistic, expressive discourse can be ideologically empowering.

Coles uses this realization that expressive discourse has both individual and social functions to great advantage. *The Plural I: The Teaching of Writing* (1978) presents a semester-long sequence of writing assignments that engages students in writing self-critical phenomenology. Through the sequence, the class, as individuals and a group, comes to agree on a set of meanings and values concerning the purpose of education, in the process achieving Coles's goal of forming his students into practicing humanists. The sequence culminates in a formal review and evaluation of the work of the course. Anticipating the reflective self-assessments that have become important in current portfolio evaluation practice, Coles's final assignment asks for formal reflection: "Where did you start this term? Where did you seem to come out? . . . [W]ho were you? Who are you now?" (258). In Kinneavy's terms, Coles is asking his students to write *apologia*, a high-level of expressive discourse.

Reception and Significance in Composition Studies

Initial Dismissal

Expressivism originated in opposition to mainstream practice, offering an alternative to current-traditional teaching. The mainstream reacted in a variety of ways. Chief among these was simple dismissal. Expressivism was labeled a fringe movement. More substantial opposition came in the form of the back-to-basics movement which, with its emphasis on grammar and standard formats, was really current traditional teaching dressed in new clothes.

Several other rhetorical schools grew up along with expressivism, all part of the renaissance in rhetoric in the 1960s and 1970s. These other schools, especially neoclassicism and cognitive rhetoric, were not averse to theory. Expressivists distrusted theory because it often distracted attention from students and teaching. Given the early expressivist aversion toward theory, it is no surprise that formal theoretical considerations of expressivism are generally critical. Covino notes the antipathy of both classicists and cognitivists, both of whom label expressivism's sense of the self and its importance irrational (4). Lately, however, cognitivists have reaffirmed the important but problematic role of the self. Bruner, who described himself as "acutely uncomfortable" with considerations of the self, concedes that merely labeling the self a cultural construct does not negate its power. He theorizes a "transactional self" (57–69) who through metacognition and reflection "penetrates knowledge for his own uses, and if he can share and negotiate the result of his penetrations, then he becomes a member of the culture-creating community" (132). Membership in such a community is the goal of much expressivist work.

Ideological Critiques and Theoretical Defenses

The strongest critiques originate in social rhetoric, specifically from Berlin and Faigley. Berlin offers an extended ideological critique. In "Contemporary Composition: The Major Pedagogical Theories," he portrays "expressionism" as an untheorized and ideologically debased form of neo-Platonism. Elsewhere he links expressivism to "Emersonian romantic" rhetoric and subsequently to the "rhetoric of liberal culture" and to Dewey and the progressive education movement. Thus he locates expressivist rhetoric among "subjective" theories of rhetoric. His critique is rich, attending in considerable detail to expressivist practices to construct a theory. His allegiance to social epistemic rhetoric, however, results in readings that, as I will continue to argue, are not verified by a close analysis of expressivist work. Berlin and the other social rhetoricians view expressivism's primary flaw as a false and otherworldly epistemology of the self that privileges individualism and rejects the material world. Faigley argues that expressivism's Romantic view of the self is philosophically and politically retrograde, making it ineffectual in postmodern times. Further, expressivism's concern with the individual and authentic voice directs students away from social and political problems in the material world.

In response to this critique, Elbow offers an extended defense of voice. In *Landmark Essays: On Voice and Writing*, Elbow collects sixteen essays by various theorists, including Bakhtin, Gibson, and Ong, as well as critics of expressivism such as Faigley and bell hooks. In an introduction, Elbow traces the voice controversy as far back as Aristotle and Plato. He equates voice and ethos and argues that because Aristotle includes techniques to, in the philosopher's own words, "make ourselves *thought to be* sensible and morally good," he thus affirms Plato's earlier declaration that ethos—good character—is the central concern in all rhetoric. Aristotle "is affirming both positions in what is in fact a common sense view: 'It's nice to *be* trustworthy; but if you're skilled you can fake it' " (xli).

"Resonant" voice, one of five empirically verifiable instances of voice, is Elbow's primary concern. Sensitive to critiques of the expressivist view of self, Elbow walks a careful theoretical line. Resonant voice manages to get a great deal of the self "*behind* the words." Discourse can never "articulate a whole person," but at times we can "find words that seem to capture the rich complexity of the unconscious . . . that somehow seem to *resonate with* or *have behind them* the unconscious as well as the conscious [Elbow's emphasis] . . . [W]ords of this sort . . . we experience as resonant—and through them we have a sense of presence with the writer" (xxxiv). As with voice, he relates "presence" to ethos in classical rhetoric.

Later in the essay Elbow connects resonant voice with self-identity and argues that voice in writing is a locus for power. From a pragmatic perspective, he argues against a binary view that opposes sentimental (expressivist) and sophisticated (postmodern) views of self; writers need to use both. The sentimental self (the believer) functions best in exploratory writing. The sophisticated self (the doubter) works well when revising with a pragmatic end in mind.

In the same volume, Freisinger's "Voicing the Self: Toward a Pedagogy of Resistance in a Postmodern Age" counters the claim that expressivism devalues social and political engagement, arguing instead that the expressivist concept of self is a starting point for resistance, as defined by Giroux. He invokes several postmodern explorations of the self, including Smith's *Discerning the Subject*. Smith argues that much postmodern social theory considers only the "cerned" self—the self in the abstract. As a result, postmodern theory cannot provide a workable concept of human agency. Such a theory is available only through considerations of the "discerned" self. Freisinger argues that expressivism's emphasis on the immediacy and peculiarity of individual experience works to create this "discerned" self. Freisinger also invokes the concept of radical reflexivity in Taylor's *The Dialogic Self* to elaborate expressivism's concern for reflective thinking as a starting point for resistance and liberation.

Expressivism's original kinship with philosophy explains a very recent defense against the ideological critiques. In "Politics and Ordinary Language: A Defense of Expressivist Rhetorics," O'Donnell questions the motivation of some ideological critics, accusing them of being more interested in teaching a particular ideology than in providing students with the tools of social and political critique. Expressivism's strength is its insistence that all concerns, whether individual, social, or political, must originate in personal experience and be documented in the student's own language. What O'Donnell calls expressivism's "unguardedness" makes it attractive to teachers concerned with raising political consciousness. He offers a defense based in ordinary language philosophy, showing how expressivist practices "facilitate investigations of political issues in unique, sometimes necessary ways" (424).

Recent Syntheses

The best index of any movement's significance is its persistence in the professional literature. By that measure, expressivism thrives. The ideological critiques inspired several volumes of expressivist theory and application. In addition, expressivism continues to receive attention in *College English*, *College Composition and Communication*, *Rhetoric Review*, and *Journal of Advanced Composition*. This last section will look briefly at this new work.

Though expressivism developed before social rhetoric, both share the same goal: raising consciousness to move people to act against injustice, whether the war in Vietnam or economic, racial, or gender injustice. This commonality of purpose has resulted in several exciting syntheses. Most prominent among these is Gradin's *Romancing Rhetorics*, whose purpose is to politicize expressivism and "establish a pedagogy of equity" in which all can contribute and be heard (121). Gradin explores a commonly overlooked connection between romanticism and expressivism by pointing to German romanticism's concern for social justice and political action and countering the claim that expressivism values individualism to the exclusion of social concerns. Rather, expressivists value autonomy as signaled in the concern to empower people through voice, and they believe that individuals can use personal awareness to act against oppressive material and psychological conditions. She also connects expressivism with feminism, noting that Elbow and his pedagogy are referenced in Belenky et al.'s *Women's Ways of Knowing*. Similarly, in *Writing from the Margins: Power and Pedagogy for Teachers of Composition*, Hill considers Elbow and other expressivists as models for building a new pedagogy of awareness and equity.

Another exciting synthesis comes in the work of Fishman and McCarthy. In a series of articles, they examine attacks on expressivism based in discourse community theory. Led by Bartholomae, these critics argue that emphasizing personal writing, as expressivism does, wastes students' time. Rather, students need training in the conventions of academic discourse so they can succeed in the institutions that will provide them access to economic and social power. Elbow critiques this charge in "Being a Writer vs. Being an Academic: A Conflict in Goals."

Fishman and McCarthy begin by asking "Is Expressivism Dead?" Answering no, they argue that expressivism does not endorse the ideal of the isolated individual. Arguing from the same socially concerned German romanticism as Gradin, they contend that expressivist techniques can be used to achieve social constructivist goals in a writing across the curriculum context. In "Community in the Expressivist Classroom," they explore the tension between conventional authoritarian and expressivist liberal and communitarian classroom ideals. Fishman claims some success in promoting student voice while teaching disciplinary conventions. However, his experience underscores the complexity of the expressivist classroom ideal, where students function as experts and teachers as learners. They conclude that this complexity, rather than the reductive either/or positions generally presented in the literature, offers significant opportunities for progress. The last piece, "Teaching for Student Change: A Deweyan Alternative to Radical Pedagogy," defends the safe and cooperative classroom championed by the expressivists against recent charges by feminists and critical teachers that expressivist pedagogy protects the status quo by encouraging a politeness that camouflages inherent conflicts in the classroom and society at large. Fishman and McCarthy offer an alternative that privileges diversity and encourages transformation for teachers who "find certain types of conflict unattractive but who seek student critique and change" (344).

BIBLIOGRAPHY

Primary Texts

Textbooks

Coles, William E., Jr. *The Plural I: The Teaching of Writing*. New York: Holt, 1978.
———. *Writing without Teachers*. New York: Oxford UP, 1973.
———. *Writing with Power*. New York: Oxford UP, 1981.
Elbow, Peter, and Pat Belanoff. *A Community of Writers: A Workshop Course in Writing*. New York: Random House, 1989.
———. *Sharing and Responding*. New York: Random House, 1989.
Macrorie, Ken. *Telling Writing*. Rochelle Park, NJ: Hayden, 1970.
Murray, Donald. *A Writer Teaches Writing*. New York: Holt, 1968.
Progoff, Ira. *At a Journal Workshop*. New York: Dialogue House, 1975.

Commentary and Metadiscourse

Elbow, Peter. "Being an Academic vs. Being a Writer. A Conflict in Goals." *College English* 46 (1995): 72–83.
———. "A Method for Teaching Writing." *College English* 30 (1968): 115–25.
———. "Toward a Phenomenology of Freewriting." *Nothing Begins with N: New Investigations of Freewriting*. Ed. Pat Belanoff, Peter Elbow, and Sheryl I. Fontaine. Carbondale: Southern Illinois UP, 1991, 189–213.
Macrorie, Ken. *Uptaught*. New York: Hayden, 1970.

————. *A Vulnerable Teacher*. Rochelle Park, NJ: Hayden, 1974.

Murray, Donald. "Writing as Process: How Writing Finds Its Own Meaning." In *Eight Approaches to Teaching Composition*. Ed. Timothy R. Donovan and Ben McClelland. Urbana, IL: NCTE, 1980, 3–20.

Major Scholarship in Composition

Belenky, Mary F., Blythe McVicker Clinchy, Nancy Rule Goldberger, and Jill Mattuck Tarule. *Women's Ways of Knowing: The Development of Self, Voice, and Mind*. New York: Basic, 1986.

Berlin, James A. "Contemporary Composition: The Major Pedagogical Theories." *College English* 44 (1982): 765–77.

————. *Rhetoric and Reality: Writing Instruction in American Colleges, 1900–1985*. Carbondale: Southern Illinois UP, 1987.

————. *Writing Instruction in Nineteenth-Century American Colleges*. Carbondale: Southern Illinois UP, 1984.

Britton, James. *Language and Learning*. New York: Penguin, 1970.

Britton, James, et al. *The Development of Writing Abilities (11–18)*. London: Macmillan, 1975.

Bruner, Jerome. *Actual Minds, Possible Worlds*. Cambridge: Harvard UP, 1986.

Burnham, Christopher C. "Expressive Rhetoric: A Source Study." In *Defining the New Rhetorics*. Ed. Theresa Enos and Stuart C. Brown. Newbury Park, CA: Sage, 1993, 154–70.

Covino, William. *Magic, Rhetoric, and Literacy*. Albany: State U of New York P, 1994.

Elbow, Peter. "Introduction: About Voice in Writing." In *Landmark Essays on Voice and Writing*. Ed. Peter Elbow. Davis, CA: Hermagoras P, 1994, xi–xlvii.

————. *Landmark Essays on Voice and Writing*. Davis, CA: Hermagoras P, 1994.

Faigley, Lester. *Fragments of Rationality: Postmodernity and the Subject of Composition*. Pittsburgh, PA: U of Pittsburgh P, 1992.

Fishman, Stephen M., and Lucille P. McCarthy. "Community in the Expressivist Classroom: Juggling Liberal and Communitarian Visions." *College English* 57 (1995): 62–81.

————. "Is Expressivism Dead? Reconsidering Its Romantic Roots and Its Relation to Social Constructionism." *College English* 54 (1992): 647–61.

————. "Teaching For Student Change: A Deweyan Alternative to Radical Pedagogy." *College Composition and Communication* 47 (1996): 342–66.

Freisinger, Randall R. "Voicing the Self: Toward a Pedagogy of Resistance in a Postmodern Age." In *Landmark Essays on Voice and Writing*. Ed. Peter Elbow. Davis, CA: Hermagoras P, 1994, 187–211.

Gradin, Sherrie L. *Romancing Rhetorics: Social Expressivist Perspectives on the Teaching of Writing*. Portsmouth, NH: Boynton/Cook, 1995.

Harris, Jeanette. *Expressive Discourse*. Dallas, TX: Southern Methodist UP, 1990.

Hill, Carolyn Erikson. *Writing from the Margins: Power and Pedagogy for Teachers of Composition*. New York: Oxford UP, 1990.

Kinneavy, James. *A Theory of Discourse*. Englewood Cliffs, NJ: Prentice-Hall, 1971.

O'Donnell, Thomas. "Politics and Ordinary Language: A Defense of Expressivist Rhetorics." *College English* 58 (1996): 423–39.

Smith, Paul. *Discerning the Subject*. Minneapolis: U of Minnesota P, 1988.

Taylor, Charles. "The Dialogic Self." In *The Interpretive Turn*. Ed. David R. Hiley,

James F. Bowman, and Richard Shusterman. Ithaca, NY: Cornell UP, 1991, 304–14.

Trimbur, John. "Consensus and Difference in Collaborative Learning." *College English* 51 (1989): 602–16.

CHRISTOPHER C. BURNHAM

F

FEMINIST THEORIES

Summary

The diversity and productive conflicts among feminist thinkers now indicate the evolution of feminist theory and practice. However, the tendency to omit, oversimplify, or collapse trains of feminist thought as if they were not fraught with difference is common. The disciplines that have most successfully and usefully appropriated feminist theory have cultivated a critical awareness of its various strands and the conflicts among its schools of thought. A simple geography might help to sketch this complicated theoretical terrain. The following five major divisions of the general landscape of feminist theory are meant to indicate some key differences among theories. They are Anglo-American, cultural, French, postcolonial, and postmodern feminist theories. Theorists' stances on issues of agency, identity, language, and culture serve as boundaries between the different theories.

Anglo-American feminist theory is rooted in liberal humanism, with its emphasis on the individual, unified "self" and on universal human experience. Human agency is a distinct possibility within this frame, and political change is wrought through changes in individuals. A women's expression of her personal experience and the consciousness-raising that accompanies it are defining characteristics of this theory whose slogan is "the personal is the political." This theory's emphasis on equity between men and women and on women's inclusion in areas dominated by men presumes a view of culture particularly American in its democratic ideal and distinguishes it from the other feminist theories discussed here, all of which problematize the forces of culture and language. These theorists have examined canon formation and images of women in texts by men and women, seeking to include and to value women.

Cultural feminist theory, in contrast to Anglo-American theory's desire to integrate, seeks to separate men from women on the levels of identity, language, and culture. These theorists define an essential set of differences between man and woman, critique the *patriarchal* history of devaluing the woman's side, and revalue her identity. A few of the binary elements often cited include the following:

Feminine/Masculine

Collaborative/Competitive

Connection/Individuation

Private/Public

Inclusive/Exclusive

Relational patterns/Linear patterns

Nurture/Combat

Body/Mind

As cultural feminism valorizes the left side of the binaries and criticizes the right, it offers utopian visions of a future culture based on woman's identity and capable of "re-visioning" the patriarchy. It often relies on the ethical and critical perspectives of outsider women as theorists who are capable of revisionary insights unavailable to insiders. This outsider status is evident in cultural feminism's experimental language practices, which link these theorists to the next territory of feminist theory.

French feminist theory rereads psychoanalytic theory in order to appropriate the body as a linguistic and stylistic locale for revolutionary practice. The female body has its own (non)language, outside of the *phallogocentric* system of language, which shapes and controls identity. Woman can gain revolutionary agency by disrupting the phallic law encoded in language. The difference between the strategic stylistic practices of the cultural feminists and those of the French—called *écriture feminine*—is the specifically psychoanalytic point of view of the French, who adopt and revise the Lacanian idea that language (the *symbolic*) shapes identity and culture at the psyche's foundation. Hélène Cixous's and Luce Irigaray's "writing the body" and Julia Kristeva's semiotic disruptions of language exemplify French feminism's practices.

Postcolonial feminist theory foregrounds cultural diversity and complicates the idea of difference as it insists on the multiple analysis of cultural forces shaping identity. The categories of race, class, gender, and sexual orientation form the basis for this analysis, which is ideologically aware and calls for activism within a multicultural politics. Postcolonial feminist theorists have rightly criticized white feminists for their exclusionary, racist attitudes toward women of color, especially those white feminists who reduce diverse women to an essentialized "Woman"—assumed to be white, heterosexual, and middle-class. Alice Walker's *womanist* criticism, Gayatri Spivak's treatment of the concept of "the Subaltern," and bell hooks's revolutionary theory and pedagogy exemplify this theory's complexity.

Postmodern feminist theory shares some important common ground with postcolonial feminist theory, both of which are engaged in the analysis of subjectivity at the defining intersection of identity and culture. At this intersection, histories and economies of race, class, gender, sexual preference, and other determining forces socially construct the subject. Agency diminishes as language bears down on subjects, molding identity. Postcolonial critics describe these forces, which shape the image of "the Other" as exotic or as erased by the promotion of white, Eurocentric universals. Postmodern theoretical moves call into question the conventional, often naturalized, notion of woman and trouble these designations. As the postmodern *subject* replaces the humanist "self," identity is seen as the rehearsals of forced scripts, the same typecasting, and the same nasty outcome.

Reception and Significance in Composition Studies

Numbers of recent feminist articles in composition studies and rhetoric have noticed the field's "feminization" and its ironically slow acceptance of feminist theory (e.g., Clark, Holbrook, Looser). But feminist compositionists have become increasingly theoretical during the 1990s and have begun consciously to ask theoretically loaded questions. Who is the object/subject of feminist theory—the essentialized Woman, the psychoanalytic feminine, the socially constructed, gendered subject? Can "essentialized" versions of women be useful politically? If so, how? What language theory is claimed by each feminism, and what pedagogies might result for the writing classroom? How do agency, identity, language, and culture weigh in as relative influences for writers writing and for teachers teaching? The tensions within feminism, especially in the last decade, regarding the contradictory readings of *woman* and *gender* as well as the politics of those many readings are evident in composition studies' reception of feminist theory.

Anglo-American feminist theory, with its emphasis on equity and inclusion and on the individual "self" coming to voice, has been adopted automatically by many feminist compositionists. For instance, *Teaching Writing: Pedagogy, Gender, and Equity*, the 1987 Caywood and Overing collection (the first devoted to feminist composition studies), includes a number of articles that reflect this theoretical attitude, for instance, this explanation of student voice: "As the student makes small choices, then important ones, she discovers her rhetorical voice along with her personal, female voice." The author says that this writing makes accessible "the genuine self behind the mask." The larger outcome is "a peaceful world" and "a new woman" (Frey, 102).

Another example of composition studies that draw on the tenants of Anglo-

American feminist theory is the early historical work of Patricia Bizzell, Cheryl Glenn, and, arguably, Susan Jarratt, though these writers have more recently launched into postmodern modes. But the projects of feminist composition studies historians often have been influenced by the liberal feminist tradition of inclusion and canon reformation. They offer critiques of standard male-authored rhetorical texts, and they propose revisions of the history of rhetoric by adding woman. Within this historical feminism, Patricia Bizzell's most radical suggestion is "to look in places not previously studied for work by women that would not have traditionally been considered as rhetoric, and to frame arguments redefining the whole notion of rhetoric in order to include this new work by women" ("Opportunities for Feminist Research," 51). This "opportunity for feminist research" might stretch beyond the liberal enterprises of recuperating women figures to add to rhetoric's historical list and practicing resisting reading of the predominately male-authored rhetoric classics. However, Miriam Brody's *Manly Writing*, Patricia Bizzell's "Praising Folly," and most of Susan Jarratt's feminist appropriation of the sophistic rhetoric stretch this categorical territory into postmodernism.

Cultural feminist theory has influenced composition studies most obviously with its characterization of woman and the feminine. Much of the feminist composition studies of the 1980s has argued that the side of the feminine should be the basis for building pedagogy because the values that women embody are superior to the manly practices of the patriarchy. These compositionists have tied the feminine to specific classroom practices that seem to grow out of women's innate and/or culturally assigned characteristics. In this way, some composition studies work has imported the binary oppositions that are the hallmark of cultural feminism.

Both Anglo-American and cultural feminist theories have had a major influence on feminist composition studies. These two theories share an ideology based on individualism, subordinating language and culture to the higher power of the "self," who is largely free to choose and direct her actions and to access her "authenticity" through her personal experience and her unique self-expression. These conceptions contrast to the next three categories of feminism, all of which share a tendency to regard language and culture as inextricable and as powerful determiners of identity and agency.

French feminist theory offers compositionists a radical stylistic alternative to academic discourse, as Lynn Worsham's "Writing against Writing: The Predicament of *Ecriture Feminine* in Composition Theories" points out. Also, compositionists such as Lillian Bridwell-Bowles make cases for experimental writing as a means to bring diversity into discourse practice. But French feminisms have not had as much influence on composition studies as postcolonial and postmodern theories have.

Postcolonial feminist theory, especially as practiced by bell hooks, and postmodern feminist theory emphasize critical pedagogy and the centrality of language as a site of struggle. Studies like Karlyn Kohrs Campbell's "Style and

Content in the Rhetoric of Early Afro-American Feminists'' work toward the ends of these feminist theories. She describes the rhetorical markers associated with feminine rhetoric: ''Consistent with their allegedly poetic and emotional natures, women tend to adopt associative, dramatic, and narrative modes of development, as opposed to deductive forms of organization. The tone tends to be personal and somewhat tentative rather than objective or authoritative'' (440). But Campbell's project is not to reinscribe these feminine traits appearing in the rhetoric of Afro-American feminists but instead to point out that these markers do not appear. This type of rhetorical analysis calls the essential characteristics assigned to women into question and furthers the postcolonial critique of a universalized figure.

Along with this kind of rhetorical analysis, composition studies feminists have found scholarly direction in postcolonial and postmodern critiques of the monolithic ethos of the academic: Linda Nicholson, in the introduction to *Feminism/ Postmodernism*, describes it as ''that which replicates 'a God's eye view' as opposed to that which expressed the perspectives of particular persons or groups.'' This is a scholarly ethos ''transcending the perspective of any one human being or group'' (4). Judith Butler characterizes the perspective that delimits academic rhetoric's ethos as a masculine, white, neutral gaze, ''which passes its own perspective off as the omniscient, one which presumes upon and enacts its own perspective as if it were no perspective at all'' (136). The ethos and topos of the racialized female body can interrupt, disrupt, and redirect this conventional perspective (which has dominated scholarship), as postcolonial and postmodern feminist theories have demonstrated.

Currently, anthologies and journals committed to thinking in composition studies have started to grapple seriously with sophisticated feminist theory. Suzanne Clark's review article, ''Women, Rhetoric, Teaching,'' concludes: ''The new visibility of feminist writing in rhetoric and composition will finally add gender as an important subject in the fund of disciplinary knowledge. The discussion about what that means has only just begun'' (122). Likewise, in ''Editor's Reflections: Vision and Interpretation,'' Louise Phelps and Janet Emig locate the rapid breakthrough of feminism into the field of composition studies with Elizabeth Flynn's publication of ''Composing as a Woman'' in 1988, a good historical point of reference (407).

Probably the most important impact that feminist theories have had on composition studies is reflected in the conflict around *essentialism*. Composition studies is starting to echo postcolonial and postmodern feminist theorists as they debate this dominant issue. Devoney Looser's ''Composing as an 'Essentialist'? New Directions for Feminist Composition Theories'' analyzes the various ''camps'' in composition studies. Her article is a take off on and critique of Elizabeth Flynn's ''Composing as a Woman.'' Looser defines the easy biologist essentialism and the trickier '' 'essentialist' tradition of descriptive gender categories'' (59) and then exemplifies these common categories, for instance, ''women as non-linear thinkers, women as more relationally oriented than men because of their mother's effect on their lives, women as having an ethic of care'' (56). In the last section of her essay, Looser asks, ''In order for feminist composition theories to gain currency or authority within or outside of the discipline, must we posit a homogeneous 'woman's way' or even a 'feminist's way' of anything—whether it be writing or teaching?'' Her answer is ''a resounding 'no' '' (65). She cites Denise Riley and Diana Fuss as antidote theorists whose ideas, she argues, can alleviate the essentialist tendencies in composition studies that she outlines in her essay. In the same vein, Anuradha Dingwaney and Lawrence Needham offer a persuasive critique of Cynthia Caywood and Gillian Overing's influential 1987 collection, *Teaching Writing: Pedagogy, Gender, and Equity*. ''As a self-conscious political strategy, essentializing women and their attitudes is to some extent necessary to create the identification and solidarity necessary for social action. As an unexamined belief . . . , essentializing women and their qualities poses difficulties for feminist theory and the feminist writing class'' (12).

Many feminist scholars in composition studies have traced and retraced the conventional feminine figure of cultural feminism—repeating her particular ''Women's Ways of Knowing,'' teaching out of those repetitions, and proclaiming those very iterations as the basis of feminist practice. For instance, in her conclusion to the 1995 collection, *Feminine Principles and Women's Experience in American Composition and Rhetoric*, edited with Janet Emig, Louise Phelps confesses in her first sentence, ''Our title for this volume has surprised and disconcerted many people, including some of our contributors'' (407). The reason for this titular agitation lies in the theoretical conflicts between the feminisms that foreground particular characteristics as essentially bound to women and those that insist on the social construction of gendered subjects. Phelps's ''feminine principles'' are reminiscent of cultural feminism's characterizations and valuation of women.

Likewise, Olivia Frey's ''Beyond Literary Darwinism: Women's Voices and Critical Discourse'' characterizes women's voices as ''personal, evocative, sensual,'' and, above all, nonadversarial, although she also claims that these voices are ''not easily categorized'' and points to exemplary writers like Gloria Anzaldúa, who are ''breaking through the boundaries of literary critical discourse that may not fit the values, the perceptual frameworks, and the ways of writing of many women in English departments across the country'' (507–8). On one hand, Frey's theory of language depends on the binary opposition between men and women and reinscribes the essential qualities of woman. But at the same time she invokes the uncategorizable—as the French and postcolonial feminists have done. Frey exemplifies many feminist composition scholars who are torn between theoretical positions and still in the process of working out their places in the geography of theory.

Unlike the compositionists, who have adopted an essentialized version of women as peaceful and, therefore, of feminist pedagogy and discursive practice as peaceful, bell hooks and Eichhorn and colleagues see conflict as productive. In *Talking Back*, hooks asserts that "Feminist education—the feminist class-room—is and should be a place where there is a sense of struggle, where there is visible acknowledgment of the union of theory and practice" (51). In "A Symposium on Feminist Experiences in the Composition Classroom," Eichhorn et al. produce a series of readings emphasizing difference and authority and capable of questioning "those pedagogical models which privilege only an at-mosphere of safety or a completely maternal climate" (299). Defined by strug-gle, social negotiation, and care to position subjects locally and specifically, this kind of "[f]eminist pedagogy is a flexible practice that . . . legitimizes struggle as positive and productive; it provides the arena to analyze contradiction, iden-tification, and resistance" (321). Likewise, Susan Jarratt, in *Contending with Words: Composition and Rhetoric in a Postmodern Age*, discusses "Feminism and Composition: The Case for Conflict": She affirms that although "early mappings of feminist pedagogy deserve praise," our goal should be "a more carefully theorized understanding of the multiple forms of power reproduced in the classroom" (113).

Along with the crucial importance of composition studies adopting a critical sense of the difference between essentialist and antiessentialist feminist theories and their views on language and identity, feminist theory has had an important impact on how feminists read the maxim "the personal is political." Jane Tomp-kins, in "Me and My Shadow," proclaims, "The criticism I would like to write would always take off from personal experience, would always be in some way a chronicle of my hours and days, would speak in a voice which can talk about anything, would reach out to a reader *like me* and touch me where I want to be touched" (173; emphasis added). But postcolonial feminist theory would prob-lematize this stance, reminding scholars that not everybody wants to be touched and that those who do want to be touched still do not necessarily want to be like Jane Tompkins! For touching may have the feel of erasure for women outside of the white middle to upper class sisterhood, which has historically represented feminism. Jacqueline Jones Royster's "When the First Voice You Hear Is Not Your Own" describes "cross-cultural misconduct. These types of close encounters that disregard dialectical views are a type of free touching of the powerless by the power-full" (32). Royster warns white academics of their inappropriate and harmful touching of "Others," recommending respect for cul-tural boundaries in such a way as to prevent "Others" from feeling themselves "subject matter but not subjects" (32). Finally, Royster calls for theoretical care as diverse scholars coexist in "areas of engagement that in all likelihood will remain contentious" (33).

Royster's comments on who can speak for whom and what speakers can do to avoid "cross-cultural misconduct" resonate with Gesa Kirsch and Joy Rit-chie's central questions in "Beyond the Personal: Theorizing a Politics of Lo-cation in Composition Research":

This new emphasis on the personal, on validating experience as a source of knowledge, raises a number of recurring questions. . . . How do we both affirm the importance of "location," and yet understand the limitations of our ability to locate ourselves and others? How do issues of power, gender, race and class shape a politics of location? (7)

As feminist composition studies has critically incorporated feminist theory from other diverse disciplines, conflicts have heated up. In response to this theoretical dissension, Janice Lauer argues that in the short history of the discipline, its strength has rested in the very politics marked as feminine, including cooperation and caring. She defends this short list of conventional descriptors of the feminine as the means by which the discipline has evolved. Furthermore, she contends that composition studies is already troubled because of its youth as a discipline and its concomitant struggles to achieve a theoretical coherence and pedagogical solidarity that would lend it authority and improve its bleak institutional economy. Within Lauer's argument lies the "essential" question for composition studies as it receives feminist theories: how can the discipline advance as an identifiable and increasingly powerful institutional entity while continuing to partake of the rich, influential, and contentious thought and debate resident in current feminisms?

BIBLIOGRAPHY

Primary Texts

Butler, Judith. *Bodies That Matter*. New York: Routledge, 1993.
Fuss, Diana. *Essentially Speaking*. New York: Routledge, 1989.
hooks, bell. *Talking Back*. Boston: South End P, 1989.
———. *Teaching to Transgress*. New York: Routledge, 1994.
Moi, Toril. *Sexual/Textual Politics*. New York: Routledge, 1985.
Nicholson, Linda, ed. *Feminism/Postmodernism*. New York: Routledge, 1990.
Riley, Denise. *Am I That Name? Feminism and the Category of "Women" in History*. Minneapolis: U of Minnesota P, 1988.
Spivak, Gayatri. *In Other Worlds*. London: Methuen, 1987.

Major Scholarship in Composition

Bizzell, Patricia. "Opportunities for Feminist Research in the History of Rhetoric." *Rhetoric Review* 2 (1992): 50–58.
———. "Praising Folly." In *Feminine Principles and Women's Experience in American Composition and Rhetoric*. Ed. Louise Phelps and Janet Emig. Pittsburgh, PA: U of Pittsburgh P, 1995, 27–42.
Bridwell-Bowles, Lillian. "Discourse and Diversity: Experimental Writing within the Academy." *College Composition and Communication* 43.3 (1992): 349–68.
Brody, Miriam. *Manly Writing: Gender, Rhetoric, and the Rise of Composition*. Carbondale: Southern Illinois UP, 1993.
Bullock, Richard, and John Trimbur, eds. *The Politics of Writing Instruction: Postsecondary*. Portsmouth, NH: Boynton/Cook, 1991.
Campbell, Karlyn Kohrs. "Style and Content in the Rhetoric of Early Afro-American Feminists." *Quarterly Journal of Speech* 72 (1986): 434–45.

Caywood, Cynthia, and Gillian Overing, eds. *Teaching Writing: Pedagogy, Gender, and Equity*. Albany: State U of New York P, 1987.

Clark, Suzanne. "Women, Rhetoric, Teaching." *College Composition and Communication* 46.1 (1995): 108–22.

Clifford, John, and John Schilb, eds. *Writing Theory and Critical Theory*. New York: MLA, 1994.

Dingwaney, Anuradha, and Lawrence Needham, "Feminist Theory and Practice in the Writing Classroom: A Critique and A Prospectus." In *Constructing Rhetorical Education*. Ed. Marie Secor and Davida Charney. Carbondale: Southern Illinois UP, 1992, 6–25.

Eichhorn, Jill, et. al. "A Symposium on Feminist Experiences in the Composition Classroom." *College Composition and Communication* 43 (1992): 297–321.

Flynn, Elizabeth. "Composing as a Woman." *College Composition and Communication* 39 (1988): 423–35.

———. "Composition Studies from a Feminist Perspective." In *The Politics of Writing Instruction*. Ed. Richard Bullock and John Trimbur. Portsmouth, NH: Boynton/Cook, 1991, 137–54.

Frey, Olivia. "Beyond Literary Darwinism: Women's Voices and Critical Discourse." *College English* 52.5 (1990): 507–26.

———. "Equity and Peace in the New Writing Class." In *Teaching Writing: Pedagogy, Gender, and Equity*. Ed. Cynthia Caywood and Gillian Overing. Albany: State U of New York P, 1987, 93–105.

Glenn, Cheryl. "Sex, Lies, and Manuscript: Refiguring Aspasia in the History of Rhetoric." *College Composition and Communication* 45 (1994): 180–99.

———. "Remapping Rhetorical Territory." *Rhetoric Review* 13 (1995): 287–303.

Harkin, Patricia, and John Schilb, eds. *Contending with Words: Composition and Rhetoric in a Postmodern Age*. New York: MLA, 1991.

Holbrook, Sue Ellen. "Women's Work: The Feminizing of Composition." *Rhetoric Review* 9 (1991): 201–29.

Jarratt, Susan. "Feminism and Composition: The Case for Conflict." In *Contending with Words*. Ed. Patricia Harkin and John Schilb. New York: MLA, 1991, 105–23.

———. *Rereading the Sophists*. Carbondale: Southern Illinois UP, 1991.

Kirsch, Gesa, and Joy Ritchie. "Beyond the Personal: Theorizing a Politics of Location in Composition Research." *College Composition and Communication* 46 (1995): 7–29.

Lauer, Janice. "The Feminization of Rhetoric and Composition Studies?" *Rhetoric Review* 13 (1995): 276–86.

Looser, Devoney. "Composing as an 'Essentialist'? New Directions for Feminist Composition Theories." *Rhetoric Review* 12 (1993): 54–69.

Olson, Gary, and Elizabeth Hirsh, eds. *Woman Writing Culture*. Albany: State U of New York P, 1996.

Phelps, Louise, and Janet Emig, eds. *Feminine Principles and Women's Experience in American Composition and Rhetoric*. Pittsburgh, PA: U of Pittsburgh P, 1995.

Royster, Jacqueline Jones. "When the First Voice You Hear Is Not Your Own." *College Composition and Communication* 47 (1996): 29–40.

Secor, Marie, and Davida Charney, eds. *Constructing Rhetorical Education*. Carbondale: Southern Illinois UP, 1992.

Tompkins, Jane. "Me and My Shadow." *New Literary History* 19 (1987): 169–78.

Walker, Alice. *In Search of Our Mothers' Gardens: Womanist Prose.* New York: Harcourt Brace, 1983.
Worsham, Lynn. "Writing against Writing: The Predicament of *Ecriture Feminine* in Composition Theories." In *Contending with Words.* Ed. Patricia Harkin and John Schilb. New York: MLA, 1991, 82–104.

VICTORIA BOYNTON

FREIREAN THEORY

Summary

From its earliest manifestations in the 1950s and 1960s—when Paulo Freire first began writing about his work with adult literacy programs in Brazil—Freirean theory has focused on and attempted to explain the intersection and interrelatedness of critical literacy, liberatory pedagogy, and cultural politics. Freire would resist the label of "Freirean theory" as a way to describe the principles and practices he has developed over the years. Consistently, he has insisted that he is "never interested just in theory, just in *praxis*, but in the relationships between them" (Olson, 161). "Freirean theory," then, is best understood as a dynamic process of reflecting and acting, and not as a static set of explanatory principles.

North American educators were first introduced to Freirean theory through *Pedagogy of the Oppressed*, which has become Freire's most widely known book. In the decades since the 1970 publication of the first English edition of this book, Freire has written a succession of books and articles that supplement and complement the tenets he begins to develop there. Central to Freire's theory is the recognition that "both humanization and dehumanization are possibilities" for individuals as "uncompleted" beings who are "conscious of [their] incompletion" (*Pedagogy* 27). Freire believes that humanity's "vocation" is to engage in the ongoing process of "humanization," characterized by men and women "yearning . . . for freedom and justice, and by their struggle to recover their lost humanity" (*Pedagogy* 28). In its fullest manifestations, Freirean theory has as one of its objectives the transformation of the world to secure social justice for all. Education and literacy are vital and necessary components in this transformative project.

For Freire, the goal of education is to enable individuals to become critically literate, "to develop the critical consciousness which would result from their intervention in the world as transformers of that world" (*Pedagogy* 60). Individuals develop critical consciousness as they learn "to perceive social, political, and economic contradictions, and to take action against the oppressive elements of reality" (*Pedagogy* 19). Freire recognizes that "[r]eading [or writing] does not consist merely of decoding [or encoding] the written word or language; rather, it is preceded by and intertwined with knowledge of the world. Language and reality are dynamically interconnected" (Freire and Macedo, 29). In a socially constructed world, individuals can be cast into roles as passive objects or they can become active agents. Freire sees critical literacy "as a set of cultural practices that promotes democratic and emancipatory change" instead of reproducing existing oppressive social and political formations (Freire and Macedo, 141).

In *Pedagogy of the Oppressed* (and in subsequent works) Freire defines education "as the practice of freedom" (60). He proposes a dialogical, liberatory pedagogy. Opposed to "banking education" which "anesthetizes and inhibits creative power, problem-posing education involves a constant unveiling of reality. The former attempts to maintain the *submersion* of consciousness; the latter strives for the *emergence* of consciousness and *critical intervention* in reality" (68). Just as educators should be always critically self-reflective, they should help students "develop their power to perceive critically *the way they exist* in the world *with which* and *in which* they find themselves." In this way, "they come to see the world not as a static reality, but as a reality in process, in transformation" (70–71). When students and teachers see the world in this way, through critical reflection, they are able to become active agents for change.

Freire understands change as a process that is always situated in specific social, cultural, and historical contexts. He recognizes that "the process of change starts exactly in the place that we would like to change," and that each time, the "place" is different. His is not a project to impose some monolithic version of constructed reality. Instead, he invites students and teachers "to strive for more and higher levels of freedom" (Olson, 155).

Reception and Significance in Composition Studies

Freirean theory in its strongest versions has not been widely embraced by compositionists. Because Freirean theory insists on making visible the political dimensions of educational practices, teachers who attempt to enact it are often characterized as ideologues, little different from the oppressors they claim to be resisting (especially in North American settings, where Freire's critique of capitalism can evoke opposition from students and teachers). Ira Shor's work represents the most visible and consistent attempt to employ Freirean theory in postsecondary composition courses. Writing teachers such as Shor and James Berlin advocate cultural studies approaches for their writing classes, often interrogating the ways in which race, class, and gender intersect to construct oppressive subjectivities and identities.

In cases where its political component is less visible, Freirean theory has been especially attractive to writing teachers because of its emphasis on pedagogy and literacy and because of its focus on the dialectical interrelations between theory and practice. Because Freirean theory comprises many of the principles and practices that are common to social-epistemic and constructivist rhetorics and to cultural studies approaches to teaching composition, it shares with these approaches a prominent position as a legitimate approach to teaching writing. In other words, because Freirean theory embodies principles and practices that are learner-centered, reflective, and constructivist, because it advocates active, independent learning, and because it sees literacy as social practice and cognitive process, Freirean theory can be said to have a strong presence in composition studies. For writing teachers and composition scholars who have turned (or returned) their attention to the social and cultural dimensions of literacy, Freirean theory is an integral part of their professional identity kit.

In addition to Ira Shor, the more active and prominent North American educators and scholars who could be seen as "Freireistas" (Victor Villanueva's label) include James Berlin, Patricia Bizzell, Victor Villanueva, bell hooks, Henry Giroux, Peter McLaren, and Stanley Aronowitz. Though not all are working only in composition studies, each of these scholars can be identified as a "transformative intellectual" who is "concerned with improving economic and social conditions in the larger society" (Berlin, *Rhetorics* 112–13).

As compositionists continue to define the role of composition studies in the larger institutional and social networks of educational practices, Freirean theory could become increasingly more important. Its attention to the relationships among pedagogy, literacy, and politics will help scholars and teachers continually situate (and resituate) their work more meaningfully in larger social and cultural contexts. Its insistence on the dynamic dialectical interrelationship of reflection and action will insure that teachers and scholars continue to define (and redefine) their roles in an educational process that is the practice of freedom.

BIBLIOGRAPHY

Primary Texts

Freire, Paulo. *Cultural Action for Freedom*. Cambridge, MA: *Harvard Educational Review* and Center for the Study of Development and Social Change, 1970.
———. *Education for Critical Consciousness*. New York: Continuum, 1996. (First English edition, 1973.)
———. *Letters to Christina: Reflections on My Life and Work*. New York: Routledge, 1996.
———. *Pedagogy in Process: The Letters to Guinea-Bissau*. New York: Seabury P, 1978.
———. *Pedagogy of Hope: Reliving Pedagogy of the Oppressed*. New York: Continuum, 1996.
———. *Pedagogy of the Oppressed*. New York: Continuum, 1990. (First English edition, 1970.)
———. *The Politics of Education: Culture, Power, and Liberation*. New York: Bergin and Garvey, 1985.
Freire, Paulo, and Antonio Faundez. *Learning to Question: A Pedagogy of Liberation*. New York: Continuum, 1989.
Freire, Paulo, and Donaldo Macedo. *Literacy: Reading the Word and the World*. New York: Bergin and Garvey, 1987.
Freire, Paulo, and Ira Shor. *A Pedagogy for Liberation: Dialogues on Transforming Education*. New York: Bergin and Garvey, 1987.

Major Scholarship in Composition

Aronowitz, Stanley, and Henry Giroux. *Postmodern Education: Politics, Culture, Social Criticism*. Minneapolis: U of Minnesota P, 1991.

Berlin, James A. "Freirean Pedagogy in the U.S.: A Response." In *(Inter)views: Cross-Disciplinary Perspectives on Rhetoric and Literacy*. Ed. Gary Olson and Irene Gale. Carbondale: Southern Illinois UP, 1991, 169–76.

———. *Rhetorics, Poetics, and Cultures*. Urbana, IL: NCTE, 1996.

Bizzell, Patricia. "Academic Discourse and Critical Consciousness: An Application of Paulo Freire." In *Academic Discourse and Critical Consciousness*. Pittsburgh, PA: U of Pittsburgh P, 1992, 129–52.

———. "Marxist Ideas in Composition Studies." In *Contending with Words: Composition and Rhetoric in a Postmodern Age*. Ed. Patricia Harkin and John Schilb. New York: MLA, 1991, 52–68.

Giroux, Henry. *Theory and Resistance in Education: A Pedagogy for the Opposition*. South Hadley, MA: Bergin and Garvey, 1983.

hooks, bell. "Paulo Freire." In *Teaching to Transgress: Education as the Practice of Freedom*. New York: Routledge, 1994, 45–58.

Knoblauch, C. H., and Lil Brannon. *Critical Teaching and the Idea of Literacy*. Portsmouth, NH: Boynton/Cook, 1993.

McLaren, Peter. *Life in Schools: An Introduction to Critical Pedagogy in the Foundations of Education*. New York: Longman, 1989.

Olson, Gary A. "History, Praxis, and Change: Paulo Freire and the Politics of Literacy." In *(Inter)views: Cross-Disciplinary Perspectives on Rhetoric and Literacy*. Ed. Gary Olson and Irene Gale. Carbondale: Southern Illinois UP, 1991, 155–68.

Shor, Ira. *Critical Teaching and Everyday Life*. Boston: South End P, 1980.

———. *Empowering Education: Critical Teaching for Social Change*. Chicago: U of Chicago P, 1992.

———, ed. *Freire for the Classroom: A Sourcebook for Liberatory Teaching*. Portsmouth, NH: Boynton/Cook, 1987.

Villanueva, Victor, Jr. *Bootstraps: From an American Academic of Color*. Urbana, IL: NCTE, 1993.

———. "Considerations for American Freireistas." In *The Politics of Writing Instruction: Postsecondary*. Ed. Richard Bullock and John Trimbur. Portsmouth, NH: Boynton/Cook, 1991, 247–62.

GLENN BLALOCK

G

GENERATIVE RHETORIC

Summary

Logically, the term ''generative rhetoric'' could encompass any structures or processes that help writers or speakers *generate* what they want to say. Among North American composition specialists, however, the term ''generative rhetoric'' is associated primarily with the work of Francis Christensen.

The crux of Christensen's generative rhetoric is the use of form—especially syntax—to generate content (i.e., not just as *dispositio*, but also as a technique for *inventio*). Various researchers, including Mina Shaughnessy, have pointed out that one distinguishing feature of sophisticated writers is their ability to stick with and develop a topic, substantiating generalizations and abstractions. Christensen asserted that students can develop this ability by working with certain sentence and paragraph structures that encourage them to generate specifics.

Christensen's approach is often juxtaposed with sentence combining because both are designed to help students write more sophisticated sentences. While sentence combining teaches students how to combine preexisting sentences (first in exercises, later in their own drafts), Christensen's generative rhetoric encourages students to expand existing sentences by generating new particulars. ''We need,'' Christensen wrote, ''a rhetoric of the sentence that will do more than combine the ideas of primer sentences. We need one that will generate ideas'' (*Notes* 26). To this end, Christensen emphasized an especially readable type of sentence he dubbed ''cumulative.''

Christensen's approach begins with the observation that where his students might write, ''We caught two bass,'' E. B. White wrote,

We caught two bass, hauling them in briskly as though they were mackerel, pulling them over the side of the boat in a businesslike manner without any landing net, and stunning them with a blow on the back of the head.

The quality of sentences like White's, Christensen observed, is located particularly in the free modifiers that specify and concretize, modifiers that are optional (in that the sentence is grammatically and conceptually complete without them). In Christensen's terminology, what E. B. White's modifiers have added to this sentence is called *texture*.

Christensen reveals the judgment that underlies his pedagogical emphasis when he asserts that "the writing of most students is thin—even threadbare"; his course teaches "strategies for adding depth to your writing, . . . working toward greater density and variety in texture as well as toward exactness and concreteness" (Christensen and Munson, *Christensen Rhetoric Program*, "Teaching Script," 20). Christensen's rhetoric helps student writers see and appreciate opportunities to create texture by adding modifiers—especially free or "loose" modifiers—to their draft sentences. By grammatical analogy, Christensen goes on to show students how to add specifying sentences to their draft paragraphs. Most paragraphs, he asserts, "are like the sentences I called 'cumulative.' " (*Notes* 78).

Christensen was not impressed by sentences that achieve complexity by sacrificing readability. He carefully distinguished cumulative sentences, which "march along effortlessly," from "non-cumulative" (periodic) sentences—like this one, written by Joseph Wood Krutch,

Those who are appalled by the prospect of living in a universe which, for the first time in several centuries, has ceased to seem comprehensible may be somewhat reassured by the reminder that it is only the novelty of the modern instances which is disturbing and that they have all along been living with other irresolvable paradoxes which did not trouble them simply because they had been for so long accepted.

Such sentences do not flow: they are "difficult to read and understand." The cumulative sentence, Christensen writes, "is far easier to read, although it might be as long as, over even longer than, the sentence that is not cumulative" (*Christensen Rhetoric Program*, "Teaching Script" 9).

Christensen's rhetoric counterbalances the standard modern bromide that "tightening" is the crucial operation for creating good sentences and paragraphs. Citing John Erskine—

When you write, you make a point, not by subtracting as though you sharpened a pencil, but by adding. . . . The noun, the verb, and the main clause serve merely as a base on which the meaning will rise. *The modifier is the essential part of any sentence.*

In so doing, Christensen directs writers' attention to what modifiers can add.

Christensen uses Eudora Welty's sentence—

Stretching away, the cotton fields, slowly emptying, were becoming the color of the sky, a deepening blue so intense that it was like darkness itself.

—to illustrate that free modifiers can be slotted into the beginning or middle as well as the end of a sentence. The initial premodifier, "stretching away," directs readers' minds forward toward "the cotton fields." The other two free modifiers direct attention back (to "the cotton fields" and "the color of the sky," respectively).

The most "natural" place to add a "loose" or free modifier, however, is in a postmodifier slot, located after the noun or verb it modifies. Physically, the sentence keeps moving across the page, but cognitively/rhetorically, the sentence pauses. As the modifier attaches to a preceding base, the "movement" or "direction of modification" is back toward that noun or verb "head." The additions placed after it move backward, as in this sentence, to modify the statement of the base clause or, more often, to explain it or add examples or details to it, so that the sentence has a flowing and ebbing movement, advancing to a new position and then pausing to consolidate it. From the structural principles of addition and direction of modification, Christensen turns to considerations of meaning with his third principle, levels of generality.

The usual function of free modifiers, Christensen asserts, is to specify (and/or concretize) what they modify.

How grateful they were for the coffee, she looking up at him, tremulous, her lips pecking at the cup, he blessing the coffee as it went down her. (John Updike)

The postmodifiers here break "they" into "she" and "he," and then concretize how each was grateful. Similarly, "her lips pecking at the cup" concretizes "tremulous." Such modifiers can also define and/or concretize an abstraction:

Oratory is the art of making pleasant sounds, which cause the header to say "Yes, Yes" in sympathy with the performer, without enquiring too closely what he means. (Sam Tucker)

For teaching purposes, Christensen diagrams levels of generality like this:

1 Joad's lips stretched tight over his long teeth a moment, and
1 he licked his lips,
    2 like a dog,
        3 two licks
            4 one in each direction from the middle.

Christensen demonstrates how these three principles produce texture (without sacrificing flow) by presenting literary passages with most modifiers deleted.

Reception and Significance in Composition Studies

Christensen's generative rhetoric had two significant impacts. Firstly, it was juxtaposed with sentence combining as a way to help students write more sophisticated syntax, to achieve what was called syntactic "fluency" or "maturity." Secondly, it was used to teach—and perhaps more significantly—to analyze discursive patterns (i.e., as the basis for a "grammar of passages").

As Eden and Michell emphasize, the central virtue of Christensen's rhetoric is that it presents writing "as a process of adding, of elaborating on what you have already said." This, they assert, makes it especially useful "as a diagnostic tool, a guide for writers revising," for it shows writers how to find in what has already been drafted "opportunities for writing more" (422).

David Karrfalt, Richard Larson, Michael Grady, Frank D'Angelo, and others have extended Christensen's analogy further, demonstrating how Christensen's rhetorical principles can be applied beyond the sentence to paragraphs, longer passages, and whole essays.

Christensen had little use for sentence combining—precisely because it is not very generative. For him, the key distinction is that sentence combining helps students write in one sentence what they or someone else has already written in several simpler sentences, whereas generative rhetoric (also known, in this context, as sentence construction) helps students generate and add new content to an existing sentence. After considerable debate (and Christensen's death), however, several textbook authors, notably Strong, Stull, and Memering and O'Hare, offered students both sentence combining and generative sentence construction as complementary techniques.

Various studies have evaluated the effectiveness of Christensen's generative rhetoric; typically, they use controlled pretest/posttest studies to demonstrate that instruction in generative sentence construction can lead students to write longer T-units (measures of syntactic complexity) with more free modifiers (e.g., Brooks, Davis, Faigley, Walshe). But generative sentence construction, like sentence-combining, lost favor after studies indicating that such gains have disappeared if the student subjects are retested a year or more after instruction.

Various researchers, including Ellen Nold and, Sarah Freedman, Brent Davis, Catharine Keech, Rebekah Caplan, Betty Cain, and myself have used the structural principles of Christensen's generative rhetoric for discourse analysis of passages. Generally, they create a kind of "grammar of passages" that analyzes passages by looking at the logical/semantic relationships, including patterns of modification, among coordinate, subordinate, and superordinate sentences.

Such analysis can be useful to researchers, teachers, and writers. By analyzing the structure of paragraphs and longer passages, it can help identify the characteristics of rhetorical communities, delineating the contrasting rhetoric of languages, discourses, and disciplines. My work, *Toward a Grammar of Passages*, for instance, reports studies by colleagues who have identified a traditional rhetorical pattern in Chinese, a recurring spiraling structure that, when transferred into English discourse, creates a problem for Chinese ESL students because it is not recognizable in current English rhetoric.

Christensen's rhetoric clearly favors particular stylistic values. Sabrina Thorne Johnson has criticized its literary bias. In fact, the bias is even more specific, favoring a readable modernist style with lots of concrete particulars—precisely the sort of stylistic bias Richard Ohmann has criticized for tending to exclude theorizing abstractions. Certainly, Christensen takes his examples sentences from modern literary narratives, and both *A New Rhetoric* and his work with Munson, *The Christensen Rhetoric Program* focus on narrative writing. Free modifiers and cumulative sentences are assuredly useful and commonly used in other sorts of prose, but not so intensively and often for purposes somewhat different from those Christensen emphasizes. My students find Christensen's lesson particularly useful when they are writing personal essays.

BIBLIOGRAPHY

Primary Texts

Christensen, Francis, and Bonnijean Christensen. *A New Rhetoric*. New York: Harper, 1976.

———. *Notes toward a New Rhetoric: 9 Essays for Teachers*, 2nd ed. New York: Harper, 1978.

Christensen, Francis, and Marilynn M. Munson. *The Christensen Rhetoric Program*. New York: Harper, 1968.

Major Scholarship in Composition

Broadhead, Glenn J., and James Berlin. "Twelve Steps to Using Generative Sentences and Sentence-Combining in the Composition Classroom." *College Composition and Communication* 32 (1981): 295–307.

Cain, Betty. *Beyond Outlining: New Approaches to Rhetorical Form*. Lanham, MD: UP of America, 1992.

Caplan, Rebekah, and Catharine Keech. *Showing-Writing: A Training Program to Help Students Be Specific*. Bay Area Writing Project Collaborative Research Study no. 2, Berkeley, CA: Bay Area Writing Project, 1980.

Coe, Richard M. *Toward a Grammar of Passages*. Carbondale: Southern Illinois UP, 1988.

D'Angelo, Frank. *A Conceptual Theory of Rhetoric*. Cambridge, MA: Winthrop, 1975.

———. "A Generative Rhetoric of the Essay." *College Composition and Communication* 25:5 (1974): 388–96.

Davis, Wesley K. "The Effects of Christensen's Generative Rhetoric of a Sentence on the Right-Branched Free Modifiers of College Freshman Writing." 1989 ERIC no. 313–706. 30 pp.

Eden, Rick, and Ruth Mitchell. "Paragraphing for the Reader." *College Composition and Communication* 27 (1986): 416–30.

Eschliman, Herbert, R. "Francis Christensen in Yoknapatawpha County." *Univ-Review* 37 (1971): 232–39.

Faigley, Lester. "Generative Rhetoric as a Way of Increasing Syntactic Fluency." *College Composition and Communication* 30 (1979): 176–81.

————. "The Influence of Generative Rhetoric on the Syntactic Maturity and Writing Effectiveness of College Freshmen." *Research in the Teaching of English* 13 (1979): 197–206.

Grady, Michael. "A Conceptual Rhetoric of the Composition." *College Composition and Communication* 22 (1971): 348–54.

————. "On Teaching Christensen Rhetoric." *English Journal* 61 (1972): 859–73, 877.

Johnson, Sabrina Thorne. "Some Tentative Strictures on Generative Rhetoric." *College English* 31 (1969): 155–65. Compare responses by Bonnijean McGuire Christensen and A.M. Tibbetts in *College English* 31 (1970).

Karrfalt, David H. "Generation of Paragraphs and Larger Units." *College Composition and Communication* 17 (1966): 82–87.

Keech, Catharine. "Apparent Regression in Student Writing Performance as a Function of Unrecognized Changes in Task Complexity." Ph.d. Diss., U of California, Berkeley, 1984.

Larson, Richard L. "Toward a Linear Rhetoric of the Essay." *College Composition and Communication* 22 (May 1971): 140–46.

Memering, Dean, and Frank O'Hare. *The Writer's Work*. Englewood Cliffs, NJ: Prentice-Hall, 1980.

Nold, Ellen W., and Brent E. Davis. "The Discourse Matrix." *College Composition and Communication* 31 (1980): 141–52.

Nold, Ellen W., and Sarah W. Freedman. "An Analysis of Readers' Responses to Essays." *Research in the Teaching of English* 11 (1977): 164–74.

Ohmann, Richard. "Use Definite, Specific, Concrete Language." *College English* 41 (1979): 390–97.

Shaughnessy, Mina. "Beyond the Sentence." In *Errors and Expectation*. New York: Oxford, 1977, 226–74.

Strong, William. *Sentence Combining: A Composing Book*. New York: Random House, 1973.

————. *Sentence Combining and Paragraph Building*. New York: Random House, 1981.

Stull, William L. *Combining and Creating: Sentence-Combining and Generative Rhetoric*. New York: Holt, 1983.

————. "Sentence Combining, Generative Rhetoric, and Concepts of Style." In *Sentence Combining: A Rhetorical Perspective*. Ed. Donald A. Daiker, Andrew Kerek, and Max Morenberg. Carbondale: Southern Illinois UP, 1985, 76–85.

Walshe, R.D. "Report on a Pilot Course on the Christensen Rhetoric Program." *College English* 32 (1971): 783–89.

Wolk, A. "The Relative Importance of the Final Free Modifier: A Quantitative Analysis." *Research in the Teaching of English* 4 (1970): 59–68.

RICHARD M. COE

GENRE THEORY: AUSTRALIAN AND NORTH AMERICAN APPROACHES

Summary

Until the late 1980s, the term *genre* was rarely used in relation to English composition. Although, like other rhetorical concepts, it was alive and well in speech communications (see Campbell and Jamieson), in English it seemed to be an arhetorical prestige term reserved largely for literature. During the 1980s, however, theorists on several continents, working independently in distinct traditions, seized on the notion of genre as central to understanding the social, functional, and pragmatic dimensions of language use. The beginnings of this movement in relation to nonliterary writing can be marked by Michael Halliday's *Language as Social Semiotic* (1978), Carolyn Miller's ''Genre as Social Action'' (1984), and the publication in English translation of Mikhail Bakhtin's *Speech Genres and Other Late Essays* (1984). A somewhat parallel development of the concept of genre also occurred in other disciplines (e.g., anthropology, linguistics, literary criticism).

The new theories of genre constitute a particularly powerful and promising approach to writing as social process. These theories are stimulating research that begins to specify how particular discourses are socially motivated, generated, and constrained. The theories and consequent research promise, moreover, defined answers to such postmodern questions as what it means to say that an individual (or small group of collaborating individuals) wrote a particular memo, article, or novel—and what it means to say that we not only write, but are written. They provide a basis for teaching/learning methods that could prepare students to handle the social constraints they will face in practical writing tasks as workers, citizens, consumers, and in other social roles. As the rebirth of rhetorical conceptions of writing led to an understanding of writing tasks as defined by rhetorical situations (classically stated as purpose, audience, and occasion), so the new genre theories direct our attention to the ways in which those purposes, audiences, and occasions recur—the ways in which writing tasks are neither totally unique nor unprecedented. That is, they direct our attention to precisely those aspects of writing from which Romantically individualistic concepts of writing deflected our attention.

The crux of the new genre theories is this: a genre is a socially standard strategy, embodied in a typical form of discourse, that has evolved for responding to a recurring type of rhetorical situation. Unlike traditional theories of genre, which focused primarily on discursive form, the new theories explain the discursive structures of a genre functionally, as standard responses of a recurring type of rhetorical situation. Although genres are still usually identified initially by structural/textual regularities (Bakhtin, 60–63), genre is now understood rather as the functional relationship between that structure and the situation. Thus, any complete description of a genre includes at least three aspects:

1. the standard form of the discourse,

2. the type of recurring situation that evokes it,

3. the functional relation, namely, (1) understood as a strategy for responding to (2).

What we may call the new rhetoric of genre inquires about the evolving, situated, motivated relationship among (1) language/style/form, (2) rhetorical situation, contexts of situation and culture, and (3) function/use/effect/ideology. It helps us understand discourse as sociocultural process, which we may both shape and be shaped by, and that directs and deflects attention, constitutes subject positions, opportunities and constraints, community, and hierarchy. For composition teachers and students, the new conception replaces the reductive formalism of traditional composition with a critical rhetoric of genre.

Writing is dialogic, not only in the sense that it responds (both to situation and to previous utterances), but also in the sense of being "addressed" (here Bakhtin and Burke share a defining word)—of anticipating readers and their responses. To make sense of a genre, we must understand it, not merely as a socially standard form, but as a socially standard rhetorical strategy for addressing a type of situation—for attempting to evoke a desired type of response. Although individual practitioners using the genre may have no conscious understanding of the form as strategy (and perhaps only tacit knowledge of the form itself), the genre has evolved (and continues to evolve) by a process of discursive selection; it exists because it works, in some sense or other, as a response to the situation. The individual journalist may or may not understand why a news report organized as an inverted pyramid satisfies her editor; the individual student probably does not understand why a five-paragraph essay leads his English teacher to respond with relatively good grades. If we want to explain a genre—or, as Bakhtin emphasizes (80), to free ourselves from the tyranny of genre—we should describe it as a functional rhetorical strategy.

The new work on genre epitomizes the significance of approaching reading and writing as social processes in which individuals participate (without necessarily being entirely conscious of how social the processes are). Like its antecedents, the new genre theory focuses primarily on *types* of texts and utterances, and only secondarily on what individualizes particular texts and utterances. Like the New Rhetoric, with which it shares intellectual roots, the new genre theory focuses primarily on symbolic action—what texts and utterances *do*—and only secondarily on what they *say*. Several of the most influential theorists (especially Halliday and, via Kenneth Burke, Miller) were specifically influenced by Bronislaw Malinowski's concept of discourse as "symbolic action" in "context of situation" and all the new genre theories approach writing as situated social action. That is to say, writing is understood, first and foremost, as an attempt to *do* something (by saying something), not as mere representation. Like any act, then, writing is situated and motivated (though there are obvious differences between the ways in which novels and memos are situated, motivated, and purposive).

Genres are both generative (heuristic) and constraining. They comprise "configurations of semantic resources that the member of the culture associates with a situation type (Halliday, 111); they are "structuring devices for realizing meaning in specific contexts" (Green in Reid, 86); they can "determine the roles taken up by the participants, and hence the kinds of texts they are required to construct" (Christie et al., 16). Although "genres are subject to free creative reformulation . . . , to use a genre freely and creatively is not the same as to create a genre from the beginning'' (Bakhtin, 80). Like other aspects of discourse community, genres are neither value-free nor neutral and often imply hierarchical social relationships (see, e.g., Gilbert and Green and Lee in Freedman and Medway). We should, therefore, ask critical, metarhetorical questions, such as

What sorts of communication does the genre encourage and, what sorts does it constrain against?

Who can—and who cannot—use this genre? Does it empower some people while silencing others?

Are its effects dysfunctional beyond their immediate context? (Cf. bureaucratese, which often serves bureaucrats well, and works within the bureaucracy but that also often oppresses those outside the bureaucracy.)

What values and beliefs are instantiated within this set of practices?

What are the political and ethical implications of the rhetorical situation constructed, persona embodied, audience invoked, and context of situation assumed by a particular genre?

From a ''cultural studies'' perspective, one could turn this analysis on its head, taking the genre, not as an object of study, but rather as a signifier about the community that uses it and asking what the genre signifies about the discourse community that uses it? (For other useful summaries, see Devitt, ''Generalizing''; Freedman, ''Show and Tell?''; and the introductions to Freedman and Medway, eds., *Learning and Teaching Genres* and *Genre and the New Rhetoric*.)

Reception and Significance in Composition Studies

As the theory itself would lead one to suspect, the new theories of genre, although based on similar premises, developed differently in different situational contexts. In Australia, for instance, genre-based approaches to teaching composition developed as an antithesis to a ''personal experience,'' expressionist approach, imported from England, for which ''creativity'' was the key term. Certain educators—most prominently Frances Christie, Jim Martin, and Joan Rothery, all of whom studied with Halliday[1]—believed this approach (like the expressionist ''freewriting'' approach in the United States) supported the existing social hierarchy and failed disadvantaged students. These educators argued that students whose parents are well educated members of the dominant culture tend to acquire tacit knowledge of the structures underlying culturally dominant discursive strategies. Thus, if these strategies and the linguistic structures needed to effect them are not taught, students who do not arrive at school with the requisite cultural knowledge and abilities are disadvantaged. Because the ability to use such strategies appropriately serves a ''gatekeeper'' function within the meritocracy, these educators urge teachers to teach the genres of power (including school genres) to disadvantaged children so that they will gain access to distributed power.

Because of their educational goals and because their approach was rooted in Halliday's systemic-functional linguistics (which locates meaning in language as a system and in text structures), these educators focused their research on textual structures and rather broadly defined genres (e.g., the scientific report). Christie et al. (1990–1992) identified the "generic structures" that appear to be involved in learning "the various school subjects" in terms that resemble traditional rhetoric's modes of development:

factual genres: procedure, description, report, explanation, and argument

narrative genres (a.k.a. recounts): personal experience; fantasy; moral tales; myths, spoofs, and serials; and thematic narratives

Although Martin, Christie, and Rothery insist that texts are produced in contexts of situation and culture (and although Martin, in "Grammaticalizing," has posited ideology as a level beyond genre), they assert that meaning is carried in the text structure and that individual language users construct reality through discursive structures. They use analytical tools and frames from systemic functional linguistics to identify the grammatical structures needed to produce genres of power, beginning with those used in "Show and Tell" (Christie, "The Morning News Genre"). They perceive genres as "staged, goal oriented social processes": "[as social processes] because members of a culture interact with each other to achieve them; as goal oriented because they have evolved to get things done; and as staged because it usually takes more than one step for participants to achieve their goals" (Martin et al., 59). They advocate an interventionist role for teachers, who should model the social purpose of the text type, jointly construct with students a model text (using appropriate grammatical structures), and consult with students during their independent construction of texts.

The Australian system-functional school of genre theory has, moreover, provoked useful insights from Australians who are not actually members of the school, such as Anne Freadman (see, e.g., "Anyone for Tennis?" in Reid), Thibault, Threadgold, Kress, Hasan, Luke, and Knapp, all of whom have challenged the model of genre and language articulated by Martin, Rothery, and Christie. Their critiques focus on a disjuncture between the claim that meaning is encapsulated in textual objects and genres are autonomous systems with a social constructionist functional model of discourse. Thibeault, for instance, argues that the instrumentalist view of genre presumes one-way causality in which genre is a means to an end, but in which the end is not ideologically built into the structure of the genre (i.e., presumes one can readily teach a genre of power without inculcating the ideological ends that shaped the genre). Knapp in 1995 perceived two broadly different interpretations of genre in Australia: the systemic-functional model and the genre as social process model. The latter is closer to the assumptions about language, discourse, rhetoric, and pedagogy of North American genre studies.

A different context of situation has taken North American genre studies along this latter path. Firstly, those developing and applying the theory have been predominantly postsecondary teachers and researchers in composition, rhetoric, and ESL, not educators concerned with school curricula and teacher education. Their work coincides with a more general tendency among North American composition specialists to understand writing as a social process that occurs within heterogeneous (and often hierarchical) discourse communities. Their teaching and research focuses, as one might expect, on academic writing, workplace writing, and English for Specific Purposes (ESP). In part because of their context of situation and in part because of the culture of postmodernism, they are much more concerned with discursive and writing process *differences* that students and graduates meet as they move from discipline to discipline, from college to workplace, and from workplace to workplace, than with finding the *common* structures of broad discourses. That is to say, they are more concerned with how students must discourse differently as they move from English to history, sociology, and biology courses than with the structures common to, say, scientific writing in general. They have been especially concerned with the varieties of workplace and other worldly writing. Recently, some have focused on the difficulty graduates have in making the transition from writing academically at university to writing professionally at work. In the process, they have problematized and called into question very basic traditional concepts, such as, audience (see Paré, ''Ushering 'Audience' Out'').

The touchstone text, which almost all North American researchers cite, is Carolyn Miller's 1984 article, ''Genre as Social Action,'' which derives from her dissertation on the genre of environmental impact statements and is conceptually based in Kenneth Burke's New Rhetoric, especially his assertion that discourse is primarily action (and only secondarily representation) and that

[c]ritical and imaginative works are answers to questions posed by the situation in which they arose. They are not merely answers, they are strategic answers, stylized answers . . . [adopting] various strategies for the encompassing of situations. These strategies size up the situations, name them in a way that [dances] an attitude toward them. (*Philosophy* 3, 9)

This leads to a focus on genres as socially defined strategies for doing, that is, for achieving particular types of purposes in particular types of situations.

Several important early studies grew from a concern with ''writing across the curriculum'' and used naturalistic research to discover the range of genres elicited by the various academic disciplines (e.g., Herrington, McCarthy). Such studies were and are animated by a recognition of the extent to which different disciplines evoke and require distinctive discourses that reflect differing ways of thinking, approaching data, and reasoning from evidence. In fact, some early theorizing and research does not use *genre* as its pivotal term, for example, Bizzell (who writes of "discursive forms"), D'Angelo, and Coe ("An Apology," "Rhetoric 2001").

Other research focuses on the initiation of newcomers in academic and workplace discourses (e.g., Berkenkotter, Huckin, and Ackerman; McCarthy and Fishman; Freedman, "Argument"). In differentiating genres, researchers have pointed beyond textual features to issues such as what counts as novelty (Kaufer and Geisler), what can be assumed as background knowledge readers share (Giltrow and Valiquette), what particular communities are prepared to recognize as persuasive (Herrington; Currie), and what is the essential social action of particular genres (Freedman, Adam, and Smart). Studies of workplace genres have examined the discourse of accountants (Devitt, "Intertextuality"), central bankers and social workers (Pare and Smart), business people (Yates, *Control*; Broadhead and Freed), lawyers and tribunes (Harper, reported in Coe, "Eco-Engineering"), scientists (Bazerman, *Shaping*; Myers, *Writing Biology*), social workers (Paré), and veterinarians (Schryer), among many others. A smaller number of studies have looked at worldly writing outside the workplace, for example, Giltrow's examination of political briefs ("Canadian Contexts").

As this research deconstructs the complex interactive dynamics among writers, texts, and situations, it discovers important implications for teaching. Bazerman, for instance, points to the many political, social, ideological, institutional, and curricular factors at play in the negotiated creation and evolution of classroom genres (in Freedman and Medway, *Learning*). Both Dias and Hunt (in Freedman and Medway, *Learning*) demonstrate how new classroom genres can be created in response to fundamental reorientations in curricular and pedagogic goals as well as by new technologies.

Others use or describe what Coe has called "eco-engineering," namely, devising or revising discursive forms as a means of motivating writers to write differently in particular situations (cf., "Eco-Engineering Workplace Genres," which summarizes a number of other studies). Thus, Paré describes how a hospital social work department responded to doctors who ignored what social workers wrote in patients' charts by reformulating the standard social work format, thereby imposing brevity and propositional discourse on social workers who preferred fullness and narrative. As early as 1974, Coe himself advocated using such formal motivation to help students develop more complex and contextual understandings of process and causality ("Rhetoric 2001"). Davis reports on a new form of introduction designed to actualize and embody a feminist reconception of objectivity.

Much research has demonstrated that genre knowledge is typically tacit (which means that experts cannot be counted upon to articulate their genre knowledge explicitly) and that it is typically acquired in situ through models (which serve as prototypes), by observing how experts revise novices' drafts, and by other "apprenticeship" processes. The literature on situated learning and practical cognition has been drawn on in particular to illuminate the processes of acquiring genre knowledge (Berkenkotter and Huckin, *Genre Knowledge*; Freedman, ''Situating.'')

This has led to considerable discussion about the efficacy of explicit teaching of particular genres, especially in isolation from authentic writing situations (cf., e.g., Freedman, ''Show and Tell?''; Coe in Freedman and Medway, *Learning*): does explicit teaching of particular genres work (and, if so, under what circumstances)? Should or should not genre knowledge be allowed to remain tacit and writing instruction be allowed to work on an apprenticeship model? Is it possible to have students learn particular genres before they enter the relevant situations and have an authentic need to use them? Should we recreate in our courses authentic writing situations (e.g., by constituting the class as a collaborative research community), thus leading students to reinvent appropriate text forms?

There does seem to be consensus that students need to understand writing as social action, as situated and strategic, and as occurring in significantly different discourses and genres. This assumption challenges the notion that there is any such universal thing as ''good writing'' except in relation to particular situations and contexts (i.e., it is more Aristotelian or Sophist than Platonic or pre-Socratic, and it is postmodern rather than modern in its assumptions). Students' attention is thus directed to difference, and they learn to expect that new rhetorical situations will often require new discursive structures and strategies. Thus they develop the rhetorical competence to work out the real expectations underlying various teachers' and supervisors' instructions and responses.

NOTE

1. Intriguingly enough, this development might have proceeded very differently and/or taken place (albeit differently, of course) in Canada had Canada Immigration not prevented Halliday from accepting a position at the University of British Columbia, thus deflecting him to Australia.

BIBLIOGRAPHY

Primary Texts

Bakhtin, M. M. ''The Problem of Speech Genres.'' In *Speech Genres and Other Late Essays*. Minneapolis: U of Minnesota P, 1984, 60–102.

Berkenkotter, Carol, and Thomas Huckin. *Genre Knowledge in Disciplinary Communication: Cognition/Culture/Power*. Hillsdale, NJ: Erlbaum. 1995.

Burke, Kenneth. *The Philosophy of Literary Form*. 1941. Rev. abr. ed. New York: Vintage, 1957.

Campbell, Karlyn Kohrs, and Kathleen Hall Jamieson, eds. *Form and Genre: Shaping Rhetorical Action*. Falls Church, VA: Speech Communication Association, 1978.

Freedman, Aviva, and Peter Medway, eds. *Genre and the New Rhetoric*. London: Taylor and Francis, 1994.

Halliday, M. A. K. *Language as Social Semiotic*. London: Edward Arnold, 1978.

Miller, Carolyn. ''Genre as Social Action.'' *Quarterly Journal of Speech* 70 (May 1984): 151–67.

Reid, Ian, ed. *The Place of Genre in Learning*. Geelong, Australia: Deakin UP, 1987. See especially Anne Freadman's "Anyone for Tennis?" (91–124).

Swales, John M. *Genre Analysis*. Cambridge: Cambridge UP, 1990.

Major Scholarship in Composition

Bazerman, Charles. *Shaping Written Knowledge*. Madison: U of Wisconsin P, 1988.

Bazerman, Charles. "Where Is the Classroom?" In *Learning and Teaching Genres*. Ed. Aviva Freedman and Peter Medway. Portsmouth, NH: Heinemann–Boynton/Cook, 1994, 25–30.

Bazerman, Charles, and James Paradis, eds. *Textual Dynamics of the Professions*. Madison: U of Wisconsin P, 1991.

Berkenkotter, Carol. "Paradigm Debates, Turf Wars, and the Conduct of Sociocognitive Inquiry in Composition." *College Composition and Communication* 42 (1991): 151–69.

Berkenkotter, Carol, Thomas Huckin, and John Ackerman. "Rethinking Genre from a Socio-Cognitive Perspective." *Written Communication* 10 (1993): 475–509.

Bizzell, Patricia. "What Happens When Basic Writers Come to College?" *College Composition and Communication* 37 (1986): 294–301.

Broadhead, Glenn, and Richard Freed. *The Variables of Composition: Process and Product in a Business Setting*. Carbondale: Southern Illinois UP, 1986.

Brosnahan, Irene, Richard Coe, and Ann Johns. "Discourse Analyses of Written Texts in an Overseas Teacher Training Program." *English Quarterly* 20.1 (Spring 1987): 16–25.

Campbell, Karlyn Kohrs, and Kathleen Hall Jamieson. "The Generic Approach." In *Methods of Rhetorical Criticism: A Twentieth Century Perspective*, 3rd ed. Ed. Bernard L. Brocks, Robert L. Scott, and James W. Chesebro. Detroit, MI: Wayne State UP, 1989, 331–60.

Christie, Frances. "Language and Schooling." In *Language, Schooling and Society*. Ed. Stephen N. Tchudi. Upper Montclair, NJ: Boynton/Cook, 1985, 21–40.

———. *Language Education*. Geelong, Australia: Deakin UP, 1985.

———. "The Morning News Genre: Using a Functional Grammar to Illuminate Educational Issues." *Australian Review of Applied Linguistics* 10.2 (1987): 182–98.

Christie, Frances, Brian Gray, Pam Gray, Mary Macken, J. R. Martin, and Joan Rothery. *Language: A Resource for Meaning*. Sydney, Australia: Harcourt, 1990–92.

Coe, Richard M. "Teaching Genre as Process." In *Learning and Teaching Genres*. Ed. Aviva Freedman and Peter Medway. Portsmouth, NH: Heinemann–Boynton/Cook, 1994, 157–69.

Coe, Richard M. "An Apology for Form; or, Who Took the Form Out of the Process?" *College English* 49.1 (1987): 13–28.

———. "Eco-Engineering Workplace Genres: A Study in the Sociology of Discourse." Presentation at the World Sociology Congress, Bielefeld, Germany, July 1994.

Currie, Pat. "What Counts as Good Writing? Enculturation and Writing Assessment." In *Learning and Teaching Genre*. Ed. Aviva Freedman and Peter Medway. Portsmouth, NH: Heinemann–Boynton/Cook, 1994, 157–69.

———. "Rhetoric 2001." *Freshman English News* 3.1 (1974): 1–13.

Colomb, Gregory G., and Joseph M. Williams. "Perceiving Structure in Professional Prose." In *Writing in Non-Academic Settings*. Ed. Lee Odell and Dixie Goswami. New York: Guilford, 1986.

D'Angelo, Frank. *A Conceptual Theory of Rhetoric*. Cambridge, MA: Winthrop, 1975. See especially Chapters 2, 5, and 6.

Davis, Fran. "A Practical Assessment of Feminist Pedagogy: Work in Progress." *Inkshed* 7.5/8.1 (November 1988): 1–3.

Devitt, Amy. "Generalizing about Genre." *College Composition and Communication* 44.4 (1993): 573–86.

———. "Intertextuality in Tax Accounting: Generic, Referential, and Functional." In *Textual Dynamics of the Professions*. Ed Charles Bazerman and James Paradis. Madison: U of Wisconsin P, 1991, 336–57.

Dias, Patrick. "Initiating Students into the Genres of Discipline-Based Reading and Writing." In *Learning and Teaching Genres*. Ed. Aviva Freedman and Peter Medway. Portsmouth, NH: Heinemann–Boynton/Cook, 1994, 193–206.

Doheny-Farina, Stephen. "Creating a Text/Creating a Company: The Role of a Text in the Rise and Decline of a New Organization." In *Textual Dynamics of the Professions*. Ed. Charles Bazerman and James Paradis. Madison: U of Wisconsin P, 1991, 306–35.

Eiler, Mary Ann. "Process and Genre." In *Worlds of Writing: Teaching and Learning in a Discourse Community of Work*. Ed. Carolyn Matalene. New York: Random House, 1986, 43–63.

Freadman, Anne, "Anyone for Tennis?" In *The Place of Genre in Learning*. Ed. Ian Reid. Geelong, Australia: Deakin UP, 1987, 91–124.

Freedman, Aviva. "Argument as Genre and Genres of Argument." In *Perspectives on Written Argumentation*. Ed. Deborah Berrill. Norfold, NJ: Hampton, forthcoming.

———. "Show and Tell? The Role of Explicit Teaching in the Learning of New Genres." *Research in the Teaching of English* 27.3 (1993): 222–51. Revised version rpt. in *Genre and the New Rhetoric*. Ed. Aviva Freedman and Peter Medway. London: Taylor and Francis, 1994.

———. "Situating Genre: A Rejoinder." *Research in the Teaching of English* 27.3 (1993): 273–82.

Freedman, Aviva, Christine Adam, and Graham Smart. "Wearing Suits to Class: Simulating Genres and Simulations as Genre." *Written Communication* 11.2 (1994): 193–226.

Freedman, Aviva, and Peter Medway, eds. *Learning and Teaching Genres*. NH: Heinemann–Boynton/Cook, 1994.

Gilbert, Pam. "Stoning the Romance: Girls as Resistant Readers and Writers." In *Learning and Teaching Genres*. Ed. Aviva Freedmann and Peter Medway. Portsmouth, NH: Heinemann–Boynton/Cook, 1994, 173–91.

Giltrow, Janet. "Canadian Contexts for Public Advocacy: Briefs as a Genre." *Technostyle* 7.3 (1988): 17–25.

Giltrow, Janet, and Michele Valiquette. "Genres and Knowledge: Students Writing in the Disciplines." In *Learning and Teaching Genres*. Ed. Aviva Freedman and Peter Medway. Portsmouth, NH: Heinemann–Boynton/Cook, 1994.

Green, Bill. "Gender, Genre, and Writing Pedagogy." In *The Place of Genre in Learning: Current Debates*. Ed. Ian Reid. Geelong, Australia: Deakin UP, 1987.

Green, Bill, and Alison Lee. "Writing Geography: Literacy, Identity, and Schooling." In *Learning and Teaching Genres*. Ed. Aviva Freedman and Peter Medway. Portsmouth, NH: Heinemann–Boynton/Cook, 1994, 207–24.

Halliday, M. A. K., and Ruqaiya Hasan. *Language, Context and Text: A Social-Semiotic Perspective*. Geelong, Australia: Deakin UP, 1985.

Halliday, M.A.K., and Jim R. Martin. *Writing Science*. London: Falmer, 1993.

Herrington, Ann. "Writing in Academic Settings: A Study of the Contexts of Writing in Two College Chemical Engineering Courses." *Research in the Teaching of English* 19 (1985): 331–61.

Hunt, Russell. "Speech Genres, Writing Genres, School Genres, and Computer Genres." In *Learning and Teaching Genres*. Ed. Aviva Freedman and Peter Medway. Portsmouth, NH: Heinemann–Boynton/Cook, 1994, 243–62.

Jamieson, Katherine M. Hall. "Antecedent Genre as Rhetorical Constraint." *Quarterly Journal of Speech* 61 (1975): 406–15.

Kaufer, David, and Cheryl Geisler. "Novelty in Academic Writing." *Written Communication* 6 (1989): 286–311.

Knapp, Peter. "The Trouble with Genre." *Idiom* 29.2 (1995): 34–41.

Lee, Alison. "Questioning the Critical: Linguistics, Literacy, and Pedagogy." In *Constructing Critical Literacies*. Ed. Peter Freebody, Sandy Muspratt, and Allan Luke. New York: Hampton, 1994.

McCarthy, Lucille. "A Stranger in Strange Lands: A College Student Writing Across the Curriculum." *Research in the Teaching of English* 21 (1987): 233–65.

McCarthy, Lucille, and Stephen Fishman. "Boundary Conversations: Conflicting Ways of Knowing in Philosophy and Interdisciplinary Reasearch." *Research in the Teaching of English* 25 (1991): 418–68.

Martin, Jim R. *Factual Writing: Exploring and Challenging Social Reality*. Geelong, Australia: Deakin UP, 1985.

Martin, Jim R., Frances Christie, and Joan Rothery. "Social Processes in Education: A Reply to Sawyer and Watson." In *The Place of Genre in Learning*. Ed. Ian Reid. Geelong, Australia: Deakin UP, 1987, 58–82.

Myers, Greg. *Writing Biology*. Madison: U of Wisconsin P, 1990.

Paré, Anthony. "Ushering 'Audience' Out." *Textual Studies in Canada* 1 (1991): 45–64.

Paré, Anthony, and Graham Smart. "Observing Genres in Action: Towards a Research Methodology." In *Genres in the New Rhetoric*. Ed. Aviva Freedman and Peter Medway. London: Taylor & Francis, 1994, 146–54.

Popken, Randall. "Genre Transfer in Developing Writers." *Focuses* 5.1 (Summer 1992): 3–17.

Prince, Michael B. "Literacy and Genre." *College English* 51 (1989): 730–49.

Schryer, Catherine F. "Records as Genre." *Written Communication* 10 (1993): 200–234.

Slevin, James F. "Genre Theory, Academic Discourse, and Writing within the Disciplines." In *Audits of Meaning*. Ed. Louise Z. Smith. Portsmouth, NH: Boynton/Cook, 1988, 3–16.

Spilka, Rachel, ed. *Writing in the Workplace: New Research Perspectives*. Carbondale: Southern Illinois UP, 1993.

Thibault, Paul. "Genre, Social Action and Pedagogy: Towards a Critical Social Semiotic Account." *Southern Review* 21 (1989): 338–62.

Threadgold, Terry. "The Genre Debate." *Southern Review* (Australia) 21.3 (1988): 315–30.

Threadgold, Terry, and Gunther Kress. "Towards a Social Theory of Genre." *Southern Review* (Australia) 21.3 (1988): 215–43.

Walzer, Arthur E. ''Articles from the 'California Divorce Project': A Case Study in the Concept of Audience.'' *College Composition and Communication* 36.2 (1985): 150–159.

Williams, Joseph, and Gregory Colomb. ''The Case for Explicit Teaching: Why What You Don't Know Won't Help You.'' *Research in the Teaching of English* 27 (1993): 252–64.

Winsor, Dorothy. ''Engineering Writing/Writing Engineering.'' *College Composition and Communication* 41 (1990): 58–82.

Yates, JoAnne. *Control through Communication.* Baltimore: Johns Hopkins UP, 1989.

RICHARD M. COE AND AVIVA FREEDMAN

H

_____

HERMENEUTICS

Summary

In Greek, *hermeneutikos* means "interpreter" (from Hermes, the Messenger God). "Hermeneutics," therefore, designates *the art or science of interpretation*. Best known in the English-speaking world as specifically biblical interpretation, hermeneutics has a long history in both Greek and Jewish culture as the science or method of construing texts of high cultural significance, especially sacred and legal documents. The term is now employed commonly as a synonym for "text interpretation" and sometimes for "literary interpretation" (when "literature" is understood inclusively as "anything written down").

Hermeneutics embraces many notions of interpretation (Crusius, 3–6), but we shall concentrate on *philosophical* (or ontological) *hermeneutics*, a postmodern development. In this context, hermeneutics is not primarily what we do when we must understand and apply the meanings of a text. Nor is it primarily an esoteric, specialized activity of theologians, legal experts, or literary critics. Rather, as "symbol-using animals" (Burke, 3), *all* human beings exist in and as interpretations, understanding self, culture, history, nature—everything that can be understood—according to traditions that always pre-exist us. We *are* the hermeneutical animal to a degree far exceeding other known species—to a degree that makes our existence qualitatively different from that of animals without language. Hence, we have developed ontological hermeneutics.

Put another way, in the older and still more common conception, hermeneutics is tool-like, an isolated art or science that we can pick up and lay down at will. In the postmodern conception, *interpretation has us, not we it*—and has us beyond our capacity for complete comprehension or control. It therefore belongs not to method, but to being.

What makes ontological hermeneutics "postmodern" in the philosophical sense of the term? From Descartes on, modernism sought Truth, a foundation for knowledge in that which was certain, beyond doubt, and beyond history—hence its preoccupation with the universal and with method, validation, and proof. In contrast, philosophical hermeneutics claims that all we have or can have is "readings" and readings of readings, without resolution in any fully adequate, finalized, or authoritative interpretation. What truths we claim are provisional, historical, subject always to revision, and subject sometimes to replacement by other claims. In turning away from the quest for a secure foundation, ontological hermeneutics belongs to postmodern philosophy (see postmodernism).

We can trace philosophical hermeneutics to Friedrich Nietszche, who clearly understood both the priority of interpretation and its all-pervading hold over us. But it was Martin Heidegger who took Nietzsche's emphasis on interpretation and transformed it into a compelling philosophy. Later, Heidegger's student, Hans-Georg Gadamer, developed philosophical hermeneutics as such, fleshing out its theory, exploring its history, and applying it in interpretations of philosophical texts. Other major philosophers have contributed as well, most notably Paul Ricoeur.

Ontological hermeneutics, then, began and continues as a philosophical school or movement. In the last decade or so, it has become a significant voice in literary theory (see Weinsheimer). About the same time, rhetoricians and composition theorists began to explore its implications for their work as well. We shall be concerned, of course, with its bearing on rhetoric, especially composition theory.

At first glance, hermeneutics appears to be only another of many "imports"—theories taken from other disciplines and applied to composition. While true so far as it goes, this understanding does not go very far. Historically, as Friedrich Schleiermacher pointed out in the early 1800s, hermeneutics and rhetoric have always been closely related, interpreting texts being the counterpart to making them. Furthermore, composition itself cannot be distinguished from interpretation. Everything that goes into a rhetorical act must be construed: the subject matter itself, what is at issue, the readership, the occasion, the lines of reasoning that might work, and so forth—none of which is simply "there" as "brute fact." Indeed, beyond the level of skill with language itself, the quality of a rhetorical act depends largely on the quality of the interpretations that the writer brings to the task and discovers as the writing unfolds. Finally, every theory of rhetoric from Aristotle on can be nothing else but an interpretation of the art. Thus, while the cues for a hermeneutical rhetoric came from outside the discipline, from contemporary philosophy, it only makes explicit what is implicit in the practice and theory of rhetoric itself. Most imports cannot make this claim.

To compose is to interpret—we begin from this self-evident proposition. It follows that composition theory must incorporate a theory of interpretation. But which? Here consensus apparently ends. Although some decry the relativism of postmodern culture, relativism is unavoidable: We are accustomed to many ways of "reading" anything interesting enough to draw collective attention. Some of these ways are represented in this volume—for example, Burkean theories of rhetoric, critical theory of the Frankfurt School, Deconstruction, and Freirean Theory. But regardless of the way of reading we prefer, what happens when we "read"—understand, interpret—anything? Less a way of reading than an inquiry into reading itself, philosophical hermeneutics seeks to answer this question. Should we find its answer compelling, perhaps we can agree about the general nature of interpretation, if not about which specific way is best.

We have said that human beings exist in and as interpretation. What does this mean? It means that interpretation is never "objective." Nothing in our experience is a "naked given" that is "just there" as an unmediated presence. Rather, we encounter everything via preunderstandings of our world, most of which are unconscious and hard to articulate. That is, we always "understand" before we realize that we have, before we can even say anything about what we know. Michael Polanyi called this always-preexisting understanding, "tacit knowledge," which is known not through propositions but through activity, through "life" (49–65). Heidegger called it "forehaving," which he distinguished from "foresight" (roughly "ideology," our general theory of the world) and "foreconception" (our specific notion of some particular something—what it is, how it functions, its value, etc.) (see Crusius, 26–30).

Because we experience everything from within a horizon of tacit knowledge, ideology in general, and more specific preconceptions, interpretation cannot be objective—but neither is it "subjective." For the most part, "my" preunderstanding of something is not "mine" at all, but belongs to my language, culture, class, occupation, family background, and so forth.

Interpretation is by nature *intersubjective*, irreducibly *collective*. It is never a grasping of the "thing itself," but an inquiry into how we have always already understood something. Consequently, our existing in and as interpretations also means that we must rehabilitate a word more misunderstood and despised than "rhetoric"—namely, "prejudice," which etymologically is "prejudgment."

Because of its association with the destructive folly of racial and ethnic hatred, the last thing we want to be called is prejudiced. And yet, even if we have no prejudice in the common use of the word, we prejudge in other ways. Far from being always negative, something to set aside or overcome, prejudice is indispensable: We have no initial experience of anything except through prejudgments of it. The Enlightenment's prejudice against prejudice is the greatest single barrier to understanding interpretation.

So what happens when we interpret something? Usually little happens—at least at the level of conscious awareness. As long as nothing challenges our prejudices, we simply assimilate what we encounter to understandings we already have. For the most part we have no awareness of constantly interpreting ourselves, others, and "the world" at all. Understanding becomes an experience when we confront the anomalous—things that do not fit our preconceptions— and when we interact with people who interpret the same thing differently.

At this point, when our prejudices are called into question, one of two things happens: either we ignore the challenge or we begin the process of "taking it in." Given our normally heavy investment in current ways of seeing things, the first possibility is the more likely. We can often write off the anomalous as just odd, inexplicable; we can often dismiss a challenge as poorly informed, motivated by ill will, and so on. But sometimes the anomalies are too numerous and too significant to brush aside; sometimes the challenge is too insistent and too persuasive to explain away. Sometimes we heed the resistance; sometimes we listen to the other. When this happens, interpretation becomes truly interesting and dynamic; the potential for change and growth is at hand.

So what happens when, as Gadamer put it, "a text begins to speak"—when we allow it to call our prejudgments into question? We begin a process akin to dialogue, an inquiry or experimental feeling of our way along toward a resolution. We try to formulate the differences, find words for what is at stake. We reformulate our thinking in an effort to find a place for the anomalies. We reject or modify part of what we thought as the cogency of the challenge sinks in. We challenge the challenger, exposing the prejudices for scrutiny that called our own into question. And so we progress, through the whole unpredictable process of dialogue. We may resolve nothing, but remain caught up in the question, the way some of Plato's dialogues "end"; alternately, we may achieve nearly complete agreement, "the fusion of horizons" Gadamer discusses (*Truth* 273–74). Most of the time we fall more or less awkwardly in the middle, partly at odds, partly on common ground—in tension. But wherever we suspend or land, "something different comes to be" (Gadamer, *Philosophical Hermeneutics* 38), something perhaps even new.

At its best, when it is most engaging and consequential, interpretation is dialogical. Note that what happens when we interpret is not changed fundamentally by strong loyalty to a certain way of reading. Marxists, for example, are still revising Marx, caught up in the ongoing dialogue about how best to understand and apply his critique of capitalism. The same can be said of Freudians or Derrideans, of any way of reading that remains a live option. Interpretation always "works" along the lines described by philosophical hermeneutics.

It is neither possible nor desirable that students of composition reach consensus about ways of reading. But we need to share a common understanding of interpretation itself, otherwise we cannot understand ourselves when we write, nor grasp what is going on as our students compose. Furthermore, rhetoric, as a general theory of composing, requires a general account of interpretation. Philosophical hermeneutics provides such an account.

Reception and Significance in Composition Studies

The earliest article by a composition theorist to address philosophical hermeneutics specifically was published in 1979, but only in the last decade at most has philosophical hermeneutics become a presence in our field. Almost all of the sources listed under "Major Scholarship in Composition" in the Bibliography introduce philosophical hermeneutics and make basic claims about its potential significance. But its advocates have not moved far beyond introducing it, and the claims advanced have not been seriously contested thus far. In the ordinary sense, then, we cannot as yet speak of a "reception"; the argument must develop more first. Nevertheless, the rudiments of a reception may be discerned in how its advocates have placed it in relation to composition theory generally.

For decades now, "process" has dominated thought about composing. This thinking, however, has relied typically on a commonsense notion of process, detached from the concept's extensive development in post-Nietzschean philosophy. Philosophical hermeneutics is one way to explore the implications of process with greater sophistication and depth. (See, for example, Kinneavy's 1987 article, which uses Heidegger's analysis of "foreconception" to criticize existing views of process and to advance a better one.)

Drawing first on linguistics and then later on psychology, especially cognitive psychology, some theorists have wanted to turn composition studies into a social science. Inspired in part by Gadamer's critique of the limitations of scientific method in *Truth and Method* and also by his explicit linkage of hermeneutics with the rhetorical tradition, hermeneutical theorists assert that what matters most in acts of composing cannot be objectified nor illuminated by empirical study. That is, if writing is not primarily "behavior" but rather action based on an author's interpretation of subject matter, readership, purpose, and so forth, and if interpretation is a never-to-be-repeated dialogue, how can method "get at" it? Philosophical hermeneutics reclaims composition for humanistic study. (See Gere, especially the chapter by Spellmeyer.)

Part of this reclamation is to situate composing and theories of it, not in abstract, invariant "structures," but rather in concrete, dynamic histories—in a contingent, never quite predictable (nor therefore controllable) world. Philosophical hermeneutics, consequently, rejects formalism in interpretation and prescriptivism in rhetoric. Method understands understanding as mastery, and hermeneutics as perpetual, always open-ended inquiry—from this difference all the characteristic emphases of hermeneutics stem, including how it receives current theory and practice in composition. No doubt how our discipline ultimately receives hermeneutics will depend largely on whether we come to find method or dialogue the more attractive.

As with reception, so it is also with the significance of philosophical hermeneutics—more potential than actuality. A small but growing group of scholars has made the theory available to the discipline at large, but assimilation is far from complete, and many wonder, not without reason, what exactly one "does" with it. Except in graduate seminars, one thing we should not do is teach it in the usual sense of the word. No sane person will assign Gadamer to students in ordinary writing classes, nor seek to fill their heads with hermeneutical terminology. Rather, its impact will be more indirect, less intrusive. It will affect our thinking about composition, our theories, and because of this, the textbooks we write and select, the classroom experience we want our students to have, and the questions we ask over drafts in student conferences (see Crusius, 74–92).

Most importantly, philosophical hermeneutics should help us see students more focally *as interpreters*, and to link their capacities as writers more consistently with how they interpret everything around them, including the writing classroom itself. As many have pointed out, we tend to take students as "patients" with "ills" that require "treatments"—which is to say, we understand them in the way method has taught us. But patients, as the root of the word itself suggests, are passive, people who must "suffer" whatever the master prescribes. Something is obviously wrong with the metaphor, since writers must be active, engaged, and in pursuit of their own authority and since no one is the master of language or the composing process. What if we began to see writing seriously as an ongoing dialogue and became genuinely engaged in dialogues with students over their texts? What if we stop pretending that we are experts and became fellow inquirers?

Clearly, the practical significance of philosophical hermeneutics has nothing to do with "teaching" it as such. What, then, of its significance beyond the writing classroom, as a way of understanding ourselves? Self-understanding in any humanistic field reduces to a few basic stances. We have traditionalists, people who see their field as defined by a great text or texts and see themselves as representing its claims. Aristotelians are an example in composition studies. We have antitraditionalists, Cartesians in effect, who would sweep the slate clean and start over from scratch—for example, those who want to make a science out of composition studies. Finally, we have the critical theorists, usually followers of Nietzsche, Marx, or Freud, who want to liberate themselves and their students from traditional attitudes and prejudices via a "deeper" understanding of human motivation.

Hermeneutical rhetoric does not understand itself in any of these ways. Given its close ties to the rhetorical tradition and its critique of method's claim to omnicompetence, it is furthest removed from the Cartesians. It sees all interpretation as arising out of traditions, but it resists the notion of "final authority" in any reading. It does not deny the possibility of "depth" in interpretation or its value, but it is suspicious of the "we know better" attitude that goes with it.

From a hermeneutical perspective, the problem with all three stances is their shared tendency toward monologue—the one voice, the one method, the one way of reading. In contrast, what matters for hermeneutics is "the conversation": with texts old and new, among people past and present. For it is in ongoing dialogues that our truths arise, where prejudices are revealed as either enabling or disabling. The very possibility of some degree of self-understanding resides in the conversation.

Hermeneutical rhetoric takes a dialogical stance. This is the key to its significance for composition studies.

BIBLIOGRAPHY

Primary Texts

Burke, Kenneth. "Definition of Man." In *Language as Symbolic Action: Essays on Life, Literature, and Method*. Berkeley: U of California P, 1966, 3–24.

Gadamer, Hans-Georg. *Philosophical Hermeneutics*. Trans. and ed. David E. Linge. Berkeley: U of California P, 1976.

———. *Truth and Method*. 2nd ed. Trans. Garrett Barden and John Cumming. Rev. trans. Joel Weinsheimer and Donald C. Marshall. New York: Crossroads, 1989.

Heidegger, Martin. "Being and Time: Introduction." In *Martin Heidegger: Basic Writings*. Ed. David Farrell Krell. New York: Harper and Row, 1977, 41–89.

Mueller-Vollmer, Kurt, ed. *The Hermeneutics Reader*. New York: Continuum, 1989.

Ricoeur, Paul. *Hermeneutics and the Human Sciences: Essays on Language, Action, and Interpretation*. Ed. John B. Thompson. New York: Cambridge UP, 1981.

Weinsheimer, Joel. *Philosophical Hermeneutics and Literary Theory*. New Haven, CT: Yale UP, 1991.

Major Scholarship in Composition

Crosswhite, James. *The Rhetoric of Reason: Writing and the Attractions of Argument*. Madison: U of Wisconsin P, 1996.

Crusius, Timothy W. *A Teacher's Introduction to Philosophical Hermeneutics*. Urbana, IL: NCTE, 1991.

Gere, Anne Ruggles, ed. *Into the Field: Sites of Composition Studies*. New York: MLA, 1993.

Kinneavy, James L. "The Process of Writing: A Philosophical Base in Hermeneutics." *Journal of Advanced Composition* 7 (1987): 1–9.

———. "The Relation of the Whole to the Part in Interpretative Theory and in the Composing Process." In *Linguistics, Stylistics, and the Teaching of Composition*. Ed. Donald McQuade. Akron, OH: U of Akron, Department of English, 1979.

Phelps, Louise W. *Composition as a Human Science: Contributions to the Self-Understanding of a Discipline*. New York: Oxford UP, 1988.

Phelps, Louise W., ed. *Ricoeur and Rhetoric*. Special issue of *Pre/Text* 4 (1983).

Polanyi, Michael. *Personal Knowledge: Towards a Post-Critical Philosophy*. Chicago: U of Chicago P, 1962.

Spellmeyer, Kurt. "Being Philosophical about Composition, Hermeneutics, and the Teaching of Writing." In *Into the Field: Sites of Composition Studies*. Ed. Anne Ruggles Gere. New York: MLA, 1993, 9–29.

TIMOTHY W. CRUSIUS

I
____

IDENTITY POLITICS AND COMPOSITION STUDIES

Summary

Identity politics is an umbrella term for a set of movements based on features of identity and their political implications—the women's movement, civil rights, gay/lesbian/biracial/transgender rights, and so forth. Representing the competing relationships that define modern society, it is the ultimate scene for understanding postmodernity. "Postmodern individuals" define themselves in multiple ways, no longer possessing a "core self" or identity or professing allegiance to a worldview generic to the society. They choose from such diverse factors as race, ethnicity, class, gender, sexuality, age, religion, spirituality, disability, regionalism, nationalism, family kinship, sports, political stances, and even hairstyles ("Big-hairs" or "Skinheads") as they define the "community(ies)" to which they belong. They may also change some identity priorities as the situation dictates, or they may identify with a particular hybrid instead of a single community—for example, "radical eco-feminists of color."

In *Yearning: Race, Gender, and Cultural Politics*, bell hooks argues for defining the self "in relation, the self not as signifier of one 'I' but the coming together of many 'I's' " (30–31). However one chooses to establish identity alliances, the defining characteristic of postmodernity, according to Jürgen Habermas, is its rejection of foundational epistemologies and grand narratives, and its assertion that "reason" and "truth" are related to power (Giroux 12: see the editor's introduction). Composition theorists who have written about identity, politics, and voice in the classroom (e.g., Ritchie, Trimbur, Schilb, Sullivan) cite a range of theorists including Bakhtin, Foucault, Spivak, West, and others listed in the primary bibliography. Many have used Mary Louise Pratt's "contact zones," "social spaces where cultures meet, clash, and grapple with each other, often in contexts of highly asymmetrical relations of power" (34), as a metaphor for writing classrooms engaged in reading and writing about identity politics.

Reception and Significance in Composition Studies

Robert Brooke introduced composition studies to "identity negotiations," combining "identity" from psychology and "negotiations" from politics and sociocultural theory. In *Writing and Sense of Self*, Brooke described a shift in focus from himself as sequencer of instruction to the students as learners. Once he made this shift, he knew he had to understand the ways in which students negotiated identities before he could engage them as learners or help them to write for a range of audiences in complex rhetorical situations. Drawing on social psychologists such as Goffman, Erikson, and R. D. Laing, Brooke demonstrated the significance of identity theory to pedagogy.

Other writers have emphasized the political side of identity politics. In the introduction to their edited collection on composition in a "postmodern world," Patricia Harkin and John Schilb announce that their purpose is to provide support for those who "believe that the study of composition and rhetoric is not merely the service component of the English department but also an inquiry into cultural values" (1). As composition studies continues to define its raison d'être, theorists have claimed the classroom as a critical scene where students can interrogate the culture into which they write, while they explore their own identities. This combination of inquiry into politics and identity is consistent with recent work in "critical pedagogy" (e.g., Paulo Freire, Henry Giroux), which provides justifications for reading and writing about what many have called the "culture wars." Susan Miller, describing composition studies as a profession argues that "those of us who are 'in' composition are uniquely placed across the border separating textual and 'real' worlds, where we might become more powerful critics of the intellectual politics that encloses each" (x). On the other hand, some academics (e.g., Pinsker, Hairston) have raised questions about the appropriateness of politically charged content in the hands of radical teachers whose classrooms may not serve the perceived purposes of the academy and the world of work.

Nonetheless, the reception of identity politics at the field's national conventions and journals is extremely positive. Several College Composition and Communication Conference chairs in the 1990s (e.g., McQuade, Cook, Bridwell-Bowles, Royster) have used autobiographical materials about identity and identity politics in their national addresses. Books by Rose, Villanueva, and Gilyard about their own identities and literacy struggles have been widely used as models for student writing. Despite much academic support for "multiculturalism" as an ideal, linguistic diversity itself is not a universally accepted goal. Lisa Delpit has questioned the widespread tolerance of dialect differences in African American students' academic writing. Early respondents to Oakland's "Ebonics" debate charged educators with "dumbing down" the curriculum for

African-American students. As gatekeepers in many institutions, composition teachers are expected to eliminate linguistic diversity and to prepare students for a national "standard" in English. Min-Zhan Lu teaches diverse styles and dialects in her classrooms and does not privilege "standard English" exclusively because the "unequal sociopolitical power of diverse discourses" is obvious to students who cannot ignore the pressure for standard English. While many in the field propose alternatives policies such as the CCCC National Language Policy, the institutions that support writing programs often openly demand a traditional curriculum.

There are three obvious reasons why identity politics has to matter to composition studies. First, composition instructors try to help students write into an academy that is struggling with postmodernity. Students have to understand that some scholars still believe in foundational truths and perspectives, while others have long since deconstructed such a worldview. Without the rhetorical tools to analyze difference and to understand the consequences of identity politics, students will be ill-equipped to write effectively.

Secondly, the notion of "voice" is central to composition studies. Its presence (or absence) is a focus in all our theories of writing (e.g., "expressivist," "rationalist," "social epistemic," etc.). Identity politics makes it necessary for students to understand where a "voice" comes from, whether their voices are singular or plural, whether voices are "inherent" or socially constructed, and whether their readers will be homogenous or diverse. Lester Faigley also argues that teachers who ignore the political problems that come with asking for "truth-telling" autobiographical essays, for example, are placing themselves in a position of privilege "because the teacher is outside of the petty interests of history but within the boundaries of universal truth" (131). He uses Foucault, as Giroux uses Habermas, to argue that such teaching is perilously close to (if not actually) an abuse of power.

Finally, identity politics is important as we attempt to understand contemporary modes of communication and writing. Foss, Foss, and Trapp explain rhetoricians' responses to identity politics this way: "Initially, the focus of a challenge is on inclusion. . . . [Then] the second step in the process of challenge involves the reconceptualization of rhetorical constructs themselves using the knowledge gained from the study of alternate rhetorics" (274). The field's interest in hypertext, for example, has been linked to a need for polyvocal writers and the lack of homogenous readers. Jay Bolter reflects on the demise of the printed book and the emergence of electronic writing:

The printed book requires a printed persona, a consistent voice to lead the reader on a journey through the text. It has been hard for me to establish and maintain such a voice. . . . Indeed, a many-voiced text that is large enough to contain and admit its own contradictions may be the only convincing form of writing." (ix)

Other authors (Ede and Lunsford) have argued that collaboration allows multiple and diverse voices to speak through writing.

BIBLIOGRAPHY

Primary Texts

Ackelsberg, Martha A. "Identity Politics, Political Identities: Thoughts toward a Multicultural Politics." *Frontiers* 16.1 (1996): 87–100.

Albrecht, Lisa, and Rose M. Brewer. *Bridges of Power: Women's Multicultural Alliances.* Philadelphia: National Women's Studies Association by New Society Publishers, 1990.

Aronowitz, Stanley. *The Politics of Identity: Class, Culture, Social Movements.* New York: Routledge, 1992.

Aronowitz, Stanley, and Henry A. Giroux. *Postmodern Education, Border Pedagogy, Politics, and Cultural Criticism.* Minneapolis: U of Minnesota P, 1991.

Bakhtin, Mikhail. *The Dialogic Imagination.* Trans. Caryl Emerson and Michael Holquist. Austin: U of Texas P, 1981.

Berube, Michael, and Cary Nelson. *Higher Education under Fire: Politics, Economics, and the Crisis of the Humanities.* New York: Routledge, 1995.

Campbell, Jane. *Disability Politics: Understanding Our Past, Changing Our Future.* New York: Routledge, 1996.

Chandler, Daniel. "The Construction of Identity in Personal Home Pages on the World-Wide Web." 5 pars. plus many links. World Wide Web, n.d. (Available http://www.aber.ac.uk/%7Edgc/munich.html.)

Ehrenreich, Barbara. *Fear of Falling: The Inner Life of the Middle Class.* New York: Pantheon, 1989.

Espiritu, Yen Le. *Asian American Panethnicity: Bridging Institutions and Identities.* Philadelphia: Temple UP, 1992.

Geismar, Kathryn, and Guitele Nicoleau, eds. *Teaching for Change: Addressing Issues of Difference in the College Classroom.* Reprint Series no. 25. Cambridge, MA: *Harvard Educational Review*, 1993.

Gergen, Kenneth J. *Realities and Relationships.* Cambridge: Harvard UP, 1994.

———. "Social Construction and the Transformation of Identity Politics." 37 pars. Online. World Wide Web, 7 April 1995. (Available http://www.swarthmore.edu/SocSci/kgergen1/text8.html/.)

Glenn, Jordan. *Cultural Politics: Class, Gender, Race, and the Postmodern World.* Oxford, UK: B. Blackwell, 1995.

Gillis, John R., ed. *Commemorations: The Politics of National Identity.* Princeton, NJ: Princeton UP, 1994.

Giroux, Henry A., ed. *Postmodernism, Feminism, and Cultural Boundaries.* Albany: State U of New York P, 1991.

hooks, bell. *Black Looks: Race and Representation.* Boston, MA: South End P, 1992.

———. *Talking Back: Thinking Feminist, Thinking Black.* Boston: South End P, 1989.

———. *Yearning: Race, Gender, and Cultural Politics.* Boston: South End P, 1990.

Journal of Aging and Identity. New York: Human Sciences P, 1996–.

Lerda, Valeria Gennaro, and Tjebbe Westendorp. *The United States South: Regionalism and Identity.* Rome: Bulzoni, 1991.

Levine, Lawrence. *Highbrow/Lowbrow: The Emergence of Cultural Hierarchy in America.* Cambridge: Harvard UP, 1988.

McCarthy, Cameron, and Warren Crichlow, eds. *Race, Identity and Representation in Education.* New York: Routledge, 1993.

Moraga, Cherrie, and Gloria Anzaldúa. *This Bridge Called My Back: Writings by Radical Women of Color*. Watertown, MA: Persephone P, 1981.

Myrsiades, Kostas, and Jerry McGuire. *Order and Partialities: Theory, Pedagogy, and the "Postcolonial."* New York: State U of New York P, 1995.

Omi, Michael, and Howard Winant. *Racial Formation in the United States: From the 1960s to the 1980s*. New York: Routledge, 1986.

O'Sullivan, Patrick. *Religion and Identity*. London: Leicester UP, 1996.

Pinsker, Sanford. "Cooling the Polemics of the Culture Warriors." *Chronicle of Higher Education* 42 (May 3, 1996): A56.

Pratt, Mary Louise. "Arts of the Contact Zone." In *Profession 91*. New York: MLA, 1991, 33–40.

Rajchman, John. *The Identity in Question*. New York: Routledge, 1995.

Sollors, Werner, ed. *The Invention of Ethnicity*. New York: Oxford UP, 1989.

Thompson, Becky W., and Sangeeta Tyagi. *Beyond a Dream Deferred: Multicultural Education and the Politics of Excellence*. Minneapolis: U of Minnesota P, 1993.

Tilly, Charles, ed. *Citizenship, Identity and Social History*. New York: Cambridge UP, 1996.

Waters, Mary C. *Ethnic Options: Choosing Identities in America*. Berkeley: U of California P, 1990.

West, Cornel. *Race Matters*. New York: Vintage Books, 1994.

Young, Robert B. *No Neutral Ground: Standing by the Values We Prize in Higher Education*. San Francisco, CA: Jossey-Bass, 1997.

Major Scholarship in Composition

Bolter, Jay David. *Writing Space: The Computer, Hypertext, and the History of Writing*. Hillsdale, NJ: Erlbaum, 1991.

Bridwell-Bowles, Lillian. "Discourse and Diversity: Experimental Writing within the Academy." *College Composition and Communication* 43 (1992): 349–68.

———. "Freedom, Form, Function: Varieties of Academic Discourse." *College Composition and Communication* 46 (1995): 46–61.

Brooke, Robert. "Modeling a Writer's Identity: Reading and Imitation in the Writing Classroom." *College Composition and Communication* 39 (1988): 23–41.

———. "Underlife and Writing Instruction." *College Composition and Communication* 38 (1987): 141–53.

———. *Writing and Sense of Self: Identity Negotiation in Writing Workshops*. Urbana, IL: NCTE, 1991.

Bulloch, Richard, and John Trimbur, ed. *The Politics of Writing Instruction*. Portsmouth, NH: Boynton/Cook, 1991.

Comfort, Juanita. "Negotiating Identity in Academic Writing: Experiences of African American Women Doctoral Students." Diss. Columbus: Ohio State U, 1995.

Cook, William. "Writing in the Spaces Left." *College Composition and Communication* 44 (1993): 9–25.

Dilpit, Lisa. *Other People's Children: Cultural Conflict in the Classroom*. New York: W.W. Norton, 1995.

Ede, Lisa, and Andrea Lunsford. *Singular Texts/Plural Authors*. Carbondale: Southern Illinois UP, 1990.

Faigley, Lester. *Fragments of Rationality: Postmodernity and the Subject of Composition*. Pittsburgh, PA: U of Pittsburgh P, 1992.

Flynn, Elizabeth. "Composing 'Composing as a Woman.' " *College Composition and Communication* 41 (1990): 83–89.

Foss, Sonja, Karen A. Foss, and Robert Trapp. *Contemporary Perspectives on Rhetoric.* 2nd ed. Prospect Heights, IL: Waveland P, 1991.

Fox, Thomas. *The Social Uses of Writing: Politics and Pedagogy.* Norwood, NJ: Ablex, 1990.

Gilyard, Keith. *Voices of the Self: A Study of Language Competence.* Detroit: Wayne State University Press, 1991.

Hairston, Maxine. "Diversity, Ideology, and Teaching Writing." *College Composition and Communication* 43 (1992): 179–93.

Harkin, Patricia, and John Schilb, eds. *Contending with Words: Composition and Rhetoric in a Postmodern Age.* New York: MLA, 1991.

Kehily, Mary Jane. "Self-Narration, Autobiography and Identity Construction." *Gender and Education* 7 (1995): 23–31.

Kirsch, Gesa E., and Joy S. Ritchie. "Beyond the Personal: Theorizing a Politics of Location in Composition Research." *College Composition and Communication* 46 (1995): 7–29.

Looser, Devoney. "Composing as an 'Essentialist'?: New Directions for Feminist Composition Theories." *Rhetoric Review* 12 (1993): 54–69.

Lu, Min-Zhan. "Professing Multiculturalism: The Politics of Style in the Contact Zone." *College Composition and Communication* 45 (1994): 442–58.

Malinowitz, Harriet. "The Rhetoric of Empowerment in Writing Programs." In *Rhetoric: Concepts, Definitions, Boundaries.* Ed. William A. Covino and David A. Jolliffe. Boston: Allyn and Bacon, 1995, 679–89.

McQuade, Donald. "Living In—and On—the Margins." *College Composition and Communication* 43 (1992): 11–22.

Miller, Richard. "Fault Lines in the Contact Zone." *College English* 56 (1994): 389–408.

Miller, Susan. *Textual Carnivals: The Politics of Composition.* Carbondale: Southern Illinois UP, 1991.

Ritchie, Joy S. "Beginning Writers: Diverse Voices and Individual Identity." *College Composition and Communication* 40: 152–74.

Rose, Mike. *Lives on the Boundary.* New York: Free P, 1989.

Rothgery, David. " 'So What Do We Do Now?' Necessary Directionality as the Writing Teacher's Response to Racist, Sexist, Homophobic Papers." *College Composition and Communication* 44 (1993): 241–47.

Royster, Jacqueline Jones. "When the First Voice You Hear Is Not Your Own." *College Composition and Communication* 47 (1996): 29–40.

Schilb, John. "Cultural Studies, Postmodernism, and Composition." In *Contending with Words: Composition and Rhetoric in a Postmodern Age.* Ed. Patricia Harkin and John Schilb. New York: MLA, 1991, 173–88.

Sullivan, Patricia A., and Donna J. Qualley, eds. *Pedagogy in the Age of Politics: Writing and Reading (in) the Academy.* Urbana, IL: NCTE, 1994.

Trimbur, John. "Literacy and the Discourse of Crisis." In *Politics of Writing Instruction.* Ed. Richard Bullock and John Trimbur. Portsmouth, NH: Boynton/Cook, 1991, 277–95.

Villanueva, Victor, Jr. *Bootstraps: From an American Academic of Color.* Urbana, IL: NCTE, 1993.

Welch, Nancy. "Revising a Writer's Identity: Reading and 'Re-modeling' in a Composition Class." *College Composition and Communication* 47 (1996): 41–61.
                                                                            LILLIAN BRIDWELL-BOWLES

INVENTION

Summary/Reception and Significance in Composition Studies

In the twentieth century, a range of fields have been debating the relationship between knowledge and discourse. Influenced by these debates, as well as by discussions of rhetoric as epistemic (Leff), postmodern ideas that all knowledge is constructed, and theories of social construction, composition theorists have articulated a range of inventional theories sensitive to these epistemological arguments. Several early theories enacted classical concepts, developing inventional arts like *status* to guide the initiation of discourse and *topoi* to construct ethical, emotional, and rational arguments appropriate for the situation and audience (Lauer, "Issues"). These arts were based on conceptions of invention as discourse based, probable, and situated, as in Edward Corbett's arguments for reintroducing the art of *status* and topics to help writers focus and develop their writing; James Kinneavy's work on *kairos* as a positioning force in writing; D'Angelo's topics, including the nonrational, in his conceptual theory of rhetoric; and Gage's arguments for the enthymeme, issues, and dialogue in composition. These theorists countered nineteenth-century treatments of invention as either absent or ensnared in modes of discourse (Berlin, *Writing Instruction*; Crowley; Johnson).

Motivated by challenges to the validity and significance of formal logic (Perelman; Toulmin), other composition theorists became interested in heuristics, a kind of thinking that characterized the inquiry of creative people in different fields. Because heuristic thinking was neither as rigorous as formal logic nor completely aleatory, composition theorists thought it promising to guide complex writing activities where unknowns were investigated. Heuristic strategies engaged intuition, yet were conscious and could be taught (Perkins; Nickerson, Perkins, and Smith; Lauer, "Heuristics"). Early studies focused on general heuristics to facilitate discovery, while later work has concentrated on discipline-specific heuristics. Disagreements continue over whether general or domain-specific heuristics are more fruitful for discoverers and learners (Perkins and Salomon; Carter).

Several composition theorists created heuristic guides for such inventional acts as the initiation of discourse, exploratory activity, and argument construction. Richard Young, Alton Becker, and Kenneth Pike constructed a modern epistemological heuristic to help writers go beyond the known. Based on the tagmemic concept of cultural difference, tagmemic rhetoric offered strategies for stating unknowns; for exploring subjects and noting their distinctive features, range of variation, and distribution; and for verifying insights. Kenneth Burke introduced another powerful strategy, the Pentad and ratios, which he conceived originally as a hermeneutic tool, but which became widely used as a heuristic strategy. Linda Flower and John Hayes also advocated the use of heuristics within their cognitive theory of writing, devising problem-solving strategies to guide problem representation, goal setting, and idea generation. Other theorists framed inventional practices such as the journal, meditation, and analogy (Rohman and Wlecke); freewriting (Elbow); and clustering, looping, cubing, and brainstorming (see Harrington et al.).

In the 1980s, drawing on social construction theory, Karen Burke LeFevre delineated a social theory of invention, differentiating four levels: Platonic, internal dialogic, collaborative, and collective.

Other compositionists studied the collaborative nature of invention (e.g., Lunsford and Ede) and described collaborative invention practices (e.g., Bosworth and Hamilton; Flower, *Construction*). Several scholars in Writing in the Disciplines investigated the situated and generic nature of invention (e.g., Bazerman, Crismore and Farnsworth); while Writing Across the Curriculum programs have introduced students to strategies for learning, and occasionally for inquiry, in a range of fields (e.g., Maimon, Nodine, and O'Connor; Gere; Herrington and Moran).

In the last decade or so, work on invention has benefited from feminist studies, cultural studies, cross-cultural rhetoric, and theories of technology. Early feminist studies of women's ways of knowing (Flynn), although subsequently critiqued for essentialism, nevertheless prompted theorists to better account for "feminine" ways of inventing. A number of composition theorists have been experimenting with different "feminine" composing practices (e.g., Phelps and Emig; Gannett). Cultural studies' efforts to increase understanding of the ways in which social, political, racial, and economic forces interpellate values and cultural assumptions led theorists like James Berlin (poststructuralism) to develop heuristics for cultural critique. Contrastive rhetoricians have been studying the composing tactics of writers from different cultures (Connor). Finally, other scholars have argued that technology radically alters our views of invention and meaning, particularly visual meaning (e.g., Sullivan; Kaplan). A more in-depth view of the rich terrain of inventional theory and practices can be found in a number of sources (e.g., Young, "Invention," "Recent Developments"; Young and Liu).

One of the touchstones for the significance of any theory in composition studies is its impact on practice. For three decades, inventional theories have infiltrated textbooks and changed instructional methods. The diverse directions into which inventional theory has migrated also demonstrate its vitality and centrality in rhetoric and composition studies, reflecting changing and complex epistemological theories.

BIBLIOGRAPHY

Primary Texts

Berlin, James. "Poststructuralism, Cultural Studies, and the Composition Classroom: Postmodern Theory and Practice." *Rhetoric Review* 11 (1992): 16–33.

Burke, Kenneth. "The Five Key Terms of Dramatism." In *Contemporary Rhetoric: A Conceptual Background with Readings*. Ed. Ross Winterowd. New York: Harcourt Brace, 1975, 155–62.

———. "Questions and Answers about the Pentad." *College Composition and Communication* 29 (1978): 330–335.

Corbett, Edward. *Classical Rhetoric for the Modern Student*. New York: Oxford UP, 1971.

D'Angelo, Frank. *A Conceptual Theory of Rhetoric*. Englewood Cliffs, NJ: Winthrop P, 1975.

Elbow, Peter. "Freewriting Exercises." In *Writing without Teachers*. New York: Oxford UP, 1973, 3–11.

Emig, Janet. "Writing as a Mode of Learning." *College Composition and Communication* 28 (1977): 122–28.

Flower, Linda. *The Construction of Negotiated Meaning: A Social Cognitive Theory of Writing*. Carbondale: Southern Illinois UP, 1994.

Flower, Linda, and John Hayes. "Problem Solving Strategies and the Writing Process." *College English* 39 (1977): 449–61.

Gage, John. "An Adequate Epistemology for Composition: Classical and Modern Perspectives." In *Essays on Classical Rhetoric and Modern Discourse*. Ed. Robert Connors, Lisa Ede, and Andrea Lunsford. Carbondale: Southern Illinois UP, 1984.

Kinneavy, James. "*Kairos*: A Neglected Concept in Classical Rhetoric." In *Rhetoric and Praxis: The Contribution of Classical Rhetoric to Practical Reasoning*. Washington, DC: Catholic UP, 1986, 79–105.

Lauer, Janice. "Heuristics and Composition." *College Composition and Communication* 21 (1970): 396–404.

LeFevre, Karen Burke. *Invention as a Social Act*. Carbondale: Southern Illinois UP, 1986.

Rohman, Gordon, and Albert O. Wlecke. *Prewriting: The Construction and Application of Model for Concept Formation in Writing*. Cooperative Research Project #2174, Cooperative Research Project of the Office of Education, U.S. Department of Health, Education, and Welfare, Washington, DC, 1964.

Young, Richard, Alton Becker, and Kenneth Pike. *Rhetoric: Discovery and Change*. New York: Harcourt, Brace, Jovanovich, 1970.

Major Scholarship in Composition

Bazerman, Charles. *Shaping Written Knowledge: The Genre and Activity of the Experimental Article in Science*. Madison: U of Wisconsin P, 1988.

Berlin, James. *Writing Instruction in Nineteenth-Century American Colleges*. Carbondale: Southern Illinois UP, 1984.

Bosworth, Kris, and Sharon Hamilton, eds. *Collaborative Learning: Underlying Process and Effective Techniques*. San Francisco, CA: Jossey-Bass, 1994.

Carter, Michael. "The Idea of Expertise: An Exploration of Cognitive and Social Dimensions of Writing." *College Composition and Communication* 41 (1990): 265–86.

Connor, Ulla. *Contrastive Rhetoric: Cross-cultural Aspects of Second-Language Writing*. Cambridge: Cambridge UP, 1996.

Crismore, Avon, and Rodney Farnsworth. "Mr. Darwin and His Readers: Exploring Interpersonal Metadiscourse as a Dimension of *Ethos*." *Rhetoric Review* 8 (1989): 91–112.

Crowley, Sharon. *The Methodical Memory: Invention in Current-Traditional Rhetoric.* Carbondale: Southern Illinois UP, 1990.

Flynn, Elizabeth. "Composing as a Woman." *College Composition and Communication* 39 (1988): 423–35.

Gannett, Cinthia. *Gender and the Journal: Diaries and Academic Discourse.* Albany: State U of New York P, 1992.

Gere, Anne, ed. *Roots in the Sawdust: Writing to Learn across the Curriculum.* Urbana, IL: NCTE, 1985.

Harrington, David, et al. " A Critical Survey of Resources for Teaching Rhetorical Invention: A Review Essay." *College English* 40 (1979): 641–61.

Herrington, Anne, and Charles Moran, eds. *Writing, Teaching, and Learning in the Disciplines.* New York: MLA, 1992.

Johnson, Nan. *Nineteenth Century Rhetoric in North America.* Carbondale: Southern Illinois UP, 1991.

Kaplan, Nancy. "Ideology, Technology, and the Future of Writing." In *Evolving Perspectives on Computers and Composition.* Ed. Gail Hawisher and Cynthia Selfe. Urbana, IL: NCTE, 1991, 11–41.

Lauer, Janice. "Issues in Rhetorical Invention." In *Essays on Classical Rhetoric and Modern Discourse.* Ed. Robert Connors, Lisa Ede, and Andrea Lunsford. Carbondale: Southern Illinois UP, 1984, 127–39, 277–80.

Leff, Michael. "In Search of Ariadne's Thread: A Review of the Recent Literature on Rhetorical Theory." *Central States Speech Journal* 29 (1978): 73–91.

Lunsford, Andrea, and Lisa Ede. *Singular Texts/Plural Authors.* Carbondale: Southern Illinois UP, 1990.

Maimon, Elaine, Barbara Nodine, and Finbarr O'Connor, eds. *Thinking, Reasoning, and Writing.* New York: Longman, 1989.

Miller, Carolyn. "Genre as Social Action." *Quarterly Journal of Speech* 70 (1984): 151–67.

Nickerson, Raymond, David Perkins, and Edward Smith. *The Teaching of Thinking.* Hillsdale, NJ: Erlbaum, 1985.

Perelman, Chaim, and Madame Olbrechts-Tyteca. *The New Rhetoric: A Treatise on Argumentation.* Trans. John Wilkinson and Purcell Weaver. Notre Dame, IN: Notre Dame P, 1969.

Perkins, David. *The Mind's Best Work.* Cambridge, MA: Harvard UP, 1981.

Perkins, David, and Gavriel Salomon. "Are Cognitive Skills Context Bound?" *Educational Researcher* 16 (1989): 16–25.

Phelps, Louise, and Janet Emig, eds. *Feminist Principles and Women's Experience in American Composition and Rhetoric.* Pittsburgh, PA: U of Pittsburgh P, 1995.

Sullivan, Patricia. "Taking Control of the Page: Electronic Writing and World Publishing." In *Evolving Perspectives on Computers and Composition.* Ed. Gail Hawisher and Cynthia Selfe. Urbana, IL: NCTE, 1991, 43–6.

Toulmin, Stephen. *The Uses of Argument.* New York: Cambridge UP, 1958.

Young, Richard E. "Invention: A Topographical Survey in Teaching Composition." In *Teaching Composition: Ten Bibliographic Essays.* Ed. Gary Tate. Fort Worth: Texas Christian UP, 1976.

———. "Recent Developments in Rhetorical Invention." In *Teaching Composition:*

Twelve Bibliographic Essays. Ed. Gary Tate. Fort Worth: Texas Christian UP, 1987, 1–38.

Young, Richard E., and Yameng Liu, eds. *Landmark Essays on Rhetorical Invention in Writing*. Davis, CA: Hermagorus P, 1994.

JANICE M. LAUER

L

LEARNING THEORY

Summary

Cognitive psychologists, such as Vygotsky, claim that learning occurs in meaningful, social, collaborative contexts and that language and the construction of meaning are closely associated. Squire notes that because language is the primary agent for thinking, it is used for a myriad of purposes, including classifying, labeling, and constructing ideas; composing, reconstructing, or comprehending them; and relating the new to the known. Language is represented symbolically by reading and writing, and so current research views them as parallel processes that are best developed together (Britton, Smith, Marshall, Wells, Graves, Teale and Sulzby, Goodman).

The anthropomorphic structures that exist in each individual's brain play a large role in how new material is learned and retained. Learning theorists, such as Ausubel, believe that cognitive structures within the brain form a hierarchy of well-organized systems of facts, concepts, and generalizations. The cognitive structure refers to the totality of knowledge that an individual possesses in any subject area, and new knowledge is acquired by linking fresh facts to already-existing structures. Ausubel further stresses that the most important influence upon what a student will learn is what he or she already knows (Novak); therefore, content only becomes meaningful if it is integrated and allowed to become part of the learner's overall cognitive organization. This view might explain why the segmented curricula that exist in many schools today could pose great difficulty for students, and why it is so hard for many of them to think critically in various subject areas.

Ausubel asserts that learning is attained by "subsumption"; that is, from general knowledge to specific information (Novak). This happens both by "integrative reconciliation," where new concepts are linked to existing cognitive structures, and by "progressive differentiation," which results when new knowledge is merged with old as a result of meaningful learning experiences. Some cognitive factors that affect the degree of learning that occurs are developmental readiness, intellectual ability, practice, and the quality of the instructional materials themselves. Learners may acquire new knowledge either gradually or suddenly, depending upon the personal importance of the material and the extent of prior knowledge that already exists within their cognitive networks. Information transfer, then, is possible only if the correct "links" (either the existing cognitive structures or the use of prepared organizers) exist to make the transfer possible (Heinen, Sherman, and Strafford).

Similarly, Rummelhart's schema theory is also formulated upon the importance of prior knowledge. A schema is a guide or a pattern for understanding an event (Woolfolk, 247). Calling schemata "the building blocks of cognition," Rummelhart asserts that all new learning is based upon the foundation that a learner already possesses. Rummelhart and Ortony have stated that schemata are the "key units of the comprehension process" (111), which function as unarticulated theories about the learner's environment. Rummelhart believes that we learn via accretion, or by refining and further developing ideas that we possess about a subject based upon our past experiences with it. For example, it is possible to learn to read in English because we already have schemata for books printed in this language; we know that the book opens from the front and that reading progresses from left to right, and top to bottom. Had we been brought up in a culture with a different schema for reading (Hebrew, for instance, where reading progresses from the back of the book to the front and from right to left), we would encounter more problems in our pursuit of English literacy activities. Rummelhart terms the process by which schemata are naturally invoked and employed without conscious thought "accretion" and believes that this is the state in which learning can most readily occur.

Bruner claims that three systems exist for processing information to construct models of the world: through action, through imagery, and through language (also referred to as the enactive, the iconic, and the symbolic). He observes that the way in which new information is integrated is an important component of problem solving (Bruner, Oliver, and Greenfield) and feels that language provides a means for both representing and transforming an experience (Smith). Furthermore, this constant manipulation of language and the resultant internalization of its metalinguistic foundation allows the student to employ these capacities with increasing skill and malleability. The ability to synthesize new and previously learned material is critical to the development of higher-level thinking strategies which, in turn, require students to integrate critical thinking, analysis, reasoning, and understanding (McGee and Richgels).

According to many cognitive psychologists, then, new learning is based upon prior knowledge, which is utilized to understand new situations; this in turn changes students' prior knowledge structures, and it can later be used to interpret other unfamiliar situations (Andre and Phye).

Reception and Significance in Composition Studies

Because fill-in-the-blank or short-answer types of assignments do not allow for the processing or "integrative reconciliation" that is necessary for legitimate learning to occur, the classroom use of essay questions, which demand reflection and integration, enables students to search through existing knowledge networks and create new knowledge. Feathers asserts that items in one's prior knowledge structures are interconnected, and so thinking about one item frequently leads the learner to consider another. Hence, one may experience the condition where writing about a subject generates new thoughts about the topic and so serves to engender more learning. This use of prior knowledge to create new meaning in literacy related tasks is known as "constructivism" (Spiro, Spivey).

Researchers have investigated new theories concerning how writing should best be taught (Emig; Flower and Hayes; Applebee; Hillocks; Bereiter and Scardamalia) and have concluded that it is imperative that it be addressed in a more comprehensive and integrated manner throughout the curriculum. Yet relatively few teachers employ writing as a means of increasing learning; rather, most administer writing assignments (particularly at the upper levels) as a means of testing student comprehension of materials.

A study of the effects of reading and writing upon critical thinking (conducted by Tierney, Soter, O'Flahavan, and McGinley) suggests that a symbiotic relationship appears to exist between reading and writing that affords students the opportunities to think more evaluatively. They note that "by criss-crossing the terrain of a topic, they [students] appear to achieve multiple perspectives and a more evaluative stance with regard to their own understanding" (168). A similar study conducted by McGinley found that the nature of reasoning and composing changed over time and that as students began composing essays from multiple sources, they worked toward restructuring the material to make it their own. He found that individual reading and writing activities provided students with overlapping but different purposes; reading tended to provide them with new information, while writing helped them to organize what they were thinking. Gillin found that writing *before* reading allowed students to think more critically during the reading process. Other researchers (Applebee, Langer and Applebee) have indicated that writing influences thinking and thus is a viable tool for cultivating learning. Murray notes that "writing is thinking, not thought recorded" (xii); likewise, Flannery O'Connor remarked that "I write because I don't know what I think until I read what I say" (quoted in Murray, 8).

BIBLIOGRAPHY

Primary Texts and Major Scholarship in Composition

Andre, T., and G. Phye. "Cognition, Learning, and Education." In *Cognitive Classroom Learning*. Ed. G. Phye and T. Andre. San Diego, CA: Academic P, 1986, 1–19.

Applebee, Arthur N. "Writing and Reasoning." *Review of Educational Research* 54 (1984): 577–96.

———. *Writing in the Secondary School*. Urbana, IL: NCTE, 1981.

Ausubel, David P. "The Use of Advance Organizers in the Learning and Retention of Meaningful Verbal Material." *Journal of Educational Psychology* 51 (1960): 267–72.

Bereiter, Carl, and Marlene Scardamalia. *The Psychology of Written Composition*. Hillsdale, NJ: Erlbaum, 1987.

Britton, James. "The Course of Cognitive Growth." *American Psychologist* 19 (1964): 1–15.

———. "The Functions of Writing." In *Research on Composing: Points of Departure*. Ed. Charles Cooper and Lee Odell. Urbana, IL: NCTE, 1978, 13–28.

———. *Language and Learning*. London: Penguin, 1970.

———. *Prospect and Retrospect: Selected Essays*. Upper Montclair, NJ: Boynton/Cook, 1982.

Bruner, Jerome, R. Oliver, and P. Greenfield. *Studies in Cognitive Growth*. New York: Wiley, 1966.

Emig, Janet. "Hand, Eye, Brain: Some 'Basics' in the Writing Process." In *Research on Composing: Points of Departure*. Ed. Charles Cooper and Lee Odell. Urbana, IL: NCTE, 1978, 59–71.

———. "Writing as a Mode of Learning." *College Composition and Communication* 28 (1977): 122–27.

Feathers, K. *Infotext*. Markham, Canada: Pippin, 1993.

Flower, Linda, and John R. Hayes. "A Cognitive Process Theory of Writing." *College Composition and Communication* 32 (1981): 365–87.

Gillin, Jeri. "The Effect of Essay Writing Strategies on Critical Thinking in Mixed-Achievement Students." Ph.D. dissertation, U of Massachusetts at Lowell, 1994.

Goodman, Kenneth. "Whole Language Research: Foundations and Development." In *What Research Has to Say about Reading Instruction*. Ed. S. Samuels and A. Farstrup. Newark, DE: International Reading Association, 1992, 46–69.

Graves, Donald. *Investigating Nonfiction*. Portsmouth, NH: Heinemann, 1989.

Heinen, J., T. Sherman, and K. Strafford. "Role of Learning Theory in Educational Psychology." *Psychological Reports* 67 (1990): 763–74.

Hillocks, George. *Research on Written Composition: New Directions for Teaching*. Urbana, IL: NCTE, 1986.

Langer, J., and Arthur Applebee. *How Writing Shapes Thinking*. NCTE Research Report #22. Urbana, IL: NCTE, 1987.

Marshall, J. "The Effects of Writing on Students' Understanding of Literary Text." *Research in the Teaching of English* 21 (1987): 31–63.

McGee, L., and D. Richgels. "Learning from Text Using Reading and Writing." In *Reading and Writing Together: New Perspectives for the Classroom*. Ed. Timothy Shanahan, Norwood, MA: Christopher Gordon, 1990, 145–68.

McGinley, W. "The Role of Reading and Writing while Composing from Sources." *Reading Research Quarterly* 27 (1992): 227–247.

Murray, Donald. *Shoptalk: Learning to Write with Writers*. Portsmouth, NH: Boynton/Cook, 1990.

Novak, John D. A *Theory of Education*. Ithaca, NY: Cornell UP, 1977.

Rummelhart, D. "Schemata: The Building Blocks of Cognition." In *Theoretical Issues in Reading Comprehension.* Ed. R. J. Spiro, B. C. Bruce, and W. F. Fuller. Hillsdale, NJ: Erlbaum, 1980, 35–58.

Rummelhart, D. E. and A. Ortony. "The Representation of Knowledge in Memory." In *Schooling and the Acquisition of Knowledge.* Ed. R. C. Anderson and R. J. Spiro. Hillsdale, NJ: Erlbaum, 1977, 99–136.

Smith, M. "Bruner on Writing." *College Composition and Communication* 28 (1977): 129–32.

Spiro, R. "Constructive Processes in Prose Recall." In *Theoretical Issues in Reading Comprehension.* Ed. R. J. Spiro, B. C. Bruce, and W. F. Fuller. Hillsdale, NJ: Erlbaum, 1980, 245–78.

Spivey, Nancy. "Construing Constructivism." *Poetics* 16 (1987): 169–92.

Squire, James. "Composing and Comprehending: Two Sides of the Same Basic Process." *Language Arts* 60 (1983): 581–89.

Teal, W., and E. Sulzby. "Emergent Literacy: New Perspectives." *Emerging Literacy: Young Children Learn to Read and Write.* Ed. S. Morrow and L. Morrow. Newark, DE: International Reading Association, 1989, 1–15.

Tierney, Robert, et al. "The Effects of Reading and Writing upon Thinking Critically." *Reading Research Quarterly* 24 (1989): 134–73.

Vygotsky, Lev. *Thought and Language.* Cambridge, MA: MIT P, 1962.

Wells, M. "The Roots of Literacy." *Psychology Today* 22 (1988): 20–22.

Woolfolk, A. *Educational Psychology.* Englewood Cliffs, NJ: Prentice-Hall, 1987.

JERI GILLIN

LESBIAN AND GAY STUDIES/QUEER THEORY

Summary

Gay and lesbian studies, like the traditional freshman composition course, began (and begins) in personal experience. The act of claiming one's sexual identity—of understanding, affirming, articulating, and proclaiming oneself as gay, lesbian, bisexual or transgendered—results (for many) in a new perspective on one's social world. Community boundaries are discovered, strengthened, or minimized as the individual explores new identities and roles. The field of lesbian and gay studies builds on this perceptual difference, establishing theoretical frameworks grounded in such experiences.

From this transformative experience come perspectives that give rise to larger abstract patterns: the personal is not only political, but theoretical. Eve Kosofsky Sedgwick points to the central importance of the closest and the self-definitional act of coming out in the experience of gay men and lesbians. Experienced variously as a loss, discovery, or shift of identity, this moment (or process) becomes, through reflection and analysis, a framework for broader social analysis.

In the political arena, such a personal perspective broadens to a communal one, depending on the individual's identification with various explicit or implicit communities and the relation of those communities with others across various structures of power. Such writers as Audre Lorde, Cherríe Moraga, and Gloria Anzaldúa link sexual identity with race, class, and gender as sites of oppression and identity. The impact of AIDS on the gay communities has opened another interpretive nexus for political and cultural analysis.

As thinking by lesbians and gay men has coalesced into a body of ideas that can be termed ''lesbian/gay theory,'' several issues have proven crucial. The central theoretical debate in lesbian and gay studies has been defined by the essentialist and the constructionist viewpoints. Essentialists identify a fundamental core in sexual identity (though not necessarily a biologically determined one), a continuity of identity and difference across historical cultures. Constructionists, following Michel Foucault, argue that all such sexual identities are socially constructed and resist a rigid dichotomy that defines homosexuality and heterosexuality as essential opposites. Most recently, a number of challenges to traditional thinking about sexual identity have constituted an approach termed ''queer theory.''

The use of the word ''queer'' to describe this emergent body of thinking can connote several distinct emphases: one may intend to reclaim a historically hurtful word; one may intend to broadly include people who may not self-identify as *gay* or *lesbian* (most notably, *bisexual* or *transgendered* persons); one may be pursuing a theoretical agenda directed away from the predominantly essentialist view that has characterized more traditional lesbian and gay studies. In this third sense, *queer* is assertively resistant to definition: ''It is not simply that queer has yet to solidify and take on a more consistent profile, but rather that its definitional indeterminacy, its elasticity, is one of its constituent characteristics'' (Jagose, 1).

The critical projects of queer theorists are diverse (even contradictory), often arising from substantially different assumptions about sexuality, gender, language and identity. Historian John D'Emilio analyzes the social context of the emergence of ''modern homosexuality.'' Judith Butler points to the effects of identity categories in limiting personal identity. Diana Fuss traces the impact of the ''outsider'' position in which lesbians and gay men have traditionally been positioned: ''Interrogating the position of 'outsiderness' is where much recent lesbian and gay theory begins, implicitly if not always directly raising the questions of the complicated processes by which sexual borders are constructed, sexual identities assigned, and sexual politics formulated'' (2). These different ways of talking about shifting identities have clear parallels to work in composition studies on the relation of multiple voices and discourse communities.

Reception and Significance in Composition Studies

These different facets of lesbian and gay thinking have affected the concerns of composition studies in very different ways. Harriet Malinowitz frames the common challenge this way: ''Which of our theories of writing *don't* explode when we consider their ramifications for gay and lesbian writers?'' (39).

Given the centrality of the coming-out experience, it is not surprising to see a body of work examining personal experiences in the contexts of composition studies. Analyzing the lives of teachers and students on both sides of the closet door illuminates both sexual identity and the field of composition. Work by

Harriet Malinowitz, Sarah-Hope Parmeter and Irene Reti, and Mary Elliot reveals how the insights of personal, practical, and theoretical reflection offer valuable perspectives on the lives of gay men and lesbians in the composition classroom.

Lesbian and gay political theory has also been useful in articulating the dimensions of personal experience. Perhaps even more dramatic has been the effect of such analyses of gay/lesbian issues on the practices of composition classes. Such issues as same-sex marriage or AIDS are now regularly included in textbooks and increasingly used in composition courses, at varying levels of political and theoretical sophistication; hard on the heels of the inclusion of such topics have come considerations of the dynamics of homophobia in the classroom, including computer-mediated classroom settings.

The most notable work to date linking lesbian and gay studies to composition studies is Harriet Malinowitz's *Textual Orientations*, linking a theoretical application of a number of strands of composition theory to the experiences of lesbian and gay students with an ethnographic analysis of a queer-centered composition course. By mapping out the congruences of composition theory and the experience of lesbian and gay people, Malinowitz suggests many avenues for future study; by tracing the implications of these congruences in the literacy development of the students in her courses, she illuminates the rich complexities of identity, language, and writing.

Beyond an expanded awareness of the particular experiences of lesbian, gay, bisexual, and transgendered students and teachers and a greater inclusiveness of lesbian and gay topics in composition textbooks and courses, neither lesbian and gay studies nor queer theory has yet had a noticeable influence on composition studies as a whole. Such awareness and inclusiveness should not be minimized, of course; the impact of these changes for queer folk engaged in the study of composition has been dramatic. As queer theory continues to pose challenges to our accepted notions of identity, gender, and language, composition studies may prove a fruitful ground for exploration and inquiry.

BIBLIOGRAPHY

Primary Texts

Anzaldúa, Gloria. *Borderlands/La Frontera: The New Mestiza*. San Francisco, CA: Aunt Lute Books, 1987.

Butler, Judith. *Gender Trouble: Feminism and the Subversion of Identity*. New York: Routledge, 1990.

D'Emilio, John. *Sexual Politics, Sexual Communities: The Making of a Homosexual Minority in the United States, 1940–1970*. Chicago: U of Chicago P, 1983.

Foucault, Michel. *The History of Sexuality*. New York: Vintage, 1980.

Fuss, Diana, ed. *Inside/Out: Lesbian Theories, Gay Theories*. New York: Routledge, 1991.

Jagose, Annamarie. *Queer Theory: An Introduction*. New York: New York UP, 1996.

Lorde, Audre. *Sister Outsider*. Freedom, CA: Crossing P, 1984.

Moraga, Cherrié, and Gloria Anzaldúa, eds. *This Bridge Called My Back: Writings by Radical Women of Color*. New York: Kitchen Table/Women of Color P, 1984.

Sedgwick, Eve Kosofsky. *Epistemology of the Closet*. Berkeley: U of California P, 1990.

Major Scholarship in Composition

Elliot, Mary. "Coming out in the Classroom: A Return to the Hard Place." *College English* 58 (1996): 693–708.

Malinowitz, Harriet. *Textual Orientations: Lesbian and Gay Students and the Making of Discourse Communities*. Portsmouth, NH: Boynton/Cook, 1995.

Parmeter, Sarah-Hope, and Irene Reti, eds. *The Lesbian in Front of the Classroom: Writings by Lesbian Teachers*. Santa Cruz, CA: HerBooks, 1988.

RANDAL WOODLAND

LITERACY-ORALITY THEORIES

Summary

In the 1980s in composition studies there were two different controversies over literacy. One was over Hirsch's "cultural literacy." The other was the debate concerning literacy-orality theory, also known as the great leap theory, the great divide theory, and the autonomous model, which was a perspective with roots, proponents, and critics in several disciplines in the humanities and social sciences. Familiarity with this controversy is assumed by serious scholars in composition.

According to Brandt (in the 1996 *Encyclopedia of Rhetoric and Composition*), the term *literacy* has come to indicate "the ways that individual acts of writing are connected to larger cultural, historical, and, social and political systems" (392). This definition derives in large part from the literacy-orality debate, since its arguments were an important part of the shift from the cognitive perspective of the 1970s and early 1980s, which saw writing as individual problem solving, to the social view predominant in the late 1980s and 1990s.

In great leap theories, literacy is not just the encoding and decoding of sound and meaning in and from graphic forms, but also includes the binary opposite of orality. Strong versions assert that simply reading and writing with a Greek-derived alphabet actually causes fundamental advances—great developmental leaps—in human cognition. These cognitive leaps then bring about alterations not only in the consciousness of individuals, but also in cultures. Literacy, in this view, marks the great divide between advanced, complex cultures and traditional ones. Literacy is seen as autonomous and acontextual, existing prior to and apart from culture.

Great leap models typically present orality and literacy as either a strict dichotomy or a single continuum, which contrasts the modes of speech, composition, behavior, and thought of orality with those of literacy. The prototype of an oral culture is held to be Havelock's description of preliterate Greece. The prototype of literacy is advanced academic literacy in modern, industrialized Western countries—that is, reading extended texts and producing theoretical expository prose.

According to Havelock in *Preface to Plato*, in preliterate Greece the knowledge and values necessary for the survival of the culture were transmitted through poetry. The content was tradition, the language formulaic. Using familiar formulas, the poet constructed the poem itself in a public oral performance wherein both bard and audience entered into an almost trance-like, or "mimetic," state, which prevented the bard from introducing new ideas and the audience from questioning or analyzing. At about the time of Plato, Havelock claims, literacy had become so internalized that the mental "energy" previously needed for the memorization of the poetry was released for other sorts of cognitive activity. With this new energy, literate persons began to compare texts and note inconsistencies, synthesize conflicting opinions, and question the authority of the oral tradition. As Havelock explains it, Plato's dialectic, a product of literacy, was a way of breaking the mimetic spell and forcing the audience to question and analyze.

Goody and Watt assert that Aristotle and the next generation of Greek thinkers used these literate modes of thought to develop systematized abstract thinking, such as the syllogism, the categories, and the taxonomies in various fields of study. Later, according to Ong, the technology of print made literacy accessible to more people and released more mental energy for abstract thinking in many new fields. Western culture underwent a recapitulation and an extension of the great leap. The climax, Olson says, came when British thinkers like John Locke learned to use the essay to explore abstract problems and to create new theoretical knowledge.

According to Ong in *Orality and Literacy*, in primary oral cultures perception is holistic; therefore, both thought and language are additive, aggregative, redundant, conservative, empathetic, participatory, and situational (37–50). In literate cultures, people see parts and relationships; thus thought and language are subordinative, analytic, exploratory, objective, distanced, and abstract (37–50). The oral personality, Ong claims, is "more communal and externalized, and less introspective" than the literate personality (69). In oral cultures, "Knowing means achieving close, empathetic, communal identification with the known, 'getting with it,' " Ong says (45–46): participation, not analysis, is the basis of knowledge in oral cultures, according to Ong ("Literacy," 4).

Reception and Significance in Composition Studies

Some compositionists, including Ong ("Literacy"), have argued that this depiction of orality is useful in describing the thought patterns and the language, particularly the written language, of first-year students, basic writers, and minorities in American colleges and universities. The most controversial articulation of this notion came in 1983 when Farrell used the great leap theory to recommend teaching "the full deployment" of the verb *to be*, which Farrell regards as a literate form, in order to help African-American students advance academically.

But disagreement came from those in composition who were reading anthropological and sociolinguistic studies that called into question certain propositions of great leap theories. Some of this research is summarized in Daniell ("Against the Great Leap") and in Rose ("Narrowing"); some is collected in volumes edited by Frawley, by Tannen, and by Kintgen, Kroll, and Rose. For example, Heath casts doubt on Ong's characterization of oral and written language by showing that oral language can have far more complex syntax than literate language with the same message, speaker, and audience. Scribner and Cole use evidence from their study of multiple literacies among the Vai people of northern Africa to argue that cognitive properties typically associated with literacy are qualities imparted by Western schooling, not by literacy per se. Freire theorizes the relationship of political and economic oppression in his native Brazil and his literacy pedagogy. These and similar works led many in composition studies to see literacy not as the cause of certain social and cultural conditions, but rather as the result.

The immediate response to Farrell was that his claims are logically untenable and his pedagogy is damaging. Other critics charge the great leap theory with ethnocentrism. Giving substance to this criticism is Ong's dismissal of writing systems such as "cuneiform, Chinese characters, Mayan script, and the Japanese syllabary, and so forth" (*Orality* 3). Still others deconstruct Ong's assertion that his term "oral" is "less invidious and more positive" than terms formerly applied to traditional societies like "savage," "primitive," and "inferior" (*Orality* 174–75). Feminists point to Ong's essentialist and explicit association of orality with stereotypical female traits, such as emotion, immediacy, and practicality (Ong, *Interfaces* 22–29). Marxists see changes in education in general and in writing instruction in particular in the nineteenth century not as part of the shift from orality to literacy, as Ong claims ("Literacy"), but as part of the shift from an agricultural economy to industrial capitalism.

Some critics point out that characteristics in Ong's portrayal of orality have typically appeared in academic research as qualities associated with the language, thought, and behavior of relatively powerless groups—women, blacks, other ethnic minorities, and the poor. Still others criticize the great leap theory for its assumption of an isomorphic relationship between thought and language and for its application of historical, cultural, and literary theories to actual individuals and groups.

The work used to refute great leap models of literacy argues that literacy is not a thing in itself, but is rather both multiple and highly contextual. By focusing on specific contexts, a number of studies in the 1980s and 1990s offered insights into various literate practices but rarely made theoretical statements that claim to be valid for literate persons or literate cultures in general. Interestingly, many of these studies are by women, and many of their subjects are women. Taking for granted Marxist and feminist critiques of language and culture, the researchers distrust narratives in which one group becomes powerful because of its adoption of a supposedly neutral technology.

One of the earliest of these studies was Radway's examination of reading by middle-class women. Subsequent work by Brodkey, Horsman, and Gere open windows into the literacy—and lives—of working-class women. Brandt's interviews with adults of various ages demonstrate the ambiguities and poignancies of acquiring and using literacy in America in this century. Other research examines the relations of literacy and religion or spirituality (Moss; Fishman; Daniell, "Composing"). This work marks the move of composition studies away from a narrow focus on classroom literacy.

Recent essays by Killingsworth and by Sreberny-Mohammadi point to what may be the real value of literacy-orality theory. Both essays demonstrate that using this theory to examine new technologies and various media can enrich and complicate our understanding of both electronic communication and the relationship of literate and oral language forms. Finally, Killingsworth situates orality and literacy and writing pedagogy against capitalism, reconceptualizing theories of composing: "Both [Romantic and social-epistemic rhetorics] are essentially reassertions of the politics of orality against the demands of an extreme literate culture" (37).

BIBLIOGRAPHY

Primary Texts

Frawley, William, ed. *Linguistics and Literacy*. New York: Plenum, 1982.

Freire, Paulo. *Pedagogy of the Oppressed*. Trans. Myra Bergman Ramos. New York: Seabury, 1970.

Goody, Jack, and Ian Watt. "The Consequences of Literacy." *Comparative Studies in Society and History* 5 (1963): 304–45.

Havelock, Eric. *Preface to Plato*. Cambridge, MA: Harvard UP, 1963.

Heath, Shirley Brice. "Protean Shapes in Literacy Events: Ever-Shifting Oral and Literate Traditions." In *Spoken and Written Language*. Ed. Deborah Tannen. Norwood, NJ: Ablex, 1982, 91–117.

Kintgen, Eugene R., Barry Kroll, and Mike Rose, eds. *Perspectives on Literacy*. Carbondale: Southern Illinois UP, 1988.

Olson, David R. "From Utterance to Text: The Bias of Language in Speech and Writing." *Harvard Educational Review* 47 (1977): 257–81.

Ong, Walter J., Jr., *Interfaces of the Word*. Ithaca, NY: Cornell UP, 1977.

———. "Literacy and Orality." *ADE Bulletin* 58 (1978): 1–7.

———. *Orality and Literacy*. London: Methuen, 1982.

Scribner, Sylvia, and Michael Cole. *The Psychology of Literacy*. Cambridge, MA: Harvard UP, 1981.

Tannen, Deborah, ed. *Spoken and Written Language*. Norwood, NJ: Ablex, 1982.

Major Scholarship in Composition

Brodkey, Linda. "On the Subject of Class and Gender in 'The Literacy Letters.' " *College English* 51 (1989): 125–41.

Brandt, Deborah. "Literacy." In *Encyclopedia of Rhetoric and Composition*. Ed. Theresa Enos. New York: Garland, 1996, 392–394.

———. "Remembering Writing, Remembering Reading." *College Composition and Communication* 45 (1994): 459–79.

Daniell, Beth. "Against the Great Leap Theory of Literacy." *Pre/Text* 7 (1986): 181–93.

———. "Composing (as) Power." *College Composition and Communication* 45 (1994): 238–46.

Farrell, Thomas J. "IQ and Standard English." *College Composition and Communication* 34 (1983): 470–84.

Fishman, Andrea. *Amish Literacy*. Portsmouth, NH: Heinemann, 1988.

Gere, Anne Ruggles. "Kitchen Tables and Rented Rooms: The Extracurriculum of Composition." *College Composition and Communication* 45 (1994): 75–91.

Hirsch, E. D., Jr. *Cultural Literacy*. Boston: Houghton, 1987.

Horsman, Jennifer. *Something in My Mind Besides the Everyday: Women and Literacy*. Toronto, Canada: Women's P, 1990.

Killingsworth, Jimmie. "Product and Process, Literacy and Orality: An Essay on Composition and Culture." *College Composition and Communication* 44 (1993): 26–39.

Moss, Beverly J. "Creating a Community: Literacy in African-American Churches." *Literacy Across Communities*. Ed. Beverly J. Moss. Creskill, NJ: Hampton P, 1994, 147–78.

Radway, Janice A. *Reading the Romance*. Chapel Hill: U of North Carolina P, 1984.

Rose, Mike. "Narrowing the Mind and Page: Remedial Writers and Cognitive Reductionism." *College Composition and Communication* 39 (1988): 267–302.

Sreberny-Mohammadi, Annabelle. "Media Integration in the Third World: An Ongian Perspective." In *Media, Consciousness, and Culture*. Ed. Bruce E. Gronbeck, Thomas J. Farrell, and Paul A. Soukup. Newbury Park, CA: Sage, 1991, 133–46.

BETH DANIELL

M

MARXIST AND NEO-MARXIST THEORIES

Summary

"The philosophers have only *interpreted* the world, in various ways; the point, however, is to *change* it" (Tucker, 145). So claims Marx in his eleventh thesis on Feuerbach. Marxism aims to change the world by overcoming the alienation of men and women from their own productive capabilities. This alienation and its conquest are central themes of Marx's *Economic and Philosophic Manuscripts of 1844*. Marx believed that human beings produce both themselves and the world surrounding them: "The *entire so-called history of the world*," he wrote, "is nothing but the begetting of man through human labour, nothing but the coming-to-be of nature for man" (Tucker, 92). Under a capitalist economy, however, human beings grow increasingly alienated from their productive powers. The relationship between worker and capitalist is an exploitative one: the worker, lacking access to the means of production, must sell her labor power to another to survive; the capitalist, in turn, hires the worker to profit from the labor she performs beyond that required to sustain herself.

The alienating powers of capitalism also appear in the structure of commodity exchange, which Marx examines in the first volume of *Capital*. Though there are "many different kinds of useful labour" (Tucker, 308), Marx advances, these many kinds become abstracted and homogenized in order to facilitate the exchange of commodities. Abstracted and homogenized, labor becomes objectified in the commodity; the commodity, thus objectified, then seems to take on a life of its own. The commodity form alienates people from their own labor and from their relationships with one another; "a definite social relation between men," Marx claims, "assumes . . . the fantastic form of a relation between things" (Tucker 321). Marx's *Capital* is, then, a critique of the situation in which human beings' "own social action takes the form of the action of objects, which rule the producers instead of being ruled by them" (Tucker 323). If we doubt that this happens, we need only to look to the stock market: "A fluctuation on the stock exchange," as Terry Eagleton notes, "can mean unemployment for thousands" (*Ideology* 85).

To understand how and why human beings remain alienated, Marxism engages in the critique of ideologies, which is to say, the examination of the connections between our feelings, ideas, and beliefs and the maintenance and reproduction of existing social relations. Following Marx's own description in the Preface to *A Contribution to the Critique of Political Economy*, Marx's understanding of ideology has often been explained (indeed, caricaturized) in terms of "base" and "superstructure." According to this view, human beings remain alienated because a "legal and political superstructure" and corresponding "forms of social consciousness" grow out of, and serve to legitimate, existing means of economic production (quoted in Eagleton, *Ideology* 80). In subsequent Marxist theorizing about ideology, the works of Antonio Gramsci and of Louis Althusser are arguably the most important. Gramsci rejects the metaphor of a material "base" determining an ideological "superstructure": "At least in the case of the most advanced States," he writes, " 'civil society' has become a very complex structure and one which is resistant to the catastrophic 'incursions' of the immediate economic element" (235). Gramsci's work is most notable for its examination of "hegemony"—the ways in which the ruling powers obtain and maintain day-to-day, lived "consent" through the mechanisms of "civil society" (families, schools, media, churches, etc.), as well as the ways in which such consent might be challenged. Althusser extends Gramsci's analysis of "civil society" by examining the roles that different "Ideological State Apparatuses" play in the reproduction of labor power (150). For Althusser, ideology "represents the imaginary relationship of individuals to their real conditions of existence" (162). Though they feel themselves to be freely acting subjects, that is, Althusser claims that *"individuals are always-already subjects"* (176), which means that they are always-already "subjected" into subject positions generated by the need to reproduce the conditions of production (182).

Other figures informed by the Marxist tradition and important to composition include Mikhail Bakhtin, whose dialogic theory appears in *Marxism and the Philosophy of Language* (published under the name of V. N. Volosinov) and elsewhere; Raymond Williams, whose work has played a seminal role in the development of cultural studies; and Jürgen Habermas, whose writings argue for the creation of consensus apart from relations of domination.

Reception and Significance in Composition Studies

Because Marxism's "terminology is not a neutral 'preparation for action' but 'inducement to action,' " it is, Kenneth Burke claims, "unsleepingly rhetorical''; because much of its persuasiveness depends on the "insistence that it is purely a science," however, Burke observes that "the Marxist persuasion is usually advanced in the name of no-rhetoric" (101–2). While traditional Marxism dismisses the rhetorical as mere inducement to false consciousness, other thinkers within the Marxist heritage have argued that Marxism suffers when it dismisses rhetoric. Frank Lentricchia, for instance, praises Burke for his "lonely American performance of 'Western Marxism' " (23) and for his emphasis on the role of the rhetorical within Marxism itself. Burke, Lentricchia claims, "was doing Gramsci's work before anyone but Gramsci (and his censors) could read what would be called the *Prison Notebooks*" (37); the "political work of the hegemonic, as well as that of a would-be counter-hegemonic culture," Lentricchia continues, "Burke saw (as Marx did not) as most effectively carried through at the level of a culture's various verbal and nonverbal languages" (24). Complementing Lentricchia's call for a rhetorically aware Marxism is Terry Eagleton's argument for rhetoric as an alternative to literary studies; Eagleton advocates the former because it sees "speaking and writing . . . as forms of *activity* inseparable from the wider social relations between writers and readers, orators and audiences, and as largely unintelligible outside the social purposes and conditions in which they [are] embedded" (*Literary Theory* 206).

Marxism's impact on composition appears most directly when composition instructors consider the ways in which their work either reproduces or challenges class and related inequalities. This issue has particular relevance for composition, which often serves a gatekeeping and indoctrinating role within the academy. The work of the Brazilian Marxist educator Paulo Freire has proven influential in such considerations, as has that of his American followers, Henry Giroux and Ira Shor. Traditional pedagogy's emphasis on memorization and repetition, Freire claims, presents knowledge as if it were timeless rather than historically and socially situated; by thus denying men's and women's roles in the creation of knowledge through interaction with the world, Freire continues, traditional pedagogy disempowers students by denying them an awareness of their ability to transform the world. Freire offers "problem-posing" education as an alternative; it aims to awaken students to their potentiality as historical agents and to facilitate a critical awareness of students' own historical and social situations. Two lines of politically oriented composition theory, Bruce Herzberg claims, have developed in the United States from Freire's example: the first, Herzberg writes, encourages "students to reflect upon their own experience . . . to see how their attitudes and knowledge have been shaped by unexamined assumptions"; the second, Herzberg continues, "attempt[s] to demystify the conventions of academic discourse" so that they are available for student use and critique (114–15). While either line risks merely reproducing existing relations by incorporating the student into the university, the "goal," Herzberg concludes, "is to move . . . to a more general awareness for students that knowledge is made by groups for their own purposes." Elsewhere, Greg Myers and John Trimbur offer important Marxian critiques of collaborative learning.

Other compositionists have drawn on Marxist theory to examine the ways in which writing instruction itself reproduces existing social relations. Richard Ohmann, for instance, has examined the ways in which writing textbooks alienate students by regarding them as ahistorical, isolated individuals. Because they elide ideology, Ohmann contends, such textbooks offer an impoverished conception of argument. "I don't deny," he writes,

that rational argument plays a role in changing minds; obviously it does. But to understand how it does, and within what limits, one must surely consider how the ideas people have relate to the ideas they *need* to have, not because of logic but because of their material and social circumstances. (158)

James Berlin extends Ohmann's critique by analyzing the different ideological work performed by cognitive, expressionistic, and social-epistemic rhetorics. Both cognitive and expressionistic rhetorics, he claims, promote "discursive practices that are compatible with dominant economic, social, and political formations" (478): the former, though offering itself as ideologically free science, participates in the "reification of technocratic science characteristic of late capitalism" (484) through its self-valorizing claims to objectivity and its unreflective promotion of problem-solving and goal-directed skills; the latter, though offering itself as an ideologically invested critique, perpetuates the status quo through the distrust of collective resistance resulting from its romantic individualism. Berlin advocates social-epistemic rhetoric, which, he argues, "supports economic, social, political, and cultural democracy" by viewing rhetoric as "a political act involving a dialectical interaction engaging the material, the social, and the individual writer, with language as the agency of mediation" (488–89). More recently, Susan Miller has critiqued composition's privileging of "process"; quoting Michael Apple, Miller writes that process-oriented curricula "require students to see language, and all reality, as a social construction, without also teaching them how 'to inquire as to *why* a particular form of social collectivity exists, *how* it is maintained, and *who* benefits from it' " (8). Though distancing itself from Ohmann's "traditional Marxism" (53), Miller's account joins post-Althusserian considerations of subjectivity with feminist and post-structuralist theories to examine the ways in which composition and literature reproduce themselves, along with those who teach and study them, within the academy.

BIBLIOGRAPHY

Primary Texts

Althusser, Louis. *Lenin and Philosophy and Other Essays*. New York: Monthly Review, 1971.
Eagleton, Terry. *Ideology: An Introduction*. New York: Verso, 1991.
——. *Literary Theory: An Introduction*. Oxford, UK: Blackwell, 1983.
Gramsci, Antonio. *Selections from the Prison Notebooks*. Ed. and trans. Quintin Hoare and Geoffrey Nowell Smith. New York: International, 1971.

Habermas, Jürgen. *The Theory of Communicative Action, Volume 1: Reason and the Rationalization of Society*. Boston: Beacon P, 1984.

Tucker, Robert C. *The Marx-Engels Reader*. Ed. Robert C. Tucker. 2nd ed. New York: Norton, 1978.

Volosinov, V. N. *Marxism and the Philosophy of Language*. New York: Seminar, 1973.

Williams, Raymond. *Marxism and Literature*. New York: Oxford, 1977.

Major Scholarship in Composition

Berlin, James. "Rhetoric and Ideology in the Writing Class." *College English* 50 (1988): 477–94.

Bullock, Richard, and John Trimbur, eds. *The Politics of Writing Instruction: Postsecondary*. Portsmouth, NH: Heinemann, 1991.

Burke, Kenneth. *A Rhetoric of Motives*. New York: Prentice-Hall, 1950.

Freire, Paulo. *Pedagogy of the Oppressed*. New York: Continuum, 1989.

Giroux, Henry. *Theory and Resistance in Education: A Pedagogy for the Opposition*. South Hadley, MA: Bergin, 1983.

Herzberg, Bruce. "Composition and the Politics of the Curriculum." In *The Politics of Writing Instruction*. Ed. Richard Bullock and John Trimbur. Portsmouth, NH: Heinemann, 1991, 97–118.

Lentricchia, Frank. *Criticism and Social Change*. Chicago: U of Chicago P, 1963.

Miller, Susan. *Textual Carnivals: The Politics of Composition*. Carbondale and Edwardsville: Southern Illinois UP, 1991.

Myers, Greg. "Reality, Consensus, and Reform in the Rhetoric of Composition Teaching." *College English* 48 (1986): 154–74.

Ohmann, Richard. *English in America*. New York: Oxford UP, 1976.

Shor, Ira. *Critical Teaching and Everyday Life*. Chicago: U of Chicago P, 1987.

Trimbur, John. "Consensus and Difference in Collaborative Learning." *College English* 51 (1989): 602–16.

JOHN MADRITCH

MEASUREMENT AND EDUCATIONAL ASSESSMENT THEORY

Summary

This entry provides a history of the development of writing assessment and the theoretical impact of educational measurement theory upon the practices used to assess student writing. Early influences on assessing writing outside a classroom context came mostly from classical test theory based upon logical positivism, which supported scientific and educational theory and practice throughout most of the twentieth century. The epistemological and theoretical influences of positivism have begun to wane during the last two decades, and more socially based notions of reality have begun to influence measurement theory, fostering the development of alternative assessment practices like authentic and performative educational assessment. Authentic assessment refers to tasks that represent a more real sense of what comprises academic achievement or skill (Wiggins). Performative assessment is often equated with authentic assessment, though both types of assessment refer to how well a student can exhibit skill in a specific area (see Black, Helton, and Sommers for definitions and discussions of the two terms). More recent developments in writing assessment have been influenced by a socially constructed notion of reality that includes the importance of individual context and personal involvement. These newer assessment practices are having an important impact on the very notion of what makes an assessment valid (Moss, "Shifting Conceptions"). This entry traces both sets of influences in trying to account for current practice in writing assessment. For purposes of clarity, I label these different theoretical influences Theory #1 and Theory #2. The numbers indicate their chronology.

Theory #1

Writing assessment initially evolved from entrance examinations instituted by Harvard and other Ivy League schools in the late 1800s. In the early twentieth century, the College Entrance Examination Board (CEEB) was formed so that students could take one exam approved by several institutions and have it count toward entrance for a number of schools connected to the board. Before that, students had to take a specific examination for each school. These early standardized exams were influenced during the 1920s by advances in educational testing, brought on by the need to classify recruits for World War I, and were used to formalize writing assessment under the auspices of such testing institutions as the CEEB and the Educational Testing Service (ETS). The development of writing assessment procedures, as we now know them, is the result of decades of research by the Test Development Staff at ETS. Building upon research started in the 1920s (Hopkins and others), the researchers at ETS systematically established the procedures for writing assessment (see Godshalk, Swineford, and Coffman for a review of this literature).

These efforts were undertaken under the auspices of classical test theory, which dictates that a measurement instrument has to be both valid and reliable. In the psychometric sense, validity designates the degree to which a test measures what it purports to measure, and reliability pertains to how consistent a test is. In order for a test to be valid, it must also be reliable: "Reliability is a necessary but not a sufficient condition for validity" (Cherry and Meyer, 110). The history of writing assessment has been predicated upon the ability to create procedures within which independent raters could agree consistently enough (interrater reliability) to make the procedures statistically viable and theoretically supportable. Classical test theory is based on a positivist philosophy, which contends "that there exists a reality *out there*, driven by immutable natural laws" (Guba, 19). Within the positivist foundation of classical test theory, it is possible to isolate a particular human ability and measure it. Positivist epistemology assumes that student ability in writing, as in anything else, is a fixed, consistent, and acontextual human trait. Our ability to measure such a trait needs to recognize these consistencies and could be built upon psychometrics, a statistical apparatus devised for use in the social sciences. Mathematics, as in physics, was conceived as the "language" of an empirical methodology that would assist in the discovery of fundamental laws governing behavior. Guba labels this science "context free" because the laws revealed by this type of scientific method are held to be independent of the observer and the particular events in which they were discovered.

The biggest stumbling block in the creation of direct assessment procedures for writing (those that included writing) was the inconsistency of raters' judgments about the same papers. As late as 1961, Diederich, French, and Carlton examined the scoring of 300 papers by 53 raters on a nine-point scale. Ninety-four percent of the papers received at least seven different scores. Because procedures involving the drafting and reading of student writing were not statistically or theoretically viable, given the need for reliability, multiple-choice tests of grammar, usage and mechanics (labeled indirect tests of writing because they contain no actual writing) flourished during the 1950s, 1960s and 1970s. The earliest and most persistent debate in writing assessment revolved around whether to use indirect measures of writing, which consisted of questions on grammar or usage, or direct tests, which included the reading and scoring of student writing. These "indirect" measures continue to be used to make important decisions about student writers. A survey of writing placement practices (Huot, "A Survey") undertaken in the 1990s revealed that half of the reporting institutions still used some indirect measure to place students into first-year writing courses. The debate about direct or indirect tests of writing was often characterized as being between testers and teachers, when in reality it was within the measurement community itself, since attaining an acceptable level of scoring consistency (interrater reliability) was the aim of both direct and indirect measures. In the composition community, reliability has been supported on practical and ethical grounds by those who see it as a means of ensuring fairness to students: "Reliability is a simple way of talking about fairness to test takers, and if we are not interested in fairness, we have no business giving tests or using test results" (White, "Holistic Scoring" 93).

A common assumption once prevalent in composition studies was that writing assessment was a practice without a theory (Gere). Faigley, Cherry, Jolliffe and Skinner elaborate this view by explaining that the pressing need to develop writing assessment procedures outstrips our ability to develop a theoretical basis for them. The theoretical foundation of writing assessment is apparent in its continuing emphasis on ensuring reliable methods for scoring student writing. Simply, interrater reliability has dominated writing assessment literature (Huot, "A Review"). It is clear from even a cursory reflection on the history of direct writing assessment that not only were current methods for evaluation created within an established theoretical framework, but, moreover, critical issues like reliability and validity exist and were defined within the context of classical test theory.

To be a viable assessment option within classical test theory, writing assessment had to meet the same requirements expected of standardized tests. Conventional writing assessment's emphasis on uniformity and test-type conditions is a product of a testing theory, which assumes that individual matters of context and rhetoric are to be overcome in favor of producing a true measure of student ability, which can only be arrived at through technical and statistical rigor. Most of the procedures and improvements in writing assessment have had as their goals either the reliability of the scoring or that of the instrument itself. For example, writing assessment requires the development of writing prompts that are similar in difficulty and suitability for the testing population. Some early writing assessment programs produced great discrepancies in scores between one year and another because the writing tasks were of such variable difficulty (Hoetker). Procedures for designing appropriate writing prompts often involve pilot testing and other measures (Ruth and Murphy) to ensure that students will perform fairly consistently on writing tasks used as part of the same, or similar, programs across different locations and times.

The bulk of writing assessment procedures are devoted to furnishing the raters with a means for agreement (Davis, Scriven, and Thomas; Myers; White, *Teaching and Assessing Writing*). Generally, raters are trained on a set of sample papers that are especially representative of particular scores on a scoring guideline or rubric. Once raters can agree consistently on scores for sample papers, they begin to score independently. Raters are periodically retrained or calibrated each day and throughout the scoring session(s) at appropriate intervals, like after breaks for meals. These practices are consistent with a theory that assumes that teachers or other experts can identify good writing when they see it, and that in order for the assessment to be valid, it must be consistent.

Theory #2

These practices and the theory that drive them have been undergoing a revolution during the last two decades or so, a revolution that is just beginning to filter down to the assessment of student writing. These changes in measurement theory should have a strong influence on writing assessment procedures because these shifts have been spurred by the same philosophical and theoretical movements in the construction of knowledge that have influenced writing pedagogy. Some extreme positions call for the dismantling of validity itself, which is the cornerstone of classical test theory. For example, Guba and Lincoln, in their book *Fourth Generation Evaluation*, posit a theory of evaluation based on the tenets of social construction in which validity is seen as just another social construct. Peter Johnston contends "that the term validity, as it is used in psychometrics, needs to be taken off life support" (510). These critiques of validity are based on the critique of a positivist notion of reality that assumes that human traits are distributed normally throughout the population and that these traits are distinct from the observer or tester and can thus be measured accurately across individual contexts. This negative influence of objectivity relates specifically to the assessment of writing, since good communication often requires the personal involvement of both writer and reader. The importance of reflection or stance in writing is antithetical to an objective approach because to assume a particular position is to be subjective (Johnston, 511).

Since the 1980s, validity has come to be defined as more than just an assessment of whether a test measures what it purports to measure. Samuel Messick and Lee Cronbach, two of the most prominent scholars of validity theory, have been revising their views throughout the last decade. For Messick, validity is "an integrated evaluative judgment of the degree to which empirical evidence and theoretical rationales support the adequacy and appropriateness of inferences and actions based on test scores or other modes of assessment" (5). In this definition there are two striking differences from traditional notions of validity. First of all, Messick includes multiple theoretical, as well as empirical, considerations. In other words, in writing assessment the validity of a test must include a recognizable and supportable theoretical foundation as well as empirical data from students' work. Second, a test's validity also includes its use. A test, for example, that is used for purposes outside a relevant theoretical foundation for the teaching of writing would be an invalid measure of writing ability. Cronbach's stance is similar. For Cronbach, validity "must link concepts, evidence, social and personal consequences and values" (4).

In both of these definitions of validity, we are asked to consider more than just empirical or technical aspects of the way we assess. In writing assessment, the technical aspects of creating rubrics, training raters, developing writing prompts, and the like have been the reasons why outside objective measures were superior to merely having teachers score student papers. These new conceptions of validity question our preoccupation with the technical aspects of writing assessment procedures. In Cronbach's terms, we will need to link together these technical features with what we know about writing and the teaching of writing.

These changing notions of validity have also had an impact on reliability. Historically, validity and reliability have existed in tension with each other. As far back as the 1950s, measurement theorists have lamented that procedures that have theoretical interest and importance are often difficult to measure precisely and consistently; on the other hand, those procedures that deliver maximum consistency and precision often lack substance and meaning for application to theoretical concepts and principles: "The concepts of theoretical interest (in education and psychology) tend to lack empirical meaning, whereas the corresponding concepts with precise empirical meaning often lack theoretical importance" (Torgerson 8).

Michael Williamson finds that this historical tension between reliability and validity has been central to the development of writing assessment procedures and sees it beautifully demonstrated in the debate over direct and indirect measures of writing assessment, in which more reliable measures like multiple-choice exams are actually less valid ways to evaluate student writing. Williamson contends that "the properties of a test which establish its reliability do not necessarily contribute to its validity'' (162). He then goes on to challenge the traditional notion that reliability is a precondition for validity: ''Thus, comparatively high reliability is neither a necessary nor a sufficient condition for establishing the validity of a measure'' (162).

While Williamson contends that reliability should be just one aspect of judging the worthwhile nature of an assessment, Pamela Moss asks the question in her title, ''Can There Be Validity without Reliability?'' Moss asserts that reliability in the psychometric sense ''requires a significant level of standardization [and that] this privileging of standardization is problematic'' (6). Moss goes on to explore what assessment procedures look like within a hermeneutic framework. She uses the example of a faculty search in which members of a committee read an entire dossier of material from perspective candidates and make hiring decisions only after a full discussion with other members of the committee. In a later article (''Enlarging the Dialogue''), Moss explores the value of drawing on the work and procedures from interpretive research traditions to increase an understanding of the importance of context in assessment. Instead of interchangeable consistency, within an interpretive tradition, reliability becomes a critical standard with which communities of knowledgeable stakeholders make important and valid decisions. Interpretive research traditions like hermeneutics support the emerging procedures in writing evaluation because they ''privilege interpretations from readers most knowledgeable about the context of assessment'' (''Can There Be Validity,'' 9). An interpretive framework supports the linguistic context within which all writing assessment should take place because it acknowledges the indeterminacy of meaning and the importance of individual and communal interpretations and values.

Reception and Significance in Composition Studies

The three main types of procedures developed during the 1960s and 1970s for the assessment of student writing were holistic, primary trait, and analytic. All of these procedures involve the reading of student writing by two or more independent judges, who arrive at a numerical score for an individual essay. Holistic procedures entail the giving of a single score for the entire essay, even though the scoring rubric or guideline may detail specific characteristics for each of the scores (usually a 4- or 6-point scale). Analytic scoring includes separate scores for specific characteristics of student writing, though more important areas like content and organization can be weighted more heavily than less important concerns like spelling or transitions. Weighted or not, analytic schemes aggregate individual scores to give an overall analytic score. The primary trait method works similarly to the analytic with raters scoring individual traits of student writing. The primary trait method, however, derives its categories from the rhetorical demands of a particular rhetorical situation. For example, in a writing prompt that asked for directions, proper sequence would be an important trait. All three methods of assessing student writing have been used for various assessment purposes, although the holistic remains the most popular due to its ability to achieve high reliability and its low cost (Veal and Hudson). The analytic method has been shown to be a slightly better predictor of writing quality (Freedman; Veal and Hudson), and the primary trait method continues to be used in the writing assessment section of the National Assessment of Educational Progress.

Portfolios are the newest and perhaps the most important form of writing assessment to be introduced. They have garnered more attention in terms of publications and conferences in the last decade than the rest of writing assessment during the last three decades. Portfolios usually involve the submission of several pieces of student writing that represent more than one genre and allow students to compose over time. Portfolios typically include reflective writing by students on the selection and composition of the writing included in the portfolio. In this sense, portfolios allow students not only to present their written products but also to give the reader some idea of the process of producing the writing itself. Unlike the other methods for assessing student writing, portfolios were developed first in the writing classroom itself (Belanoff and Dickson; Burnham; Black et al.; Ford and Larkin; Yancey; and others).

Within the last few years, methods to assess student writing have been developed outside of the psychometric auspices of classical test theory. William L. Smith developed procedures for placing students into first-year college writing classrooms in which readers were hired in pairs to represent each of the possible courses into which students could be placed. Readers were deemed expert for a specific course after they had achieved extensive and recent experience in teaching a particular course. In such a system, raters make one decision as to whether or not students should be placed in the course they represent. Richard Haswell and Susan Wyche-Smith (''Adventuring''; ''Two-Tiered Rating Procedure'') report on procedures in which the majority of students are placed in first-year courses through the reading of a single reader. Teresa Lowe and Brian Huot report on procedures that adapt these two methods in a pilot project in which raters read state-mandated high school portfolios to place students into first-year writing classes. Russel Durst, Lucille Schwartz, and Marjorie Raymer report on procedures using portfolios to exit students from first year writing classes in which readers make a consensus decision based upon a discussion they have about individual portfolios. These emergent procedures for assessing student writing are being supported by the development of new theories of measurement that recognize the importance of the individual learner and her or his specific educational context. Such radical shifts in measurement theory should provide composition teachers and administrators with many opportunities to develop writing assessment procedures that reflect classroom practice in the teaching of writing.

BIBLIOGRAPHY

Primary Texts and Major Scholarship in Composition

Belanoff, Patricia, and Marcia Dickson, eds. *Portfolios: Process and Product.* Portsmouth, NH: Boynton/Cook, 1991.

Black, Laurel, Edwina Helton, and Jeffrey Sommers. *New Directions in Writing Assessment*. Portsmouth, NH: Boynton/Cook, 1994.

Burnham, Christopher. "Portfolio Evaluation: Room to Breathe and Grow." In *Training the New Teacher of College Composition*. Ed. Charles Bridges. Urbana, IL: NCTE, 1986, 125–38.

Carini Patricia F. "An Essay on Standards, Judgement and Writing." *Assessing Writing* 1 (1994): 29–66.

Cherry, Roger, and Paul Meyer. "Reliability Issues in Holistic Assessment." In *Validating Holistic Scoring for Writing Assessment: Theoretical and Empirical Foundations*. Ed. Michael M. Williamson and Brian Huot. Cresskill, NJ: Hampton, 1993, 109–41.

Cronbach, Lee J. "Five Perspectives on Validity Argument." In *Test Validity*. Ed. Harold Wainer. Hillsdale, NJ: Erlbaum, 1988, 3–17.

Davis, Barbara Gross, Michael Scriven, and Susan Thomas. *The Evaluation of Composition Instruction*. 2nd ed. New York: Teachers College P, 1987.

Diederich, Paul, John W. French, and Sydell T. Carlton. *Factors in Judgments of Writing Quality*. RB no. 61-15. Princeton, NJ: Educational Testing Service, 1961. (ERIC no. ED 002–172.)

Durst, Russel K., Marjorie Roemer, and Lucille Schultz. "Portfolio Negotiations: Acts of Speech." In *New Directions in Portfolio Assessment*. Ed. Laurel Black, Donald A. Daiker, Jeffrey Sommers, and Gail Stygall. Portsmouth, NH: Boynton/Cook, 1994.

Faigley, Lester, Roger Cherry, David A. Jolliffe, and Anna M. Skinner. *Assessing Writers' Knowledge and Processes of Composing*. Norwood, NJ: Ablex, 1985.

Ford, James, and Gregory Larkin. "The Portfolio System: An End to Backsliding Standards." *College English* 39 (1978): 950–55.

Freedman, Sarah. "The Registers of Student and Professional Expository Writing: Influences on Teachers' Responses." In *New Directions in Composition Research*. Ed. Richard Beach and Lillian Bridwell. New York: Guilford, 1984, 334–47.

Gere, Anne R. "Written Composition: Toward a Theory of Evaluation." *College English* 42 (1980): 44–58.

Godshalk, Fred I., Frances Swineford, and William E. Coffman. *The Measurement of Writing Ability*. CEEB RM no. 6. Princeton, NJ: Educational Testing Service, 1966.

Greenberg, Karen L., Harvey S. Wiener, and Richard A. Donovan. *Writing Assessment: Issues and Strategies*. New York: Longman, 1986.

Guba, Egon G. "The Alternative Paradigm Dialog." In *The Paradigm Dialog*. Ed. Egon G. Guba. Newbury Park, CA: Sage, 1990, 17–27.

Guba, Evon G., and Yvonna S. Lincoln. *Fourth Generation Evaluation*. Newbury Park, CA: Sage, 1989.

Haswell, Richard, and Susan Wyche-Smith. "Adventuring into Writing Assessment." *College Composition and Communication* 45 (1994): 220–36.

———. "A Two-Tiered Rating Procedure for Placement Essays." In *Assessment in Practice: Putting Principles to Work on College Campuses*. Ed. Trudy Banta. San Francisco, CA: Jossey-Bass, 1995, 204–7.

Hoetker, James. "Essay Examination Topics and Students' Writing." *College Composition and Communication* 33 (1982): 377–92.

Hopkins, Thomas L. "The Marking System of the College Entrance Examination

Board.'' *Harvard Monographs in Education* (Cambridge, MA), series 1, no. 2 (1921).

Huot, Brian. ''The Literature of Direct Writing Assessment: Major Concerns and Prevailing Trends.'' *Review of Educational Research* 60 (1990): 237–63.

———. ''A Survey of College and University Writing Placement Practices.'' *WPA: Writing Program Administration* 17 (1994): 49–67.

Johnston, Peter. ''Constructive Evaluation and the Improvement of Teaching and Learning.'' *Teachers College Record* 90 (1989): 509–28.

Lowe, Teresa J., and Brian Huot. ''Using KIRIS Portfolios to Place Students in First-Year Composition at the U of Louisville.'' *Kentucky English Bulletin* (forthcoming).

Messick, Samuel. ''Meaning and Values in Test Validation: The Science and Ethics of Assessment.'' *Educational Researcher* 18.2 (1989): 5–11.

Moss, Pamela A. ''Can There Be Validity Without Reliability?'' *Educational Researcher* 23.2 (1994): 5–12.

———. ''Enlarging the Dialogue in Educational Measurement: Voices from Interpretive Research Traditions.'' *Educational Researcher* 25.1 (1996): 20–28.

———. ''Shifting Conceptions of Validity in Educational Measurement: Implications for Performance Assessment.'' *Review of Educational Research* 62 (1992): 229–58.

Myers, Miles. *A Procedure for Writing Assessment and Holistic Scoring.* Urbana, IL: NCTE, 1980.

Ruth, Leo, and Sanda Murphy. *Designing Writing Tasks for the Assessment of Writing.* Norwood, NJ: Ablex, 1988.

Smith, William L. ''Assessing the Reliability and Adequacy of Using Holistic Scoring of Essays as a College Composition Placement Program Technique.'' In *Validating Holistic Scoring for Writing Assessment: Theoretical and Empirical Foundations.* Ed. Michael M. Williamson and Brian Huot. Cresskill, NJ: Hampton, 1993, 142–205.

Torgerson, Warren S. *Theory and Methods of Scaling.* New York: Wiley, 1958.

Veal, Ramon L., and Sally A. Hudson. ''Direct and Indirect Measures for the Large-Scale Evaluation of Writing.'' *Research in the Teaching of English* 17 (1983): 285–96.

White, Edward M. ''Holistic Scoring: Past Triumphs and Future Challenges.'' In *Validating Holistic Scoring for Writing Assessment: Theoretical and Empirical Foundations.* Ed. Michael M. Williamson and Brian Huot. Cresskill, NJ: Hampton, 1993, 79–108.

———. *Teaching and Assessing Writing.* 2nd ed. San Francisco: Jossey-Bass, 1994.

Wiggins, Grant. *Assessing Student Performance.* San Francisco: Jossey-Bass, 1993.

Williamson, Michael M. ''The Worship of Efficiency: Untangling Theoretical and Practical Considerations in Writing Assessment.'' *Assessing Writing* 1 (1994): 147–74.

Yancey, Kathleen Blake. *Portfolios in the Writing Classroom.* Urbana, IL: NCTE, 1992.

BRIAN HUOT

N

NARRATIVE THEORY

Summary

An important branch of contemporary narrative theory emerged in the 1960s and early 1970s in the work of Todorov, Genette, and Barthes, among others, who pioneered "narratology," as Todorov named it in 1969. Inspired by Lévi-Strauss's work on myths (*Anthropologie Structurale*, 1958) and Propp's on folk-tales (1920s), they approached their study with scientific rigor and a faith that narratives—written, told, or otherwise presented—have common features and deep structures born of universal workings of the human mind. They named variously the features particular to narrative—types of characters, actions, and points of view, but all emphasized the important distinction between "what" is told—the story or narrative—and the "way" it is told—the narration. They believed that identifying these elements in their virtually limitless arrangements, which they conceived as a kind of grammar, would allow scholars to understand all narratives as particular manifestations of shared structural systems.

Narratology was deeply indebted to the linguistic structuralism of Saussure's *Cours de linguistique générale* (1915, translated into English in 1959), not least for the belief that stories, through universal systems of signs, "construct" reality. Whether seen as rigorously objective and penetrating or as reductive, static, and antihumanistic, narratology effectively banished from narrative criticism any sense of stories as transparent vehicles for discernible realities or, in the more romantic view, as unproblematic visions of individually animated minds creating their own meanings. However, such interest as narrative scholars held in uncovering universal deep structures began to wane in the late 1970s; they became convinced that structures could not explain everything about the power of stories, which James Phelan characterizes (in *Narrative As Rhetoric*) as their ability "to communicate knowledge, feelings, values, and beliefs to an audience" (18).

Informing this loss of faith were several theoretical shifts that highlighted ways in which the very telling of stories—dependent on highly mutable contexts and the transforming nature of time and of language itself—threatens to subvert them. Phelan says we owe to deconstruction "the wide acceptance of the principles that language is inherently unstable, that there is no transcendental anchor to textual meanings, and that textual meanings are more likely to be at odds with one another than not" (8), ideas that clearly challenged the structuralist assumptions of narratology. In *Literary Theory: An Introduction*, Terry Eagleton says that poststructuralism represented a shift "from seeing the poem or novel as a closed entity, . . . to seeing it as irreducibly plural, an endless play of signifiers" (138).

Eagleton captures other growing theoretical concerns of the 1980s as well: "Was language really all there was? What about labour, sexuality, political power?" (111). Even if the old idea of the "soul" of the writer is irrecoverable, still, Eagleton writes, language "in some way involves human subjects and their intentions" (113). Appreciating the limitations of structuralism and deconstruction too, narrative scholars increasingly perceived stories less as closed or self-perpetuating systems and more as entities by and about human subjects influenced by cultural contexts, historical times, ideologies, and the distribution of power within heterogeneous communities. Consequently, much current narrative theory focuses on the discourse of stories—the ways in which their tellers enact culture in communicating with readers or listeners. Theorists speak of the rhetoric of narrative, construing its impact through a problematized and, Phelan says, "endlessly recursive relationship" among "author, text, and reader" (xii). If the structuralist principles of narratology decentered the intentional storyteller and overthrew faith in an objective reality, the theories that followed refigured narrative meanings as unstable, plural, profoundly contextualized, and interactive.

Current narrative theory is informed by a dizzying variety, not only of critical schools but also of disciplines—linguistics, anthropology, psychoanalysis, sociology, and so on. Also, though most thoroughly at home in literature departments, it has touched an increasing range of fields by turning critics' attention away from the esthetics—some would say the surface features—of literature toward features that all narrative discourses share. Even literary critics are likely to speak of "narrative," rather than "fiction." And stories from anthropology to history, medicine, and film—from the psychoanalyst's office to the courtroom, advertisement, and talk show host—open themselves to narrative inquiry; Christopher Nash's *Narrative in Culture*, with its contributions from theorists in economics, legal discourse, psychoanalysis, and genetics, nicely illustrates the present reach of narrative theory. In addition, the work of contemporary narrative theorists has certainly been enriched by and may also have fostered the practice of writers who mix stories of history, autobiography, fiction, and fantasy and who create such new genres as "literary" or "creative nonfiction" and the "academic autobiography."

Reception and Significance in Composition Studies

Composition teachers certainly ask students to read and write narratives with increasing frequency, partly because of heightened interest in multicultural education. But Judith Summerfield is probably right when she guesses, in "Is There a Life in This Text? Reimagining Narrative," that most writing teachers present narrative assignments to students "uncritically and unproblematically" (182). A survey of the literature confirms her hunch. One reason why narrative theory has not been more widely and explicitly embraced by those in composition studies is, doubtless, the beholden nature of writing programs to institutions with conventional ideas about writing instruction. Also, whatever their intellectual sympathies, writing teachers may well think that "doing" theory in the classroom undermines much that they have always stressed about good writing: in expository and argumentative writing, clear and authoritatively expressed theses and "objective" support and, in personal narrative, "authentic" voice. An even greater challenge is to ask students to see their own personal essays and the narrative elements of their expository and argumentative writing as multivoiced, as hiding as much as they reveal, as particular to time and culture, as provisional.

Still, narrative theory has had subtle effects on composition studies: in scholars' appreciation for threads common to the decisions writers make as they "compose" argument, exposition, personal narration, and fiction; in courses in which students read and write a mix of—and sometimes mixed—genres; in renewed interest in essays as Montaigne conceived them—as nonlinear, nondefinitive forays which blend the personal and the empirical.

And a few composition scholars engage narrative theory explicitly in the classroom. In "Essays and Experience, Time and Rhetoric," Douglas Hesse articulates the relation between "discursive" and "presentational" writing. He believes that increased interest in the narrative essay grows in part from a wish to protect, against the forces of theory, the "enabling fiction of the autonomous essayist rendering personal truths" (210). Hesse says that such essays as Orwell's, Woolf's, and Dillard's are stories whose narrators present "themselves as readers of their own experience" (199). And he explains how essay narratives persuade, offering "truth not as timeless, logical, and stable but always situational, constructed in experience, their tar paper and sheetrock showing" (199).

Judith Summerfield offers rich possibilities for applying narrative theory to the classroom. She contends that "questions—of memory, of the present reworking the past, . . . of witnesses and versions . . . —enter the writing classroom as opportunities, considerations, invitations for writing, and for writing about writing" (186). She urges colleagues not to ask students whether, even in their personal narratives, they are "telling the truth" and to act instead as if there were a life in their story independent of its highly contextualized telling.

She acknowledges that her approach can meet resistance, as from a student who protested, 'This is *my* story.... It's not *a* story, it's *the* story'' (193). Still, she challenges students to "subjunctivize" the situations about which they write, to try on roles, to read and write different genres that deal "with the 'same' material," "to try their different waters" (186), and to "understand the pervasiveness of fiction as argument" (192). Composition scholars like Hesse and Summerfield suggest how to treat narratives in class in ways theorists deem effective: appreciating their plurality of voices, their multiple stories, and their various ways of telling—all representing countless ways of knowing.

BIBLIOGRAPHY

Primary Texts

Bal, Mieke. *Narratology: Introduction to the Theory of Narrative*. Trans. Christine van Boheemen. Toronto: U of Toronto P, 1985.

Barthes, Roland. *Mythologies*. Trans. Annette Lavers. New York: Noonday Press, 1972.

Booth, Wayne C. *The Rhetoric of Fiction*. 2nd ed. Chicago: U of Chicago P, 1983.

Bruner, Jerome. *Acts of Meaning*. Cambridge: Harvard UP, 1990.

———. *Actual Minds, Possible Worlds*. Cambridge: Harvard UP, 1986.

Coste, Didier. *Narrative as Communication*. Minneapolis: U of Minnesota P, 1989.

Eagleton, Terry. *Literary Theory, An Introduction*. Minneapolis: U of Minnesota P, 1983.

Genette, Gérard. *Narrative Discourse: An Essay in Method*. Ithaca, NY: Cornell UP, 1980.

Lévi-Strauss, Claude. *Structural Anthropology*. Trans. Claire Jacobson and Brooke Grundfest Schoepf. New York: Basic Books, 1963.

Martin, Wallace. *Recent Theories of Narrative*. Ithaca, NY: Cornell UP, 1986.

Miller, J. Hillis. "Narrative." In *Critical Terms for Literary Study*. Ed. Thomas McLaughlin and Frank Lentricchia. Chicago: U of Chicago P, 1990, 67–79.

Nash, Christopher, ed. *Narrative in Culture*. London: Routledge, 1990.

Phelan, James. *Narrative as Rhetoric*. Columbus: Ohio State UP, 1996.

Phelan, James, and Peter J. Rabinowitz, eds. *Understanding Narrative*. Columbus: Ohio State UP, 1994.

Prince, Gerald. *A Dictionary of Narratology*. Lincoln: U of Nebraska P, 1987.

Propp, Vladimir. *Morphology of the Folktale*. Trans. Laurence Scott. Ed. Svatava Pirkova-Jacobson. Austin: U of Texas P, 1968.

Ricoeur, Paul. *Time and Narrative*, 3 vols. Chicago: U of Chicago P, 1984–1986.

Saussure, Ferdinand de. *Course in General Linguistics*. Trans. Wade Baskin. Eds. Albert Sechehaye and Albert Reidlinger. New York: Philosophical Library, 1959.

Todorov, Tzvetan. *Grammaire du Décaméron*. The Hague: Mouton, 1969.

———. *The Poetics of Prose*. Ithaca, NY: Cornell UP, 1977.

Winterowd, W. Ross. *The Rhetoric of the "Other" Literature*. Carbondale: Southern Illinois UP, 1990.

Major Scholarship in Composition

Brodkey, Linda. "Making a Federal Case Out of Difference: The Politics of Pedagogy, Publicity, and Postponement." In *Writing Theory and Critical Theory*. Eds. John Clifford and John Schilb. New York: MLA, 1994, 236–61.

DiPardo, Anne. "Narrative Knowers, Expository Knowledge: Discourse as a Dialectic." *Written Communication* 7 (1990): 59–95.

Hesse, Douglas. "Essays and Experience, Time and Rhetoric." In *Writing Theory and Critical Theory*. Ed. John Clifford and John Schilb. New York: MLA, 1994, 236–61.

Summerfield, Judith. "Is There a Life in This Text? Reimagining Narrative." In *Writing Theory and Critical Theory*. Eds. John Clifford and John Schilb. New York: MLA, 1994, 179–93.

CATHERINE S. PENNER

NEOPRAGMATISM

Summary

Neopragmatism loosely designates the revival of interest during the 1980s in the traditional pragmatism of philosophers such as Charles Sanders Peirce, William James, and John Dewey. Neopragmatism shares pragmatism's emphasis on agency, or process, and thus both describe the world in terms of *how* it works, not in terms of what it *is*, in the foundational sense. What distinguishes neopragmatism from its predecessor is its heightened awareness of the rhetorical nature of any systematic inquiry, the idea that our knowledge of how the world works is mediated, if not controlled, by the social nature of language.

The pragmatism of James and Dewey has had the most influence on the neopragmatists. James saw pragmatism as a method of justification, believing that one validated metaphysical systems and their corresponding values by equating their practical effects with their "truth content." In James's *Pragmatism*, the truth of an idea was its "practical cash-value," and it was useful to the extent that it indicated "ways in which existing realities may be *changed*" (46). Rather than viewing ideas as commodities, James saw them as strategies for naming and thus constituting experience. In *The Quest for Certainty* (1929), Dewey saw pragmatism as a useful means of critiquing rationalist philosophy, whose truth value was wrongly judged by its internal consistency, instead of by its practical consequences (i.e., by "what works"). Essentially, how well ideas or things work in the world is a measure of their truth, and thus, their value.

Neopragmatism, whose most prominent advocate is Richard Rorty, holds that pragmatism is a method both of understanding and of justification, but denies that any proposition about the universe has some intrinsic value by nature of its commensurability with some metaphysical reality. Rorty argues in *Philosophy and the Mirror of Nature* (1979) that "pragmatic philosophers are skeptical primarily *about systematic philosophy*, about the whole project of universal commensuration" (368). His premise is that vocabularies acquire their status from people who use them rather than from their transparency to the real. So instead, the neopragmatist aims to characterize fully the agency of interpretation and its consequences. Giles Gunn calls this "a hermeneutic model of critical inquiry as a form of conversation or dialogue" (65). Rorty's version of neopragmatism is thus a metanarrative on the possibility and conduct of philosophy, in whatever contexts that philosophy may be exercised. Rather than theorizing better explanations of the world, Rorty sees wisdom as consisting in the ability to sustain a conversation about human beings as both "described objects and describing subjects" (378).

Other strands of neopragmatism not only value the dialogic nature of philosophical epistemology but also place more stress than Rorty does on the speaking subject (the writer or philosopher), who is always already encrypted by history and culture. Frank Lentricchia's *Criticism and Social Change* (1982) and Giles Gunn's *The Culture of Criticism and the Criticism of Culture* (1987) agree that philosophy has no representational authority, yet they adamantly argue that this incommensurability is not simply a consequence of the discord between signifier and signified. Lentricchia, for instance, wants to describe the cluster of social and material conditions that inscribe critical theory and that make it a rhetorical as well as an epistemological endeavor. Using Kenneth Burke's battles with Marxists in the 1930s as its central anecdote, Lentricchia's 1982 book examines the ideological conditions that determine the consequences, and even the generation, of criticism. The truth or value of an idea cannot be measured by its practical consequences alone because those consequences (and the critics who induce them) are subject to the normalizing forces of ideology. In other words, there is a codeterminative relationship between philosophical principles and social life. From this perspective, Rorty's call for extending the conversation could be seen as a reaffirmation of the status quo, since social circumstances regulate the form and direction such a conversation might take.

Giles Gunn sees in neopragmatism a way out of (or around) the nihilism of poststructuralism, and he frequently cites Burke's insight that philosophies may "work" in spite of inherent structural or conceptual contradictions and thus provide us with the will to believe despite the acknowledged absence of transcendental signifieds and metaphysical presence. It may be true that classical philosophy's claims to truth no longer have any demonstrable validity. Nevertheless, our nature compels us to act, and to act together, and in doing so we create cultural forms that are, from a poststructuralist point of view, artificial and self-serving constructs. Still, Gunn argues, philosophical perspectives can, and often do, make differences in the world of experience, contradictory or not, and he sees Burke as a comic theorist who uses puns, perspective by incongruity, and the proverbial, to "outmaneuver language" so that our terministic screens "do not become the prisonhouse of thought" (Gunn, 85). As Gunn sees it, the neopragmatist cannot rely on the goodwill of those involved to extend the conversation, but must find ways in, and through, language to redirect the conversation's momentum away from premature consensus.

Reception and Significance in Composition Studies

While neopragmatism has a pervasive but general influence not only on composition studies but on the character of modern thought (as does pragmatism), as a theory its specific impact begins with Kenneth A. Bruffee's essay, "Col-

laborative Learning and the Conversation of Mankind'' (1984) and his bibliographical essay, ''Social Construction, Language, and the Authority of
Knowledge'' (1986), both of which were published in *College English* and generated considerable debate. Bruffee cites Rorty on the point that knowledge is
communally constructed, and uses it to argue that writing, as a form of reflective
thought, is internalized social conversation. Also citing figures like Thomas
Kuhn, Michael Oakeshott, and Clifford Geertz, Bruffee concludes that when we
teach writing, we should construct our classrooms in such a way as to imitate
the process by which knowledge is socially constructed: through peer group
negotiation, argument, hypothesis testing, and ultimately, consensus building,
with the teacher acting as facilitator. Bruffee's ideas have had an enormous
influence in composition studies, but his detractors are numerous. They include
Greg Myers, whose ''Reality, Consensus, and Reform in the Rhetoric of Composition Teaching'' (1986) echoes Lentricchia's call for a form of pragmatism
that recognizes the material and cultural forces that affect ''knowing,'' something Myers argues that Bruffee does not address. Some claim that at worst,
Bruffee's model encourages students to merely imitate Orwellian groupthink,
without sufficient appreciation for the value of dissensus in extending reflection,
a charge John Trimbur addresses in ''Consensus and Difference in Collaborative
Learning'' (1989). It is important to note, however, that as this debate over the
merits of social construction as a pedagogical model has evolved in composition
studies, it has become increasingly distant from neopragmatism as articulated
by Rorty and others.

Burke, of course, has had an enormous impact on composition studies, and
although his studies of symbolic action have yet to be adequately associated
with either the new or old pragmatism, the work by Gunn and Lentricchia to
this end has helped draw out this emphasis in Burke. Work by W. Ross Winterowd, William A. Covino, Timothy Crusius, Tilly Warnock, Richard Coe, and
others enact a pragmatic rhetoric that is, at crucial junctures, guided by Burkean
insights. In this regard, neopragmatism functions in composition studies, through
Burke's influence, as an attitude of what Gunn calls ''pragmatic wariness'' (86).

The significance of Rorty's version of neopragmatism in composition studies
was dealt a serious blow after Gary Olson's interview with Rorty for the *Journal
of Advanced Composition* (1989; rpt., 1991). There, Rorty claimed to have no
knowledge of social constructionism, saw writing across the curriculum as a
terrible idea, and trivialized the teaching of composition. John Schilb notes in
his response to the interview that it highlights what Bruffee and Rorty have in
common: both neglect ''configurations of power based on gender, race, and
class'' (239). Neopragmatism *can* be a significant way of theorizing composition
to the extent that it helps us recognize the ways in which material and social
conditions impact the production and exchange of discourse, not only across
fields of study, but also across sociopolitical boundaries. Its fundamental insights—ones best articulated and developed by Burke, Lentricchia, and Gunn—

have yet to be assimilated *as* neopragmatic, though it is likely that they have already appeared in other guises, in the form of social-epistemic rhetoric.

BIBLIOGRAPHY

Primary Texts

Burke, Kenneth. *The Philosophy of Literary Form.* 1941. Rpt. Berkeley: U of California P, 1973.

Dewey, John. *The Quest for Certainty.* New York: Minton, Balch, and Co., 1929.

Geertz, Clifford. *The Interpretation of Cultures.* New York: Basic Books, 1971.

Gunn, Giles. *The Culture of Criticism and the Criticism of Culture.* New York: Oxford UP, 1987.

James, William. *Pragmatism.* 1907. Rpt. Cleveland, OH: World Publishing, 1963.

Kuhn, Thomas. *The Structure of Scientific Revolutions.* 2nd ed. Chicago: U of Chicago P, 1970.

Lentricchia, Frank. *Criticism and Social Change.* Chicago: U of Chicago P, 1982.

Oakeshott, Michael. *Rationalism in Politics.* New York: Basic Books, 1962.

Olson, Gary A. "Social Construction and Composition Theory: An Interview with Richard Rorty." *Journal of Advanced Composition* 9.1–2 (1989): 1–9. Rpt. In *(Inter)views: Cross-Disciplinary Perspectives on Rhetoric and Literacy.* Ed. Gary A. Olson and Irene Gale. Carbondale: Southern Illinois UP, 1991, 227–35.

Pierce, Charles Sanders. *The Essential Writings.* Ed. Edward C. Moore. New York: Harper and Row, 1992.

Rorty, Richard. *Philosophy and the Mirror of Nature.* Princeton, NJ: Princeton UP, 1979.

Schilb, John. "On Personally Constructing 'Social Construction': A Response to Richard Rorty." *Journal of Advanced Composition* 10.1 (1990): 146–49. Rpt. In *(Inter)views: Cross-Disciplinary Perspectives on Rhetoric and Literacy.* Ed. Gary A. Olson and Irene Gale. Carbondale: Southern Illinois UP, 1991. 238–240.

Major Scholarship in Composition

Bruffee, Kenneth A. "Collaborative Learning and the Conversation of Mankind." *College English* 46.7 (1984): 635–52.

———. "Social Construction, Language, and the Authority of Knowledge: A Bibliographical Essay." *College English* 48.8 (1986): 773–90.

Coe, Richard M. *Toward a Grammar of Passages.* Carbondale: Southern Illinois UP, 1988.

Covino, William A. *The Elements of Persuasion.* Boston: Allyn and Bacon, 1998.

Crusius, Timothy W. "A Case for Kenneth Burke's Dialectic and Rhetoric." *Philosophy and Rhetoric* 19.1 (1986): 23–37.

Myers, Greg. "Reality, Consensus, and Reform in the Rhetoric of Composition Teaching." *College English* 48.2 (1986): 154–74.

Olson, Gary A., and Irene Gale. *(Inter)views: Cross-Disciplinary Perspectives on Rhetoric and Literacy.* Carbondale: Southern Illinois UP, 1991.

Trimbur, John. "Consensus and Difference in Collaborative Learning." *College English* 51.6 (1989): 602–16.

Warnock, Tilly. "Reading Kenneth Burke: 'Ways In, Ways Out, Ways Roundabout.' " *College English* 48.1 (1986): 62–75.

Winterowd, W. Ross. *Compostition/Rhetoric: A Synthesis*. Carbondale: Southern Illinois UP, 1986.

DAVID BLAKESLEY

NEW CRITICISM

Summary

Richard Beach defines New Criticism as a

. . . critical approach beginning in the 1940s that emphasizes a quasi-"scientific," close reading of the text's language. . . . Advocates of this approach assume that the meaning of a text is "in" the language of the text. The reader's task is to carefully explicate that use of techniques such as figurative language, point of view, meter, and rhyme. . . . [New Critics] reject the idea that meaning varies according to the unique transaction between individual readers and text in particular contexts. (164)

Born of the British move from belle-lettristic literary response during the first decades of the twentieth century, New Criticism finds its origins in the call for a less subjective "practical criticism" and "close reading" designed to reveal a text's validity from a formal rather than a cultural perspective. Two major influences in the move toward this sort of textual explication are I. A. Richards's *Principles of Literary Criticism* (1926) and *Practical Criticism* (1929). In each of these texts, Richards calls for reading protocols that compel a reader to discover a text's greatness in the tensions and interrelationships between tropes, linguistic structures, images, symbols, and the like, rather than in the author's intentions or the text's effect on the reader.

In its prescriptive approach toward critical reading, "practical criticism's" uniform aesthetics worked to remove literature from the hands of the academic elitism that had previously controlled how the profession evaluated texts. However, in this action, the pendulum was to swing to the alternate extreme: from ultimately subjective belle-lettrism to abject, objective analysis. Generally associated with the American literary critics John Crowe Ransom, Cleanth Brooks, W. K. Wimsatt, and M. C. Beardsley, to name but a few prominent figures, the New Criticism, as we know it today, emerged as an efficient and uniform means by which a reader might understand a literary text through its linguistic complexities while neglecting any sense of historical, cultural, or personal investigation. While it was a means to efficient classroom evaluation and formulaic text production in the college writing course, New Criticism's rigid focus on form over content and product over process threatened to stifle a student's personal involvement in language-oriented studies. Perhaps the most influential American texts regarding the New Critical relationship between literary studies and composition studies are Cleanth Brooks and Robert Penn Warren, *Understanding Poetry: An Anthology for College Students* (1938), and their composition textbook, *Modern Rhetoric* (1949). By concentrating on terms like *tension*, *ambiguity*, *irony*, *coherence*, and *unity*, Brooks and Warren were able to transfer

New Critical protocols into the teaching of writing and, as James Berlin observes, to place poetry (i.e., canonical literature) above any other sort of writing—including student texts. Foremost here was the idea that formal structure, planning, and product orientation were as much the foundations of "correct" writing as they were of "correct" reading.

W. K. Wimsatt and Monroe C. Beardsley established two major New Critical terms that further entrenched New Criticism in the American English department. In their influential essays, "The Intentional Fallacy" (1946) and "The Affective Fallacy" (1949), they efficiently removed both the author and the reader from interpretive reading. The term *intentional fallacy* suggests that it is a mistake to read a text in search of the author's intent and that the text, once written, holds a meaning specific to itself and not in what the author might have meant to convey through it. The term *affective fallacy* maintains that the reader should not be concerned with any personal or emotional investment in the text. By efficiently removing both the author and the reader from the critical formula, the New Critics encouraged impersonal, singular "correct" readings and writings based in form and function. Both of these contentions crossed over into the contemporary composition class and threatened to alienate young writers from their own texts. If the author *and* the reader are to be removed from the official text of literature, where, we might ask, is the place of the student writer in her or his own writing? New Criticism would have to answer: in the acquiescence to formal codes, mechanics, and convention—no more; no less. In the New Critical orientation, propriety and correctness precluded process in favor of a well-wrought product.

Reception and Significance in Composition Studies

New Criticism has not fared well with contemporary compositionists. As W. Ross Winterowd, Robert Scholes, and Stanley B. Straw, among others, observe, composition studies finds its origins in the traditional English department and thus shares with the department its overall critical and theoretical foundations. Yet, the whole premise of New Criticism tends to go against the grain of an efficient, process-oriented composition theory in general. Thus, contemporary composition's general theoretical disposition can be seen in its departure from its New Critical beginnings. Ann Berthoff's observation that a teacher will teach writing according to her or his own perspective on language holds true here. Since the teaching of writing fell to the English department early on, it was the New Critics, torn from their true goals of literary espousal, who were compelled to design and promote courses in synch with their own literary theories. Because, as Scholes and Winterowd observe, many of these literature-based teachers saw composition as a menial "service" course, they formulated product-based formulae designed to stratify the generally dynamic act of writing for purposes of uniform teaching techniques and consensual standards for evaluation.

In his important essay, "The Purification of Literature and Rhetoric" (1987), Winterowd observes composition's service orientation and the negative effect it has on student writers. Steven Lynn, in "A Passage into Critical Theory" (1990), recognizes the service orientation as well, noting that, "New Criticism and Current-Traditional-Rhetoric are product oriented and thus concerned with error" (262). This infatuation with correctness is where contemporary compositionists part with the formalistic close readings on which New Criticism insists in both literary and student texts. James Berlin observes that New Criticism's assumption that there is a correct way to present and read a text has passed over into the writing classroom to create current-traditional rhetoric, as addressed by Lynn. This negative traditionalism dictates prescriptive, text-centered pedagogies that stifle student writers with strict, formulaic rules rather than encouraging them to break out and try new and dynamic ways to bring their own textuality to the fore. The move from current-traditionalism to Berlin's "rhetoric of liberal culture" can best be seen in the move toward process-oriented composition pedagogy and reader-response theory. And it is in these areas that the most prominent research concerning the relationship between New Criticism and composition studies can be found.

From the contemporary compositionists' point of view, New Criticism is prescriptive, static, and outdated. Simply put, it is something we should not do. However, New Criticism's earlier call for practical criticism and close reading cannot be neglected. Close reading is necessary to interpretive reading and writing. An understanding of how a text's form and structure work upon the reader—a recognition of aesthetic tropal relationships, tension, irony, and so on—can help the reader into a further understanding of the text on other terms; and in the spirit of close reading, a writer can develop the sort of investigative writing activity prominent in Peter Elbow's freewriting exercises or the reader-response theorists' phenomenological approaches. In this case, we see that close reading, as an activity, is a positive part of interpretation if it is directed contextually rather than isolated within a formal model of static meaning.

Composition's relationship with New Criticism can be seen most readily in the work of "crossover" theorists like Louise Rosenblatt, Ann Berthoff, Kenneth Burke, Wayne Booth, Frank Lentriccia, and various other proponents of the "New Rhetoric" and reader-response theories. Both of these theoretical positions offer to diffuse New Critical prescriptivism by reuniting writing and reading as alternately related, interdependent, interpretive processes. Inasmuch as reading and writing are inseparable, contemporary composition studies tend toward a goal of a unified theory that might bring a wholeness to the traditional English department. Patricia Bizzell notes this concern in her essay, "On the Possibility of a Unified Theory of Composition and Literature." Likewise, Robert Scholes addresses the need for a juncture between the "proletarian" compositionists and the "elitist" literature specialists in *Textual Power*, while Terry Eagleton sums up the problem by calling for rhetoric as the main concern in all English studies.

We might say that the popular debate between process and product begins with New Criticism's emergence on the American academic scene. Significantly, the contemporary academy's move away from New Critical influences in the writing/reading classroom has helped to (re)unite reading and writing through process orientations and reader-response theory. In the final analysis, contemporary composition's answer to the New Criticism offers what I. A. Richards's practical criticism set out to do in the first place: offer the reader/writer the tools necessary to discover the aesthetics of textual experience. In a postindustrial milieu, close reading remains necessary; however, at this juncture, it might well be seen ironically, as a means to restore to literature and student writing the soul that New Criticism's formal objectivity threatened to obscure.

BIBLIOGRAPHY

Primary Texts

Booth, Wayne. *The Rhetoric of Fiction.* Chicago: U of Chicago P, 1961.
Brooks, Cleanth. *The Well Wrought Urn: Studies in the Structure of Poetry.* 1947. Rpt. London: Methuen, 1968.
Brooks, Cleanth, and Robert Penn Warren. *Modern Rhetoric.* New York: Harcourt, 1949.
———, eds. *Understanding Poetry: An Anthology for College Students.* New York: Henry Holt, 1938.
Empson, William. *Seven Types of Ambiguity.* 1930. Rpt. Hammondsworth, UK: Penguin, 1966.
Eagleton, Terry. "The Rise of English." In *Literary Theory: An Introduction.* Minneapolis: U of Minnesota P, 1983.
Lentriccia, Frank. *After the New Criticism.* Chicago: U of Chicago P, 1980.
Ransom, John Crowe. *The New Criticism.* Norfolk, CT: New Directions, 1941.
Richards, I. A. *Principles of Literary Criticism.* 1924. Rpt. New York: Harcourt Brace, 1961.
———. *Practical Criticism.* 1929. Rpt. London: Routledge, 1964.
Wellek, René, and Austin Warren. *Theory of Literature.* Hammondsworth: Penguin, 1949.
Wimsatt, W. K., *The Verbal Icon: Studies in the Meaning of Poetry.* London: Methuen, 1970.
Wimsatt, W. K., and Monroe, C. Beardsley. "The Affective Fallacy." In *The Verbal Icon: Studies in the Meaning of Poetry.* Ed. W. K. Winsatt. London: Methuen, 1970.
———. "The Intentional Fallacy." In *The Verbal Icon: Studies in the Meaning of Poetry.* Ed. W. K. Wimsatt. London: Methuen, 1970.

Major Scholarship in Composition

Aycock, Colleen. "New Critical Rhetoric and Composition." Los Angeles, CA: Ph.D. dissertation, U of Southern California, 1984.
Beach, Richard. *A Teacher's Introduction to Reader-Response Theories.* Urbana, IL: NCTE, 1993.
Berlin, James. *Rhetoric and Reality: Writing Instruction in American Colleges, 1900–1985.* Carbondale: Southern Illinois UP, 1987.
Berlin, James, and Robert Inkster. "Current-Traditional Rhetoric: Paradigm and Practice." *Freshman English News* 8 (1980): 1–4, 13–14.

Berthoff, Ann E. *The Making of Meaning: Metaphors, Models, and Maxims for Writing Teachers*. Montclair, NJ: Boynton/Cook, 1981.

———, ed. *Richards on Rhetoric: I. A. Richards, Selected Essays 1929–1974*. New York: Oxford UP, 1991.

Bizzell, Patricia. "On the Possibility of a Unified Theory of Composition and Literature." *Rhetoric Review* 4.2 (1986): 202–17.

Burke, Kenneth. *Counter-Statement*. Berkeley: U of California P, 1968.

———. *Language as Symbolic Action*. Berkeley: U of California P, 1966.

———. *The Philosophy of Literary Form*. Berkeley: U of California P, 1973.

Clifford, John, and John Shilb. "Composition Theory and Literary Theory." In *Perspectives on Research in Composition*. Ed. Ben W. McClelland and Timothy R. Donovan. New York: MLA, 1985, 45–67.

Fogarty, Daniel. *Roots for a New Rhetoric*. New York: Columbia U, Teacher's College, Bureau of Publication, 1959. Rpt. New York: Russell and Russell, 1968.

Lynn, Steven. "A Passage into Critical Theory." *College English* 15.3 (1990): 258–67.

Rosenblatt, Louise. *Literature as Exploration*. New York: Appleton-Century, 1938.

———. *The Reader, the Text, the Poem: The Transactional Theory of the Literary Work*. Carbondale: Southern Illinois UP, 1978.

Scholes, Robert. *Textual Power: Literary Theory and the Teaching of English*. New Haven, CT: Yale UP, 1985.

Straw, Stanley, B. "Challenging Communication: Readers Reading for Actualization." In *Beyond Communication: Reading Comprehension and Criticism*. Ed. Deanne Bogdan and Stanley B. Straw. Portsmouth, NH: Boynton/Cook, 1988.

Winterowd, W. Ross. "The Purification of Literature and Rhetoric." *College English* 49.3 (1987): 257–73.

———, and Jack Blum. *A Teacher's Introduction to Composition in the Rhetorical Tradition*. Urbana, IL: NCTE, 1994.

DENNIS CIESIELSKI

NEW HISTORICISM

Summary

Whether the work of the "Historian community in Composition" is represented as "pedagogical history" or "institutional history" (North, 66–67), as "intellectual" or "social" history (Schilb, "History of Rhetoric" 20–21), as "traditional 'big' histories" or "new," "more naturalistic" histories (Miller, "Composition," 19), or as "Traditional, Revisionary, and Sub/Versive" (Vitanza, "Notes," 85), compositionists have recognized the necessity of "a kind of knowledge that must be natural in any new field, knowledge about who and what has come before." (Re)constructing this knowledge has been an important part of the larger project of defining composition studies as "both the oldest and the newest of the humanities" (Connors, "Writing," 49). History has been a central concern for compositionists, and New Historicism has been an especially useful theoretical approach.

Since Stephen Greenblatt used the phrase in the early 1980s, "New Historicism" has come to represent a complex combination of theory and practice. Emerging first as an approach to reading and interpreting literary texts, New

Historicism developed further with "its use of poststructuralism to deconstruct existing literary histories and its desire to reconstruct more representative ones" (Thomas, 21). These latter applications of New Historicist theory have traveled to composition studies as part of the larger migration of theories from literary and cultural studies. However, unlike their counterparts in literary studies, historians in composition share a "joint project, a proselytizing intellectual agenda for the field as a whole." Not only do they seek to establish composition as a legitimate academic field of study, but they also wish to "encourage change in actual . . . ways of conceiving of writing instruction" (Miller, "Composition," 19–20).

As it is employed in literary studies, "New Historicism sets aside the potted history of ideas," the totalizing grand narrative, "the theory of economic stages, . . . and the study of authorial influence." In place of these views, New Historicists explore how "social and cultural events commingle messily." As a result, they can make a valid claim to have established new ways of studying history and a new awareness of how history and culture define each other" (Veeser, xiii). Louis Montrose describes New Historicism as "[t]he post-structuralist orientation to history," and he characterizes it "as a reciprocal concern with the historicity of texts and the textuality of history." Montrose explains further:

By "the historicity of texts," I mean to suggest the cultural specificity, the social embedment, of all modes of writing—not only the texts that critics study but also the texts in which we study them. By "the textuality of history," I mean to suggest, firstly, that we can have no access to a full and authentic past, a lived material existence, unmediated by the surviving textual traces of the society in question . . . ; and secondly, that those textual traces themselves are subject to subsequent textual mediations when they are construed as the "documents" upon which historians ground their own texts, called "histories." As Hayden White has forcefully reminded us, such textual histories necessarily but always incompletely constitute in their narrative and rhetorical forms the "History" to which they offer access. (Montrose, 20)

To acknowledge the textuality of history means also to recognize what John Schilb calls the "rhetoricity of history" ("The History of Rhetoric" 240). Accounts of histories are always already situated in complex webs of discourse, in several ways. The individual who constructs a history is situated in cultural and social contexts; she or he either "chooses a politics or is chosen by a politics" (Berlin, "Postmodernism," 171). Recognizing their situatedness, New Historicists seek to "foreground the politics of their perspective" (185). Further, the materials or events that historians choose to represent are also products of and participants in specific cultural contexts. New Historicism helps make visible the various "terministic screens" that both reflect and deflect reality (Burke, 45).

Reception and Significance in Composition Studies

Historians of composition and rhetoric embraced New Historicism soon after it emerged in literary and cultural studies, although the extent to which they have employed the strongest political, cultural, or materialist versions of the theory has varied. Building on the tradition established in preceding decades by historians such as Kitzhaber, Corbett, Murphy, and Kennedy, compositionists have continued to construct histories of several different kinds. Tracing composition's connection to classical rhetoric continues to be an important function of histories. The various historical accounts that have emerged range from those that are less revisionist and "Sub/Versive" to those that are explicitly political. The works of Lunsford, Glenn, Crowley, or Covino, for instance, though clearly reconstructing the rhetorical tradition, are not as openly political as the works of Jarratt or Bizzell and Herzberg.

The writing of institutional, curricular, and pedagogical histories of twentieth-century composition has flourished, and for the most part, these works are more readily identifiable as stronger versions of New Historicism. Berlin's and Vitanza's works (including the journal *Pre/Text*, which Vitanza launched in 1980) serve as exemplars of the ways in which New Historicism enables scholars to radically "refigure" composition studies and composition teaching. Harris, Faigley, Lu, Horner, Salvatori, and Miller also exemplify applications of New Historicist theory that are more explicitly political. In less overtly political ways, the work of scholars such as Connors, Brereton, and Johnson also contribute to the evolving historical portraits of composition studies.

The value of New Historicism resides in part in its attention to the intersections of theory, practice, and cultural and social contexts. Of equal value is its resistance to closure. New Historicism can assist us in the ongoing project that James Berlin defines in *Rhetorics, Poetics, and Cultures*: "It is time all reading and writing teachers situate their activities within the contexts of the larger profession as well as the contexts of economic and political concerns. We have much to gain working together, much to lose working alone" (180).

BIBLIOGRAPHY

Primary Texts

Berlin, James A. "Postmodernism, Politics, and Histories of Rhetoric." *Pre/Text* 11 (1990): 170–87.
———. "Revisionary History: The Dialectical Method." *Pre/Text* 8 (1987): 47–61.
Burke, Kenneth. *Language as Symbolic Action: Essays on Life, Literature and Method*. Berkeley: U of California P, 1966.
Connors, Robert J. "Writing the History of Our Discipline." In *An Introduction to Composition Studies*. Ed. Erika Lindemann and Gary Tate. New York: Oxford UP, 1991, 49–71.
Greenblatt, Stephen. "Towards a Poetics of Culture." In *The New Historian*. Ed. H Aram Veeser. New York: Routledge, 1989, 1–14.
Jarratt, Susan C. "Toward a Sophistic Historiography." *Pre/Text* 8 (1987): 9–26.
Miller, Susan. "Composition as a Cultural Artifact: Rethinking History as Theory." In *Writing Theory and Critical Theory*. Ed. John Clifford and John Schilb. New York: MLA, 1994, 19–32.

Montrose, Louis A. "Professing the Renaissance: The Poetics and Politics of Culture."
     In *The New Historian*. Ed. H Aram Veeser. New York: Routledge, 1989, 15–36.
Murphy, James J., James Berlin, Robert Connors, Sharon Crowley, Richard Enos, Susan
     Jarratt, Nan Johnson, Jan Swearingen, and Victor Vitanza. "Octalog: The Politics
     of Historiography." *Rhetoric Review* 7 (1988): 5–49.
Schilb, John. "Differences, Displacements, and Disruptions: Toward Revisionary His-
     tories of Rhetoric." *Pre/Text* 8 (1987): 29–44.
———. "The History of Rhetoric and the Rhetoric of History." Reprinted in *Pre/Text:
     The First Decade*. Ed. Victor Vitanza. Pittsburgh, PA: U of Pittsburgh P, 1993,
     237–262.
Thomas, Brook. *The New Historicism and Other Old-Fashioned Topics*. Princeton, NJ:
     Princeton UP, 1991.
Veeser, H. Aram, ed. *The New Historicism*. New York: Routledge, 1989.
Vitanza, Victor J. " 'Notes' towards Historiographies of Rhetorics; or, Rhetorics of the
     Histories of Rhetorics: Traditional, Revisionary, and Sub/Versive." *Pre/Text* 8
     (1987): 63–125.
———. *Writing Histories of Rhetoric*. Carbondale: Southern Illinois UP, 1994.
White, Hayden. *Metahistory: The Historical Imagination in Nineteenth-Century Europe*.
     Baltimore: Johns Hopkins UP, 1975.

Major Scholarship in Composition

Bartholomae, David. "The Tidy House: Basic Writing in the American Curriculum."
     Journal of Basic Writing 12 (1993): 4–21.
Berlin, James A. *Rhetoric and Reality: Writing Instruction in American Colleges, 1900–
     1985*. Carbondale: Southern Illinois UP, 1987.
———. *Rhetorics, Poetics, and Cultures: Refiguring College English Studies*. Urbana,
     IL: NCTE, 1996.
———. *Writing Instruction in Nineteenth-Century American Colleges*. Carbondale:
     Southern Illinois UP, 1984.
Bizzell, Patricia, and Bruce Herzberg, eds. *The Rhetorical Tradition: Readings from
     Classical Times to the Present*. Boston: Bedford, 1990.
Brereton, John, ed. *The Origins of Composition Studies in the American College, 1875–
     1925: A Documentary History*. Pittsburgh, PA: U of Pittsburgh P, 1995.
Campbell, Joann, ed. *Toward a Feminist Rhetoric: The Writing of Gertrude Buck*. Pitts-
     burgh, PA: U of Pittsburgh P, 1996.
Connors, Robert J. "The Rise and Fall of the Modes of Discourse." *College Composition
     and Communication* 32 (1981): 444–63.
Connors, Robert J., Lisa S. Ede, and Andrea A. Lunsford, eds. *Essays on Classical
     Rhetoric and Modern Discourse*. Carbondale: Southern Illinois UP, 1985.
Corbett, Edward P. J. *Classical Rhetoric for the Modern Student*. New York: Oxford UP,
     1965; 3rd ed., 1990.
Covino, William A. *The Art of Wondering: A Revisionist Return to the History of Rhet-
     oric*. Portsmouth, NH: Boynton/Cook, 1988.
Crowley, Sharon. *The Methodical Memory: Invention in Current Traditional Rhetoric*.
     Carbondale: Southern Illinois UP, 1990.
Enos, Theresa, and Stuart C. Brown, eds. *Professing the New Rhetorics*. Englewood
     Cliffs, NJ: Blair, 1994.
Faigley, Lester. *Fragments of Rationality*. Pittsburgh, PA: U of Pittsburgh P, 1992.

Gere, Anne Ruggles. *Writing Groups: History, Theory, and Implications.* Carbondale: Southern Illinois UP, 1987.

Glenn, Cheryl. *Rhetoric Retold: Regendering the Tradition from Antiquity through the Renaissance.* Carbondale: Southern Illinois UP, 1997.

———. "Sex, Lies, and Manuscript: Refiguring Aspasia in the History of Rhetoric." *College Composition and Communication* 45 (1994): 180–99.

Harris, Joseph. *A Teaching Subject: Composition since 1966.* Upper Saddle River, NJ: Prentice-Hall, 1996.

Hawisher, Gail E., Paul LeBlanc, Charles Moran, and Cynthia L. Selfe. *Computers and the Teaching of Writing in American Higher Education, 1979–1994: A History.* Norwood, NJ: Ablex, 1996.

Horner, Bruce. "Discoursing Basic Writing." *College Composition and Communication* 47 (1996): 199–222.

Horner, Winifred Bryan. *Nineteenth-Century Scottish Rhetoric: The American Connection.* Carbondale: Southern Illinois UP, 1993.

Jarratt, Susan. *Rereading the Sophists: Classical Rhetoric Refigured.* Carbondale: Southern Illinois UP, 1991.

Johnson, Nan. *Nineteenth-Century Rhetoric in North America.* Carbondale: Southern Illinois UP, 1991.

Kitzhaber, Albert. *Rhetoric in American Colleges, 1850–1900.* Dallas: Southern Methodist UP, 1990.

Lu, Min-Zhan. "Conflict and Struggle: The Enemies or Preconditions of Basic Writing?" *College English* 54 (1992): 887–913.

———. "Redefining the Legacy of Mina Shaughnessy: A Critique of the Politics of Linguistic Innocence." *Journal of Basic Writing* 10 (1991): 26–40.

Lunsford, Andrea, ed. *Reclaiming Rhetorica: Women in the Rhetorical Tradition.* Pittsburgh, PA: U of Pittsburgh P, 1995.

Miller, Susan. *Rescuing the Subject: A Critical Introduction to Rhetoric and the Writer.* Carbondale: Southern Illinois UP, 1989.

———. *Textual Carnivals: The Politics of Composition.* Carbondale: Southern Illinois UP, 1991.

Neel, Jasper. *Aristotle's Voice: Rhetoric, Theory, and Writing in America.* Carbondale: Southern Illinois UP, 1995.

———. *Plato, Derrida, and Writing.* Carbondale: Southern Illinois UP, 1988.

North, Stephen. *The Making of Knowledge in Composition: Portrait of an Emerging Field.* Upper Montclair, NJ: Boynton/Cook, 1987.

Russell, David R. *Writing in the Academic Disciplines, 1870–1990: A Curricular History.* Carbondale: Southern Illinois UP, 1991.

Salvatori, Mariolina, ed. *Pedagogy: Disturbing History, 1819–1929.* Pittsburgh, PA: U of Pittsburgh P, 1996.

Swearingen, C. Jan. *Rhetoric and Irony: Western Literacy and Western Lies.* New York: Oxford UP, 1991.

Varnum, Robin. *Fencing with Words: A History of Writing Instruction at Amherst College during the Era of Theodore Baird, 1938–1966.* Urbana, IL: NCTE, 1996.

GLENN BLALOCK

P

PHENOMENOLOGICAL CRITICISM

Summary

The concerns that distinguish phenomenological criticism in crucial ways parallel those inherent in composition studies. Composition studies reveals in its complexity the dynamics of creating and conversing with ontic, historical "things"—written texts—that are, at the same time, only made present through the processes of those beings who animate such texts: the diverse experiences of readers and writers. In the same way, the transactions, obstacles, and ambiguities characteristic of that animation are the subjects of phenomenological criticism, in particular the phenomenological literary theory of Polish philosopher Roman Ingarden (1893–1970).

Ingarden, who is considered the originator of phenomenological aesthetics, offers a phenomenological response to the question, "What is the literary work of art?" His two seminal texts, *The Literary Work of Art* (1931) and *The Cognition of the Literary Work of Art* (1937) are both general in their phenomenological descriptions and serve best as points of departure or a grounding for more particular literary critical study; *The Literary Work of Art* deals with the conditions necessary for a work of literature to exist *as* literature, and *The Cognition of the Literary Work of Art* cleaves more to defining "the psychic subject during a reading" (*The Literary Work of Art* 333). Ingarden obeys in his investigation the organicism of the entity under examination in a fashion typical of phenomenological inquiry. He describes the literary work of art without co-opting terminology analogous to or suggestive of any other philosophical description. In their exhaustive rigor, Ingarden's texts are reminiscent of Husserl's *Ideas I* (1913) and Heidegger's *Being and Time* (1927), in particular referring to Husserl's writings throughout. Ingarden offers an analysis of the mode of being characteristic of any literary work. He delineates the properties that distinguish such entities from other objects, considering both the ontic nature of the work—its physicality in paper, binding, and ink—and those traits constitutive of its literary nature, in particular its four interrelated "strata": word sounds; meaning units such as nouns, verbs, and sentences; "schematized aspects," or the intricate design of characters, places, or things given to readers through which states of being are presented; and represented objectivities, or the realities the words and sentences make present. A fifth stratum, "ideas" or "metaphysical qualities," is operative in some of the finest literary works of art, but, Ingarden asserts, this stratum is not essential to the description of a work per se. The work as a whole is "schematic," with the various strata at once interactive, interdependent, and yielding potential meanings for the text. However, "the literary work is never *fully* grasped in *all* its strata and components but always only partially, always, so to speak, in only a *perspectival foreshortening*" (*The Literary Work of Art* 334). This qualification echoes a similar claim by Heidegger in *Being and Time* that, because of the human mode of being's ability to "be open" toward entities in a focused, but limited fashion (a human being cannot see a thing in all ways at once), entities reveal only parts of themselves at a given time, concealing the remainder. What is revealed is contingent upon the thinker's perspective in relation to an entity. Ingarden's notion of perspectival foreshortening is, then, consistent with other phenomenological descriptions of what it is to be human.

Ingarden also describes the ways in which the literary work presents itself as an *experience* through the combined intentions of both an author, as creator, and a reader, as the animator of the text. While Ingarden's description "is at once a study in ontology and a study of essence" (D. M. Levin, Foreword to *The Literary Work of Art* xxiv), these concerns do not elevate Ingarden's consideration of the literary work to purely metaphysical speculation; instead, like all phenomenological inquiry, the essential being of the work is pursued in the "logically necessary and sufficient conditions" (Levin, Foreword to *The Literary Work of Art* xxiv) that constitute a real-life reading experience. Ingarden's phenomenology, like that of the hermeneuticists Heidegger and Gadamer, is continually rooted in and delimited by the real.

Several dichotomies become apparent in Ingarden's description. First, the literary work offers both differentiation and unity. Ingarden's strata reveal distinctively different conditions at the sound, word, sentence, and paragraph levels; however, he claims that "the value qualities that are constituted in the individual strata . . . [which] in their totality bring about a polyphonic harmony" (*The Literary Work of Art* 369): the distinction of the parts ultimately lends only to pleasing unity of the whole. (As an aside, reader-response theorist Wolfgang Iser has criticized Ingarden's valorizing of harmony as indicative of the latter's inability to overcome his own grounding in classical aesthetics.) Ingarden also defines the balance between the literary work's ontic and animated modes of being. Regardless of the authorial genius that brings it into being, the literary work, as an object in itself, has no power, no life. Only through a reader's attention does the work exist, but the text, holding in reserve a potential for experiences, transcends any one particular reading. This relationship inspires an important term in Ingarden's phenomenological account: the literary work's *heteronomy*. As Paul B. Armstrong notes in his discussion of Ingarden in *The Johns Hopkins Guide to Literary Theory and Criticism*, the literary work

has its origin in the acts of consciousness of its creator that are preserved in writing or through other physical means [such as the performance of drama], and these acts are then reanimated (although not precisely duplicated) by the consciousness of the reader [or, in the case of drama, the spectator]. The work is not reducible to the psychology of either the author or the reader, however. It has a history that goes beyond the consciousness of any individual reader. The existence of a work transcends any particular, momentary experience of it, even though it came into being and continues to exist only through various acts of consciousness. . . .[The work] is neither autonomous of nor completely dependent on the consciousness of the author and the reader; rather, it is paradoxically based on them as it transcends them. (564)

In the manner Armstrong delineates, the literary work is both contingent in its dependency upon what Ingarden terms as "concretizations" or "actualizations"—real acts of consciousness performed by readers reading—and, at the same time, transcendent of any single concretization, thus availing itself to other readings. These concretizations are never to be confused with embodying the actual literary work itself because, in "aesthetic apprehension of the work," the reader

usually *goes beyond* what is simply presented by the text (or projected by it) and in various respects *completes* the represented objectivities, so that at least some of the spots of indeterminacy are removed and are frequently replaced by determinations that not only are not determined by the text but, what is more, are not in agreement with the positively determined objective moments. (Ingarden, *The Literary Work of Art* 252).

Alive only as it is experienced in manifold actualizations but yet never fully grasped by them, appearing ontic yet transcendent, the literary work as "an intersubjective intentional object" (Ingarden, *Cognition* 14) is

a true wonder. It exists and lives and works on us, it enriches our lives to an extraordinary degree, it gives us hours of delight, and it allows us to descend into the very depths of existence, and yet it is only an ontically heteronomous formation which in terms of ontic autonomy is a nothing. If we wish to apprehend it theoretically, it shows a complexity and many-sidedness that can hardly be taken in; and yet it stands before us in aesthetic experience as a unity which allows this complex structure to shine through. It has an ontically heteronomous existence that seems to be completely passive and to suffer defenselessly all our operations; and yet by its concretizations it evokes deep changes in our life; it broadens it, raises it above the flatness of everyday existence, and gives it a lovely radiance. It is a "nothing" and yet a wonderful world in itself—even though it comes into being and exists only by our grace. (Ingarden, *The Literary Work of Art* 373)

While Ingarden has helped to characterize the interdependence of relationships among the text, the author, and the reader in reader-response theories (see Magliola's *Phenomenology and Literature*, 107–40), his impact on composition studies has yet to be articulated. However, despite the arcane nature of much of his writing, Ingarden's insights do address current issues in composition studies. For example, his phenomenological methodology has the potential to reveal the nature of texts in a way that invites the interplay, and not the exclusivity, of expressivist and social-epistemic theories of knowledge construction. He acknowledges the psychic privacy of the individual's response to a text but, at the same time, notes the variety of readings from diverse, historical individuals that are necessary for maintaining the text's vitality. Knowledge of the text is negotiated by the one and the many over time and in concert. In addition, Ingarden's work foregrounds the reconciliation of both consensus and dissensus about textual meaning; a text regarded negatively, for Ingarden, simply may not have found the correct or appreciative audience. Ingarden also characterizes the defining freedom of the text to transcend all readings: the generality of his phenomenological description returns to texts an ineffability denied them in more narrow determinations of their being as psychologistic projections of culturally situated authors or audiences. Paradoxically, he unbinds texts from those beings who are responsible for their continued existence.

Reception and Significance in Composition Studies

In more pragmatic classroom use, Ingarden's definition of the literary work's properties has particular attractiveness in emphasizing for students the synergy of a text's structure and intention: how strata of meaning are interdependent, interactive, and differently animated with each "reconstruction" (*The Literary Work of Art* 337), as Ingarden calls the conscious acts of readers reading. A change at one level of textual strategy profoundly affects the reader's encounter with the next. A distillation of Ingarden's theories about the literary work could become best animated when applied to the construction and analyses of students' *own* texts. Ingarden provides a framework of concerns for novice writers: they must think seriously about choices of words and sentence patterns, about the indeterminacy available in even their most defined prose, and about the ways in which their readers will fill in those "spots." Teachers, as readers and evaluators of students' texts, are no less immune to textual indeterminacy, frequently intending meanings far different from those of the authors. Ingarden, like the composition specialists in Anson's 1989 *Writing and Response*—particularly Wall and Hull in their chapter, "The Semantics of Error"—acknowledges that the written text's own potential for ambiguity promotes such divergence. At best, Ingarden provides a disposition toward the life of language that sharply diverges from the reduction thereof to equipmental facility as an "instrument" of communication. The dynamic union of text and writer (or reader) that Ingarden defines could reveal to students both their complicity in the gamble of meaning *and* that of the work. Perhaps Ingarden's phenomenological description may yield a protocol for constructing texts, at once emphasizing formal features and imbuing structure with a concomitant intersubjective, transactional energy of its own—a life rooted both in the real experiences of readers reading and in the transcendent realm of ideas.

BIBLIOGRAPHY

Primary Texts

Ingarden, Roman. *The Cognition of the Literary Work of Art*. 1937. Rpt. Trans. Ruth Ann Crowley and Kenneth R. Olson. Evanston, IL: Northwestern UP, 1973.
————. *The Literary Work of Art*. 1931. Rpt. Trans. George G. Grabowicz. Evanston, IL: Northwestern UP, 1973.

Major Scholarship in Composition

(*Note*: A review of current composition scholarship revealed neither books nor articles applying Ingarden's theories to composition studies. The works dealing with Ingarden noted here, however, focus on issues of concern for composition specialists and tangentially may serve the purpose of integrating Ingarden's perspective into the field of composition studies.)

Anson, Chris M. *Writing and Response, Practice and Research*. Urbana, IL: NCTE, 1989.
Armstrong, Paul B. "Phenomenology." In *The Johns Hopkins Guide to Literary Theory and Criticism*. Ed. Michael Groden and Martin Kreiswirth. Baltimore, MD: Johns Hopkins UP, 562–66.
Hausman, Carl. "Language and Metaphysics: The Ontology of Metaphor." *Philosophy and Rhetoric* 24.1 (1991): 25–42.
Magliola, Robert R. *Phenomenology and Literature*. West Lafayette, IN: Purdue UP, 1977.
Murray, Michael. "Ingarden and the End of Phenomenological Aesthetics." *Research in Phenomenology* 19 (1989): 171–79.
Olmsted, Wendy Raudenbush. "The Uses of Rhetoric: Indeterminacy in Legal Reasoning, Practical Thinking and the Interpretation of Literary Figures." *Philosophy and Rhetoric* 24.1 (1991): 1–24.
Shusterman, R. "Ingarden, Inscription and Literary Ontology." *Journal of the British Society for Phenomenology* 18.2 (1987): 103–19.
Steeves, H. Peter. "Phenomenology and the Possibility of Narrative." *CLIO* 24 (Fall 1994): 21–36.
Ulicka, D. "Language and Experience: The Object and Method of Ingarden's Philosophy." *Pamietnik Literacki* 77.3 (1986): 117–42.
————. "Mimesis and Literary Character: Ingarden's Concept of Language in the Literary Work." *Pamietnik Literacki* 79.2 (1988): 143–76.
Wall, Susan V., and Glynda A. Hull. "The Semiotics of Error: What Do Teachers Know?" In *Writing and Response*. Ed. Chris M. Anson. Urbana, IL: NCTE, 1989, 261–92.

Wellek, René. *Four Critics: Croce, Valery, Lukacs, and Ingarden.* Seattle: U of Washington P, 1982.

JUDITH HALDEN-SULLIVAN

POSTMODERNISM

Summary

No definition could adequately embrace the contradictions and diverse perspectives associated with postmodernism, and critics have argued that the term itself
resists definition. Jean Baudrillard describes the postmodern as

the characteristic of a universe where no more definitions are possible. . . . It all revolves
around an impossible definition. One is no longer in a history of art or a history of forms.
. . . The extreme limit of these possibilities has been reached. . . . All that remains . . . is
to play with the pieces. Playing with the pieces—that is postmodern. (''Interview,'' 24).

Some critics argue that this indefinite quality of postmodernism is positive and
provocative: ''There is no way of working quickly through the contradictions
described in discussions of postmodernity. . . . Indeed, asserting that there is no
satisfactory definition of postmodernism is a positive expression. . . . When it
can be defined, the provocativeness of postmodernism will have long since
ended'' (Faigley, 3–4). Even so, postmodernism has frequently been associated
with a number of recurring themes:

1. Indeterminacy, including linguistic ambiguity, irony, and uncertainty.
2. Fragmentation, including the effects of anarchy, chaos, and chance.
3. Delegitimation and antifoundationalism, including skepticism toward master codes,
   metanarratives, totalization, the unity of the individual subject, and universal claims
   about ''absolute truths'' and the ''nature of reality.''
4. Ephemerality and immanent change, including a sense that the pervasive fluidity of
   appearances and innovation have erased distinctions of ''high and low culture,'' ''surface and depth,'' ''representation and object,'' and historical periodization.
5. Heterogeneity and carnivalization, including pluralistic styles, pastiche, hybridization,
   inversion, parody, absurdity, and decanonization.
6. Resistance to rationalized and dominant socioeconomic structures, especially patriarchy, capitalism, and phallologocentrism. ''Phallologocentism'' extends ''logocentrism,'' the idea that Western discourse has been centered on and has valorized ''logos'' as a privileged form of speech and reason limited by the Platonic metaphysics
   of presence, by aligning the centrality of the logos with the image of the ''phallus''
   as a metonymy of male-dominated discourse in Western political traditions of patriarchy.

   Critics began using the term ''postmodernism'' in the 1940s as a synonym
for ''ultramodern'' and to describe antirationalist reactions to abstract art, while
''Post-Modern'' architecture later emerged as an eclectic and pastiche style that

borrows indiscriminately from previous styles (Rose, *Parody* 196). In literary criticism, Ihab Hassan argues that postmodernism constitutes a radical break with modernism's hierarchical, formalist, and totalizing tendencies: ''Postmodernism veers toward . . . open, playful, provisional, disjunctive, and indeterminate forms, a discourse of ironies and fragments'' (*Dismemberment* 271). From the late 1960s onward, postmodernism is variously applied to any endeavor that breaks with formal codes of representation in favor of mixed modes or a radical departure from normalized conventions. Similarly, the rhetorical gesture of the ''post-'' prefix attempts to get beyond the codified and known by opening up a linguistic space for the as-yet unknown and unexplored—a gesture that continues to gather a plurality of ''post-'' signifiers under its umbrella: postindustrial, poststructuralism, post-Marxism, postcapitalism, postcolonial, and so forth.

Some critics view the fragmentation and emphemerality of postmodernism as symptoms of the historical exhaustion of modernist innovations, which have degenerated into an impoverished mass culture of kitsch, relativism, and nihilism in which ''anything goes.'' Jürgen Habermas rejects both postmodernism and the ''exhaustion of modernism'' critique as ''neoconservative'' political reactions that abandon the unfinished Enlightenment ''project of modernity,'' and he calls for a renewal of the Enlightenment ideals of political emancipation through a reasoned consensus of ''communicative rationality'' (''Modernity,'' in Foster, 8). Andreas Huyssen, however, counters that such negative views of postmodernism betray a nostalgia for the modernist hegemony of high art over and against mass culture and that poststructuralism, which critically informed postmodernism with academic theories of linguistic self-limitation and intertextuality in the 1970s (see entries on ''Poststructuralism'' and ''Deconstruction'' in this volume), brought closure to modernist aesthetics and opened postmodernism to a new horizon of ''productive tension between the political and the aesthetic, between history and the text, between engagement and the mission of art'' (221).

Jean-Francois Lyotard provides a forceful example of the postmodern theme of deligitimation by questioning the grand narratives of Enlightenment modernism and human progress: ''I define postmodern as incredulity toward metanarratives'' (xxiv). Lyotard attacks Habermas's notion of consensus and communicative rationality as a totalizing discourse of self-legitimation; he embraces ''paralogy'' instead, and he characterizes postmodern knowledges as partial, contingent, and localized. Consensus, then, becomes a suspect value that seeks rational closure, while postmodern knowledges remain open to the pragmatic differences of heterogeneous language games, or a dissensus of competing ''little narratives'' (Lyotard 64–67). Such cultural critics as Richard Rorty pursue a similar antifoundationalist position but view the pragmatics of language games as a means of preserving a balance among competing interpretive communities, the radical dissensus of diverging beliefs, and the desire for intellectual freedom.

Neo-Marxist and materialist thinkers express concern about postmodernism's tendency to depoliticize discourse, and they call upon "resistance postmodernism" to provide the political vitality required to reassert a utopian vision of social justice. Hal Foster identifies "resistant postmodernism" as an anti-aesthetic that deconstructs the modernist tradition of "art for art's sake" and reinscribes alternative cultural forms in a "practice, cross-disciplinary in nature, that is sensitive to cultural forms engaged in a politic (e.g., feminist art) or rooted in the vernacular" (xii–xv). Similarly, Fredric Jameson criticizes postmodern tendencies toward passivity, alienation, and the erasure of depth, historicity, and affect as symptoms of "the cultural logic of late capitalism," which must be resisted. He posits an "aesthetic of cognitive mapping" which would enable individuals to re-locate and rehistoricize their subject positions as agents of change within the global displacements of international capitalism (54, 409). Other proponents of resistance postmodernism, including feminist theorists, view Jameson's position as a return to modernist aesthetics that occludes the heterogeneity and diversity of postmodern politics. Donna Haraway, for example, draws upon and surpasses Marxist and antifoundational themes in "A Cyborg Manifesto," where she rejects naturalized categories of representation in favor of an "experimental ethnography" that transgresses the semiotic boundaries between humans and machines and requires regeneration through "a powerful infidel heteroglossia . . . that means both building and destroying machines, identities, categories, relationships, space stories" (181). Similarly, in "Gender Trouble," Judith Butler resists the "category of women" itself as "foundational" and "normative," and she suggests that such categories limit feminist experience and exclude women whose emancipation must also be considered along "class, color, age, and ethnic lines" (in Nicholson, 325–27). Teresa Ebert, on the other hand, calls for a renewal of historical materialism and an ideological critique of the continuing exploitation of women by international, patriarchal capitalism. Ebert specifically criticizes "ludic postmodernists" and "ludic feminists" (including Haraway and Butler) for being seduced by poststructuralist aesthetics and its assumptions about linguistic play, and she advocates Marxist feminism as a means reestablishing the emancipatory project of feminism (3–15).

Reception and Significance in Composition Studies

Postmodernism's reception in composition theory reflects many of the same enthusiasms, divisions, and contradictions described earlier for critical theorists in general. For example, some have embraced postmodernism's "incredulity toward metanarratives" and its potential for valuing localized narratives, dissensus, and personal histories. Other compositionists worry that postmodernism's skepticism toward metanarratives and attention to dissensus and the incommensurability of discourses may contribute to the decline of public discourse, ultimately subverting the hard-won Enlightenment values of emancipation and social justice. John Schilb, for example, notes that "just as modernism still elicits diverse moral and political judgements, so it remains undecided whether we should celebrate or disdain postmodernism'' (in Harkin and Schilb, 174). The question of postmodernism has complicated the evolution of composition theory and elicited intense debate around several themes, including the following:

1. The incredulity toward metanarratives has increased skepticism toward foundational theories for unifying composition research and pedagogy, or what Victor Vitanza calls ''the will to systematize [the] language of [composing]'' (in Harkin and Schilb, 144–47). Such skepticism toward unifying theories may encourage compositionists' historic tendency to draw upon theoretical models from other disciplines, borrow procedures from disparate modes of inquiry, and view writing pedagogy as a dispersed collection of diverse and localized practices.

2. The heterogeneity and fragmentation of traditionally unified concepts such as author, intention, purpose, message, voice, and so on have reshaped the concepts of the writing and reading subjects as contradictory sites of competing psychological and political forces: for example, writers may now occupy diverse ''subject positions'' overdetermined by heterogeneous cultural, political, and economic claims, while readers may be constructed as occupying an intersection of overlapping and competing discourse communities (Faigley, 225).

3. Decanonization and the acceptance of mass or ''popular'' culture has decentered the master narratives of modernist aesthetics and traditional writerly authority, allowing the languages of women and minorities, student writing, peer collaboration, and visual and electronic media to become serious objects of theoretical study and alternative pedagogical practices. As a corollary to decentered writerly authority, the hegemony of teacherly and institutional authorities have also been called into question by composition theorists (Gale, 1–32).

4. Resistance postmodernism foregrounds cultural critique, argumentation, and political commitment as critical writing practices dedicated to exposing the contradictions and limitations imposed on composition as a modernist discipline (Worsham and Jarratt in Harkin and Schilb, 84–104, 105–138). This would include, for example, a critique of college composition programs as rationalized and oppressive economic structures that reinforce the subservient roles of women as pedagogical laborers and thus reproduce, rather than resist, the dominant discourses of hegemonic culture.

Postmodernism has had a pervasive influence on composition theory and practice. On the one hand, it challenges compositionists' assumptions about the possibility of a unified theoretical ground for making claims about writing instruction, their desire for a common pedagogical concept of the ''writing student'' as a unified and rational subject, and the political viability of using the institutionalized standards of ''academic discourse'' as a means for assimilating students into the dominant culture and its discourse. On the other hand, postmodernism offers multiple and heterogeneous points of departure for rethinking modernist tendencies in composition theory and for opening writing pedagogy to diverse modes of resistance, counterpractice, critical inquiry, and ethical subjectivity.

BIBLIOGRAPHY

Primary Texts

Aronowitz, Stanley, and Henry A. Giroux. *Postmodern Education: Politics, Culture, and Social Criticism*. Minneapolis: U of Minnesota P, 1991.

Baudrillard, Jean. "Interview: Game with Vestiges." *On the Beach* 5 (1984): 19–25.

———. *Simulacra and Simulation*. Trans. Sheila Faria Glaser. Ann Arbor: U of Michigan P, 1994.

Butler, Judith. "Gender Trouble, Feminist Theory, and Psychoanalytic Discourse." In *Feminism/Postmodernism*. Ed. Linda Nicholson. New York: Routledge, 1990.

Calinescu, Matei. *Five Faces of Modernity*. Durham, NC: Duke UP, 1987.

Conner, Steven. *Postmodernist Culture: An Introduction to Theories of the Contemporary*. Oxford, U.K.: Basil Blackwell, 1989.

Ebert, Theresa L. *Ludic Feminism and After: Postmodernism, Desire, and Labor in Late Capitalism*. Ann Arbor: U of Michigan P, 1996.

Foster, Hal, ed. *The Anti-Aesthetic: Essays on Postmodern Culture*. Port Townsend, WA: Bay P, 1983.

Giroux, Henry A. ed. *Postmodernism, Feminism, and Cultural Politics: Redrawing Educational Boundaries*. Albany: State U of New York P, 1991.

Habermas, Jürgen. "Modernity—An Incomplete Project." In *The Anti-Aesthetic: Essays on Postmodern Culture*. Ed. Hal Foster. Port Townsend, WA: Bay P, 1983; republished as *Postmodern Culture*. London, 1985, 3–15.

Harvey, David. *The Condition of Postmodernity: An Enquiry into Cultural Change*. Oxford, U.K.: Blackwell, 1989.

Haraway, Donna J. "A Cyborg Manifesto: Science, Technology, and Socialist-Feminism in the Late Twentieth Century." In *Simians, Cyborgs, and Women: The Reinvention of Nature*. By Donna J. Haraway. New York: Routledge, 1991, 149–81.

———. *Simians, Cyborgs, and Women: The Reinvention of Nature*. New York: Routledge, 1991.

Hassan, Ihab. *The Dismemberment of Orpheus: Toward a Postmodern Literature*. Madison: U of Wisconsin P, 1982.

———. *The Postmodern Turn: Essays in Postmodern Culture and Theory*. Columbus: Ohio State UP, 1987.

Hoeveler, J. David. *The Postmodernist Turn*. New York: Twayne, 1996.

Hutcheon, Linda. *The Politics of Postmodernism*. London: Routledge, 1989.

Huyssen, Andreas. *After the Great Divide: Modernism, Mass Culture, and Postmodernism*. Bloomington: Indiana UP, 1986.

Jameson, Fredric. *Postmodernism, or, The Cultural Logic of Late Capitalism*. Durham, NC: Duke UP, 1991.

Jencks, Charles. *The Language of Post-Modern Architecture*. 1977. Rpt. London: Academy, 1991.

Kellner, Douglas. *Jean Baudrillard: From Marxism to Postmodernism and Beyond*. Stanford, CA: Stanford UP, 1989.

Lyotard, Jean-Francois. *The Postmodern Condition: A Report on Knowledge*. Minneapolis: U of Minnesota P, 1984.

———. *The Postmodern Explained*. Minneapolis: U of Minnesota P, 1992.

McGown, John. *Postmodernism and Its Critics*. Ithaca, NY: Cornell UP, 1991.

Nicholson, Linda, ed. *Feminism/Postmodernism*. New York: Routledge, 1990.

Rorty, Richard. *Contingency, Irony, and Solidarity*. Cambridge: Cambridge UP, 1989.

Rose, Margaret A. *Parody: Ancient, Modern, and Post-Modern*. Cambridge: Cambridge UP, 1993.

———. *The Post-Modern and the Post-Industrial*. Cambridge: Cambridge UP, 1991.

Waugh, Patricia. *Practicing Postmodernism, Reading Modernism*. New York: Edward Arnold, 1992.

Major Scholarship in Composition

Faigley, Lester. *Fragments of Rationality: Postmodernity and the Subject of Composition*. Pittsburgh, PA: U of Pittsburgh P, 1992.

Gale, Xin Liu. *Teachers, Discourses and Authority in the Postmodern Composition Classroom*. Albany: State U of New York P, 1996.

Harkin, Patricia, and John Schilb, eds. *Contending with Words: Composition and Rhetoric in a Postmodern Age*. New York: MLA, 1991.

Jarratt, Susan. "Feminism and Composition: The Case for Conflict." In *Contending with Words: Composition and Rhetoric in a Postmodern Age*. Ed. Patricia Harkin and John Schilb. New York: MLA, 1991, 105–23.

Kent, Thomas. *Paralogic Rhetoric: A Theory of Communicative Interaction*. Lewisberg, PA: Bucknell UP, 1993.

Olson, Gary A., and Sidney I. Dobrin, eds. *Composition Theory for the Postmodern Classroom*. Albany: State U of New York P, 1995.

Schilb, John. "Cultural Studies, Postmodernism, and Composition." In *Contending with Words: Composition and Rhetoric in a Postmodern Age*. Ed. Patricia Harkin and John Schilb. New York: MLA, 1991, 173–88.

Vitanza, Victor. "Three Countertheses: Or, a Critical In(ter)vention into Composition Theories and Pedagogies." In *Contending with Words: Composition and Rhetoric in a Postmodern Age*. Ed. Patricia Harkin and John Schilb. New York: MLA, 1991, 139–72.

Worsham, Lynn. "Writing against Writing: The Predicament of *Ecriture Féminine* in Composition Studies." In *Contending with Words: Composition and Rhetoric in a Postmodern Age*. Ed. Patricia Harkin and John Schilb. New York: MLA, 1991, 82–104.

WILLIAM V. VAN PELT

POSTSTRUCTURALISM

Summary

Poststructuralism should be considered not so much a unified theory as an umbrella term for a variety of theories that historically followed structuralism and New Criticism and have now given way to postmodernism, a larger umbrella term. Several of these include but are in no way limited to deconstruction, reader-response theory, New Historicism, postcolonialism, social constructionism, and the writings of Michel Foucault, Jacques Derrida, Roland Barthes, Jacques Lacan, Stanley Fish, and Julia Kristeva. Arguably, cultural studies and ideological criticism may also be said to have their roots in some of the analyses of language that poststructuralism warrants, but it is the wallowing in language that distinguishes these avenues from poststructuralism. As such, poststructuralism has at least four central tenants: (1) no speaking subject determines meaning; (2) language regulates the order of discursive formations; (3) divisions between traditional oppositions are weakened; and (4) meanings are dispersed and exist only in relation to each other.

Meaning, for poststructuralism, is not bound by a speaking subject or author in the sense that the author would determine meaning. Although New Criticism similarly would limit the author's role in determining the meaning of a text, poststructuralism argues for the significance of the reader (particularly in reader-response theory, from Barthes) and the author-function (from Foucault). For Barthes, in "From Work to Text," "the *I* that writes the text is never, itself, anything more than a paper *I*" (79). Barthes argues in "The Death of the Author" that the meaning of a text does not depend on the intentions of the writer but rather the interpretation of the reader. In "What Is an Author?" Foucault argues that the subject "should be reconsidered, not to restore the theme of an originating subject, but to seize its functions, its intervention in discourse, and its system of dependencies" (137). Further, he contends that "the rules of formation operate not only in the mind or the consciousness of individuals, but in discourse itself" (*Archaeology* 63). In this way, the poststructural subject might be said to have several subject positions that are supplied by discourse, which also works to subject (i.e., to make one follow certain rules). For Lacan, the individual is an amalgam of society.

The construction of subjects works through language, and Foucault says that language regulates the order of discursive formations, which are complex groups of relations that function as a rule. Foucault says that a discursive formation occurs "whenever one can describe, between a number of statements, such a system of dispersion, whenever, between objects, types of statement, concepts, or thematic choices, one can define a regularity" (*Archaeology* 38). For poststructuralism, these regularities construct practice, largely determining what can be said and how. In part, Fish's description of the interpretive community rests on understanding language as a system determined by social and cultural forces.

For deconstruction in particular, poststructuralism weakens divisions between traditional oppositions, such as between signifier and signified and between reader and writer. For Eagleton, "deconstruction tries to show how such oppositions, in order to hold themselves in place, are sometimes betrayed into inverting or collapsing themselves, or need to banish to the text's margins certain niggling details which can be made to return and plague them" (133). Derrida describes these oppositions for what he calls their "differance": that is, the way they differ in space and defer in time. In his argument in *Of Grammatology* and elsewhere, Derrida explains why it is possible to deconstruct these oppositions by showing that they are constituted by discourse and "elevated by social ideologies to a privileged position, or made the centres around which other meanings are forced to turn" (Eagleton, 131).

Rather, for poststructuralists, meanings are dispersed in texts in a "web-like complexity of signs"(Eagleton, 132) and "a continual flickering, spilling and defusing of meaning" (Eagleton, 134). For Derrida, in "Structure, Sign and Play in the Discourse of the Human Sciences," the theory of the supplement allows texts to never be closed but rather always keeps them both lacking in some way and needing supplementary material (289). In "Signature Event Context," Derrida says that all texts are iterable and capable of being grafted onto other texts, like a plant onto another plant (317). Meanings, then, are scattered and not housed in one particular place, but are always capable of being cited in any context (320). Foucault considers statements dispersed in discourse, arguing that his own discourse "is trying to operate a [decentering] that leaves no privilege to any [center]" (*Archaeology* 205). Statements exist only in relation to each other. Such work informs Kristeva's intertextual theory.

Reception and Significance in Composition Studies

It might be said that as literary studies turned to poststructural theory, so did composition studies. In his *Fragments of Rationality*, Lester Faigley comments that in the early 1980s some English department faculty recognized how deconstructive analyses and process pedagogies both "undermined the fixed, authoritative text" that was the subject of traditional literary analysis (37). Deconstructionists, he comments, see meaning as open and "ever spreading," while process pedagogues look at texts as "endlessly revised" (37). Even more so, Edward M. White finds a "general hospitality" from composition teachers toward poststructuralist theories "because they reflect with considerable accuracy the world within which we grade our papers, work through holistic essay readings, and confer with more or less inarticulate undergraduates" (187).

But the response to poststructuralism within composition has been really more mixed than White suggests. Several years after White's article was published, John Schilb comments, "To me—with the substantial benefit of hindsight!—the overall reception [to poststructuralism] has wound up being mixed to negative" ("Composition and Poststructuralism," 440). In "Composition and Poststructuralism: A Tale of Two Conferences," Schilb compares two influential conferences—one the 1963 College Composition and Communication Conference meeting, which helped to institutionalize composition, and the other the 1966 Johns Hopkins University meeting, at which several influential French literary critics described their views. After imagining exchanges between Edward Corbett and Roland Barthes, Francis Christensen and Jacques Lacan, and Wayne Booth and Jacques Derrida, Schilb argues that English departments should engage in a similar conversation to allow poststructural and literary theory to inform each other. Similarly, Jack Blum writes that "poststructuralism provides ample opportunity to make theoretical connections between literary studies and composition" (93). Further, he argues, "poststructuralism reinstates a strong emphasis upon reading as a central commitment of the composition classroom" (94), a close reading that questions the assumptions a text makes and asserts that students have something of value to say.

On the other hand, W. Ross Winterowd comments: "Derrida's work is profoundly interesting, utterly provocative, and, in my own view, often totally wrongheaded. Nonetheless, we should think about consequences'' (84). Winterowd argues that the composition teacher will have a problem with indeterminate meanings because he or she will not be able to claim knowledge of what the student is trying to say in a paper. ''In fact, if we give up the idea that meaning is determinate, we pretty much reduce teaching composition to mechanics'' (85). The imitation of difficult, opaque literary theory will be most valued, he warns, and Faigley echoes that by the end of the 1980s, ''more disturbing versions of deconstruction had come to composition studies, questioning the advice given in composition textbooks to use thesis statements, topic sentences, headings, and other cues to the reader'' (*Fragments* 37).

Several poststructural literary theorists have also commented on composition and its use of poststructuralism. J. Hillis Miller, in his essay, ''Composition and Decomposition: Deconstruction and the Teaching of Writing,'' argues that deconstructive reading—the rhetoric of tropes—and composition instruction—the rhetoric of persuasion—must inform each other. ''We should take the most advanced insights into language from both sides and attempt to work out commensurate pedagogies'' (55). Jacques Derrida, in an interview with Gary A. Olson, comments that writers should write for the appropriate discipline: ''You can't teach writing simply as a formal technique. Each technique is determined by the specific content of the field'' (Olson, 6–7). Moreover, he argues that a deconstructive composition pedagogy would pay special attention to situation, including audience and the purpose for writing. In this way, new ways of composing might develop. But he notes that his own teaching is ''very traditional'' (10): he teaches the great, canonical texts, and says, ''There's no deconstruction without the memory of the tradition'' (12).

And, finally, Stanley Fish argues that the trend in composition theory to consider antifoundational theories, which he says teach ''that questions of fact, truth, correctness, validity, and clarity can neither be posed nor answered in reference to some extracontextual, ahistorical, nonsituational reality, or rule, or law or value'' (67), may be wrongheaded. Antifoundationalists, of which Fish counts himself as one, focus instead on the situated meaning—whether in paradigm, community, or context. But he contends that composition teachers like Patricia Bizzell, Richard Lanham, and Kenneth Bruffee are wrong to believe that an understanding of situation would lead to better judgments, better democracy, and better writing. Fish calls the desire to escape our situatedness, to self-consciously consider it, and to teach students to do the same an antifoundationalist ''theory hope.''

Probably in part because of the lack of clear agreement about just what poststructuralism should include, composition theory has used the term in discussions of a variety of topics, including pedagogy, reading strategies, and writing exercises. Below, articles are organized in the same way in which characteristics of the theory were described: (1) no speaking subject determines meaning; (2) language regulates the order of discursive formations; (3) divisions between traditional oppositions are weakened; and (4) meanings are dispersed and exist only in relation to each other.

Much of the work that has talked about poststructuralism in composition has focused on the way in which the speaking subject no longer determines his or her own meaning. James Berlin, in "Poststructuralism, Cultural Studies, and the Composition Classroom: Postmodern Theory in Practice," says that in this theory the subject is "the product of social and material conditions— . . . the construction of the various signifying practices, the uses of language, of a given historical moment" (18). We are "made up of various competing discourses, conflicted and contradictory scripts, that make our consciousness anything but unified, coherent, and autonomous" (18). Berlin notes how social-epistemic rhetoric might provide poststructuralism with ways to talk about the production and reception of texts. In this way, "the classroom becomes the point at which theory and practice engage in a dialectical interaction, working out a rhetoric more adequate to the historical moment and the actual conditions of teacher and students" (25).

In referencing Foucault's "Discourse on Language," Linda Brodkey considers how "we are at once constituted and unified as subjects in language and discourse" (125). Teachers, she argues, need to learn more about how students construct social reality in their text. Brodkey offers an analysis of a series of letters written by between English teachers and their adult, working-class students. She finds that

the teachers' markedly inept responses to their correspondents' narratives suggest that the hegemony of educational discourse warrants teachers not only to represent themselves as subjects unified by the internal conflicts like guilt that preoccupy professionals, but to disclaim narratives that represent a subject alternatively unified in its conflicts with an external material reality. (130)

Lori H. Lefkovitz advocates the teaching of poststructuralist theory in composition classes so that students can learn more about their subject positions and the discourse that "subjects" them, and thus be able to challenge their marginalization. Similarly, Ronda Leathers Dively encourages the active study and critique of students' religious faiths. Poststructuralism, she says, offers students a means for understanding how they have been constructed by their religious experience and how dualisms affect this construction.

On the other hand, Jasper Neel argues in *Plato, Derrida, and Writing* that the last thing writing leads to is self-discovery (124). Rather, writing allows for the evaluation of life, but that life is the *writing* itself. Like Neel, Sharon Crowley, in *A Teacher's Introduction to Deconstruction*, finds that poststructuralism rejects self-aware consciousness. She explains deconstruction, describes its reception in English studies, and argues that it supports a process pedagogy, saying that "a deconstructive attitude toward writing pedagogy will focus its attention away from the individual authors and toward the language currently in use in the community served by the pedagogy'' (33). Engaging students in a community of readers and specific situations is most important, she argues.

Crowley, in ''writing and Writing,'' encourages teachers to consider how authority might be given to the text rather than to an individual ''author.'' ''Poststructural thought—for all of its avowed occulting of the author—assumes that writing is a manifestation of desire, is a reach for author-ity. Invention begins in the encounter with one's own text or with those of others'' (98). Jeffrey Carroll contends that the idea that students ''own'' the writing that they take care to produce sets up a materialist concept that runs counter to current poststructural theory. If writing is dialogic and depends upon the commentary of others in a writing workshop, the authority of the writer must be viewed more as an ''author-function,'' as Foucault describes.

Schilb argues in ''Poststructuralism, Politics, and the Subject of Pedagogy'' that teachers who engage in theory need to consider how their teaching practices make ''subjects'' of their students. Praising feminist pedagogies in particular, which he says encourage the active, dialogical pursuit of knowledge, he criticizes several articles that encourage deconstructive critiques without acknowledging their own contradictions. In an application of deconstruction to composition theory itself, Robert Brooke deconstructs work by Linda Flower, which, he argues, ''is directly concerned with the development of control in the dynamics of composing'' (405). He compares her work to Derrida's concept of ''arche-writing,'' which Brooke describes as ''the potentiality or possibility of consciousness, meaning, and intention existing in language-understood-as-arche-writing'' (414). Since writing forces us to confront the subject of writing, Brooke argues that teachers should encourage students to view themselves as changing in dynamic ways.

Perhaps the most influential poststructural theory that has come to composition has been the idea of the discourse community. Lester Faigley in ''Competing Theories of Process: A Critique and a Proposal'' comments that the development of discourse communities by Patricia Bizzell and David Bartholomae is poststructural because, for Foucault, language regulates the order of discursive formations. Patricia Bizzell defines the discourse community as ''a group of people who share certain language-using practices'' (222) and notes its origin in the speech community and the interpretive community. David Bartholomae, in ''Inventing the University,'' quotes Foucault and says that students must become ''insiders'' in a particular discourse community by imitation and parody of the writings of that community. ''Leading students to believe that they are responsible for something new or original, unless they understand what those words mean with regard to writing, is a dangerous and counterproductive practice'' (143). Rather, Bartholomae argues that students are invented by the discourses they practice.

Similarly, in ''Intertextuality and the Discourse Community,'' James E. Porter considers how intertextuality comes out of poststructuralist thought and argues that it suggests that students should be taught to write for a particular discourse community. "According to this view, authorial intention is less significant than social context: the writer is simply a part of a discourse tradition, a member of a team, and a participant in a community of discourse that creates its own collective meaning" (35). And in another use of Foucault, Carol Snyder applies Foucault's system of classifications in *The Archaeology of Knowledge* and elsewhere in order to show students how such classifications structure the way in which we think about our world. She offers a series of questions and provocations for students to consider in an exercise on classifying.

Several composition theorists have looked at deconstruction as a way to better their students' habits of reading by studying and breaking down oppositions in popular essays and their own writings. Jon Harned argues that expressivist pedagogies assume a reality outside of language and that writing, and he encourages instruction in writing deconstructive analyses of texts to question that assumption. Similarly, David Kaufer and Gary Waller recommend teaching students to subvert their own language and question their own ideologies in order to see how reading and writing come together. They offer a series of writing tasks that encourage students to think more about grammar and audience.

Schilb argues, though, that deconstructive readings can aid students in writing, but not if they suggest to students that all writing is continuously deconstructing *itself.* Through his own deconstructive analysis of an essay by Joan Didion and a description of how a class might fruitfully use such a reading, Schilb argues that this kind of reading can help students to better see how their writing is a negotiation between their own choices and what they see as their readers' interests.

Deconstruction's emphasis on questioning a text's apparent oppositions between referentiality and textuality, the literal and the figural, cause and effect, and inside and outside can lead students to develop a better sense of how a writer like Didion doesn't simply imitate the world but instead perceives, analyzes, and plots it through her own particular perspective and through the medium of language. ("Deconstructing Didion," 278)

Another series of articles, though, has used that thread of poststructuralism that sees meanings as dispersed and intertextual, which has led some composition theorists to question the merit of teaching about discourse communities and using deconstruction as a tool of process pedagogy. In "The Plural Text/The Plural Self: Roland Barthes and William Coles," Joseph Harris compares the work by Coles and Barthes who, he says, both advocate a complexity of writing to open up a plurality of meanings and see the self in relation to other discourses. "What is at issue is not simply how clear or correct its phrasings are, but who is speaking in it—how much we hear in it of its author and how much of the more familiar languages of school or authority" (166).

In "Foucault and the Freshman Writer: Considering the Self in Discourse," Kurt Spellmeyer points to the different forces pulling at a student writer, who must choose between following the norms of institutional discourse or not. He rebukes Porter for positing Foucault as wishing a stable discursive formation: "We must recognize instead that empowerment within discourse is a special form of intrusiveness, a strategic act of resistance to the totalizing force of conventions, which should not be confused with ignoring or rejecting all conventions out of hand" (726–27). Peter Vandenberg and Colette Morrow similarly argue that the "endless and uncircumscribed context" (18) that intertextuality implies runs afoul of descriptions of the discourse community like those by Porter, Bizzell, and Bruffee. Moreover, they comment, "a writing pedagogy that attempts to prepare students for communities by privileging particular sets of epistemological and discursive conventions both reifies and co-opts a descriptive theory we label intertextuality" (21).

Bruce Herzberg describes Foucault's theories about discursive statements and practices as central to the rhetorical critique of how power and knowledge get constructed. For composition teachers, he comments, critique must be made of how and why certain strategies are seen as socially constructed; for instance, Herzberg argues that collaborative pedagogies mimic social situations but fail to reproduce them. "If, with Foucault, we reject the theory that language is the servant of knowledge in favor of the theory that discourse constitutes knowledge and its powers, we may be able to reconstitute our composition courses under the rubric of a new rhetoric" (81). Paul Heilker uses Foucault's *Discipline and Punish* to consider the ways in which some of the strategies of the process-centered paradigm serve to empower writing teachers and composition as a field while also improving students' writing. But Heilker finds "that the paradigm shift did not fundamentally improve the lot of students, but rather only increased the disparity in their power relations with their instructors: exactly the opposite of its ostensible, advertised aim and commonly construed results" (12).

For John Clifford, "Poststructuralism . . . decenters writing as well as the self, seeing both not only as the effect of language patterns but as the result of multiple discourses already in place, already overdetermined by historical and social meanings in constant internal struggle" (40). But Clifford argues that the teaching of writing is an "ideological act" in which culture produces subjects, "creating accommodating students who are eager to fill designated positions of influence" (39). By instructing in grammar and using the process approach, he suggests, teachers position their students as the subjects of power who write "correct" academic papers but lose their capacity to resist.

Knoper summarizes several articles about deconstruction and composition, finding deconstruction "tucked into familiar writing theories and teaching orthodoxies" (128). By emphasizing deconstruction more as a method of reading, he contends that some composition exercises are leaving "familiar and unexamined aims of 'improvement' toward 'better' writing intact" (132). Though he notes that most academic journals still do not do it, "writing in our profession nonetheless includes, or is moving toward (or returning to), a writing of uncertainty, recursiveness, complexity, a writing that is especially and obviously *written*. Do we not have a responsibility to teach students this thinking-writing?"

(138). Similarly, Schwartz argues that the use of deconstruction in composition still allows students to view the world as unproblematic as students are encouraged "to read complicatedly but to write clearly" (63). Rather, "[t]he apparent failure to be clear, then, may actually be an intentional refusal-to-say, one that demands an active effort from the reader to 'complete' the text's meaning" (65). She encourages writing " 'against the grain' of commonsense" (70).

BIBLIOGRAPHY

Primary Texts

Barthes, Roland. "The Death of the Author." In *Image-Music-Text*. New York: Hill and Wang, 1977, 142–48.

―――. "From Work to Text." In *Textual Strategies*. Ed. Josue Harari. Ithaca, NY: Cornell UP, 1977, 73–81.

―――. "The Old Rhetoric: An Aide-Memoire." In *The Semiotic Challenge*. Trans. Richard Howard. New York: Hill and Wang, 1988, 11–94.

―――. *S/Z*. Trans. Richard Miller. New York: Hill and Wang, 1974.

―――. "To Write: An Intransitive Verb?" In *The Structuralist Controversy: The Languages of Criticism and the Sciences of Man*. Ed. Richard Macksey and Eugenio Donato. Baltimore: Johns Hopkins UP, 1972, 134–45.

Derrida, Jacques. *Dissemination*. Trans. Barbara Johnson. Chicago: U of Chicago P, 1981.

―――. *Of Grammatology*. Trans. Gayatri Chakravorty Spivak. Baltimore, MD: Johns Hopkins UP, 1976.

―――. "Signature Event Context." In *Margins of Philosophy*. Trans. Alan Bass. Chicago: U of Chicago P, 1982, 309–30.

―――. "Structure, Sign and Play in the Discourse of the Human Sciences." In *Writing and Difference*. Trans. Alan Bass. Chicago: U of Chicago P, 1978, 278–93.

―――. "White Mythology: Metaphor in the Text of Philosophy." In *Margins of Philosophy*. Trans. Alan Bass. Chicago: U of Chicago P, 1982, 207–71.

Eagleton, Terry. *Literary Theory: An Introduction*. Minneapolis: U of Minnesota P, 1983.

Fish, Stanley. *Is There a Text in This Class? The Authority of Interpretive Communities*. Cambridge, MA: Harvard UP, 1980.

Foucault, Michel. *The Archaeology of Knowledge and the Discourse on Language*. Trans. A. M. Sheridan Smith. New York: Pantheon, 1972.

―――. *Discipline and Punish: The Birth of the Prison*. Trans. Alan Sheridan. New York: Vintage, 1979.

―――. "What Is an Author?" In *Language, Counter-Memory, Practice*. Trans. Donald F. Bouchard and Sherry Simon. Ed. Donald F. Bouchard. Ithaca, NY: Cornell UP, 1977, 113–38.

Kristeva, Julia. *Desire in Language: A Semiotic Approach to Literature and Art*. Trans. Thomas Gora, Alice Jardine, and Leon S. Roudiez. Ed. Leon S. Roudiez. New York: Columbia UP, 1980.

Lacan, Jacques. *Ecrits: A Selection*. London: Tavistock, 1977.

―――. "Of Structure as an Inmixing of an Otherness Prerequisite to Any Subject Whatever." In *The Structuralist Controversy: The Languages of Criticism and the Sciences of Man*. Ed. Richard Macksey and Eugenio Donato. Baltimore: Johns Hopkins UP, 1972, 186–95.

Major Scholarship in Composition

Atkins, G. Douglas, and Michael Johnson, eds. *Writing and Reading Differently: Deconstruction and the Teaching of Composition and Literature.* Lawrence: UP of Kansas, 1985.

Bartholomae, David. "Inventing the University." In *When a Writer Can't Write.* Ed. Mike Rose. New York: Guilford, 1985, 134–65.

Berlin, James A. "Poststructuralism, Cultural Studies, and the Composition Classroom: Postmodern Theory in Practice." *Rhetoric Review* 11.1 (1992): 16–33.

Bizzell, Patricia. *Academic Discourse and Critical Consciousness.* Pittsburgh, PA: U of Pittsburgh P, 1992.

———. "Cognition, Convention, and Certainty: What We Need to Know about Writing." *Pre/Text* 3.3 (1982): 213–43.

Blum, Jack. "Poststructural Theories and the Postmodern Attitude in Contemporary Composition." In *A Teacher's Introduction to Composition in the Rhetorical Tradition.* Ed. W. Ross Winterowd and Jack Blum. Urbana, IL: NCTE, 1994, 92–111.

Booth, Wayne. *Critical Understanding: The Powers and Limits of Pluralism.* Chicago: U of Chicago P, 1979.

———. "The Rhetorical Stance." *College Composition and Communication* 14 (1963): 139–45.

Brodkey, Linda. "On the Subjects of Class and Gender in 'The Literacy Letters.'" *College English* 51.2 (1989): 125–41.

Brooke, Robert. "Control in Writing: Flower, Derrida, and Images of the Writer." *College English* 51.4 (1989): 405–17.

Bruffee, Kenneth. "Collaborative Learning and the Conversation of Mankind.'" *College English* 46 (1984): 635–52.

———. Liberal Education and the Social Justification of Belief." *Liberal Education* 68.2 (1982): 95–114.

Carroll, Jeffrey. "Giving and Taking: A Note on Ownership." *Writing Instructor* 11.1 (1991): 17–22.

Christensen, Francis. "A Generative Rhetoric of the Sentence." *College Composition and Communication* 14 (1963):155–61.

Clifford, John. "The Subject in Discourse." In *Contending with Words: Composition and Rhetoric in a Postmodern Age.* Ed. Patricia Harkin and John Schilb. New York: MLA, 1991, 38–51.

Corbett, Edward P. J. "Literature and Composition: Allies or Rivals in the Classroom?" In *Composition and Literature: Bridging the Gap.* Ed. Winifred Bryan Horner. Chicago: U of Chicago P, 1983, 168–84.

———. "The Usefulness of Classical Rhetoric." *College Composition and Communication* 14 (1963): 162–64.

Crowley, Sharon. *A Teacher's Introduction to Deconstruction.* Urbana, IL: NCTE, 1989.

———. "writing and Writing." In *Writing and Reading Differently.* Ed. G. Douglas Atkins and Michael Johnson. Lawrence: UP of Kansas, 93–100.

Dively, Ronda Leathers. "Religious Discourse in the Academy: Creating a Space by Means of Poststructuralist Theories of Subjectivity." *Composition Studies/Freshman English News* 21.2 (1993): 91–101.

Faigley, Lester. "Competing Theories of Process: A Critique and a Proposal." *College English* 48.6 (1986): 527–42.

———. *Fragments of Rationality: Postmodernity and the Subject of Composition*. Pittsburgh, PA: U of Pittsburgh P, 1992.

Fish, Stanley. "Anti-Foundationalism, Theory Hope, and the Teaching of Composition." In *The Current in Criticism: Essays on the Present and Future of Literary Theory*. Ed. Clayton Koelb and Virgil Lokke. West Lafayette, IN: Purdue UP, 1987, 65–79.

Flower, Linda. "The Construction of Purpose in Writing and Reading." *College English* 50 (1988): 528–50.

Harned, Jon. "Post-Structuralism and the Teaching of Composition." *Freshman English News* 15 (1986): 10–16.

Harris, Joseph. "The Plural Text/The Plural Self: Roland Barthes and William Coles." *College English* 49.2 (1987): 158–70.

Heilker, Paul. "*Discipline and Punish* and Process and Paradigms (or Foucault, Visibility, (Dis)Empowerment, and the Construction of Composition Studies)." *Composition Studies/Freshman English News* 22.1 (1994): 4–13.

Herzberg, Bruce. "Michel Foucault's Rhetorical Theory." In *Contending with Words: Compostion and Rhetoric in a Postmodern Age*. Ed. Patricia Harkin and John Schilb. New York: MLA, 1991, 69–81.

Kaufer, David, and Gary Waller. "To Write Is to Read Is to Write, Right?" In *Writing and Reading Differently*. Ed. G. Douglas Atkins and Michael Johnson. Lawrence: UP of Kansas, 66–92.

Knoper, Randall. "Deconstruction, Process, Writing." In *Reclaiming Pedagogy: The Rhetoric of the Classroom*. Ed. Patricia Donahue and Ellen Quandahl. Carbondale: Southern Illinois UP, 1989, 128–43.

Lanham, Richard. "One, Two, Three." In *Composition and Literature: Bridging the Gap*. Ed. Winifred Bryan Horner. Chicago: U of Chicago P, 1983, 1–29.

Lefkovitz, Lori H. "The Subject of Writing within the Margins." In *Reorientations: Critical Theories and Pedagogies*. Ed. Bruce Henricksen and Thais E. Morgan. Urbana: U of Illinois P, 1990, 165–78.

Miller, J. Hillis. "Composition and Decomposition: Deconstruction and the Teaching of Writing." In *Composition and Literature: Bridging the Gap*. Ed. Winifred Bryan Horner. Chicago: U of Chicago P, 1983, 38–56.

Neel, Jasper. *Plato, Derrida, and Writing*. Carbondale: Southern Illinois UP, 1988.

Olson, Gary A. "Jacques Derrida on Rhetoric and Composition: A Conversation." *Journal of Advanced Composition* 10.1 (1990): 1–21.

Porter, James E. "Intertextuality and the Discourse Community." *Rhetoric Review* 5.1 (1986): 34–47.

Schilb, John. "Composition and Poststructuralism: A Tale of Two Conferences." *College Composition and Communication* 40.4 (1989): 422–43.

———. "Deconstructing Didion: Poststructuralist Rhetorical Theory in the Composition Class." In *Literary Nonfiction: Theory, Criticism, Pedagogy*. Ed. C. Anderson. Carbondale: Southern Illinois UP, 1989, 262–86.

———. "Poststructuralism, Politics, and the Subject of Pedagogy." In *Pedagogy Is Politics: Literary Theory and Critical Teaching*. Urbana: U of Illinois P, 1992, 48–69.

Schwartz, Nina. "Conversations with the Social Text." In *Reclaiming Pedagogy: The Rhetoric of the Classroom*. Ed. Patricia Donahue and Ellen Quandahl. Carbondale: Southern Illinois UP, 1990, 60–71.

Snyder, Carol. "Analyzing Classifications: Foucault for Advanced Writing." *College Composition and Communication* 35.2 (1984): 209–16.

Spellmeyer, Kurt. "Foucault and the Freshman Writer: Considering the Self in Discourse." *College English* 51.7 (1989): 715–29.

Vandenberg, Peter, and Colette Morrow. "*Inter*textuality or *Intra*textuality? Rethinking Discourse Community Pedagogy." *Writing Instructor* 14.1 (1994): 17–24.

White, Edward M. "Post-Structural Literary Criticism and the Response to Student Writing." *College Composition and Communication* 35.2 (1984): 186–95.

Winterowd, W. Ross. "Post-Structuralism and Composition." *Pre/Text* 4.1 (1983): 79–92.

DAVID R. LEIGHT

PRAGMATIC SEMIOTICS

Summary

The pragmatic semiotics of C. S. (Charles Sanders) Peirce differs from other pragmatic philosophies and other systems of semiotics in several particulars, but its central uniqueness comes from its grounding of all philosophy in semiotics. Peirce's semiotic system in turn both incorporates and generates a metaphysic that Peirce called "ideal-realism": a belief that ideas and reality are continual and triadic, not dichotomous. Direct knowledge or communication of reality, then, is not so much "impossible" as it is a fundamentally false concept, based on a false assumption that reality and knowledge are dichotomous and in need of reconnection. Knowledge and reality both being semiotic, they are always partial and subject to further interpretation, just as language is.

What makes this highly abstract foundation "pragmatic" is that it seeks to account for the otherwise unlikely efficacy of language in practical affairs without lapsing into either a naive positivism or a jaded relativism. Peirce contended that only a provisional faith in the possibility of universal agreement about reality offered the optimism and meaningfulness that made philosophy—and indeed all human endeavor—worth pursuing. Thus, he developed his dialectical mottoes of "provisional optimism," "contrite fallibilism," and refusing to "pretend to doubt in our philosophy what we do not doubt in our hearts" (Brent, 1–25). That is, while we should remain contritely aware of our perpetual fallibility, we should remain provisionally optimistic about the ability to improve our practical knowledge; and we should not pretend to claim philosophical doubt if it contradicts beliefs upon which we still act. Given fallibility, Peirce advocates the self-conscious resort to communities of inquiry as the best means to enhance the coherence of all interpretations. While this sounds very much like "discourse community" theory, there is a subtle difference: communities that do not themselves practice Peirce's maxims might all agree on an interpretation of reality but still be fundamentally wrong, and in ways that would be revealed by the results of their practices.

Peirce's semiotics renders his metaphysics coherent with the dialectic of these pragmatic maxims. With semiosis, knowledge, and reality all entirely bound up in each other, interpretation is not a "misreading" of an external reality, but the only kind of access there is to anything. The workings of this semiotic are necessarily triadic, according to Peirce, for multiple reasons that defy complete description in a brief entry. Indeed, the full range of possible triadic relations among signs is in turn complex beyond what can be addressed here (Spinks, *Peirce and Triadomania*). Most importantly for composition theorists, though, a triadic semiotics escapes the twin "meaninglessness" traps of semiotic dualism—that either there is language that "gets it right" or else "everything is right." There are, in Peirce's system, more or less fallible interpretations, to be reviewed according to triadic analysis. Berthoff, the foremost exponent of Peirce's pragmatism within composition theory, points out the main consequence of triadicity:

Taking triadicity seriously means understanding interpretation as a logical, not a merely psychological, concept and understanding representation not as a substitution or abridgment or some kind of simple-minded mimesis but as the representation of relationships. . . . Accepting triadicity as a fundamental principle means giving up the concept of "the right meaning" and focusing instead on "the right procedure." ("I. A. Richards," 74)

Other philosophers—most notably James and Dewey—carried on the banner of pragmatism, and others—most notably A. N. Whitehead, Susanne Langer, Willard O. V. Quine, and Umberto Eco—have worked carefully with Peirce's semiotics. Peirce's own central focus on pragmatic semiotics, though, remains a distinctive project.

Both the complexity of his thought and the oddities of his publication career complicate the task of understanding and applying Peirce's pragmatic semiotics. Though controversial in its particulars, Brent's biography of Peirce explains the disarray of Peirce's original writings and greatly assists entry to Peirce's own work. Once the extensive new compilation of Peirce's work has been completed (*Writings*), the remarkable clarity and power of his best work may begin to overshadow the sheer density, mass, and chaos of his opus as a whole, rendering his ideas more accessible to composition scholars. Though there are many good collections of selected articles by Peirce, Hoopes best combines an awareness of recent understandings, an attention to issues of interest to composition scholars, and an understanding that such a work can be only a beginning for more thorough inquiry.

Reception and Significance in Composition Studies

Despite the difficulties of Peirce scholarship, Berthoff has been an astute translator of Peirce's ideas into composition practice. Though in her work she refers rather more often to Richards, Langer, and Freire than to Peirce, Berthoff has long urged the fundamental value of Peirce's theories. Her landmark 1981 book, *The Making of Meaning*, gives Peirce's pragmatic semiotics a central place as the philosophical test of other valuable theories and their applications. The next year, her seminal article "I. A. Richards and the Audit of Meaning" similarly touted Richards, in significant part for his understanding of Peirce's triadic semiotics. While many other composition scholars have applied James's more psychological pragmatism and Dewey's more politicized pragmatism to their theories, and while others use the neopragmatisms of Rorty or Davidson, Berthoff has had Peirce's pragmatic semiotics nearly to herself. Even Berthoff rarely features extensive Peircean analysis, emphasizing instead the consequences of triadicity: that psychology and politics are always dynamically related through language and that treating either psychology or politics as foundational leads inevitably to positivist or mystic interpretations.

Berthoff's use of Peirce does not seem to have had a strong impact on composition scholarship. Berthoff's readers—and especially her opponents—often misperceive her philosophical difference, leading to persistent misinterpretations of her positions as simply being opposed to, alternately, empirical psychology or political activism. Further, while Berthoff's work has been prominently published, highly praised, and often cited, there has been surprisingly little effort by other composition theorists to extend her Peircean line of inquiry. Only one book by an author other than Berthoff openly undertakes to extend her uses of Peirce into new areas (Ronald and Roskelly). Even in a Festschrift in her honor featuring many prominent national voices (Smith), only colleagues of hers at the University of Massachusetts, Boston, clearly built articles directly on Berthoff's own ideas. Further, though Berthoff is cited frequently in composition articles, her own ground in Peirce's triadic semiotics is often excluded from the discussion of her ideas. Indeed, even the plain fact of her mutually agreed common cause with Paulo Freire—and his agreement that it is her "philosophical rigor" (Freire, xi) that impresses him about her work, has not brought a serious consideration of Berthoff's philosophy into play in the burgeoning field of Freirean scholarship. Berthoff has recently found arguably greater scholarly approval within literary studies ("Walker Percy's Castaways") and semiotics ("Sapir"; "Semiotics") than within composition studies.

Perhaps most inexplicable, though, is the branch of misunderstanding of Berthoff that declares her so philosophical as to be disinterested in the politics of economy and gender. From early on, her most fundamental question has been, "Can we change the social context in which English composition is taught by the way we teach English composition?" ("Problem," 240). Berthoff simply maintains that politics must be viewed in a dynamic that equally includes language and psychology, for reasons that a philosophical grounding in pragmatic semiotics can explain. Many American "radical" theorists seem unaware that Freire agrees quite amicably with Berthoff about the philosophy of literacy and learning. Peirce's underlying theory being designed to foster effective and sound action, Berthoff's abiding interest in social transformation should be more easily perceived if a more complete understanding of the former becomes more common in composition scholarship.

A smattering of other scholars have applied Peirce's pragmatic semiotics in areas at least touching on composition. Corse applies ideas of Peirce and other semioticians to composition, though oddly with no mention of Berthoff's work. Pine very carefully analyzes Berthoff's Peircean philosophy as applied to teacher research. Lyne sketches the largely unrealized potential of Peirce's speculations about rhetoric. Meanwhile, as Winner indicates, potential uses of Peirce's ideas within poststructural literary studies could be extraordinarily fruitful. Rosenblatt, of course, has long applied Peirce's triadic semiotic to problems of literary pedagogy in ways quite consistent with Berthoff's work.

The greatest significance of Peirce's pragmatic semiotics remains unrealized in scholarly work in composition. As Ronald and Roskelly point out in *Farther Along*, the theories of Peirce and Berthoff have a potential to take us beyond current dichotomies, productively reopening arguments currently marked mainly by frozen positions. No other work yet published seems to have taken *Farther Along* any farther, however.

Perhaps fittingly, Berthoff's practical applications of Peirce's theory have been taken up more enthusiastically. The double-entry journal is now a standard tool in the new-traditional writing process toolbox, and Berthoff's acronym, HDWDWW—for "how does who do what and where?"—is at least in the second tier of standard invention heuristics. Colleagues at the University of Massachusetts, Boston, have extended Berthoff's thinking successfully into practical applications for writing tutors (Meyer and Smith) and for language arts teachers (Kutz and Roskelly). Any random survey of courses for future composition theorists will find steady use of Berthoff's texts, especially her most overtly Peircean text, *The Making of Meaning*. Peirce's pragmatic semiotics may have a very wide influence in composition practice, despite the relative lack of attention in composition scholarship. Still, if Berthoff's acclaimed methods do indeed grow from her philosophy, the limited exploration of Peirce's ideas within composition scholarship indicates further untapped potential. Moreover, if Berthoff and Freire are then mutually right about the coherence of their visions, Peirce's ideas might contribute to a vigorous and hardy liberatory pedagogy for American composition educators.

BIBLIOGRAPHY

Primary Texts

Brent, Joseph. *Charles Sanders Peirce: A Life*. Bloomington and Indianapolis: Indiana UP, 1993.

Hoopes, James, ed. *Peirce on Signs*. Chapel Hill: U of North Carolina P, 1991.

Peirce, C. S. *Collected Papers of Charles Sanders Peirce*. Cambridge: Harvard UP, 1931–35. Rpt. Cambridge: Harvard UP, 1938.

———. *Writings of Charles S. Peirce*. Bloomington: Indiana UP, 1982–.

Spinks, C. W. *Peirce and Triadomania; A Walk in the Semiotic Wilderness*. Approaches to Semiotics 103. Berlin and New York: Mouton de Gruyter, 1991.

Major Scholarship in Composition

Berthoff, Ann E. Foreword. In *Literacy: Reading the Word and the World*. By Paulo
    Freire and Donald Macedo. Westport, CT: Bergin and Garvey, 1987, xi–xxiii.
———. *Forming/Thinking/Writing: The Composing Imagination*. 1978. 2nd ed. Ports-
    mouth, NH: Boynton/Cook, 1982.
———. "From Problem-Solving to a Theory of Imagination." *College English* 33
    (1972): 636–49.
———. "How Philosophy Can Help Us." *Pre/Text* 9 (1988): 61–90. A Polylog with
    John Schilb, Patricia Harkin, and C. Jan Swearingen.
———. "I. A. Richards and the Audit of Meaning." *New Literary History* 14 (1982):
    63–79.
———. *The Making of Meaning*. Upper Montclair, NJ: Boynton/Cook, 1981.
———. "Problem-Dissolving by Triadic Means." *College English* 58 (1996): 9–21.
———. The Problem of Problem Solving." *College Composition and Communication*
    22 (1971): 237–42.
———. "Rhetoric as Hermeneutic." *College Composition and Communication* 42
    (1991): 279–87.
———. "Sapir and the Two Tasks of Language." *Semiotica* 71 (1988): 1–47.
———. "Semiotics and Edward Sapir." In *The Semiotic Web 1990*. Ed. Thomas A.
    Sebeok, Jean Umiker-Sebeok and Evan P. Young. Berlin: Mouton de Gruyter,
    1991, 47–59.
———. *The Sense of Learning*. Portsmouth, NH: Boynton/Cook, 1990.
———. "Walker Percy's Castaways." *Sewanee Review* 102 (1994): 409–23.
———. "What Works? How Do We Know?" *Journal of Basic Writing* 12.2 (Spring/
    Summer 1993): 3–17.
———, ed. *Reclaiming the Imagination*. Portsmouth, NH: Boynton/Cook, 1984.
Corse, Sandra. "The Nonverbal Interplay in Written Texts." *Teaching English in the
    Two-Year College* 14 (1987): 181–86.
Freire, Paulo. Foreword. In *Audits of Meaning*. Ed. Louise Z. Smith. Portsmouth, NH:
    Boynton/Cook, 1988, xi–xii.
Kutz, Eleanor, and Hepzibah Roskelly. *An Unquiet Pedagogy*. Portsmouth, NH: Boynton/
    Cook, 1991.
Lyne, John R. "C. S. Peirce's Philosophy of Rhetoric." In *Rhetoric Revalued*. Ed. Brian
    Vickers. Binghamton, NY: Medieval and Renaissance Texts and Studies, 1982,
    267–76.
Meyer, Emily, and Louise Z. Smith. *The Practical Tutor*. New York: Oxford UP, 1987.
Pine, Nancy. "Three Personal Theories That Suggest Models for Teacher Research."
    Teachers College Record 93 (1992): 656–72.
Richards, I. A. *Richards on Rhetoric: I. A. Richards, Selected Essays, 1929–74*. Ed. Ann
    E. Berthoff. New York: Oxford UP, 1991.
Ronald, Kate, and Hepzibah Roskelly. *Farther Along: Transforming Dichotomies in
    Rhetoric and Composition*. Portsmouth, NH: Boynton/Cook, 1990.
Rosenblatt, Louise M. *Literature as Exploration*. 1938. 4th ed. New York: MLA, 1983.
———. "The Transactional Theory: Against Dualisms." *College English* 55 (1993):
    377–86.
———. "Viewpoints: Transaction Versus Interaction—A Terminological Rescue Op-
    eration." *Research in the Teaching of English* 19 (1985): 96–107.

Smith, Louise Z., ed. *Audits of Meaning*. Festschrift in honor of Ann E. Berthoff. Portsmouth, NH: Boynton/Cook, 1988.

Winner, Thomas G. "Peirce and Literary Studies with Special Emphasis on the Theories of the Prague Linguistic Circle." *Peirce and Value Theory: On Peircean Ethics and Aesthetics*. Ed. Herman Parret. Amsterdam: Benjamins, 1994, 277–99.

KEITH RHODES

PRAGMATISM AND INSTRUMENTALISM

Summary

America's only indigenous philosophical movement had its origin in the work of Charles Sanders Peirce (1839–1914). Peirce inspired his contemporaries, including William James and two of his students at Johns Hopkins University: John Dewey and Josiah Royce. Peirce's pragmatism was also developed by Clarence Irving Lewis and George Herbert Mead.

James is largely responsible for establishing Peirce, his lifelong friend, as the father of pragmatism. The affinity of Peirce and James can be seen in pragmatism's doctrine of meaning. Many formulations of this doctrine might be noted, but Peirce's pragmatic maxim in *Baldwin's Dictionary of Philosophy and Psychology* (1902) is concise: "Consider what effects, that might conceivably have practical bearings, we conceive the object of our conception to have. Then our conception of these effects is the whole of our conception of the object" (Peirce, 48). James adds, "To trace and compare their respective consequences is an admirable way of establishing the differing meanings of different conceptions" (48–49).

But the pragmatic doctrine of meaning is only a part of the theory about inquiry and experience. Dewey's "instrumentalism" takes the process of inquiry as experimentation. "Inquiry," he says, "is the controlled or directed transformation of an indeterminate situation into one that is so determinate in its constituent distinctions and relations as to convert the elements of the original situation into a unified whole" ("Pattern," 320). The *instrumental* quality of this response to indeterminacy involves the way inquiry functions as a tool to intelligently direct one's experience. Instrumentalism replaces static notions like stimulus and response (see Dewey's early paper, "The Reflex Arc Concept in Psychology") with the dynamic language of organism, emphasizing function and purpose as guides to inquiry, from the problematic to the resolved. For Dewey, science epitomized the way theory and practice cooperate in experience.

Pragmatism rejected what Dewey called the "epistemology industry," the tradition from Locke to Kant that focused so much attention on knowing about knowing as a precondition for philosophizing. The pragmatists pointed out that we begin philosophizing, not as blank slates nor armed with indubitable propositions, but rather chock-full of beliefs and attitudes; indeed, we are equipped with a great deal of knowledge about our world from the pre-philosophic outset. The pragmatists reconceived the notion of experience to account for this richer, thicker phenomenology of experience we discover in ordinary experience. The reconception of experience is among Dewey's fundamental contributions to philosophy.

A New View of Experience

Dewey titles the second chapter of *Experience and Education*, "The Need of a Theory of Experience." The need to reconceive experience led the pragmatists to think of experience as a dynamic process, comprising many aspects of the organic environment, including sense perception.

The pragmatists rejected the British empiricists' view that sense perception and reason are separate domains because sense perception then is a veil between the perceiver and the external world. In contrast, the pragmatists asserted the primacy of experience and denied that we only experience ideas or language and not the world. James describes experience in its fullness as an event or a drop, drawing attention even to its spatial character:

A conscious field *plus* its object as felt or thought of *plus* an attitude toward the object *plus* the sense of a self to whom the attitude belongs—such a concrete bit of personal experience may be a small bit, but it is a solid bit as long as it lasts. . . . It is a *full* fact, even though it be an insignificant fact; it is of the *kind* to which all realities whatsoever must belong: the motor currents of the world run though the like of it; it is on the line connecting real events with real events. (489)

Sensation is not a mediator, but part of that concrete and voluminous bit of experience. Dewey reconceives of experience this way:

Experience . . . recognizes in its primary integrity no division between act and material, subject and object, but contains them both in an unanalyzed totality. . . . Now empirical method is the only method which can do justice to this inclusive integrity of "experience." It alone takes this integrated unity as the starting point for philosophic thought. (*Experience and Nature* 10–11).

Whitehead similarly states: "Experience is not a relation of an experient to something external to it, but is itself the 'inclusive whole' which is the required connectedness of 'many in one' " (233). Thus the pragmatists refuse to reduce experience to any single element—consciousness or sensation—instead substituting the "full fact" characterized by attention, adjustment, intelligence, growth.

The classical period of American philosophy extends from the Civil War to the 1930s. Although the pragmatic strain can be identified in Jonathan Edwards, Ralph Waldo Emerson, and other early Americans, not until Peirce, James, and Dewey was there an American response to the modernist tradition—challenges and developments that are still discussed a century later.

Reception and Significance in Composition Studies

Pragmatism worked through many of modernism's inherent philosophic problems. Postmodernist and neopragmatist responses to modernism have instigated a reconsideration of classic pragmatism and a fresh appreciation of its original way of responding to composition's inherited modernist difficulties. Pragmatism's presence has, until very recently, been tacit yet tangible. Emig is correct: "John Dewey is everywhere in our work" (12). At mid-century, Dewey's view of experience influenced Louise Rosenblatt's pioneering work in reader response criticism, and her transactional view of the poem influenced attitudes about student writing.

Thomas Newkirk observed in 1989 that studies of the writing process have too often been ahistorical: "Most glaring is the almost complete absence of references to John Dewey" (178). Yet Dewey influenced the late nineteenth-century, process-oriented pedagogy of Fred Newton Scott (see Russell, *Writing* 199). Mara Holt has described the conflicts that accompanied applications of Dewey's ideas in the 1920s.

More recently, Stephen Fishman and Donald Jones both portrayed the writing process theorists like Donald Murray and Peter Elbow as practitioners of Dewey's instrumentalism. They have tried to prove Newkirk's assertion that the cardinal principles of process pedagogies (the primacy of experience, the constructive model of thought, the social nature of learning, the relationship of classroom learning to democratic values) are Deweyan.

Fishman's "Explicating Our Tacit Tradition" grounds contemporary expressivism in three Deweyan principles: the social goal of education, community experience and purpose, and the nature of perception. After Fishman, Jones's "The Postmodern Impasse of Agency" and Fishman and McCarthy's "Teaching for Student Change" are the two most recent investigations of Dewey and composition studies. Jones argues that pragmatism's relevance has only begun to be noticed (98). He identifies four Deweyan principles in Murray's process pedagogies and then argues that this tacit tradition, once articulated, can answer postmodern questions about agency. By theorizing a Deweyan, nonfoundational concept of agency, Jones synthesizes the best aspects of competing pedagogies: writing process and postmodern composition instruction.

Peter Elbow's "The Uses of Binary Thinking" expands the pragmatic epistemology he suggested in his appendix to *Writing without Teachers*. Elbow presents a Deweyan view of experience in his notion of the "believing game" or what he calls, "the dialectic of experience" (*Writing* 149). Elbow speaks of ideas, language, and concepts as working hypotheses that help us bring reality into focus. His dialectic of experience is pragmatism's replacement of the quest for certainty with the adventure of discovery.

In addition to the research already mentioned, Thomas Kent (1992) and David Russell (1993) have made explicit appeal to Dewey or to neopragmatism. Louise Phelps's *Composition as a Human Science* is imbued with American pragmatism. This book, and her 1985 chapter, "Rhythm and Pattern in a Composing Life," bring together important aspects of the pragmatic-process tradition such as philosophical realism, phenomenology, and lived experience as the initial source and final check on refined theory.

The significance of pragmatism and Dewey's instrumentalism was felt before it was spoken. As Elbow, Murray, Phelps, and others have practiced phenomenology by articulating and generalizing the structure of their experience as writers, they have come under the instrumental sway that Dewey also felt: *the need for a theory of experience.* Several movements in early twentieth-century philosophy (phenomenology, process philosophy, existentialism) have been guided by the same need and moved in a similar direction, but none with the completeness of pragmatism.

The recent interest in phenomenology, though it is still nascent in composition studies, is a good sign for classical pragmatism—a sign that interest in a theory of experience (guided by the description of experience) is rising to greater importance. As such theory develops, its kindred movement, pragmatism, will also grow in importance because of its philosophical power to overcome the impasses that exist in postmodern thought. Any time theory begins to market its own importance, it is time to heed Dewey's admonition to "return the refined products back to the context of actual experience, there to receive their check, inherit their full content of meaning, and give illumination and guidance in the immediate perplexities which originally occasioned reflection" (*Nature* 31). The significance of pragmatism for composition studies lies in the possibilities beyond these perplexities through which it has just begun to guide us.

BIBLIOGRAPHY

Primary Texts

Dewey, John. *Art as Experience.* New York: Capricorn, 1934.
———. *Experience and Education.* New York: Collier, 1938.
———. *Experience and Nature.* 2nd ed. La Salle, IL: Open Court, 1929.
———. "The Pattern of Inquiry." In *Pragmatism.* Ed. H. S. Thayer. Indianapolis, IN: Hacket, 1982, 316–34.
———. "The Reflex Arc Concept in Psychology." In *Pragmatism.* Ed. H. S. Thayer. Indianapolis, IN: Hacket, 1982, 262–74.
James, William. *The Varieties of Religious Experience: A Study in Human Nature.* 1902. Rpt. New York: Modern Library, 1929.
Peirce, Charles Sanders. "A Definition of Pragmatic and Pragmatism." 1902 Rpt. In *Pragmatism.* Ed. H. S. Thayer. Indianapolis, IN: Hacket, 1982, 48–60.
Thayer, H. S., ed. *Pragmatism: The Classic Writings.* Indianapolis, IN: Hacket, 1982.
Whitehead, Alfred North. *Adventures of Ideas.* New York: Free P, 1933.

Major Scholarship in Composition

Elbow, Peter. "The Uses of Binary Thinking." *Journal of Advanced Composition* 12 (1993): 51–78.
———. *Writing without Teachers.* New York: Oxford UP, 1973.
Emig, Janet. "The Tacit Tradition: The Inevitability of a Multi-Disciplinary Approach

to Writing Research.'' In *The Web of Meaning: Essays on Writing, Teaching, Learning and Thinking*. Ed. Aviva Freedman and Ian Pringle. Ottawa, Ontario: CCTE, 1980, 9–17.

Fishman, Stephen M. ''Explicating Our Tacit Tradition: John Dewey and Composition Studies.'' *College Composition and Communication* 44.3 (1993): 315–30.

Fishman, Stephen M., and Lucille Parkinson McCarthy. ''Teaching for Student Change: A Deweyan Alternative to Radical Pedagogy.'' *College Composition and Communication* 47 (1996): 342–66.

Holt, Mara. ''Dewey and the 'Cult of Efficiency': Competing Ideologies in the Collaborative Pedagogies of the 1920s.'' *Journal of Advanced Composition* 14 (1994): 73–92.

Jones, Donald C. ''The Postmodern Impasse of Agency: The Resounding Relevance of John Dewey's Tacit Tradition.'' *Journal of Advanced Composition* 16 (1996): 81–102.

Kent, Thomas. ''Externalism and the Production of Discourse.'' *Journal of Advanced Composition* 12 (1992): 57–74.

Murray, Donald. *Learning by Teaching: Selected Articles on Writing and Teaching*. Portsmouth, NH: Boynton/Cook, 1982.

Newkirk, Thomas. *More Than Stories*. Portsmouth, NH: Heinemann, 1989.

Phelps, Louise W. *Composition as a Human Science*. New York: Oxford UP, 1988.

———. ''Rhythm and Pattern in a Composing Life.'' In *Writers on Writing*. Ed. Tom Waldrep. New York: Random House, 1985, 241–58.

Rosenblatt, Louise. ''The Transactional Theory: Against Dualisms.'' *College English* 55 (1993): 377–86.

Russell, David. ''Vygotsky, Dewey, and Externalism: Beyond the Student/Discipline Dichotomy.'' *Journal of Advanced Composition* 13 (1993): 173–98.

———. *Writing in the Academic Disciplines, 1870–1990*. Carbondale: Southern Illinois UP, 1991.

DANIEL J. ROYER

PROCESS THEORY OF WRITING

Summary

''Process theory'' makes the assumption that writing is more than the sum of its formal textual parts—which is to say, more than its lexical, syntactic, and semantic structures. Rather, writing is a manifestation of complex and interpenetrating cognitive, social, and cultural processes reflecting the literate meaning making of writers. Texts are shaped by these processes and help shape the processes in turn. To understand writing is to understand these processes, and describing and interpreting them can serve writing, teaching, and learning.

While several process theories of writing have evolved over the past few decades, ''process theory'' is most often associated with the cognitive process theories of writing that flourished in the 1970s and early 1980s. These theories represent structuralist attempts to account for writers' underlying thinking strategies during composing. According to these theories, all composing can be pegged to these underlying strategies, and examining these strategies can yield explanations of how and why individual writers write as they do in given writing situations. While in more recent years process theories of writing have begun to reflect poststructuralist assumptions about the social and cultural influences on writers' thinking and text production and the writer's influence on the broader social and cultural world, it is cognitive process theory that many feel revolutionized writing research and practice and associate with "process instruction."

Several cognitive process theorists have offered explanations of writers' thinking during composing (see Scardamalia and Bereiter, "Research on Written Composition"). But the most enduring and influential cognitive process theory of writing is that of Flower and Hayes (for example, "A Cognitive Process Theory of Writing"; Hayes and Flower, "Identifying the Organization of Writing Processes"). The Hayes/Flower theory "rests on four key points" ("A Cognitive Process Theory," 366), the primary being that "the process of writing is best understood as a set of distinctive thinking processes which writers orchestrate or organize during the act of composing" (366). These thinking processes fall into three general categories: (a) planning, (b) translating, and (c) reviewing. Planning includes generating ideas, setting goals, and organizing and can occur either on a global level (including, for example, setting broad rhetorical purposes and goals) or on a more local, text level (for example, deciding what to do next). Translating involves turning ideational plans—which may or may not be fully articulated, and may indeed be only "felt" or in other ways envisioned—into written language. And reviewing includes evaluating and revising plans and already written texts. This three-part thinking process is constrained by two influences. The first is the writer's task environment, which is comprised of the writer's overall rhetorical problem (that is, the given topic, audience, and rhetorical exigency) and the text produced so far. The second is the writer's long-term memory, including her or his stored knowledge of the topic, audience, and writing plans.

Another key point in this theory of writing is that the thinking processes involved in writing are hierarchical and embedded. That is, writing is not a linear process; it does not move from planning to translating and then to reviewing, while never looking back: One does not abandon planning at a particular time in the process, for example, even though planning would seem to come "first" and to be followed by the other strategies. Rather, writers' thinking strategies (for example, the strategies of generating ideas or revising) can and do encompass any or all other strategies. In generating ideas, for example, writers may simultaneously evaluate and revise these ideas, this process perhaps resulting in new rhetorical plans which are themselves evaluated and may be revised at any point in the composing process. Most of the time, writers are unaware of this complex thinking activity.

The other key points in the theory are that the composing process is, at bottom, a goal-directed process and that writers create goals by generating multilevel goals and changing them based on what they have learned in the act of writing itself.

This process theory not only explains writers' thinking strategies while composing. It also gives researchers a template or model for examining the nature of these strategies for different writers and across writing tasks. With this model of the composing process, researchers can begin to account for the differences between novice and expert writers; among student writers in the same classroom; among the tasks of creating different text genres, for example, narrative compared to expository essays; and across different instructional environments, for example, when assignments specify purpose and audience and when they do not, or when teachers provide in-class time for the process to unfold compared to when this provision is not made.

Several criticisms have been made of cognitive process theories of writing. One of the foremost is that the empirical evidence for the theories was gathered largely in the "laboratory" as individuals composed aloud to a researcher audience on a researcher-provided topic (see, for example, Smagorinsky, "Think-Aloud Protocol Analysis"). Most of this composing, moreover, was done by college-level or professional writers. Thus, the model of composing that has come to stand for cognitive process theory is based on a relatively narrowly defined (though large in number) sample of writers composing under special conditions. Claims about the ways writers write based on this model are deemed necessarily limited.

Other criticisms have targeted the emphases and implications inherent in the composing model itself. Nystrand, Greene, and Wiemelt ("Where Did Composition Studies Come From"), for example, argue that the thinking strategy of "translation," which is prominent in the three-part Hayes/Flower model, presupposes that ideas always exist "somewhere" before they are turned into language. The model, that is, does not appear to allow for the distinct probability that language itself is generative, helping to shape and beget ideas as writers write. Also criticizing the model, Bizzell ("Composing Processes") argues that it emphasizes the activities inside the writer's head at the expense of contextual considerations. Contexts of composing (the task environment and the writer's long-term memory) are cast simply as ground or frame, rather than assuming importance on their own right.

Addressing many of these criticisms, social and cultural perspectives on writing have broadened the scope of cognitive theories, attempting to account for the role of cultural practices and social situations in writers' composing. Not surprisingly, social and cultural perspectives on the writing process have flourished and taken shape as empirical evidence for the nature of writing is increasingly taken from natural literacy and learning environments, including both school and nonschool environments, that encompass diverse populations of writers.

With these emerging perspectives has come much attention to the relationship between the individual writer and others in the social/cultural world. In attempting to account for the writing process, social and cultural theorists, for example, emphasize writers' social and cultural backgrounds and the diverse experiences and discourse practices they bring to literate acts (for example, Bizzell, "Composing Processes''; Dyson, *Social Worlds*; Heath, *Ways with Words*). Many theorists, relatedly, also explain writing as a dialogic process between writers and their social/cultural worlds: In Dyson's words, learning to write means "learning to interpret—and potentially, to reinterpret—the social world and one's place in it" (*Social Worlds*, 5–6). From this perspective, the emphasis in composing is not on orchestrating a series of thinking processes but on perceiving how one's language reflects and makes sense in a larger social and cultural context.

With this changing emphasis, Flower (for example, in *The Construction of Negotiated Meaning*) has extended her early composing model to better account for the influence on the writer of the culture's literate practices, the social environment of writing, and the reader's role in contributing to the meaning of a text. Interestingly, Flower's newer process theory speaks, not of the process of "composing," but rather of the process of "discourse construction" and, in doing so, recognizes that there is no meaning making apart from the way text functions—the way it is used and interpreted by different people in different social-cultural contexts:

[B]oth writers and readers construct meaning within the broader context of a social and cultural context, of language, of discourse conventions. . . . These form an outer circle of influence in conjunction with and often produced through a more immediate circle of general purposes, specific goals, and activated knowledge linked to the task at hand. In the model, both readers and writers build socially shaped, individually formed meanings. (52–53)

This theory of discourse construction reflects the current social-cognitive urge in composition studies in general. It is not surprising that a central question in this social-cognitive "revolution" is not about writers' mental processes but about the nature of writers' contexts. Regarding context, for example, one critical question asked by theorists is whether context is exterior to the writer, pushing on the writer as it were, as Flower suggests, or whether context is realized or accomplished by writers and readers dialogically, "created and justified" (Nystrand et al., "Where Did Composition Studies Come From") in the literate act. (On this point, see also Brandt, *Literacy as Involvement*). The opposition of these two questions may be counterproductive both for theory and for scholarship, however. Ways to reconcile them would seem necessary if the composition community is to develop a process theory of writing that understands composing as both a contextualized and contextualizing act.

Reception and Significance in Composition Studies

The impact of process theory in composition studies has been substantial. Process theory and studies of process-oriented teaching have been the topic of scholarly work for well over two decades with no promise of ending soon. While criticisms and concerns exist (for example, the recent research in genre theory), scholarship reflected in leading professional journals and texts devoted to composition and the teaching and learning of English and language arts have centered, sometimes almost exclusively, on issues of process theory and process-oriented pedagogy.

However, the composition community has tended to shape process theory to its own (sometimes differing) ends and may generally be said to have conceived of the writing process in a range of ways, depending on which aspects of the process scholars have chosen to highlight. Distinctions have been made, in particular, among the developmental, expressive, and social aspects of the process (see Gere, Fairbanks, Howes, Roop, and Schaafsma, *Language and Reflection*). Those emphasizing the developmental aspects of the writing process have focused on the ways in which individual students learn through instruction aimed at their composing strategies (for example, instruction aimed at generating ideas, developing awareness of audience, revising texts), especially through scaffolding techniques that build on and extend students' own writing skills and information (for example, the work of Arthur Applebee and Judith Langer). Those emphasizing the expressive aspects of the writing process have addressed the ways students can or do draw on their own experiences and beliefs to engage with their topics in personally meaningful ways (for example, the work of Nancie Atwell, David Bleich, Peter Elbow). Those who emphasize the social aspects of the writing process have addressed the ways interactions in the classroom—for example, teacher-student or student-student conversations—shape students' ideas, skills, and the values and beliefs they develop about how writing functions in particular contexts (for example, the work of Anne Haas Dyson, Shirley Brice Heath, Martin Nystrand).

In the research community, process theories of writing have spawned, and been shaped by, major lines of research in both composition and pedagogy. Many early studies focused on manipulating the writer's task environment—altering assignments to differently frame students' relationships with the audience, for example—to see the effects of such manipulations on different student writers and their writing. Other studies investigated the thinking and learning involved in producing different types of texts.

As social and cultural perspectives have begun to take hold on process theory, research has been increasingly concerned with the contexts of writing, both in school and out of school, and the ways different writers negotiate in and interpret these contexts. These studies have tended to follow case study and other qualitative—rather than experimental—approaches. They have also been increasingly conducted in socially and culturally diverse settings, not a condition exploited by earlier cognitive studies.

Within the burgeoning body of school-based studies in particular, these more socially influenced investigations have tended to look at the ways in which process-oriented teaching strategies operate in different settings, how different teachers interpret them, and how different students make sense of them as they write and learn. Looking at process-oriented teaching events against larger classroom contexts, studies have examined the place in students' learning of teacher-student writing conferences, peer response groups, peer-editing groups, writing exchanges within and between classrooms, whole-classroom interactive lessons, spontaneous peer talk, students working together on computers, and peer collaborations. These studies frequently indicate that students' thinking and learning during different social interactions depend largely on the nature of the greater classroom community in which the interactions occur as well as on the social and cultural backgrounds of the students.

In many of these studies, attention has been paid to the social community created by student writers interacting during different teaching events with their peers and teachers. One critical question related to teaching and learning in process-oriented classrooms has been whether involved and interactive classroom communities by their very nature shape classroom events that foster students' thinking and learning. While some research has indicated that such is the case, enough exceptions have been found, especially among cultural- and language-minority students, that the research on the contexts of process pedagogy seems only to have scratched the surface for understanding how and whether students from diverse social and cultural backgrounds are learning to write in process-oriented classrooms. While process theory has pressed researchers to make explicit the thinking and contextual forces involved in writing, these forces remain implicit in natural teaching and learning situations unless teachers make efforts to reveal them to students and exploit them in the service of the students' learning. (For full reviews of research on writing and writing pedagogy that reflect process theories of writing, see DiPardo and Freedman, "Peer Response Groups"; Durst, "The Mongoose and the Rat"; Dyson and Freedman, "Writing"; Nystrand et al., "Where Did Composition Studies Come From?"; Smagorinsky and Smith, "The Nature of Knowledge"; Sperling, "Revisiting the Speaking-Writing Connection").

BIBLIOGRAPHY

Primary Texts and Major Scholarship in Composition

Applebee, Arthur, and Judith Langer. "Instructional Scaffolding: Reading and Writing as Natural Language Activities." *Language Arts* 60 (1983): 168–75.

Atwell, Nancie. *In the Middle: Writing, Reading, and Learning with Adolescents.* Portsmouth, NH: Boynton/Cook, 1987.

Bizzell, Patricia. "Composing Processes: An Overview." In *The Teaching of Writing: Eighty-Fifth Yearbook of the National Society for the Study of Education.* Ed. Anthony R. Petrosky and David Bartholomae. Chicago: U of Chicago P, 1986, 49–70.

Bleich, David. *Readings and Feelings: An Introduction to Subjective Criticism.* Urbana, IL: NCTE, 1975.

Brandt, Deborah. *Literacy as Involvement: The Acts of Writers, Readers, and Texts.* Carbondale: Southern Illinois UP, 1990.

DiPardo, Anne, and Sarah Warshauer Freedman. "Peer Response Groups in the Writing Classroom: Theoretic Foundations and New Directions." *Review of Educational Research* 58 (1988): 119–49.

Durst, Russel K. "The Mongoose and the Rat in Composition Research: Insights from the *RTE* Annotated Bibliography." *College Composition and Communication* 41 (1990): 393–408.

Dyson, Anne Haas. *Social Worlds of Children Learning to Write in an Urban Primary School*. New York: Teacher's College P, 1993.

Dyson, Anne Haas, and Sarah Warshauer Freedman. "Writing." In *Handbook of Research on Teaching the English Language Arts*. Ed. James Flood, Julie Jensen, Dianne Lapp, and James Squire. New York: Macmillan, 1991, 754–74.

Elbow, Peter. *Writing with Power: Techniques for Mastering the Writing Process*. New York: Oxford University Press, 1981.

Flower, Linda. *The Construction of Negotiated Meaning: A Social Cognitive Theory of Writing*. Carbondale: Southern Illinois UP, 1994.

Flower, Linda, and John R. Hayes. "A Cognitive Process Theory of Writing." *College Composition and Communication* 32 (1981): 365–87.

Gere, Anne Ruggles, Colleen Fairbanks, Alan Howes, Laura Roop, and David Schaafsma. *Language and Reflection: An Integrated Approach to Teaching English*. New York: Macmillan, 1992.

Hayes, John R., and Linda Flower. "Identifying the Organization of Writing Processes." In *Cognitive Process in Writing: An Interdisciplinary Approach*. Ed. Lee Gregg and Erwin Steinberg. Hillsdale, NJ: Erlbaum, 1980, 3–30.

Heath, Shirley Brice. *Ways with Words*. Cambridge: Cambridge UP, 1983.

Nystrand, Martin, Stuart Greene, and Jeffrey Wiemelt. "Where Did Composition Studies Come From? An Intellectual History." *Written Communication* 10 (1993): 267–333.

Scardamalia, Marlene, and Carl Bereiter. "Research on Written Composition." In *Handbook of Research on Teaching*. Ed. M. Wittrock. New York: Macmillan, 1986, 778–803.

Smagorinsky, Peter. "Think-Aloud Protocol Analysis: Beyond the Black Box." In *Speaking About Writing: Reflections on Research Methodology*. Ed. Peter Smagorinsky. Thousand Oaks, CA: Sage, 1994, 3–19.

Smagorinsky, Peter, and Michael Smith. "The Nature of Knowledge in Composition and Literary Understanding: The Question of Specificity." *Review of Educational Research* 62 (1992): 279–305.

Sperling, Melanie. "Revisiting the Speaking-Writing Connection: Challenges for Research on Writing and Writing Instruction." *Review of Educational Research* 66 (1996): 53–86.

MELANIE SPERLING

PSYCHOANALYTIC THEORY

Summary

Psychoanalytic theory, or Depth Psychology, begins with the theorizing of Sigmund Freud (influenced by his friend Wilhelm Fliess) around the turn of the century. Freud's recognition of the unconscious and the subsequent development of psychotherapy, his great contribution, created a new field of scientific inquiry. He profoundly influenced modern culture, redefining and altering contemporary understanding of what it is to be human. Patrick Mahoney observes that "the documentation on Freud already amassed is said to surpass in specificity and depth of insight the extant material on any other human being in history'' (1). Freud's own twenty-four volumes of writing dominate the psychoanalytic movement.

Another major stream of psychoanalytic theory evolved through Carl Gustav Jung, the heir apparent to Freud until their famous split in 1913. Jung hypothesized that the complexes of the psyche were not necessarily always evidence of pathology. Instead, Jung placed greater reliance on enabling the growth of consciousness to take place in the individual. He explained that "the aim of individuation is nothing less than to divest the self of the false wrappings of the persona [that self presented to the outside world] on the one hand, and of the suggestive power of primordial images [universal patterns or motifs] on the other'' (*Collected Works* 7:174). Jung also differed from Freud in terms of interpretation. For Freud the meaning of a dream or story was always latent and waiting to be broken up logically. But Jung did not distinguish between manifest and latent; instead, he advocated a logic of narrative.

In *Revisioning Writer's Talk*, Mary Ann Cain explains that the logic of narrative is one of "representing and interpreting experiential knowledge'' (10). She explains that it is a "mode of knowing'' in which "stories become the events they narrate'' (11). Jung, musing on his conversations with Ochiay Biano, chief of the Taos, New Mexico, Pueblo, wrote about the power of narrative exhibited in the stories of the Pueblo religion. Without their stories, Jung believed, the Pueblos would cease to exist as a people. Their stories, he felt, simultaneously created a cosmology and the myth of the Pueblo people's importance in the world (*Memories* 246–53).

The "French Freud,'' Jacques Lacan, has exerted a growing influence on American literary theory and social thought since his death in 1981. Lacan extended Freud's theories in terms of the psychological and social. For Lacan, the social cannot be separated from the personal. The personal "I'' always remains decentered and permanently fragmented. This shifts psychoanalysis away from Freud's commitment to increase consciousness and individual autonomy. Lacan rejected the autonomous ego as an illusion. He saw the unconscious as structured like language, with its gaps, incapacities, resistance, and disobedience—as the discourse of the Other.

In the United States and Great Britain, psychoanalytic theory, through its Freudian lineage, has evolved into many branches. Two of the better known divisions are ego psychology (Anna Freud), which emphasizes the ego as controlling impulses, and object-relations theory (Harry Stack Sullivan, Melanie Klein, Nancy Chodorow), which stresses the effects of very early family and social relations on the individual.

For rhetoric and composition, psychoanalytic theory offers ways to articulate the connections between knowledge, rhetoric, and the production of written discourse as it evolves through interior dialogues of the self into the language of the exterior world.

Reception and Significance in Composition Studies

The rhetorical theory underlying composition studies has always been deeply implicated with psychology. Aristotle's second book of the *Rhetoric* concerns the psychology of audience. In the eighteenth century George Campbell and Hugh Blair and in the nineteenth century Richard Whately and Alexander Bain turned rhetoric firmly in the direction of psychology. With the initiation of process theory in the 1960s, composition theory turned to psychology for its language, theory, and methodology. The concentration on process has involved theorists, teachers, and researchers not only in the various phases of writing, but also in the different individual levels of social and cognitive development that students bring to the classroom.

To teach composition is to directly encounter student problems of resistance and the transference of both negative and positive projections. This was the subject of a special double issue, "Psychoanalysis and Pedagogy," of *College English* in 1987. Robert Con Davis, guest editor, posited in his introduction that "the problematics of psychoanalytic therapy (defined by 'resistance,' 'transference,' and 'repression') are the same as 'the problematics of teaching' " (622). The articles contained in the special issue articulated the theories of Freud and Lacan in terms of application to literary criticism and composition pedagogy.

In 1995 the *Journal of the Assembly for Expanded Perspectives on Learning* (JAEPL) was created to focus on nontraditional approaches to learning, language use, and teaching grounded beyond the cognitive domain as traditionally defined.

Because psychoanalytic theory deals with the individual, it has been most directly influential in expressive views of process theory. Psychiatrists such as C. G. Jung, Rollo May, Abraham Maslow, and Carl Rogers have been influential in the work of James Moffett especially, and also in the writing of Ann Berthoff, Frank D'Angelo, Peter Elbow, Janet Emig, Donald Graves, and Ken Macrorie.

Because psychoanalytic theory was the first science to recognize the importance of gender in the formation of human personality, both Freud's and Jung's theories on the engendering of self and Other underlie much of feminist theory and indirectly influence the arguments of feminist historiographers such as Susan Jarratt, C. Jan Swearingen, and Kathleen Welch. For example, Welch's discussion of interior dialogue is deeply psychological.

Both psychoanalytic theory and the formulation of rhetorical theory trace their beginning to the Greeks. The central motif inaugurating psychoanalytic theory, Freud's Oedipus complex, goes back to a Greek myth of the psyche. While rhetoric describes the production of discourse, psychoanalytic theory attempts to describe the production of consciousness—and therefore, the unconscious motivations—that lie behind that production of discourse. Thus, psychoanalysis helps composition theory speak to aspects of mentation beyond the cognitive.

Page duBois has called psychoanalysis "one of the most valuable instruments we have for describing the processes of the mind, sexuality, gendering, the production of the unconscious, and the historically specific metaphysical binarism that determines our hierarchical logic" (8).

Used rhetorically to analyze contemporary consciousness, psychoanalytic theory offers a way to comprehend the deeper levels of language and psyche. In practice, as a form of discourse analysis, it offers a way through the surface opacity of rational language to underlying profound levels of the psyche. As James Baumlin and Tita French Baumlin characterize it, "psychoanalysis has become literally the study of a patient's rhetoric, an explication of one's defensive tropes and schemes" (246). It also points to the possibility of turning inward and of using the powerful tool of writing as an instrument to enhance awareness, to critique the conditions and terms of one's own life, and to hypothesize the symbiotic internal relationship of self and Other.

While process (prewriting, drafting, and rewriting) in composition theory has long been used, ways to interpret these modes coming from the context of the language of the unconscious—with its often mythical dimensions—offers composition theory a way to deepen its theoretical stance. Working with internal images, whether evoked in dreams, meditations, or dialogues, it draws upon the inherent resources of the subconscious. Perhaps this means combining such rhetorical concepts as the cognitive (language as a tool for acquiring knowledge), the expressionistic (language as a medium for inner growth), and the epistemic, (language as knowledge and knowledge as language) into an expanded paradigm of balance along a continuum instead of the Aristotelian contrastive bipolarities of mind and body, intellect and spirit.

Kathleen Welch reconceptualizes standard process composition pedagogical techniques as serving to "embrace the unconscious as a primary aspect of writing" (138). These techniques reemphasize and demonstrate the reality language as a "kind of flux" and so they require fluidity in the classroom. An awareness of the larger dimensions of consciousness helps to psychically produce change, articulate multiple perspectives, create a deeper self-consciousness, and thereby introduce new possibilities of being.

As a form of discourse analysis, psychoanalytic theory, creates a deepening self-reflexivity. Our words and the written discourses of our students are often pregnant with unconscious meaning. For example, the stories that emerge from journals are not linear, chronological accounts, for the most part, because the psyche does not perceive reality as clock reality. The fact that each night we spend approximately one-third of our existence in sleep and outside of chronological reality as we have constructed the daily logic of it indicates that clock time and linear rationality govern only part of our lives and consciousness.

Psychoanalytic theory does not privilege the irrational at the expense of the rational, but reminds us of the ever-present subtext of deeper meaning. By offering ways to theorize the relationship of internal and external discourse, it opens possibilities to formulate a dialogic relationship between body, self, and society. It promotes the possibility of a composition reflective of the amplitude of consciousness and being.

BIBLIOGRAPHY

Primary Texts

Chodorow, Nancy J. *Feminism and Psychoanalytic Theory*. New Haven, CT: Yale UP, 1989.

Freud, Anna. *The Ego and the Mechanism of Defence*. Trans. Cecil Baines. New York: International Universities P, 1964.

Freud, Sigmund. *The Origins of Psychoanalysis: Letters to Wilhelm Fliess*. London: Imago, 1954.

———. *The Standard Edition of the Complete Psychological Works of Sigmund Freud*. Trans. James Strachey with Anna Freud. 24 vols. London: Hogarth P, 1953–66.

Jung, Carl G. *The Collected Works of C. G. Jung*. Trans. R. F. C. Hull. Ed. Herbert Read, Michael Fordham, Gerhard Adler. 20 vols. Princeton, NJ: Princeton UP, 1953–79.

———. *Memories, Dreams, Reflections*. Trans. Richard and Clara Winston. Ed. Aniela Jaffe. New York: Pantheon, 1963.

Kugler, Paul. *The Alchemy of Discourse: An Archetypal Approach to Language*. Lewisburg, PA: Bucknell UP, 1982.

Lacan, Jacques. *Ecrits*. Paris: Seuil, 1966.

———. *Ecrits: A Selection*. Trans. Alan Sheridan. London: Tavistock, 1977.

Mahoney, Patrick. *Freud as a Writer*. New York: International Universities P, 1982.

Maslow, Abraham H. *Motivation and Personality*. New York: Harper, 1970.

May, Rollo. *Existential Psychology*. New York: Random House, 1961.

Moore, Burness, and Bernard D. Fine. *Psychoanalysis: The Major Concepts*. New Haven, CT: Yale UP, 1995.

Rogers, Carl R. *On Becoming a Person*. Boston: Houghton, 1961.

Sullivan, Harry Stack. *The Interpersonal Theory of Psychiatry*. Ed. Helen Swick Perry and Mary Ladd Gawel. New York: Norton, 1953.

Major Scholarship in Composition

Baumlin, James S., and Tita French Baumlin. "Psyche/Logos: Mapping the Terrains of Mind and Rhetoric." *College English* 51 (1989): 245–61.

Berthoff, Ann E. *Forming/Thinking/Writing: The Composing Imagination*. Portsmouth, NJ: Boynton/Cook, 1978; 2nd ed., 1982.

Brand, Alice Glarden, and Richard L. Graves. *Presence of Mind: Writing and the Domain beyond the Cognitive*. Portsmouth, NH: Boynton, 1994.

Cain, Mary Ann. *Revisioning Writer's Talk: Gender and Culture in Acts of Composing*. Albany: State U of New York P, 1995.

D'Angelo, Frank J. *A Conceptual Theory of Rhetoric*. Cambridge, MA: Winthrop, 1975.

Davis, Robert Con, ed. "Psychoanalysis and Pedagogy, I, II." *College English* 49 (1987): 621–49, 749–76.

duBois, Page. *Sowing the Body: Psychoanalysis and Ancient Representations of Women*. Chicago: U of Chicago P, 1988.

Elbow, Peter. *Writing Without Teachers*. New York: Oxford UP, 1973.

Emig, Janet. "The Uses of the Unconscious in Composing." *College Composition and Communication* 15 (1964): 6–11.

Harkin, Patricia, and John Schilb, eds. *Contending with Words: Composition and Rhetoric in a Postmodern Age*. New York: MLA, 1991.

Graves, Donald. *Writing: Teachers and Children at Work*. Exeter, NH: Heinemann, 1983.

———, ed. *A Researcher Learns to Write: Selected Articles and Monographs*. Exeter, NH: Heinemann, 1984.

Jarratt, Susan. *Rereading the Sophists*. Carbondale: Southern Illinois UP, 1991.

Journal of the Assembly for Expanded Perspectives on Learning (various issues).

Kalamaras, George. *Reclaiming the Tacit Dimension: Symbolic Form in the Rhetoric of Silence*. Albany: State U of New York P, 1994.

Macrorie, Ken. *Telling Writing*. Rochelle Park, NJ: Hayden, 1970.

———. *Uptaught*. New York: Hayden, 1970.

Moffett, James. *Teaching the Universe of Discourse*. Boston: Houghton, 1983.

———. *The Universal Schoolhouse: Spiritualizing Society*. San Francisco, CA: Jossey-Bass, 1994.

Rogers, Carl R. *On Becoming a Person*. Boston: Houghton, 1961.

Swearingen, C. Jan. *Rhetoric and Irony: Western Literacy and Western Lies*. New York: Oxford UP, 1991.

Welch, Kathleen. *The Contemporary Reception of Classical Rhetoric*. Hillsdale, NJ: Erlbaum, 1990, 113–41.

Vipond, Douglas. *Writing and Psychology: Understanding Writing and Its Teaching from the Perspective of Composition Studies*. Westport, CT: Praeger, 1993.

Young, Richard E., Alton L. Becker, and Kenneth L. Pike. *Rhetoric: Discovery and Change*. New York: Harcourt, 1970.

ROBERTA ANN BINKLEY

R

READER RECEPTION THEORY

Summary

Reader reception theory is one version of the audience-centered literary criticism that emerged in Europe in the late 1960s (the other being reader response theory). Audience-centered criticism emphasizes the prominent role of the reader or audience in determining the meaning of a literary text or dramatic work of art. Reception theory had its origins in Germany as a critical trend termed *Rezeptionstheorie*, and it arose in close proximity to larger social and political changes in Europe and America during the late 1960s. Students and younger literary scholars called for a reform of the traditional methods found in what they felt was a highly restrictive system of higher education. Formalist criticism, from New Criticism to structuralism, which had dominated literary criticism for several decades, seemed to the young literary theorists as a narrow, elitist, and politically conservative approach to literature. Formalist critics had largely ruled out discussions of personal feelings or responses in an effort to emulate scientific objectivity and rigor. Audience-centered criticism, on the other hand, argued that meaning resided, not in the text itself, but in the interaction between the text, the reader, and the cultural context.

Two versions of audience-centered criticism emerged from this critical movement. Reader-response criticism, as exemplified by the work of Wolfgang Iser, Stanley Fish, and Louise Rosenblatt, pays attention to the ways in which individual readers make meaning. An "ideal" reader may be projected by the critic, as in Fish's projections of his own reading experiences, or a critic may look for the ways in which a reader fills in gaps in the text, as in Iser's model. Reader reception theory, in contrast, emphasizes the historical and sociological context of works of art, as exemplified by the writing of Hans Robert Jauss. Jauss believed that the reception of a general audience, contemporary with a historical period in which a work was produced, could be adequately reimagined and compared with contemporary responses. Reception theory, because of its emphasis on audience reception, lent itself to oral and dramatic forms addressed to large public audiences (including film and television) as well as to readers' receptions of written literature. Both theories, however, shifted the focus away from the text and toward the reader or audience, thus legitimizing as never before the inclusion of personal responses to literature and the dramatic arts.

Reception and Significance in Composition Studies

Reception theory, because of its emphasis on audience, bore a close resemblance to much of the rhetorical work of compositionists in the 1970s. For example, Walter Ong, in his award-winning article "The Writer's Audience Is Always a Fiction," raised the question of "readers' roles called for by a written text" (9). Although he did not mention directly the work of the German critics, the issues that Ong broaches are the same: "the history of the ways in which readers have been called on to relate to texts before them" (9). Ong also mentions in his article the work of Wayne Booth and Walker Gibson, who "come quite close to the present study in their treatment of the 'mock reader' " (Ong, 9). These rhetoricians, because of their interest in issues of audience, come the closest to the German reader reception critics in their approaches to the study of language and literature.

As Jane Tompkins noted in her chapter "The Reader in History," in her 1980 edited collection on reader-response criticism, more recent versions of audience-centered criticism include the notion of social constructionism: "Instead of protecting literature from unfavorable comparisons with science[,] . . . response-centered theory, in its most recent formulations, denies the existence of any reality prior to language and claims for poetic and scientific discourse exactly the same relation to the real—namely, that of socially constructed versions of it" (224). Furthermore, Tompkins points out that this socially constructed view of language placed contemporary literary critics in a position "very similar to, if not the same as, that of the Greek rhetoricians for whom mastery of the language meant mastery of the state" (226). Her insight as expressed in this chapter foreshadowed much of the social constructionist rhetoric and its similarity to parallel movements in literary criticism, which has occupied compositionists for much of the last decade. Contemporary critical theory, and the criticism (rhetoric) of antiquity both have at their heart "the common perception of language as a form of power" (226).

The significance of reader reception theory to the field of composition and rhetoric lies in the shift toward an emphasis on audience and, subsequently, to the social constructionism it promulgated, thus laying the groundwork for much of the current theories and practices in the composition field. Reception theory is also significant because issues of audience reception have brought contemporary literary criticism and contemporary rhetorical theory very much closer together, with common arenas of critical concern. Articles in composition journals and, indeed, the entire journal *Reader* show the ongoing interest of the composition field in the issues of audience and reader reception. Recent works that explore these issues include Kathleen McCormick's book, *The Culture of Reading and the Teaching of English* and Kirsch and Roen's collection, *A Sense of Audience in Written Communication*. Subsequent works by compositionists in social constructionism reveal the logical extension, in both rhetoric and critical theory, of audience issues toward reflections on historical and social contexts and their influence on both creating and understanding "meaning" in texts.

BIBLIOGRAPHY

Primary Texts

Iser, Wolfgang. *The Act of Reading: A Theory of Aesthetic Response.* Baltimore, MD: Johns Hopkins UP, 1978.

Jauss, Hans Robert. *Toward an Aesthetic of Reception.* Trans. Timothy Bahti. Intro. by Paul de Man. Minneapolis: U of Minnesota P, 1982.

Tompkins, Jane P. "The Reader in History: The Changing Shape of Literary Response," and "Bibliography." In *Reader-Response Criticism: From Formalism to Post-Structuralism.* Ed. Jane P. Thompkins. Baltimore, MD: Johns Hopkins UP, 1980, 201–72.

Major Scholarship in Composition

Bogdan, Deanne, and Stanley B. Straw, eds. *Beyond Communication: Reading Comprehension and Criticism.* Portsmouth, NH: Boynton/Cook, 1990.

Booth, Wayne C. *The Rhetoric of Fiction.* Chicago: U of Chicago P, 1961.

Bruffee, Kenneth A. "Social Construction, Language, and the Authority of Knowledge: A Bibliographical Essay." *College English* 48 (1986): 773–90.

Ede, Lisa, and Andrea Lunsford. "Audience Addressed/Audience Invoked: The Role of Audience in Composition Theory and Pedagogy." *College Composition and Communication* 35 (1984): 155–71.

Fish, Stanley. *Is There a Text in This Class? The Authority of Interpretive Communities.* Cambridge: Harvard UP, 1980.

Gibson, Walker. "Authors, Speakers, Readers, and Mock Readers." *College English* 11 (February 1950): 265–69.

Kirsch, Gesa, and Duane H. Roen, eds. *A Sense of Audience in Written Communication.* Newbury Park, CA: Sage, 1990.

McCormick, Kathleen. *The Culture of Reading and the Teaching of English.* Manchester, U.K.: Manchester UP, 1994.

Ong, Walter J., "The Writer's Audience Is Always a Fiction." *PMLA* 90 (January 1975): 9–21.

Rosenblatt, Louise. *The Reader, the Text, the Poem: The Transactional Theory of the Literary Work.* Carbondale: Southern Illinois UP, 1978.

Winterowd, W. Ross. " The Rhetorical Transaction of Reading." *College Composition and Communication* 27 (1976): 185–91.

CHRISTINE A. HULT

READER-RESPONSE CRITICISM

Summary

Reader-response criticism holds that the object of knowledge cannot be separated from the knower—that the meaning of a text cannot be determined apart from its effects upon a specific reader. Although there is no consensus about the degree to which either the reader or the text contributes to the making of meaning, reader-response theorists believe that "meaning" is not "within" a text but comes about during the "transaction" between an active reader and a text. "Interpretation," then, according to Stanley Fish, "is not the art of construing but of constructing" (*Text* 327). As Jane Tompkins explains, Fish's version of reader-response criticism "focuses on the reader's moment-to-moment reactions to the language of the text" (xvi); similarly, Joseph Comprone refers to Fish's emphasis on a reader's "immediate perceptual processing of literary syntax" (276). Initially, Fish argued that meaning arose temporally from "a succession of decisions made by readers about an author's intentions" (*Text* 161); later he theorized that a text's meaning emanates from the practices of specific social group, or "interpretive community," into which a reader has been socialized. His emphasis on the cognitive and the social contrasts with Bleich's and Holland's emphases on subjectivity.

Norman Holland's assertion that "interpretation is a function of identity" ("Unity," 815) suggests the psychoanalytic dynamic of his reader-response method. Holland believes that individuals respond to texts "in terms of [their] own 'lifestyle,' " by which he means "an individual's characteristic way of dealing with the demands of outer and inner reality" (*5 Readers* 8). These "identity themes" bring to bear that person's "defenses, expectations, and fantasies" upon the act of interpretation (McCormick, 155). Likewise David Bleich's psychological version of reader-response theory sees reading and interpreting as "a wholly subjective process" that is "determined by the rules of the personality of the perceiver" (*Readings* 3). Bleich relies upon written "response statements" to generate students' perceptions of the text, as well as the "motivating feeling" that generated that perception (*Subjective Criticism* 148). These perceptions are negotiated in a community that then produces knowledge through subjective synthesis.

Reception and Significance in Composition Studies

As John Clifford and John Schilb note, reader-response critics' "collective emphasis on reading as a dynamic interaction of reader and text corresponds with the emphasis of composition researchers on writing as a recursive process that helps writers make and remake meaning" ("Composition Theory," 46). Indeed, as early as 1982, Anthony Petrosky argued that the work of reader-response theorists like Louise Rosenblatt, Bleich, and Holland suggests the same sort of "composing" that was at the time being advocated by process compositionists like David Bartholomae (20). Adopting the language of compositionists, Kathleen McCormick classifies reader-response theorists as promoting an "expressive" model of reading, wherein reading is seen "primarily as an activity in which readers create their own 'personal' or 'subjective' meanings from the texts they read" (30).

Clifford and Schilb suggest that Bleich's theories are "especially congenial to teachers of writing" because of his emphasis upon "written self-reflection" and "group inquiry akin to the give-and-take of peer groups in composition classes" ("Composition Theory" 47; see also Comprone, 312). Likewise, Comprone notes Holland's use of written responses to texts and the "implied strategy of teaching students to revise their more expressive response drafts into more transactional pieces of criticism" (308), a practice that has become commonplace in composition classrooms and which McCormick claims originates with Bleich (McCormick, 155).

Fish's reception in composition studies has been influential, but problematic. While he has popularized the idea of "interpretive communities" and their impact upon readers and writers (see *Doing What Comes Naturally* 315–41), that concept has been charged with "conceptual relativism" (Dasenbrock). Additionally, many compositionists have been unreceptive to his idea that theory does not impact practice (Bizzell; Roemer; Schilb).

Reader-response theories, according to Tompkins, provide "a way of conceiving texts and readers that reorganizes the distinctions between them" so that, in essence, "[r]eading and writing join hands, change places, and finally become distinguishable only as two names for the same activity" (x). Reader response theory "still thrives in composition," according to Clifford and Schilb; however, "under the surging influence of feminism, neo-Marxism, minority perspectives, postcolonial thought, and the work of Michel Foucault, reader-response theorists . . . have increasingly turned to ideological critique. They see readers and writers not as free, individual agents but, rather, as the products of discourses that frequently serve the state" ("Introduction," 5). Many reader-response theorists now view "individual reading and writing performances" as potential "modes of subjection and resistance to dominant institutions" ("Introduction," 5). By downplaying the political, Holland has retained less prominence in composition studies. And as Richard Beach points out, Holland's theories suggest a "unity in the reader's self" that current thought tends to discount (Beach, 97).

Both Bleich and Fish, however, do currently theorize a socially constructed reader (Flynn, 317). In Bleich's most recent work, he has continued to explore reading through such frameworks as collaboration and gender. Fish's recent scholarship, which is less concerned with theories of reading, has made him a subject of critique in composition studies because of his controversial claim that "[t]heory's day is dying . . . and the only thing left for a theorist to do is to say so" (*Doing* 341).

BIBLIOGRAPHY

Primary Texts

Bleich, David. *The Double Perspective: Language, Literacy, and Social Relations*. New York: Oxford UP, 1988.

———. *Readings and Feelings: An Introduction to Subjective Criticism*. Urbana, IL: NCTE, 1975.

———. *Subjective Criticism*. Baltimore, MD: Johns Hopkins UP, 1978.

Fish, Stanley. *Doing What Comes Naturally: Change, Rhetoric, and the Practice of Theory in Literary and Legal Studies*. Durham, NC: Duke UP, 1989.

———. *Is There a Text in This Class? The Authority of Interpretive Communities*. Cambridge: Harvard UP, 1980.

Holland, Norman. *The Critical I*. New York: Columbia UP, 1992.

———. *5 Readers Reading*. New Haven, CT: Yale UP, 1975.

———. "Unity Identity Text Self." *PMLA* 90 (1975): 813–22.

Rosenblatt, Louise. *The Reader, the Text, the Poem: The Transactional Theory of the Literary Work*. Carbondale: Southern Illinois UP, 1978.

Major Scholarship in Composition

Bartholomae, David. "Teaching Basic Writing: An Alternative to Basic Skills." *Journal of Basic Writing* 2 (1979): 85–109.

Beach, Richard. *A Teacher's Introduction to Reader-Response Theories*. Urbana, IL: NCTE, 1993.

Bizzell, Patricia. "Foundationalism and Anti-Foundationalism in Composition Studies." In *Academic Discourse and Critical Consciousness*. Pittsburgh, PA: U Pittsburgh P, 1992, 202–21.

Clifford, John, and John Schilb. "Composition Theory and Literary Theory." In *Perspectives on Research and Scholarship in Composition*. Ed. Ben W. McClelland and Timothy R. Donovan. New York: MLA, 1985, 45–67.

———. Introduction. In *Writing Theory and Critical Theory*. Ed. John Clifford and John Schilb. New York: MLA, 1994, 1–15.

Comprone, Joseph J. "Literary Theory and Composition." In *Teaching Composition: Twelve Bibliographical Essays*. Ed. Gary Tate. Revised and enlarged ed. Fort Worth: Texas Christian UP, 1987, 291–330.

Dasenbrock, Reed Way. "Do We Write the Text We Read?" *College English* 53 (1991): 7–18.

Flynn, Elizabeth A. " 'Gender and Reading' Revisited." In *Writing Theory and Critical Theory*. Ed. John Clifford and John Schilb. New York: MLA, 1994, 313–18.

McCormick, Kathleen. *The Culture of Reading and the Teaching of English*. Manchester, U.K.: Manchester UP, 1994.

Petrosky, Anthony R. "From Story to Essay: Reading and Writing." *College Composition and Communication* 33 (1982): 19–36.

Roemer, Marjorie Godlin. "Which Reader's Response?" *College English* 49 (1987): 911–21.

Schilb, John. *Between the Lines: Relating Composition Theory and Literary Theory*. Portsmouth, NH: Boynton/Cook, 1996.

Tompkins, Jane P., ed. *Reader-Response Criticism: From Formalism to Post-Structuralism*. Baltimore, MD: Johns Hopkins UP, 1980.

DON BUSHMAN AND JOHN CLIFFORD

READER-RESPONSE THEORY

Summary

The key to the reader-response theory of Louise Rosenblatt is the word *transaction*, a term she adopted from John Dewey, who used it to describe relationships between reciprocally conditioned elements (Rosenblatt, "Retrospect," 104). She chose this term rather than one like *interaction*, which "is tied to a dualistic paradigm that treats human beings/nature, subject/object, and knower/known as separate entities." For Rosenblatt, then, *transaction* characterizes the reader-text relationship as one "in which each element, instead of being fixed and predefined, conditions and is conditioned by the other. . . . No sharp separation between perceiver and perception can be made, since the observer is part of the observation" ("Transactional Theory," 380). Her articulation of this theory emerged through a half-century of research and practice and the publication of her two major works, *Literature as Exploration*, in 1938, and *The Reader, the Text, the Poem*, in 1978.

In *Literature as Exploration*, a book about classroom pedagogy as much as literary theory, she argued that the same personal, social and cultural factors that affect how a person perceives the world "will inevitably affect the equation represented by book plus reader. His past experience and present preoccupations may actively condition his primary spontaneous response" (79). While acknowledging that some personal associations may distort or limit literary response, Rosenblatt insisted that personal connections are crucial to the literary experience—that every reading is a recreation or performance of the work by a unique reader.

With the publication of *The Reader, the Text, the Poem: The Transactional Theory of the Literary Work* in 1978, Rosenblatt built on her earlier work but shifted her focus from classroom pedagogy to the act of literary reading itself. Here she distinguished between literary, or *aesthetic*, and nonliterary, or *efferent*, reading. The difference, she suggested, is in the reader's stance or "focus of attention during the reading event." In *efferent* or non-literary reading, "the reader's attention is focused primarily on what will remain as the residue after the reading—the information to be acquired, the logical solution to a problem, the actions to be carried out" (23–24). By contrast, in *aesthetic*, or literary, reading, "the reader's primary concern is what happens during the actual reading event. . . . Attention is centered directly on what he is living through during his relationship with that particular text." The essential factor, then, is not the text but the stance the reader takes toward the text; thus, the same text may be read either efferently or aesthetically (24–25).

Derived as it is from classroom experience, her theory continues to have a greater impact on classroom teachers than on literary critics. If the literary experience is the creation of an active reader in concert with the text, examination of either the text or the reader alone cannot account for the literary work. Attention must be paid to the *transaction*—the reciprocity of reader and text. In the classroom, she insisted, "a free, uninhibited emotional reaction to a work of art or literature is an absolutely *necessary* condition of sound literary judgment" (75). Beyond this, it remains the teacher's responsibility "to initiate a process through which the student can clarify and enlarge his response to the work. This entails complementary objectives: on the one hand, a critical awareness of his own reactions, and on the other hand, a keener and more adequate perception of all that the text offers" (77).

Reception and Significance in Composition Studies

Rosenblatt is acknowledged to be "the first among the present generation of critics to describe empirically the way readers' reactions to a poem are responsible for any subsequent interpretation of it" (Tompkins, xxvi). But this acknowledgment came slowly. Her early work was overshadowed by the emergence of New Criticism. So, too, her emphasis on pedagogy rather than literary theory seemed to remove her work from the attention given mainstream criticism. It was not until the 1970s that a popular shift away from formalist criticism brought Rosenblatt's work the reconsideration, respect, and attention it deserved.

While her work is generally revered by other reader-response theorists, her choice of terms to describe the reader-text relationship is viewed by some as problematic. David Bleich argues that her words seem to imply an active nature to the text (145). Norman Holland, too, says that he differs from Rosenblatt in that she indicates that "the text's causal role in the transaction equaled the perceiver's" (qtd. in Bleich 146). Ann Berthoff believes much of this disagreement is caused by a weakness in the term *transaction*. She suggests that "some may interpret it as tending to reify the text, to suggest a power and position equal to that of the reader . . . , [i]t may imply two parties of equal status . . . and seem to represent a dyadic semiotics." In actuality, she says, Rosenblatt's work emphasizes the "interdependency of openness and selection" and her "hermeneutics, like her semiotics, is triadic and pragmatic" (80–81).

Rosenblatt is quick to point out her differences with other reader-response theorists. She believes that most still see the reader and the text in traditional ways—as separate entities acting independently on one another. They place "meaning" in either the reader or the text rather than recognizing the reciprocal nature of the relationship. She argues that psychoanalytic reader-response theories overemphasize and treat responses to literature as no more than interpretations of self. Poststructuralists or deconstructionists, she believes, overemphasize the text and ignore the unique nature of each reader and reading experience ("Retrospective," 105–6).

Like much composition theory, Rosenblatt's philosophy springs from the progressive, pragmatic tradition of William James and John Dewey. It shares an "expressivist" model of teaching and learning with the work of writing theorists like James Moffett and Peter Elbow. Her work, like theirs, provides an alternative to objectivist, cognitively based models. Whether creating the texts students read or the texts they write, it recognizes the authority of each student's voice and vision. Finally, it promotes similar classroom practices: the use of freewriting, journals, and reading logs to evoke and to examine initial responses; the exploration of multiple perspectives in student discussion; and the need for reflection, revision, and substantiation in the development and support of interpretation.

BIBLIOGRAPHY

Primary Texts, Major Scholarship in Composition, and Works Cited

Berthoff, Anne E. "Democratic Practice, Pragmatic Vistas: Louise Rosenblatt and the Reader's Response." In *The Experience of Reading: Louise Rosenblatt and Reader Response Theory*. Ed. John Clifford. Portsmouth NH: Boynton/Cook, 1991, 77–84.

Bleich, David. "Epistemological Assumptions in the Study of Response." In *Reader Response Criticism: From Formalism to Post-Structuralism*. Ed. Jane P. Tompkins. Baltimore, MD: Johns Hopkins UP, 1980, 134–63.

Rosenblatt, Louise. *Literature as Exploration*. 1938. 4th ed. New York: MLA, 1983.

———. "The Poem as Event." *College English* 26.2 (1964): 123–28.

———. *The Reader, the Text, the Poem: The Transactional Theory of the Literary Work*. Carbondale: Southern Illinois UP, 1978.

———. "Retrospect." In *Transactions with Literature*. Ed. Edmund J. Farrell and James R. Squire. Urbana, IL: NCTE, 1990, 97–107.

———. "The Transactional Theory: Against Dualisms." *College English* 55 (1993): 377–86.

Tompkins, Jane P. Introduction. In *Reader Response Criticism: From Formalism to Post-Structuralism*. Ed. Jane P. Tompkins. Baltimore: Johns Hopkins UP, 1980.

FRANK MADDEN

ROGERIAN RHETORIC

Summary

Rogerian rhetoric was introduced by Young, Becker, and Pike in their 1970 textbook, *Rhetoric: Discovery and Change*. Traditional rhetoric, Young, Becker, and Pike claimed, assumes an adversarial relationship in which the rhetor uses modes of persuasion to break down the audience's resistance to the claims presented. This rhetoric may work when the audience has a dispassionate desire to seek truth through argument or is an objective third party such as a judge. In emotionally charged situations, however, the audience will hold more strongly to its beliefs as those beliefs are challenged more strongly.

Young, Becker, and Pike suggest breaking these barriers to communication by using a variant of Carl Rogers's nondirective therapy. In "Communication: Its Blocking and Its Facilitation," Rogers suggests that in emotional disputes, neither party should put forward a position until she or he has carefully, nonjudgmentally, and with the maximum possible empathy restated the position of the other, *to the other's satisfaction*. This will convey to the other the sense that he or she is understood and that the two parties are more similar than different, thereby creating a context for communication.

Young, Becker, and Pike admit that this is not as easy to accomplish in writing as it is in face-to-face discussion. However, they claim that a writer can approximate Rogerian discussion through a strategy with the following general stages:

1. An introduction to the problem and a demonstration that the opponent's position is understood.
2. A statement of the contexts in which the opponent's position may be valid.
3. A statement of the writer's position, including the contexts in which it is valid.
4. A statement of how the opponent's position would benefit if he were to adopt elements of the writer's position. If the writer can show that the positions complement each other, that each supplies what the other lacks, so much the better. (283)

It is vital that when the rhetor imagines and restates the audience's perspective, she or he does so, not to find holes in it or even to make partial concessions as in traditional debate, but genuinely to search for areas of validity.

Reception and Significance in Composition Studies

Rogerian rhetoric was controversial from its beginning. While some, like Bator and Hairston, embraced it immediately, others argued that it is nothing but warmed-over Aristotelian rhetoric (Lunsford), that persuasion and non-directive therapy are fundamentally incompatible (Ede), or that it ignores the fundamentally conflict-laden processes of history (Pounds). Lassner suggests that, while it may be legitimate for a man to surrender some of his traditional rhetorical power, a woman will find such a surrender too much like returning to the passive rhetorical position occupied by women ever since Aristotle asserted that public speaking would damage a woman's uterus. Finally, I have argued (Brent, "Young, Becker and Pike's 'Rogerian Rhetoric' ") that Rogerian rhetoric in its original form is grounded in a wish, traceable to General Semantics, to transcend language in order to obtain an objective, value-neutral stance, which we now believe to be impossible.

Because of such theoretical objections, combined with the practical difficulty of conveying empathy without sounding like a politician trying to buy votes, Rogerian rhetoric has had difficulty achieving unqualified acceptance. Yet it has had an uncanny persistence. For many scholars, the turn toward dialogism, collaborative learning, and the social construction of knowledge makes Rogerian rhetoric more rather than less interesting, despite problems with its earliest formulations. Teich's 1992 collection, *Rogerian Perspectives: Collaborative Rhetoric for Oral and Written Communication*, brings together a number of long-term supporters of Rogerian rhetoric (Coe, Bator, Zappen, Teich, and Young himself) with newer scholars to offer ways in which Rogerian rhetoric can still be relevant in the 1990s.

Rogerian rhetoric may have been handicapped by a tendency to see it merely as a persuasive technique, in which capacity it is inadequate or contradictory.

Rogerian argument is perhaps best seen not as a persuasive strategy, but as an invention heuristic that encourages writers to begin by imagining the world as others see it (Brent, ''Rogerian Rhetoric''). Rogerian rhetoric may have retained its appeal in composition studies not so much because it helps students win arguments as because it may help them grow into more tolerant, more inclusive, and more dialogic human beings.

BIBLIOGRAPHY

Primary Texts

Rogers, Carl R. ''Communication: Its Blocking and Its Facilitation.'' In *On Becoming a Person*. Boston: Houghton, 1961, 329–37.

Young, Richard E., Alton L. Becker, and Kenneth L. Pike. *Rhetoric: Discovery and Change*. New York: Harcourt, 1970.

Major Scholarship in Composition

Bator, Paul. ''Aristotelian and Rogerian Rhetoric.'' *College Composition and Communication* 31(1980): 427–32.

Brent, Doug. ''Rogerian Rhetoric: Ethical Growth through Alternative Forms of Argumentation.'' In *Argument Revisited, Argument Redefined: Negotiating Meaning in the Composition Classroom*. Ed. Barbara Emmel, Paula Resch, and Deborah Tenney. Thousand Oaks, CA: Sage, 1996, 73–96.

———. ''Young, Becker and Pike's 'Rogerian Rhetoric': A Twenty-Year Reassessment.'' *College English* 53 (1991): 452–66.

Ede, Lisa. ''Is Rogerian Rhetoric Really Rogerian?'' *Rhetoric Review* 3 (1984): 40–48.

Hairston, Maxine. ''Carl Rogers' Alternative to Traditional Rhetoric.'' *College Composition and Communication* 27 (1976): 373–77.

Lassner, Phyllis. ''Feminist Responses to Rogerian Argument.'' *Rhetoric Review* 8 (1990): 220–32.

Lunsford, Andrea A. ''Aristotelian vs. Rogerian Argument: A Reassessment.'' *College Composition and Communication* 30 (1979): 146–51.

Pounds, Wayne. ''The Context of No Context: A Burkean Critique of Rogerian Rhetoric.'' *Rhetoric Society Quarterly* 17 (1987): 45–59.

Teich, Nathanial, ed. *Rogerian Perspectives: Collaborative Rhetoric for Oral and Written Communication*. Norwood, NJ: Ablex, 1992.

Textbooks Incorporating Rogerian Rhetoric

Coe, Richard M. *Process, Form, and Substance: A Rhetoric for Advanced Writers*. 2nd ed. Englewood Cliffs, NJ: Prentice-Hall, 1990.

Flower, Linda. *Problem-Solving Strategies for Writers*. 4th ed. Fort Worth, TX: Harcourt Brace Jovanovich, 1993.

Hairston, Maxine. *A Contemporary Rhetoric*. 3rd ed. Boston: Houghton, 1982.

DOUG BRENT

RUSSIAN ACTIVITY THEORY

Summary

Activity theory was developed out of L. S. Vygotsky's cultural-historical theory by one of his two main collaborators, A. N. Leont'ev, beginning in the late

1930s. It has evolved into a major direction in Russian social psychology and now has adherents worldwide, influencing studies in education, language socialization, computer interface design, and expert work, among others. (It is not to be confused with the classroom Activity Approach of the Deweyan progressives in the United States.)

Activity theory embraces many versions. Here I summarize Leont'ev's version, as developed by Engeström. This version explains human behavior, including writing, through three levels or lenses: activity system, action, and operation.

First, the *activity system* is the basic unit of analysis for both groups' and individuals' behavior. An activity system is any ongoing, object-directed, historically conditioned, dialectically structured, tool-mediated human interaction: a family, a religious organization, an advocacy group, a political movement, a course of study, a school, a discipline, a research laboratory, a profession, and so on. These activity systems are mutually (re)constructed by participants using certain material tools in certain ways and not others, including discursive tools such as speech sounds and inscriptions (speaking and listening, reading and writing).

An activity system might be thought of as a triangle with three interacting constituents. Activity theory analyzes the way (1) some subject—individual or collective—uses (2) concrete tools (including the inscriptions called writing) to pursue (3) an object and a motive.

Tools are material objects in use by some individual or group for some object/motive; that is, tools-in-use. The uses of a single material thing may differ over time and across different activity systems.

The object/motive refers to the "raw material" upon which the subject(s) brings to bear various tools, the "object of study" of some discipline, for example (e.g., cells in cytology, literary works in literary criticism) *and* the direction of that activity, its purpose (e.g., analyzing cells, analyzing literary works). That is, the object of an activity system also incorporates an object*ive*, a motive.

An activity system (and human behavior generally) must be understood historically. The identity of the subjects, the purpose (object/motive) of their actions, and their tools-in-use are historically (re)constructed over time. Like other species, humans act purposefully and have biological motives for their activity. But human behavior may differ radically among groups. The use of tools (including vocalizing and marking) and—most importantly—the division of labor that tools allow *mediates* humans' interactions, separating the biological motive from the object of activity. With the division of labor, a range of ongoing activity systems arises. The use of tools mediates the activity in specific and objective ways that are realized *historically*, through a developing cooperation and/or competition (division of labor) in the use of tools.

Contradictions in people's objects and motives arise as activity systems stretch out in space and time, multiplying through the division of labor to become large, powerful, and immensely varied—as their histories unfold variously and dynamically. These deep contradictions are played out in changing power relations among individuals and groups, which can be analyzed at both the micro and macro levels by tracing the variable uses of discursive and other tools to mediate the contradictions and transform activity systems. For example, students doing an internship may find it extremely difficult or even troubling to write on the job, because they feel the contradiction between school writing, with the object/ motive of a grade, and writing for an organization with another object/motive, where the relations with others mediated by writing are longer-term and the stakes are higher (Winsor; Dias et al.).

Second, specific, time-bound *actions* make up activity systems. Subjects take specific actions that are directed toward specific goals, which realize the ongoing object/motive of a collective activity system. These actions are usually conscious.

Third, actions are realized through *operations*, specific ways of taking actions toward goals within certain conditions. Over time, an action may be operationalized as a routine way of accomplishing some goal and may become unconscious—until conditions change. For example, the first time one uses an automobile stick shift, it is a conscious action, but with repeated use the action becomes a routine operation, which will remain unconscious until conditions change (e.g., driving a vehicle with a different shift pattern). Similarly, learning to write involves a range of actions that may be operationalized in various activity systems as conventions and genres of discourse. However, operations may be *appropriated* from one activity system to another (e.g., beginning sentences with a capital letter).

Reception and Significance in Composition Studies

Activity theory, as a distinct branch of Vygotskian theory, has only recently begun to influence composition studies. It has been most widely used in research on the acquisition of disciplinary discourses, with attendant issues of identity and authority (e.g., Dias et al.; Prior). These uses have come mainly through its intersection with North American genre theory, where genres are seen as dynamic, local realizations of specific social purposes of intersecting groups (re)negotiating power. And it has been used to explain the micro-level relations between institutions of schooling and the macro-level social practices (activity systems) with which classrooms and curricula interact (e.g., Russell).

The growing significance of activity theory in composition studies lies in its ability to analyze the dynamic social interactions mediated by writing at both the micro level (psychological and interpersonal) and the macro level (sociological or cultural). Writing is seen as one material tool among many through which identity, authority, and power relations are (re)negotiated. Concepts of "discourse community" and Bakhtinian "dialogism" are thus broadened and the gaps between the analysis of individual and social behavior—as well as gaps between the behavior of various groups—can be bridged in an overarching theory.

BIBLIOGRAPHY

Primary Texts

Engeström, Yrjö. "Developmental Studies of Work as a Test Bench of Activity Theory: The Case of Primary Care Medical Practice." In *Understanding Practice: Perspectives on Activity and Context*. Ed. Seth Chaiklin and Jean Lave. New York: Cambridge UP, 1993, 64–103.

———. *Learning by Expanding*. Helsinki, Finland: Orienta-Konsultit Oy, 1987.

Leont'ev, A. N. *Problems of the Development of Mind*. Moscow: Progress, 1981.

Wertsch, James V., ed. *The Concept of Activity in Soviet Psychology*. Armonk, NY: Sharpe, 1979.

Major Scholarship in Composition

Dias, Patrick X., Aviva Freedman, Peter Medway, and Anthony Paré. *Worlds Apart: Acting and Writing in Academic and Workplace Context*. Hillsdale, NJ: Erlbaum, 1998.

Prior, Paul. *Writing/Disciplinarity: A Sociohistoric Account of Literate Activity in the Academy*. Hillsdale, NJ: Erlbaum, forthcoming.

Purves, Alan C., and William C. Purves. "Viewpoints: Cultures, Text Models, and the Activity of Writing." *Research in the Teaching of English* 20 (1986): 174–96.

Russell, David R. "Activity Theory and Its Implications for Writing Instruction." In *Reconceiving Writing, Rethinking Writing Instruction*. Ed. Joseph Petraglia. Hillsdale, NJ: Erlbaum, 1995, 51–77.

Winsor, Dorothy A. *Writing like an Engineer: A Rhetorical Education*. Hillsdale, NJ: Erlbaum, 1996.

DAVID R. RUSSELL

S

SCHEMA THEORY

Summary

Schema theory refers to the collection of models that represent how humans comprehend and transform knowledge. A schema is a collection of ideas and the relationships among ideas that can be filled out with particular instances. For example, we "comprehend" the eyes of a stranger by drawing upon an abstract knowledge of eyes accumulated through the years. We then fill in the abstraction with particulars: the stranger's eyes are blue or brown, round or oval, and so on. Schemata for eyes may be derived from clusters, or schema, of blue, green, or brown, oval or round, eyes. The schemata of a face may be derived from a schema of eyes, a schema of mouths, and so on. According to schema theorists, each new face, and each new set of eyes transforms how we comprehend both eyes and faces. Thus, we are constantly processing new schema and transforming prototypes, which can then be filled out with particulars that contribute to new transformations.

Schemata take some of the following forms: prototypes of concepts, such as the human face; an action, such as striking a nail; scripts or sequences of events, such as making an introduction; and plans or goals, such as grocery shopping. Although initially conceived as somewhat static, hierarchical clusters of abstractions, schema theorists have advanced the notion of schema to include some flexibility within the hierarchies to allow for each new transformation. As a result, schema models currently fall into three overlapping, comprehension-oriented categories: the first emphasizes how information is stored or represented in memory; the second, how stored information is used to guide comprehension of incoming information (recall); and the third, how new information transforms previous schema (operational). No matter what the emphasis, however, schema and schemata generally fit the following definition: prototypical abstractions, hierarchically organized in memory, formed from numerous experiences, with properties that can be recognized as variable, that by inductive reasoning form a generic concept that allows for predictions from incomplete information (Thorndyke).

The definition for schema is so general that it can encompass any attempt to organize and explain some aspect of comprehension. If schema are defined as patterns or "places" for organization and recall, for example, then Aristotle's *topoi* can be seen as schema. Most psychologists, however, trace the notion of schema from Kant's categories of experiences and then through Piaget's (1926) definition of schema as properties or intelligent acts at a given stage of mental growth and his categorization of schemata for encoding the observed stages of human development, beginning with the preverbal, sensorimotor schemas at ages 18–24 months. After Piaget, as cognitive psychologists began to focus on the constant tranformation of knowledge that occurs within categories, researchers in problem solving began to view schemata as solution methods guiding the problem solver's behavior (Bertz). Contemporary researchers now use schema theory to support the encoding of semantic knowledge via syntactic grammars in linguistics and list processing in computer science and to explain reading processes, justify writing across the curriculum, and construct reading/writing models for hypertexts.

Reception and Significance in Composition Studies

The first composition specialist to draw upon schema theory was Linda Flower, whose problem-solving strategies reflected a general interest in the ways in which cognitive psychologists studied how human beings process their growing experience and knowledge of the world. Working from invention strategies in traditional rhetoric, contemporary process approaches to writing, and schema theory, Flower articulated general strategies to assist novice writers in analyzing a problem, recalling information, and organizing that information to respond to reader expectations. In her introduction to *Problem Solving Strategies for Writing*, Flower supported her strategies by stating that she wanted students "to understand their own thinking processes" and "to comprehend and remember fully what they have to say" (vii). Shortly after the publication of Flower's *Strategies*, Bazerman attempted to unravel the ways in which expert readers and writers use prior schema both to guide comprehension and to transform knowledge. Bazerman's "Physicists Reading Physics: Schema-laden Purposes and Purpose-laden Schema" contributed to a growing body of reading research suggesting that as much as 85–90 percent of information used to comprehend an article comes from schema outside the text (Egan). As a result of this research, schema and schema theory began to figure prominently in writing across the curriculum articles as specialists attempted to articulate the discipline-specific schema (local knowledge) that would assist novice writers in reading and writing in the discipline: recognition of the rich body of outside knowledge needed to comprehend and write in the discipline generated discussions of the merits of general composition versus the more specialized writing across the disciplines courses. Most recently, schema theory has been used to support a writing curriculum that addresses both general knowledge (cognitive strategies that transfer from one field to another) and local knowledge (social knowledge) of the field (Foertsch).

In addition to supporting writing across the curriculum, schema theory has been used to argue the merits of hypertext. In Selfe and Hilligoss's recent book on literacy and computers, the chapter by Davida Charney uses schema theory to argue for a structured, hierarchical approach to representing information in hypertext. Emphasizing the problem solving approach to writing, Charney comments, "The romantic view of hypertext that aims at enabling imaginative leaps and connections between disparate texts, facts, and images thus puts enormous technological and creative effort at the service of preserving what might be quite rare and ephemeral associations" (251). In response to Charney, Catherine Smith argues that writing involves more than problem solving. For Smith, the "thin cognition" of problem solving, as supported by the hierarchical concepts of schema theory, does not compare to the "thick cognition," of comprehending, which accounts for orderly logical capabilities as well as other "more anarchistic elements of—doubt, contradiction, intuition, recollection, forgetfulness, denial, tacit knowledge, partial awareness—the full, mixed baggage of consciousness" (265). For Smith, the associative properties of neural net theory are more suitable for modeling the "structural representation of the thinking process through various sources and moments of understanding" (269) than the hierarchical structure of schema theory. The differing views of Charney and Smith illustrate the difficulty of operationalizing the interplay of analytical and intuitive processes that characterize all writing tasks and explain why some composition practitioners view intelligent computer systems, psychological models, and syntactic grammars as having little to do with the teaching of writing. In spite of the practitioners' reservations, however, if we agree that the strength of schema lay in the way they [schema] "function as instructions for what to perceive, how to interpret it, and what to do then" (Flower, "Negotiating," 271), then it would seem that schema and schema theory will continue to influence composition and rhetoric research and pedagogy in the future.

BIBLIOGRAPHY

Primary Texts and Major Scholarship in Composition

Arbib, Michael A., Jeffrey Conklin, and Jane C. Hill. *From Schema Theory to Language.* New York: Oxford UP, 1987.

Bazerman, Charles. "Physicists Reading Physics: Schema-laden Purposes and Purpose-laden Schema." *Written Communication* 2 (1985): 3–23.

Betz, W. *Zeitschrift fur Angewandte Psychologie* 41 (1932): 166–78.

Charney, Davida. "The Effect of Hypertext on Processes of Reading and Writing." In *Literacy and Computers: The Complications of Teaching and Learning with Technology.* Ed. Cynthia Selfe and Susan Hilligoss. New York: MLA, 1994, 238–63.

Egan, Margaret. "Capitalizing on Reader's Strengths." *Journal of Reading* 37.8 (1994): 636–40.

Flower, Linda. "Negotiating Academic Discourse." In *Reading-to-Write.* Ed. Linda Flower et al. New York: Oxford UP, 1990, 221–52.

———. *Problem Solving Strategies for Writing.* New York: Harcourt, 1981.

Foertsch, Julie. "Where Cognitive Psychology Applies: How Theories about Memory and Transfer Can Influence Composition Pedagogy." *Written Communication* 12.3 (1995): 360–83.

Kant, Immanuel. *Critique of Pure Reason.* 1787. Rpt. Trans. Norman K. Smith. London: Macmillan, 1963.

Kintsch, Walter, and Edward Greene. "The Role of Culture-specific Schemata in the Comprehension and Recall of Stories." *Discourse Processes* 1 (1978): 1–13.

Kintsch, Walter, and Teun van Dijk. "Toward a Model of Text Comprehension and Production." *Psychological Review* 85 (1978): 363–94.

Piaget, Jean. *The Language and Thought of the Child.* New York: Harcourt, 1926.

Rummelhart, David E., and Andrew Ortony. "The Representation of Knowledge in Memory." In *Schooling and the Acquisition of Knowledge.* Ed. Richard C. Anderson, Rand J. Spiro, and William E. Montague. Hillsdale, NJ: Erlbaum, 1977, 99–135.

Shank, Roger, and Robert P. Abelson. *Scripts Plans, Goals, and Understanding.* Hillsdale, NJ: Erlbaum, 1997.

Smith, Catherine F. "Hypertextual Thinking." In *Literacy and Computers: The Complications of Teaching and Learning with Technology.* Ed. Cynthia Selfe and Susan Hilligoss. New York: MLA, 1994, 264–81.

Thorndyke, Perry. "Applications of Schema Theory in Cognitive Research." In *Tutorials in Learning and Memory; Essays in Honor of Gordon Bower.* Ed. John R. Anderson and Stephen M. Kosslyn. New York: Freeman, 1984, 167–92.

Thorndyke, Perry, and Frederick Hayes-Roth. "The Use of Schemata in the Acquisition and Transfer of Knowledge." *Cognitive Psychology* 11 (1979): 82–106.

Thorndyke, Perry, and Frank R. Yekovich. "A Critique of Schema-based Theories of Human Story Memory." *Poetics* 9 (1980): 23–49.

Winograd, Terry. "A Framework for Understanding Discourse." In *Cognitive Processes in Comprehension.* Eds. Marcel A. Just and Patricia A. Carpenter. Hillsdale, NJ: Erlbaum, 1977, 63–88.

EMILY GOLSON

SCHOOL WRITING TASKS: THEORIES OF COMPOSING AND LEARNING

Summary

"We classify at our peril," begin Britton, Burgess, Martin, MacLeod, and Rosen in their report on *The Development of Writing Abilities (11–18).* However, the classification of writing tasks that emerged from the London School in the mid-1970s has become one of the most widely used systems for studying school writing. The classification system has also undergone modifications as well as critiques, leading to the construction of a significant theoretical tool for the study and teaching of school writing. In developing a discourse scheme for understanding the cognitive and linguistic demands of school writing, Britton and his colleagues based their theory on language function, that is, the universe of possible uses of language in general and written language in particular. Writing teachers are perhaps more familiar with the traditional modes of discourse—narration, description, exposition, argumentation, and sometimes poetry. Because these categories of writing assignments are based largely on fully formed, preordained structure rather than the nature of the task itself or the demands it makes on the writer, Britton and colleagues looked to extant theories of language function and intention to explore the intellectual value and complexities of school writing. For them, writing within a particular function (e.g., to tell a story, to report on an event) enables writers to organize meaning around intention and language use.

Jakobson's theory of the hierarchy of speech functions provided a key principle in helping Britton et al. construct the system: the idea that although there might be several functions operating within a single text, there is one primary function. Defining the function of the written text in this manner became a basic tenet in his theory of discourse. Beginning with the "great divide" between informational uses of writing on the one hand and poetic or literary uses on the other, Britton et al.'s system proposed three main categories: transaction, expressive, and poetic. The transaction function includes expository and persuasive writing, with subcategories that constitute an abstractive scale from reporting to summarizing, analyzing, and theorizing. The expressive function is best understood as corresponding to informal talk among friends, where the rules of use are relaxed. The poetic function is essentially the literary uses of language as in poetry, fictional narratives, drama used to represent the writer's experiences, and, in turn, to represent a virtual experience for the reader. Applebee (*Writing in the Secondary School; Contexts for Learning to Write*), in his adaptation of Britton et al.'s system, renamed the three overall categories to "informational," "personal," and "imaginative." He also refined and extended the system to include subcategories for both personal and imaginative writing, and streamlined and reconceptualized the subcategories for informational writing to characterize more accurately writing in American schools. Because his classroom observations and survey research revealed that a great deal of school writing required no composing, Applebee also added a category for "restricted" uses of writing such as multiple choice and short answer exercises.

Reception and Significance in Composition Studies

In the area of written composition, the work of Britton et al. has been instrumental in countering the "current-traditional" approach (Young's term) emphasizing the use of worksheets, mastery of grammar and punctuation skills, and teaching static "modes" of discourse. Britton and colleagues stressed instead the use of writing as a tool for learning and communicating. Because they are English, their work focuses primarily on schooling in Great Britain; however, their writings have enjoyed substantial attention in the United States as well. In light of current developments in American education, particularly the growing emphasis on the learning of cultural facts and on minimal competency testing, the work of Britton et al. has considerable relevance to contemporary issues of education in the United States, particularly in the area of school literacy. Their function categories have been used in empirical studies as well as in writing curricula and textbooks. In addition, a number of theoretical studies (Harris, "The Spectator as Theorist") have critiqued the function system and its applications. Those critiques have focused on issues such as the system's developmental claims, the meaning of the categories themselves, and their reliability and validity.

Britton's and Applebee's categories, when presented with instructions for their use, illustrative examples, and accompanying reliability data, have made for a major contribution to writing research. A comprehensive search of journals, books, the Educational Resources Information Center (ERIC) system, and *Dissertation Abstracts International* from 1970 through 1989 showed that the categories have been used in 26 studies of writing and eleven critiques of the system (Durst and Newell, "The Uses of Function"). In this section three areas of research using the theory of school tasks are examined: (a) the nature of school writing, (b) connections between writing and learning, and (c) critiques of the function system.

Although Britton's concern for school writing was shaped by his involvement in issues of evaluation and his interest in language development and linguistic theory, a key impetus of his research program was the restricted role he felt that writing played in school learning. That is, Britton saw writing being used primarily as a means for evaluating students' previous learning rather than for extending or reformulating that learning. When Britton and his colleagues applied the function categories to over 2,000 pieces of student writing, they found that transactional or informational writing accounted for 63 percent of the writing, with a steady increase in this proportion as students moved into the upper years of secondary school. Although their results indicated that students did little poetic or imaginative writing (18 percent), the most disappointing result was the small proportion of expressive writing (5.5 percent), a type of writing that, they pointed out, is "best adapted to exploration and discovery" (*Development*, 197). After reconceptualizing Britton's category system to include "restricted" writing and to increase interrater reliability, Applebee studied writing in U.S. schools as well as writing activities in content area textbooks. The function categories proved valuable in conceptualizing both the limits and possibilities of school writing, about which little was known prior to Applebee's work. Interestingly, Applebee's (*Writing in the Secondary Schools*) survey of writing in U.S. schools revealed similar patterns of school writing as Britton and his colleagues in Great Britain. As a result of their surveys of school writing tasks, both Britton and

Applebee expressed concerns over what counts as learning and what students must do to demonstrate knowledge in various content areas.

As every writer and writing instructor knows, different writing tasks ask students to engage with ideas, information, and experiences in differing ways—for example, outlining the contents of a book chapter is typically less demanding than selecting specific ideas from the same chapter for critical analysis. Consequently, writing research (Durst; Greene; Langer and Applebee; Marshall; Newell) has examined under what conditions students learn from writing, including the reasoning processes that accompany the generation and reformulation of ideas that enable them to understand and remember the information they read. Restricted writing tasks, such as answering study questions, summary writing, and analytic writing, are not only assigned often in secondary schools but at the broad level that writing can serve, they also represent three distinct ways to engage students in thinking and reasoning about what they are assigned to read in various content areas. The underlying assumption that frames this discussion is that the extent to which information is manipulated enhances topic understanding. For example, writing tasks require more active engagement with the content of a reading passage than do nonwriting tasks such as mental review. The kind of understanding referred to here is conceptual, that is, it involves a knowledge of concepts gleaned from reading passages in a range of content areas.

In answering study questions (assigned by the teacher or included in a textbook), students are usually asked to do so with a brief statement that suggests specific information in the passage. As a learning tool per se, answering study questions is more appropriate for the short-term retention of facts used to prepare for a more conceptually demanding task. Summary writing can also provide the classroom teacher with a tool for reviewing previous learning or preparing for new tasks. However, when summarizing, students must consider text-based information somewhat differently than what is required when answering study questions. Two types of plans are necessary: plans for combining and integrating information from the text, and plans for representing the organization of the text in a succinct way. Although summarizing enables students to get a comprehensive feel, or "bird's eye view," of the information, such tasks tend to represent only the major ideas in a temporal order (as they occur in the reading passage), leading to only the short-term retention of those ideas. With analytic writing, students have access to a different tool for understanding new ideas and information: a focused examination of relations among ideas and events. Across a series of studies, a consistent pattern has emerged of the kinds of thinking and reasoning fostered by analytic writing, which involves a complex manipulation of ideas as a result of marshaling an argument to support a point of view and selecting language for representing it. Although analytic writing focuses on a narrower range of content in the reading passage when compared to tasks such as answering study questions or summarizing, a more lasting intellectual representation of that content seems to develop through an integration and reformulation of ideas.

Although the function system has been used extensively in research on writing, there is a considerable body of work that critiques the system itself. Critical studies began to appear in the late 1970s and have persisted up to the present, giving evidence of the continuing interest in and controversy over the function categories. One of the most persistent debates has focused on the distinction between participant and spectator roles, a distinction that underlies the function system. "Role" refers to the stance a reader or writer takes toward language, whereas "function" refers to the use of language reflected in a particular text. In the participant role, language is used to get things done: to buy, sell, persuade, inform, and so forth. In the spectator role, language is used to come to grips with experiences and feelings through a "verbal object" or work of literature. Though intended as a way of differentiating literary and nonliterary approaches to writing, the participant/spectator distinction has been criticized for dichotomizing the complex roles of language into two mutually exclusive and overly simplified categories.

Nevertheless, reference to participant and spectator roles remains useful for three reasons: (1) they are theoretically powerful descriptions of how we use language to represent the world to ourselves; (2) the terms differentiate language use in ways that lead to important research issues such as how students negotiate the complexities of various tasks; and (3) Britton's theory of writing tasks and Applebee's refinements of the categories and subcategories capture distinctions made within the context of school literacy. Accordingly, the function system represents one of the most significant contributions to studies of school writing.

BIBLIOGRAPHY

Primary Texts

Applebee, Arthur N. *Contexts for Learning to Write*. Norwood, NJ: Ablex, 1984.
―――. *Writing in the Secondary School: English and the Content Areas*. Urbana, IL: NCTE, 1981.
Britton, James N. *Language and Learning*. Middlesex, England: Penguin, 1970.
Britton, James, Tony Burgess, Nancy Martin, Alex McLeod, and Harold Rosen. *The Development of Writing Abilities (11–18)*. London: Macmillan, 1975.

Major Scholarship in Composition

Britton, James N. "Viewpoints: The Distinctions between Participant and Spectator Role Language in Research and Practice." *Research in the Teaching of English* 18 (1984): 320–31.
Durst, Russel K. "Cognitive and Linguistic Demands of Analytic Writing." *Research in the Teaching of English* 21 (1987): 347–76.
Durst, Russel K., and George E. Newell. "The Uses of Function: James Britton's Category System and Research on Writing." *Review of Educational Research* 59 (1989): 375–95.
Greene, Stuart. "The Role of Task in the Development of Academic Thinking through

Reading and Writing in a College History Course." *Research in the Teaching of English* 27 (1993): 46–75.

Harris, Joseph. "The Spectator as Theorist: Britton and the Functions of Writing," *English Education* 20 (1988): 41–50.

Jakobson, Roman. "Linguistics and Poetics." In *Style in Language*. Ed. T. A. Sebeok. Cambridge, MA: MIT P, 1960, 350–77.

Langer, Judith, and Arthur N. Applebee. *How Writing Shapes Thinking*. Urbana, IL: NCTE, 1987.

Marshall, James D. "The Effects of Writing on Students' Understanding of Literary Texts." *Research in the Teaching of English* 21 (1987): 30–63.

Martin, Nancy, Pat D'Arcy, Brian Newton, and Robert Parker. *Writing and Learning across the Curriculum (11–16)*. Montclair, NJ: Boynton/Cook, 1976.

Newell, George E. "Learning from Writing in Two Content Areas: A Case Study/Protocol Analysis." *Research in the Teaching of English* 18 (1984): 265–87.

Young, Richard E. "Paradigms and Problems: Needed Research in Rhetorical Invention." In *Research on Composing*. Ed. C. R. Cooper and L. Odell. Urbana, IL: NCTE, 1978, 29–48.

GEORGE E. NEWELL

SECOND LANGUAGE WRITING THEORY

Summary

There is no single theory of writing in a second language. The purpose of this discussion, therefore, is to provide a historical review of paradigm shifts that have shaped second language writing theory and practice. These shifts have been framed by changing conceptions of language in the field of linguistics and of learning in the field of psychology.

Throughout the earlier part of the century, the dominant conception of language was structural in character. In the American context, this approach aimed for a close accounting of the phonological, morphological, and syntactic structures found in languages through detailed fieldwork, which placed an emphasis on oral forms. This conception of language, tied to behaviorist psychology, yielded a distinct brand of language pedagogy. Specifically, language learning was viewed as a process of habit formation in which the structural patterns of language could be learned through operant conditioning. The primacy of oral language meant that literacy was used mainly to reinforce oral patterns. For example, in beginning and intermediate language courses, literacy practices often were limited to completing sentence drills and other grammar-based exercises. Once students learned to correctly control oral patterns, attention was paid to increasingly longer chunks of text through "controlled" composition activities (e.g., Paulston and Dykstra). The movement of instruction from the sentence level to the paragraph level, and finally to the essay level was informed by research in the area of contrastive rhetoric. For example, Robert Kaplan suggested that the writing of second language learners (L2) may seem out of focus because L2 writers are employing or "transferring" rhetorical conventions associated with norms from their linguistic and cultural backgrounds—conventions that are not linear and explicit in ways that English academic writing is. Kaplan's suggestion for practice involved L2 writers analyzing and practicing rhetorical structures representative of English thought patterns.

By the late 1950s, Noam Chomsky had challenged many of the assumptions of structural linguistics and behaviorist theories of language learning. He suggested that language learning is more complex than the formation of verbal habits. As a point of departure, Chomsky posited the existence of an innate language learning faculty capable of extracting a finite set of linguistic rules from exposure to natural speech. Chomsky's theory of language, coupled with prevailing theories of learning from cognitive psychology, suggested that attention should be paid to the internal cognitive processes through which individuals understand their complex environments. Collectively, these trends resulted in a paradigm shift away from a focus on the formal properties of texts in favor of a focus on the internal cognitive processes of meaning construction in the minds of writer/readers. Following the work of Janet Emig, Linda Flower, and John Hayes (Emig; Flower and Hayes), who studied the composing process of writers in their first language, L2 theorists such as Vivian Zamel investigated the writing process of second language learners. These investigations revealed a number of findings regarding the ways in which L2 writers discover meaning and solve problems of form and function. Specifically, studies suggested the composing process of L2 writers, like that of first language (L1) writers, is nonformulaic, exploratory, recursive, and generative. In classroom practice, these findings urged teachers to instruct students in planning, drafting, reviewing, revising, and editing (e.g., Krapels).

Critics of the cognitive perspective, such as John Swales, argued that the process approach focuses too much on the individual writer and the cognitive relationship between the writer and the writer's internal world, at the expense of understanding the social context in which he or she is situated. With theoretical antecedents to the work of Dell Hymes in linguistics and Lev Vygotsky in psychology, Swales and others suggest a more social orientation to understanding writing. Specifically, James Gee argued that language and learning should not be cast as an intrapersonal cognitive phenomenon but rather as a set of interpersonal, socially constructed, situated practices. Attention to the social context of writing yielded a new approach to understanding L2 composition. That is, theorists framed learning to write as a process of socialization into the literacy practices of a specific group or discourse community. Given this perspective, the task of the composition instructor is to apprentice a newcomer into a discourse community by analyzing the patterns of language use and thought common to a specified discipline. Such a perspective has given rise to a renewed interest in contrastive rhetoric and genre theory as well as a number of instructional programs focusing on "English for Specific Purposes" (ESP) or "English for Academic Purposes" (EAP). Critics of EAP and ESP, such as Patricia Bizzell, argued that it falsely positions second language writers as novices and native speaking readers as experts, when in fact they represent competing social classes. In a similar vein, Nystrand, Greene, and Wiemelt suggested that it is specious to assume students can gain entry into disciplines if they merely learn the right forms and conventions. Researchers who are more wedded to a process perspective (e.g., Raimes) counter that a genre perspective rarefies discourse structures as well as power structures and leads to instruction that is overly form driven.

Reception and Significance in Composition Studies

A review of the literature suggests three issues. First, as Ann Raimes highlights, too many discussions of L2 literacy construct the L2 writer in "generalized" terms that gloss over important differences regarding L1 literacy, L2 language proficiency, age, gender, and cultural background (420). Tony Silva raises a second concern in a discussion of the overextended assumption that L1 and L2 writing are essentially the same phenomenon (657). Third is the extent to which L2 writing theorists have adequately addressed the connection between orality and literacy and the role L2 writing development plays in a general theoretical accounting of second language acquisition.

Shifting paradigms regarding the nature of L2 writing have had the most impact on classrooms at the postsecondary level but current debates have added a needed political dimension to a discussion of L2 writing theory. Such debates provide new terrain for exploring the connection between L2 literacy practices and issues of power and identity (e.g., Weinstein-Shr).

BIBLIOGRAPHY

Primary Texts and Major Scholarship in Composition

Bizzell, Patricia. "Language and Literacy." In *A Source Book for Basic Writing Teachers*. Ed. Theresa Enos. New York: Random House, 1987, 125–37.

Chomsky, Noam. *Aspects of the Theory of Syntax*. Cambridge, MA: MIT P, 1965.

Emig, Janet. *The Composing Process of Twelfth Graders*. Urbana, IL: NCTE, 1971.

Flower, Linda, and John Hayes. "A Cognitive Process Theory of Writing." *College Composition and Communication* 32.4 (1981): 365–87.

Gee, James. "Orality and Literacy: From the Savage Mind to Ways with Words." *TESOL Quarterly* 20.4 (1986): 719–46.

Hymes, Dell. *Foundations in Sociolinguistics*. Philadelphia: U of Pennsylvania P, 1974.

Kaplan, Robert. "Cultural Thought Patterns in Inter-Cultural Education." *Language Learning* 16 (1966): 1–20.

Krapels, Alexandra. "An Overview of Second Language Writing Process Research." In *Second Language Writing*. Ed. Barbara Kroll. Cambridge: Cambridge UP, 1990, 37–56.

Nystrand, Martin, Stuart Greene, and Jeffrey Wiemelt. "Where Did Composition Studies Come From?" *Written Communication* 10.3 (1993): 267–333.

Paulston, Christina Bratt, and Gerald Dykstra. *Controlled Composition in English as a Second Language*. New York: Regents, 1973.

Raimes, Ann. "Out of the Woods: Emerging Traditions in the Teaching of Writing." *TESOL Quarterly* 25.3 (1991): 407–30.

Silva, Tony. "Towards an Understanding of the Distinct Nature of L2 Writing: The ESL Research and Its Implications." *TESOL Quarterly* 27.4 (1993): 657–73.

Swales, John. *Genre Analysis*. Cambridge: Cambridge UP, 1990.

Vygotsky, Lev. *Mind in Society*. Cambridge: Harvard UP, 1978.

Weinstein-Shr, Gail. "Literacy and Social Process." In *Cross Cultural Approaches to Literacy*. Ed. Brian Street. Cambridge: Cambridge UP, 1993, 272–93.

Zamel, Vivian. "The Composing Process of Advanced ESL Students: Six Case Studies." *TESOL Quarterly* 17.2 (1983): 165–87.

MEG L. GEBHARD

SEMIOTICS/CONSTRUCTIVIST SEMIOTICS/ SOCIAL SEMIOTICS

Summary

Understood as the study and science of sign systems in language, *semiotics* is derived from Greek *simeion* (sign) and *semeiotikos* (one who interprets or divines the meaning of signs). Traditionally, sign study is divided into three areas—syntactics, the study of grammar; semantics, the study of meaning; and pragmatics, the study of the actual purposes and effects of meaningful utterances. In the twentieth century, the theories of Charles Sanders Peirce and Ferdinand de Saussure most significantly influenced the evolution and direction of contemporary semiotics. In the 1950s, the discipline developed a sociopolitical dimension when Roland Barthes applied semiotics to French popular culture, identifying the underlying ideological and mythological power of signs. Arguing for American language instruction that emphasizes critical reading and writing skills to serve as a foundation for participation in public life, James Berlin proposed that composition courses must surely include an analysis of cultural phenomena using semiotic strategies to uncover the interested and ideological nature of discourse.

In general, a *sign* is any information-bearing entity, such as road signs, maps, mathematical equations, animal sounds, and so on. Signs contain two distinct, inseparable parts—the signifier (a set of marks on a page, speech sounds, or hand signals) and the signified (the concept, idea, and meaning). Swiss structural linguist Ferdinand de Saussure (1857–1913) defined the study of signs within society, or *semiology*, as the contrast between elements and relationships as embodied in language. Because a sign derives its meaning and significance from its relationship to other signs within an entire system, it is the *difference* between the objective structure of signs and their governing laws that become the focus of Saussure's oeuvre. Thus, *langue*, or formal language, is the domain of linguistics. Recognizing that the relationship between the signifier and the signified is arbitrary and unnatural, signs derive their communicative power from socially established, rule-governed rituals. In addition, language use, as organized through a system of formal relations, is not arbitrary. The relationship between the signifier and signified is usually socially, historically, and culturally determined. Therefore, the actual use of language in communication, or *parole*, which is always contextually determined and in constant flux, is the domain of psychology. Saussure's propensity for studying the systematic coherency of formal language underscores his conception of language in static or synchronic terms; he neglects its historical or diachronic dimensions.

American pragmatist philosopher, physicist, and mathematician, Charles Sanders Peirce (1839–1914), formulated the basic principles for the contemporary study of signs. Arguing that signs can never approximate or contain any definite meaning, Peirce defined a sign as "something that stands for something in some respect or capacity." Signs have three distinct, inseparable parts—the *sign* or *representamen* (which stands for something in the mind of the interpreter); the *object* (the thing it stands for); and the *interpretant* (the thought or concept generated in relation to the sign and object). Recognizing the arbitrary relationship between signs and objects, Peirce differentiates among three kinds of signs: a *symbol* or *conventional sign* lacks any resemblance or correspondence to which the entity refers, depending on social and cultural custom for meaning (for example, a red traffic light means "Stop"); an *index* or *natural sign* is causally correlated with its object, resulting from an associative but unintentional relationship (for example, a yawn indicates sleepiness or boredom); and an *icon* resembles and corresponds with its conceptual object or some characteristic of its object (for example, a photograph captures the likeness of the person, and similarly, a sunburst logo is identified with the *CCC* journal). According to Peirce, the study of signs or the process of sign interpretation must not be limited to the decoding and the substitution of certain signs for others. Rather, the study of signs extends to three areas—speculative grammar, the classification of various possible sign functions; critical logic, the analysis of circumstances surrounding truth, reality, and knowledge; and speculative rhetoric, the identification of patterns of communication and the interpretation of relationships among signs.

The area of speculative rhetoric is most relevant to composition studies. Because signs are both tools of communication and a system of relationships resulting from language use, they become the mediating factor among subject, reality, and community. Therefore, a community's linguistic habits and rituals fulfill both communicative and regulatory functions. Thus, an understanding of a community's patterns of signification will permit an understanding of human thought and behavior. In order to uncover a community's patterns of signification, one must have speculative instruments like those developed by literary theorist I. A. (Ivor Armstrong) Richards (1893–1979). Although overlooked, the work of American philosopher and critic Susanne Langer (1895–1985), who scrutinizes the human inclination for signification and the natural ability for abstraction, should be considered. Langer highlights human beings' natural tendency for abstraction and symbolization: "The basic need, which is certainly obvious only in man, is the need of symbolization" (42). Symbols, "instruments of thought," are central to all human understanding and knowledge making. Applying her study of signs to subjects such as art, music, and religion, Langer explains that symbols derive their communicative effectiveness and significance not individually but in their discursive ability to organize, define, conceptualize, and communicate our humanity. Therefore, symbols are "not proxy of their objects, but are *vehicles for the conception of objects*" (61).

By investigating "how words work," Richards finds that the study of signs includes "the study of misunderstanding and its remedies" ("Philosophy of Rhetoric" 3–4). Richards maintains that language is the key to understanding human cognition, thus developing speculative instruments or tools to aid thinking; after all, "language is an instrument for controlling our becoming" (*Speculative* 9). Since words are "notoriously uncontrollable," Richards emphasizes the need for a "systematic study of *the inherent and necessary opportunities for misunderstanding*" in language (74). Because of the inherent metaphorical dimension in language and the "interanimations" among words, Richards introduces protocols for understanding how meaning is constructed. These protocols were later redeveloped to aid in the teaching of writing and reading by Ann E. Berthoff. In collaboration with C. K. Ogden (Ogden and Richards, *The Meaning of Meaning*), Richards places language at the center of Aristotle's communication triangle, making it the primary consideration when examining and redefining the dialectical relationships among symbol, referent, and thought/reference.

In the late 1950s, French semiologist and social critic Roland Barthes (1915–1980) applied Saussure's theories on the study of signs to his investigations of popular culture. Unlike Saussure, Barthes underscored the political and ideological dimensions in semiotic analysis, highlighting how all signs simultaneously reveal and conceal some interest, usually the underlying worldview of the dominant power. Stressing that semiotics cannot focus on simply uncovering the linguistic relationships between signs and symbols, Barthes advocated that the study of signs, especially in popular culture, involves a critical attention to ideology and the operations of mythology. Through analyses of subjects like wrestling and fashion, Barthes analyzed how emerging signifying systems build on already existing systems, which are usually influenced by class interests and values.

Reception and Significance in Composition Studies

The principal proponents for connecting semiotics with composition studies are Ann E. Berthoff and James Berlin. Synthesizing and explaining the work of Peirce, Langer, and Richards, Berthoff focuses on the inventive powers of language, discussing how signs allow writers to clarify and articulate relationships, to transform information into meaning. Insisting that language underscores personal conceptions and social contexts, Berthoff advocates for a heuristic that integrates the writer's cognitive, affective, and rational processes. Defining writing as the purposeful activity of meaning making, Berthoff introduces ways for developing rigorous thinking habits through close rhetorical reading of texts and careful development of rhetorically aware texts. Because she has transformed the study to the production of meaningful signs in the writing classroom, Berthoff has been recognized for her scholarship, which underscores a systematic pedagogy and sequence of assignments that aid in critical thinking.

In the late 1980s, the dominant trajectory for semiotics involves cultural studies, as advocated by James Berlin. Building on the theories of Robert Hodge and Gunther Kress as well as the work of British author Raymond Williams, Berlin offers a strong rationale for emphasizing semiotics, popular culture, and ideology in the writing classroom. Focusing on the social aspects of meaning making, Berlin argues that writing classes should move beyond issues of linguistic correctness (grammar and mechanics) in order to concentrate on the struggles and tensions that lead to the emergence of meaning. In other words, semiotic analyses must confront the ''set of rules prescribing the conditions for the production and reception of meanings, which specify who can claim to initiate (produce, communicate) or know (receive, understand) meanings about what topics under what circumstances and with what modalities (how, when, why)'' (Hodge and Kress, 4). Arguing against a pedagogy that focuses exclusively on the production of academic texts, Berlin maintains that ''students must come to see that the languages they are expected to speak, write and embrace as ways of thinking and acting are never disinterested, always bringing with them strictures on the existent, the good, the possible, and regimes of power'' (''Post-Structuralism,'' 144). Thus, the teaching of reading and writing must surely involve lessons in the ''methods for describing and analyzing the operations of signification'' (144). Berlin's rationale is situated in his definition of the intellectual whose role takes on an important social and political dimension. Describing the writing classroom as the site for preparing students for critical involvement in public life, competent readers and writers are ones who are aware of cultural codes, competing discourses, linguistic subjectivities (race, class, gender formations), and the utilization of language to bring about ''more democratic and personally humane economic, social, and political arrangements'' (146). Using topics such as advertising, work, play, education, gender, and individuality, Berlin's students are asked to identify hierarchies, binaries, narrative patterns, discursive rituals in their semiotic analyses.

Finally, Sonia Maasik and Jack Solomon identify in their first year composition reader two sections that draw on semiotics: first, prominent and dominant images in contemporary American popular culture (usually media dominated); and second, social and political issues of contemporary importance, including controversies that affect the quality of American life (for example, multiculturalism, AIDS, gender). In order to endeavor a semiotic analysis, students are asked to take a number of steps: go beyond what a sign is to explain what it means; identify what that sign may be related to within a system, including differences and similarities; recognize which systems of belief or ''mythologies'' are being evoked; and investigate the mythologies that shape our values and perceptions and influence our interpretation (3–14).

BIBLIOGRAPHY

Primary Texts

Barthes, Roland. *Elements of Semiotics.* Trans. Anetto Lavers and Colin Smith. New York: Hill and Wang, 1968.

————. *The Semiotic Challenge.* Trans. Richard Howard. New York: Hill and Wang, 1988.

Berger, Arthur Asa. *Signs in Contemporary Culture: An Introduction to Semiotics.* Salem, WI: Sheffield, 1989.

Eco, Umberto. *A Theory of Semiotics.* Bloomington: Indiana UP, 1976.

Gottdiener, M. *Postmodern Semiotics: Material Culture and the Forms of Postmodern Life.* Cambridge: Blackwell, 1995.

Hodge, Robert, and Gunther Kress. *Social Semiotics.* Ithaca, NY: Cornell UP, 1988.

Langer, Susanne. *Philosophy in a New Key.* Cambridge, MA: Harvard UP, 1942.

Nöth, Winifred. *Handbook of Semiotics.* Bloomington: Indiana UP, 1990.

Ogden, C. K., and I. A. Richards. *The Meaning of Meaning.* New York: Harcourt, 1923.

Peirce, Charles Sanders. *Charles S. Peirce: Selected Writings.* Ed. P. O. Wiener. New York: Dover, 1958.

Richards, I. A. *Philosophy of Rhetoric.* New York: Oxford UP, 1936.

————. *Speculative Instruments.* New York: Harcourt, 1955.

Saussure, Ferdinand de. *Course in General Linguistics.* Trans. Wade Baskin. Ed. Charles Bally and Albert Reidlinger. New York: Philosophical Library, 1959.

Sebeok, Thomas A. *Semiotics in the United States.* Bloomington: Indiana UP, 1991.

Silverman, Kaja. *The Subject of Semiotics.* New York: Oxford UP, 1983.

Williams, Raymond. *Keywords: A Vocabulary of Culture and Society.* Rev. ed. New York: Oxford UP, 1983.

Major Scholarship in Composition

Berlin, James. "Post-Structuralism, Semiotics, and Social-Epistemic Rhetoric." In *Defining New Rhetorics.* Ed. Theresa Enos and Stuart C. Brown. Newbury Park, CA: Sage, 1993, 137–53.

————. *Rhetorics, Poetics, and Cultures: Refiguring College English Studies.* Urbana, IL: NCTE, 1996.

Berlin, James, and Michael Vivion, eds. *Cultural Studies in the English Classroom.* Portsmouth, NH: Boynton/Cook, 1992.

Berthoff, Ann E. *Forming/Thinking/Writing: The Composing Imagination.* Portsmouth, NH: Boynton/Cook, 1988.

————. *The Making of Meaning: Metaphors, Models, and Maxims for Writing Teachers.* Portsmouth, NH: Boynton/Cook, 1981.

————. *Richards on Rhetoric: Selected Essays of I. A. Richards (1929–1974).* New York: Oxford UP, 1991.

Fitts, Karen, and Alan France, eds. *Left Margins: Cultural Studies and Composition Pedagogy.* Albany: State U of New York P, 1995.

Lyne, John R. "Rhetoric and Semiotic in C. S. Peirce." *Quarterly Journal of Speech* 66 (1980): 155–68.

Maasik, Sonia, and Jack Solomon, eds. *Signs of Life in the USA.* 2nd ed. Boston: Bedford, 1997.

SUE HUM

SOCIAL CONSTRUCTIONISM
Summary

Social constructionism challenges traditional epistemological assumptions, specifically, the view that our knowledge of the world is the outcome of direct and unfiltered access to reality. Rather, social constructionists argue, we view the world through a social filter: prevailing ideologies, social and cultural constructs such as community beliefs and assumptions—or, less broadly, for a body of scientists, shared paradigms—all direct our interpretation of reality. To be specific, it is our discourse about the world, imbued as language is with the beliefs and assumptions of ourselves and others, the continually emerging product of historical and social contingencies, that mediates our understandings of what is "out there." In other words, for social constructionists the world comes to us through language. As Berlin puts it, the "individual never responds to things in themselves but to discursive formations of things in themselves" ("Composition Studies," 108). In *Metaphors We Live By*, Lakoff and Johnson identify several root metaphors, and thereby the versions of reality, that are implicit in our everyday use of English. Thus, social constructionists regard language as interested and invested rather than as a transparent conduit conveying truth. Our knowledge, especially because it registers in and most often operates through language, is accordingly a consequence of social processes rather than directly given to or constructed by the individual.

Bruffee's bibliographical essay on social constructionism ("Social Construction") provides an informative account of this theory, its antecedents, and its relevance for composition studies:

A social constructionist position in any discipline assumes that entities we normally call reality, knowledge, thought, facts, texts, selves, and so on are constructs generated by communities of like-minded peers. Social construction understands reality, knowledge, thought, facts, texts, selves, and so on as community-generated and community-maintained linguistic entities—or, more broadly speaking, symbolic entities—that define or "constitute" the communities that generate them. (774)

Community is a grounding concept in accounts of social constructionism. Knowledge is both produced in and reciprocally reproduces human communities. "Communities of like-minded peers" may put far too harmonious and accommodating a face on the knowledge making practices of a discourse community, implying an absence of conflict, of social positioning and opposing ideologies. For instance, lab reports or ethnographic accounts, which appear to provide a transparent window on reality, are in effect representations shaped by discourse practices of institutions and communities, and driven (however tacitly) "not simply by empirical reality but by a battery of desires, repressions, investments, and projections," to borrow Edward Said's trenchant formulation (cited by Herndl, "Writing Ethnography," 322). In practice, disciplinary knowledge is not always consensual, coherent, or focused; it is often in flux, open to negotiation, and, despite a seemingly univocal surface, fissured and conflicted.

While early social-constructionist accounts of knowledge making have accounted for the formation of social beliefs, which constitute our everyday, taken-for-granted accounts of reality (Berger and Luckman), later developments have taken increasingly to examining disciplinary knowledge making as the construction of belief systems. Thus, in setting the ground for his account of revolutions in basic scientific concepts, Thomas Kuhn asserts that an "apparently arbitrary element, compounded of personal and historical accident, is always a formative ingredient of the beliefs espoused by a given scientific community at a given time" (4). He goes on to speak of scientific research as "a strenuous and devoted attempt to force nature into the conceptual boxes supplied by professional education" and of how the activity of normal science is "predicated on the assumption that the scientific community knows what the world is like" (5).

A philosophical position closely linked with social constructionism is anti-foundationalism, the position associated with philosopher Richard Rorty. According to Stanley Fish, anti-foundationalism "teaches that questions of fact, truth, correctness, validity, and clarity . . . are intelligible and debatable only within the precincts of the contexts or situations or paradigms or communities that give them their local and changeable shape" (344). Thus anti-foundationalism accords with the kind of social-constructionist inquiry that is attentive to "local knowledge," which is anthropologist Clifford Geertz's term for the traditional, situated knowledge that is current and active in a community and functions as interpretive lens. Geertz would add that researchers in such an orientation also ought to be aware of how they themselves are "positioned" (see Bizzell, *Academic Discourse* 202–21, and Smit for discussions concerning anti-foundationalism and writing).

Allan Luke cites the work of Michel Foucault on how discourse "actually defines, constructs, and positions human subjects" and how "discourses [in Foucault's words] 'systematically form the objects about which they speak,' shaping grids and hierarchies for the institutional categorization and treatment of people" (8). Social constructionist oriented research may thus examine practices that create a certain social reality, for instance, reports—generally accepted as factual—on literacy levels, crime rates, or what constitutes mental illness in our society. In the latter case, a study by McCarthy and Gerring is particularly instructive. Their analysis of the processes involved in the revision of a major manual concerned with the classification of mental disorders bears out their view of "texts, including scientific ones, not as neutral transporters of information but as reflections of social and political forces, at once shaped by these forces and, at the same time, shaping them" (151). Moreover, while the finished document "appears to present well-entrenched consensual knowledge, it actually floats on currents of debate and dispute" (151). Such reality-constructing practices are manifest and consequential in nondiscursive activities as well: in prevailing understandings that direct everyday decisions as to what constitutes a "pass" or a "fail" or the definition of "standards" in academic circles or again, in a social worker's determination of a client's eligibility for social assistance or in a culture's understanding of childhood, family, or even the self. All such notions derive their meaning from within the social practices in which they are employed. As Gergen ("The Social Constructionist Movement") argues, such definitions are not open to empirical validation and are continually shifting: "Whether an act is defined as envy, flirtation, or anger floats on a sea of social interchange" (268).

But social constructionism is only one among several such attempts to explain the formation of human knowledge. If beliefs about the construction of knowledge are ranged along a continuum, Berlin's and Bruffee's accounts of social constructionism, for instance, represent one polar node of such a continuum. Toward the other node range views which are known in the sociology of knowledge as "constructivist" (see the entry on constructivist theory in this volume). Both paradigms—constructivism and social constructionism—deny that knowledge mirrors an objective reality independent of the knower or that knowledge somehow exists fully formed, ready to be acquired; rather, they maintain, the construction of knowledge is an active process. However, constructivists and social constructionists diverge in where they locate the site of such knowledge making: *inner-directed*, on the one hand, in the sense that constructivists regard individuals as more or less autonomous agents of knowledge, focusing on their cognitive operations as they interact with physical and social reality; or *outer-directed*, on the other hand, in that social constructionists assign knowledge making to communities and subcommunities, focusing on how human knowledge in general is constructed as a product of social interaction and regarding discourse and discourse production as the proper sites for understanding human actions and mental processes (the constructs of "inner-directed" and "outer-directed" are drawn from Bizzell, 75–103).

The constructivist paradigm, which is essentially a psychological theory, focuses on an individual constructing empirically viable internal models of reality or accommodations, alone or while working with others, whereas social constructionism regards knowledge as socially negotiated and constituted in discourse, which registers shared assumptions and beliefs, in a socially emerging view of the world. Thus, Piaget's account of childhood learning is constructivist in orientation, while Vygotsky's sociocultural approach in his account of the development of higher mental functions may be regarded as approaching the constructionist. By Vygotsky's account, those functions emerge first in social interaction before they are internalized by the individual. Because Vygotsky specifies both the social interaction and the internal processes of the individual, commentators such as Gergen ("Social Construction") argue that Vygotsky's orientation is only partially social constructionist.

On account of its nearly exclusive concern with social processes, the social constructionist account has been criticized as being disembodied and agentless, obscuring "the fact that meaning and the work of construction are still located in the minds of individual agents'' (Flower, 62–63). A counterargument to such criticism would be one drawn by D. C. Phillips from philosopher Helen Longino, who ''attacks the assumption made within traditional individualized epistemology that a knower can be conceived validly as being an isolated individual, stripped of interests, motives, biases, and other socially determined traits.'' According to Phillips, Longino's argument is that an individual's assumptions and knowledge claims need to be scrutinized and validated in community, using communal standards within an interactive, dialogic framework (10).

Nystrand, Greene, and Wiemelt suggest that neither the social nor the individual perspective is, in itself, sufficient as an explanation of knowledge and discourse production, and that, following Bakhtin, we ought to regard discourse as

a forum where the forces of individual cognition, on the one hand, and social ideology and convention, on the other, ''dialectically interpenetrate'' each other. . . . In other words, the individual and the social provide neither competing nor even alternative perspectives on meaning in discourse; rather, context and cognition operate always and only in an interpenetrating, co-constitutive relationship. (295)

Although Bakhtin is often invoked in social constructionist discussion, particularly his notions of *dialogism* and *heteroglossia* (see the entry on Dialogism/ Bakhtinian theory in this volume), the position suggested by his concept of *answerability* does not get sufficient play, quite likely because *answerability* summons up the argument that participants in Bakhtin's dialogue are answerable (in the sense of being individually accountable), which is an incompatible position if individual agency is discounted in knowledge making (see Rothschild Ewald 339).

Reception and Significance in Composition Studies

Social constructionist theory enters the field of composition as part of the larger movement away from the view of the writer as a solitary, autonomous individual and toward an understanding of the situatedness of writers and writing. It provides a theoretical frame for studying writers and writing as socially situated. No longer is knowledge unquestioningly viewed as objective or writing regarded as a form of information processing. Berlin, Bruffee, Bizzell, Faigley, Lefevre, and Myers are among composition theorists most often cited as social constructionist in orientation.

The division between constructivism and social constructionism replicates to a large extent some of the main divergences in composition theory. Applied to prevailing theoretical models of composition, the constructivist perspective supports the cognitivist focus on the internal processes of individual writers and the operations involved in reading and writing as acts of construction and co-construction, negotiating meaning, and the production of written text. Thus success or failure in writing can be attributed to individuals' cognitive operations, and interventions can be pointed in that direction rather than in the direction of the contexts in which writing is deployed. But constructivists *do* acknowledge a social dimension in acts of composing, considering how other readers, other texts, and cowriters are involved in the individual's construction of meaning (Flower; Spivey). To an extent, a constructivist stance is also in accord with an expressivist or Romantic view of writers with the concomitant task of the teacher to help students discover and express what is latent.

Social constructionist discussions of writing, on the other hand, are preoccupied with discourse as socially constructed. The perspective is global, the concept of discourse communities rather than individual agency figuring largely in such discussion. The focus is on how such a community defines writers and writing; how texts represent that community; how the community, its discourse, and disciplinary knowledge are constituted and reconstituted; and how participants in discursive practices form and are formed by these practices and the disciplinary and professional formations in which they participate.

Socially constructed knowledge is not treated as absolute, but as continually revisable through social exchange: "temporary locations in dialogic space—samples of discourse that are accorded status as 'knowledgeable tellings' on given occasions" (Gergen, "Social Construction," 30); a "social artifact" (Bruffee, "Collaborative Learning"). Because it is seen as replicating the social processes by which knowledge is made, collaborative writing is the preferred mode in social constructionist teaching. Collaborative writing goes beyond coauthoring (as division of labor) and peer editing toward writing interdependently within contexts that necessitate rather than merely structure or assign working in groups. It is literally writing together, jointly inquiring and constructing, dialogically with others and others' texts (see Reither and Vipond). One might note in passing how electronic conversations on the World Wide Web are a vibrant example of our realization of knowledge, not as personal possession but as the continually emerging and shared outcome of discursive exchange.

Within a social constructionist perspective, such collaborative work can make as its main preoccupation the need to critically examine discourse practices within relevant disciplines and professions with the goal of uncovering, for instance, how certain textual practices enable reporting as objective representation what are essentially subjective and interpretive accounts. Students may inquire how knowledge is constituted in specific disciplines and workplaces, whose interests are served by the dominant discourse, and which positions are excluded. They may analyze professional discourse, remaining aware at the same time how such discourse is contingent and institutionally implicated and what their options are as participants in such practices.

However, school-based writers do not operate with the kinds of exigencies and motives that drive knowledge making in the workplace (see Dias et al.). Collaborative classrooms may replicate only some aspects of workplace knowledge making practices. The expectation in some collaborative practices that groups ought to work toward consensus suggests to critics a denial of the personal and subjective response. In nonschool settings, writers may not always work consensually and dissent may frequently generate productive dialogue. Moreover, while tentativeness may be valued as a learning strategy in school, writing in workplaces, more often than not, is production rather than learning oriented. Often, participation for established members of such formations has become routinized and automatic as "the way we do things here"; for aspiring members, joining is a matter of adjustment and habituation to "their way of doing things."

Thus students may quite likely regard their interests are best served by learning and cultivating institutionally preferred discourses, without regard to the ideologies embodied in those discourses. It is often suggested that students ought to be introduced to the paradigms, norms, conventions, and practices of relevant disciplinary and professional discourse communities (to analyze or emulate them, or both). While such fixing of conventions and practices in flux may breach the anti-foundationalist orientation of social constructionists, Bazerman argues that "the issue is whether we write within any stable social regularities with stable social tools to achieve stable social effects. Or are social relations ad hoc, fluid, unpredictable, and thus to be constructed new every time?" (*Constructing Experience* 126). Current genre theory casts some light on this quandary: rules or regularities in writing are an outcome of regularities in contexts, are therefore situation generated, and a product of a community's ongoing genre making (see the entry on Genre theory in this volume).

Collaboration, however, can be justified for reasons other than that it emulates workplace knowledge making practices. Maybe collaboration is a timely acknowledgment of the need to provide for multivoicedness, multicultural classrooms, and diverse perspectives—all-in-all, the need to enable people at the margins to bring their unique perspectives to knowledge construction. Collaborative writing need not be invariably, as its detractors say, an attempt to silence the individual in order to promote social skills, or to adopt the consensual and production-oriented practices of the business world at the expense of the questioning that supports learning and inquiry in the classroom.

Both Gergen ("The Social Constructionist Movement") and Phillips point out how the social constructionist orientation to knowledge making is far more congenial to contemporary feminist thinking than is the empiricist, particularly because of the social constructionist bias toward communal rather than individual endeavor, and the consequent redistribution of power and the social empowerment of the underprivileged. As Belenky et al. point out, recognizing the constructedness of experience is a liberating experience for women: "Theories become not truth but models for evaluating experience" (138). The notion of knowledge as constructed implies a position "in which all women view knowledge as contextual, experience themselves as creators of knowledge, and value both subjective and objective strategies for knowing" (15), with a corresponding decline in the deference accorded to the expert. However, Belenky et al. appear to have adopted a social constructivist rather than constructionist position in that they stress the power of the individual as knowledge creator rather than membership in a group and social exchange.

A social constructionist approach to composition teaching tends to raise uncomfortable questions about practices that normally go unexamined. We might ask, for instance, as Baardman does, whether we can continue to hold a belief in ownership of writing and treat it almost exclusively as a record of students' thinking (2). We might also ask how we might acknowledge and deal with the fact that students' interpretations of teachers' requests may be constituted differently from the ways teachers intend them? As Johnston (with school children in mind) points out, "Teachers (and other adults involved in children's literacy development) imbue children's behavior with meaning differently, depending on how they have constructed their own knowledge of children and of literate activity" (7). Eventually, our questions merge into the broader question of how discourse communities construct what counts as knowledge and what it takes to be regarded as knowledgeable.

Social constructionism as it is applied to composition has had its share of detractors. Unlike expressive and cognitive approaches, its theory does not so clearly suggest its classroom applications or their likely outcomes. Thus, one can be engaged by the theory yet not be driven to transform practice. We tend not to look within ourselves or at our own writing for socially constructed knowledge, which instead comes to us in its published documents; consequently, socially constructed knowledge is more read than written, and is therefore more the subject of study than it is of practice. One powerful hindrance to its classroom application is that it does not satisfy the pedagogical imperative that seeks, in Faigley's terms, "a rational, coherent student subject." The main pedagogical approach it promotes, collaborative learning, is dismissed by its critics as trading intrasubjectivity for intersubjectivity, personal knowledge for group knowledge, individual expression and authenticity for group hegemony, and academic inquiry for workplace practices.

A fairer criticism is that in its exclusive concern with discourse as mediating knowledge, it fails to recognize an affective dimension to cognition or to consider entities other than the linguistic or symbolic as having knowledge making potential (see Petraglia). Moreover, while it effectively deconstructs "objective" knowledge, it suggests no obvious means of evaluating knowledge claims other than rhetorical persuasion.

BIBLIOGRAPHY

Primary Texts

Bakhtin, M. M. *The Dialogic Imagination*. Trans. Caryl Emerson and Michael Holquist. Ed. Michael Holquist. Austin: U of Texas P, 1981.

Berger, Peter L., and Thomas Luckman. *The Social Construction of Reality: A Treatise in the Sociology of Knowledge*. New York: Anchor, 1967.

Foucault, Michel. *The Archaeology of Knowledge*. Trans. A. M. Sheridan Smith. New York: Harper, 1976.

Geertz, Clifford. *Local Knowledge: Further Essays in Interpretive Anthropology.* New York: Basic, 1983.

Gergen, Kenneth J. "Social Construction and the Educational Process." In *Constructivism in Education.* Ed. Leslie Steffe and Jerry Gale. Hillsdale, NJ: Erlbaum, 1995, 17–39.

———. "The Social Constructionist Movement in Modern Psychology." *American Psychologist* 40 (1985): 266–75.

Kuhn, Thomas S. *The Structure of Scientific Revolutions.* Chicago: U of Chicago P, 1962.

Longino, Helen. *Science as Social Knowledge.* Princeton, NJ: Princeton UP, 1990.

Phillips, D. C. "The Good, the Bad, and the Ugly: The Many Faces of Constructivism." *Educational Researcher* 24 (1995): 5–12.

Piaget, Jean. *The Construction of Reality in the Child.* New York: Ballantine, 1954.

Rorty, Richard. *Philosophy and the Mirror of Nature.* Princeton, NJ: Princeton UP, 1979.

Said, Edward. *Orientalism.* New York: Pantheon, 1978.

Steffe, Leslie, and Jerry Gale, eds. *Constructivism in Education.* Hillsdale, NJ: Erlbaum, 1995.

Vygotsky, Lev. *Mind in Society: The Development of Higher Psychological Processes.* Ed. Michael Cole. Cambridge, MA: Harvard UP, 1978.

Major Scholarship in Composition

Baardman, Sandy. "Shifting Perspectives: Developing Social Conceptualizations of Writing." In *Social Reflections on Writing: To Reach and Realize.* Ed. Sandy Baardman, Stanley Straw, and Laura Atkinson. Winnipeg, MN: Literacy Publications, 1994, 1–11.

Bazerman, Charles. *Constructing Experience.* Carbondale and Edwardsville: Southern Illinois UP, 1994.

———. *Shaping Written Knowledge: The Genre and Activity of the Experimental Article in Science.* Madison: U of Wisconsin P, 1988.

Belenky, Mary F., et al. *Women's Ways of Knowing: The Development of Self, Voice, and Mind.* New York: Basic, 1986.

Berlin, James A. "Composition Studies and Cultural Studies: Collapsing Boundaries." In *Into the Field: Sites of Composition Studies.* Ed. Anne Ruggles Gere. New York: MLA, 1993, 99–116.

———. *Rhetorics, Poetics, and Cultures: Refiguring College English Studies.* Urbana, IL: NCTE, 1996

Bizzell, Patricia. *Academic Discourse and Critical Consciousness.* Pittsburgh, PA: U of Pittsburgh P, 1992.

Bruffee, Kenneth. A. "Collaborative Learning and the 'Conversation of Mankind.' " *College English* 46 (1984): 635–52.

———. "Social Construction, Language, and the Authority of Knowledge: A Bibliographical Essay." *College English* 48 (1986): 773–90.

Clark, Gregory. *Dialogue, Dialectic, and Conversation: A Social Perspective on the Function of Writing.* Carbondale and Edwardsville: Southern Illinois UP, 1990.

Dias, Patrick, Aviva Freedman, Peter Medway, and Anthony Paré. *Worlds Apart: Acting and Writing in Academic and Workplace Contexts.* Hillsdale, NJ: Erlbaum, 1998.

Faigley, Lester. *Fragments of Rationality: Postmodernity and the Subject of Composition.* Pittsburgh, PA: U of Pittsburgh P, 1992.

Fish, Stanley. "Anti-Foundationalism, Theory Hope, and the Teaching of Composition."

In *Doing What Comes Naturally: Change, Rhetoric, and the Practice of Theory in Literary and Legal Studies*. Durham, NC: Duke UP, 1989, 342–55.

Flower, Linda. *The Construction of Negotiated Meaning: A Social Cognitive Theory of Writing*. Carbondale and Edwardsville: Southern Illinois UP, 1994.

Herndl, Carl G. "Writing Ethnography: Representation, Rhetoric, and Institutional Practices." *College English* 53 (1991): 320–32.

Johnston, Peter H. *Constructive Evaluation of Literate Activity*. White Plains, NY: Longman, 1992.

Lakoff, George, and Mark Johnson. *Metaphors We Live By*. Chicago: U of Chicago P, 1980.

LeFevre, Karen Burke. *Invention as a Social Act*. Carbondale: Southern Illinois UP, 1987.

Luke, Allan. "Text and Discourse in Education: An Introduction to Critical Discourse Analysis." In *Review of Research in Education* 21 (1995–1996). Ed. Michael Apple. Washington, DC: AERA, 1995, 3–48.

McCarthy, Lucille Parkinson, and Joan Page Gerring. "Revising Psychiatry's Charter Document: DSM-IV." *Written Communication* 11 (1994): 147–92.

Myers, Greg. "The Social Construction of Two Biologists' Proposals." *Written Communication* 2 (1985): 219–45.

———. *Writing Biology: Texts in the Social Construction of Knowledge*. Madison: U of Wisconsin P, 1990.

Nystrand, Martin, Stuart Greene, and Jeffrey Wiemelt. "Where Did Composition Studies Come From? An Intellectual History." *Written Communication* 10 (1993): 267–83.

Petraglia, Joseph. "Interrupting the Conversation: The Constructionist Dialogue in Composition." *Journal of Advanced Composition* 11 (1991): 37–55.

Reither, James and Douglas Vipond. "Writing as Collaboration." *College English* 51 (1989): 855–67.

Rothschild Ewald, H. "Waiting for Answerability: Bakhtin and Composition Studies." *College Composition and Communication* 44 (1993): 331–48.

Smit, David. "Hall of Mirrors: Antifoundationalist Theory and the Teaching of Writing." *Journal of Advanced Composition* 15 (1995): 35–52.

Spivey, Nancy. "Written Discourse: A Constructivist Perspective." In *Constructivism in Education*. Ed. Leslie Steffe and Jerry Gale. Hillsdale, NJ: Erlbaum, 1995, 313–29.

PATRICK DIAS

SOCIO-COGNITIVE THEORY AND COGNITIVE RHETORIC

Summary

Socio-cognitive theories of literate acts seek to reconcile two often-conflicting camps within the still-youthful field of composition studies—the "cognitive process" empiricists and the "hermeneutically trained" social constructivists (Brandt, 317; Berkenkotter, "Paradigm" 151). Linda Flower, perhaps the most prominent of all the cognitive researchers investigating written composition, has characterized socio-cognitive theory as striving to develop an "integrated . . . vision which can explain how context cues cognition" during the performance of reading and writing ("Cognition, Context," 289).

The research informing socio-cognitive theory, says Flower, should be empirical in its rigor and skepticism, and rhetorical in its eschewing of a search for "Truth" and building of "probabilistic arguments about controversial subjects" ("Cognitive Rhetoric," 173). The term "cognitive rhetoric," therefore, is meant to suggest both a mode of inquiry and potential classroom practices that would go beyond heuristics and a sensitivity to context "to include the thinking strategies of writers and the comprehension strategies of readers" (Flower, *Construction* 121).

The felt need for a theoretical linking of empirical and hermeneutic approaches followed a period of more than a decade in which research into the cognitive activities of writers had stirred considerable enthusiasm and controversy. During the 1970s and early 1980s, several controlled studies yielded useful observations concerning the thinking patterns of both "basic" and experienced writers. Bereiter and Scardamalia noted the absence among young children first learning to write of an "executive routine" for controlling planning and invention strategies ("Conversation," 46). Flower and Hayes's models of the composing process, derived from "think-aloud" protocols, supported Sommers's finding that writing activities such as planning and revision were often recursive and performed in combination, thus challenging the sequential "stages" found in the earlier process models of Rohman (106) and Britton et al. (22–37).

Fault lines soon appeared, however, between what Bizzell called "outer-directed" (socially oriented) and "inner-directed" (cognitively oriented) theorists (217). Dobrin suggested that the scope of Flower and Hayes's inquiries was unnecessarily limited by the strong influence of research into artificial intelligence on their work. By considering problem solving as the primary impetus for writing, Dobrin argued, Flower and Hayes made the same mistake as artificial intelligence researcher Herbert Simon, who was trying to increase the problem-solving capabilities of computers by examining human methods (Dobrin, 713).

Critics were skeptical of any generalizations about writing processes derived from laboratory-based studies. They were strongly influenced by the research of Vygotsky, Luria, Scribner and Cole, Heath, Dyson, and Bazerman, which appeared to make it increasingly clear that a writer's cognitive activities could not be described without taking into account the "discourse community" in which the writing took place and the rhetorical situation which prompted it. "In sum, literacy is not simply a set of skills"; Dyson announced at the end of the article publicizing her study, "it is a social activity" ("Learning," 262).

"Think-aloud" protocols, the methodology of choice among cognitively oriented researchers, also came under heavy attack during the 1980s. Cooper and Holzman, Dobrin, and Geisler charged that protocols were both inappropriate for studying writing and misused by those who employed them. At the same time, Geisler staunchly defended the use of "think aloud" protocols, contending that when properly obtained, they have "ecological validity" during a subject's reading and writing and provide "indirect evidence of cognition" (110–11; see also Ericsson and Simon). Recent socio-cognitive research has modified the applications of protocols. Geisler combined protocols with interviews and written drafts to categorize participants' activities "in terms of the cultural products ... they consulted and produced" as they developed their positions regarding an issue in ethics (170). Brandt has used Garfinkel's ethnomethodology to analyze protocols as "accounts" of thinking inseparable from the social awareness that induced it.

To sum up, scholars involved in developing recent socio-cognitive theories of composition have clearly taken earlier criticisms of cognitive research seriously, while resisting capitulation to the social constructivist position. Berkenkotter, whose research first took protocols out of the "laboratory" and into more "naturalistic" settings ("Decisions"), has characterized the social-cognitive split as something of a "turf war," since research of both orientations has been empirical in nature. "Meaning making" involves acts of conscious intent on the part of a writer, Flower continues to insist, and not just "the brush of discourses passing in the night" (*Construction* 41). "Context," she declared in a 1989 essay, "does not produce a text through immaculate conception" ("Cognition, Context," 289). Only a theory that allows for and considers individual agency can yield knowledge about how such agency takes place, thus enabling teachers to effectively intervene in the development of particular student writers.

Emerging Theories

The editorial constraints dictated by the nature of this book prohibit detailed description of the multiple forms empirical research and socio-cognitive theory building have taken in the past decade. Briefly summarizing representative ideas put forth by Cheryl Geisler, Linda Flower, and Deborah Brandt, however, could provide a sense of the direction the inquiry has taken. One clear trend has been a shift in the focus of hypotheses from the differences between experienced or accomplished and "basic" writers, which often seemed to assume the distinction held no matter what kind of discourse was being produced, towards the differences between expert and naive writers within a particular content field.

Geisler argues that the "great divide" in academic literacy is between an institutionally induced naiveté that regards text as an autonomous reflection of external reality and a knowing expertise that regards text as an adaptation of abstracted information for specific audiences (89–90). Bereiter and Scardamalia have traced that naiveté to Alfred North Whitehead's concept of "inert ideas"— those propositions that often dominate school instruction and which are imparted to students with no other discernible use than later recitation and testing (*Psychology* 180).

Geisler has concluded that the transformation of novice writers into experts is dependent upon the unmasking of textual autonomy through "localized accounts of how something is actually accomplished" and the development of students' ability to engage in "meta-discourse," namely, to reflect upon the social, epistemological and rhetorical situations in which they read and write texts (238). Interestingly, Geisler also advocates the value of "amateur perspectives" for academic disciplines, since "expertise in academic literacy" involves not just negotiation between "domain content" and the "rhetorical world of abstract authorial conversation," as identified by Bereiter and Scardamalia, but also negotiation among those two "worlds" and a "narrated world of everyday experience" similar to that identified by Dyson (Geisler, 240; Dyson, "Negotiating").

A second trend involves a necessary increase in the complexity of models of compositional cognition, as can be clearly seen in the recent work of Flower, who has made the most extended efforts to articulate a comprehensive socio-cognitive theory.

One model evolves from the 1984 "multiple representation hypotheses" developed by Flower and Hayes ("Images, Plans, and Prose") and a "connectivist" theory of memory developed by Bechtel and Abrahamson (Flower, *Construction* 95). Writers construct meaning through ongoing reconfigurations of mental representations in "modes" that extend "from imagery, to metaphors and schemas, to abstract conceptual propositions, to prose" (Flower and Hayes, "Images" 129) rather than by logically manipulating "static symbols" (Flower, *Construction* 97). Flower accommodates constructivist thinking within this model by identifying some networked memory "nodes" as "voiced" or "talking" representations of "the writer's prior experiences with the language" and "the socioideological belief system in which that language emerged in the first place" (*Construction* 99). But the tension between the social and cognitive is ever present and Brandt has argued that Flower's metaphor characterizing "writing as an 'interaction' between context and cognition" still creates a separation of the individual from the social sphere that is "not viable" (325).

Brandt advocates analyzing cognitive data such as "think-aloud" protocols using the ethnomethodology developed by sociologist Harold Garfinkel. A "domain of inquiry" rather than a research technique, Brandt claims ethnomethodology eliminates the split in socio-cognitive theorizing through its regard of human utterances as "accounts" which simultaneously reflect thought and social awareness (326). People explain what they are doing and why because questions regarding their activities are either voiced or implicit within their social environment (333). Rather than revealing the "un-" or "sub"conscious, an ethnomethodological examination of composing perceives the writer's consciousness of a "self" only identifiable in relation to the social and cultural contexts in which composing takes place. Individual agency is preserved because the writer interprets perceived circumstances, and in acting upon those interpretations seeks to alter the circumstances (Heritage, 131–32).

Reception and Significance in Composition Studies

The significance of any theory can be best measured by its impact on classroom practice. Cognitive research into composing behaviors, combined with the pioneering work of Janet Emig (*Composing*), Donald Graves and his colleagues, and various others, was the driving force behind the "process" movement in writing instruction during the late 1970s and early 1980s. Social constructivist theory has spawned, over the last decade or so, thousands of undergraduate and secondary classrooms that identify themselves as "communities of writers" and feature various collaborative activities and "authentic" invitations to engage in writing. Efforts to develop a comprehensive socio-cognitive theory of written composition are less than a decade old. As the "new kid on the block" (Flower, "Cognitive Rhetoric," 171), it obviously remains to be seen just what impact such theorizing will have on future research and practice.

Socio-cognitive inquiry may be of use in addressing two significant teaching problems in composition. One problem involves the gradual immersion of student writers in discourse communities "defined by certain domain-specific knowledge" (Carter, 281). Socio-cognitive theorists and researchers could construct answers to the following two questions: Are there general writing strategies that can be applied and modified as students move from naiveté to expertise? If there are, then how might teachers encourage students to employ such strategies at various stages in the evolution of student writers?

Carter has argued that the most beneficial way to regard the development of communicative expertise is by characterizing student writers as moving along a continuum from the application of "culturally generated" global strategies (281) to eventual acquisition of local writing knowledge. He recommends a "cognitive apprenticeship" in which students would first learn strategies "specific to writing" and then applicable to "a variety of writing domains" (282), thus "providing a 'scaffolding' so that students could begin working in each domain by focusing on both the knowledge peculiar to that domain and the general strategies that carry over from other domains" (284). Foertsch modifies the sequential nature of Carter's model, pointing out that recent research in cognitive psychology indicates "general knowledge and specialized knowledge arise from the same pool of memories, the same set of learning experiences" (364). No learning within composition can be decontextualized because all generalizations are derived from "particular context-dependent episodes" (368).

The second teaching problem socio-cognitive inquiry may address involves accommodating a variety of culturally based cognitive styles, representative of both dominant and historically oppressed cultures, within writing classrooms operating under tight instructional time constraints (Delpit, "Silenced Dialogue," 283; Foertsch 370). Despite the emphasis on "diversity," Flower warns that past apprenticeship models based primarily on constructivist theory have tended to favor the "most prepared" (*Construction* 124). The "most prepared" for such instructional models in writing, according to African-American educator Lisa Delpit, have usually been upper-class and middle-class white students already familiar with the "linguistic forms" and "communicative strategies" of the dominant culture ("Silenced Dialogue," 283). Delpit argues that, while such pedagogies emphasize the development of fluency, Black students already possess fluency but lack knowledge of "standard, generally acceptable literary forms" ("Skills," 383–84). They start out as "remedial" within writing process classrooms, and need "explicit presentation" because they lack "the leisure of a lifetime of 'immersion' " ("Silenced Dialogue," 283).

Flower contends that composition teachers working within a constructivist instructional model have often devised "fictions of cognition" to explain the supposedly errant thinking of their least successful students (*Construction* 123–24). Socio-cognitive research, she suggests, could provide insights into the thinking of students shaped within a variety of social milieu, insights that would dispel the above-mentioned fictions while helping teachers decide when "the sharing of insider knowledge" would be appropriate (*Construction* 125).

Whatever the eventual impact of socio-cognitive theorizing on composition studies, Delpit's description of the estrangement during the eighties between African-American teachers and local writing process projects is certainly an argument for the inclusive impulse currently driving the theory's proponents ("Skills," 382–83). As Charney has recently written: "The only way to progress as a discipline is to undertake the hard task of inter-connecting our work" (591); those currently constructing socio-cognitive theories of writing have taken that mandate seriously.

BIBLIOGRAPHY

Primary Texts

Bechtel, William, and Adele Abrahamson. *Connectionism and the Mind*. Cambridge, MA: Basil Blackwell, 1991.

Ericsson, K. Anders, and Herbert A. Simon. *Protocol Analysis*. Cambridge, MA: MIT P, 1985.

Garfinkel, Harold. *Studies in Ethnomethodology*. Englwood Cliffs, NJ: Prentice-Hall, 1967.

Heritage, John. *Garfinkel and Ethnomethodology*. Cambridge, MA: Basil Blackwell, 1984.

Luria, A. R. *Cognitive Development: Its Cultural and Social Foundations*. Trans. Martin Lopez-Morillas and Lynn Solotaroff. Ed. Michael Cole. Cambridge, MA: Harvard UP, 1976.

Newell, Allen, and Herbert A. Simon. "Computer Science as Empirical Inquiry: Symbols and Search." In *Mind Design: Philosophy, Psychology, Artificial Intelligence*. Ed. John Haugeland. Cambridge, MA: MIT Press, 1981.

———. *Human Problem Solving*. Englewood Cliffs, NJ: Prentice-Hall, 1972.

Scribner, Sylvia, and Michael Cole. *The Psychology of Literacy*. Cambridge, MA: Harvard UP, 1981.

Simon, Herbert A. *The Sciences of the Artificial*. 2nd ed. Cambridge, MA: MIT Press, 1981.

Vygotsky, Lev S. *Thought and Language*. Ed. and trans. Eugenia Hanfmann and Gertrude Vakar. Cambridge, MA: MIT P, 1962.

Whitehead, Alfred North. *The Aim of Education and Other Essays*. New York: Macmillan, 1929.

Major Scholarship in Composition

Ackerman, John M. "Reading, Writing, and Knowing: The Role of Disciplinary Knowledge in Comprehension and Composing." *Research in the Teaching of English* 25 (1991): 133–78.

Bazerman, Charles. "What Written Knowledge Does: Three Examples of Academic Discourse." *Philosophy of the Social Sciences* 11 (1981): 361–87.

Bereiter, Carl, and Marlene Scardamalia. "From Conversation to Composition: The Role of Instruction in a Developmental Process." In *Advances in Instructional Psychology.* Ed. Robert Glaser. Vol. 2. Hillsdale, NJ: Erlbaum, 1982, 1–64.

———. *The Psychology of Written Composition.* Hillsdale, NJ: Erlbaum, 1987.

Berkenkotter, Carol. "Decisions and Revisions: The Planning Strategies of a Publishing Writer." *College Composition and Communication* 34 (1983): 156–69.

———. "Paradigm Debates, Turf Wars, and the Conduct of Socio-Cognitive Inquiry in Composition." *College Composition and Communication* 42 (1991): 151–69.

Bizzell, Patricia. "Cognition, Convention, and Certainty." *Pre/Text* 3 (1982): 213–43.

Brandt, Deborah. "The Cognitive as the Social: An Ethnomethodological Approach to Writing Process Research." *Written Communication* 9 (1992): 315–55.

Britton, James, et al. *The Development of Writing Abilities (11–18).* London: Macmillan, 1975.

Carter, Michael. "The Idea of Expertise: An Exploration of Cognitive and Social Dimensions of Writing." *College Composition and Communication* 41 (1990): 265–86.

Charney, Davida. "Empiricism Is Not a Four-Letter Word." *College Composition and Communication* 47 (1996): 567–93.

Cooper, Marilyn and Michael Holzman. "Counterstatement: Reply to Flower and Hayes." *College Composition and Communication* 36 (1985): 97–100.

———. "Talking about Protocols." *College Composition and Communication* 34 (1983): 288–93.

Delpit, Lisa D. "The Silenced Dialogue: Power and Pedagogy in Educating Other People's Children." *Harvard Educational Review* 58 (1988): 280–98.

———. "Skills and Other Dilemmas of a Progressive Black Educator." *Harvard Educational Review* 56 (1986): 379–85.

Dobrin, David N. "Protocols Once More." *College English* 48 (1986): 713–25.

Dyson, Anne Haas. "Learning to Write/Learning to Do School: Emergent Writers' Interpretations of School Literacy Tasks." *Research in the Teaching of English* 18 (1984): 233–64.

———. "Negotiating Multiple Worlds: The Space/Time Dimensions of Young Children's Composing." *Research in the Teaching of English* 22 (1988): 355–90.

Emig, Janet. *The Composing Process of Twelfth Graders.* Urbana, IL: NCTE, 1971.

———. "Inquiry Paradigms and Writing." *College Composition and Communication* 33 (1982): 64–75.

Flower, Linda. "Cognition, Context, and Theory Building." *College Composition and Communication* 40 (1989): 282–311.

———. "Cognitive Rhetoric: Inquiry into the Art of Inquiry." In *Defining the New Rhetorics* Ed. Theresa Enos and Stuart C. Brown. Newbury Park, CA: Sage, 1993, 171–90.

———. *The Construction of Negotiated Meaning.* Carbondale: Southern Illinois UP, 1994.

Flower, Linda, and John R. Hayes. "The Cognition of Discovery: Defining a Rhetorical Problem." *College Composition and Communication* 31 (1980): 21–32.

———. "A Cognitive Process Theory of Writing." *College Composition and Communication* 32 (1981): 365–87.

———. "The Dynamics of Composing: Making Plans and Juggling Constraints." In

Cognitive Processes in Writing Eds. Lee W. Greg and Erin R. Steinberg. Hillsdale, NJ: Erlbaum, 1980, 31–50.

————. "Images, Plans, and Prose: The Representation of Meaning in Writing." *Written Communication* 1 (1984): 120–60.

Flower, Linda, et al. *Reading-to-Write: Exploring a Cognitive and Social Process.* New York: Oxford UP, 1990.

Foertsch, Julie. "Where Cognitive Psychology Applies: How Theories about Memory and Transfer Can Influence Composition Pedagogy." *Written Communication* 12 (1995): 360–83.

Geisler, Cheryl. *Academic Literacy and the Nature of Expertise.* Hillsdale, NJ: Erlbaum, 1994.

Graves, Donald. *Writing: Teachers and Children at Work.* Portsmouth, NH: Heinemann, 1983.

Greene, Stuart. "The Role of Task in the Development of Academic Thinking through Reading and Writing in a College History Course." *Research in the Teaching of English* 27 (1993): 46–75.

Heath, Shirley Brice. *Ways with Words.* Cambridge: Cambridge UP, 1983.

Rohman, Gordon. "Pre-Writing: The Stage of Discovery in the Writing Process." *College Composition and Communication* 16 (1965): 106–12.

Sommers, Nancy. "Revision Strategies of Student Writers and Experienced Adult Writers." *College Composition and Communication* 31 (1980): 378–88.

CORNELIUS COSGROVE

SOPHISTIC RHETORIC

Summary

Over the last couple decades, a growing number of scholars in composition and rhetoric have embraced the title "Sophist," acknowledging that the ideologies and pedagogies in postmodern theories of composition and rhetoric reflect the teachings of the fifth-century B.C. Sophists of ancient Greece. Indeed, various scholars have suggested that much of the "rhetorical turn" that has gripped the humanities can be seen as a return to Sophism and a turning away from the philosophical rhetorics of Plato and Aristotle (Vitanza, Fish). Rhetoricians, among them Vitanza, Jarratt, and Neel, even suggest that we may be entering a "New Sophistic" in which long-held foundationalist assumptions about reality, language, and morality are giving way to Sophism's inherent pragmatism and civic humanism. What unites contemporary Sophists together is a rejection of the "philosophical" tradition in rhetorical theory, inspired by Plato and Aristotle, that has dominated the history of rhetoric in Western culture (Vitanza, 53–54). The contemporary Sophistic movement is attempting to reclaim rhetoric from the guardianship and suppression of philosophy, restoring the pluralism, anarchism, and playfulness that were once valued qualities of rhetoric.

From the earliest texts in ancient Greece, the word "Sophist," despite its derogatory undertones today, was broadly applied to anyone who had expertise in a particular field of study. For this reason, intellectuals as diverse in background and opinion as Pythagoras, Protagoras, and Socrates were commonly referred to as "Sophists" in recognition of their mastery of academic areas. During the fifth-century, however, the meaning of the word "Sophist" became narrower in scope, and reserved for professional teachers of rhetoric who trained young Athenians to succeed in civic arenas, such as the legislature, the law courts, and the marketplace. With the rise of democracy in fifth-century Athens, these "older" Sophists—among whom historians count Protagoras, Gorgias, Hippias, Prodicus, and various other minor figures-filled the demand for instructors who could educate students beyond the traditional Greek curricula of literature, grammar, arithmetic, and athletics. Indeed, H. I. Marrou, a scholar of ancient Greek education, claims that the Sophists' greatest contribution to Greek culture was the "invention" of teaching as a profession (49).

A few critics of the contemporary Sophistic movement have pointed out that the ancient Sophists did not follow a common ideology or pedagogy (see Schiappa). Nevertheless, there are some interesting commonalties among the ancient Sophists that allow us to identify them as a coherent group with a common ideology (Untersteiner, xv; Guthrie, 44). First, the Sophists believed strongly in the power of education to mold young people into successful individuals and citizens of the state. Second, the Sophists stressed the importance of socially invented law, custom, and convention (*nomos*) over absolute natural law or natural order (*physis*). Third, the Sophists believed that they could teach *arete* (i.e., virtue, excellence, values). Finally, the Sophists aided and supported the rise of democracy by teaching Athenians how to use verbal advocacy and counteradvocacy to solve problems that faced the community. The Sophists recognized that democracy required persuasive advocacy and counteradvocacy in the legislature and law courts (Jarratt, 104).

What we find in both ancient Sophism and contemporary Sophistic rhetoric is a basic faith in civic humanism and a pragmatic approach to civic life. Neel, in *Aristotle's Voice*, however, points out that the contemporary Sophistic movement is not dependent on what the ancient Sophists may or may not have believed or taught. Rather, Neel argues, contemporary Sophism should "inhabit the (human) discourse that Plato and Aristotle excluded under the name of Sophistry, regardless of whether that excluded and debased discourse correctly reproduces what anyone else in ancient Athens may have advocated" (190). In other words, the mission of contemporary Sophism is not to figure out what the ancient Sophists believed and practiced, but rather to develop concepts that allow us to turn away from the absolutism of Western philosophy.

Contemporary Sophism, however, has been mainly occupied with the historical restoration of Sophistic beliefs and practices, using concepts from postmodernism to patch together and flesh out a coherent Sophistic perspective. The primary assumption of contemporary Sophism, like ancient Sophism, is the notion that reality is ever-changing and changeable. Whereas "philosophical" rhetorics from Plato to Campbell are explicitly or implicitly grounded on the concept of Being—the assumption that truth is ultimately static and absolute—Sophistic rhetoric sees reality as always "coming to be," or dynamic, playful, and evolving. Sophism assumes that language is restless; consequently, metaphor, irony, and other tropes keep language (and reality) indeterminate, ambiguous, playful, paradoxical, and somewhat less than rational. Sophism assumes that attempts to describe "the way things are" are ultimately tragic, because reality and language are always in flux, slipping away just when one believes that the truth is finally pinned down.

Some of the pivotal concepts that make up Sophistic rhetoric offer a sense of what contemporary Sophism is about.

Logos

The rhetorical turn brought about by Nietzsche, Heidegger, Lyotard, Derrida, Lanham, Feyerabend, and Rorty, to name a few among many, has in many ways revived the Sophists' understanding of *logos*. The description of *logos* in Aristotle's *Rhetoric*, which is familiar to all of us, offers merely a shadow of the meaning this word held for the Sophists and other pre-Socratics. Kerferd demonstrates that the word *logos* had three applications in ancient Greece: (1) language, speech, discourse, arguments; (2) thought, mental processes, reasoning; and (3) the world about which we speak, including structural principles and natural laws (83). In Sophistic rhetoric, *logos* is far more fluid and all-encompassing than Plato or Aristotle would have allowed. Sophists believe that logos is what is accepted as reality; consequently, one's *logos* is always open to change. Richard Lanham best describes the contemporary Sophistic view of logos: "Rhetorical man is trained not to discover reality but to manipulate it. Reality is what is accepted as reality, what is useful" (4).

Dissoi Logoi

The concept of contrary arguments is a cornerstone of Sophistic ideology and rhetoric, including antilogic, eristic, paralogy, and dialectic. As defined by Protagoras, *dissoi logoi* is the assumption that "there are at least two accounts (*logoi*) opposed to each other in any situation" (quoted by Diogenes Laertius). In essence, *dissoi logoi* posits that one side (*logos*) of an argument defines the existence of the other, creating a rhetorical situation in which at least two *logoi* struggle for dominance. In contrast, Western culture's implicit assumption that argument is about truth or falsity urges one to assume that one side of the argument is true or more accurate and that other accounts are false or less accurate. Quite differently, Sophists acknowledge that one side of the argument might in a particular context represent the "stronger" *logos* and others the "weaker," but this does not preclude a weaker *logos* from becoming the stronger in a different or future context. Sophism assumes that the stronger *logos*, no matter how strong, will never completely overcome competing *logoi* and earn the title of absolute truth. Rather—and this is the heart of *dissoi logoi*— at least one other perspective is always available to serve as an other to the stronger argument.

Nomos

Sophistic rhetoric assumes that the beliefs people accept as true are inescapably socially situated. The *nomoi* (i.e., norms, conventions, beliefs) of a particular community, Sophists teach their students, are socially invented; therefore, truths are contingent on a time and place and are always contextualized within the community that believes in them. Moreover, Sophism recognizes that *nomoi* can be revised to suit the changing rhetorical situations that face a community. Sophists assume that commonly held truths, values, and conventions are inventions that spin out of attempts to make sense of a changing reality and allow people to get along in the world. Accordingly, Sophists recognize that the identification of held beliefs, customs, and conventions is an essential step toward being persuasive in a particular community. Today, as in ancient Greece, contemporary Sophists teach their students to locate communal conventions and values, so students can be persuasive in their own communities and communities they wish to join.

Kairos

Eric White characterizes *kairos* as "a passing instant when an opening appears which must be driven through with force if success is to be achieved" (13). White's definition captures the dynamic spirit of the Sophistic notion of *kairos* better than this word's more common definition, "the right time and place," derived from Aristotle. The Sophistic understanding of *kairos* assumes that rhetors are "thrown into" the moment, always interpreting and shaping the evolving features of the rhetorical situation around them. *Kairos* ensures that a person cannot get "outside" the rhetorical situation to assess the situation objectively. Rather, the rhetor is always situated, opportunistically looking for the right place and moment to drive home an argument. Untersteiner suggests that for Gorgias, *kairos* exacted a decision point at which the rhetor's will must overcome the other features of the situation, imposing "one of the two alternatives" available (161).

This survey of Sophistic concepts illustrates how the notion of "coming to be" and civic humanism serve as the basis of Sophistic rhetoric. Unlike Platonic or Aristotelian notions of one absolute *logos*, Sophism posits that a *logos* is ever-changing and changeable, and that multiple *logoi* are available in any given rhetorical situation. Meanwhile, truth, made up of a community's *nomoi*, is socially invented, open-ended, and subject to change. Sophism rejects static absolutism for an evolving reality that forces rhetors to always act and react in the moment.

Reception and Significance in Composition Studies

Sophism is more an awakening than a revolution in the fields of composition and rhetoric. It is a revival of the civic humanism that was overcome by the absolutism of Platonism and Aristotelianism. Consequently, Sophism's significance to the field of rhetoric has been more subtle than the typical bandwagon theories that rumble through the disciplines of composition and rhetoric every five or ten years. Leff, in "Modern Sophistic and the Unity of Rhetoric," writes that "the most obvious feature of this approach [Sophism] is its rejection of global generalizations, grand theories, and synthetic methodologies" (22). If so, then the contemporary Sophistic movement is a rejection of a long tradition of foundationalism and the pursuit of absolute truth. The movement represents a change in how one perceives and discourses about reality, not simply a change in methodology or teaching practices. Granted, Sophism does change how one goes about doing his or her work and how one teaches her or his classes. But in the end, a conversion to Sophism is the realization that the foundationalist beliefs at the basis of classical rhetoric are out of line with contemporary needs and values.

BIBLIOGRAPHY

Primary Texts

Campbell, George. *The Philosophy of Rhetoric*. New York: Leavitt, 1834.
Derrida, Jacques. *Of Grammatology*. Baltimore: Johns Hopkins UP, 1976.
Feyerabend, Paul. *Against Method*. New York: Verso, 1988.
Heidegger, Martin. *Being and Time*. New York: Harper, 1962.
Isocrates. *Isocrates*. Trans. G. Norlin. Cambridge, MA: Harvard UP, 1968.
Lyotard, Jean Francois. *The Postmodern Condition*. Trans. G. Bennington and B. Massumi. Minneapolis: U of Minnesota P, 1984.
Nietzsche, Friedrich. *The Will to Power*. Trans. W. Kaufmann and R. Hollingdale. New York: Random–Vintage, 1966.
Rorty, Richard. *Objectivity, Relativism, and Truth*. New York: Cambridge UP, 1991.
Sprague, Rosamond, ed. *The Older Sophists*. Columbia: U of South Carolina P, 1972. A collection of fragments from the fifth-century Greek Sophists.

Major Scholarship in Composition

Fish, Stanley. *Doing What Comes Naturally*. Durham, NC: Duke UP, 1989.
Guthrie, W. K. C. *The Sophists*. Cambridge: Cambridge UP, 1971.
Jarratt, Susan. *Rereading the Sophists*. Carbondale: Southern Illinois UP, 1991.
Kerferd, G. B. *The Sophistic Movement*. Cambridge: Cambridge UP, 1981.
Lanham, Richard. *The Motives of Eloquence*. New Haven, CT: Yale UP, 1976.
Leff, Michael. "Modern Sophistic and the Unity of Rhetoric." In *The Rhetoric of the Human Sciences*. Ed. J. Nelson, A. Megill, and D. McCloskey. Madison: U of Wisconsin P, 1987, 19–37.
Marrou, H. I. *A History of Education in Antiquity*. Trans. G. Lamb. Madison: U of Wisconsin P, 1956.
Neel, Jasper. *Aristotle's Voice*. Carbondale: Southern Illinois UP, 1994.
Schiappa, Edward. "Neosophistic Rhetorical Criticism in the Historical Reconstruction of Sophistic Doctrines?" *Philosophy and Rhetoric* 23 (1990): 192–217.
Untersteiner, Mario. *The Sophists*. Trans. K. Freeman. Oxford, U.K.: Basil Blackwell, 1954.
Vitanza, Victor. "Critical Sub/Versions of the History of Philosophical Rhetoric." *Rhetoric Review* 6 (1987): 41–65.
White, Eric Charles. *Kaironomia: On the Will to Invent*. Ithaca, NY: Cornell UP, 1987.

RICHARD D. JOHNSON-SHEEHAN

SPEECH ACT THEORY

Summary

Speech act theory, the study of language viewed as actions, is generally considered to have begun in the 1950s with a series of lectures by the British philosopher J. L. Austin that were published as *How To Do Things with Words*. We know, however, through references in Aristotle's *Poetics* (249) and in *The Lives of Eminent Philosophers* of Diogenes Laertius (IX.53) to specific observations by the philosopher and contemporary of Socrates, Protagoras, that similar lines of inquiry were part of the rhetorical and linguistic investigations of the Sophists in the fifth-century B.C.E.

Philosophy of Language and Speech Act Theory

Austin began his inquiry by examining certain types of statements, such as, "I now pronounce you husband and wife," in a marriage ceremony, which he labels *performatives*. In speaking or writing a series of words in these situations, he observes, a individual does not represent states of affairs, he or she creates them. Unlike the representational statements commonly studied by philosophers of language, performative utterances cannot be judged as "true or false." Instead, such statements are either appropriate or inappropriate, operative or inoperative, successful or unsuccessful, or in Austin's terminology, *felicitous* or *infelicitous*. Austin then develops a schema of the specific conditions necessary for the successful execution of each of these acts. These requirements concern such issues as the speaker's intention and his or her role within a specific social or institutional context.

By the end of the argument, however, Austin retracts his original distinction between performatives and declarative statements and concludes that all types of written and spoken utterances contain many of the same characteristics as the special case with which he started his discussion. Using the statement, "France is hexagonal," as an example, Austin demonstrates that this sentence, like all other utterances, is true and appropriate for "certain intents and purposes," but not for others. "It is good enough for a top ranking general, perhaps, but not for a geographer" (143).

Austin, John Searle, and other speech act philosophers and linguists have developed various but similar descriptions of the linguistic levels contained in any speech act. The following schema is adapted from Kent Bach and Robert Harnish's *Linguistic Communication and Speech Acts* (3–38):

Utterance Act: Speaking or writing a syntactically correct string of works in a given language and within a specific context

Locutionary Act: Employing the string of words to represent a specific logical proposition

Illocutionary Act: Using the proposition to perform a specific speech act (e.g., asserting, demanding, promising, requesting, or appointing)

Perlocutionary Act: A listener or reader performing the expected response to a specific illocutionary act (e.g., believing, performing, or not performing something).

At a farm, for example, someone may utter to someone else, the string of words or utterance act, "The bull is in the field." This utterance also constitutes a locutionary or propositional act, containing a reference, "the bull," and a predicate describing an action or state of affairs, in this case, "is in the field." However, a central point of speech act analyses is that, in actual use, all locutionary acts are simultaneously illocutionary acts. In uttering, "The bull is in the field," a speaker is not only representing a state of affairs but is simultaneously, warning, asserting, or even possibly (if, for example, the audience is a matador) inviting. In addition, illocutionary acts are usually made with the intention of producing some sort of response from the listener or reader, such as, in the example, stopping people from endangering themselves, changing their belief from "the bull is in the barn" to "it is in the field," or having them accept an invitation for bullfight practice.

There have been numerous attempts to classify the general types of illocutionary acts. Searle's taxonomy (*Expression and Meaning* 1–29) is the most widely known and is based on such criteria as the speaker's intention in performing the act, the speaker's expressed psychological state, and whether the utterance represents or brings about a state of affairs. Searle proposes the following five classes of illocutionary acts:

Assertives, statements, such as *claiming* or *hypothesizing*, that assert, in different degrees, the truth of the proposition contained in the utterance, and are made by a speaker or writer with the intention of causing the audience to believe the assertion

Directives, utterances made by a speaker, such as *commanding* or *begging*, that have the intention of causing the audience to perform one or more specific actions

Commissives, utterances, such as *promising* or *threatening*, in which a speaker or writer commits to perform one or specific actions

Expressives, statements, such as *thanking* or *apologizing*, in which a speaker or writer's primary intention is to express a psychological state

Declarations, utterances, such as *appointing* or *declaring*, that, when appropriately performed, create a new state-of-affairs

As Searle notes (*Expression* 17) this final category is similar to Austin's original definition of *performatives*. Both Searle (19–20) and Bach and Harnish (108–34) note that specific institutional rules or conventions always inform these kinds of speech acts. Both also note that there are two distinct subtypes: those that by their utterance make a representation a state of affairs into an institutional fact, such as an umpire calling a pitch a "strike," and those, such as appointing or resigning, that do not represent existing facts but rather create a new ones.

There have been a number of subsequent attempts to develop taxonomies for illocutionary acts and also to classify *performative verbs*, the verbs in a language that explicitly indicate the speech act being performed, such as the verb *to advise* in the sentence, "I advise you not to order the chicken salad sandwich."

Indirect Speech Acts and Grice's Cooperative Principle and Conversational Maxims

A central issue in speech act theory has been the analysis of *indirect speech acts*, the common linguistic phenomenon of sentences that have the grammatical form of one type of illocutionary act while possessing the illocutionary force of another. As mentioned previously, the sentence, "The bull is in the field," has the grammatical form of what Searle defines as *assertives* but could have the illocutionary force of two very different types of *directives, inviting* or *warning*. The sentence, "Can you please stop talking," spoken by a teacher to a student has the grammatical form of a question or request, but may be clearly meant by the speaker and understood by the student to be a command. Searle, among others, has attempted to describe the procedures a listener or reader uses to determine the correct illocutionary force of an utterance (*Expression* 30–57).

H. Paul Grice, a colleague of both Austin and Searle, explains *indirect speech acts* through his theory of *conversational implicature*. Rather than formulating his analysis as specific linguistic rules analogous to syntactical, phonological, or morphological rules, Grice views the principles governing the cooperative use of language "as a special case or variety of [any human] purposive, indeed rational, behavior" ("Logic and Conversation," 47). In most conversations, he argues, "Each participant recognizes . . . a common purpose or set of purposes, or at least a mutually accepted direction." Furthermore, he states, "At each stage [of the conversation] some possible conversational moves would be excluded as conversationally unsuitable" ("Logic and Conversation," 45). He calls this general principle implicitly governing language interaction, the *cooperative principle*, and, borrowing from Kant, derives from this general principle, four categories of maxims that govern most conversational uses of language ("Logic and Conversation," 45–46):

Quantity
>   Make your contribution as informative as is required (for the current purposes of the exchange).
>   Do not make your contribution more informative than is required.

Quality
>   Try to make your contribution one that is true.
>   Do not say what you believe to be false.
>   Do not say that for which you lack adequate evidence.

Relation
>   Be relevant.

Manner
>   Avoid obscurity of expression.
>   Avoid ambiguity.

Be brief (avoid unnecessary prolixity).
Be orderly.

An indirect speech act occurs when a speaker intentionally violates one of the conversational maxims, creating an implicature that makes what is meant radically different from what is said.

Consider the example of an employer asking one of her employees if a coworker who works next to her has been coming to work on time. The employee flouts the Maxim of Relation by praising some of the coworker's daily actions instead of answering the employer's question. In many discourse situations, such a response means more than just an evaluation of some specific acts; it also implies that the coworker has been late to work but that she performs valuable work nonetheless. Similarly, a response that violates the Maxim of Quantity by listing each day the coworker has come to work on time might imply that the coworker has been late all other times. Grice notes that common rhetorical and literary figures are produced by the flouting of maxims. Irony, for example, is produced by the intentional flouting of one or more maxims, such as in Mark Twain's famous remark, "Reports of my death have been greatly exaggerated."

Reception and Significance in Composition Studies

Speech act theory has influenced rhetorical theory, composition pedagogy, and the theory and practice of writing across the disciplines. Reed Way Dasenbrock has offered J. L. Austin's original formulation of speech act theory as a foundation for the construction of a new rhetorical theory that both maintains the traditional emphasis on the rhetorical nature of language and provides relevant and contemporary frameworks for examining argumentation and style. Walter H. Beale incorporated Austin's exploration of the representational and performative dimensions of discourse into his *Pragmatic Theory of Rhetoric* (63–67). Marilyn Cooper has employed speech act theory along with other theoretical models to propose an "ecological model of writing," arguing that writing should be viewed not only as a cognitive process but also as a complex system of formal and informal social interactions. In a similar approach, Les Perelman, in "The Context of Classroom Writing," questioned the viability of "personal" writing in a classroom, arguing that classroom writing, like many other forms of writing is largely institution based, being informed and governed by specific institutional rules and conventions.

Specific aspects of speech act theory and related pragmatic theory have been used to develop effective pedagogical tools. Kim B. Lovejoy, for example, employed Grice's Conversational Maxims to develop an effective heuristic for student revision. Speech act and pragmatic analyses have been particularly useful in developing strategies for identifying and addressing specific pragmatic and related cultural issues of different groups of language speakers.

Finally, speech act analysis, especially Grice's less formal conversational analysis, has been widely used in the theory and practice of writing in the disciplines. The very generality of Grice's maxims allows them to be useful guidelines for discovering the more specific institutional rules and conventions governing quality, quantity, relevance, and manner in a variety of discourse communities.

BIBLIOGRAPHY

Primary Texts and Major Scholarship in Composition

Aristotle. *Poetics*. Trans. Ingram Bywater. In *Aristotle's Rhetoric and Poetics*. New York: Modern Library, 1954.

Austin, J. L. *How to Do Things with Words*. 2nd ed. Ed. J. O. Urmson and Marina Sbisà. Cambridge, MA: Harvard UP, 1975.

Bach, Kent, and Robert M. Harnish. *Linguistic Communication and Speech Acts*. Cambridge, MA: MIT P, 1982.

Beale, Walter H. *A Pragmatic Theory of Rhetoric*. Carbondale: Southern Illinios UP, 1987.

Cooper, Marilyn M. "The Ecology of Writing." *College English* 48 (1986): 364–75.

Coulthard, Michael. *An Introduction to Discourse Analysis*. London: Longman, 1977.

Dasenbrock, Reed Way. "J. L. Austin and the Articulation of a New Rhetoric." *College Composition and Communication* 38 (1987): 291–305.

Diogenes Laertius. *Lives of the Philosophers*. Ed. and trans. R. D. Hicks. Cambridge, MA: Harvard UP, 1979.

Grice, H. Paul. "Logic and Conversation." In *Syntax and Semantics: Speech Acts*. Ed. Peter Cole and Jerry L. Morgan. New York: Academic P, 1975, 41–58.

———. *Studies in the Way of Words*. Cambridge, MA: Harvard UP, 1989.

Leech, Geoffrey N. *Principles of Pragmatics*. London: Longman, 1983.

Levinson, Stephen C. *Pragmatics*. Cambridge: Cambridge UP, 1983.

Lovejoy, Kim B. "The Gricean Model: A Revising Rubric." *Journal of Teaching Writing* 6 (1987): 9–18.

Perelman, Les. "The Context of Classroom Writing." *College English* 48 (1986): 471–79.

Searle, John R. *Expression and Meaning: Studies in the Theory of Speech Acts*. Cambridge: Cambridge UP, 1979.

———. *Intentionality: An Essay in the Philosophy of Mind*. Cambridge: Cambridge UP, 1983.

———. *Speech Acts: An Essay in the Philosophy of Language*. Cambridge: Cambridge UP, 1969.

Sperber, Dan, and Deirdre Wilson. *Relevance*. Cambridge, MA: Harvard UP, 1986.

Stubbs, Michael. *Discourse Analysis: The Sociolinguistic Analysis of Natural Language*. Oxford, U.K.: Basil Blackwell, 1983.

LESLIE C. PERELMAN

STASIS THEORY

Summary

Stasis theory is a collection of concepts, drawn from ancient rhetoric, that lead a rhetor to determine the central issue in a rhetorical situation—the question that initiates and motivates the argument. Compared with other inventional systems derived from classical rhetoric, stasis theory has received relatively little attention in composition studies. Contemporary work involving stasis theory, however, is sound, challenging, and capable of generating additional scholarship.

The term *stasis* is Greek for "a stand." The term made its way into Latin in the verb *sto, stare* ("to stand") and its cognates, for example, *status* and *constitutio*. Given the origins of rhetoric as *techne* in fifth-century B.C.E. courts, it is not surprising that stasis theory was "in the air" enough to appear in early Greek handbooks. Aristotle mentions it in passing in Book III of the *Rhetoric*, but it was the post-Aristotelian Hellenist, Hermagoras of Temnos, in the second century B.C.E. who developed the first full treatment of stasis theory as an inventional system. Hermagoras's work, which forms the basis of all later classical treatments is, unfortunately, lost. Modern scholars, however (notably George Kennedy and Ray Nadeau), have reconstructed Hermagorean theory from references in later works. Both Cicero (*De Inventione*) and the author of the *Rhetorica ad Herennium* knew stasis theory thoroughly, and Quintilian summarizes the extant treatments in Book III of the first-century C.E. *Institutio Oratoria*. Hermogenes of Tarsus wrote the classical period's most extensive treatment of stasis in 176 C.E.

Stasis theory guides a rhetor to determine in a particular case the issue where agreement ends and, thus, where an argument must begin. A case involving a particular question, or *hypothesis* (in contrast to a general question, or *thesis*), is generated by a conflict between the prosecutor's charge, the *kataphasis*, and the defendant's denial, the *apophasis*. Out of this conflict comes the matter under judgment, the *synechon*. Using stasis theory, the rhetor proceeds through a hierarchy of four questions (or *stases*) until she or he determines where the disagreement lies. The first stasis (*stochasmos*) conjectures about fact: Did something occur? Is there an act to be considered? Does this thing generally occur? The second stasis (*horos*) raises the question of definition: What should this act be called? How can this thing be defined? The third stasis (*poiotes*) concerns the quality of the act: How serious is this act? How should this thing be evaluated? The fourth and final stasis (*metalepsis*) calls for a procedural question: Is this act being considered in the proper venue? Does this thing call for some other kind of formal procedure?

Stasis theory as taught by Hermagoras changed very little in the nearly two millennia since it was codified. Hermogenes's alterations to it were not significant: While Hermagoras applied it in all three types of discourse situations recognized in antiquity—judicial, deliberative, and epideictic—Hermogenes saw the theory's use only in judicial and deliberative speeches. Hermogenes listed thirteen different stases, but they were essentially amplifications of Hermagoras's basic four.

Two contemporary rhetorical theorists have proposed significant changes in stasis theory. Jeanne Fahnestock and Marie Secor, in a 1985 article ("Toward a Modern Version of Stasis"), list five stases: fact, definition, cause, value, and policy or action. They explain that traditional stasis theory would have subsumed cause under definition, but the changes in epistemology wrought by the rise of science mandate a separate stasis for cause. They maintain that *value* is a more operational term than *quality*, and they see arguments that call for action plans coming from their final stasis.

Reception and Significance in Composition Studies

Perhaps because its hierarchical nature seems at odds with many of the opportunistic, intuitive invention techniques inscribed in the process movement, stasis theory has been invoked very seldom in contemporary composition pedagogy, and only a handful of scholars have used it centrally in their research. Composition textbooks that treat argument specifically, such as John Gage's *The Shape of Reason*, or that see all writing as essentially argumentative, such as Sharon Crowley's *Ancient Rhetorics for Contemporary Students*, do teach stasis theory as a means of inventing and refining a thesis.

Two studies are noteworthy for their use of stasis as a central component in current composition theory and research. Michael Carter sees stasis as one of two concepts from classical rhetoric (along with *kairos*) that both forecast and underlie the contemporary view of composition as social constructionism. Describing the theory's heuristic power to point a rhetor to appropriate *topoi*, to generate an impetus for rhetorical action, to structure inquiry, and to resolve conflict, Carter sees stasis "not [as] individualistic and internal; instead, it represent[s] a community-oriented rhetoric" (101). Fahnestock and Secor, in a 1988 article ("The Stases in Scientific and Literary Argument") analyzing the stases in scientific and literary scholarship, laud "the power of the stases as a teachable invention technique in the classroom":

[T]he stases tell the writer "where to think," not "what to think." They do not dictate or predict the precise claims that attempt to answer the [stases'] questions; that will be a function of the particular arguer, audience, and available evidence. The stases simply describe the logic inherent in the development of an issue. (428–29)

BIBLIOGRAPHY

Primary Texts

Aristotle. *On Rhetoric*. Trans. George A. Kennedy. New York: Oxford UP, 1991.

Cicero. *De Inventione; De Optimo Genere Oratorum; Topica*. Trans. H. M. Hubbell. Cambridge, MA: Harvard UP, 1949.

Nadeau, Ray. "Hermogenes *On Stasis*: A Translation with an Introduction." *Speech Monographs* 31 (1964): 361–424.

Pseudo-Cicero. *Rhetorica ad Herennium*. Trans. Harry Caplan. Cambridge, MA: Harvard UP, 1981.

Quintilian. *Institutio Oratoria*. 4 vols. Trans. H. E. Butler. Cambridge, MA: Harvard UP, 1980.

Major Scholarship in Composition

Carter, Michael. "*Stasis* and *Kairos*: Principles of Social Construction in Classical Rhetoric." *Rhetoric Review* 7 (1988): 97–112.

Crowley, Sharon. *Ancient Rhetorics for Contemporary Students.* New York: Macmillan, 1994.

Fahnestock, Jeanne, and Marie Secor. "The Stases in Scientific and Literary Argument." *Written Communication* 5 (1988): 427–44.

———. "Toward a Modern Version of Stasis." In *Oldspeak/Newspeak: Rhetorical Transformations.* Ed. Charles Kneupper. Arlington, TX: Rhetoric Society of America, 1985, 217–26.

Gage, John. *The Shape of Reason.* New York: Macmillan, 1987.

Kennedy, George A. *The Art of Persuasion in Greece.* Princeton, NJ: Princeton UP, 1963.

Nadeau, Ray. "Classical Systems of Stases in Greek: Hermagoras to Hermogenes." *Greek, Roman, and Byzantine Studies* 2 (1959): 51–71.

DAVID A. JOLLIFFE

STRUCTURALISM

Summary

Despite Ferdinand de Saussure's few written theoretical publications, the joint compilation of his lectures on general linguistics by his students at the University of Geneva in 1915 (published as the *Cours de Linguistique Générale*) set the stage for modern linguistic study. In his course, Saussure coins the term *semiology* and suggests a scientific study of language based on a synchronic rather than diachronic model of language. Thus, he maintains that all the tools necessary for understanding a given language system are present at any given moment; historical study of a language's development is unnecessary. He further divides language into *parole*, the individual utterance of a speaker, and *langue*, an abstract system of rules governing language use. In the now-famous metaphor of the chess game, Saussure explains that *langue* can be seen as the universally agreed upon rules of chess, while *parole* is equivalent to any particular game played. Besides offering these broad structures of language, Saussure also suggests several axioms that govern the operation of language.

Saussure replaces the "word" as the basic unit of language with the "sign." He defines the sign as the composite of the signified, the idea or image being expressed, and the signifier, the phonic articulation of that idea. The relationship of the signifier to the signified is arbitrary or "unmotivated"; Saussure argues there is no necessary relationship between any given object or idea and the term used to represent it. However, this arbitrariness does not suggest that signifiers can be freed from their signifieds. The relationship, though unmotivated, is *fixed* within a given language. Thus, no individual speaker, no particular expression of *parole*, can alter the sign. For example, the word "tree" cannot suddenly be applied to the object in the world known as "table," and yet "tree's" relationship to the physical object we call tree is arbitrary. There is no inherent "tree"ness in the utterance "tree." This causes greater complexity on the level of ideas; for example, concepts such as "liberty" possess neither a clear sign nor a clear signified.

In light of this gap between signifier and signified, Saussure argues "in language there are only differences *without positive terms*" (emphasis in original). Since no signifier has meaning in and of itself, it can only draw meaning in contrast to what it is not. The word "tree" only carries meaning insofar as it is not "bush" or "house." This notion applies to signifieds as well as signifiers. Like the terms that represent signifieds, objects and ideas possess linguistic meaning only through contrast.

Reception and Significance in Composition Studies

Although not published in English until 1959, *Course in General Linguistics* gained rapid acceptance among European linguists and literary theorists. Roman Jakobson (Russian formalist), Claude Lévi-Strauss (a noted French anthropologist), as well as other literary and cultural theorists adopted Saussure's semiology as the foundation for what would become structuralism. Structuralism sought to discover the underlying order of thought, language, and culture. Content was regarded as secondary; instead, language analysis became the model for interpreting the human experience.

While there is little research connecting Saussure's work with linguistics to composition studies directly, *Structuralism de Saussure* has permeated early twentieth-century language theory. Structuralism in composition has been associated with traditional rhetorical analysis, which de-emphasizes content in favor of form. It also has been used more recently to explain the word's ability to represent something else in terms of metaphor and metonymy. Those who today favor Saussurean analysis are foundationalists, maintaining a Platonic separation between language and idea. By arguing the distinction between signifier and signified, they believe de facto the word exists after the idea. Those who are anti-foundationalists embrace the poststructuralist concept that there is nothing outside of language. In one such example from the *Journal for Advanced Composition*, "Hall of Mirrors: Anti-Foundationalist Theory and the Teaching of Writing," David W. Smit questions the implications for the teaching of writing that derive directly from this debate. The theories of Saussure serve as the centerpiece for both the foundational and anti-foundational arguments.

BIBLIOGRAPHY

Primary Texts

de Saussure, Ferdinand. *Course in General Linguistics*. Ed. Charles Bally and Albert Sechehaye. Trans. Wade Baskin. New York: McGraw-Hill, 1959.

Major Scholarship in Composition

Aarsleff, Hans. *From Locke to Saussure: Essays on the Study of Language and Intellectual History*. Minneapolis: U of Minnesota P, 1982.

Berthoff, Ann E. "Problem-Dissolving by Triadic Means." *College English* 58.1 (1996): 9–21.

Culler, Jonathan. *Ferdinand de Saussure*. Ithaca, NY: Cornell UP, 1986.

de George, Richard T. *The Structuralists: From Marx to Lévi-Strauss*. Ed. Richard T. De George and Fernande M. De George. Garden City, NY: Anchor, 1972.

Evans, Rick. "Masks: Literacy, Ideology, and Hegemony." *Rhetoric Review* 14.1 (1995): 88–103.

Harlos, Christopher. "Rhetoric, Structuralism, and Figurative Discourse: Gerard Genette's Concept of Rhetoric." *Philosophy and Rhetoric* 19.4 (1986): 209–23.

Harris, Roy. *Reading Saussure*. La Salle, IL: Open Court, 1987.

Hawkes, Terence. *Structuralism and Semiotics*. Berkeley and Los Angeles: U of California P, 1977.

Holdcroft, David. *Saussure: Signs, System and Arbitrariness*. New York: Cambridge UP, 1991.

Holland, Norman N. *The Critical I*. New York: Columbia UP, 1992.

Jakobson, Roman. "Closing Statement: Linguistics and Poetics." In *Style in Language*. Ed. Thomas Sebeok. Cambridge, MA: MIT P, 1960, 350–77.

Koerner, E. F. K. *Bibliographia Saussureana: 1870–1970*. Metuchen, NJ: Scarecrow P, 1972.

Smit, David W. "Hall of Mirrors: Anti-Foundationalist Theory and the Teaching of Writing." *Journal of Advanced Composition* 15.1 (1995): 35–54.

Sullivan, Francis J. "Critical Theory and Systemic Linguistics: Textualizing the Contact Zone." *Journal of Advanced Composition* 15.3 (1995): 411–34.

KAREN ADELE LEMKE BATES AND MARTIN T. BUINICKI

STYLISTICS

Summary

Simply put, stylistics is the study of style. Divisible into two levels of inquiry, stylistics is a methodological and scientific discipline based on quantitative linguistics, as well as the examination of the style of a text, writer, speaker, or period using the methods and claims of that discipline. Stylistics examines the expressive language of a text and, in a sense, any close text reading such as New Criticism is a kind of stylistics. Stylistics supports a rigorous quantitative methodology, identifying texts' phonetic, lexical, and syntactical features either manually or via computer. Its goal may be to describe and interpret author intention and a text's meaning, or it may have specific aims such as determining authorship or compiling an inventory of the particular resources of a language, author, group, or period.

Stylistics is a practical, not theoretical, field. One central claim is that there is such a thing as style, describable as expression of choices in relation to a norm and measured by comparing linguistic units. The range of "quantitative" and "impressionistic" stylistics is illustrated by the conceptual resources and methodologies of two early schools. Charles Bally, the French founder of modern stylistics, attempted to create a science of style, identifying a norm through observation and classification against which stylistic deviation, the "affective element" in language, could be measured. In contrast, Leo Spitzer, of the German *Stilforschung*, intuited which stylistic features were significant in literary texts, using his "philological circle" to move from a specific feature toward a work's central spirit. A literary work represented the creative expression of an individual or culture.

Since then, schools of stylistics have been revolutionized by linguistics and the computer. The principles, methods, and vocabularies of modern linguistics have made it possible to describe stylistic features with precision, beyond impressionistic labels as "heavy" or "clear." This vocabulary allows focus on small units of style (phomene, morpheme), larger conceptual arrangements (grammar, syntax, semantics), or even the deep structure of language, via Chomsky's generative grammar.

In practice, stylistics is an interdependent discipline, relying on tools of linguistics and drafted for literary criticism. Quantitative linguistic stylistics compares the frequency of stylistic variations to an external aggregate norm. Michael Riffaterre's important articles theorizing about stylistic methodologies declare "a linguistic norm is virtually unobtainable [and] . . . irrelevant" ("Criteria," 168). His norm becomes the "context" of the text itself; stylistic devices are features surprising his average reader. Richard Ohmann extends the concept of style as choice by declaring "the stream of experience is the background against which 'choice' is a meaningful concept"(9). His claim that style can be understood as epistemic choice implies that stylistic study can uncover a writer's epistemology. Thus stylistics becomes entangled with the interpretive aims of literary criticism, where its ability to illustrate how different connotative effects are achieved has made it a powerful critical tool. In addition, stylistics has proved useful in author attribution cases such as those on the Junius Letters and the Federalist Papers.

Computers have provided a wealth of raw data essential for advances in quantitative stylistics. Large concordances have been created, linguistic features have been inventoried, and software has been developed. However, the revolutionary impact of this technology on practical stylistics is accompanied by a realization that "computer systems have proven to be very poorly suited to . . . refined analysis of complex language" (Olsen, 309).

Reception and Significance in Composition Studies

When composition was "born" as a discipline in 1963, the current-traditional paradigm emphasized the composed product. Stylistics, as attention to word choice and syntax, was central under the rubric of editing.

During the product/process paradigm shift of the 1970s and 1980s, stylistics flourished in composition's two arenas: reading/interpreting texts (theoretical stylistics) and generating texts (pedagogical stylistics). Composition teachers developed sequences for teaching stylistic analysis with the goal of benefiting composing. Louis Milic explains that stylistic study advances progress in composition by illustrating "the principle of synonymity, the crucial theorem of stylistics . . . in a rational and gradual manner" ("Composition," 198). Essays by Edward Corbett, John Fleischauer, and Winston Weathers outlined stylistic exercises, analyzing expert writers' choices and then students' compositions.

The discipline of stylistics does not have a generative arm; composition importantly explored this potential both in pedagogy and rationale. Transformational grammar in particular prompted teachers and researchers to experiment with pedagogies which would test the resources of stylistics. Ohmann's pivotal essay, "Generative Grammars and the Concept of Literary Style," outlined how transformational grammar furnishes a "grammar that provided certain relationships, formally statable, of alternativeness among constructions" (265). His demonstration of the embedded deep structure of sentences was enormously influential, leading to sentence-combining exercises aimed at increasing syntactic maturity.

By 1983, W. Ross Winterowd could attempt to theorize about the rationale of sentence-combining and accessibility as "pedagogical stylistics," claiming such exercises "give students access to the tacit knowledge in their reservoir of competence and thus allow them to develop *technique*" (83). Sentence-combining pedagogies by Francis Christensen, John Mellon, and Frank O'Hare were extended to the paragraph by Christensen, Alton Becker, and Frank D'Angelo, on the (later discredited) premise that sentence syntactic complexity is a microcosm of the paragraph and the composition as a whole. Although revitalizing, these approaches have been criticized as prescriptive, affecting linguistic choice most at the point of revision. In addition, Joseph Williams notes that this text-centered approach to generating stylistic alternatives does not relate single sentences to each other or illustrate how stylistic choices may be shaped by context (177).

Thus stylistics, central to composition as editing in 1963, matured in the next 20 years in pedagogies for sentence/paragraph combining and imitation. Although not part of composition theorizing, transformational grammar was drafted to develop a productive arm of stylistics. A more promising application from linguistics for stylistics may come from the speech act theory of John Searle and John Austin which considers units larger than a sentence, and could holistically relate stylistic features to author, audience, and discourse community. However, this has not yet flowered in composition classrooms.

In 1976, Edward Corbett claimed that "stylistic study is the most advanced and flourishing area of the so-called 'new rhetoric' " ("Approaches," 83). Stylistics is key to this orientation, in which reality is created through a dialect of writer, audience, language, and context. In this regard, the significance of stylistics as a analytic tool is secure even when visible in some classrooms and absent from others.

However, the significance of stylistics as a generative tool is far from certain. By 1985 Elizabeth Rankin noted that there "has been a noticeable decline in the status of style as a pedagogical concept" (8). For stylistics to have continuing importance for composition, it must formulate a sustained and specific answer to composition's formidable question: "To what extent and by what means can the writing behavior of the student be influenced to change?" (Milic, "Theories," 67). Conversations about its significance hinge on the nature and teachability of style. Milic states, "for teaching, a dualistic theory [of style] seems to be essential . . . unashamedly concerned with form and not with content'' (''Theories,'' 126). In this ''ornamental'' theory of style, the normative resources of a language provide linguistic choices so a ''thing'' can be expressed in a variety of ''ways.'' The pedagogical implication is that style can be taught, suggesting potential for stylistics. The contrasting position, ''monism,'' understands style to be the unique expression of each individual; thus the individual, not the language system, is the source of style. Style springs from ''native competence,'' not ''learned rules'' (Pringle, 94), which effectively removes stylistics as a generative pedagogical tool from a teacher's pantry of resources.

John Gage counters that composition teachers actually ''straddle the fence between the monistic and dualistic.'' Stressing revision advocates ''a separation between the way a thing is said . . . and the ideas themselves''; while stressing ''clarity and the 'plain style' . . . we seem to call upon precisely the opposite assumption, namely that there is one ideally suited linguistic formula for each idea'' (619–20). For stylistics to develop as a generative and theorizable part of composition, it must develop a theory and pedagogy which will recognize that ''both of these powers—of language and of intention—at are work . . . when we compose'' (621).

Rankin explores these deeper questions affecting stylistics, noting that the new rhetoric has not ''offered us a sound, complete, and adequate theory of style'' (8). Such a theory should, first, offer a flexible definition of style as both product and process, ''both a set of observable features of a finished text and a way of discovering what that text will become'' (Rankin, 12). It should also recognize that style involves both conscious ''rhetorical choices'' and unconscious ''stylistic options'' (Milic, ''Rhetorical,'' 87).

All theories of style have implications for pedagogy and for whether stylistics may be plumbed for process-oriented, generative methodologies. Gage and Rankin's observations suggest stylistics should still be used during revision, but could be expanded to explore the role of voice in individual texts and discourse communities. That composition remains interested in the expressive and the constructed individual voice, as well as the social voice of a discourse community, suggests that stylistics will need to address features that deviate from a norm, as well as normative language use or stylistics as appropriateness.

BIBLIOGRAPHY

Primary Texts

Bally, Charles. *Traité de Stylistique Française*. 3rd ed. 2 vols. Geneva: Georg, 1951.

Ellegard, Alvar. *A Statistical Method for Determining Authorship: The Junius Letters, 1769–1772*. Göteborg, Sweden: Acta Universitatis Gothoburgensis, 1962.

Enkvist, Nils Erik. *Linguistic Stylistics*. The Hague, Holland, and Paris: Mouton de Gruyter, 1973.

Leitner, Gerhard, ed. *New Directions in English-Language Corpora*. Berlin: Mouton de Gruyter, 1992.

Milic, Louis. ''Rhetorical Choice and Stylistic Option.'' In *Literary Style: A Symposium*. Ed. Seymour Chatman. London: Oxford UP, 1971, 77–88.

Ohmann, Richard. "Prolegomena to the Analysis of Prose Style." In *Style in Prose Fiction*. Ed. Harold C. Martin. New York: Columbia UP, 1959, 1–24.

Olsen, Mark. "Signs, Symbols, and Discourses." *Computers and the Humanities* 27 (1993–94): 309–14.

Riffaterre, Michael. "Criteria for Style Analysis." *Word* 15.1 (1959): 154–74.

———. "Stylistic Context." *Word* 16.2 (1960): 207–18.

Spitzer, Leo. *Linguistics and Literary History*. Princeton, NJ: Princeton UP, 1948.

Major Scholarship in Composition

Austin, L. L. *How to Do Things with Words*. Ed. J. O. Urmson and Marina Sbisà. Cambridge, MA: Harvard University Press, 1975.

Becker, Alton. "A Tagmemic Approach to Paragraphic Analysis." *College Composition and Communication* 16 (1965): 237–42.

Christensen, Francis. "A Generative Rhetoric of the Sentence." *College Composition and Communication* 14 (1963): 155–61.

Corbett, Edward P. J. "Approaches to the Study of Style." In *Teaching Composition: Twelve Bibliographical Essays*. Ed. Gary Tate. Forth Worth: Texas Christian UP, 1987, 83–130.

———. "Teaching Style." In *The Territory of Language*. Ed. Donald A. McQuade. Carbondale: Southern Illinois UP, 1986, 23–33.

D'Angelo, Frank J. "Style as Structure." *Style* 8 (Spring 1974): 322–64.

Fleischauer, John F. "James Baldwin's Style: A Prospectus for the Classroom." *College Composition and Communication* 26 (1975): 141–48.

Gage, John T. "Philosophies of Style and Their Implications for Composition." *College English* 41 (1980): 615–22.

McQuade, Donald A., ed. *The Territory of Language: Linguistics, Stylistics, and the Teaching of Composition*. Carbondale: Southern Illinois UP, 1986.

Mellon, John C. *Transformational Sentence-Combining: A Method for Enhancing the Development of Syntactic Fluency in English Composition*. Champaign, IL: National Council of Teachers of English, 1969.

Milic, Louis T. "Composition via Stylistics." In *The Territory of Language*. Ed. Donald A. McQuade. Carbondale: Southern Illinois UP, 1986, 192–203.

———. "Theories of Style and Their Implications for the Teaching of Composition." *College Composition and Communication* 16 (1965): 66–69, 126.

O'Hare, Frank. *Sentence Combining: Improving Student Writing Without Formal Grammar Instruction*. Urbana, IL: National Council of Teachers of English, 1973.

Ohmann, Richard. "Generative Grammars and the Concept of Literary Style." In *Teaching Freshman Composition*. Ed. Gary Tate and Edward P. J. Corbett. New York: Oxford UP, 1967, 261–77.

Pringle, Ian. "Why Teach Style? A Review-Essay." *College Composition and Communication* 34 (1983): 91–98.

Rankin, Elizabeth D. "Revitalizing Style: Toward a New Theory and Pedagogy." *Freshman English News* 14 (1985): 8–13.

Searle, John R. *Speech Acts: An Essay in the Philosophy of Language*. London: Cambridge UP, 1969.

Weathers, Winston. "Grammars of Style: New Option in Composition." *Freshman English News* (Winter 1976). Rpt. in *Rhetoric and Composition: A Sourcebook for*

Teachers and Writers. Ed. Richard L. Graves. Portsmouth, NH: Boynton/Cook, 1990, 200–214.

Williams, Joseph M. "Non-Linguistic Linguistics and the Teaching of Style." In *The Territory of Language.* Ed. Donald A. McQuade. Carbondale: Southern Illinois UP, 1986, 174–91.

Winterowd, W. Ross. "Prolegomenon to Pedagogical Stylistics." *College Composition and Communication* 34 (1983): 80–90.

Yoos, George and Philip Keith. "Style, Invention, and Indirection: Aphorisms." In *Composition in Context.* Ed. W. Ross Winterowd and Vincent Gillespie. Carbondale: Southern Illinois UP, 1994, 390–97.

LINDA VAVRA

T

TAGMEMIC INVENTION

Summary

Tagmemic invention is a method of inquiry and reflective thinking. To understand how tagmemic invention works, it is important to understand the aims of tagmemic analysis theory. Tagmemic analysis theory assumes that all constituents of discourse simultaneously make up and are made up of hierarchical structures. To identify instances of these structures in sentences, Pike designed the "tagmeme," a "composite of a functional slot in a grammatical pattern, with an accompanying generalized plot element, plus a class of appropriate fillers, manifested by one chosen member of the class" (Young, Becker, and Pike, 295). For example, the sentence, *The police arrested my roommate*, can be analyzed as follows:

Discourse unit: "The police arrested my roommate."

Tagmeme of interest: *my roommate*

Other units: *The police arrested*

Analysis:

1. The grammatical pattern in which the tagmeme is situated is a *sentence*.

2. The tagmeme's functional slot is that of *object*.

3. The object is being acted upon; "*Affected*" is thus the generalized plot element.

4. The class of appropriate fillers is "things that can be 'arrested' by 'The police.' "

5. The phrase "my roommate" is the filler.

The purpose of tagmemic analysis is to situate units of discourse in linguistic and conceptual hierarchies. Tagmemic invention extends the goal of tagmemic analysis by expanding the domain of objects analyzed beyond units of discourse to include any problem of knowledge. Young, Becker, and Pike, for example, have adapted the notions of hierarchy, slots, and fillers, to a heuristic that is useful in deepening written accounts of experience. The key terms of the heuristic are *particle*, *wave*, and *field*. With these terms, we can describe a tree, for example, as follows:

Particle. The tree is a discrete unit that can be seen, photographed, recalled.

Wave. The tree has a life span—it grows and dies.

Field. The tree is a system made up of smaller units—leaves, roots, bark.

All sorts of subjective experiences—problems, feelings, values, and so on—can be analyzed tagmemically. Young, Becker, and Pike were particularly interested in problems of knowledge and decision making. We can view a problem of diplomacy, for example, as a particle (because it is a unique historical situation), as a wave (because it develops in response to changing political conditions), and as a field (because to be considered a problem by someone, it must comprise a set of actual conditions coming into contact with a value matrix). Although no special methods are required to study this kind of problem closely and thoroughly, tagmemic analysis provides a solid framework for deepening our perspective.

The pedagogy of tagmemic invention includes steps beyond the tagmemic analysis of an experience. The writer must also persuade an audience to understand this experience by discovering points of contact—cultural, conceptual, linguistic—with members of the audience. This is especially important when the writer wishes to address a problem of knowledge or decision making. While these strategies for identification with one's audience do not follow directly from tagmemic analysis, they are important components of tagmemic invention, reflecting Young, Becker, and Pike's interest in the pragmatic philosophy and cognitive psychology of such figures as Dewey and Herbert Simon. For tagmemic invention is meant to be used as a powerful but flexible heuristic for thinking through problems, not merely as a tool for generating discourse. And "problems," as Young, Becker, and Pike would argue, are not merely technical knots to be untied in various forms of life and action, but rather are the essential motivating forces behind all meaningful human activity.

Reception and Significance in Composition Studies

As a general approach to the problem of invention, tagmemic invention is an historically important alternative to classical and Romantic approaches. But its complexity has hindered its acceptance in the writing classroom. Hillocks, for instance, has found that efforts to teach tagmemic invention have had mixed results, possibly due to this complexity. Although Hillocks and others (e.g.,

Kneupper) have offered simplified versions of the heuristic in an effort to make the method more teachable, the pedagogical potential of tagmemic invention has not been studied extensively. It may be fair to say, then, that the impact of tagmemic invention on the practice of writing pedagogy has been small, its impact on the thinking of composition theorists has been somewhat more significant, and its long-term value in composition theory and pedagogy has yet to be determined.

The best introduction to tagmemic invention is Bruce Edwards Jr.'s essay, "The Tagmemic Contribution to Composition Teaching" (Manhattan: Kansas State University *Occasional Papers in Composition History and Theory*, 1979). Other useful works are listed below.

BIBLIOGRAPHY

Primary Texts and Major Scholarship in Composition

Dewey, James. *How We Think*. Boston: D.C. Heath, 1910.

Edwards, Bruce, Jr. "The Tagmemic Contribution to Composition Teaching." In *Occasional Papers in Composition History and Theory*. Manhattan: Kansas State University, 1979.

Hillocks, George. "Inquiry and the Composing Process: Theory and Research." *College English* 44 (1982): 659–73.

Kneupper, Charles W. "Revising the Tagmemic Heuristic: Theoretical and Pedagogical Considerations." *College Communication and Composition* 31 (1980): 160–68.

Pike, Kenneth L. *Linguistic Concepts: An Introduction to Tagmemics*. Lincoln: U of Nebraska P, 1982.

Young, Richard E. "Recent Developments in Rhetorical Invention." In *Teaching Composition: 12 Bibliographical Essays*. Ed. Gary Tate. Forth Worth: Texas Christian UP. 1987, 1–38. See especially the section on "Pedagogy and Methods of Invention" (25–34).

———. "Methodizing Nature: The Tagmemic Discovery Procedure." In *Rhetoric and Change*. Ed. William E. Tanner and Jimmy Dean Bishop. Mesquite, TX: Ide House. 1982, 126–37.

Young, Richard E., Alton Becker, and Kenneth L. Pike. *Rhetoric: Discovery and Change*. New York: Harcourt, 1970.

JAY L. GORDON

TEXT ANALYSIS

Summary

The goals of text analysis are as diverse as the many disciplines and subdisciplines whose scholarship it informs: rhetoric, psychology, education, linguistics, and literary criticism, to name but a few. At the heart of all forms and methods of text analysis, however, is a common theoretical principle: that some examination of the nature and organization of a written text can yield linguistic insights that either extend or stand beyond the propositional "content" or meaning of the text. This assumption itself is problematic because, as reader-response theorists have pointed out, meaning (literal or nonliteral) resides partly in readers and is a function of what they bring to a text; it is not only what exists in some essential way in the text itself. An analysis of meaning, then, cannot come purely from the text itself because one has no access to potential readers' constructions. This paradox is somewhat weakened by the argument that the infinite interpretive possibilities in a text are constrained by its linguistic structures and conventions—or, as Huckin points out, that "texts contain observable patterns of language usage that come to mean certain things to the members of a given community" (86). At some level, then, text analysis proceeds from the assumption that the application of specific tools or methods of analysis can explain meaning based on semantic, lexical, syntactic, and organizational features; as Cooper puts it, text analysis is "the characterization or schematization of whole texts" (287).

In this sense, text analysis has affinities with discourse analysis (see Coulthard), the two terms often being used synonymously. Text analysis may be distinguished from discourse analysis, however, on the basis of medium: whereas discourse analysis may include the analysis of conversational interaction (phone calls, business meetings), text analysis is more likely to apply to written texts in somewhat conventionalized genres such as narratives, student essays, corporate memos, lab reports, tests of writing used in large-scale assessments, and the like. For reasons of focus, this overview will limit itself to written text, which itself is most relevant to scholarship in composition studies. All texts, however, as de Beaugrande and Dressler have argued, must be understood as text *types* in discursive contexts—communicative occurrences involving, at some level, the function of human interaction (3).

Text-analytical methods are extremely diverse and tend to be highly complex and elaborate, requiring a good deal of linguistic apparatus, knowledge of formal logic, and plentiful examples from natural and artificial texts. For this reason, even a list of text-analytical methods is beyond the scope of the present overview (but for a more comprehensive introduction to text linguistics, see de Beaugrande and Dressler). Instead, a sketch of a few interrelated methods of contemporary text analysis may be instructive.

The linguistic method perhaps most fully applied to the field of composition studies is what is generally called *cohesion analysis*. According to a comprehensive treatment of this method—Michael Halliday and Ruqaiya Hasan's *Cohesion in English*—cohesion is a semantic concept that "occurs where the interpretation of some element in the discourse is dependent on that of another" (4). It is a particularly apt example of contemporary methods in text analysis because of how, by showing the way that parts of text are bridged to each other and to their larger semantic contexts, it tries to distinguish the concept of a text from what might otherwise be a "collection of unrelated sentences" (1). At its simplest, cohesion refers to the ways in which texts are "stuck together"—the ways in which sentences are linked or connected by various linguistic and semantic ties. Cohesion occurs, Halliday and Hasan explain, "when interpretation of some element in the discourse depends on that of another. The one presupposes the other, in the sense that it cannot be effectively decoded except by recourse to it" (4). Because grammatical dependencies "often obtain among elements not directly adjacent to each other" (de Beaugrande and Dressler, 49), cohesion is achieved through the use of various elements such as repetition, parallelism, ellipsis, co-reference, conjunction, and lexical cohesion (linking words that are synonymous or in lexical sets). In the domain of reference, for example, an item in a text may have some exophoric (situational) reference to something beyond the text; it may have endophoric reference to something that has already been introduced in preceding text; or it may have endophoric reference to something not yet introduced in the text. Texts are cohesive to the extent that these sorts of references can reasonably be recovered—that "the thing referred to has [been] identified somehow" (Halliday and Hasan, *Cohesion* 33). Text analysis focusing on reference is therefore preoccupied with the types and extent of reference chains, especially because the frequency of each type of reference may vary across registers and genres. Cohesion analysis more generally, then, examines texts from many of the perspectives that explain the relationships between and among sentences, relationships that give rise to continuous, extended discourse.

A second theoretical perspective for text analysis, *functional sentence perspective*, was developed by members of the Prague school of linguistics (see Chafe; Danes). In the early 1970s, Prague School linguists were interested in the ways that writers manage or "stage" the information in a text. Texts proceed partly through a balance of "given" information (what has already been introduced) and "new" information (what has not yet been introduced). Sentences also contain "topics" or "themes" which usually appear first, followed by "comments" or "rhemes," which are glosses on the topics. The theme is the focus (what the writer wants to emphasize), and its placement acts as a guide to the reader for the direction of the discourse. Analysis of information management proceeds, then, by specifying clauses according to the categories old/new and topic/comment, and then identifying the focus of the information in a sentence and the syntactic strategies for shifting or managing it (see Cooper, 298).

A third domain of text analysis, *propositional analysis*, developed at the intersections of psychology, reading research, and linguistics. This theory is perhaps best exemplified by the work of Walter Kintsch and Teun van Dijk (individually and collaboratively). The goal of propositional analysis is to explain the relationship between the information contained explicitly in a text's semantic propositions (as well as that which is logically inferred or entailed from those propositions) and its organization in reading, memory, and retrieval. Readers, van Dijk explains, "cannot, and need not, store all the propositional information of a given discourse in verbal processing. Hence, this information will, at least in part, be reduced to macrostructures"—a semantic representation of a group of sentences (137–38). Macrostructures are said to facilitate comprehension; they have certain definable linguistic properties and help to "determine for a discourse or part of it the range of possible concepts which may be used and thus are a global constraint on lexical insertion'' (152). A text about a man running into a bank with a gun may end, for example, with the sentence ''The holdup did not last longer than three minutes,'' yet a holdup was not explicitly mentioned in the prior text. The previous passage, then, must have contained an argument or predicate ''which is coreferential with respect to the same event as the word *holdup*'' (151). The goals of propositional analysis are initially to specify the propositional and macrostructural organization of texts and then, through empirical research, validate this analysis through processing and recall studies. The relationship between the human processing of text and the organization of the text itself thus serves to enhance the scholarship in each domain— as experiments on prose recall have already accomplished (see van Dijk, 157).

As suggested in these three general methods, contemporary text analysis offers the field of composition studies important interdisciplinary directions by connecting studies of textuality (formal linguistics), studies of the ways in which readers process written text (psycholinguistics), and studies of the strategies involved in text production among people with varying writing abilities (composition). By developing methods for describing what makes texts ''readable'' or ''understandable,'' text analysis suggests specific lines of research on text production as well as specific practical strategies for classroom instruction.

Reception and Significance in Composition Studies

In its emergent stages, composition studies adopted ''traditional'' methods of analyzing or describing texts, methods inherited from structural linguistics or prescriptive grammar. This tendency is well illustrated in D'Angelo's ''bibliographic survey of the principal developments of the sentence from the nineteenth century to the present, with particular emphasis on the relationship of the sentence to composition theory and practice'' (303). With the exception of a brief focus on work in sentence combining and the ''generative rhetoric of the sentence'' (which draws from transformational-generative approaches to syntax), D'Angelo's survey characterizes a field relatively uninformed by newer advances in the analysis of texts and the important relationships of sentences to their surrounding linguistic and rhetorical contexts.

Such methods of text analysis, which are framed in the assumptions of traditional grammar, focused largely on the features of written texts to the exclusion of context and the divergent interpretations of meaning necessitated in the reading process. The project of traditional analysis was to describe specific, verifiable characteristics of certain kinds of texts. The intellectual context in which this work took place stressed empiricism and linguistic fact, and was dominated by modernist assumptions about truth, validity, and the inherent properties of human and natural artifacts (see Faigley). Chomskyan linguistics, which argued for abstract underlying principles of language initially at the cost of variability in language use, strongly influenced assumptions about the appropriate methods and goals of text analysis. The concept of underlying (deep) and surface structures—a hallmark of transformational-generative theory—led to attempts within the field of composition to find parallels to the manipulation of basic syntactic constructions into various surface forms, particularly in an area of research now known as sentence combining.

Beginning in the mid-1970s, the field of written composition shifted its focus quite dramatically, in its pedagogical manifestations, away from textual types, modes, and the characteristics of "good writing" and toward the processes of text production. This "process movement," as it is now generally called, had the effect of creating for text analysis what Huckin has described as a "decade of relative neglect" (84). The preoccupation with the analysis of moment-by-moment processes of writing and the creation of underlying cognitive models of text production shifted many researchers' attention away from static features. Simultaneously, the advent of new technologies, particularly the use of word processing, created an intellectual and pedagogical climate that brought the revising process into sharper focus.

During this time, the analysis of text could not disappear, in part because texts themselves remained both the goal (or outcome) of composing and a significant component of the "data" for most composition-related research—even the most qualitative. In studies of composing and revising, for example, specific kinds of textual decisions had to be described and analyzed with reference to the emerging (or changing) text itself. For the most part, however, such descriptions lacked reference to the principles of text analysis developing in more linguistically oriented areas of written communication. As critics of process-oriented research have pointed out, the texts themselves seemed relatively unimportant next to the writer's cognitive processes as they might be revealed through, for example, "think-aloud" protocols.

Some scholars, notably Haswell ("Textual Research"), have pointed to deeper intellectual and disciplinary conflicts between the goals of text analysis and competing strands of research. Text analysis appears to some scholars mindful of the complex social nature of writing as lacking in context, too preoccupied with minutiae. Others criticize what appears to be the traditionally empirical foundations of text analysis—the statistical analysis of frequency or the way in which text analysis often figures in controlled experimental research. Still others claim that comparative text analysis often lacks validity, especially when it does not account for the complex human variables of the writer's context, social goals, and background knowledge.

Some interest in applying the theories and methods of text analysis to the field of written composition was, however, expressed in the mid-1980s, although in competition with the flourishing of scholarship on the writing process. In a review of various methods of text analysis newly developed in linguistics, structuralism, and rhetorical theory, Cooper tried to show how examinations of textual characteristics could supplement and enhance other scholarship in composition studies. This new work, he pointed out, takes us "beyond the sentence, to which we have been bound in developmental studies for over sixty years'' (287). Clearly focused on an understanding of writing *development*, Cooper's aim in adapting text analysis to composition studies was to ''seek out procedures that may inform us about the development of discourse competence, procedures useful for analyzing the texts of children and older novice writers'' (292).

Borrowing from the major works in text analysis, Cooper's review explains the underlying assumptions and methods of a number of text-analytical perspectives, including cohesion analysis, information management, functional sentence perspective, thematic structure, narrative analysis, and analysis of persuasion. While not restricted entirely to linguistic perspectives, Cooper's contribution suggests some central ways in which the principles of text analysis could be used in both research and pedagogy in the field. His enthusiasm for the application of text linguistics to scholarship in composition was echoed soon after by William Strong, who urged compositionists to ''translate new linguistic insights into activities that reveal, by induction and indirection, what we want students to internalize and transfer to their prose'' (86).

In spite of these and other optimistic proposals, as well as sporadic attempts to carry them out in composition research, text analysis has remained relatively peripheral to the goals and focus of scholarship in the field. Recently, however, some scholars have tried to revive interest in text analysis by suggesting ways it can be made more sensitive to social context. As Huckin puts it, the field of composition studies is experiencing a reemergence of text analysis ''that includes not only the cognitive and expressive aspects so closely associated with the process movement but sociological and cultural dimensions as well'' (85). Existing and perhaps undiscovered methods of text analysis can be used to further illuminate the ''communities and individuals involved [in writing] and how the tensions and relations between them affect the composing process'' (85). Huckin's argument for the usefulness of text analysis suggests some degree of methodological consistency: whereas the tools, terms, and focus of text analysis continue to evolve, as a significant component of research on written communication it can hardly be threatened with extinction as long as texts themselves are, at some level, the object of inquiry.

In spite of the recent influence of postmodernism in composition, which has ruptured many essentialist notions of writing and textuality, it would appear foolhardy to abandon belief in the idea that texts rely on socially constructed, recognized, reified, and communicatively significant features. As we continue to make new discoveries about the processes of text production, the nature of texts in various disciplinary and social communities, and the properties that characterize particular kinds of texts, we must be informed about various methods and perspectives for analysis. We must be ready to adopt text-analytical strategies when these are useful (as so many researchers have done, for example, with the concept of the T-unit, a measure of syntactic complexity); at the same time, we must be willing to critique, refine, or reject those methods when they lose their explanatory power or fail to reflect the full complexity of writing in its situated use.

The potential for computer analyses of text is still relatively untapped, in part because of the difficulty of computers to operate at much more than simplistic levels of recognition and parsing. However, as advances are made in artificial intelligence and natural-language processing by computers, we may experience a renaissance of interest in text analysis as a means to provide information about the structures and linguistic/rhetorical features of written texts. In turn, this new information could advance our knowledge of how children and adults learn to write—and practice writing—in a variety of settings.

As noted, applications of formal text analysis to composition studies have been sporadic, most appearing in print in the 1980s. Perhaps because of its obvious connections to the writing process or to the assessment of "quality" in student writing, cohesion analysis prompted a burst of activity in composition scholarship. Witte and Faigley, for example, in a study of essays rated as high or low in quality, found a strong relationship between the ratings and the number and type of cohesive ties in the students' texts. In a study of the relationships between cohesion, coherence, and the quality of students' writing, McCulley also found that cohesion contributed in important ways to the coherence of texts of equal length, which in turn related to ratings of quality. Other studies of cohesion include those by Stotsky, Haswell, and Bamberg. Markels's book-length work on cohesion proposes a methodology for determining the coherence of a text, based on four structures in expository paragraphs. She then applies this methodology to an analysis of various texts and proposes some pedagogical applications.

Other connections between methods of text analysis and the analysis of student writing, both speculative and research-based, appeared from time to time throughout this period, including Horning's attempt ("Propositional Analysis") to apply Kintsch's propositional analysis to the teaching of composition. Ultimately, however, text analysis was overshadowed in composition scholarship by the preoccupation with studies of the writing process and, at the end of the 1980s, a new interest in context—especially in the analysis of text production and reception across discursive communities. Part of the reluctance to pursue text analysis with greater vigor may have stemmed from its rather contradictory findings, as Haswell ably documents in his review of cohesion research (Textual 313–17).

In spite of the ultimate goals of composition scholarship—to lead to improved pedagogy and improved student writing—text analysis seems to have made almost no contribution to textbooks. Notable exceptions include work by Vande Kopple, a compositionist with an enduring interest in linguistic theory and text analysis (see *Clear and Coherent Prose*). The great majority of handbooks and rhetorics continue to revert to traditional concepts and terminology when describing methods for creating coherent, cohesive, readable, and stylistically appealing prose.

BIBLIOGRAPHY

Primary Texts

Chafe, Wallace. *Meaning and the Structure of Language.* Chicago: U of Chicago P, 1970.

Coulthard, Malcolm. *An Introduction to Discourse Analysis.* London: Longman, 1977.

Danes, Frantisek, ed. *Papers on Functional Sentence Perspective.* Prague, Czech Republic: Academia, 1974.

de Beaugrande, Robert. *Text, Discourse, and Process: Toward a Multidisciplinary Science of Texts.* Norwood, NJ: Ablex, 1980.

———. *Text Production: Toward a Science of Composition.* New York: Ablex, 1984.

de Beaugrande, Robert, and Wolfgang Dressler. *Introduction to Text Linguistics.* New York: Longman, 1981.

Francis, W. Nelson, and Henry Kucera. *Frequency Analysis of English Usage: Lexicon and Grammar.* Boston: Houghton Mifflin, 1982.

Halliday, M. A. K., and Ruqaiya Hasan. *Cohesion in English.* New York: Longman, 1976.

———. *Language, Context, and Text: Aspects of Language in a Social-Semiotic Perspective.* New York: Oxford UP, 1989.

Kintsch, Walter. *The Representation of Meaning in Memory.* Hillsdale, NJ: Erlbaum, 1979.

van Dijk, Teun A. *Text and Context: Explorations in the Semantics and Pragmatics of Discourse.* New York: Longman, 1977.

van Dijk, Teun A., and Walter Kintsch. *Strategies of Discourse Comprehension.* New York: Academic P, 1983.

Major Scholarship in Composition

Bamberg, Betty. "What Makes a Text Coherent?" *College Composition and Communication* 34 (1983): 417–29.

Cooper, Charles R. "Procedures for Describing Written Texts." In *Research on Writing: Principles and Methods.* Ed. Peter Mosenthal, Lynn Tamor, and Sean A. Walmsley. New York: Longman, 1983, 287–313.

D'Angelo, Frank J. "The Sentence." In *Research in Composition and Rhetoric: A Bibliographic Sourcebook.* Ed. Michael G. Moran and Ronald F. Lunsford. Westport, CT: Greenwood, 1984, 303–17.

Dillon, George. *Constructing Texts: Elements of a Theory of Composition and Style.* Bloomington: Indiana UP, 1981.

Fahnestock, Jean. "Semantic and Lexical Coherence." *College Composition and Communication* 34 (1983): 400–416.

Faigley, Lester. *Fragments of Rationality: Postmodernity and the Subject of Composition.* Pittsburgh, PA: U of Pittsburgh P, 1992.

Haswell, Richard. "Length of Text and Measurement of Cohesion." *Research in the Teaching of English* 22 (1988): 428–33.

———. "Textual Research and Coherence: Findings, Intuition, Application." *College English* 51 (1989): 305–19.

Horning, Alice S. "Propositional Analysis and the Teaching of Reading 'with' Writing." *Journal of Advanced Compostion* 6 (1985–86): 49–64.

———. *The Psycholinguistics of Readable Writing: A Multidisciplinary Exploration.* Norwood, NJ: Ablex, 1993.

Huckin, Thomas N. "Context-Sensitive Text Analysis." In *Methods and Methodology in Composition Research*. Ed. Gesa Kirsch and Patricia A. Sullivan. Carbondale: Southern Illinois UP, 1992, 84–104.

Markels, Robin Bell. "Cohesion Paradigms in Paragraphs." *College English* 45 (1983): 450–64.

———. *A New Perspective on Cohesion in Expository Paragraphs*. Carbondale: Southern Illinois UP, 1984.

McCulley, George A. "Writing Quality, Coherence, and Cohesion." Ph.D. dissertation, Utah State U, Logan, UT, 1983.

Slater, Wayne H., Michael Graves, and Sherry B. Scott. "Discourse Structure and College Freshmen's Recall and Production of Expository Text." *Research in the Teaching of English* 22 (1988): 45–61.

Strong, William. "Linguistics and Writing." In *Perspectives on Research and Scholarship in Composition*. Ed. Ben W. McClelland and Timothy R. Donovan. New York: MLA, 1985, 68–86.

Stotsky, Sandra. "Types of Lexical Cohesion in Expository Writing: Implications for Developing the Vocabulary of Academic Discourse." *College Composition and Communication* 33 (1983): 430–46.

Vande Kopple, William. *Clear and Coherent Prose*. New York: Scott, Foresman, 1989.

———. "Given and New Information and Some Aspects of the Structures, Semantics, and Pragmatics of Written Texts." In *Studying Writing: Linguistic Approaches*. Ed. Charles Cooper and Sidney Greenbaum. Beverly Hills, CA: Sage, 1986, 72–111.

Winterowd, Ross. "The Grammar of Coherence." *College English* 31 (1970): 828–35.

Witte, Stephen, and Lester Faigley. "Coherence, Cohesion, and Writing Quality." *College Composition and Communication* 32 (1981): 189–204.

CHRIS M. ANSON

V

VYGOTSKIAN THEORY

Summary

Lev Semyonovich Vygotsky (1896–1934), psychologist of the early Russian Soviet period, has had continuing (though politically troubled) influence in Russia since the late 1920s, and since the mid-1960s has been gaining increased attention in the United States and throughout the world. Particularly relevant to writing is his interest in the higher psychological functions, developed in the use of symbolic tools.

Starting out as a teacher of language and literature prior to the revolution, Vygotsky became interested in how structured texts can foster particular complex states of mind in the reader. The revolution, perceived to offer a radical break in human history by providing new conditions for the development of human personality, oriented his inquiry into the social formation of mind. This work appeared in its matured form in the last four years of his life, and is best known in the English-speaking world in the translated volumes *Thought and Language* and *Mind in Society*.

Vygotsky examined how minds develop within social interaction, transforming the individual's biological legacy through the group's cultural legacy. External forms of activity and social relationships he saw internalized as human mental activity; with the social nature of any psychological function preserved when it becomes internalized. Symmetrically, he saw culturally transmitted tools as the externalization of psychological functions. The cultural legacy he found expressed in tools developed to aid us in activities, which we deploy purposefully in tasks at hand. These tools are symbolic tools as well as material. A string around the finger or an alarm clock can act as an aid to memory. An abacus helps us remember and manipulate quantities, and thereby calculate financial transactions. Language helps us coordinate work and experiences with others, provide each other with guidance in the pursuit of tasks, and share representations of present, distant, or imagined worlds.

We learn to think using these tools. Without tools we are limited to acting and thinking with those things immediately at hand, and are thus, in essence, slaves to the visual field. A major leap is made when an ape or a human, seeing a piece of inaccessible fruit, remembers that a stick (not immediately present) could be used as an aid, and then seeks the stick to serve as a tool. The imaginative perception of a mental object then influences the material unfolding of the situation, through transformed perception and action. Mind is created in the pursuit of action, considering the material and symbolic tools available; and the development of individual human minds occurs through a history of participations in tool-mediated activities.

Language provides the most extensive tools for developing shared attention, working with others, and intervening in our own mental processes. Language is learned in human interaction, through which it develops its meanings, so that a parent and child in playing a game create ranges of mutual intelligibility and shared attention through negotiations of language, that negotiation being carried out by continuing interpretation and action on each other's part. Language learned in interaction then provides an individual means of controlling one's own attention, as when a child, in reenacting a hiding game by her- or himself, repeats the phrase, "Where is?" initially uttered by an adult play-partner. Vygotsky considers the development of a private, internal language as these traces of social language remain only in fragmentary internalized form, directing attention and cognition. What appears on the intramental plane of the individual first appears on the intermental plane of social interaction. As one learns, in practical apprenticeship, to use the cultural-historical legacy of the carpenter's tool kit within the circumstances and tasks where the tools are demonstrated to be useful, so one learns to use, in daily interaction, the cultural-historical legacy of the language tool kit one is introduced to as a social medium; one then learns, through internalization, to use the language tool kit as the individualized medium of cognition.

What an individual may then be able to accomplish by oneself contains the residue of many previous interactions in the form of memories and tools, as well as the cultural memory built into the tools. What that person can do in new circumstances is further expanded by coordination with a partner who brings a different set of tools and memories to that task. The extent of coordination is as well affected by the tools of coordination—that is how flexibly and well one can talk and work with the partner. This new coordination allows one to reach beyond oneself in doing new tasks, learning new skills, imagining new thoughts.

This area of interaction Vygotsky calls the Zone of Proximal Development. One's ability as a learner, for example is not to be measured simply by what one already knows, but by the extensiveness of the new situations one is able to enter into successfully and thus learn from. Similarly, to make learning available for students, instructors must bring new material and skills into a zone of intelligibility, possible participation, and motivated interaction. Students recognize and incorporate the new tools only insofar as they help direct and shape attention and motives already forming in pursuit of some desired object. Vygotsky originally conceived the Zone of Proximal Development in terms of the dyad of a learner and an adult or more skilled peer, such that the zone was defined entirely by the larger knowledge and competence of a dominant matured person. We can, however, also think of a more open space of responsiveness as any two individuals of different skills, knowledge, and perception meet over a shared task, provide communicative challenges to each other, or together explore new tasks and situations. That is, learning through interaction can occur in a variety of circumstances that are not predetermined by finite, known skills embodied in a teacher.

Language in its abstract representations radically extends the reach of our imaginations, and allows others to bring to our mind nonpresent objects, not only from our shared prior memories (''the lunch we had last Tuesday''), but from the experience of one but not the other (''the fabulous restaurant I went to last week that I must tell you about''), or even reported events that neither shared (''the recipes Yasmin told me about, which she had learned from her family'').

Vygotsky was particularly interested in how the cultural heritage of organized concepts transmitted in school (usually translated unfortunately as ''scientific concepts'') transformed the mind and thought of adolescents. Within his particular historical moment, Vygotsky did not, however, relativize or otherwise problematize official learning as embodied in school subjects, nor did he doubt univocal progress in science; rather, he saw the immediate challenge as educating an unschooled and poor peasantry. Nor did Vygotsky consider the other organized discourses that shape the character of interaction and cognition within other social institutions, such as scriptural religions, law, medicine, or commerce, even though such culturally organized discourses, with their particular sets of discursive tools, equally provide sites for individual development and transformation. Further, communal knowledge and memory are potentially expandable to all things reportable within the sociolinguistic communication systems we have developed; however, this knowledge is only transmitted through the differentiated social groupings, situations, and sociolinguistic media by which we encounter the utterances of others. That is, the linguistic resources and sites for social interaction may be fractured and multiple.

Vygotsky, in discussing the development of children's ability to use literate signs, considers how written language might differ from spoken language as a tool along with writing's consequences for human cognition. He points out that alphabetic writing is a second-order sign, or a sign of a sign. A picture can directly suggest an object, event, situation or memory. A word can directly call to mind the referent of the word. A spelled, alphabetic word, however, only represents the sounds of the spoken word. Writing is also further removed from the interlocutor than is speech. The abstraction of written language from experience presents special challenges for learning and motivation. Furthermore, the distance writing creates between experience and representation and between utterer and audience encourages reflection upon and fascination with written signs as a system in themselves, both for good and for ill.

Value of the Theory for Writing and the Teaching of Writing

Vygotsky thus presents an account of mental growth in relation to language learning and participation. He points to the use of written language as a tool that extends our mental reach and provides opportunities for more extensive interactions. Texts provide resources that can potentially extend the Zone of Proximal Development if students are brought into interaction with those texts in pursuit of their own objects—whether to build a model airplane, to articulate an understanding of oneself and one's world, or to argue to change an obnoxious policy. The act of writing then can be seen as speaking to rich interactive environments drawing on the discursive resources provided by the environment, both as previously internalized by the writer and as newly sought and brought to bear on the occasion.

For writing teachers, Vygotsky draws our attention to the importance of constructing social and problem environments that will draw students into tasks that will extend their language competences. We need to attend both to the motives that impel our students and to the situations and resources we establish in the classroom that will provide the tools and opportunities for student growth.

Further, Vygotsky points us toward the use of language for monitoring and self-regulating our behavior, so that meta-languages of writing instruction, whether rules, instructions, guidelines, rhetorical concepts, or other reflective vocabulary, can assist with choice making in writing. However, such meta-languages are useful only when they coordinate with the students' own motives and perceptions, so that they become internalized into students' minds and thoughts in orienting to writing situations. That is, the meta-languages of language of instruction only provide positive educational value when brought into a Zone of Proximal Development formed around motivated student writing tasks.

Reception and Significance in Composition Studies

The richness and depth of Vygotsky's thoughts have inspired a great variety of work, and lie behind such now familiar and widely used concepts as situated cognition, distributed cognition, guided participation, scaffolding, cognitive apprenticeship, legitimate peripheral participation, and communities of practice. The ideas of Vygotsky and his followers have been increasingly influential in education studies (see Dyson, Moll, and Smagorinsky), and related ideas have been elaborated under the rubric of Activity Theory (see Russian activity theory in this volume). Among compositionists who have drawn directly on the work of Vygotsky are Bazerman, Berkenkotter and Huckin, Dias et al., Nystrand,

Prior, and Zebroski. Within composition studies, Vygotsky's ideas are often linked to the dialogism of Mikhail Bakhtin (see Dialogism/Bakhtinian Theory in this volume), but they also stand behind much of the work in genre theory and the study of specialized discourses. Of great importance in understanding the psychology of literacy is the work of Scribner and Cole.

BIBLIOGRAPHY

Primary Texts

Vygotsky, Lev S. *Collected Works.* Vol 2: *The Fundamentals of Defectology.* New York: Plenum P, 1993.

———. *Mind in Society.* Cambridge, MA: Harvard UP, 1978.

———. *Psychology of Art.* Cambridge, MA: MIT P, 1971.

———. *Thought and Language.* Cambridge, MA: MIT P, 1986.

Vygotsky, Lev S., and A. R. Luria. *Studies on the History of Behavior: Ape, Primitive, and Child.* Hillsdale, NJ: Erlbaum, 1993.

Selected Secondary Texts

Kozulin, Alex. *Vygotsky's Psychology.* Cambridge, MA: Harvard UP, 1990.

van der Veer, René, and Jan Valsiner. *Understanding Vygotsky.* Oxford, U.K.: Blackwell, 1991.

Wertsch, James, ed. *Culture, Communication, and Cognition: Vygotskian Perspectives.* Cambridge: Cambridge UP, 1985.

Major Scholarship in Composition

Bazerman, Charles. *Constructing Experience.* Carbondale: Southern Illinois UP, 1994.

———. *Shaping Written Knowledge.* Madison: U of Wisconsin P, 1988.

Berkenkotter, Carol, and Tom Huckin. *Genre Knowledge.* Mahwah, NJ: Erlbaum, 1994.

Dias, Patrick, Aviva Freedman, Peter Medway, and Anthony Paré. *Worlds Apart: Acting and Writing in Academic and Workplace Contexts.* Mahwah, NJ: Erlbaum, 1998.

Dyson, Anne H. *Social Worlds of Children Learning to Write in an Urban Primary School.* New York: Teachers College P, 1993.

Moll, Luis C., ed. *Vygotsky and Education.* New York: Cambridge UP, 1990.

Nystrand, Martin. *The Structure of Written Communication.* Orlando, FL: Academic P, 1986.

Prior, Paul. *Writing/Disciplinarity.* Mahwah, NJ: Erlbaum, 1998.

Scribner, Sylvia, and Michael Cole. *The Psychology of Literacy.* Cambridge, MA: Harvard UP, 1981.

Smagorinsky, Peter. "Personal Growth in Social Context." *Written Communication* 14.1 (1997): 63–105.

Zebroski, James. *Thinking through Theory.* Portsmouth, NH: Boynton/Cook, 1994.

CHARLES BAZERMAN

W

WHOLE LANGUAGE: A PHILOSOPHY OF LANGUAGE LEARNING AND TEACHING

Summary

Whole language, a grassroots movement in education, developed as part of a shift in education away from the traditional behaviorist model of teaching and learning. While the term *whole language* may be relatively new, the philosophy of education upon which it is based is not. As early as the seventeenth century, educator John Amos Comenius, an influence on Jean Piaget, argued that learning should be pleasurable and grounded in students' real lives. Unfortunately, no simple definition exists for the term *whole language*. One theorist, Dorothy Watson, who has revised her definition many times over the years, expressed it this way in 1989: "Whole language is a perspective on education that is supported by beliefs about learners and learning, teachers and teaching, language and curriculum" (132). To those who think of whole language as a methodology or a set of activities, Watson's definition seems quite vague. But whole language is a philosophy, a set of beliefs, a perspective based on a theory of language learning. Whole language affirms that language is best learned in authentic, meaningful situations, ones in which language is not separated into parts, but remains whole, integrating reading, writing, listening, and speaking. Whole language defines the role of the teacher as one of facilitator and the role of the student as one of active participant in a community of learners. As Judith Newman says, "*Whole language* is a shorthand way of referring to a set of beliefs about curriculum, not just language arts curriculum, but about everything that goes on in a classroom. . . . *Whole language* is a philosophical stance" (1).

Whole language can trace its roots to the progressive education movement, a theoretical position developed from Jean Jacques Rousseau's eighteenth-century Romantic naturalism and John Dewey's twentieth-century pragmatism. Progressive education opposed social conformity, classroom authoritarianism, and imposition of an academic curriculum as restraints upon the natural curiosity of learners. Whole language embraces the Progressive ideals of teaching students rather than teaching subject matter and respecting students as individual learners, each blessed with unique needs and abilities. Thus, whole language classrooms are student-centered rather than teacher-directed places of learning, in which the curriculum is an organic entity, growing with and out of teachable moments as they exist in individual classrooms.

In 1963, Thomas Kuhn's *The Nature of Scientific Revolutions* had an unforeseen influence on education theory. In the book, the physicist argued that paradigms or belief systems shift due to unexplainable anomalies, inconsistencies between beliefs held and evidence uncovered in a particular field or academic discipline. Thus, a system remains stable, in Kuhn's terms, until research presents overwhelming evidence to contradict accepted practice or enough shocks to the system to cause what was the traditional way of viewing the discipline to become unreliable, unsatisfactory, and generally perceived as being out-of-date. It is only then that a paradigm shift can occur.

In education, much of what was being done prior to the rise of whole language was based on the "taxonomy of learning" developed by Benjamin Bloom, a follower of B. F. Skinner, the founder of behavioral psychology. Early educational psychologists had turned to behavioral psychology to explain the psychology of learning because they perceived it to be scientific, employing, as it did, the measurement of variables with controls as the basis of its experimental designs. Behaviorists regarded observation and inductive knowledge as unacceptable scientific research methods. Instead, the type of research deemed "scientific" in the behavioral sense was based on the study of animals—not human children—"learning" to pass through mazes and press buttons necessary to release food pellets, in controlled laboratory settings—not in home settings or real classrooms. In general, behavioral psychology supports the premise that learning takes place from part to whole, and such studies concluded that motivation and reinforcement were necessary for the rote memorization and recall that behaviorists believed constituted learning. Classrooms in high schools and universities are still stamped by a behaviorist orientation in which students are expected to memorize information and regurgitate facts and ideas transmitted to them through lectures and textbooks. In a behavioral paradigm, an educated person is said to be one who is culturally literate, having learned the necessary "facts" that the dominant culture deems important.

As much as other fields of inquiry, education found itself questioning existing beliefs which had become unstable in the light of new findings. Cognitive psychologists made discoveries about how the human mind learns. For example, cognitive psychologists such as George Mandler found that although emotion is an intrinsic part of learning, because it is unpredictable, it had been excluded as a variable in experimental laboratory situations. Developmental psychologists studied the importance of early childhood learning, development which takes place between birth and the beginning of formal schooling. The research of Ingrid Ylisto and David Doake showed that young children approach written language expecting it to make sense. The research of Jerome Harste, Virginia Woodward, and Carolyn Burke ("Examining Our Assumptions") showed that the reading and writing of three- to six-year-old children was not dependent on stages but on strategies, the same strategies that characterize the literacy expectations of adult language users, specifically text intent, negotiability, risk taking, and fine-tuning of language with language. Dolores Durkin and Melinda Clark suggested that children's literacy development depended on the literacy experiences available both at home and at school: students are more apt to use reading and writing strategies if they are immersed in an environment in which they see people—both adults and children—reading and writing.

Whole language teachers owe a great deal of what they know about the learning process to extensive research in fields and disciplines as diverse as cognitive psychology, psycholinguistics, sociolinguistics, language acquisition, education, sociology, anthropology, linguistics, developmental psychology, composition studies, literacy theory, and semiotics. Psycholinguistic researchers such as Noam Chomsky, Frank Smith, and George Miller found important connections between thought and language, previously claimed as the domain of philosophers, that caused a rethinking of how language is written and read. Smith continued Miller's research on language learning and, in his first edition of *Understanding Reading*, published in 1972, looked at the process of reading as a combination of psychological and social influences. Michael Halliday, a British linguist, pointed out that children do not learn to talk the way linguists learn language. Learning to talk is not an abstract system that can later be used to fulfill a variety of purposes as linguistics can. He points out, as does Gordon Wells, that children learn language and its uses simultaneously.

Literary theorists such as Louise Rosenblatt, Stanley Fish, and Wolfgang Iser redefined reading, looking at how readers construct meaning from text. Rosenblatt's 1978 book, *The Reader, the Text, the Poem*, analyzed the role of the reader in recreating and interpreting a literary work of art. Fish's belief that "interpretation is not the art of construing but the art of constructing" (327) echoed Rosenblatt's conception of reading as an event in which meaning is constructed. Iser, in *The Act of Reading*, speaks of meaning as being located somewhere between the text and the reader, actualized as a result of the transaction between the two.

Sociolinguists Lev Vygotsky, Courtney Cazden, and Dell Hymes looked at the social aspects of language and learning. Russian psychologist Vygotsky, a contemporary of Piaget, stressed the social aspects of learning and the importance of community in the learning process. Cazden's research looked at the role of "teacher talk" and student response in the classroom and the influence of oral speech on learning. Hymes's research studied the influence of culture on language.

Whole language arose in part as a Kuhnian reaction to anomalies unexplained by behavioral psychology. Research on emerging literacy, along with the work of sociopsycholinguists such as Frank Smith, Constance Weaver, and Kenneth Goodman, led to a new view of the teaching and learning—one that is holistic as well as scientific and naturalistic—in which reading is conceived of as a search for meaning, concentrating on the whole rather than the parts, and writing is conceived of as an act of discovery for preschool children, as it is for all writers. As a result, over the past 30 years, the paradigm in education has begun to shift away from a *transmission* model of teaching—behaviorist-based instruction in which teachers are basically nothing more than what Weaver calls "scripted technicians," or hired hands whose job it is to pass on a curriculum established by people outside the classroom. The paradigm has begun to move toward a *transactional* mode of learning, based on a philosophy of whole language, in which learners actively engage with their teachers, their classmates, and their environment in order to actively create their curriculum.

While no one text elucidates the whole language philosophy completely, there are several works that might be considered seminal. Kenneth Goodman's *What's Whole in Whole Language?* is the book that brought the complex theory underpinning whole language to the public by summarizing its premises. Many teachers found this an accessible book to suggest to colleagues and parents. Many see Frank Smith's *Understanding Reading*, originally published in 1972 and now in its fifth edition, as the one that explicated the reading process as a sociopsycholinguistic act, thereby laying the groundwork for a new perspective on teaching and learning language. Donald Graves's 1983 work, *Writing: Teachers and Children at Work*, added the writing process to the whole language discussion by his presentation of the process approach to writing in a workshop classroom. Jerome Harste, Virginia Woodward, and Carolyn Burke's 1984 *Language Stories and Literacy Lessons* demonstrated how language is acquired and therefore how its acquisition can be supported by parents and teachers. Harste, Woodward, and Burke found that young children transact with a variety of text, including environmental print, in a cyclical process that leads to new levels of psycholinguistic and sociolinguistic activity and that continues throughout life, resulting in an ever-changing nature of literacy.

Because the term *whole language* has been misunderstood and misused, it may help to mention some of the most common misconceptions about whole language. Some believe whole language is applicable to elementary grades only. It is true that whole language has been implemented more extensively in elementary grades, yet because whole language is a philosophy of learning, its tenets apply to learners of all ages and at all stages, including ESL students and those labeled as "special" in a variety of ways. Stephen Krashen claims that his model for language acquisition by second language learners is identical to the whole language model of language learning developed by Goodman and

Smith: language acquisition occurs when learners encounter new aspects of language, including sound-spelling correspondences, new vocabulary, and new grammar, that they have not yet acquired but are developmentally ready to acquire. Another misconception is that whole language teachers let students control the class, doing whatever they please. Because whole language teachers do not view lecturing and transmitting isolated bits of information to students as teaching, they believe that students readily learn skills when they are engaged in authentic reading and writing activities. Some mistakenly believe whole language classrooms lack structure because groups of students talk and work together while their teacher conferences with students singly or in groups. There is a difference between structure and control. What might seem unstructured to those used to straight rows of quiet students is actually the structure of a student-centered class. Such classes are well-structured, with students aware of their responsibilities as learners and classroom procedures that facilitate learning in a community where all participants are learners and teachers. Another mistaken belief is that whole language teachers accept whatever students produce, regardless of quality. Assessment and evaluation are important parts of a whole language classroom, yet they are not defined as stanines and percentile scores. Process as well as product is an integral part of assessment. Whole language teachers are observers who are constantly assessing students' strengths and needs in order to provide experiences which will build on students' strengths, rather than concentrate on their weaknesses.

Reception and Significance in Composition Studies

It is difficult to judge the reception of whole language theory in composition and its significance in the field of composition. Whole language and composition studies are intertwined; composition studies are a part of whole language, and theories of composition influence whole language theory. Both theories draw on similar sources and have a shared sense of corresponding research. Theorists and practitioners in whole language and composition studies look to similar subject areas and research for their foundation—collaboration, cooperative learning, feminism, Marxism, social constructivism, poststructuralism, language acquisition, reader-response, and language development. As composition specialist Beth Daniell has written, "What defines composition studies . . . is the belief that our central task is to help human beings use language—the one phenomenon that more than any other defines our identity—to create meaning" (134).

The paradigm shift in education that gave rise to the whole language philosophy was also felt in composition studies. The features of a traditional behaviorist program for the teaching of writing have been characterized by Richard Young as having an "emphasis on the composed product rather than on the composing process; [showing a] strong concern with usage . . . and . . . style; [and a] preoccupation with the informal essay and research paper" (31). Maxine Hairston, in her landmark 1982 article, "The Winds of Change: Thomas Kuhn and the Revolution in the Teaching of Writing,'' added three more features to Young's description: traditional teachers believe "that competent writers know what they are going to say before they begin to write, thus, their most important task [before writing is] to organize their content, . . . that the composing process is linear, . . . [and] that teaching editing is teaching writing'' (78). In such classes, when students write, they write essays on assigned topics, in prescribed formats such as "comparison and contrast,'' with a prescribed length assigned in numbers of words, and they write for a known audience—their teacher. That approach to teaching is based on a behaviorist paradigm of stimulus/ response: learning language from smallest part to whole, emphasizing product over process, and imposing purpose and style on the writing task. The classes often begin with lessons which focus on grammar, mechanics, spelling, and vocabulary lists, followed by numerous skills exercises, each having one correct answer. The textbooks used in traditional composition classes are often grammar handbooks, variations on such classics as *Warriner's* or Strunk and White's *Elements of Style*, supplemented with workbooks and dittos for the practice of skills.

Whole language, as a philosophy of learning, holds various beliefs about language and learning that correspond with many of the changes that have taken place in the composition classroom. A whole language perspective on composition "emphasizes the importance of engaging students in authentic communication, speaking and writing experiences that have the students communicating to real audiences for real purposes'' (Golub, 2).

As a philosophy grounded in research studying how people become literate, whole language has changed educators' beliefs about the nature of reading and writing and learning. From this combined research, whole language has come to embrace certain beliefs about language learning in general and composition studies in particular, such as:

1. Students learn by constructing meaning from the world around them, learning what is worthwhile, useful, and easiest to learn, a view quite different from a behaviorist view of learning by stimulus/response, in which students are believed to learn by listening to lectures, copying notes, memorizing information, and reproducing items on a test.

2. Reading and writing skills develop simultaneously along with oral language skills. In a behaviorist classroom, language learning is thought to be sequential, reading taught through direct instruction as a progression of objectively tested skills, writing taught through drill and the practice of the subskills of spelling, grammar, and sentence structure. Judging by the intensity with which some schools still cling to behavioral learning, it is hard to believe that, in 1957, Noam Chomsky's *Syntactic Structures* demonstrated that language learning is too complex to be regarded as "habit learning'' and that a behaviorist approach trivializes language and learning.

3. Curriculum in a whole language classroom is not a prescribed course of study, unlike a behaviorist view of learning, in which teachers assume that their students will perform according to their plan and schedule, meeting or exceeding

the prescribed limits of the teacher's own expectations. Instead, whole language theorists believe learning occurs when students are engaged in transactions with print and encouraged to think and create and when their teachers provide experiences that allow them to develop improved language competence and content knowledge.

4. Although error is inherent in the learning process, real learning is best developed when students are given opportunities to make mistakes as they move toward true discovery and are supported in an atmosphere of respect and mutual engagement, one encouraging risk taking.

5. Reading and writing are context specific and are reflections of unique situations. Because young children expect language to make sense, they learn to read and develop as writers. As students progress in their reading, their experience with language and life helps them build the schema needed to adjust their expectations about conventions and patterns of language and characters as they broaden their understanding of how the world works.

6. Whole language includes all aspects of language learning—students learn to read while they are writing and they learn about writing by reading. Classroom talk is another vehicle for learning; students learn to listen by speaking and to speak by listening. Students may also learn about reading and writing while listening, but not when forced to listen exclusively to class lectures by their teacher, an activity designed to exercise the language abilities of the teacher, not the students.

Whole language theory informs a classroom environment. Whole language theorist Donald Graves lamented in an address at the 1996 National Council of Teachers of English conference that if asked to imagine oneself standing in a doorway to any classroom in the United States, the majority of people, when asked what they see when they look inside, will see the teacher front and center, students in rows, with notebooks open on their desks and their attention focused on the teacher. This is not what whole language teachers want their classrooms to look like. Pedagogical practices that are consistent with whole language philosophy are highly interactive and social in nature, thus helping the students in these classrooms acquire the social skills necessary to function in most learning and life situations.

A composition classroom informed by whole language has a noticeable look to it, one reflecting a different sense of the teacher and students' roles. Some principles of a whole language composition classroom are:

1. Whole language theory keeps language whole. Literacy acts in the composition classroom are taught in context, with an emphasis on meaning and "making sense" in oral and written communication. Whole language theory maintains that grammar, usage, and editing skills be taught in the composition classroom in the context of the students' language use rather than as isolated exercises.

2. Whole language theory promotes a literate environment in the composition classroom: It suggests that teachers act as facilitators rather than dispensers of

knowledge, demonstrating what it means to be literate by reading and writing in and out of the classroom, sharing their literacy experiences with their students. Whole language teachers advocate reading and writing every day in the composition classroom, allowing students to choose what they read and write about from a variety of texts written by adult and student authors. In a workshop environment students are encouraged to work cooperatively in groups (which form for varied reasons, including shared interests), supporting each other as a community of writers. Their teacher becomes a part of this writing community, modeling, supporting, and most importantly, writing with students. Whole language learners are surrounded by literacy and literature as the impetus to writing about their world. Whole language learners in a composition classroom take risks in their writing and thinking.

3. Whole language theory advocates teachers' use of observation in the composition classroom to evaluate and assess student progress, focusing on what students are capable of doing, rather than looking at students' shortcomings. In composition classes influenced by progressive education and whole language theorists, students' growing conception of themselves as readers and writers is evidence that learning is occurring. It is only natural that composition researchers turn to techniques derived from ethnographic and naturalistic research to chart their students' growing conception, doing case studies, action research, and micro-ethnographies of classrooms. These forms of research have much in common with a research technique favored by whole language practitioners—called "kidwatching" by Yetta Goodman, an assessment technique that observes how actual students—"kids"—learn, using classroom research as a tool to drive instruction. Whole language theorists come to "rely on more naturalistic procedures and the paradigm which undergirds the naturalistic approach to research" (Harste, Woodward, and Burke, "Examining Our Assumptions," 87). For the same reason that composition teachers listen and question during writing conferences, whole language teachers listen, observe, and question as they support student learners in all areas of the curriculum.

Whole language theorist Kenneth Goodman would suggest that students in composition classes read for information and for enjoyment, so they can interact with the texts that surround their lives, and write about what happens to them, so that they can share their experiences with others. To paraphrase Goodman, composition teachers should invite their students to use language to write about the stories that their lives tell and use language to demonstrate the cycle of inquiry—writing questions about that which they seek to understand, reacting to answers, and responding to questions in writing. Kenneth Goodman believes that whole language brings together literacy learning—"the language, the culture, the community, the learner, and the teacher" ("Why Whole Language," 363).

BIBLIOGRAPHY

Primary Texts and Works Cited

Bloom, Benjamin. *Taxonomy of Educational Objectives. Handbook I: Cognitive Domain.* New York: McKay, 1956.

Cazden, Courtney. *Classroom Discourse: The Language of Teaching and Learning.* Portsmouth, NH: Heinemann, 1988.

Chomsky, Noam. *Syntactic Structures.* The Hague, Holland: Mouton, 1957.

Clark, Melinda M. *Young Fluent Readers.* London: Heinemann, 1976.

Comenius, John Amos. *John Amos Comenius on Education.* Intro. Jean Piaget. New York: Teacher's College P, 1957.

Daniell, Beth. "Theory, Theory Talk, and Composition." In *Writing Theory and Critical Theory.* Ed. John Clifford and John Schilb. New York: MLA, 1994, 127–40.

Dewey, John. *Democracy in Education.* New York: Macmillan, 1916.

Doake, David. "Book Experience and Emergent Reading Behavior." Paper Presented at the Annual Meeting of the International Reading Association, Atlanta, GA, 1979.

Durkin, Dolores. *Children Who Read Early.* New York: Teacher's College P, 1966.

Fish, Stanley. *Is There a Text in This Class? The Authority of Interpretive Communities.* Cambridge, MA: Harvard UP, 1980.

Golub, Jeff. "The Voices We Hear." *English Leadership Quarterly* 15.2 (1993): 2–4.

Goodman, Kenneth. *What's Whole in Whole Language?* Portsmouth, NH: Heinemann, 1986.

———. "Why Whole Language Is Today's Agenda in Education." *Language Arts* 69 (1992): 354–63.

Goodman, Yetta. "Kid Watching: An Alternative to Testing." *National Elementary Principals Journal* 57 (1978): 41–45.

Graves, Donald. "The Debate That Won't Go Away: Cultural Battles and Curricular Experience." Presentation at the Annual Meeting of the National Council of Teachers of English, Chicago, IL, November 23, 1996.

———. *Writing: Teachers and Children at Work.* Portsmouth, NH: Heinemann, 1983.

Hairston, Maxine. "The Winds of Change: Thomas Kuhn and the Revolution in the Teaching of Writing." *College Composition and Communication* 33 (1982): 76–88.

Halliday, Michael. *The Linguistic Sciences and Language Teaching.* Bloomington: Indiana UP, 1965.

Harste, Jerome, Virginia Woodward, and Carolyn Burke. "Examining Our Assumptions: A Transactional View of Literacy and Learning." *Research in the Teaching of English* 18.1 (1984): 84–108.

———. *Language Stories and Literacy Lessons.* Portsmouth, NH: Heinemann, 1984.

Hymes, Dell. *Foundations on Sociolinguistics: An Ethnographic Approach.* Philadelphia: U of Pennsylvania P, 1974.

Iser, Wolfgang. *The Act of Reading: A Theory of Aesthetic Response.* Baltimore: Johns Hopkins UP, 1979.

Krashen, Stephen. "Issues in Literacy Development." Testimony Presented to the California Framework on Language Arts Committee, Sacramento, CA, October 25, 1996.

Kuhn, Thomas. *The Structure of Scientific Revolutions.* Chicago: U of Chicago P, 1963.

Mandler, George. *Cognitive Psychology.* Hillsdale, NJ: Erlbaum, 1985.

Miller, George. *The Psychology of Communication*. New York: Basic Books, 1967.

Newman, Judith, ed. *Whole Language: Theory in Use*. Portsmouth, NH: Heinemann, 1985.

Rosenblatt, Louise. *The Reader, the Text, the Poem*. Carbondale: Southern Illinois UP, 1978.

Rousseau, Jean Jacques. *Emile*. Everyman's Library no. 518. Trans. Barbara Foxley. New York: Dutton, 1911.

Skinner, B. F. *Science and Human Behavior*. New York: Macmillan, 1953.

Smith, Frank. *Understanding Reading*. 1972. Rpt. 5th ed. Hillsdale, NJ: Erlbaum, 1994.

Vygotsky, Lev. *Mind in Society*. Ed. M. Cole, V. J. Steiner, S. Scribner, and E. Souberman. Cambridge, MA: Harvard UP, 1978.

Vygotsky, Lev. *Mind in Society: The Development of Higher Psychological Processes*. Ed. Michael Cole. Cambridge, MA: Harvard UP, 1978.

Watson, Dorothy J. "Defining and Describing Whole Language." *Elementary School Journal* 90 (1989): 129–42.

Weaver, Constance. *Reading Process and Practice: From Socio-Psycholinguistics to Whole Language*. Portsmouth, NH: Heinemann, 1988.

————. *Understanding Whole Language: From Principles to Practice*. Portsmouth, NH: Heinemann, 1990.

Wells, Gordon. *The Meaning Makers: Children Learning Language and Using Language to Learn*. Portsmouth, NH: Heinemann, 1986.

Ylisto, Ingrid. "Early Reading Responses of Young Finnish Children." *Reading Teacher* 31 (1977): 167–72.

Young, Richard. "Paradigms and Problems: Needed Research in Rhetorical Invention." In *Research on Composing*. Ed. Charles R. Cooper and Lee Odell. Urbana, IL: NCTE, 1978, 29–47.

Major Scholarship in Composition

Atwell, Nancie. *In the Middle: Writing, Reading, and Learning with Adolescents*. Portsmouth, NH: Heinemann–Boynton/Cook, 1987.

Claggett, Fran. *A Measure of Success: From Assignment to Assessment in English Language Arts*. Portsmouth, NH: Heinemann–Boynton/Cook, 1996.

Golub, Jeffrey N. *Activities for an Interactive Classroom*. Urbana, IL: NCTE, 1994.

Graves, Donald. *A Fresh Look at Writing*. Portsmouth, NH: Heinemann, 1994.

Hurlbert, Mark C., and Michael Blitz, eds. *Composition and Resistance*. Portsmouth, NH: Heinemann–Boynton/Cook, 1991.

Kirby, Dan, Tom Liner, and Ruth Vinz. *Inside Out: Developmental Strategies for Teaching Writing*. 2nd ed. Portsmouth, NH: Heinemann–Boynton/Cook, 1988.

Kutz, Eleanor, and Hepzibah Roskelly. *An Unquiet Pedagogy: Transforming Practice in the English Classroom*. Portsmouth, NH: Heinemann–Boynton/Cook, 1991.

Probst, Robert. *Response and Analysis: Teaching Literature in Junior and Senior High School*. Portsmouth, NH: Heinemann–Boynton/Cook, 1988.

Romano, Tom. *Clearing the Way: Working with Teenage Writers*. Portsmouth, NH: Heinemann, 1987.

Schilb, John. *Between the Lines: Relating Composition Theory and Literary Theory*. Portsmouth, NH: Heinemann–Boynton/Cook, 1996.

Spandel and Stiggins. *Creating Writers: Linking Assessment and Writing Instruction.* 2nd ed. New York: Longman, 1997.

Strickland, Kathleen. *Literacy, Not Labels: Celebrating Students' Strengths through Whole Language.* Portsmouth, NH: Heinemann–Boynton/Cook, 1995.

Strickland, Kathleen and James Strickland. *Un-Covering the Curriculum: Whole Language in Secondary and Post-Secondary Classrooms.* Portsmouth, NH: Heinemann–Boynton/Cook, 1993.

Zebroski, James. *Thinking through Theory: Vygotskian Perspectives on the Teaching of Writing.* Portsmouth, NH: Heinemann–Boynton/Cook, 1994.

Zemelman, Steven, and Harvey Daniels. *A Community of Writers: Teaching Writing in the Junior and Senior High School.* Portsmouth, NH: Heinemann, 1988.

KATHLEEN M. STRICKLAND AND JAMES STRICKLAND

THE WORLD WIDE WEB AND COMPOSITION THEORY

Summary

The impact of the World Wide Web (WWW) on writing closely parallels the impact of hypertext upon writing. In both cases, traditional linear text is changed into a text that need not read from top to bottom, left to right, but which may be read via a variety of different paths provided, or provided for, by the writer. Thus, as with hypertextual systems of writing, the reader of Webbed writing has a variety of paths to choose, or not choose, to take and a part in creating the meaning made by the Webbed text, as she or he determines the flow of the text and, in basic terms, "what happens next." This entry will discuss the basic elements of Webbed writing; it will look at its implications in three areas: non-linearity, multimediation, and interactivity; and it will raise the important issue (as of this writing in 1997) of access to hypertext.

The Web may perhaps have a more popular and widespread application than hypertext applications such as HyperCard or StorySpace. Thus, the Web is for many, including students, the primary introduction to hypertext. In addition, it represents, if more proletarian, then also a more accessible and perhaps affordable inroad into hypertextuality for many persons. It is relatively simple to write HyperText Markup Language (HTML) formatting for Web pages; many current programs automate many complex formatting functions; many Internet service providers offer Web page storage as part of one's monthly fee; some provide assistance in Web page creation, as well. Finally, it is relatively simple to serve Web pages oneself; Web servers are available as freeware and shareware on the Web itself; at this writing, Microsoft Office 97 is reported to contain a native Web server.

The emergence of the World Wide Web (the interrelated system of text and graphic sites served from Internet-connected computers first brought out in 1991 by Tim Berners-Lee of CERN) had an immediate impact on writing and its teaching. Hypertext (coined originally by Ted Nelson in 1961) (Melrod 570) had existed for decades; the Web brought together the nonlinearity of hypertext and the connectivity of the Internet. The introduction of graphical browsers such as Mosaic and, later, Netscape and Microsoft Internet Explorer brought hypertext to a far broader audience than had previously been able to access or understand it; with the elevation of the Internet to near-cult status at the end of the 1990s, it is possible that more people know more about the basic workings of hypertext than know about the basic workings of their own automobiles. With the advent of free or low-cost browsers and access to the Web, two things have happened: many Internet account holders put their own Web pages onto their access providers' (and their own) servers, and many writing teachers have made hypertext an easier reality in the classroom—and arguably, as easily usable a tool as a blackboard and chalk.

Writing a Web page is not computer programming; it is neither quite the same procedure as creating a "standalone" hypertext (such as in Hypercard or StorySpace). HTML, the system used to create Web pages, is not a computer "language" at all but a set of formatting conventions that, when read by a "browser" (e.g., Netscape et al.—a program that accesses the Web and navigates, selects, and displays the HTML file) displays it as a hypertextual, multimedia document. The Web site writer specifies through HTML tags what she or he wants the text to do—or what she or he wants to add to the text. HTML also brings images and sound to documents and creates hypertextual links. These tags thus create the three primary characteristics of a Webbed page (and thus a Webbed rhetoric): the potential for *nonlinearity, multimediation,* and *interactivity.*

Nonlinearity

Webbed writing is not the only nonlinear writing, of course. Johndan Johnson-Eilola reminds that nonelectronic texts can be nonlinear—dictionaries, encyclopedias, or footnotes, for example (201). Nor need Webbed writing be nonlinear. HTML lends itself equally well to the idea of simple display as well as to that of connectivity. Plain text can and often is placed on the Web. Indeed, the Web serves as a powerful preserving agent and repository of thousands of traditional texts in sites such as the Online Book Initiative, the Oxford Text Archive, or Project Gutenberg. (Further evidence of the traditionality evident in the Web may be seen in the thousands of Web advertisements touting goods and services that differ little, if any, from thousands of their cognate roadside billboards in the noncyber world; see also Sidler).

When hypertextual, Webbed documents can be both creative and adaptive. These terms are used to describe two different kinds of hypertexts—the one the ab initio creation of hypertext for the Web, and the other the adaptation of extant traditional text with hypertextual links. Many documents on the Web are arguably the former; the latter, though, abound in increasing numbers, often in educational Web venues. See, for example, the Jane Austen Web site at the University of Texas (http://uts.cc.utexas.edu/~churchh/janeinfo.html).

The nonlinearity of Web documents is both eminently possible and often hard to find; many, if not most, writers are still conditioned into thinking in a "linear" (i.e., beginning, middle/end, thesis, body/conclusion) structure (Martin E. Rosenberg argues that the pervasive "linearity of logocentric argumentation" is difficult if not impossible to escape; see pages 291–93). A computer document, therefore, is easily apprehended as a scrolled version of the traditionally paginated vertical (i.e., traditional) text. Indeed, it is easiest to write HTML by first typing in the vertical text in the traditional way, and then adding the HTML tags which link the document to other documents as a planned afterthought. The result is that many documents on the Web that are text-and-link-primary adhere in some degree vertical linearity; hyperlinks therein function often as markers, "page"-turners, or end-links to related documents.

One of HTML's greatest advantages is the way it can bring text together (or split it apart) in associative, thematic, or other patterns. With hypertextual links, one can bring related or interesting Web documents, either those created by oneself or others, into contact with one's own, in whatever pattern or sequence one wishes. In this way, hypertext is reshaping notions of coherence and linearity in writing.

Assume, for example, a student assignment on the War between the States, in which a student finds, in her research, links to text and photography of the Manassas battlefield just after the battle in the Web site of a museum in another state. Her site might contain the following:

Another battle that caused the South to have a high opinion of its own arms early in the war was that of <a href="http://www.dixie.edu/WBTS/Manassas/overview.htm> Manassas</a>.

Selecting the word *Manassas* would take the reader to the second site, one specifically discussing and providing pictures of the battle.

The most obvious difference between traditional text and Web document (or hypertext document) is that the traditional text exists in a vertical, unmoving form. Webbed rhetoric makes stasis subordinate, using linearity only when it suits the purpose of the document. The role of the document creator for a Web document is one of multi- and mixed-media artist as well as author. Rather than planning a beginning-middle-end document, she or he plans a construct that exists in many planes of space. Think, for example, of a simple four-dimensional cube drawing (something, by the way, that is simple to provide on a Web document but cumbersome to describe in words and possible but difficult to provide in a traditional, vertical printed book such as this one). Each side exists on a different plane from each other side. So do the nodes in a Webbed document. One node can be the "home" page, beginning the project; another can literally be a thousands of miles away, leading in a liminally related but also different direction. A third node can issue from a word in the document, expanding in a separate note on the meaning and other associations of the word—

a hyperannotation; another may be the starting point for a completely new but arguably related document.

Hypertext (and this includes Webbed text) provides the possibility for fractioning the text into nodes having their own lives, separate in physical (at least on the screen) and epistemological (for the moment of the reading, at least) space. Webbed rhetoric, though, raises the issue of "ultimate connectivity." It's been mentioned many times that every document on the Web is connected to every other document on the Web (a sort of cyberspace *Six Degrees of Separation*). This constant imperative—that, literally, the rest of the (cyber) world exists a few short clicks from the page one is creating, has created, or is reading, is what charges the Webbed page to a different degree than a freestanding hypertext.

Martin Rosenberg asserts that hypertext (he mentions StorySpace and Hypercard) is not "free" because it still has an element of "containment"—the geographic containment of the block of text, the implicit "logocentric" tradition of the individual text elements, and the fact that the existence of an individual hypertextual story is often limited to the physical medium of the diskette, CD-ROM, or computer hard drive (274). This finitude is both not an issue and exactly the issue with a Webbed document. If, for example, the nonlinearity of a diskette-based hypertext is confusing or disturbing, then what of the concept of a Web page? Does, for example, the act of writing a Web page imply knowledge of the Web? It does not, because a Web page can be displayed independent of the Web through a browser. But what of the choice of placing the page, or allowing or requesting it to be placed, on a server serving to an Intranet or the Web itself? Placement of a Webbed text *on the Web* has a very real effect on the piece of writing. What, too, are the relationships of a single Web page to the pages "nearest" it (the pages it was intentionally linked to)? What is the relationship of the original Web document to the pages that *those* pages are linked to? In hypertext on the Web, one makes an initial conscious choice for both the limitation (or theme, thesis, focus, or other conscious "framing" of the text) and the illimitability of our creation. One can choose the links that will lead in one direction—but can one check every link of every other Web site that the site links to? And all *their* links to other sites, and all *their* links, ad infinitum? The answer is a very real No—because most humans have neither time nor willingness to check thousands and thousands of pages; because Web links change—expire, get added to, move to other sites on the Web, to other servers—a singular difference from the limitable hypertext of Rosenberg's assertion. The fundamental nature of Web rhetoric, then, is a series of dualities: the empowering nature of the hypertext (Knievel, 5) and the lack of power over the links of others that one chooses to link to one's own; the plan of one's site and the chaos of the Web; the voice of one's own becoming part of a gigantic universal Whitmanesque yawp. Unless the hypertext is entirely self-contained or links only to self-contained hypertexts, it enters into indeterminacy by its author's acts of textual determination.

Multimediation

Russel Wiebe and Robert S. Dornsife, Jr. state that "computer composition" will become a transformed, separate discipline only when the "notion of a 'text' [is] broadened to everything from conventional essays, to paintings, photographs, videos, and hybrids that we have yet to imagine" (133). Their concept of "collage" (135) is apt for considerations of Webbed hypertext, for it is the graphic and other multimediated possibilities of the Web, and the ease of acquiring and implementing them that make creating Web pages so appealing. Multimediation makes the Webbed document different from both traditional texts and hypertext qua hypertext. A WWW document has traditional texts, *and* hypertext, *and* graphics. Look, for example, at a personal Web site—one whose primary purpose is to introduce, promote, or otherwise show oneself—and one will likely see images of several types: photographic images, images scanned onto a disk, digital images created in the computer, or others. There can even be sound or full-motion video or animated clips (assuming that the computer reading it has the hardware and software to play the clip). Wiebe and Dornsife assert that multimediation can begin and occur in noncomputer venues (135). But Webbed writing can bring these disparate rhetorical venue into one cyberspace venue.

This has made writers more aware of the appearance of a text as well as its substance and structure. Far more than the traditional black ink on white tree product, the Web document now has texture and depth. This added complexity can cause a few raised eyebrows when some Web pages are viewed, or can cause real pleasure when others are called to the screen. In addition, too, is a perceived "revival of orality," according to L. M. Dryden, wherein "elements of the orality that predated the printing press may resound" in presentations of student multimedia projects (291).

Interactivity

The effect of nonlinearity in web hypertexts is that the reader now shares part of the duty of determining the meaning with the author. Thus the nonlinearity and the multimediation themselves play a part in making the text interactive (though Douglas Eyman asserts that this is a relatively "superficial" collaboration). The reader chooses his or her own path through the site, and out of the site (which pathway has now become *part* of the site, by virtue of its being the pathway *away from*, but still associated with, the site). She or he can stop, double back, explore, retrace steps, save pieces (either as HTML files or as Bookmark notations, to be returned to later—making the potentially ephemeral more permanent), follow the Forward and Back buttons on the browser (or those in the nest of Web pages)—in terms of setting the pace and direction of the reading, the reader has considerably more control than the reader of a traditional vertical text. He or she may even create a self-index text of his or her own by using a Web search engine to create an annotated index derived from input keywords; at that, point, then, the hypertext is no longer the locus, or even the origination point, of the journey, but only one point, one annotation, on a larger treasure map of the Web.

The reader may respond to the document or even add to the document. For example, many Web pages have fill-in forms wherein the reader can add text and even hyperlinks to the document; a hyperfiction can ask readers to supply alternative endings (or beginnings, or middles, or any other part for that matter) to the story. The reader, rather than assumed to be passive, now is invited, is begged, is coerced, cajoled, welcomed into the text-creating process. In addition, the addition to these texts—indeed, the creation of hypertext and placing it on the Web—is a collaborative act in that the writer has placed her or his text in the ultimate public environment and tacitly inviting comment (see also Eyman).

Reception and Significance in Composition Studies

Weibe and Dornsife state that "what matters most [in the transformation of composition] is that we invite our students to think, read, and to compose across the whole range of media that make up their (and our) daily lives" (135). Multimediation, nonlinearity, and interactivity can certainly achieve this. If employment by many English teachers in a short period of time is any measure of the validity of either a theoretical position or a pedagogical approach, then Webbed writing is a popular and seemingly valid approach.

The newness, though, of Webbed writing raises its own issues, issues to be expected of both a technologically based system and of a system so clearly and recently expansive of its predecessor. As Paul Leblanc asserts, "New network and hypertext technologies are re-inventing writing and outpacing both our theory and pedagogy" (7). Multimediation, for example, has engendered its own set of questions. Susan Lang writes:

One issue facing writing instructors who have students browsing or composing in webbed environments is whether or not to incorporate discussion of the use of the image in webbed composition instruction, and if so, how? Questions instructors may ask themselves to clarify this issue include:

- What, after all, is an image . . . [and] how does one categorize video and animation?
- How do student generated images versus those acquired from other sources fit into discussions of webbed composing? Are there differences to be considered?
- For instructional purposes, how can the relationship between image and text be defined?

That these questions are not fully answered, that teachers and students alike are working them out together, can also be the cause of quite a bit of epistemological head-scratching. Johnson-Eilola notes that the "unfamiliarity [with the obvious nonlinearity of hypertext] can become a site of insurmountable difficulty rather than empowerment and learning" and that "hypertext is clearly a technology that should not be blindly applied to writing and reading instruction" (202). Whether a teacher uses Webbed writing in a class will inevitably depend on a number of factors, including the teacher's own theoretical position and praxis within that position, the age and preparation of the students, the kind of writing class she or he teaches, and a variety of other inputs. As Lang implies, there are still many questions to be answered before the profession, or for that matter any individual teacher, makes a decision about the efficacy of Webbed writing. Michelle Sidler, for example, provides a critical analysis of Webbed writing in her praxis; finding that Webbed writing is "imagistic and two-dimensional" as well as "decontextualized," "combin[ing] editorial information and advertising" alike, she asserts that "writing teachers and researchers must develop strategies to help students recognize and evaluate 'webomercials' when we teach web research and other activities that employ the Web."

One very important question to be asked is the question of access to the technology. It was stated earlier that Webbed writing is easily accessible. However, Webbed rhetoric is completely technology-dependent; traditional linear rhetoric is not. At this writing, many school systems do not have Web access; many of these schools lack computer technology to make Web access possible. The reasons are many—cost, administrative structure, social or cultural priorities, fear of the immense clutter of the Web, desire to "protect" students, and many others. It is not the place of this entry to criticize these reasons, or to prefer one pedagogical method over another. However, Webbed writing cannot be liberatory to those who have no access to it; likewise, it seems clear that a failure to examine and understand the reasons a school or school system chooses not to, or is unable to, employ Webbed writing will have the effect of ignoring a very large segment of the audience the Web arguably seeks to affect. In this, then, Webbed writing is, and will likely remain in the foreseeable future, apart from the mainstream of the majority of pedagogical systems.

BIBLIOGRAPHY

Primary Texts and Major Scholarship in Composition

Note: The works in "Works Cited," plus these sources, are representative of extant Web studies or relevant hypertextual studies. In addition, commercial texts on writing for the World Wide Web abound.

Douglas, J. Yellowlees. "The Audience Made Real: Hypertext and the Teaching of Writing." *Educators' Tech Exchange* 1.4 (Winter 1993): 17–22.

Joyce, Michael. *Of Two Minds: Hypertext Pedagogy and Poetics*. Ann Arbor: U of Michigan P, 1995.

Kairos: A Journal for Teachers of Writing in Webbed Environments. http://english.ttu.edu/kairos/.

Landow, George P., ed. *Hyper/Text/Theory*. Baltimore, MD: Johns Hopkins UP, 1994.

Nielsen, Jakob. *Hypertext and Hypermedia*. Boston: Academic, 1993.

Selfe, Cynthia L, and Susan Hilligoss, eds. *Literacy and Computers: The Complications of Teaching and Learning with Technology*. New York: MLA, 1994.

Slatin, John. "Reading Hypertext: Order and Coherence in a New Medium." *College English* 52.8 (1990): 871–83.

Works Cited

Dryden, L. M. "First Response: Hypermedia Environments." In *Literacy and Computers: The Complications of Teaching and Learning with Technology.* Ed. Cynthia L. Selfe and Susan Hilligoss. New York: MLA, 1994, 282–304.

Eyman, Douglas. "Hypertext And/As Collaboration in the Computer-Facilitated Writing Classroom." *Kairos: A Journal for Teachers of Writing in Webbed Environments.* http://english.ttu.edu/kairos/1.2/features/eyman/bridge.html.

Johnson-Eilola, Johndan. "Reading and Writing in Hypertext: Vertigo and Euphoria." In *Literacy and Computers: The Complications of Teaching and Learning with Technology.* Ed. Cynthia L. Selfe and Susan Hilligoss. New York: MLA, 1994, 195–219.

Knievel, Michael. "Restoration of Authorship in Computer-Aided Composition: Usurping the Throne of the Anonymous Author." Unpublished manuscript. Omaha, NE: Creighton U, 1997.

Lang, Susan. "Review of *Cultures of Vision: Images, Media, and the Imaginary* by Ron Burnett." *Kairos: A Journal for Teachers of Writing in Webbed Environments.* http://english.ttu.edu/kairos/1.2/reviews/pedissue.html.

Leblanc, Paul. "Reinventing Writing in the Virtual Age." *Educators' Tech Exchange* 1.4 (Winter 1993): 7–13.

Melrod, George. "Digital Unbound." In *The Press of Ideas: Readings for Writers on Print Culture and the Information Age.* Ed. Julie Bates Dock. Boston: Bedford, 1996, 570–79.

Rosenberg, Martin E. "Physics and Hypertext: Liberation and Complicity in Art and Pedagogy." In *Hyper/Text/Theory.* Ed. George P. Landow. Baltimore, MD: Johns Hopkins UP, 1994, 268–98.

Sidler, Michelle. "Hyped Up for *Friends*: Cultural Studies and Web Research in Composition." *Kairos: A Journal for Teachers of Writing in Webbed Environments.* http://english.ttu.edu/kairos/1.3/features/sidler/bridge.html.

Wiebe, Russel, and Robert S. Dornsife, Jr. "The Metaphor of Collage: Beyond Computer Composition." *Journal of Advanced Composition* 15.1 (1995): 131–37.

ROBERT WHIPPLE, JR.

WRITING ACROSS THE CURRICULUM

Summary/Reception and Significance in Composition Studies

The term "writing across the curriculum" (WAC) usually refers to two related, but distinct phenomena. The first is writing as it is carried out and appears in diverse forms within the many disciplines that make up a school or college curriculum; the term "writing in the disciplines"(WID) is often applied to this phenomenon. The second is the organized effort to spread responsibility for teaching writing and critical thinking among those many disciplines. While David Russell (1991) has catalogued examples of related efforts in the United States from 1870, the term itself, as name for a self-conscious movement, came into widespread use in the late 1970s and is still used to refer primarily to cross-disciplinary faculty development projects, the first of which is usually dated to 1970 (Russell). As Nancy Martin (1992) has pointed out, "WAC" has been an American phenomenon, an attempt to redress the gradual, century-long displace-

ment of writing from most courses in American secondary schools and universities and its consequent isolation in required English courses at the high school
level and in required courses (sometimes as few as one) in English composition
in the university (Berlin). This displacement had been largely the result of the
popularity in the United States of testing methods which had substituted so-
called "objective" measures (Applebee) for the more complex "subjective"
products of writing.

WAC therefore differed from its influential British counterpart, "language
across the curriculum" (LAC; *A Language for Life*), the subject of government-
sponsored research in the United Kingdom from 1965 to 1975. First, the American focus on writing narrowed the British emphasis on overall language
development. Second, the British LAC research centered from the outset on the
relationship between language use, written and oral, and the growth of children's
cognitive and social abilities (Barnes et al.; Britton; Britton et al.). This emphasis
on intellectual and social growth, which came into American WAC through the
work of Emig, Fulwiler, and others and which has been known by the phrase
"writing to learn," has from the outset of the American movement been somewhat less central to WAC than the emphasis on structural and syntactic writing
skills ("learning to write").

WAC's primary emphasis on "learning to write," at first narrowly defined
in terms of organizational patterns and use of syntax and spelling in so-called
"standard" English (Shaughnessy), derived from national preoccupation in the
1970s with the consequences of expanding opportunity in higher education to
African Americans and to non-native speakers of English. A *Newsweek* cover
story from December 1975, "Why Johnny Can't Write," catalyzed attention to
the disregard of writing at all educational levels, especially in the climate created
by equal educational opportunity.

A broader theory of "learning to write," based on the British research and
the work of such Americans as Mina Shaughnessy, Janet Emig, Peter Elbow,
Ken Macrorie, Linda Flower, and Nancy Sommers, would take hold at the end
of the decade and influence WAC just as it influenced instruction in the English
department composition courses. Of particular importance to WAC programs
has been "process" theory, which was exemplified in the 1970s by Emig
(1983), Flower, and Sommers in their studies of the writing habits of inexpe-
rienced and experienced writers. Shaughnessy's theory of "fluency" as more
basic than "correctness," similar to James Britton et al.'s (1975) developmental
progression from the "expressive" to the "transactional," directly addressed
the needs of the nontraditional students rapidly becoming the norm in American
colleges and universities. As WAC grew in the 1980s, "learning to write" came
to mean typically a process that moved the student, regardless of the discipline,
from relatively informal writings, in "journals" (Fulwiler, 1980, 1987) for example, toward formal writings characteristic of academic or workplace prose
situated in the student's discipline.

That WAC became one popular way to address the "literacy crisis" of the

1970s was attributable to several persons and events. At Beaver College (PA), Elaine Maimon began rhetoric seminars for faculty across disciplines in 1975, an initiative that became a program-development model in 1977 when the Beaver program received the first of many federal (e.g., National Endowment for the Humanities) and private (e.g., Ford Foundation) start-up grants for WAC (see Maimon). Equally significant was the founding of the Bay Area Writing Project (CA) by James Gray of the University of California (Berkeley) in 1974. Among its innovations in advanced training of teachers at all levels was reliance on the theories that had grown out of the British research. Since its methodology was cross-curricular, the LAC research provided a precedent for involving teachers from diverse disciplines. Moreover, since LAC *assumed* (correctly, in Great Britain) that writing was assigned in all disciplines, the books of Britton, Martin (*Writing and Learning Across the Curriculum, 11–16*), and their colleagues provided impetus and rationale for making writing a part of all subjects in the United States. When National Endowment for the Humanities (NEH) funding made the Bay Area project the National Writing Project (NWP) in 1977, with matching funds for new sites across the United States, the British model began to flourish on this side of the Atlantic.

A third inspiration for WAC came from the writing of Janet Emig, the first director of the New Jersey site of the NWP, whose 1977 essay "Writing as a Mode of Learning" (which appeared in *College Composition and Communication*) explicitly connected the theoretical sources of the British work (e.g., Vygotsky, Piaget) with the concerns of American academics. "Writing to learn" thus became the second theoretical pillar of WAC.

With "learning to write" and "writing to learn" the pedagogical goals of WAC, the drive to apply these principles across institutions depended on theories of institutional change. Walvoord (1996) has analyzed WAC as conforming to the "social movement" paradigm (McAdam, McCarthy, and Zald; Benford), featuring a "shift in public perception: something that has always seemed tolerable must now seem intolerable" (59). For WAC, what occurred that made the isolation of writing in composition courses intolerable and the reemergence of writing in many disciplinary curricula desirable? While the "literacy crisis" served as a catalyst for the movement, it can be argued that for WAC much of its early success in gaining supporters from across disciplines came from the application of faculty-development principles central to the National Writing Project. Such WAC program leaders as Toby Fulwiler, Anne Gere, Keith Tandy, Chris Thaiss, Barbara Walvoord, and Art Young, all of whom began WAC work in the 1970s, directed or helped direct early NWP sites. Two NWP principles: (1) that teachers learn best from other teachers, rather than primarily from outside experts, and (2) that by writing themselves teachers understand the value of writing and gain insight into how to help others learn to write (Gray and Myers), became central, if often implicit, parts of the open or invitational "workshop" (Magnotto and Stout; Soven; Thaiss, 1997) that remains the basic strategy of WAC faculty development. Perhaps ironically, it was as consultants—"outside experts"—to numerous institutions that these individuals and others applied these theories in the workshops they coordinated.

This teacher-and-writing-centered philosophy of WAC growth, while it has sparked amazing acceptance of the concept over three decades, has also meant tremendous diversity in adaptations of the concept —as well as lack of any commonly accepted standard for either "learning to write" or "writing to learn." It is no accident that the most influential WAC publications have been eclectic in nature, offering a plethora of local adaptations rather than arguing for standards. The important volumes have been edited collections of teaching practices across disciplines (e.g., Fulwiler's *The Journal Book*, 1987), collections of program models and methods (e.g., Susan McLeod's *Strengthening Programs for Writing across the Curriculum*, 1988; McLeod and Soven's *Writing across the Curriculum: A Guide to Developing Programs*, 1992), localized qualitative research studies (e.g., Walvoord and McCarthy's *Thinking and Writing in College*, 1990), and combinations of these forms (e.g., C. W. Griffin's *Teaching Writing in All Disciplines*, 1982; Fulwiler and Young's *Programs That Work*, 1990; Farrell-Childers, Gere, and Young's *Programs and Practices: Writing across the Secondary School Curriculum*, 1994).

Given the theoretical resistance to close definitions and detailed standards, it is not surprising that attention to assessment of WAC did not occur until well into the 1980s, and the first books dedicated to the topic did not appear until 1997: Brian Huot and Kathleen Yancey's *Assessing Writing across the Curriculum: Diverse Approaches and Practices* and *In the Long Run: A Study of Faculty in Three WAC Programs*, by Walvoord, Linda Hunt, H. Fil Dowling Jr., and Joan McMahon. But even these two books, as the title of the first indicates, resist positing norms for assessment, either of student writing and learning or of program effectiveness. Indeed, *In the Long Run* argues against the program administrator's defining standards; it opts instead for program and assessment designs that encourage faculty to decide for themselves "What works" and how to measure it (139).

If assessment per se has been a relatively recent WAC thread, research into teaching and discourse within disciplines has been ongoing since the early 1980s. Methodology has varied greatly in style and sophistication, with many early reports from practitioners (e.g., Fulwiler and Young, 1982; Thaiss, 1983) describing teachers' pedagogical goals and assignments than generalizing about outcomes. Other collections, e.g., Gallehr et al.(1982), used a variety of empirical and naturalistic methods. Later in the decade, David Jolliffe's collection, *Writing in Academic Disciplines* (1988), analyzed discourse to speculate about writers' knowledge in particular fields and the functions of written knowledge. Walvoord and Lucille McCarthy's (1990) *Thinking and Writing in College: A Naturalistic Study of Students in Four Disciplines* attempted to see diverse disciplines within a coherent framework of collaborative research among disciplinary faculty and rhetoricians. Other rhetoricians (e.g., Herrington, 1985; Myers;

Henry) have qualitatively studied discourse in such fields as chemical engineering, biology, and architecture.

For a concept that has become so widely known and that manifests itself in budgeted programs at the local level, it is perhaps ironic that there is no clearly defined central national "office" for WAC. The National Network of WAC Programs, coordinated by Christopher Thaiss, has existed as a Special Interest Group of National Council of Teachers of English (NCTE) and College Composition and Communication Conference (CCCC) since 1981, but in keeping with the teacher-centered model, the network does not make policy statements nor attempt to restrict the definition of "writing across the curriculum." Its semiannual national meetings operate as discussions of issues that interested parties bring to the meetings, these discussions moderated by a ten-member board of veteran WAC program leaders (Thaiss, 1989). Moreover, while WAC has flourished as a topic of panels and workshops at NCTE and CCCC conventions for years, only in 1993 did the first national conference on WAC occur (in Charleston, SC). Two other biennial conferences have since occurred, the number of participants growing to 650; again corroborating the nonrestrictive theory of WAC growth, the aim of the conference organizers has been to showcase the diversity of disciplines and initiatives rather than narrowly define WAC (Gamboa, Lovitt, and Williams).

Serial publications reinforce the theory of divergence and inclusion. A particular WAC phenomenon has been the large number of in-house newsletters (Thaiss, 1994), while a national serial devoted to WAC, the *Journal of Language and Learning across the Disciplines*, did not emerge until 1994. A further manifestation of the divergence model has been the rapid growth of Internet web sites for individual WAC programs. Indeed, "hypertext" network theory (Landow; Turkle) is particularly congenial to the expansionist WAC theory of institutional change as it has been manifest locally and nationally.

Nevertheless, occasional critiques of non-restrictive WAC have been made. Daniel Mahala (1991) argued that WAC programs' tendency to accept local disciplinary definitions of effective writing betrayed what he saw as composition's responsibility to critique hegemonic discourse. Similarly, in several works Charles Bazerman has called for serious attention by both rhetoricians and disciplinary practitioners to the complex, socially constructed discourses of the fields. Teaching students how to evaluate these discourses "provides [them] means to rethink the ends of the discourse and offers a wide array of means to carry the discourse in new directions" (1992, 65). Exemplifying this discipline-based rhetorical critique have been a series of essays by Lucille McCarthy ("A Stranger in Strange Lands," 1987), Stephen Fishman (1985, 1989, 1993), and McCarthy and Fishman (1991; among their topics have been writing in the philosophy curriculum and the impact of such philosophers as John Dewey on currents in composition study.

Implicit and perhaps unwitting opposition to the theory of institutional change that characterized early WAC growth has been demonstrated by the increase since the mid-1980s in what Thaiss (1988) called "top-down decrees": imposition—without prior WAC faculty development—of responsibility for assignment of writing on faculty across disciplines, often in the form of "writing-intensive" requirements (Latona; Farris and Smith). While such adaptations of WAC are not surprising, given the popularity of the pedagogical concepts and the desire of institutions to emulate success, they should be recognized as departing from early WAC theory. McLeod, in 1989, posited the idea of a "second stage" of WAC, this stage indicated by an institution's moving from the primary strategy, the workshop, to curricular requirements of various types. "Stage" WAC theory presupposes a core of faculty across fields who have already adopted WAC pedagogy and who can serve as change agents among colleagues (again, similar to the "teacher/consultant" model that had informed the National Writing Project). WAC theorists (Thaiss, 1997) have barely begun to confront changes in the pedagogy that result from inversion of the stages.

As the phenomenon known as "writing across the curriculum" moves into the new millennium, theorists are attempting to address the convergences between WAC and several recent trends in education. A new volume edited by McLeod, Miraglia, Soven, and Thaiss will include essays on such heretofore underexplored themes as the impact of electronic technology on WAC, the relationship between WAC and so-called "service learning" (Fischer), writing in interdisciplinary "learning communities," and the relationship between WAC pedagogy and the writing of non-native speakers of English. As long as WAC continues to be guided by an expansionist, inclusionary vision, the number of new themes for theory will continue to grow. Even the critics of nonrestrictive WAC can be seen as adding dimensions to the definition of the term, since their work has greatly increased the number of potential sites for discourse analysis.

BIBLIOGRAPHY

Primary Texts

Bazerman, Charles. "From Cultural Criticism to Disciplinary Participation: Living with Powerful Words." In *Writing, Teaching, and Learning in the Disciplines.* Ed. Anne Herrington and Charles Moran. New York: MLA, 1992, 61–68.

———. *Shaping Written Knowledge: The Genre and Activity of the Experimental Article in Science.* Madison: U of Wisconsin P, 1988.

Britton, James. *Language and Learning.* Harmondsworth, England: Penguin, 1970.

Britton, James, Tony Burgess, Nancy Martin, Alex McLeod, and Harold Rosen. *The Development of Writing Abilities (11–18).* London: Macmillan, 1975.

Emig, Janet. "Writing as a Mode of Learning." *College Composition and Communication* 28 (1977): 122–28.

Gray, James, and Miles Myers. "The Bay Area Writing Project." *Phi Delta Kappan* (February 1978): 410–13.

Griffin, C. Williams, ed. *Teaching Writing in All Disciplines.* No. 12, *New Directions for Teaching and Learning.* San Francisco, CA: Jossey-Bass, 1982.

Herrington, Anne, and Charles Moran, eds. *Writing, Teaching, and Learning in the Disciplines.* New York: MLA, 1992.

Martin, Nancy, Pat D'Arcy, Brian Newton, and Robert Parker. *Writing and Learning across the Curriculum, 11–16.* London: Ward Lock, 1976.

McCarthy, Lucille. "A Stranger in Strange Lands: A College Student Writing across the Curriculum." *Research in the Teaching of English* 21 (1987): 233–65.

McLeod, Susan. "Writing across the Curriculum: The Second Stage, and Beyond." *College Composition and Communication* 40 (1989): 337–43.

———, ed. *Strengthening Programs for Writing across the Curriculum.* San Francisco, CA: Jossey-Bass, 1988.

McLeod, Susan, and Margot Soven, eds. *Writing across the Curriculum: A Guide to Developing Programs.* Thousand Oaks, CA: Sage, 1992.

Russell, David. *Writing in the Academic Disciplines: 1870–1990.* Carbondale: Southern Illinois UP, 1991.

Shaughnessy, Mina. *Errors and Expectations.* New York: Oxford UP, 1977.

Thaiss, Christopher. "The Future of Writing across the Curriculum." In *Strengthening Programs for Writing across the Curriculum.* Ed. Susan MacLeod. San Francisco, CA: Jossey-Bass, 1988, 91–102.

Vygotsky, Lev. *Thought and Language.* 1928; Rpt. Trans. Cambridge, MA: MIT P, 1962.

Walvoord, Barbara. "The Future of WAC." *College English* 58 (1996): 58–79.

Walvoord, Barbara, and Lucille McCarthy. *Thinking and Writing in College: A Naturalistic Study of Students in Four Disciplines.* Urbana, IL: NCTE, 1990.

Major Scholarship in Composition

Farrell-Childers, Pamela, Anne Gere, and Art Young, eds. *Programs and Practices: Writing across the Secondary School Curriculum.* Portsmouth, NH: Heinemann, 1994.

Farris, Christine, and Raymond Smith. "Writing-Intensive Courses: Tools for Curricular Change." In *Writing across the Curriculum.* Ed. Susan McLeod and Margot Soven. Thousand Oaks, CA: Sage, 1992, 71–86.

Fishman, Stephen. "Explicating Our Tacit Tradition: John Dewey and Composition Studies." *College Composition and Communication* 44 (1993): 315–30.

———. "Writing to Learn in Philosophy." *Teaching Philosophy* 8 (1985): 331–34.

———. "Writing and Philosophy." *Teaching Philosophy* 12 (1989): 361–74.

Fulwiler, Toby. *The Journal Book.* Portsmouth, NH: Heinemann–Boynton/Cook, 1987.

———. "Journals across the Curriculum." *English Journal* 69 (1980): 14–19.

Fulwiler, Toby, and Art Young, eds. *Language Connections: Writing across the Curriculum.* Urbana, IL: NCTE, 1982.

———. *Programs That Work: Methods and Models in Writing across the Curriculum.* Portsmouth, NH: Heinemann–Boynton/Cook, 1990.

Gallehr, Donald, et al., eds. *Writing Processes of College Students.* Fairfax: Northern Virginia Writing Project, 1982.

Gere, Anne, ed. *Roots in the Sawdust: Writing to Learn across the Disciplines.* Urbana, IL: NCTE, 1985.

Henry, Jim. "A Narratological Analysis of WAC Authorship." *College English* 56 (1994): 810–24.

Huot, Brian, and Kathleen Yancey, eds. *Assessing Programs in Writing across the Curriculum: Diverse Approaches and Practices.* Norwood, NJ: Ablex, 1997.

Jolliffe, David, ed. *Writing in Academic Disciplines.* Norwood, NJ: Ablex, 1988.

Magnotto, Joyce, and Barbara Stout. "Faculty Workshops." In *Writing across the Curriculum*. Ed. Susan McLeod and Margot Soven. Thousand Oaks, CA: Sage, 1992, 32–46.

McCarthy, Lucille, and Stephen Fishman. "Boundary Conversations: Conflicting Ways of Knowing in Philosophy and Interdisciplinary Research." *Research in the Teaching of English* 25 (1991): 419–68.

Quiroz, Sharon, and Michael Pemberton, eds. *The Journal of Language and Learning across the Disciplines* (quarterly publication of the Illinois Institute of Technology), 1994–.

Soven, Margot. "Beyond the First Workshop: What Else Can You Do to Help Faculty?" In *Strengthening Programs for Writing across the Curriculum*. Ed. Susan McLeod. San Francisco, CA: Jossey-Bass, 1988, 13–20.

———. *Write to Learn: A Guide to Writing across the Curriculum*. Cincinnati, OH: South-Western Publishing Company, 1996.

Thaiss, Christopher. *The Harcourt Brace Guide to Writing across the Curriculum*. Fort Worth, TX: Harcourt Brace, 1997.

———, ed. *Writing to Learn: Essays and Reflections on Writing across the Curriculum*. Dubuque, IA: Kendall-Hunt, 1983.

Townsend, Martha. "Instituting Changes in Curriculum and Teaching Style in Liberal Arts Programs: A Study of Nineteen Ford Foundation Projects." *DAI* 52 (1991): 06A (University Microfilms no. 91–34, 898).

Walvoord, Barbara, Linda Hunt, H. Fil Dowling, Jr., and Joan McMahon. *In the Long Run: A Study of Faculty in Three Writing-across-the-Curriculum Programs*. Urbana, IL: NCTE, 1997.

Other Works Cited

Applebee, Arthur. *Tradition and Reform in the Teaching of English: A History*. Urbana, IL: NCTE, 1974.

Barnes, Douglas, James Britton, and Harold Rosen. *Language, the Learner, and the School*. Harmondsworth, England: Penguin, 1969.

Bazerman, Charles. "What Written Knowledge Does: Three Examples of Academic Prose." *Philosophy of Social Science* 11 (1981): 361–87.

Benford, Robert. "Social Movements." *The Encyclopedia of Sociology*, Ed. Edgar F. Borgatta. Vol. 4, 1880–1887. New York: Macmillan, 1992.

Berlin, James. *Rhetoric and Reality: Writing Instruction in American Colleges, 1900–1985*. Carbondale: Southern Illinois UP, 1987.

Bullock Committee. *Language for Life, A Report of the Bullock Committee*. London: HMSO, 1975.

Elbow, Peter. *Writing without Teachers*. New York: Oxford UP, 1973.

Fischer, Ruth. "Writing across/beyond the Curriculum: Connecting Experience with Concept in the Community Service Link." In *Proceedings of the Third National Conference on Writing across the Curriculum*. Ed. Sylvia Gamboa, Carl Lovitt, and Angela Williams. Charleston, SC: College of Charleston, 1997.

Flower, Linda. "Writer-Based Prose: A Cognitive Basis for Problems in Writing." *College English* 41 (1979): 19–33.

Gamboa, Sylvia, Carl Lovitt, and Angela Williams, eds. *Proceedings of the Third National Conference on Writing across the Curriculum*. Charleston, SC: College of Charleston, Lightsey Conference Center, 1997.

Herrington, Anne. "Writing in Academic Settings: A Study of the Contexts for Writing in Two College Chemical Engineering Courses." *Research in the Teaching of English* 19 (1985): 331–61.

Landow, George. *Hypertext—The Convergence of Contemporary Critical Theory and Technology.* Baltimore, MD: Johns Hopkins UP, 1992.

Latona, John. "What Do We Mean by 'Writing Intensive'?" *Composition Chronicle* 4 (October 1991): 8–9.

Macrorie, Ken. *Telling Writing.* Upper Montclair, NJ: Boynton, 1976.

Mahala, Daniel. "Writing Utopias: Writing across the Curriculum and the Promise of Reform." *College English* 53 (1991): 773–89.

Maimon, Elaine. "Writing across the Curriculum: Past, Present, and Future." In *Teaching Writing in All Disciplines.* Ed. C. Williams Griffin. San Francisco, CA: Jossey-Bass, 1982, 67–74.

Martin, Nancy. "Language across the Curriculum: Where It Began and What It Promises." In *Writing, Teaching, and Learning in the Disciplines.* Ed. Anne Herrington and Charles Moran. New York: MLA, 1992, 6–21.

McAdam, Doug, John D. McCarthy, and Mayer N. Zald. "Social Movements." In *Handbook of Sociology,* Ed. Neil Smelser. Newbury Park, CA: Sage, 1988.

McLeod, Susan, Eric Miraglia, Margot Soven, and Christopher Thaiss, eds. *WAC for the New Millennium: Strategies for/of Continuing Writing across the Curriculum Programs* (manuscript in preparation).

Myers, Greg. "The Social Construction of Two Biologists' Proposals." *Written Communication* 2 (1985): 219–45.

Piaget, Jean. *The Language and Thought of the Child.* 3rd ed. London: Routledge, 1959.

Sommers, Nancy. "Revision Strategies of Student Writers and Experienced Adult Writers." *College Composition and Communication* 31 (1980): 378–88.

Tandy, Keith. "Continuing Funding, Coping with Less." In *Strengthening Programs for Writing across the Curriculum.* Ed. Susan McLeod. Thousand Oaks, CA: Sage, 1992, 55–60.

Thaiss, Christopher. "The National Network of Writing across the Curriculum Programs." *Composition Chronicle* 2 (March 1989): 9–10.

———. "WAC Newsletters: Communicating on and beyond the Campus." *The Composition Chronicle* 7 (September 1994): 8–10.

Turkle, Sherry. *The Second Self: Computers and the Human Spirit.* New York: Simon, 1984.

"Why Johnny Can't Write." *Newsweek,* 9 December 1975: 58–65.

                                                    CHRISTOPHER J. THAISS

WRITING CENTER THEORY AND SCHOLARSHIP

Summary

Writing center theorizing is a rich stew of intertwined discussion that can be only partially teased out into seemingly distinct strands. In part, there is the paradoxical problem that writing centers are positioned as different from composition classrooms while, at the same time, working within the same goals and theoretical frameworks of composition theorizing. Thus theorizing has focused on identifying the place of writing center instruction within, but distinct from, general composition instruction while as Peter Carino notes, "any theorizing must consider the center's place within the larger context of academe, where centers are not valued for their disciplinarity status but for the effect of their practice on such matters as grades, retention, and service" ("Theorizing," 24). Carino finds writing center theorizing as "a project fraught with the tensions of trying to juggle two agendas, first elucidating practice through theory, theory's usual role; second, using theory politically to define the center's relationship to composition studies and to establish the center's disciplinary status and place within the institution" (24). Others in writing center studies see theory as arising from practice and look to writing center lore and stories as more powerful sources of knowledge making. From another perspective, as Irene Clark and Eric Hobson both argue, writing centers should put aside the need for unified theories, accept the recognition of multiple theories, and reshape theory to fit their needs. Moreover, as Dave Healy notes, the highly contextualized nature of any writing center forces all discussions to be local and particularized.

Historical/Collaboration Theories

The dominant theorizing in writing center studies consists of two strands— one built from an historical perspective that explicates the origins, growth, and subsequent development of writing centers and the second that places collaboration theory at the heart of writing center work—that are too closely intertwined to be either separated or understood as isolated theoretical groundings. The historical dimension ties the development of writing centers to the evolution of composition theory and follows James Berlin's paradigm of moving composition from an older current-traditional mode emphasizing product and grammatical correctness to newer process orientations stressing expressivism that locates knowledge within the writer and social construction theory premised on socially constructed knowledge. Collaboration theory, as articulated by Kenneth Bruffee, is seen as integral to producing socially constructed knowledge, knowledge that tutor and student build together in their conversation. Collaboration theory in writing center studies, whether seen as independent or as integral to the framework of social constructionism, draws on the work of Mikhail Bakhtin and invokes Bruffee's view of the tutorial as a social transaction in which peers work toward production of academic discourse. The student brings to the conversation knowledge of the assignment and of what is to be written about and the tutor brings knowledge about conventions of discourse and standard written English (Bruffee, "Peer Tutoring," 10).

Literacy Theories

Writing center theorizing is difficult to separate from political considerations because writing centers are often defined in terms of service and viewed as existing on the margins of institutions and of composition studies. Challenged to declare their disciplinarity as well as their legitimacy in the face of such marginalization, some work on writing center theorizing has drawn on literacy studies, casting writing centers as sites of literacy but also as marginalized sites because their work with literacy is generally seen as subordinate service work for the institution. Nancy Grimm calls for writing centers to recognize their role as dealing with heterogeneity, students whose first language is not English, who use nondominant dialects, have learning disabilities, and can't follow writing assignments. Grimm notes that "[c]omposition scholars theorize about difference, but the social differences that discursive practices create and maintain are contained and silenced in the writing center" (524). Grimm challenges the role of writing centers to prepare students to participate in the mainstream and calls instead to work within heterogeneity rather than manage or eliminate it, to contribute to a dialogue about difference and to move away from accepting the assumption of literacy studies that the goal is to mainstream students. To re-articulate the relationship of writing centers to their institutions, Grimm calls on principles of popular self-help literature on relationship building to initiate dialogue with composition studies. Marilyn Cooper, also concerned with the writing center's role in working against institutional constraints and definitions of literacy, contends that writing centers can provide a space for different literacies. While Cynthia Hayes-Burton views writing centers as mediators between the discourses of dominant and dominated cultures, Carol Severino characterizes writing centers as borderlands or "contact zones" where competing dialects and cultures clash. Nancy Welch, drawing on Julia Kristeva's work, characterizes the disjuncture as "providing critical distance from, rather than immersion in, those social conversations—as a space of critical exile for students and teachers alike" (4).

Feminist Theories

One area of feminist theorizing that writing center theory and pedagogy draw on is Mary Belenky's work on women's ways of knowing. As Susan Monroe Nugent notes, this offers writing center theorists a perspective on the intellectual development of students in the writing center setting. Feminist pedagogy, a source of strength in Madeleine Grumet's work on the nurturant practices that promote learning, is transferred to the writing center in Barbara Cambridge's studies. But feminist pedagogy can also be a site of conflict as demonstrated by Meg Woolbright in her examination of feminist tutorial practices set within the patriarch system of the academy. Other feminist thinking focuses on what Mary Trachsel, drawing on the work of Joan Tronto, calls "[n]urturant activity— directed toward the end of an other's survival, growth, and social development— [which] thus constitutes the duty—the work—of the caring self" (33). Caregiving as well as offering supportive and beneficial assistance to others' growth of understanding is a gendered role so closely allied with the work of writing centers that feminist thought pervades and illuminates writing center studies. However, Trachsel calls for a recognition that writing center pedagogy "theorizes learning as a social, interdependent process through which human selves develop in relationships with others" (42), thus connecting writing center pedagogy to a nongendered basis in human language learning.

Reception and Significance in Composition Studies

The evolutionary model constructed in historical studies underlies *Writing Centers: New Directions*, edited by Ray Wallace and Jeanne Simpson, who announce as their goal the identification of new roles, constituencies, and methodologies for writing centers as they evolve from their origins in remedial work and reinvent themselves. Writing centers in this view are presented as having emerged from being product-oriented, fix-it stations to centers of collaborative learning, a view that has some acceptance in the field, particularly by those eager to identify their centers as having moved beyond product-based grammar instruction, but is more generally seen as somewhat simplistic and historically inaccurate, as evident in Lou Kelly's early articulation of the writing center model emphasizing writing process and collaboration. Peter Carino finds the historical model inadequate and moves to a cultural model that draws on "the post-structural assumptions and moves of recent cultural criticism and new historicism" ("Open Admissions," 30) and gives a richer description than the traditional models, which he calls "evolutionary" (the remedial center in the current-traditional mode) and the "dialectic" (the rejection of roots in product orientation in favor of a student-centered pedagogy of collaboration).

Expressivist views of the writing center, placing knowledge within the writer and seeking to nurture individual writers by helping them find their voices, are articulated by John Warnock and Tilly Warnock who champion the writers' authority and ability "to speak what they think" in contrast to the classroom where students are viewed as the ones who do not know (20). Similarly, Lil Brannon and C. H. Knoblauch see tutor questioning as enabling writers to reconceive ideas and evaluate strategies (45). Still current in discussions of process pedagogy in tutoring, expressivism reaffirms the student-centered role of the writing center in helping to free the writer to unlock and surface her own knowledge, and tutorial pedagogy focusing on questioning as the needed catalyst to encourage writers to find knowledge within themselves remains at its heart expressivist. Mick Kennedy argues for both expressionism and social constructionist theory as part of tutorial practice because "expressionism and social constructionism seem to form a dyad. . . . I would argue that almost any tutorial practice contains overlapping aspects of the two." This perception is echoed by Art Young who also argues that writing center theorizing must account for the expressionistic and social constructionist theories of meaning making.

Lisa Ede and Andrea Lunsford call for a comprehensive theory to place writing center scholarship within social construction work in composition scholarship. Lunsford, seeking a grand unified theory of writing centers, casts Berlin's divisions of theoretical approaches into metaphors for writing center practice and calls for an alignment with social construction theory. She identifies three kinds of writing centers: storehouses (current-traditional sites where tutors dole out information); garrets (expressionist centers that nurture individual writers

and help them find their voices); and Burkean Parlors (sites of socially constructed meaning). Rejecting the storehouse and garret models, Lunsford calls
for a more substantive recognition of writing centers as Burkean Parlors. Ede,
seeking to banish expressionist theory, evokes Bakhtin and looks to social construction theory to buy respectability for writing centers because "the time is
right . . . to place our work in a rich theoretical context" (5) and issues a call
to practitioners to join in the conversation and build on theories of collaborative
learning and on writing as a social process. From Alice Gillam's perspective,
Lunsford's account is missing contextualized illustrations of relationships between practice and theory, and so Gillam looks at social constructionist positions
in terms of their limitations in tutorial practice ("Collaborative Learning Theory"). Gillam further explores how to balance theory (the dialogic) and institutional politics and practice ("Writing Center Ecology"). Another writing
center scholar sounding a note of caution in advocating a total immersion in
social construction theory is Christina Murphy who explains that "social construction provides a paradigm that explains many aspects of writing instruction,
but doesn't provide all the answers or even enough of the answers to devalue
other theories" (36). However, Hobson calls the alliance of social construction
and collaboration theories, which place knowledge production within the dialog
of the negotiating group, "the perceived mainstay of writing center theory" (4).

Calling upon these interlaced theories, writing centers now generally disavow
a role in working with product or grammar-based instruction allied to current-
traditional theories and view their expanding roles as dynamic (Harris, "What's
Up"). Further, as can be seen in mission statements, tutor training manuals, and
articles on writing center pedagogy (hundreds of which are listed and annotated
in the bibliography compiled by Christina Murphy, Joe Law, and Steve Sherwood), writing centers state that they do not proofread student writing or focus
exclusively on grammar. A mantra of tutoring goals and tutor training is Stephen
North's statement that tutors work with writers, not their writing. Carino, who
calls North's article "[p]erhaps the most revered and oft-cited piece of writing
center discourse ever written" ("Theorizing," 27), notes that it "is finally the
statement of a practitioner who, though unable to articulate a theory for center
work, nevertheless has faith in practice" ("Theorizing," 28). Tutor training
manual discussions of pedagogy and studies of writing center collaboration all
reflect the virtually unchallenged underlying assumption that collaboration informs and defines tutorial instruction and is different in kind from classroom
collaboration (Harris, "Collaboration"). Minimalist tutoring, as defined by Jeff
Brooks, offers strategies for focusing collaborative efforts on improving the
writer and turning the responsibility and ownership of the paper over to the
writer. Though Linda Shamoon and Deborah Burns critique nondirective tutoring and call for more directiveness, they are minority voices in noting weaknesses of expressivist tutoring as expressivism continues to underpin
collaboration methods designed to free students to express their own ideas. Es-

says and training manuals on tutorial conversation stress strategies such as questioning, listening, and reflecting either, in the expressivist view, to assist the student in verbalizing the knowledge locked within or, in the social constructionist view, to make meaning through dialogue.

While writing centers are generally perceived as operating outside the normal institutional hierarchy, many such as Welch find this freedom from "the constraints of a predetermined curriculum and the normative force of grades" (5) liberating. Grimm's view of the center as a place to challenge institutional missions is not accepted by those who work compatibly within their institution's goals and find their mission integral to the work of the institution. As noted by Trachsel, "It is precisely the feminized ethos of the writing center that makes writing center work seem antithetical to scholarship . . . the 'men's work' of the academy—conceptualized . . . as a version of the traditionally masculine exploits of exploration, combat, and conquest" (32–33). This devaluing of nonscholarly work feeds into problems of marginalization while simultaneously providing the framework within which tutors are trained to work with students and to understand their roles as tutors. As Lisa Birnbaum notes, even the selection process of tutors displays this feminization as directors seek ideal tutors embued with empathy, patience, sensitivity, diplomacy, friendliness, intuition, supportiveness, responsiveness, and care-giving, all qualities seen as "feminine." This nurturant nature of writing center work is generally accepted both within writing centers and, more generally, in composition studies, for as Trachsel notes, "within the patriarchal institution of the American academy, writing centers are often socially constructed as feminine sites where something like the domestic, caregiving service of the academic community is carried out" (27). Offering a compatible pedagogy as well as insights into tutorial interaction and relationality, feminist studies illuminate, in useful ways, the work of writing centers.

BIBLIOGRAPHY

Primary Texts

Belenky, Mary Field, Blythe McVicker Clinchy, Nancy Rule Goldberger, and Jill Mattuck Tarule. *Women's Ways of Knowing*. New York: Basic, 1986.

Berlin, James. *Rhetoric and Reality: Writing Instruction in American Colleges, 1900–1985*. Carbondale: Southern Illinois UP, 1987.

Bruffee, Kenneth. "The Brooklyn Plan: Attaining Intellectual Growth Through Peer-Group Tutoring." *Liberal Education* 64 (1978): 447–68.

———. "Peer Tutoring and the 'Conversation of Mankind.' " In *Writing Center Theory and Administration*. Ed. Gary Olson. Urbana, IL: NCTE, 1984, 3–15.

Grumet, Madeleine. *Bitter Milk: Women and Teaching*. Amherst: U of Massachusetts, 1988.

Kristeva, Julia. "A New Type of Intellectual: The Dissident." In *The Kristeva Reader*. Ed. Toril Moi. Trans. Sean Hand. New York: Columbia UP, 1986. 292–300.

Tronto, Joan. *Moral Boundaries: A Political Argument for an Ethic of Care*. New York: Routledge, 1993.

Major Scholarship in Composition

Birnbaum, Lisa C. "Toward a Gender-Balanced Staff in the Writing Center." *Writing Lab Newsletter* 19.8 (1995): 6–7.

Brannon, Lil, and C. H. Knoblauch. "A Philosophical Perspective on Writing Centers and the Teaching of Writing." In *Writing Center Theory and Administration*. Ed. Gary Olson. Urbana, IL: NCTE, 1984, 36–47.

Brooks, Jeff. "Minimalist Tutoring: Making the Student Do All the Work." *Writing Lab Newsletter* 15.6 (1991): 1–4.

Cambridge, Barbara. "Bitter Milk: Lessons for the Writing Center." *Writing Center Journal* 14.1 (1993): 75–80.

Carino, Peter. "Early Writing Centers: Toward a History." *Writing Center Journal* 15.2 (1995): 103–15.

———. "Open Admissions and the Construction of Writing Center History: A Tale of Three Models." *Writing Center Journal* 17.1 (1996): 30–48.

———. "Theorizing the Writing Center: An Uneasy Task." *Dialogue* 2.1 (1995): 23–37.

Clark, Irene Lurkis. "Maintaining Chaos in the Writing Center: A Critical Perspective on Writing Center Dogma." *Writing Center Journal* 11.1 (1990): 81–93.

Cooper, Marilyn M. "Really Useful Knowledge: A Cultural Studies Agenda for Writing Centers." *Writing Center Journal* 14.2 (1994): 97–111.

Ede, Lisa. "Writing as Social Process: A Theoretical Foundation for Writing Centers?" *Writing Center Journal* 9.2 (1989): 3–13.

Gillam, Alice. "Collaborative Learning Theory and Peer Tutoring Practice." In *Intersections*. Ed. Joan A. Millin and Ray Wallace. Urbana, IL: NCTE, 1994, 39–53.

———. "Writing Center Ecology: A Bakhtinian Perspective." *Writing Center Journal* 11.2 (1991): 3–11.

Grimm, Nancy. "Rearticulating the Work of the Writing Center." *College Composition and Communication* 47.4 (1996): 523–48.

Harris, Muriel. "Collaboration Is Not Collaboration Is Not Collaboration: Writing Center Tutorials vs. Peer Response Groups." *College Composition and Communication* 43 (1992): 369–83.

———. "What's Up and What's In: Trends and Traditions in Writing Centers." *Writing Center Journal* 11.1 (1990): 15–25.

Hayes-Burton, Cynthia. " 'Hanging Your Alias on Their Scene': Writing Centers, Graffiti, and Style." *Writing Center Journal* 14.2 (1994): 122–24.

Healy, Dave. "In the Temple of the Familiar: The Writing Center as Church." In *Writing Center Perspectives*. Ed. Byron Stay, Christina Murphy, and Eric Hobson. Emmitsburg, MD: NWCA, 1995. 12–25.

Hobson, Eric. "Writing Center Practice Often Counters Its Theory. So What?" In *Intersections*. Ed. Joan A. Millin and Ray Wallace. Urbana, UL: NCTE, 1984, 1–10.

Kelly, Lou. "One-on-One, Iowa City Style: Fifty Years of Individualized Instruction in Writing." *Writing Center Journal* 1.1 (1980): 4–19.

Kennedy, Mick. "Expressionism and Social Constructionism in the Writing Center: How Do They Benefit Students?" *Writing Lab Newsletter* 22.3 (1997): 5–8.

Lunsford, Andrea. "Collaboration, Control, and the Idea of a Writing Center." *Writing Center Journal* 12.1 (1991): 3–10.

Millin, Joan A., and Ray Wallace, eds. *Intersections.* Urbana, IL: NCTE, 1984.

Murphy, Christina. "The Writing Center and Social Constructionist Theory." In *Intersections.* Ed. Joan A. Millin and Ray Wallace. Urbana, IL: NCTE, 1984, 25–38.

Murphy, Christina, Joe Law, and Steve Sherwood. *Writing Centers: An Annotated Bibliography.* Westport, CT: Greenwood P, 1996.

North, Stephen. "The Idea of a Writing Center." *College English* 46 (1984): 433–46.

Nugent, Susan Monroe. "One Woman's Ways of Knowing." *Writing Center Journal* 10.2 (1990): 17–29.

Olson, Gary, ed. *Writing Center Theory and Administration.* Urbana, IL: NCTE, 1984.

Severino, Carol. "Writing Centers as Linguistic Contact Zones and Borderlands." *Writing Lab Newsletter* 19.4 (1994): 1–5.

Shamoon, Linda K., and Deborah H. Burns. "A Critique of Pure Tutoring." *Writing Center Journal* 15.2 (1995): 134–51.

Trachsel, Mary. "Nurturant Ethics and Academic Ideals: Convergence in the Writing Center." *Writing Center Journal* 16.1 (1995): 24–45.

Wallace, Ray, and Jeanne Simpson. *Writing Centers: New Directions.* New York: Garland, 1991.

Warnock, John, and Tilly Warnock. "Liberatory Writing Centers: Restoring Authority to Writers." In *Writing Center Theory and Administration.* Ed. Gary Olson. Urbana, IL: NCTE, 1984, 16–23.

Welch, Nancy. "From Silence to Noise: The Writing Center as Critical Exile." *Writing Center Journal* 14.1 (1993): 3–15.

Woolbright, Meg. "The Politics of Tutoring: Feminism within the Patriarchy." *Writing Center Journal* 13.1 (1992): 16–30.

Young, Art. "College Culture and the Challenge of Collaboration." *Writing Center Journal* 13.1 (1992): 3–15.

MURIEL HARRIS

WRITING PROGRAM ADMINISTRATION THEORIES

Summary/Reception and Significance in Composition Studies

The theorizing of writing program administration followed the theorizing of our classroom teaching. Unlike other kinds of administrators, leaders of writing programs must contend both with practical and theoretical matters (e.g., working within the budget as well as developing the pedagogical foundation of the program). In order to do the job well, we are bound to examine the philosophical ground from which we conduct our programs of writing instruction. Evidence that writing program administrators both worked from theoretical knowledge and dealt with the practical realities of campus life came as early as 1986 in Carol Hartzog's study of over 40 writing programs. Hartzog characterized the programs as "different structural solutions to the problem of what a writing program should be" (*Composition* 135). She found that each program was "governed by theoretical assumptions about the 'discipline,' as well as by the practical realities of campus life" (*Composition* 135). These two factors—theory and local pragmatics—are two themes that appear throughout the literature. In much of the earlier work, theory related primarily to pedagogy and to defining programs. Theory sometimes received less attention than practical "how-to" details of program development. Wendy Bishop contributed to our early definition of a writing program administrator (WPA). In 1990 Irene Gale presented a case study in administration, demonstrating the need for congruence and communication between a program's theory and its administrative conduct.

While WPAs may have seen themselves as academic pioneers in the 1960s and 1970s, by the time of the Wyoming Conference Resolution (the late 1980s), there was serious consideration of WPAs' implicatedness in the politics of writing programs. The power of the administrator and the writing program's political situation have been explored in publications since the mid-1980s. Hartzog candidly assessed WPAs as "not yet . . . good politicians" ("Freshman," 14). In 1985 Linda Polin and Ed White surveyed WPAs, finding that they possessed relatively little power on significant matters of policy. Indeed, many WPAs were themselves in tenuous (i.e., untenured) positions. In 1989, Gary Olson and Joseph Moxley revisited WPAs' significantly challenged authority, showing English Department chairs' relatively low estimate of WPAs and fervently calling for "a reconceptualization of the role" of the WPA (58). Marcia Dickson wrote from a feminist perspective about the relative powerlessness of WPAs. In 1991 White further explored some problematics of WPAs and campus power. While he found "much power inherent in the position," White also learned that "new WPAs at the WPA summer workshops" were not only unaware of the importance of using power, they were "resistant to it" ("Use It," 11, 5). He concluded, advising, "Administrators, including WPAs, cannot afford the luxury of powerlessness. The only way to do the job of a WPA is to be aware of the power relationships we necessarily conduct, and to use the considerable power we have to the good of our program" ("Use It," 12).

Recently, colleagues have made a call for radical reform of governance models. Jeanne Gunner penned a critique of the "WPA-centric administrative model" (9) of one person as the program leader, calling for more sharing of authority, control, and power by "decentering the WPA and democratizing program administration" (14). Gunner earnestly called on WPAs "to cede to subordinates a share of whatever power they have attained" (15). Not to do so, Gunner contended, is to sustain an oppressive system. Christine Hult analyzed the conditions of administration from traditional political classifications of governance: monarchy, dictatorship, oligarchy, anarchy, and constitutional democracy. Hult, too, called for democracy in administration, though, she admitted, "there are several barriers that may prevent writing programs from becoming representative democracies" ("Politics Redux," 50). Barbara Cambridge and Ben McClelland also challenged traditional assumptions about WPA identity, suggesting "a more radical redefinition of the WPA, a redefinition that involves changing the basic architecture of leadership and the responsibilities of the WPA" (155). They argued for a partnership between the WPA and faculty members in joint responsibility, "shared administrative and organizational structure" (157). John Trimbur called on WPAs to resist traditional professionalization as a discipline; reading aspects of our work through Foucauldian and Marxian lenses, Trimbur suggested that WPAs "grapple daily with the persistent conflicts between building individual careers and popularizing expertise for broader social purposes" (145). Hildy Miller proposed a "postmasculinist" approach, a combination of both feminist and masculinist orientations. To sustain a postmasculinist approach an administrator must adopt a "bi-epistemological stance . . . [which] is not just a matter of replacing masculinist with feminist, but rather of somehow doing both or creating a space for one to exist within the other" (58). These various proposals, utopian in vision, lead us into the twenty-first century with reform very much at the heart of our thinking, if not yet our daily work.

In 1995, Joseph Janangelo and Kristine Hansen published *Resituating Writing: Constructing and Administering Writing Programs,* a collection of articles focusing on administration from scholarly or theoretical perspectives. In the lead article, Janangelo carried out a Derridean analysis of "the complex relations that simultaneously compose and constrain writing programs" ("Theorizing Difference," 3). He made numerous suggestions "intended to help writing programs continually reinvent ourselves through dialogue . . . so that we can avoid taking a self-destructive, adversarial stance toward our institutions" ("Theorizing Difference," 18). Christine Hult provided an analysis of the innovative kind of scholarship produced by WPAs. Hult defined the scholarship of administration as "the systematic, theory-based production and oversight of a dynamic program (as opposed to traditional scholarship which is generally defined as the production of 'texts')" ("Scholarship," 126). Ed White advised that WPAs see program assessment as a rhetorical problem of presenting information to a "skeptical audience" ("Rhetorical Problem," 148). White concluded by urging WPAs to view evaluation as an opportunity for "constructive change," rather than as a "mere measurement issue, unrelated to conceptual, contextual, and curricular issues that define the writing program" ("Rhetorical Problem," 149). In another collection on writing programs, Anne Gere reiterates innovative thinking about WPAs, especially the concepts of collaborative administration and administrative work as knowledge production.

Three documents issued by professional associations have influenced our thinking about writing program administration. In 1989 the Conference on College Composition and Communication issued a report that dealt with the concerns raised by the Wyoming Conference Resolution. The report offered a statement of principles and standards for the postsecondary teaching of writing. In 1992, after long months of collaborative writing, guidelines for writing program administrator positions were issued by the Council of WPA. This is a pragmatic rather than a theoretical document, one that offers an approach to developing reasonable work situations for program administrators. Following upon that is another collaborative document, "Evaluating the Intellectual Work of Writing Program Administrators," which calls for having the WPAs' work recognized as applied scholarship. Still a work in progress, the text appeared in draft form in the fall–winter 1996 issue of the *WPA Journal*. These documents have been well received by writing colleagues. If they have not yet materially changed much of our working conditions, they have given us a theoretical foundation for arguing issues of administrative power, professional standards, and educational quality.

BIBLIOGRAPHY

Primary Texts and Major Scholarship in Composition

Bishop, Wendy. "Toward a Definition of a Writing Program Administrator: Expanding Roles and Evolving Responsibilities." *Freshman English News* 16 (Fall 1987): 11–14.

Cambridge, Barbara L., and Ben W. McClelland. "From Icon to Partner: Repositioning the Writing Program Administrator." In *Resituating Writing: Constructing and Administering Writing Programs.* Ed. Joseph Janangelo and Kristine Hansen. Portsmouth, NH: Boynton/Cook–Heinemann, 1995, 151–59.

"CCCC Committee on Professional Standards for Quality Education." *College Composition and Communication* 40 (1989): 61–72.

"Council of Writing Program Administrators: Guidelines for Writing Program Administrator (WPA) Positions." *WPA: Writing Program Administration* 16.1–2 (Fall–Winter 1992): 89–94.

Dickson, Marcia. "Directing without Power: Adventures in Constructing a Model of Feminist Writing Programs Administration." In *Writing Ourselves into the Story: Unheard Voices from Composition Studies.* Ed. Sheryl I. Fontaine and Susan Hunter. Carbondale: Southern Illinois UP, 1993, 140–53.

"Evaluating the Intellectual Work of Writing Program Administrators: A Draft." *WPA: Writing Program Administration* 20.1–2 (Fall–Winter 1996): 92–103.

Gale, Irene. "Conflicting Paradigms: Theoretical and Administrative Tensions in Writing Program Administration." *WPA: Writing Program Administration* 14.1–2 (Fall–Winter 1990): 41–51.

Gere, Anne Ruggles. "The Long Revolution in Composition." In *Composition in the Twenty-First Century: Crisis and Change.* Ed. Lynn Z. Bloom, Donald A. Daiker, and Edward M. White. Carbondale: Southern Illinois UP, 1996, 119–32.

Gunner, Jeanne. "Decentering the WPA." *WPA: Writing Program Administration* 18.1–2 (Fall–Winter 1994): 8–15.

Hartzog, Carol P. *Composition and the Academy: A Study of Writing Program Administration.* New York: MLA, 1986.

———. "Freshman English 1984: Politics and Administrative Process." *WPA: Writing Program Administration* 8.1–2 (Fall–Winter 1991): 7–15.

Hult, Christine. "Politics Redux: The Organization and Administration of Writing Programs." *WPA: Writing Program Administration* 18.3 (Spring 1995): 44–52.

———. "The Scholarship of Administration." In *Resituating Writing: Constructing and Administering Writing Programs.* Ed. Joseph Janangelo and Kristine Hansen. Portsmouth, NH: Boynton/Cook–Heinemann, 1995, 119–31.

Janangelo, Joseph. "Theorizing Difference and Negotiating Differends: (Un)naming Writing Programs' Many Complexities and Strengths." In *Resituating Writing: Constructing and Administering Writing Programs.* Ed. Joseph Janangelo and Kristine Hansen. Portsmouth, NH: Boynton/Cook–Heinemann, 1995, 3–22.

Janangelo, Joseph, and Kristine Hansen, eds. *Resituating Writing: Constructing and Administering Writing Programs.* Portsmouth, NH: Boynton/Cook–Heinemann, 1995.

Miller, Hildy. "Postmasculinist Directions in Writing Program Administration." *WPA: Writing Program Administration* 20.1–2 (Fall–Winter 1996): 49–61.

Olson, Gary A., and Joseph M. Moxley. "Directing Freshman Composition: The Limits of Authority." *College Composition and Communication* 40 (1989): 51–59.

Polin, Linda G., and Edward M. White. "Speaking Frankly: Writing Program Administrators Look at Instructional Goals and Faculty Retraining." *WPA: Writing Program Administration* 9.1–2 (Fall–Winter 1985): 19–30.

Trimbur, John. "Writing Instruction and the Politics of Professionalization." In *Composition in the Twenty-First Century: Crisis and Change.* Ed. Lynn Z. Bloom, Donald A. Daiker, and Edward M. White. Carbondale: Southern Illinois UP, 1996, 119–32.

White, Edward M. "The Rhetorical Problem of Program Evaluation and the WPA." In *Resituating Writing: Constructing and Administering Writing Programs.* Ed. Joseph Janangelo and Kristine Hansen. Portsmouth, NH: Boynton/Cook–Heinemann, 1995, 132–50.

———. "Use It or Lose It: Power and the WPA." *WPA: Writing Program Administration* 15.1–2 (Fall–Winter 1991): 44–52.

BEN W. McCLELLAND

Selected General
Bibliography

Beach, Richard. *A Teacher's Introduction to Reader-Response Theories*. Urbana, IL: NCTE, 1993.

Berlin, James. "Contemporary Composition: The Major Pedagogical Theories." *College English* 44 (1982): 765–77.

Bizzell, Patricia. *Academic Discourse and Critical Consciousness*. Pittsburgh, PA: U of Pittsburgh P, 1992.

Clifford, John, and John Schilb, eds. *Writing Theory and Critical Theory*. New York: MLA, 1994.

Covino, William A. *The Art of Wondering: A Revisionist Return to the History of Rhetoric*. Portsmouth, NH: Boynton, 1988.

Crowley, Sharon. *A Teacher's Introduction to Deconstruction*. Urbana, IL: NCTE, 1989.

Crusius, Timothy W. *A Teacher's Introduction to Philosophical Hermeneutics*. Urbana, IL: NCTE, 1991.

Dobrin, Sidney I. *Constructing Knowledges: The Politics of Theory-Building and Pedagogy in Composition*. Albany, NY: State U of New York P, 1997.

Enos, Theresa, ed. *Encyclopedia of Rhetoric and Composition: Communication from Ancient Times to the Information Age*. New York: Garland, 1995.

Faigley, Lester. *Fragments of Rationality: Postmodernity and the Subject of Composition*. Pittsburgh, PA: U of Pittsburgh P, 1992.

Gere, Anne Ruggles, ed. *Into the Field: Sites of Composition Studies*. New York: MLA, 1993.

Harkin, Patricia, and John Schilb, eds. *Contending with Words: Composition and Rhetoric in a Postmodern Age*. New York: MLA, 1991.

Harris, Joseph. *A Teaching Subject: Composition since 1966*. Upper Saddle River, NJ: Prentice-Hall, 1997.

Heilker, Paul, and Peter Vandenberg, eds. *Keywords in Composition Studies*. Portsmouth, NH: Boynton, 1997.

Knoblauch, C. H., and Lil Brannon. *Rhetorical Traditions and the Teaching of Writing.* Upper Montclair, NJ: Boynton, 1984.

Linn, Ray. *A Teacher's Introduction to Postmodernism.* Urbana, IL: NCTE, 1996.

North, Stephen M. *The Making of Knowledge in Composition: Portrait of an Emerging Field.* Upper Montclair, NJ: Boynton, 1987.

Nystrand, Martin, Stuart Greene, and Jeffrey Wiemelt. "Where Did Composition Studies Come From? An Intellectual History." *Written Communication* 10 (1993): 267–83.

Odell, Lee. *Theory and Practice in the Teaching of Writing: Rethinking the Discipline.* Carbondale: Southern Illinois UP, 1993.

Olson, Gary A., and Sidney I. Dobrin, eds. *Composition Theory for the Postmodern Classroom.* Albany: State U of New York P, 1995.

Phelps, Louise. "Images of Student Writing: The Deep Structure of Teacher Response." In *Writing and Response: Theory, Practice, and Research.* Ed. Chris M. Anson. Urbana, IL: NCTE, 1989, 37–67.

Ray, Ruth E. *The Practice of Theory: Teacher Research in Composition.* Urbana, IL: NCTE, 1993.

Schilb, John. *Between the Lines: Relating Composition Theory and Literary Theory.* Portsmouth, NH: Heinemann–Boynton/Cook, 1996.

Villanueva, Victor, Jr., ed. *Cross Talk in Comp Theory.* Urbana, IL: NCTE, 1997.

Winterowd, W. Ross, and Jack Blum. *A Teacher's Introduction to Composition in the Rhetorical Tradition.* Urbana, IL: NCTE, 1994.

Index

About the Contributors

CHRIS M. ANSON is Morse-Alumni Distinguished Teaching Professor in the Department of English at the University of Minnesota. He has received numerous awards for teaching, including the State of Minnesota's Teaching Excellence Award. Among his authored, coauthored, and edited books are *Writing in Context* (1988), *Writing and Response: Theory, Practice and Research* (1989), *A Field Guide to Writing* (1991), *Writing across the Curriculum* (Greenwood, 1993), *Scenarios for Teaching Writing: Contexts for Discussion and Reflective Practice* (1993), *Using Journals in the Classroom: Writing to Learn* (1995), *The Longman Handbook for Writers and Readers* (1996), and *Composition Research as Critical Practice* (in preparation). His articles have appeared in numerous journals and edited collections.

RONALD G. ASHCROFT teaches writing and literature at the State University of New York at Cortland. He is a doctoral candidate in English at the State University of New York at Binghamton. His previous experiences include high school teaching and technical writing.

KAREN ADELE LEMKE BATES teaches writing at the University of Northern Colorado. Her structural approach is informed by her research in computers and writing.

CHARLES BAZERMAN is Professor of English at the University of California, Santa Barbara. His books include *Constructing Experience*, *Shaping Written Knowledge: The Genre and Activity of the Experimental Article in Science*; *Involved: Writing for College*; *Writing for Your Self*; and *The Informed Writer*. He has just completed a book examining the rhetorical and representational work that made incandescent lighting a social reality, which is entitled *The Languages of Edison's Light*. He also coedited *Textual Dynamics of the Professions* and *Landmark Essays in Writing across the Curriculum*.

ROBERTA ANN BINKLEY is Assistant Professor in the Department of Humanities at the University of Tennessee at Chattanooga.

DAVID BLAKESLEY is Associate Professor of English at Southern Illinois University, Carbondale, where he serves as the Director of Writing Studies. His current projects include an edited collection on the rhetorical nature of film and film theory and a book on Kenneth Burke's rhetoric. He has published articles on literacy, the history of rhetoric, Kenneth Burke, pedagogy, and film.

GLENN BLALOCK is Assistant Professor in the Department of English at Stephen F. Austin (SFA) State University in Nacogdoches, Texas. He teaches various courses in the writing program and in composition theory and pedagogy. In addition, he teaches methods courses for prospective secondary English teachers and serves on NCTE's Standing Committee for Teacher Preparation and Certification. At SFA, he coordinates the Writing Program committee and the new program for promoting Language and Learning in the Disciplines.

VICTORIA BOYNTON publishes and teaches at the intersection of composition, feminist theory, and women's literature. Her essays on Leslie Silko, Kate Chopin, and Collaborative Pedagogy have appeared in recent journals and essay collections. She is a faculty member at the State University of New York at Cortland.

DOUG BRENT received his doctorate in rhetoric and composition from the University of British Columbia in 1988. He is Associate Professor in the Faculty of General Studies at the University of Calgary, where he teaches courses in rhetoric, communications studies, and information technology. He is also Director of the Undergraduate Program in Communications Studies and of the Effective Writing Program. He has published articles in journals such as *College English*, *Textual Studies in Canada*, and *English Journal* and has published a monograph entitled *Reading as Rhetorical Invention: Knowledge, Persuasion and the Teaching of Research-Based Writing*.

LILLIAN BRIDWELL-BOWLES is Morse-Alumni Distinguished Professor of English and Women's Studies at the University of Minnesota, where she directs the Center for Interdisciplinary Studies of Writing. She is a past Chair of the Conference on College Composition and Communication and author of numerous books, chapters, and articles on composition theory and research, as well as feminist rhetoric.

MARTIN T. BUINICKI teaches composition and rhetoric at the University of Iowa. His recent research centers on structural and poststructural theories and approaches to literature and composition.

CHRISTOPHER C. BURNHAM, Professor, Associate Department Head, and Writing Program Administrator, teaches courses in rhetorical theory and composition in the English department at New Mexico State University in Las Cruces. His primary areas of interest include expressive rhetoric, liberatory pedagogy, evaluation, and writing and learning.

DON BUSHMAN is Assistant Professor of English and Director of Composition at the University of North Carolina at Wilmington. He teaches a variety of writing classes, from first-year composition to graduate-level courses on composition theory and pedagogy.

GUANJUN CAI is a Ph.D. candidate in Rhetoric, Composition, and the Teaching of English, with an ESL minor, at the University of Arizona. He has taught developmental writing, first-year composition, and technical writing. He has published articles on contrastive rhetoric and ESL writing and coedited *A Student's Guide to First-Year Composition*.

KERMIT ERNEST CAMPBELL is Assistant Professor in the Division of Rhetoric and Composition at the University of Texas at Austin, where he teaches graduate and undergraduate courses in composition, rhetorical theory, African American studies, and American literature. He has published articles and given numerous national and international conference presentations on African American vernacular tradition and academic writing. He is currently working on a book that intersects the study of rhetoric with issues of race and urban vernacular expression (i.e., hip hop).

SUSAN BROWN CARLTON, Associate Professor of English, teaches writing, women's studies, rhetoric and composition, and postmodern theory. She also directs the Writing Center and the Writing across the Curriculum program at Pacific Lutheran University. Her articles and essays on composition's disciplinary status, rhetoric and feminism, composition and critical theory, and rhetoric and poetics have appeared in rhetoric and composition journals and edited collections.

DENNIS CIESIELSKI is Assistant Professor of English at the University of Wisconsin at Platteville. He is author of *Between Philosophy and Rhetoric: Making Meaning in the Postmodern Composition Classroom* (1997). He has just completed a chapter, "Secular Pragmatism: Kenneth Burke and the [re]Socialization of Literary Theory," in Bernard Brock's *Kenneth Burke in the 21st Century* (forthcoming) and has also written "[Re]Presenting Writing across the Curriculum: A Case for Faculty Dialogue and Development.'' Ciesielski is currently working on an evaluative investigation of the implications of socio-epistemic theory and cultural studies in the first-year writing classroom.

JOHN CLIFFORD is Professor of English at the University of North Carolina, Wilmington, where he teaches writing, literature, and theory.

RICHARD M. COE has taught in Canada, China, and the United States. He has published numerous articles on rhetoric, literacy, composition, drama, popular culture, and literary critical method, including the prize-winning essay ''Rhetoric 2001.'' His *Toward a Grammar of Passages* (1988), based on Christensen's generative rhetoric and Burke's new rhetorical conception of form as both constraining and generative social factors in the writing process, introduced an instrument for studying generic structures. In 1990, a thoroughly revised edition of his innovative textbook was published under a new title, *Process, Form, and Substance: A Rhetoric for Advanced Writers.* Coe, who chaired the Canadian Council of Teachers of English Commission on Public Doublespeak until 1990 and then served three years on the Board of Directors of British Columbia's Plain Language Institute, is Professor at Simon Fraser University, where he won a teaching excellence award in 1984.

CORNELIUS COSGROVE is Associate Professor of English at Slippery Rock University of Pennsylvania, where he teaches courses in first-year composition, writing instruction, rhetoric, and technical writing. A former director of the writing centers at Slippery Rock and the State University of New York at Buffalo, he has published book chapters and articles in such journals as *Teaching English in the Two-Year College*, *English Leadership Quarterly*, and *English Journal*.

TIMOTHY W. CRUSIUS is Associate Professor of English at Southern Methodist University. He is author of *Discourse: A Critique and Synthesis of Recent Theories*, *A Teacher's Introduction to Philosophical Hermeneutics*, and *The Aims of Argument: A Rhetoric and Reader*. He has also published many articles on Kenneth Burke and modern rhetorical theory.

BETH DANIELL is Associate Professor of English and Director of Composition at Clemson University in South Carolina. She has published on literacy issues in *PreText*, *CCCC*, *Rhetoric Society Quarterly*, *Language Arts*, *Composition Chronicle*, *Journal of Advanced Composition*, *Journal of Teaching Writing*, the *Encyclopedia of Rhetoric and Composition*, *Literacy Networks*, and Lunsford, Moglen, and Slevin's *Right to Literacy*. Her current project is a study of how one group of women uses literacy in their spiritual lives.

DENISE DAVID is an Associate Professor of English and coordinates the English program at Niagara County Community College. She teaches courses in first-year composition, creative nonfiction, and contemporary literature. She is the recipient of a State University of New York Chancellor's Award for Excellence in Teaching.

PATRICK DIAS is Emeritus Professor of Education at McGill University. Until 1992, he was the director of McGill's Center for the Study and Teaching of Writing, which he founded in 1980. His writing is mainly in the area of adolescent response to literature and writing. Forthcoming books include: (with Freedman, Medway, and Paré), *Worlds Apart: Acting and Writing in Academic and Workplace Contexts* (1998) and (with Paré) *Transitions: Writing in Academic and Workplace Settings*. In 1991, the Canadian Council of Teachers of English awarded Dias the Merron Chorney Award for his outstanding contribution to the teaching of English in Canada.

KARIN EVANS completed her Ph.D. in a discourse community known as the Rhetoric and Composition Program at Purdue University. Her scholarly and curriculum work focuses on the implications of social theory in teaching composition. She is a member of the English faculty at Elmhurst College in Elmhurst, IL.

AVIVA FREEDMAN is Professor of Linguistics and Applied Language Studies at Carleton University, Ottawa, Canada, where her teaching focuses on writing research and theory. Her recent research and publications have involved issues relating to genre theory, acquisition, and pedagogy. In addition to articles and chapters in books on this subject, she has coedited two collections of essays (with Peter Medway), *Learning and Teaching Genre* and *Genre in the New Rhetoric*. She is also coauthor (along with Patrick Dias, Peter Medway, and Anthony Paré) of *Worlds Apart: Academic and Workplace Writing*.

MEG L. GEBHARD is a Ph.D. candidate at the University of California at Berkeley. Her research interests focus on the contextual factors of second language literacy development and the professional development of second language educators. She has taught ESL at the middle-school level and ESL composition at Syracuse University, and has conducted research in a variety of settings, including schools and workplaces.

ALICE GILLAM is Associate Professor of English at the University of Wisconsin-Milwaukee, where she directs the Composition Program. She regularly teaches graduate courses in classical rhetoric and has recently developed and taught two undergraduate courses in classical rhetoric.

JERI GILLIN is Assistant Professor of Education at Providence College in Providence, RI, where she teaches methods courses in reading and language arts at both the undergraduate and graduate levels. Previously, she was the director of Academic Support Services at Roger Williams University in Bristol, RI, where she taught composition and developmental reading courses. She has taught at all grade levels, including elementary, high school, adult basic education, ESL, and college.

GREGORY R. GLAU received his Ph.D. in rhetoric, composition, and the teaching of English from the University of Arizona. He currently directs the "Stretch" and Summer Bridge Programs at Arizona State University. Glau has published in the *Arizona English Bulletin, English Journal, Issues in Writing, Rhetoric Review, WPA: Writing Program Administration*, and others. Glau currently is working (with Craig Jacobsen) on a textbook, *Scenarios for Writing*, due to be published in 1999.

EMILY GOLSON is Associate Professor at the University of Northern Colorado, where she trains teaching assistants, directs a writing center, and integrates technology into writing courses. She has published in *JAC, Computers and Composition*, and several essay collections.

JAY L. GORDON is a doctoral candidate in Carnegie Mellon's Rhetoric program. He has a broad range of research interests, including the history of rhetoric, literacy, psychology, and philosophy.

JUDITH HALDEN-SULLIVAN is Associate Professor of English at the State University of West Georgia, where she serves as Director of Writing. She has published articles on modern and contemporary American literature and on composition, in particular, "The Phenomenology of Process," a chapter in Anne Ruggles Gere's *Into the Field: Sites of Composition Studies* (1993); an article entitled "Reconsidering Assessment: From Checklist to Dialectic," in *Assessing Writing* (1996); a forthcoming article, "Writing to Learn, *Assessing* to Learn," in *Language and Learning across the Disciplines*; and the article "Poetry Language, Thought: The Verse of Stephen Ratcliffe," forthcoming in *Sagetrieb*. She is currently preparing her second book, *The Turning*, which examines avant-garde American poetry's interrogation of the nature of language. Halden-Sullivan's own verse, a recent extension of her creative work, has been published in several experimental poetry journals.

MURIEL HARRIS is professor of English and Director of the Writing Lab at Purdue University. She edits the *Writing Lab Newsletter* and has authored and edited several books on writing center theory and practice as well as a brief grammar handbook, *The Prentice-Hall Reference Guide to Grammar and Usage*, third edition (1997). She has written numerous book chapters and articles, presented papers on writing center administration, theory, and practice, and coordinated the development of the Online Writing Lab (OWL) at Purdue.

BARBARA HEIFFERON is a doctoral student at the University of Arizona. She specializes in the rhetoric of science but also minored in literary theory. She has published articles in *Science and Engineering Ethics* and *Arizona English Bulletin* and edited two student guides and two teachers' guides for the Composition Program at the University of Arizona.

REBECCA MOORE HOWARD is Associate Professor of English and Director of Composition at Texas Christian University. She works in writing across the curriculum and writing program administration, but her scholarship focuses on print culture studies. Her articles have appeared in the *Journal of Teaching Writing, WPA: Writing Program Administration, JAC: A Journal of Composition Theory, Computers and Composition*, and *College English*. She is coauthor of *The Bedford Guide to Teaching Writing in the Disciplines* and has two forthcoming books: *Standing in the Shadow of Giants* and *Roadmaps for College Writers*.

CHRISTINE A. HULT is Professor and Associate Department Head in the English Department at Utah State University. She served as the editor for the *WPA* journal for six years and is on the WPA Board of Consultant-Evaluators. Her research interests are reflected in recent publications in *Computers in Composition* and the *Journal of Advanced Composition*, as well as in several textbooks, including *Researching and Writing across the Curriculum* and a series of research texts on writing in the disciplines. She recently edited a collection for NCTE called *Evaluating Teachers of Writing* and served as guest editor for a special issue of *Computers and Composition*.

SUE HUM is Assistant Professor of English at the University of Akron. Her research interests include composition historiography, cultural identities and literacy, and Zen Buddhism.

BRIAN HUOT is Associate Professor of English at the University of Louisville, where he directs the Composition Program. His most recent work has appeared in *College Composition and Communication* (1996), *Computers and Composition* (1996), and *Situating Portfolios: Four Perspectives* (1997), a collection of essays. With Kathleen Yancey (also in this volume), he founded and continues to edit *Assessing Writing*, the only journal devoted to writing assessment. He and Yancey have an edited collection, *Assessing Writing across the Curriculum: Diverse Approaches and Practices* (forthcoming).

CAROL JAMIESON is Professor of English and Chair of the Division of Humanities at Niagara County Community College, where she regularly teaches freshman English. She is the recipient of the State University of New York (SUNY) Chancellor's Award for Excellence in Professional Service.

RICHARD D. JOHNSON-SHEEHAN is a Professor of Language and Rhetoric at the University of New Mexico, where he teaches historical, theoretical, and applied rhetoric at the graduate and undergraduate level.

DAVID A. JOLLIFFE is Professor of English and Director of Writing Programs at DePaul University in Chicago. With William Covino, he is coauthor of *Rhetoric: Concepts, Definitions, Boundaries* (1995).

MARY LYNCH KENNEDY is Professor of English and Director of Composition at the State University of New York (SUNY) at Cortland. She has received numerous teaching awards, including the SUNY Chancellor's Award for Excellence in Teaching. She has coauthored *Writing in the Disciplines: A Reader for Writers*, 3rd ed. (1996); *Reading and Writing in the Academic Community* (1994); *Writing in the Disciplines: A Reader for Writers*, 2nd ed. (1990); *Word Processing for College Writers* (1989); and *Academic Writing* (1986).

JANICE M. LAUER is Reece McGee Distinguished Professor of English at Purdue University, where she directs the graduate program in rhetoric and composition. She is the coauthor of *Four Worlds of Writing*, *Composition Research*, and forthcoming, *In Context: Writing as Inquiry and Action*. She has also published articles on rhetorical invention, composition studies, and argument. She coordinates the Consortium of Doctoral Programs in Rhetoric and Composition, has been Chair of the College Section of NCTE, and has served on the executive committees of CCCC and the MLA Division of the History and Theory of Rhetoric. For thirteen years she directed the summer rhetoric seminar, "Current Theories of Teaching Composition."

DAVID R. LEIGHT is a Ph.D. candidate in Rhetoric and Communication at Temple University, Philadelphia. He is an adjunct instructor at Lehigh University in Bethlehem, PA; Lafayette College in Easton, PA; and Bucks County Community College in Newtown, PA. He has published articles in *Clearing House* and *Virginia English Bulletin* and presented conference papers at CCCCs.

FRANK MADDEN has a Ph.D. from New York University and is Professor and Chair of the English Department at State University of New York (SUNY) Westchester Community College. He is a recipient of the SUNY Chancellor's Award for Excellence in Teaching and the Foundation for Westchester Community College Faculty Award for Excellence in Scholarship. He is Chair of the College Section of the National Council of Teachers of English and a member of the Executive Committees of the NCTE, the MLA Association of Departments of English, and the SUNY Council on Writing. He has received research grants from the SUNY Research Council, IBM, and the League for Innovation in the Community College. His articles and chapters about literature, teaching, assessment, and educational computing have appeared in a variety of books and journals. He is also author of a reader-response–based literature text, *Literature, Composition, and Critical Thinking.*

JOHN MADRITCH teaches writing at Lehigh University, where he is a Ph.D. candidate in English.

PAULA MATHIEU is a doctoral student in language, literacy, and rhetoric at the University of Illinois at Chicago, where she also serves as assistant director of English Composition.

WILLIAM J. McCLEARY has taught English at Trotwood Madison Junior High (OH), Fairview High School (CO), Genesee Community College (NY), and SUNY at Cortland, plus short stints at other schools. He is author of *Writing All the Way* and coauthor of *Writing in the Liberal Arts Tradition.* He was editor/ publisher of *Composition Chronicle* from 1988 to 1997.

BEN W. McCLELLAND is Professor of English and Holder of the Ottillie Schillig Chair of English Composition at the University of Mississippi. He directs the university's comprehensive writing program, including the Freshman English Program, the Writing Center, and the Writing Project. Among his book publications are a freshman English textbook, *The New American Rhetoric,* (1993) (with Timothy R. Donovan), *Perspectives on Research and Scholarship in Composition* (1985), *Writing Practice: A Rhetoric of the Writing Process* (1984), and (also with Timothy R. Donovan) *Eight Approaches to Teaching Composition* (1980). McClelland also contributed to *Twelve Readers Reading,* edited by Ronald Lunsford and Rick Straub (1993), and *Writing Theory and Critical Theory,* edited by John Clifford and John Schilb (1994). McClelland is a Past President of the Council of Writing Program Administrators and the Director of its Consultant-Evaluator Board.

RICHARD McNABB teaches undergraduate courses in writing and rhetoric at the University of Arizona. He is the associate editor of *Rhetoric Review* and coeditor of *Making and Unmaking the Prospects for Rhetoric.*

JERRY MIRSKIN has been Assistant Professor at Ithaca College since 1992, where he teaches both academic and creative writing. He has delivered papers at CCCC and other conferences, and a recent paper, ''Writing as a Process of Valuing,'' appeared in *CCC.*

GEORGE E. NEWELL is Associate Professor of English education in the College of Education at Ohio State University. He was recognized for Promising

Research in the Teaching of English by the National Council of Teachers of English. He has published numerous articles exploring the interrelationship of writing and learning in journals such as *Research in the Teaching of English*, *English Education*, *Written Communication*, *Journal of Literacy Research*, and *Review of Educational Research*, and he coedited (with Russel Durst) *Exploring Texts: The Role of Discussion and Writing in the Teaching and Learning of Literature*.

CATHERINE S. PENNER received her doctorate in English literature from Syracuse University in 1973. An Associate Professor at Ithaca College in New York, she has for more than twenty years taught a variety of writing courses: personal narration, humorous writing, technical writing, exposition, and argument. She chaired the College's Writing Program from 1985–1995.

LESLIE C. PERELMAN is Associate Dean, Undergraduate Academic Affairs, Director of the Writing Requirement, and Co-Director of the Writing Initiative at the Massachusetts Institute of Technology, where he also teaches classes in technical communication. Before coming to MIT, he taught at the University of Southern California and directed the Freshman Writing Program at Tulane University. He has written on technical communication, the history of rhetoric, sociolinguistic theory, and medieval literature.

KEITH RHODES is Assistant Professor and Coordinator of Composition at Northwest Missouri State University. He has articles published and forthcoming on liberatory pedagogy and ethnographic research.

DANIEL J. ROYER is Assistant Professor of English and Director of Composition at Grand Valley State University in Allendale, Michigan. His publications include discussions of philosophical issues in rhetoric and composition studies. He has published in a variety of composition and education journals and recently contributed to *Reconceiving Writing, Rethinking Writing Instruction*.

DAVID R. RUSSELL is Associate Professor of English at Iowa State University, where he teaches in the Ph.D. program in Rhetoric and Professional Communication. His book *Writing in the Academic Disciplines, 1970–1990: A Curricular History* examines the history of American writing instruction outside of composition courses. He has published many articles on writing across the curriculum and coedited (with Charles Bazerman) *Landmark Essays in Writing across the Curriculum*. He is currently collaborating on communication across the curriculum programs in agriculture and biology, writing a book on Activity Theory and genre acquisition, and editing a collection of essays describing the uses of writing in nine national education systems.

PHYLLIS MENTZELL RYDER has published articles about social epistemic rhetoric in *JAC: Journal of Composition Theory* and in the revised anthology *Evaluating Writing*, and she also writes poetry and nonfiction prose.

JAMES J. SOSNOSKI is a professor of English at the University of Illinois at Chicago. He is the author of *Token Professionals and Master Critics: A Critique of Orthodoxy in Literary Studies* and *Modern Skeletons in Postmodern Closets: A Cultural Studies Alternative*, as well as various essays on literary and pedagogical theory, computer-assisted pedagogy, and on-line collaboration. With David Downing, he coedited "The Geography of Cyberspace" and the "Conversations in Honor of James Berlin" (both special issues of *Works and Days*). He was the Executive Director of the Society for Critical Exchange (1982–1986) and the Director of the Group for Research into the Institutionalization and Professionalization of Literary Studies (1982–1984). He has been a member of the MLA's Delegate Assembly, Ethics Committee, and Emerging Technologies Committee. At present, he is the Director of e-works, an emerging virtual department, and its Cycles and TicToc projects.

MELANIE SPERLING is Assistant Professor in the School of Education at Stanford University, where she studies and teaches in the area of writing and literacy. She has published in a number of professional journals, including *Research in the Teaching of English*, *Review of Educational Research*, and *Written Communication*, and has contributed chapters to a number of edited volumes, including the yearbook of the National Society for the Study of Education and the *Handbook of Research on Teaching*.

MICHAEL SPOONER is Director of the Utah State University Press. Best known as an editor and publisher of scholarly books, he also contributes chapters and articles to various venues in composition studies. He has collaborated with Kathleen Yancey on several articles (published in print and electronically) addressing issues of collaboration, textuality, and technology.

JAMES STRICKLAND, Professor of English at Slippery Rock University of Pennsylvania, teaches undergraduate and graduate courses in composition and rhetoric. He recently published *From Disk to Hard Copy: Teaching Writing with Computers*, and he is the former editor of *English Leadership Quarterly*, a publication of the NCTE Conference on English Leadership. He is coauthor, with his wife, Kathleen, of *UN-Covering the Curriculum: Whole Language in the Secondary and Post-Secondary Classroom*; they are currently working on *Reflections on Learning: The Role of Assessment and Evaluation in Secondary Classrooms*. Together the Stricklands have written several chapters for edited collections and published an article in *English Journal* (February 1996), "I Do Whole Language on Fridays."

KATHLEEN M. STRICKLAND, Associate Professor of Education at Slippery Rock University of Pennsylvania, teaches undergraduate and graduate courses in reading, language arts, and teacher research. She recently published *Literacy, Not Labels: Celebrating Students' Strengths through Whole Language*. She is coauthor, with her husband, James, of *UN-Covering the Curriculum: Whole Language in the Secondary and Post-Secondary Classroom*; they are currently working on *Reflections on Learning: The Role of Assessment and Evaluation in Secondary Classrooms*. Together the Stricklands have written several chapters for edited collections and published an article in *English Journal* (February 1996), "I Do Whole Language on Fridays."

CHRISTOPHER J. THAISS is Professor of English at George Mason University, where he directs the composition and writing across the curriculum programs. Active in the development of cross-curricular writing since 1978, Thaiss coordinates the National Network of WAC Programs, consults frequently for colleges and universities, and works with teachers in elementary, middle, and high schools through the Northern Virginia Writing Project. Books he has written or edited include *The Harcourt Brace Guide to Writing across the Curriculum*; *Writing to Learn: Essays and Reflections*; *Speaking and Writing, K–12* (with Charles Suhor); *Language across the Curriculum in the Elementary Grades*; and two textbooks for writing classes, *Write to the Limit* and *A Sense of Value* (with Ann Jeffries Thaiss). Current projects include a series of writing guides for specific disciplines and an anthology of essays on WAC program development.

WILLIAM V. VAN PELT is Associate Professor of English at the University of Wisconsin-Milwaukee, where he teaches Romantic literature, rhetoric, and technical writing. He is the author of several articles on writing instruction and computer technology and is the coeditor, with Charles Schuster, of *Speculations: Readings in Culture, Identity, and Values* (1995). During 1996–1997, he was a Research Fellow at the Center for Twentieth Century Studies in Milwaukee, where he engaged in research on how new communication technologies such as the Internet and World Wide Web are altering cultural images of literacy and the body.

LINDA VAVRA is a doctoral candidate in the Language, Literacy, and Rhetoric Program at the University of Illinois at Chicago. She was a contributing author to *Rhetoric: Concepts, Definitions, Boundaries* (edited by William A. Covino and David Jolliffe) and serves as coeditor of *H-Rhetor*, an electronic discussion list on the history of rhetoric and communication, and the H-Rhetor Book Review Project.

TILLY WARNOCK is an Associate Professor in the Rhetoric, Composition, and Teaching of English Program in the Department of English at the University of Arizona (UA). She is a former director of composition at UA and director of the Wyoming Writing Project, the Wyoming Conference on English, and the Wyoming Writing Center. She has published articles on rhetoric, composition, and administration; a composition textbook, *Writing Is Critical Action*; and a collection of essays with Joe Trimmer, *Understanding Others: Cultural and Cross-Cultural Studies and the Teaching of Literature*.

ROBERT WHIPPLE, JR. is Associate Professor of English and Director of Composition at Creighton University in Omaha, Nebraska. He has written on Socrates, writing centers, computer-mediated communication, popular fiction, and national teaching standards. He teaches composition, classical rhetoric, the history of writing instruction, and technical writing.

A. LEE WILLIAMS is Assistant Professor of Literacy in the Elementary/Early Childhood Department at Slippery Rock University of Pennsylvania. She focuses on undergraduate and graduate, literacy-related teacher education in both her teaching and research. Some of her previous publications concerning constructivism include a chapter in *Reflective Teaching: The Study of Your Constructivist Practices* and a chapter coauthored with Richard Vacca in *The Administration and Supervision of School Reading Programs*, 2nd ed.

RANDAL WOODLAND is Associate Professor of Composition and Rhetoric at the University of Michigan at Dearborn, where he directs the Writing Program. He is the coauthor of *Twenty Questions for the Writer* (6th ed.) and has published articles on gay/lesbian on-line spaces and the structure of electronic texts.

KATHLEEN BLAKE YANCEY is Associate Professor of English at the University of North Carolina at Charlotte, where she teaches courses ranging from first-year composition to graduate courses in rhetorical theory and writing assessment. With Brian Huot, she founded and edits the journal *Assessing Writing*. She has edited or coedited five collections of essays, including the most recently released, *Situating Portfolios: Four Perspectives*. Her current projects include a book-length volume on reflective practice, tentatively titled *A Rhetoric of Reflection*, forthcoming in 1998.

DAVID ZAUHAR is a doctoral candidate at the University of Illinois at Chicago.